For Rod and Cameron

GREENS CONCISE SCOTS LAW

PUBLIC LAW IN SCOTLAND

By

Jane Munro

*Brodies, Intrant, Faculty of Advocates,
Former Lecturer in Law, University of Edinburgh*

Published in 2003 by W. Green & Son Limited
21 Alva Street
Edinburgh EH2 4PS

Typeset by J.P. Price, Chilcompton, Somerset

Printed and bound in Great Britain by
Creative Print and Design, (Wales) Ebbw Vale

No natural forests were destroyed to make this product;
only farmed timber was used and replanted.

A CIP catalogue record of this book is available from the
British Library

ISBN 0 414 015 185

© 2003 W. Green & Son Limited

The moral rights of the author have been asserted

CONTENTS

TABLE OF CASES

TABLE OF STATUTES

TABLE OF STATUTORY INSTRUMENTS

CHAPTER 1

SOURCES

"A constitution is a thing antecedent to government, and a **1–01** government is only the creature of a constitution."[1] Clearly, this will not do to describe the British constitution.[2] We do not have a single authoritative document identifying the principal institutions of the state and the powers held by each[3]; and even where, as in the United States, a system has a constitution in this sense, it does not offer a complete description of that system's constitutional law. It is not correct, however, to say that the British constitution is "unwritten".[4] Our constitution is the aggregate of many diverse sources, some written, some not; some legal in character, others non-legal in the sense of not being judicially enforceable or of deriving rather from the realms of legal and political theory. The enactment of the Scotland Act 1998[5] and the Human Rights Act 1998[6] has cast the most salient recent developments in constitutional law in written, legislative form. But the unwritten (or at least, non-statutory) remains as significant as the written: both the Scotland Act and the Human Rights Act are, on the face of it, ordinary statutes enacted in the ordinary way and bearing no imprint of "constitutional" status, but, as we shall see, it is likely that the courts will ascribe to these and other statutes a superior

---

[1] T. Paine, *The Rights of Man*.
[2] Although there is something of Paine's idea in the arguments of those who suggest that the UK does possess an "antecedent" constitution in the form of the Acts and Treaty of Union of 1707: see, *e.g.* T. B. Smith, "The Union of 1707 as Fundamental Law" [1957] P.L. 99; D. N. MacCormick, "Does the United Kingdom have a Constitution?" (1978) 29 N.I.L.O. 1; M. Upton, "Marriage Vows of the Elephant" (1989) 105 L.Q.R. 79.
[3] Although, up to a point, the Scotland Act 1998 may be said to serve as such for Scotland.
[4] Prof. Colin Munro has rightly described the distinction between "written" and "unwritten" constitutions, and the consequences thought to flow from that distinction, as misleading and inexact: C. R. Munro, "What is a Constitution?" [1983] P.L. 563.
[5] Hereinafter "SA 1998". Together with the other devolution statutes, the Government of Wales Act 1998, the Northern Ireland Act 1998 and (albeit less significantly) the Regional Development Agencies Act 1998.
[6] Hereinafter "HRA 1998".

status by virtue of their subject-matter, and as a matter of the common law.

Already, then, we have identified two sources of those norms which go to make up our constitutional law: the law of Parliament as enacted in legislation, and the common law as expounded and applied by the courts. These take up much of, but do not exhaust, the field. Inter- and intra-institutional relations are very much the province of any system of constitutional law, and here we must look less at legal rules and more to what are known as constitutional conventions, to the law and custom of Parliament and indeed to broader concepts of legal and political theory, such as the separation of powers and the rule of law, from which certain conclusions about the appropriate balance of power between the institutions of the state may be drawn.[7] It would also be inappropriate to ignore claims to "popular sovereignty" or "the will of the people" which, if they have not made much impact on constitutional law and practice hitherto, are now being asserted with greater vigour and which may in the future illuminate not only political choices (*e.g.* as to the appropriateness of this or that piece of legislation) but also judicial decisions (*e.g.* as to the relationship between national law and EU law, or as to the legality of Westminster legislation trenching upon the legislative competence devolved to the Scottish Parliament). Finally, one should never be insular in looking for the sources of constitutional law. True it is that the term "the United Kingdom constitution" implies a strong connection between a constitution, or constitutional law, and the state. But just as the monolithic conception of the state has been weakened from within, by the asymmetric devolution of power from the central legislative and/or executive authorities of the United Kingdom to Scotland, Wales and Northern Ireland, so too has it been weakened from without. Most obviously, this has been a consequence of the United Kingdom's membership of what is now known as the European Union. But it has also been the consequence of the United Kingdom's wider engagement in the global community, wherein the state is increasingly in competition with other authoritative sites of power.[8] These developments have posed significant challenges to British constitutional traditions, and the process of accommodating those challenges within our constitutional law is continuing.

---

[7] Although the precise content of those conclusions varies according to the conceptions of the separation of powers and the rule of law one adopts.

[8] See C. M. G. Himsworth, "In a State No Longer: The end of constitutionalism?" [1996] P.L. 639; N. Walker, "Beyond the Unitary Conception of the United Kingdom Constitution" [2000] P.L. 384; N. MacCormick, *Questioning Sovereignty: Law, State and Nation in the European Commonwealth* (Oxford University Press, Oxford, 1999).

LEGISLATION

Let us begin, at any rate, with legislation—Acts of Parliament—as **1–02** a source of constitutional law, and let us begin, as it were, at the beginning.[9] Parliament, meaning the UK Parliament at Westminster, is in its present form the creation of legislation, which legislation might in that sense be described as "constitutive".[10] Before 1707 there were separate Scottish and English Parliaments. After 1707 there was a Parliament of Great Britain: by the Acts and Treaty of Union, the separate legislatures provided for their own extinction and the creation of a new entity.[11] That entity was enlarged again by the Union with Ireland Act 1800, the effects of which were reversed in large part by the legislation providing for the establishment of the Irish Free State.[12] Over the years, the Parliament thus established progressively redefined its internal composition by means of the Reform Acts,[13] the legislation to modify the power of the House of Lords to block legislation approved by the Commons[14] and, latterly, the legislation to remove altogether the right of hereditary peers to sit and vote in the

---

[9] Although even this is not going back far enough. Pre-Union enactments of the English and Scottish Parliaments which remain in force include, most importantly, the Bill of Rights 1689 and Claim of Right 1688, whereby the Parliaments finally refuted the claims of the Stuart monarchs to govern by prerogative right; and the Act of Settlement 1700 (extended to Scotland by the Treaty of Union in 1707), which regulated succession to the Crown. As to the status of pre-Union legislation, while many Acts of the Scottish Parliament were repealed pursuant to the Treaty of Union, many were not, and unless subsequently repealed (see, *e.g.* the Statute Law Revision (Scotland) Acts of 1906 and 1964) or in desuetude, continue in force.

[10] Although the legislation was sometimes subtractive in effect.

[11] Upton, (1989) 105 L.Q.R. 79, suggests that the Union involved a delegation of authority by the Scottish and English Parliaments, and that even if, after the Union, there was no need for the old Parliaments, this did not mean that they were "abolished" or that it would be legally impossible to recall them. Suffice to say for the present that, despite the rhetoric attending the first meeting of the new Scottish Parliament on May 12, 1999, that body was indeed new, the creation of an Act of the Westminster Parliament on the terms therein contained, and not the revival of the body dormant since 1707.

[12] Government of Ireland Act 1920, Irish Free State (Constitution) Act 1922 and Irish Free State (Agreement) Act 1922. These provided for the establishment of the Irish Free State as a Dominion within the Commonwealth subject to a mechanism—promptly utilised—allowing the six counties of Ulster to opt out. The Irish Free State (or Eire) declared itself a sovereign independent state in the Irish Constitution of 1937; the UK recognised this independence in the Ireland Act 1949.

[13] Notably the Representation of the People Acts 1832, 1867 and 1918. The law relating to the franchise is now contained in the Representation of the People Act 1983. Important provision is made in relation to the conduct of elections and the regulation of political parties by the Political Parties, Elections and Referendums Act 2000.

[14] Parliament Acts 1911 and 1949.

Lords.[15] By the European Communities Act 1972, Parliament incorporated into national law the whole body of Community (now EU) law, including future accretions thereto, and, whether intentionally or not, made possible recognition by the courts of the primacy of Community law over inconsistent national law.[16] Most recently, in the Human Rights Act 1998, Parliament ordained all courts to read and give effect to its enactments, existing and future, in a manner compatible with the "Convention rights",[17] so far as possible; and in the event of impossibility, conferred on the higher courts jurisdiction to make "declarations of incompatibility" in respect of the offending statutory provision(s). In the same session, Parliament made provision for the devolution of legislative competence in relation to Scotland to the Scottish Parliament, subject to various reservations and conditions, and for different forms of devolution to the National Assembly for Wales and Northern Ireland Assembly.

In their different ways—because they are constitutive or definitional, or concern the fundamental rights and freedoms of the individual, or confer authority on new constitutional actors—all of these statutes may be described as "constitutional" in a general sense. The question is whether this carries with it any higher legal status. Traditional constitutional doctrine has it that it does not.[18] The purest (or, according to taste, most dogmatic) expression of that doctrine is found in Professor Wade's classic article, in the following terms:

> "[N]o Act of the sovereign legislature (composed of the Queen, Lords and Commons) [can] be invalid in the eyes of

---

[15] House of Lords Act 1999. Section 1 of the Act is qualified, however, by s.2, which "saves" the right of the Earl Marshal, Lord Great Chamberlain and 90 other hereditary peers elected by their fellows to sit and vote pending further reform of the House of Lords. The exact nature of that reform remains unresolved: for the latest consultation on the subject see, *Constitutional Reform: Next Steps for the House of Lords,* published by the Department of Constitutional Affairs in September 2003.

[16] For discussion of the meaning of the "primacy" of EU law, see further below at para. 2–05. As to whether Parliament knew what it was about in 1972, see D. Nicol, *EC Membership and the Judicialisation of Politics* (Oxford University Press, Oxford, 1999). The author contends that, despite the explicit assertions by the ECJ of the autonomy and primacy of Community law, M.P.s did *not* appreciate the legal and constitutional consequences of accession.

[17] Namely, the rights listed in HRA 1998, Sch.1 (European Convention on Human Rights), Arts 2–12, 14 and 16–18; First Protocol, Arts 1–3; and Sixth Protocol, Arts 1 and 2.

[18] Some take issue with the label "traditional" as applied to this branch of constitutional doctrine, arguing that in fact it is a view of relatively modern provenance, and one which neglects the deeper traditions of the common law: see, *e.g.* P. Craig, "Public Law, Political Theory and Legal Theory" [2000] P.L. 211.

the courts; . . . it [is] always open to the legislature, so constituted, to repeal any legislation whatever; . . . therefore no Parliament [can] bind its successors; and . . . the legislature [has] only one process for enacting legislation, whereby it is declared to be the joint Act of the Crown, Lords and Commons in Parliament assembled. . . . [It] is an invariable rule that in case of conflict between two Acts of Parliament, the latter repeals the earlier."[19]

In other words, there is no difference in status between (for instance) the Acts of Union on the one hand and the Dentists Act on the other. This is because, on the above reasoning, the only thing that the Westminster Parliament cannot do is detract from its own continuing sovereignty, its ability to make or unmake any law whatever. That being so, any attempt to "entrench" legislation regarded as "constitutional" or otherwise significant would be an exercise in futility: that statute would remain as vulnerable as any other to repeal (express or implied) by a subsequent statute passed in the ordinary way.

The deficiencies of this view we examine later on. For now, it **1–03** suffices to note that it may no longer occupy the position of impregnability it once enjoyed. In particular, there has been judicial recognition that the status of Acts of Parliament does differ, according to whether they are "ordinary" or "constitutional". The occasion for this recognition was *Thoburn v Sunderland City Council*.[20] It was argued that provisions of the European Communities Act 1972 had been impliedly repealed by a subsequent, inconsistent Act of Parliament. Laws L.J. held that this was not possible[21]:

"Ordinary statutes may be impliedly repealed. Constitutional statutes may not. For the repeal of a constitutional Act or the abrogation of a fundamental right to be effected by statute,

---

[19] H. W. R. Wade, "The Basis of Legal Sovereignty" [1955] C.L.J. 172.
[20] [2003] Q.B. 151.
[21] *Thoburn*, above, para.63. This conclusion was in fact implicit in the earlier decision of the House of Lords in *R v S of S for Transport, ex p. Factortame Ltd (No.2)* [1991] 1 A.C. 603, although their Lordships avoided saying so in terms. The conclusion reached in *Thoburn* was also presaged by the approach taken in *R v Lord Chancellor, ex p. Witham* [1998] Q.B. 575, where Laws L.J. held that Parliament could not, other than by express statutory words, abrogate a "common law constitutional right" (there, access to the courts). This approach was followed in a number of House of Lords decisions, subject to the rider that a statute might infringe upon common law constitutional rights by necessary implication as well as expressly: see, *e.g. R v S of S for the Home Dept, ex p. Pierson* [1998] A.C. 539, *R v S of S for the Home Dept, ex p. Simms* [2000] 2 A.C. 115.

the court would apply this test: is it shown that the legislature's *actual*—not imputed, constructive or presumed—intention was to effect the repeal or abrogation? I think the test could only be met by express words in the later statute, or by words so specific that the inference of an actual determination to effect the result contended for was irresistible. The ordinary rule of implied repeal does not satisfy this test. Accordingly it has no application to constitutional statutes."

If this is so—if "constitutional" statutes are entrenched against implied override—the question is, what qualifies as a constitutional statute? Laws L.J. gave some examples: Magna Carta, the Bill of Rights 1689, the Act of Union,[22] the Reform Acts, the European Communities Act 1972, the Human Rights Act 1998 and the devolution statutes. More broadly, his Lordship described constitutional statutes as those which "either condition the legal relationship between citizen and state in some general, overarching manner, or enlarge or diminish the scope of what we would now regard as fundamental constitutional rights." This definition is not without difficulties.[23] Nonetheless, at the present stage of the development of the common law, and its understanding of the relationship between Parliament and the courts, it is not anticipated that there will be significant dissent from the assertions of Laws L.J. We may, therefore, safely speak of a category of constitutional statutes (albeit a somewhat open-ended one), which are resistant to repeal by anything other than express terms or the (strictly) necessary intendment of a later Act of Parliament.[24]

---

[22] Laws L.J. did not refer to the Scottish Act of Union, or for that matter to the Claim of Right 1688. This is presumably not because his Lordship would deny either constitutional status, but perhaps because, as a matter of judicial comity, it must in the first instance be for the Scottish courts to pronounce on the present status of pre-Union Acts of the Scottish Parliament. In any event, the analysis of Laws LJ in *Thoburn*, above, does no harm to the view that the Acts and Treaty of Union counted as "fundamental law", although it would not (yet) actually deny the United Kingdom Parliament competence to repeal portions of the Union legislation.

[23] See G. Marshall, "Metric Measures and Martyrdom by Henry VIII Clause" [2002] 118 L.Q.R. 493.

[24] It has been suggested, moreover, under reference not only to *Thoburn*, above, but also to the judgment of the ubiquitous Laws L.J. in *International Transport Roth GmbH v S of S for the Home Dept* [2003] Q.B. 728 (see especially para.71), that *Thoburn* represents but a staging post *en route* to recognition that there are "certain constitutional values or constitutional arrangements whose normative value is so great as to place them beyond any interference—specific or otherwise—by Parliament": see M. Elliott, "Embracing 'Constitutional' Legislation: Towards Fundamental Law?" (2003) 54 N.I.L.Q. 25.

COMMON LAW

This leads conveniently to a discussion of the common law as a **1–04** source of constitutional law. Professor Mitchell noted the importance of judicial decisions "either as an original source of principle or as a secondary source, when the courts are interpreting a statute."[25] To these categories (which overlap) might be added a third: determining the scope of prerogative power, which is recognised by but not founded as such on the common law, and supervising the manner of its exercise. Consideration of the prerogative also requires us to reflect on the nature of the Crown, for in many respects the confusion surrounding this concept (confusion exacerbated by historically differing approaches in Scots and English law to the liability of the Crown to be proceeded against in the courts) continues to disfigure if not entirely disable common law control of the executive.

Dicey was referring to the courts as the source of original principles when, in his account of the rule of law, he wrote that "the general principles of the constitution (as, for example, the right to public liberty, or the right of public meeting) are with us the result of judicial decisions."[26] In fact, this was a highly questionable proposition. The courts would intervene to protect invasions of individual liberty for which there was no lawful authority.[27] But the common law was subordinate to the law enacted by Parliament, at least after 1688–89,[28] and it was less accurate to speak of "rights" of liberty, speech, property, assembly and so on than of such residue of liberty as remained after subtracting all the statutory (and common law) restrictions placed upon it. To be sure, the courts had the task of interpreting statutes, and might be more or less protective of the liberty of the subject in doing so.[29] But it is only relatively recently that the courts have begun to speak in terms of "common law constitutional rights", and even there draw as much, if not more, inspiration from the post-war human rights movement, in particular the European

---

[25] Mitchell, *Constitutional Law, op.cit.*, p.23.

[26] Dicey, *Introduction to the Law of the Constitution, op.cit.*, p.195.

[27] The classic exemplar being *Entick v Carrington* (1765) 19 *State Trials* 1029.

[28] *cf. Dr Bonham's Case* (1610) 8 Co. Rep. 121, where Coke C.J. asserted that "when an Act of Parliament is against common right and reason, or repugnant, or impossible to be performed, the common law will control it, and adjudge such Act to be void."

[29] With probably the least tolerance being shown to statutory provisions purporting to authorise invasions of rights of property: see, *e.g. Cooper v Wandsworth Board of Works* (1863) 14 C.B. (NS) 180. It has been suggested that *Entick v Carrington*, above, itself is less a ringing assertion of the subjection of government to law than part of this property-fixated tradition: see K. D. Ewing, "The Politics of the British Constitution" [2000] P.L. 405.

Public Law

Convention on Human Rights,[30] as from the ancient traditions of the common law itself.[31]

The subjection of the common law to the law of Parliament was a corollary of the asserted supremacy of Parliament, as explained (in differing terms) by writers such as Blackstone and Dicey.[32] It is important to note that at the time Blackstone and (to a lesser extent) Dicey were writing, the law of Parliament encroached upon fewer areas of life than it does today.[33] In that sense, the role of the courts was as much a creative as an interpretive one, for in all the areas untouched by legislation, the common law was the law of the land.[34] This state of affairs did not last. The powers of the state and its organs increased exponentially in the nineteenth and, particularly, twentieth centuries. This was not necessarily for sinister reasons: the establishment and development of the welfare state, for one thing, and the prosecution of two world wars for another, required it, and it came about at the behest of a legislature which was (at least after 1928) elected on the basis of universal adult suffrage. Its consequence, however, was that the role of the courts in developing the common law became less important than their role in interpreting and applying statutes and instruments made under them.

The interpretive role is not carried out in a vacuum, nor is it a value-neutral exercise, and we may identify two strands of criticism (not necessarily mutually exclusive) levelled at the courts for the way in which they have performed this task. One school depicts the courts as ever apt to thwart the intentions of the legislature when its enactments conflict with the values—or class prejudices—of the

---

[30] Hereinafter "the Convention".

[31] For an instructive blending of the two traditions, see Lord Browne-Wilkinson, "The Infiltration of a Bill of Rights" [1992] P.L. 397, in which his Lordship suggested that the restrictive approach taken by the courts to the construction of penal and taxing statutes—which threaten, respectively, the liberty and property of the individual—be applied equally to statutes impinging upon other rights as enshrined in the ECHR.

[32] See P. Craig, "The Sovereignty of the United Kingdom Parliament after *Factortame*" [1991] YBEL 221.

[33] Dicey's *Law of the Constitution* was first published in 1885. The same year, H. S. Maine published *Popular Government*, which deplored both the increasing reach of statute law and the increasing domination of Parliament by the executive.

[34] The reference to the common law must include, in Scotland, reference to the civil law, which was a major influence on the development of Scots private law, if not of its public law. Likewise, the institutional writers are regarded as a source of law in Scotland, in the absence of subsequent judicial decisions to the contrary; but as Prof. Mitchell notes, the great institutional writers tended not to discuss public law so fully as private law or criminal law. Most constitutional "books of authority" are the works of English writers, and may carry less authority north of the border in consequence: see, generally, J. D. B. Mitchell, *Constitutional Law, op.cit.*, pp.19–26.

judiciary.[35] Others are more concerned with the apparent readiness of the courts (at least in the past) to allow the claims of administrative efficiency and convenience to prevail over the protection of individual freedoms.[36] Associated with the latter if not the former has been a growing perception that the protection of what might be termed "constitutional values" could no longer be left to Parliament alone, or even primarily, given the subordination of Parliament to the executive through the latter's command—in normal circumstances—of a majority in the House of Commons.[37] The judicial response to this has fused, in a sense, the function of expounding original principle and the function of statutory inter-pretation,[38] for in a number of cases in the past decade the courts have held that, in construing legislation, it is to be presumed, absent express words or necessary implication to the contrary, that Parliament intended no infringement of certain "fundamental" rights.[39] In this way, whether or not one approves of it, the courts firmly reasserted the authority of the common law as a source of constitutional norms, to such an extent that one commentator has discerned a "new and still emerging constitutional paradigm, no longer of Dicey's supreme Parliament to whose will the rule of law must finally bend, but of a bi-polar sovereignty of the Crown in Parliament and the Crown in its courts."[40]

---

[35] This school is particularly associated with Prof. Griffith (see J. A. G. Griffith, *The Politics of the Judiciary* (5th ed., 1997)) and is exemplified by the more or less continuous enactment, and outflanking, of legislation in the fields of trades union immunity and labour law in the first half of the 20th century. See also, *e.g.* K. D. Ewing, "The Politics of the British Constitution" [2000] P.L. 405 and "A Bill of Rights: Lessons from the Privy Council" in *Edinburgh Essays in Public Law* (Finnie, Himsworth and Walker eds, 1991), p.231.

[36] See in particular the surveys by Sir Stephen Sedley, "The Sound of Silence: Constitutional law without a constitution" (1994) 110 L.Q.R. 270 and "Human Rights: A twenty-first century agenda" [1995] P.L. 386. Sir Stephen attributes the "long sleep" of public law in the earlier part of the 20th century to the coincidence of the two great 19th century Reform Acts and the overhaul of the civil service, which "replaced ministers' placemen with an intellectual and administrative elite from the same schools, universities and clubs as the judges themselves, encouraging the judiciary to retreat from its prickly Victorian invigilation of the executive into a passivity which had, by the 1950s, allowed executive and local government an unprecedented measure of unchallenged power." There is probably little in this with which certain members of the first school would disagree: see, *e.g.* K. D. Ewing and C. Gearty, *The Struggle for Civil Liberties* (Oxford University Press, Oxford, 2000).

[37] By the 1990s, this perception had been strengthened by the apparent breakdown of democratic constraint on the executive residing in the fact that one party had been able, for close on 20 years, to control the legislature.

[38] A development greeted with misgiving by commentators of the first school, whose doubts about the legitimacy and accountability of the judiciary remain unassuaged.

[39] See, *inter alia*, the cases referred to at n.21.

[40] Sir Stephen Sedley, "Human Rights: A twenty-first century agenda" [1995] P.L. 386 at 389.

1–05   There is another, discrete sense in which the common law is important as a source of constitutional doctrine, and that is in its treatment of the Crown and prerogative powers. The nature of the Crown and of the prerogative is considered in greater detail in Chapter 5; suffice to say for now that the courts have successively denied the Crown any autonomous legislative authority,[41] affirmed the pre-eminence of statute over the prerogative,[42] and asserted the subjection of the prerogative to the supervisory jurisdiction of the courts provided its exercise raises justiciable questions.[43] As we shall see, despite all this, the subjection of the prerogative to law is often more a matter of principle than reality. That is not always, or necessarily, a matter of concern, for in certain circumstances political rather than legal control is apposite. What is problematic is the fact that "tradition" (and not necessarily Scottish tradition either) still shelters the exercise of government power from the full reach of the law where legal control *is* appropriate.[44] The shelter has been broken down somewhat in recent years, but not uniformly and only then by resort to reasoning which itself "groans under an unnecessary burden of history and myth."[45] The law and custom of Parliament raises similar questions.[46] Like the prerogative, the privileges of Parliament are rooted in custom,[47] but may be said to exist within the common law in the sense that they are recognised by the courts and (so far as the courts are concerned) are subject to the common law, for while the courts concede Parliament's exclusive jurisdiction in matters of privilege where properly claimed, they assert for themselves the last word on where the outer limits of privilege lie.

CONSTITUTIONAL CONVENTION

1–06 In his account of our constitutional rules, Dicey distinguished the legal rules—statutory and common law—from another set of rules consisting of the:

---

[41] *The Case of Proclamations* (1611) 12 Co. Rep. 74 and, in Scotland, *Grieve v Edinburgh and District Water Trs*, 1918 S.C. 700.

[42] *Attorney-General v De Keyser's Royal Hotel Ltd* [1920] A.C. 508.

[43] *Council of Civil Service Unions v Minister for the Civil Service* [1985] A.C. 374.

[44] Imperfect understanding of the scope of surviving prerogative powers—what Tony Benn has described as their "subterranean nature"—may also inhibit effective *political* control of their exercise.

[45] Sir Stephen Sedley, "The Crown in its own Courts" in *The Golden Metwand and the Crooked Cord: Essays on Public law in honour of Sir William Wade Q.C.* (Forsyth and Hare eds, Oxford University Press, Oxford, 1998), p.262.

[46] A number of the privileges as developed at Westminster have been extended to the Scottish Parliament by virtue of SA 1998.

[47] Although the privilege of freedom of speech was given statutory force by the Bill of Rights 1689, art.9.

"conventions, understandings, habits or practices which, though they may regulate the conduct of the several members of the sovereign power, of the ministry, or of their officials, are not in reality laws at all since they are not enforced by the courts. This portion of constitutional law may, for the sake of distinction, be termed the 'conventions of the constitution' or 'constitutional morality'."[48]

For Dicey, the central significance of constitutional conventions was that they prescribed the manner in which the prerogatives of the Crown (or of ministers or servants of the Crown) fell to be exercised. This far from exhausts the field, but it is certainly true that these are the most important, or most clearly established, conventions, and chief amongst them is the convention which requires that the Queen act only on the advice of her ministers. Yet, as we shall see, even this rule may admit of exceptions in certain circumstances, which begs the question: how is it possible to speak of conventions as "rules" of the constitution at all, if it is neither necessary that they be always obeyed nor possible (through recourse to the courts) to enforce their observance?[49]

In putting these questions, one risks falling into the error of equating conventions with legal rules. They are not legal rules, by definition. Legal rules are the product of sources we recognise as law-constitutive: the Queen in Parliament, the Scottish Parliament acting within the sphere of its competence, and the courts. Conventions, by contrast, are founded on practice and precedent. Breach of a legal rule—stealing, speeding, committing murder—does not invalidate the rule. Breach of a convention, on the other hand, may have a destructive effect, depending on the "degree of stringency and definiteness" the convention possesses.[50] Short of that, the breach may restrict the range of circumstances over which the convention is felt to hold sway, or diminish its binding force within its allotted sphere.[51] What is critical to the crystallisation and survival of a convention, however, is that it has this binding quality: as Professor Munro puts it, "feeling obliged" is a necessary condition for the existence of a convention, but neither a necessary nor a sufficient condition for the existence of a legal rule.[52] This observation may also help us to clarify what we mean

---

[48] Dicey, *An Introduction to the Law of the Constitution, op.cit.*, p.24. His insight was not a new one. Prof. Mitchell's *Constitutional Law*, for example, cites Gilbert Stuart who wrote in his *Public Law of Scotland* (1779) that "habits tend to establish a rule, and custom is often as effectual as law."

[49] As to the judicial non-enforceability of convention, see *Attorney-General v Jonathan Cape Ltd* [1976] 1 Q.B. 752.

[50] See F. W. Maitland, *The Constitutional History of England* (1908), p.398.

[51] See J. Jaconelli, "The Nature of Constitutional Convention" [1999] L.S. 24 at 33.

[52] C. R. Munro, *Studies in Constitutional Law* (2nd ed., Butterworths, London, 1999), pp.78–87.

when we speak of "breaches" of convention. The very language betrays a sense of being obliged to act in a particular way, whether or not one does so act, and an expectation of criticism if one acts otherwise. It also suggests that a constitutional actor who acts in a manner other than that ordained by convention will have thought long and hard before doing so, and will probably feel (rightly or wrongly) that he has a good reason for acting in the way he has chosen.[53] For these reasons, the term "breach" may not always, or necessarily, be apposite: "conventions are always emerging, crystallising and dissolving, and it is sometimes questionable whether a convention has been broken or has simply changed."[54] Like morality in a general sense, conventions as the morality of the constitution are a restraint on constitutional behaviour, but a more or less elastic one depending on the sanctity of the convention and the circumstances in which it falls to be applied.

This is amply illustrated by reference to the cardinal convention of the constitution noted above, whereby the Queen is required to exercise her personal prerogatives—assenting to legislation, dissolving Parliament, appointing a Prime Minister and so on—only on ministerial advice. Constitutional practice is consistent (if not altogether without ambiguity) and the reasons for it can be located in the importance we attach to such values as responsible government and democratic accountability. Thus in normal circumstances, the Queen will dissolve Parliament when advised to do so by the Prime Minister, and cause the writs to be issued accordingly for a general election. Following the election, she will appoint as Prime Minister the leader of the party having an overall majority of seats in the House of Commons, on the basis that the Prime Minister must be able to command the confidence of the Commons. The crunch comes, however, where no one party has an overall majority of seats: where Parliament, to put it another way, is hung. Does the Queen then exercise a personal discretion? The answer, provided all constitutional actors behave in a suitably statesmanlike way and follow the guidance provided by the precedents, should be "no". If there is misbehaviour on the part of political leaders, however, then the answer may be "yes".

---

[53] Jaconelli, above, discusses this point under reference to Ronald Dworkin's account of the nature of practices in *Law's Empire* (Fontana, London, 1986), which holds that practices have an element of uncertainty which is open to interpretative dispute. On this view, it is not enough to act solely on the basis of the "raw empirical data" consisting in past precedents; rather, one must supplement the data with questions of the rationale for applying the convention in the present circumstances.

[54] C. Turpin, *British Government and the Constitution: Texts, Cases and Materials* (5th ed., Butterworths, London, 2002), p.116.

The question has arisen on numerous occasions in the past **1–07** century.[55] In December 1923, Stanley Baldwin lost his overall majority in the Commons, although his remained the largest party. As the incumbent, he continued in office as Prime Minister and waited to meet Parliament. He was then defeated in the vote on the King's Speech, at which point, being plainly incapable of commanding the confidence of the Commons, he resigned. The King sent for Ramsay Macdonald, leader of the Labour Party, and invited him to form a government (the first Labour government, and a minority government, but one that might be expected to survive for a reasonable period with Liberal support).[56] By 1929, Baldwin was back in office "but got out again ere long".[57] As in 1923, no one party had an overall majority; but this time, the Conservatives were no longer the largest party in the House. Baldwin resigned immediately and, as before, the King sent for Macdonald. In neither case was royal discretion involved; political circumstances dictated the outcome.

There was no possibility of Baldwin forming a minority or coalition government in 1929, but had there been he would have been entitled to remain in office in order to explore it. So Edward Heath spent the four days following the general election of February 1974 sounding out the Liberal Party about a coalition government containing Liberal M.P.s, and only resigned when those negotiations foundered. The Labour Party was the largest party in the Commons by five seats, though lacking an overall majority, and had already declared its willingness to form a government with no support from any other party. The Queen duly sent for Harold Wilson.[58]

---

[55] It appears that some thought was given "in the usual circles" to the possibility of a hung Parliament prior to the 1992 general election, for on the state of the opinion polls it seemed a probable outcome. In the event, John Major was returned as P.M. with a majority of 19; during the course of his rather ill-starred premiership, that majority evaporated (latterly by withdrawal of the Conservative whip from 12 "Tory rebels") and by the end the P.M. was reliant on the support of Ulster Unionist M.P.s.

[56] The party balance after the Dec. 1923 election was 258 seats for the Conservatives under Baldwin, 191 seats for Labour and 159 for the Liberals. The fault line between the Conservatives, on the one hand, and Labour and the Liberals, on the other, turned on free trade.

[57] M. Spark, *The Prime of Miss Jean Brodie*.

[58] More problematic was the Queen's role not in the choice of a P.M. directly, but indirectly through her active role in the choice of leader of the Conservative Party following Anthony Eden's resignation on grounds of ill-health in 1957 and Harold Macmillan's resignation, on the same grounds, in 1963. There was no general election in either case, and no need of one, since whoever emerged (and the word is apt) as party leader would have been able to command the confidence of the Commons. But both episodes were regarded as having drawn the Queen further into matters of political controversy than was appropriate, and in 1965 the Conservatives adopted a leadership election procedure to deal with such situations.

In none of these situations was the role of the Sovereign anything other than formal. But what if, instead of resigning in 1974, Heath had advised the Queen to dissolve the newly elected Parliament on the grounds that, as it stood, it was incapable of sustaining a government in office? In such a situation, there is much force in the view that the Queen would be entitled to make her own assessment of the political landscape and reject the advice tendered if she found it wanting.[59] As King George VI's Private Secretary put it in a letter to *The Times* in 1951:

"The Sovereign could properly refuse a dissolution if satisfied that: a) the existing Parliament is still vital, viable and capable of doing its job; b) a general election would be detrimental to the national economy; c) he could rely on finding another Prime Minister who could carry on his government for a reasonable period with a working majority."

As it was, Mr Heath behaved with impeccable constitutional propriety, leaving Mr Wilson to soldier on at the head of a minority administration. Wilson assumed that a dissolution was his for the asking at a time of his choice, with or without defeat on a motion of confidence, and in the unusually volatile circumstances of 1974 he was probably right.[60] But he might not have been right if, in the meantime, the Conservatives and Liberals had managed to agree on some form of coalition, because then an administration could have been formed from the existing Parliament.

1–08   What does this tell us about the conventions surrounding the dissolution of Parliament and choice of Prime Minister? It gives the lie to arguments that the Sovereign is always, absolutely bound to adhere to the advice given by her ministers. That is not to say that the personal prerogatives should be exercised in the face of advice in anything other than the most exceptional circumstances, if for no other reason than the damage done to the reputation of the monarchy by incautious intervention. Thus in 1926, the minority Liberal Prime Minister in Canada requested a dissolution from the Sovereign's representative, the Governor-General. The Governor-General believed that the Conservative leader could

---

[59] Even then, however, she would act on advice. Note, *e.g.* that not only the P.M. and Cabinet members, but also the Leader of the Opposition and other senior parliamentarians are appointed Privy Councillors, and might as such be consulted on "privy council" terms, which is to say in complete secrecy.

[60] Mr Wilson requested a dissolution in Oct. 1974, and was returned with an overall majority of five. He resigned in 1976, handing over to James Callaghan, who found himself in a position not unlike that of Mr Major nearly 20 years later, reliant (while it lasted) on the "Lib-Lab Pact". His administration was finally brought down by the loss (by one vote) of a motion of no confidence tabled by the SNP members in Apr. 1979.

form a government having majority support in the existing Parliament, and refused. The Prime Minister resigned and the Governor-General appointed the Conservative leader in his place. Days later, the new government was defeated on a motion of confidence, leading to the dissolution which had been denied to its Liberal predecessor. In the general election that followed, the Liberals were returned with a convincing majority. Again, in 1975, the Governor-General of Australia was moved to exercise the prerogative of dismissing a Prime Minister and his government.[61] The Australian Senate (in which the opposition has a majority) refused to pass money bills authorising government expenditure, which led to a rapid depletion in the funds available to maintain public services. The Prime Minister, Gough Whitlam, requested the Governor-General to dissolve the Senate. The Governor-General insisted on a full dissolution so that a general election could be held. When Mr Whitlam refused to change his advice, the Governor-General dismissed him and his government and appointed the Leader of the Opposition, Mr Fraser, in his place on condition that he would guarantee supply and advise a dissolution and general election.[62]

It is not obvious that the circumstances of either case were so extreme as to justify departure from the normal convention. In the Whitlam case, for instance, the more astute course would have been to follow the advice given and let the electorate decide, in the fullness of time, whether Mr Whitlam's advice had been sound. Resolution of the crisis would then have rested where it properly belonged, firmly in the arena of democratic politics. On this view, the Sovereign should only exercise her prerogatives personally and without advice where the advice tendered is clearly an abuse of the system or where necessary to safeguard the parliamentary and democratic bases of the constitution.[63] The point remains that even this convention is less than absolute in its terms, and does not altogether exclude the possibility of the Sovereign exercising effective political power. This may not commend itself to those of republican bent. On the other hand, it works, and it is not as

---

[61] Although the exercise of the prerogative of dismissal had been described not so very long before as "not being within the scope of practical politics": *Adegbenro v Akintola* [1964] A.C. 614 at 631, *per* Lord Radcliffe.

[62] The subsequent election was convincingly won by the opposition Country and Liberal parties, which formed a coalition government under Fraser. See, generally, Turpin, *British Government and the Constitution*, *op.cit.*, pp.202, 203.

[63] *e.g.* where a government failed to seek a dissolution after the expiry of the five-year period prescribed in the Parliament Act 1911 as the maximum duration of any Parliament. Another example, suggested by H. Calvert, *Constitutional Law in Northern Ireland* (1968), envisages (improbably, in the present writer's view) the Queen refusing Royal Assent to a bill to alter the position of NI as part of the UK without the consent of the people of NI.

though the alternative solutions to such occasional crises are themselves free of problems.[64]

1–09   Other conventions are less prescriptive still, perhaps not least the convention of ministerial responsibility. This has a collective and an individual dimension. Collective ministerial responsibility dictates that a minister must publicly defend the policies of the government collectively agreed upon, and must resign office if he is unable to do so. Individual ministerial responsibility in its classic form involves the minister in charge of a government department assuming responsibility for all that is done by his officials in his name, such that an official's mistake is deemed to be the minister's mistake and, if sufficiently serious, warrant for his resignation. The sanction attaching to a lapse from collective ministerial responsibility is clear enough: the minister may simply be sacked. The sanction attaching to a departure from the strictures of individual ministerial responsibility, however, is less clear. In the days when Parliament was less apt to operate on rigid party lines, M.P.s might have forced an incompetent minister's resignation by withdrawing their confidence from him. Now, this is virtually inconceivable provided the government has majority support: government backbenchers are unlikely, to put it mildly, to force the resignation of one of their own. Is there, then, evidence that ministers resign in circumstances of departmental failure through a sense of obligation to do so? Professor Finer doubted it.[65] Having studied the instances of ministerial resignation over the course of the preceding century, he concluded that:

> "All [the convention] says (on examination) is that if the minister is yielding, his Prime Minister unbending and his party out for his blood—no matter how serious or trivial the reason—the minister will find himself without parliamentary support. [But] that is a statement of fact, not a code."

It is true that ministers do not routinely fall on their swords in the manner the convention seems to prescribe.[66] In 1954, Sir Thomas Dugdale resigned as Minister of Agriculture after an inquiry found maladministration by officials in his department. Again in 1982, the

---

[64] See A. Tomkins, "In Defence of the Political Constitution" [2002] 22 O.J.L.S. 157. The author contrasts the British constitutional handling of a hung Parliament with the débâcle that followed the American Presidential election in 2000, suggesting that the latter demonstrates the futility and undesirability of seeking to find the answer to all political disputes in law (see *Bush v Gore* (2000) 121 S. Ct 525).

[65] S. E. Finer, "The Individual Responsibility of Ministers" [1956] 34 *Public Administration* 377.

[66] Resignation on grounds of personal or financial embarrassment is far more common, but has little if anything to do with departmental failure.

Foreign Secretary, Lord Carrington, and two Foreign Office ministers resigned after it was claimed that the Foreign Office had
culpably misinterpreted signals of Argentinian intention in the
period preceding the Falklands conflict[67]; and in 1986, the Home
Secretary, Leon Brittan M.P., resigned after one of his officials
leaked confidential legal advice to the press. It is a patchy record of
compliance. But these ministers at least felt an obligation to resign,
and "in everyday political discourse, too, the rule continues to be
treated as if it had practical content."[68] Thus we need not accept
Finer's conclusion that there is no convention of resignation at all,
even if we concede that it is not a convention of great "stringency
and definiteness". But, as we shall see in Chapter 5, it does not
necessarily do to focus exclusively on the "blame and sanction"
aspect of the convention of ministerial responsibility. It has been
forcefully argued that the convention has had a strong influence on
the internal structuring of government.[69] Moreover, in point of
fact, ministers do answer to Parliament for the actions and
decisions of their departments, and do not routinely or sys-
tematically mislead Parliament in doing so. Viewed thus, ministerial plank-walking may be less important than the adequacy (or
otherwise) of the convention as a vehicle for securing the accountability of the executive to Parliament.

So far we have been talking about the operation of constitutional **1-10**
conventions at the UK level. To what extent may it be said that
conventions have developed in the context of the devolved Scottish
institutions? It may still be too soon to speak of "indigenous"
conventions, the products of consistent and uniform practice. But
two aspects of the devolution settlement are interesting in this
regard. First, the Scotland Act clothes in the language of legislation
the conventions that, at Westminster, govern the dissolution of
Parliament and choice of Prime Minister.[70] The First Minister is
denied the luxury of choosing, at a time advantageous to his party's
electoral prospects, when to advise a dissolution: under section
2(2) of the Act, a general election will ordinarily be held on the

---

[67] This despite the fact that the P.M. was reluctant to let them go, and despite an
official inquiry which dismissed the allegations made against the Foreign Office.
[68] C. R. Munro, *Studies, op.cit.*, p.86.
[69] T. Daintith and A. Page, *The Executive in the Constitution* (Oxford University
Press, Oxford, 1999).
[70] This translation of conventional rules into legal rules is not unknown at the UK
level. Possibly the most prominent instance is found in the Parliament Act 1911,
which abrogated the power of the House of Lords to suspend the enactment of a
"money bill" for more than one month, and dispensed with the consent of the
Lords to other public bills other than a bill to extend the life of Parliament
provided the measure was approved afresh by the Commons in the two
subsequent sessions (reduced to one session by the Parliament Act 1949). The
1911 Act was triggered by the House of Lords' refusal to approve the Liberal
budget of 1909, in breach of convention.

first Thursday in May every four years, in which event the
Parliament will be dissolved at the beginning of a period specified
by the Secretary of State by order under section 12[71] and is
required to meet within seven days of the date of the poll. A
limited measure of flexibility is provided by section 2(5), whereby
the Presiding Officer of the Scottish Parliament may propose a
date other than the first Thursday in May, but within one month of
that date, as the day for the holding of the poll. If the Presiding
Officer does propose a different date, the Queen *may* by proclamation dissolve the Parliament and require the election to be held on
the date proposed. The provision preserves the Queen's discretion,
and while no doubt the intention is that she would follow advice in
the ordinary way, the preservation—just in case?—of that discretion is noteworthy.[72] In the event that an extraordinary general
election requires to be held,[73] it is, again, for the Presiding Officer
to propose a date, and for the Queen by proclamation to give
effect to that proposal; but again the language is permissive. As to
the choice of First Minister, the appointment is made by the
Queen from among the members of the Scottish Parliament.
Section 46(4) of the Scotland Act provides that the Presiding
Officer shall recommend to the Queen the appointment of that
MSP who is nominated by the Parliament in accordance with the
section. Nowhere does the Act state in terms that the nomination
must be accepted, but the intention of the section is clear; whatever
arguments might be made about the strict legal position, here at
least we can probably speak of a convention, even at this stage, that
the Queen will act in this matter on the advice of the Presiding
Officer alone.

Secondly, there is said to be a convention—the "Sewel
convention"—whereby Westminster is obliged to seek the consent
of the Scottish Parliament before proceeding to enact legislation
touching on devolved matters.[74] This is at variance with section

---

[71] s.12 confers power on the Secretary of State to make provision in relation to
Scottish elections.

[72] The power is a statutory power, albeit that it covers the same ground as the
Queen's prerogative of dissolution at Westminster. It should not be thought,
however, that the placing of the power on a statutory footing renders its exercise
any more susceptible to judicial review. While as a matter of principle it is likely
that a court would accept it had jurisdiction to entertain an application for review
of the exercise or non-exercise of the Queen's power under s.5(2), it is equally
likely that it would regard the subject matter of the power as non-justiciable.

[73] In terms of SA 1998, s.3(1), where the Parliament resolves that it should be
dissolved (by a two-thirds majority vote if the resolution is passed on a division)
or where the prescribed period (normally 28 days) elapses without the nomination of a First Minister.

[74] See B. Winetrobe, "Counter-devolution? The Sewel convention on devolved
legislation at Westminster" (2001) 6 SLPQ 286; N. Burrows, "It's Scotland's
Parliament: Let Scotland's Parliament Legislate", 2002 J.R. 213; A. Page and A.
Batey, "Scotland's Other Parliament: Westminster Legislation about Devolved
Matters in Scotland since Devolution" [2002] P.L. 501.

28(7) of the Scotland Act, which provides that the devolution of legislative competence to the Scottish Parliament "does not affect the power of the United Kingdom Parliament to make laws for Scotland." The Sewel convention is named for the Scottish Office Minister who, during the parliamentary debates on the Scotland Bill, sought to assuage concern that, after devolution, Westminster would exploit its unimpaired legislative competence to frustrate the work of the Scottish Parliament: "The government would expect a convention to be established that Westminster would not normally legislate with regard to devolved matters in Scotland without the consent of the Scottish Parliament."[75] This principle was endorsed by the House of Commons Select Committee on Procedure in 1999,[76] and further reinforced by guidance concerning its operation in the Memorandum of Understanding between the UK government and Scottish Executive and documents issued by the Privy Council Office in 1999 and by the Constitution and Parliamentary Secretariat in 2001. Where consent is required, it is sought by way of a "Sewel motion" laid before the Scottish Parliament by the appropriate Scottish Minister following consultation between the UK government and the Scottish Executive.

It was not anticipated that Sewel motions would be used **1–11** routinely. In fact, they are commonplace. In such circumstances, it is difficult to speak of an emergent convention whereby Westminster refrains from legislating *at all* within the sphere of devolved competence. At most, the expectation is that on each occasion it does so, Westminster will first obtain the consent of the Scottish Parliament (and refrain from legislating if such consent is refused). So far, Westminster has sought, and obtained, the Scottish Parliament's consent each time it has wished to enact legislation dealing with devolved matters. We have both consistent practice and good reasons therefor. But the Sewel convention raises interesting doctrinal points. First, does it merit the name? Is it possible for a convention in the true sense of the term to "spring fully armed from the head of a particular procedure"?[77] Jaconelli suggests that, even if ultimately we may trace the emergence of a convention back to a particular event, such as a statement made in the legislature, the statement "attains that status in truth only when [it has] set in motion a chain of actions and expectations based on [its] observance." Certainly, Lord Sewel's original statement was followed by various endorsements, but their value may be questioned. The memorandum of understanding is in the nature of an agreement between two governments of near identical political stripe.

---

[75] *Hansard*, HL Vol.???, col. 791 (July 21, 1998).
[76] *Report on the Procedural Consequences of Devolution* 592.
[77] J. Jaconelli, "The Nature of Constitutional Convention" [1999] L.S. 24 at 33.

Would a memorandum of understanding between a Conservative government in London and an SNP Executive in Scotland be worded in quite the same way?[78] As a rule, agreements are regarded as binding only those who are party to them; but the essence of a constitutional convention is that it binds constitutional actors whether they like it or not. The same sort of objection might be levelled at the 1999 and 2001 guidance (if not at the conclusions of the Select Committee on Procedure): they reflect an inter-governmental comity born out of the coincidence of political control, but that it necessarily contingent.

Secondly, the terms in which Sewel tends to be discussed suggest not only that we take its force as a constitutional convention for granted but that we place it on the spectrum of "stringency and definiteness" rather further towards the convention obliging the Queen to act on ministerial advice than to, say, the convention of ministerial resignation. Does either conclusion follow? If "feeling obliged" is a necessary component of a constitutional convention, we might wish to pause before ascribing that status to Lord Sewel's dictum. What if a future Scottish Parliament with a majority of nationalist members were to refuse all Sewel motions on principle,[79] even where the arguments for UK-wide legislation were compelling? Would Westminster "feel obliged" to refrain from legislating within the sphere of devolved competence? We may not yet have reached the point at which it is possible to say so conclusively. The real test of a convention comes when it constrains constitutional actors to behave in a way other than that which they would, left to themselves, have chosen; and Sewel has still to be tested in this way.[80]

INTERNATIONAL LAW

1–12 As a Member State of the European Union, the United Kingdom is obliged to give effect to and apply directly effective norms of EU law, and that obligation is discharged through the medium of the European Communities Act 1972. The incorporation of EU law

---

[78] Would there even *be* a Memorandum of Understanding?

[79] Assuming the UK government even bothered to seek its consent.

[80] As to the question whether an Act of the Westminster Parliament trenching on the devolved competence of the Scottish Parliament would alter the devolution settlement—by "impliedly repealing or amending" the SA 1998, Sch.5 (see Burrows, n.74)—I have argued elsewhere that it would not, and that the Scottish Parliament would be quite entitled to enact legislation depriving the Westminster Act of its effect north of the border: see J. Munro, "Thoughts on the Sewel Convention", 2003 S.L.T. (News) 194. If Westminster wishes to alter the devolution settlement, in other words, it would require to do expressly, either by way of primary legislation or an Order in Council in terms of SA 1998, s.30.

has had momentous consequences for our constitutional law, as we shall see in chapter 2. But to what extent might other international legal norms serve as a source of domestic constitutional law?

Rules of *customary* international law, the product of consistent and uniform state practice which comes to reflect an *opinio juris* that particular conduct is proscribed or, as the case may be, required by international law, constitute rules of Scots law, whether or not codified in international treaties.[81] Thus, established principles of international humanitarian law on the prohibition of torture and other crimes against humanity would form part of Scots law independently of their incorporation (or otherwise) into national law by statutes. Rules of international law derived from treaties (unless they have customary law status) differ. Some constitutional systems, which are described as "monist", hold that, when a state signs and ratifies an international treaty, the contents of that treaty automatically become part of its domestic law, directly enforceable as such before its courts. The United Kingdom, however, subscribes to the "dualist" position, which holds that a treaty does not form part of national law unless and until incorporated into the law by legislation. That failing, the treaty cannot create rights or duties enforceable before the national courts. The rationale for this is that the making of a treaty is an executive, not a legislative, act, and the government should not be permitted to burden citizens with obligations unsanctioned by Parliament.[82] Lord Steyn has noted, extra-curially, that this reasoning is quite beside the point in relation to human rights treaties, which by definition do not impose burdens on individuals.[83]

---

[81] *Lord Advocate's Ref. (No.1 of 2000)*, 2001 S.C.C.R. 296. Thus it follows that, whereas questions of foreign law (including English law) constitute questions of fact on which evidence may be led, questions of customary international law constitute questions of law for the judge to determine.

[82] See *J. H. Rayner (Mincing Lane) Ltd v Dept of Trade and Industry* [1990] 2 A.C. 418 at 500, *per* Lord Oliver (the *International Tin Council* case).

[83] Lord Steyn, "Democracy Through Law" [2002] E.H.R.L.R. 723. Under reference to *Thomas v Baptiste* [2000] 2 A.C. 1 and *Lewis v Attorney-General of Jamaica* [2000] 3 W.L.R. 1785, in which the Judicial Committee of the Privy Council held that condemned men in Caribbean countries could not be executed until the determination of their appeals to the Inter-American Human Rights Committee, a body whose jurisdiction depends upon an unincorporated treaty, Lord Steyn suggests that there is "scope for the evolution of a more realistic notion", which would place human rights treaties in a special category. This may be unduly optimistic. It should however be noted that the ECtHR may take account of the terms of unincorporated international treaties to which the UK is party in reaching its decision on whether there has been a violation of the Convention rights: see *e.g. Wilson v United Kingdom* (2002) 35 E.H.R.R. 523, where regard was had to the European Social Charter 1961 and ILO Conventions Nos 87 and 98.

Nonetheless, the weight of authority remains firmly in favour of dualist orthodoxy.[84]

This is not to say that international treaties have been denied any domestic legal effect. As Diplock L.J. held in *Salomon v Commissioners of Customs and Excise*[85]:

> "There is a *prima facie* presumption that Parliament does not intend to act in breach of international law, including therein specified treaty obligations; and if one of the meanings that can reasonably be attributed to the legislation is consonant with the treaty obligations and another or others are not, the meaning which is so consonant is to be preferred."

Thus where a statutory provision was ambiguous, international treaties to which the United Kingdom was party could be relied on as an aid to construction. As we shall see, prior to the incorporation of the "Convention rights" by the Human Rights Act 1998, the European Convention on Human Rights was particularly influential in this respect.[86] But there is no reason in principle why exactly the same approach should not apply in relation to other, as yet unincorporated, treaty provisions[87]; nor any reason why international legal norms, even though unincorporated, should not continue to influence the development of the common law in appropriate circumstances.

1–13   A technique of more recent provenance (and perhaps questionable status) is to treat the executive act of entering into an international treaty, absent any indications to the contrary, as the

---

[84] See, in addition to the *International Tin Council* case ([1990] 2 A.C. 418), *R v Lyons* [2002] 3 W.L.R. 1562, paras 27, 28, *per* Lord Hoffmann; and *Whaley v Lord Advocate*, June 20, 2003, paras 41–44, *per* Lord Brodie.

[85] [1967] 2 QB 116 at 143.

[86] If only latterly in Scotland. It was held in *Kaur v Lord Advocate*, 1980 S.C. 319 that, "as the Convention was not part of the municipal law of the United Kingdom, the court was not, so far as Scotland was concerned, entitled to have regard to the Convention either as an aid to construction or otherwise" (at 330, *per* Lord Ross). This remained the position in Scots law until the First Division held in *T, Petr*, 1997 S.L.T. 724, that it could no longer be justified and should be departed from. S.3 of the HRA 1998 now requires the courts to read and give effect to all legislation, whenever enacted, consistently with the Convention rights so far as possible to do so; s.4 authorises certain higher courts to make declarations of incompatibility in respect of provisions of primary legislation which cannot be so construed (and it should be noted that provisions of Acts of the Scottish Parliament which are incompatible with the Convention rights are invalid and may be struck down accordingly).

[87] Indeed reference is regularly made to such treaties as the Universal Declaration of Human Rights, the International Covenant on Civil and Political Rights and the UN Convention on the Rights of the Child: see R. Clayton and H. Tomlinson, *The Law of Human Rights* (Oxford University Press, Oxford, 2000), paras 2.09–2.60.

foundation for a "legitimate expectation" that the government and its agencies will thereafter act in accordance with the treaty. This approach is derived from the decision of the High Court of Australia in *Minister for Immigration and Ethnic Affairs v Teoh*,[88] as approved by the English courts on a number of occasions[89] and latterly also by the Court of Session in Scotland.[90] There is a certain logic to the proposition: on ordinary principles,[91] a legitimate expectation may be created by the clear, unambiguous and unqualified representation (which may be implied by conduct) of a public authority, and there is no obvious reason why the act of signing and ratifying a treaty should not have that quality. On the other hand, as Laws L.J. noted in *R (European Roma Rights Centre) v Immigration Officer at Prague Airport*,[92] the nub of the argument is that an international treaty may have distinct and enforceable effects in domestic law independently of its incorporation by Parliament, and "that is a constitutional solecism".[93] Unless there is a fundamental reappraisal of our dualist tradition, it is difficult to disagree with this conclusion.

---

[88] (1995) 183 C.L.R. 273 at 291, *per* Mason and Deane JJ.
[89] See in particular *R v S of S for the Home Dept, ex p. Ahmed and Patel* [1999] Imm A.R. 22; *R v Uxbridge Mags Ct, ex p. Adimi* [2001] Q.B. 667.
[90] See *Ibrahim v S of S for the Home Dept*, Mar. 20, 2002 (unreported); *Khairandish v S of S for the Home Dept*, Apr. 23, 2003 (unreported).
[91] As to which, see Ch.12.
[92] [2003] All E.R. (D) 260, para.99.
[93] Simon Brown L.J., who approved and applied the *Teoh*, n.88, approach in *Adimi*, above, similarly expressed doubts about the validity of that approach in *European Roma Rights Centre*, n.92 (see para.51). It emerged in the latter case that the Court of Appeal had already rejected the *Teoh* approach in *Chundrawadra v Immigration Appeal Tribunal* [1988] Imm A.R. 161 and again in *Behluli v S of S for the Home Dept* [1998] Imm A.R. 407, neither of which was cited in *Ahmed and Patel*, n.89, or *Adimi*.

CHAPTER 2

FOUNDATIONS

PARLIAMENTARY SUPREMACY

2–01   The Diceyan doctrine of parliamentary sovereignty, or supremacy, means two things: "Parliament . . . has . . . the right to make or unmake any law whatever; and . . . no person or body is recognised . . . as having a right to override or set aside the legislation of Parliament."[1] There is a wealth of practice, precedent and authority to support both propositions. As to the first, it is of course true that "one does not establish that Parliament can do anything merely by pointing to a number of things that it has done, however impressive",[2] but at least some support for Dicey's thesis may be drawn from the many statutes, before and since Dicey's time, whereby Parliament has effected important constitutional changes, or enacted retrospective or extra-territorial legislation. As to the second, the evidence is stronger. The courts have persistently rebuffed invitations by litigants to question the validity of statutes, whether the arguments for invalidity are advanced on substantive or procedural grounds. In the first case, where it is contended that the content of an enactment is in some sense beyond the powers of Parliament, the courts have made clear that "what the statute itself enacts cannot be unlawful . . . and it is not for the court to say that a parliamentary enactment, the highest law in this country, is illegal."[3] In the second, the argument is that because of some defect in parliamentary procedure, what purports to be an Act of Parliament is not in fact an Act of Parliament at all, and as such is liable to judicial control. The inconsistency of the argument with

---

[1] A. V. Dicey, *The Law of the Constitution* (10th ed., Macmillan, London, 1959), pp.39, 40.

[2] C.R. Munro, *Studies in Constitutional Law* (2nd ed., Butterworths, London, 1999), p.13.

[3] *Cheney v Conn* [1968] 1 W.L.R. 242 at 247, *per* Ungoed-Thomas J. The argument there was that assessments of tax made under a Finance Act were unlawful as being in part for a purpose contrary to international law (namely, the maintenance of nuclear weapons). See to similar effect the full bench decision of the Inner House of the Court of Session in *Mortensen v Peters* (1906) 8 F. (J.) 93, the continuing force of which was affirmed by Lord Brodie in *Whaley v Lord Advocate*, Outer House, June 20, 2003 (not yet reported).

parliamentary privilege, in particular that aspect of privilege whereby Parliament claims exclusive jurisdiction over its own internal affairs, is plain; and although the courts have been prepared to defy assertions of privilege they consider to be ill-founded in law,[4] they have acquiesced here. As Lord Campbell put it in *Edinburgh & Dalkeith Ry v Wauchope*:

> "All that a Court of Justice can do is look to the Parliamentary Roll; if from that it should appear that a Bill has passed both Houses and received the Royal Assent, no Court of Justice can inquire into the mode in which it was introduced into Parliament, not into what was done previous to its introduction, or what passed in Parliament during its progress through Parliament."[5]

But Dicey took matters further, arguing that it was implicit in all of this that sovereignty resided in the Parliament for the time being: "a sovereign power cannot, while retaining its sovereign character, restrict its own powers". Sovereignty was continuing, and indeed, on Dicey's logic, inescapable short of revolution. It followed that there could be no difference in the "ranking" of Acts of Parliament. Consequently, any conflict between an Act of the current Parliament and an Act of one of its predecessors must be resolved in favour of the former: the later statute impliedly repeals the earlier. Again, there is judicial support for this view:

> "The legislature cannot . . . bind itself as to the form of subsequent legislation, and it is impossible for Parliament to enact that in a subsequent statute dealing with the same subject matter there can be no implied repeal. If in a subsequent Act Parliament chooses to make it plain that the earlier statute is being to some extent repealed, effect must be given to that intention just because it is the will of Parliament."[6]

---

[4] See most notably the stand-off between courts and Parliament in *Stockdale v Hansard* (1839) 9 Ad. & El. 1.

[5] (1842) 8 C.I. & F. 710, *per* Lord Campbell. For similar statements of what is termed the "enrolled bill rule" see *Lee v Bude and Torrington Junction Ry* (1871) L.R. 6 C.P. 576, *per* Willes J. ("If an Act of Parliament has been obtained improperly it is for the legislature to correct it by repealing it; but so long as it exists in law, the courts are bound to obey it") and, more recently, *Pickin v British Railways Board* [1974] A.C. 765, in which the House of Lords confirmed that the courts had no power to disregard an Act of Parliament, whether public or private, or to inquire into parliamentary procedures, even where, as here, it was alleged that the enactment of a private Act had been procured by fraud.

[6] *Ellen Street Estates Ltd v Minister of Health* [1934] 1 K.B. 590 at 597, *per* Maugham L.J. See also *Vauxhall Estates Ltd v Liverpool Corp.* [1932] 1 K.B. 733.

For Dicey, this inability to bind its successors was the only limitation on Parliament's otherwise absolute legislative authority. If correct, it carries a number of consequences. It implies that legally if not politically Parliament can revoke the irrevocable. It implies that Parliament can override earlier legislation however fundamental, even constitutive, it may be. It also implies that, were a Parliament to adopt legislation which it wished to "entrench", or protect from subsequent repeal or amendment, it could not do so effectively, because the courts will always look for and give effect to the latest expression of the will of Parliament. Does all of this really follow?

2–02   It has been argued that Parliament *did* bind its successors when legislating for the independence of former British colonies. For example, section 4 of the Statute of Westminster 1931 provided that no subsequent Act of Parliament would extend or be deemed to extend to a Dominion unless it was expressly declared in the Act that the Dominion had requested and consented to its enactment. Did Parliament thereby deprive itself of the competence to legislate for a Dominion even without the Dominion's request and consent? In *British Coal Corporation v R.*,[7] Lord Sankey L.C. described the notion that Parliament could repeal or disregard section 4 as "theory [having] no relation to realities"; in *Ndlwana v Hofmeyr*,[8] Stratford ACJ insisted that "freedom once conferred cannot be revoked." And that, without doubt, is true so far as it describes the effect before the courts of a former colony of an Act of the UK Parliament purporting to reassume legislative sovereignty over that colony. But the doctrine of parliamentary supremacy as Dicey stated it concerns what is legally valid, not what is politically possible, and in that regard concerns the relationship between Parliament and the UK courts, not the courts of any other jurisdiction. Such authority as exists suggests that the UK courts would treat such a resumption of legislative competence as valid. In 1965, the government of Southern Rhodesia unilaterally declared independence. Westminster reasserted its right to legislate for the territory in the Southern Rhodesia Act 1965, and in *Madzimbamuto v Lardner-Burke*,[9] the Judicial Committee of the Privy Council held that emergency regulations made by the rebel regime were void and that the provisions of UK statutes continued to have full legal force in Rhodesia. The Rhodesian courts refused to recognise the decisions of the Privy Council as binding on them, and in *R. v Ndhlovu*[10] held that the revolutionary constitution of 1965 was now the only lawful constitution of Rhodesia. But that

[7] [1935] A.C. 500.
[8] 1937 A.D. 229.
[9] [1969] 1 A.C. 645.
[10] (1968) 4 S.A. 515.

does not alter the fact that any Acts enacted by the UK Parliament for application to Rhodesia would have been recognised by the UK courts as valid and, so far as possible, enforceable. The same point emerges from the judgment of Sir Robert Megarry V.-C. in *Manuel v Attorney-General*,[11] in which Canadian Indian chiefs argued that the Canada Act 1982, an Act of the Westminster Parliament which "patriated" the Canadian constitution, was *ultra vires* and void. His Lordship held:

> "I have grave doubts about the theory of the transfer of sovereignty as affecting the competence of Parliament. . . . As a matter of law the courts recognise Parliament as being omnipotent in all save the power to destroy its own omnipotence. Under the authority of Parliament the courts of a territory may be released from their legal duty to obey Parliament, but that does not trench on the acceptance by the courts of all that Parliament does. Nor must validity in law be confused with practical enforceability."

If the end of the Empire did not impose constraints on the competence of the Westminster Parliament, would not logic suggest that Parliament's own constitutive instruments might have done so? Drawing on the special nature of the Acts and Treaty of Union as fundamental law, and upon indications in the language of the Union legislation that parts of it at least were intended to be unalterable, some have argued that Parliament cannot enjoy unfettered legislative competence because it was "born unfree".[12] Dicey conceded that the framers of the Union legislation might have sought to give certain provisions more than the ordinary effect of statutes, but refuted any suggestion that this was what they achieved: "the history of legislation in respect of these very Acts affords the strongest proof of the futility inherent in every attempt of one sovereign legislature to restrain the action of another equally sovereign legislature."[13] Here Dicey was referring to the Anglo-Irish as well as the Anglo-Scottish union legislation. The Union with Ireland Act 1800 contained language similar to that of the 1707 Treaty. Quite clearly, it failed to have the desired effect: the union itself was dissolved (partially) by an ordinary statute, the Irish Free State (Constitution) Act 1922. While the Anglo-Scottish union remains intact, it is nonetheless true that nearly all of the

---

[11] [1982] 3 W.L.R. 821 at 832.
[12] See *e.g.* T. B. Smith, "The Union of 1707 as Fundamental Law" [1957] P.L. 99; J. D. B. Mitchell, *Constitutional Law* (2nd ed., W. Green, Edinburgh, 1968), pp.93–98; N. MacCormick, "Does the United Kingdom Have a Constitution?" (1978) 29 N.I.L.Q. 1.
[13] Dicey, *The Law of the Constitution, op.cit.*, p.65.

provisions of the 1707 Treaty have been repealed or amended. In answer to this it has been said that Parliament has in the past refrained from legislating in a manner contrary to the Union agreement; and that where Parliament has enacted legislation in breach of the Union agreement,[14] it has done so only with the consent of the Scottish people.[15] The short answer to the first is: so what? Dicey never suggested that Parliament was unfettered by political or moral considerations; he argues, rather, for a lack of legally enforceable restraints on Parliament's competence.[16] As for the second argument, it seems to undermine the very fundamental status it seeks to attribute to the Union legislation: like any other statute, it may be changed of consent as signified in accordance with the procedures prescribed for that purpose for the time being.

It *is* true that some Scottish cases contain dicta sympathetic to the fundamental law argument. In *MacCormick* v *Lord Advocate*,[17] Lord President Cooper observed:

"The principle of the unlimited sovereignty of Parliament is a distinctively English principle which has no counterpart in Scottish constitutional law. . . . I have difficulty in seeing why it should have been supposed that the new Parliament of Great Britain must inherit all the peculiar characteristics of the English Parliament but none of the Scottish Parliament, as if all that happened in 1707 was that Scottish representatives were admitted to the Parliament of England. That is not what was done."

But, having apparently accepted that certain provisions of the Treaty were to be regarded as unalterable, his Lordship then seemed to doubt whether an allegation of breach of that funda-mental law would be "determinable as a justiciable issue in the

---

[14] There is some dubiety about how often Westminster has legislated in breach of the Union legislation (see M. Upton, " Marriage Vows of the Elephant: The constitution of 1707" (1989) 105 L.Q.R. 79), but "even the staunchest defender of [its] fundamental status would have to concede that this happened at least in the case of the Universities (Scotland) Act 1853" (which abolished the requirement that university teachers should subscribe to the Presbyterian Confession of Faith): N. Walker, *Stair Memorial Encyclopaedia* Reissue, *Constitutional Law*, para.63.

[15] In what manner this consent was supposed to be signified is never made clear, but presumably denotes the "consent" - so far as it goes - of Scottish MPs and peers at Westminster (in which case it is the consent of the Scottish people only in a fairly remote sense).

[16] See Munro, *Studies in Constitutional Law, op.cit.*, pp.135, 136; E. Wicks, "A New Constitution for a New State? The 1707 Union of England and Scotland" (2001) 117 L.Q.R. 109.

[17] 1953 S.C. 393 at 411.

courts of either Scotland or England."[18] Similarly in *Gibson v Lord Advocate*,[19] Lord Keith reserved his opinion as to the effect of hypothetical Acts of Parliament purporting to abolish the Church of Scotland or the Court of Session, but held that arguments about whether changes to Scots private law were "for the evident utility" of the subjects in Scotland in accordance with Article XVIII of the Treaty of Union would not be justiciable. More explicitly, Lord Kirkwood stated in *Murray v Rogers* that "there is . . . no machinery whereby the validity of an Act of Parliament can be brought under review by the courts."[20] If that is correct, then it closes the argument in Dicey's favour: if the courts are unwilling to entertain challenges to the conformity of new legislation with the Union agreement, then the fundamental law argument is significant only for its symbolism.[21] It may be hazarded, however, that if the courts would still decline to pronounce on the *validity* of an Act of Parliament said to be inconsistent with the Union agreement, they might now be prepared to pronounce on the issue of *compatibility* were it to be brought to their notice by someone having title and interest to do so. Indeed, as we shall see, the courts are now rather habituated to reviewing the compatibility of primary legislation with the Convention rights and Community law; that being so, there is no obvious reason why they should be less willing to review the compatibility of an Act of Parliament with some other "higher order" instrument.[22]

Some of Dicey's serried critics conceded that Parliament could **2–03** not bind itself as to the *content* of the future legislation, but insisted that it could bind itself as to the *manner and form* in which such legislation were to be passed. On this view, should Parliament wish to entrench a particular statute, it could provide in the Act that none of its provisions might be repealed or amended without, for example, a two-thirds majority vote in both Houses of Parliament.[23] The evidence relied on for this "new view" of

[18] Moreover, as has been said, the Lord President's conclusion in *MacCormick v Lord Advocate*, 1953 S.C. 393 that "the principle of the unlimited sovereignty of Parliament [has] no counterpart in Scottish constitutional law does not necessarily offer definitive guidance as to where, alternatively, sovereignty may be found within the Scottish constitution": see S. Tierney, "Constitutionalising the Role of the Judge: Scotland and the new order" in *Human Rights and Scots Law* (Boyle *et al*. eds, Hart Publishing, Oxford, 2002), p.72.
[19] 1975 SLT 134.
[20] 1992 SLT 221 at 228.
[21] As Walker puts it, "another resource to add to the normative argument about the venerability and continuing resilience of the Scottish claim to self government": *Stair Memorial Encyclopaedia* Reissue, *Constitutional Law*, para.65. On this score, see M. Addo and V. Smith, "The Relevance of Historical Fact to Certain Arguments relating to the Legal Significance of the Acts of Union" 1998 J.R. 37.
[22] On the "higher order" status of the Union legislation, see *Thoburn v Sunderland City Council* [2003] Q.B. 151 at paras 63–65, *per* Laws L.J., and above at pp.5–6.
[23] See, *e.g.* Sir Ivor Jennings, *The Law and the Constitution* (5th ed., 1959), pp.152–159; R. V. Heuston, *Essays in Constitutional Law* (2nd ed., 1964), Ch.1.

parliamentary supremacy is derived primarily from Commonwealth cases, notably *Attorney-General for New South Wales v Trethowan*[24] and *Bribery Commissioner v Ranasinghe*,[25] both decisions of the Privy Council; and the South African case of *Harris v Minister of the Interior*.[26]

Harris concerned the Separate Representation of Voters Act 1951, passed pursuant to the new *apartheid* policy by the Union Parliament of South Africa, acting by simple majority, both Houses sitting separately. Voters thereby deprived of their voting rights argued that the Act was invalid because contrary to the South Africa Act 1909, s.35 (an Act of the UK Parliament). Section 35 required certain legislation of the South African Parliament, including the 1951 Act, to be "passed by both Houses of Parliament *sitting together*, and at third reading . . . *agreed to by not less than two-thirds of the total number of members of both Houses*."[27] The South African government argued that the Union Parliament had since 1909 acquired full legislative sovereignty and so was free to disregard purported limitations on its sovereignty contained in section 35. Unanimously, the court rejected this argument and held the 1951 Act *ultra vires* and void. Centlivres C.J. stated that:

> "A State can unquestionably be sovereign although it has no legislature which is completely sovereign. . . . In the case of the Union, legal sovereignty is or may be divided between Parliament as ordinarily constituted and Parliament as constituted under [s.35]. Such a division of legislative powers is no derogation from the sovereignty of the Union and the mere fact that that division was enacted in a British statute which is still in force in the Union cannot affect the question in issue. . . . The South Africa Act . . . created the Parliament of the Union. It is that Act . . . which prescribes the manner in which the constituent elements of Parliament must function for the purpose of passing legislation. . . . [I]t follows that . . . courts of law have the power to declare the Act of 1951 invalid on the ground that it was not passed in conformity with the provisions of section 35."

This passage illustrates the nub of the manner and form argument. In identifying expressions of the sovereign will as an Act of Parliament, the courts need a rule, or rules, of recognition. Among other things, they need a rule defining what we mean by "Parliament" if they are correctly to identify one of its Acts. In *Harris*, the

---

[24] [1932] A.C. 526.
[25] [1965] A.C. 172.
[26] [1952] 1 T.L.R. 1245.
[27] Emphasis added.

constituent instrument of the Union Parliament contained such rules for the guidance of the courts in particular instances. Thus where an "Act of Parliament" is enacted by simple majority, both Houses sitting separately, in an area where the governing instrument defines "Parliament" as both Houses sitting together and acting by two-thirds majority, it is both right and logical for the courts to hold that what purports to be an "Act of Parliament" is *not*, in this instance, an Act of Parliament at all.

So far as it goes, this tells us little about the UK Parliament **2–04** because, as Lord Pearce put it in *Ranasinghe*, "in the United Kingdom there is no governing instrument which prescribes the law-making powers and the forms which are essential to those powers."[28] But the manner and form argument goes further. If the "UK Parliament" is bound by no definitions in any constituent instrument, its meaning is nonetheless subject to *common law* rules relied on by the courts in the identification of statutes. As a matter of common law, the courts accept that whatever the Queen in Parliament enacts, both Houses of Parliament sitting separately and acting by simple majority, is law. We know, however, that Parliament can change the common law. It must therefore follow that Parliament can change this common law rule and, in certain circumstances, substitute a different definition of what Parliament is for the purpose of identifying a valid Act of Parliament.

In truth, however, it may not so follow. As Wade wrote in 1955:

> "[T]he rule that the courts obey Acts of Parliament ... is above and beyond the reach of statute ... because it is itself the source of authority of statute. This puts it into a class by itself among rules of the common law. ... The rule of judicial obedience is in one sense a rule of common law, but in another sense—which applies to no other rule of common law—it is the ultimate *political* fact upon which the whole system of legislation hangs. Legislation owes its authority to the rule: the rule does not owe its authority to legislation. To say that Parliament can change the rule ... is to put the cart before the horse. ... The rule is unique in being unchangeable by Parliament- it is changed by revolution, not by legislation; it lies in the keeping of the courts and no Act of Parliament can take it from them."[29]

Such a revolution occurred in Rhodesia, when the Rhodesian courts ceased to recognise British statutes as supreme and relocated their rules of recognition—their criteria of legal validity—in

---

[28] *Bribery Commissioner v Ranasinghe* [1965] A.C. 172 at 195.
[29] H. W. R. Wade, "The Basis of Legal Sovereignty" (1955) C.L.J. 172 at 187 (an analysis approved by Lord Denning M.R. in *Blackburn v Attorney-General* [1971] 2 All E.R. 1380 at 1387).

the revolutionary constitution of 1965. The same sort of process occurred in the Glorious Revolution of 1688, where James VII (or II of England) was deposed, William and Mary were offered the Crown and the English and Scottish Parliaments asserted their pre-eminence in, respectively, the Bill of Rights and the Claim of Right. By the standards of the time, all of these acts were illegal. Yet in 1688 the pre-existing legal order was comprehensively overturned. By what standard then can it be said that what happened in 1688, and what has happened since, is legal? The answer to this lies in the acquiescence of the courts in the "break in legal continuity" occasioned by new political realities and in their acceptance of a new criterion of legal validity, namely the legal supremacy of Parliament.

Does this mean that, however much Parliament may wish to entrench a measure in the future, it is simply unable to do so, or unable to do so without a "revolution"? Professor Wade himself refuted this notion:

> "Even without a [break in legal continuity] there might be a shift in judicial loyalty if we take into account the dimension of time. . . . [N]ew generations of judges might come to accept that there had been a new constitutional settlement based on common consent and long usage, and that the old doctrine of sovereignty was ancient history . . . . The judges would then be adjusting their doctrine to the facts of constitutional life, as they have done throughout history."[30]

2–05 Now on three fronts at least, the monolithic character of Diceyan orthodoxy has indeed in recent years come under strain.[31] The first significant breach in the unity of the Diceyan conception of sovereignty was made by the decision of the House of Lords in the *Factortame* case,[32] and what is perhaps curious about *Factortame* is that it was so long coming. The United Kingdom became a member of the European Communities, as the European Union was then known, on January 1, 1973. In so doing, it signed up to a body of law derived from the founding treaties, including the law of

---

[30] H. W. R. Wade, *Constitutional Fundamentals (Hamlyn Lectures)* (Sweet & Maxwell, London, 1989).

[31] It may be said that the uncompromising logic of that orthodoxy has had an inhibiting effect on British constitutional development in the past. Having secured a bill of rights and a devolution settlement, it is easy to forget that at one time one of the most persuasive arguments (or so it was thought) against such reforms was that they would be pointless and ineffective in so far as any later, inconsistent Act of Parliament would override the parent legislation to the extent of any conflict between the two.

[32] *R. v S of S for Transport, ex p. Factortame Ltd (No. 1)* [1990] 2 A.C. 85; *R. v S of S for Transport, ex p. Factortame Ltd (No. 2)* [1991] 1 A.C. 603.

the Communities as expounded by the European Court of Justice. It has been argued that, at the time, the potential for conflict between traditional conceptions of parliamentary supremacy and Community law was not widely appreciated.[33] If so,[34] that is itself strange, for the Court of Justice had made no bones about asserting the unique nature of Community law. As the Court held in *Van Gend en Loos v Nederlandse Administratie der Belastingen*,[35] "the Community constitutes a new legal order of international law for the benefit of which states have limited their sovereign rights." Again, in *Costa v ENEL*[36]:

> "The transfer by the states from their domestic legal systems to the Community legal system of the rights and obligations arising under the Treaty carries with it a permanent limitation of their sovereign rights, against which a subsequent unilateral act incompatible with the concept of the Community cannot prevail."

Thus, as the Court of Justice confirmed in *Internationale Handelsgesellschaft MbH v Einfuhr und Vorratsstelle für Getreide und Futtermittel*,[37] Community law in all its forms prevails over national law, including national constitutional norms. All of this was clearly established in the jurisprudence of the Court of Justice before the United Kingdom gave effect to its duty to "take all appropriate measures . . . to ensure fulfilment of the obligations arising out of this Treaty or resulting from actions taken by the institutions of the Community" by enacting the European Communities Act 1972 (and for the avoidance of doubt, the Court of Justice subsequently held that in the event of a conflict between national and Community law, the national court must "apply Community law in its entirety and protect rights which the latter confers on individuals, *and must accordingly set aside any provision of national law which may conflict with it, whether prior or subsequent to the Community rule*").[38]

The challenge posed by Community law and the provisions of **2–06** the European Communities Act 1972 to Diceyan orthodoxy—that Parliament has unlimited legislative competence, and no court is able to question or set aside an Act of Parliament—is abundantly

---

[33] D. Nicol, *EC Membership and the Judicialisation of Politics* (Oxford University Press, Oxford, 1999).

[34] *cf.* J. D. B. Mitchell, "British Law and British Membership" [1971] *Europarecht* 97.

[35] [1963] E.C.R. 1 at 12.

[36] [1964] E.C.R. 1141.

[37] [1970] E.C.R. 1125.

[38] *Amministrazione delle Finanze dello Stato v Simmenthal SpA (No.2)* [1978] E.C.R. 629 (emphasis added).

clear. What was not clear, for some time, was how Community law
and our constitutional tradition might be reconciled, assuming such
a thing to be possible. It is true that, without the 1972 Act,
Community law would never have entered into national law at all.
It was that Act which, by incorporating Community law, made it
domestically binding and enforceable. But if the role of the
national courts is to give effect to the latest expression of the
sovereign will of Parliament, would it not follow that a subsequent
statute conflicting with Community law took precedence both over
the Community norm and (by way of implied repeal) over the 1972
Act itself? To argue otherwise requires one to accept that, contrary
to Dicey's theory, the European Communities Act has some
superior quality to other statutes which enables it to resist implied
repeal. It was this question which was not conclusively resolved
until *Factortame*, although there were indications of the way the
wind was blowing prior to that. For example, in *Macarthys Ltd v
Smith*,[39] which involved a conflict between Article 119 of the Treaty
of Rome and section 1 of the Equal Pay Act 1970, Lord Denning
M.R. held as follows:

> "Under section 2(1) and (4) of the European Communities
> Act 1972, the principles laid down in the Treaty are 'without
> further enactment' to be given legal effect in the United
> Kingdom; and have priority over any enactment 'passed or to
> be passed' by our Parliament. . . . In construing our statute, we
> are entitled to look to the Treaty as an aid to its construction;
> but not only as an aid but as an overriding force. If . . . it
> should appear that our legislation is deficient or is inconsistent
> with Community law by some oversight of our draftsmen then
> it is our bounden duty to give priority to Community law. Such
> is the result of section 2(1) and (4) of the European Commu-
> nities Act 1972."

This approach evades the issue of whether Community law is
actually superior in status to primary legislation by treating the
1972 Act as prescribing a special rule of statutory construction,
whereby any inconsistency with Community law is presumed,
absent express indication to the contrary, to have been unintended
and accidental. The courts are therefore doing no more than
fulfilling Parliament's real and genuine intention in construing the
domestic provision consistently with Community law. But in *Macarthys*, the incompatibility was contained in a statute pre-dating the
European Communities Act 1972; a traditionalist might therefore
argue that section 1 of the Equal Pay Act 1970 had been impliedly

---

[39] [1979] 3 All E.R. 325 at 329.

repealed by the 1972 Act and, as such, by Community law. More important is the question—the question in *Factortame*—of how the courts treat a *subsequent* statute that conflicts with Community law.

The facts of the *Factortame* case were as follows. A number of English companies whose management and shareholders were primarily Spanish nationals lost their right to exploit the UK's fishing quota when the Merchant Shipping Act 1988 made the right conditional on nationality requirements they were unable to meet. The companies argued that the Act was unlawful as being in breach of the Treaty of Rome. The House of Lords referred the case to the Court of Justice for a preliminary ruling; the Court of Justice duly held that the 1988 Act was incompatible with Community law.[40] The case returned to the House of Lords, where Lord Bridge held:

> "Some public comments on the decision of the Court of Justice . . . have suggested that this was a novel and dangerous invasion by a Community institution of the sovereignty of the United Kingdom Parliament. But such comments are based on a misconception. If the supremacy within the European Community of Community law over the national law of Member States was not always inherent in the EEC Treaty it was certainly well established in the jurisprudence of the Court of Justice long before the United Kingdom joined the Community. *Thus whatever limitation of its sovereignty Parliament accepted when it enacted the European Communities Act 1972 was entirely voluntary.* Under the terms of the 1972 Act it has always been clear that it was the duty of a United Kingdom court, when delivering final judgment, to override any rule of national law found to be in conflict with any directly enforceable rule of Community law."[41]

This passage is significant for two things. First, it speaks of a "limitation of sovereignty"—something Diceyan tradition holds to be inconsistent with the very notion of sovereignty. Secondly, however, Lord Bridge qualified any perceived radicalism by carefully ascribing this limitation of sovereignty to Parliament's own

---

[40] A separate issue in the case, which also required a preliminary ruling from the ECJ, was whether the UK courts were obliged to make available a remedy by way of interim injunction (in Scotland, interdict) to restrain a Minister of the Crown from bringing the 1988 Act into force. The Crown Proceedings Act 1947, s.21, provides that the courts may not grant coercive remedies such as injunction or interdict in proceedings against a Minister of the Crown; Community law, on the other hand, requires national legal systems to accord effective protection to Community law rights. To the extent that the bar on injunction/interdict diminished the effectiveness of national legal protection, it required to be disapplied.

[41] *Factortame (No.2)*, n.32, pp.658, 659 (emphasis added).

choice.[42] The same sense of the constitutional proprieties under-pins the later decision of the House of Lords in *R. v Secretary of State for Employment, ex parte Equal Opportunities Commission*,[43] which confirmed that the UK courts had jurisdiction to review primary legislation said to be in breach of Community law. If the argument is made out, however, the courts do not strike the Act of Parliament down as they would an administrative act. They confine themselves, rather, to declaring that an incompatibility exists. It is then for government and Parliament to rectify the matter, should they choose to do so. The strict legal truth of Diceyan doctrine is thus maintained (even if at some cost to its substance).

What *Factortame* established was that, whether enacted prior or subsequent to the relevant Community norm, an Act of Parliament cannot prevail over Community law if there is inconsistency between the two. In either case, it is presumed that Parliament did not intend to contravene Community law. Thus it is not open to Parliament *impliedly* to repeal Community law or, for that matter, the European Communities Act 1972. The Diceyan doctrine of parliamentary supremacy was therefore modified to this extent: after *Factortame*, we had to recognise that Parliament has unlimited legislative competence and no court may question or set aside an Act of Parliament *except* where Community law applies, in which case Community law prevails and the courts have jurisdiction to declare an Act of Parliament to be incompatible with Com-munity law. What *Factortame* left open was, first, whether Parlia-ment might expressly derogate from Community law; and secondly, whether what was true of the European Communities Act 1972 might also be true of other statutes. Lord Denning M.R. addressed the first of these questions in *Macarthys Ltd v Smith*[44]:

> "If the time should come when our Parliament deliberately passes an Act with the intention of repudiating the Treaty or any provision of it or intentionally of acting inconsistently with it and says so in express terms then I should have thought that it would be the duty of our courts to follows the statute of our Parliament."

2–08   The contrary view is that Parliament cannot lawfully depart from Community law expressly or otherwise: if the United Kingdom wishes to depart from its obligations as a Member State, it must negotiate for release from the Community and for the restoration of the sovereignty it is said to have transferred to the Community

---

[42] In contrast to Wade's argument that any qualification of the doctrine of unlimited parliamentary sovereignty lies in the keeping of the courts.
[43] [1995] 1 A.C. 1.
[44] [1979] 3 All E.R. 325 at 329.

on accession. In the meantime, the obligation of the courts to disapply incompatible legislation remains live. Arguments akin to this were advanced by counsel for the respondents in *Thoburn v Sunderland City Council*,[45] in suggesting that by dint of Community law the doctrine of implied repeal had no application to the European Communities Act 1972. Laws L.J. agreed that the provisions of the 1972 Act could not be impliedly repealed, but did not consider that this was a consequence of Community law. Rather, it was the result of national law itself. Drawing on some of the salient decisions in a period of unparalleled judicial creativity in the field of public law,[46] which the *Factortame* decision may have prompted and certainly did not discourage, Laws L.J. held:

> "The common law has in recent years allowed, or rather created, exceptions to the doctrine of implied repeal, a doctrine which was always the common law's own creature. There are now classes or types of legislative provision which cannot be repealed by mere implication. These instances are given, and can only be given, by our own courts, to which the scope and nature of parliamentary sovereignty are ultimately confided. The courts may say—have said—that there are certain circumstances in which the legislature may only enact what it desires to enact if it does so by express, or at any rate specific, provision. The courts have in effect so held in the field of European law itself in [*Factortame*]."[47]

Accordingly, if it is Parliament's conscious intention to legislate contrary to Community law, it must make its intention plain in express statutory words or "words so specific that the inference of an actual determination to effect the result contended for [is] irresistible."[48] But if it does so, the duty of the courts of the United Kingdom is to submit to the expression of the legislative will, because "the fundamental legal basis of the United Kingdom's relationship with the European Union rests with the domestic, not the European, legal powers."[49]

In developing this reasoning, Laws L.J. also answered the second question posited above: whether it is the European Communities Act 1972 alone that benefits from this dispensation from implied repeal. According to *Thoburn*, the 1972 Act is only one of a family of "constitutional statutes" resistant as such to implied repeal:

---

[45] [2003] Q.B. 151.
[46] In particular, *Derbyshire C v Times Newspapers Ltd* [1993] A.C. 534; *R. v S of S for the Home Dept, ex p. Leech* [1994] Q.B. 198; *R. v S of S for the Home Dept, ex p. Pierson* [1998] A.C. 539; *R. v Lord Chancellor, ex p. Witham* [1998] Q.B. 575; and *R. v Secretary of State for the Home Department, ex p. Simms* [2000] 2 A.C. 115.
[47] *Thoburn v Sunderland CC* [2003] Q.B. 151, para.60.
[48] *ibid.*, para.63.
[49] *ibid.*, para.69.

"In the present state of its maturity the common law has come to recognise that there exist rights which should properly be classified as constitutional or fundamental. And from this a further insight follows. We should recognise a hierarchy of Acts of Parliament: as it were, "ordinary" statutes and "constitutional" statutes. The two categories must be distinguished on a principled basis. In my opinion a constitutional statute is one which (a) conditions the legal relationship between citizen and state in some general, overarching manner, or (b) enlarges or diminishes the scope of what we would now regard as fundamental constitutional rights. . . . Ordinary statutes may be impliedly repealed. Constitutional statutes may not."[50]

2–09   *Thoburn v Sunderland City Council*[51] belongs to a family of cases—the second anti-Dicey front—that may be seen as asserting a second locus of sovereign power alongside the sovereignty of Parliament.[52] So far as that goes, it is not necessarily a radical departure: the will of the sovereign legislature falls to be interpreted and applied by the courts, and in that regard the courts have often failed to observe the unquestioning fidelity to legislative intent that Diceyan orthodoxy would seem to involve. In *Nairn v University of St Andrews*,[53] for example, the House of Lords held that the Universities (Scotland) Act 1889, which provided for the conferment of university degrees on women, did not impliedly repeal the Representation of the People (Scotland) Act 1868 so as to confer on women registered at a university the right to vote.[54] Other cases may exhibit a more striking tendency, in so far as the courts effectively override the law as stated in a statute. For Nicholas Barber, this is far from uncommon. He cites as examples the long-running battle between Parliament and the courts over trade union immunities,[55]

---

[50] *ibid.*, paras 62, 63. Included in the family, in the opinion of Laws L.J., are the Union with Scotland Act 1706 (meaning the Act of the pre-Union English Parliament; one presumes that his Lordship would regard the Scottish Act of Union as having the same constitutional status); the legislation to distribute and enlarge the franchise, including the Great Reform Act 1832; and the Human Rights Act and Scotland Act of 1998.

[51] [2003] Q.B. 151

[52] Which Sir Stephen Sedley has described as "a new constitutional paradigm . . . of a bi-polar sovereignty of the Crown in Parliament and the Crown in its courts": "Human Rights: A twenty-first century agenda" [1995] P.L. 386 at 389.

[53] [1909] A.C. 147.

[54] See N. Barber, "Sovereignty Re-examined: The courts, Parliament and statutes" [2000] 20 O.J.L.S. 131 at 145–146. Together with *Nairn v University of St Andrews* [1909] A.C. 147 Barber identifies *Attorney-General v Wilts United Dairies* [1921] 37 T.L.R. 884 and *Factortame*, n.32, itself as cases in which the courts have preferred an earlier Act of Parliament to a later one, in apparent defiance of the doctrine of implied repeal, but still "according to Parliament the position of supreme legal source within the constitutional system."

[55] See, *e.g. Quinn v Leathem* [1901] A.C. 495 and *Rookes v Barnard* [1964] A.C. 1129.

cases in which the courts have disregarded statutory provisions purporting to oust the jurisdiction of the courts,[56] and cases in which the courts have reinterpreted legislation to achieve results that are regarded are just and appropriate by contemporary standards however remote from the intention of the legislature.[57] On this basis, Barber suggests that in some situations at least the courts "appear to be accorded political authority by the constitutional system to make decisions contrary to the existing law . . . and when they exercise that authority, they are obeyed."[58] Approaching this from the sovereignty perspective—and bearing in mind that the concept of sovereignty serves to identify the highest point in a legal system's hierarchy of norms—it may be objected that "there cannot be an infinite regress of lawmakers able to impose limits on the authority of each one in turn."[59] Barber's response is to refute the assumption that there must be a decisive ranking of legal sources within the constitution. But the question of which legal source prevails in the event of a conflict remains.

As we shall presently see, some exponents of "common law constitutionalism" have asserted that "the constitution" must prevail over the will of Parliament in the event of a conflict between the two. Such arguments were developed prior to the enactment of the Human Rights Act 1998 (although it should not be thought that this has taken all the wind out of their sails) by way of a response to the perceived inability of Parliament to secure the protection of fundamental rights. The Human Rights Act—which is the third limb of the contemporary reappraisal of Diceyan tradition—now confers on the courts explicit statutory authority to read and give effect to Acts of Parliament, whenever enacted, in a manner compatible with certain "Convention rights" and, where this is impossible, empowers the higher courts to make "declarations of incompatibility" in respect of the statutory provisions

---

[56] See, *e.g. Anisminic Ltd v Foreign Compensation Commission* [1969] 2 A.C. 147.

[57] Thus in *R. v R* [1992] 1 A.C. 599, the House of Lords reinterpreted the Sexual Offences (Amendment) Act 1956, s.1, to include marital rape within its scope (in Scotland, the same result was achieved by judicial development of the common law in *S v H.M. Advocate*, 1989 SLT 469). Contrast this approach with that of the New Zealand Court of Appeal in *Quilter v Attorney-General of New Zealand* [1998] 1 NZLR 523: even with the aid of the New Zealand Bill of Rights Act 1990, which requires the courts in that jurisdiction to construe legislation consistently with protected rights if possible, the Court declined to interpret the Marriage Act in such a way as to permit marriage between persons of the same sex, on the grounds that such a reading would plainly be contrary to the legislature's intent.

[58] N. Barber, "Sovereignty Re-examined: The courts, Parliament and statutes" [2000] 20 O.J.L.S. 131, p.151. For Mr Barber's analysis of the legitimacy of this authority and its exercise, see "Prelude to the Separation of Powers" (2001) 60 C.L.J. 59.

[59] J. Goldsworthy, "Legislative Sovereignty and the Rule of Law" in *Sceptical Essays on Human Rights* (Campbell, Ewing and Tomkins eds, Oxford University Press, Oxford, 2001), Ch.4.

concerned. But it also explicitly denies the courts any power to invalidate primary legislation: a declaration of incompatibility is exactly that, and has no effect on the validity, continuing operation or enforcement of the provision in respect of which it is made. Thus the Convention rights, together with directly effective Community law norms, provide criteria for the review of primary legislation. But they have that status not by virtue of "the constitution" but by virtue of two Acts of Parliament; and what Parliament has given, Parliament may also take away (if only, according to *Thoburn*, by express words or irresistible implication).[60] An autonomous jurisdiction might fall to the courts in the interstices—as where, for instance, it is claimed that a provision of directly applicable Community law conflicts with one or more of the Convention rights—but in no sense would this involve a competence to set aside an Act of Parliament as being "unconstitutional". Thus, even allowing for the indeterminacy of statutory language, which may necessitate a certain amount of judicial creativity in interpretation (and certainly leaves room for judicial discretion), we are far indeed from recognising that the supremacy of Parliament has been supplanted, or even supplemented, by a competing sovereignty reposing in the courts. Provided Parliament speaks clearly, it remains free to make or unmake any law whatever, and although the courts may pronounce on the compatibility of its enactments with Community law and the Convention rights, they cannot set those enactments aside. Thus there has indeed been an adjustment in the doctrine of parliamentary supremacy.[61] But it does not amount to the "break in legal continuity" that would be required to deprive the supremacy of Parliament of its status as the "top rule" of our constitutional law.

THE RULE OF LAW

2–10 For Dicey, the rule of law stood with the legislative supremacy of Parliament as a fundamental principle of the constitution. Few would take issue with this assertion of the importance of the rule of

---

[60] It would not therefore be open to a UK court to follow the reasoning of Iacobucci J. in *Vriend v Alberta* [1998] 1 S.C.R. 493 at 563: "When the [Canadian Charter of Rights and Freedoms] was introduced, Canada went ... from a system of parliamentary supremacy to a system of constitutional supremacy. . . . Simply put, each Canadian was given individual rights and freedoms which no government or legislature could take away."

[61] And (*contra* Wade) not merely a judicial adjustment. While the courts may indeed have the last word on the content of the doctrine, so that in that sense its meaning does "lie in their keeping", Parliament itself created the conditions in which the adjustment took place, much as Lord Bridge indicated in *Factortame*, n.32.

law in our constitutional arrangements. Equally few would defend Dicey's particular conception of the rule of law, at least in all its elements. What, then, does the rule of law mean? At its narrowest, it involves the subjection of governmental power to law; and that this "principle of legality" is included within the idea of the rule of law is uncontroversial. Thus in *Entick v Carrington*,[62] the court rejected the argument that "state necessity" was sufficient warrant for authorising the King's Messengers to break in to Entick's house and seize his books and papers:

> "Every invasion of private property is a trespass. No man can set his foot upon my ground without my licence, but he is liable to an action. . . . If he admits the fact, he is bound to show by way of justification that some positive law has empowered or excused him. The justification is submitted to the judges, who are to look into the books, and see if such a justification can be maintained by the text of the statute law, or principles of the common law. . . . It is said that it is necessary for the ends of government to lodge such a power [of search and seizure] with a state officer . . . but with respect to the argument of state necessity, or to a distinction that has been aimed at between state offences and others, the common law does not understand that kind of reasoning, nor do our books take notice of any such distinctions."

In fact, even the principle of legality was imperfectly realised in the United Kingdom. The courts did not[63] require governmental bodies to found on positive legal authority for all that they did; rather, such authority was only required where necessary to validate what would otherwise constitute a legal wrong—typically, the violation of rights of personal liberty or, perhaps especially, property. Thus in *Malone v Metropolitan Police Commissioner*,[64] the police were not obliged to qualify their authority for tapping Mr Malone's telephone, since tapping telephones involved no wrong known to domestic law.[65] But even the fuller expression of the principle of legality—the idea that all the rule of law requires is the clothing of government acts with legal authority—is felt by many to lack robustness: iniquitous legal systems, such as those of Nazi Germany and South Africa under apartheid, could be punctilious in their observance of legal form and so may be said to have

---

[62] (1765) *State Trials* 1030.
[63] And do not, except where the Convention rights are in issue.
[64] [1979] Ch. 344.
[65] Whereas, before the ECHR, the absence of legal base for the actions of the police was fatal to its compatibility with ECHR, Art.8: see *Malone v United Kingdom* (1984) 7 E.H.R.R. 14.

complied with the rule of law in this sense. It was precisely this which, in the post-war period, prompted many to reject unmodified legal positivism and limited conceptions of the rule of law in favour of more prescriptive criteria. Most would now agree, therefore, that the principle of legality does not provide a complete account of the rule of law; but at this point, consensus evaporates. Speaking very broadly, writers on the subject tend to fall into two camps. On the one hand, there are those who favour a formal conception of the rule of law, which supplements the bare notion of legality with certain morally neutral values to which any legal system worthy of the name should aspire. On the other hand, there are those who, while they accept the values embodied in formal conceptions, wish to take the rule of law further and read into it a variety of substantive rights with which a constitution under the rule of law must conform.[66] A key element of the British debate between the different schools of thought relates to what the rule of law means in terms of institutional design. Often if not invariably, subscribers to the substantive rule of law argue that the rule of law is irreconcilable with the sovereignty of Parliament, and that the latter must yield to the former. Opponents of this view contend that the rule of law does not dictate particular forms of constitutional ordering—and, specifically, does not dictate constitutional review of primary legislation—and insist that the rule of law should not be confused with, or be seen to require, other attributes (democracy, social justice, equality, the protection of human rights) to which a "good" constitution ought to aspire.

2–11　　The foregoing is intended to illustrate the main parameters of the debate, and in doing so risks oversimplification. In fact it is difficult to draw a hard and fast line between the competing standpoints, and no one exemplifies this better than Dicey himself, whose account of the rule of law has been described both as formal[67] and substantive.[68] There are three facets to Dicey's

---

[66] There is probably also a third camp, which doubts the very relevance and utility of the rule of law. For some, the rule of law is simply a label, albeit a label of considerable resonance and moral persuasion, which, being intrinsically empty of content, is apt to be harnessed to the particular political preferences of whoever happens to be writing about it. For others, the concept is positively harmful, being little more than a device to bestow legitimacy on a legal system whilst blinding us to real, substantive inequality in society and so shoring up the control of a political elite. If it restrains power, it also "prevents power's benevolent exercise"; if it insists on formal equality, it reinforces "substantive inequality . . . by promoting procedural justice, it enables the shrewd, the calculating and the wealthy to manipulate its forms to their own advantage": M. Horowitz, "The Rule of Law: An Unqualified Human Good?" (1977) 86 Yale L.J. 561.

[67] See, *e.g.* P. Craig, "Formal and Substantive Conceptions of the Rule of Law: An analytical framework" [1997] P.L. 467.

[68] Perhaps most trenchantly by Sir Ivor Jennings, *The Law and the Constitution* (5th ed., 1959).

conception of the rule of law, above and beyond the basic principle of legality, which are worth exploring in order to show where he went wrong but also to tease out what it was that Dicey got right, or which, at least, endures. First, Dicey took the rule of law to mean "the absolute supremacy or predominance of regular law as opposed to the influence of arbitrary power."[69] Arbitrariness, prerogative, even "wide discretionary authority on the part of government" was, for Dicey, incompatible with the rule of law. Secondly, the rule of law required "the equal subjection of all classes to the ordinary law of the land, administered by the ordinary law courts."[70] In this respect, Dicey contrasted British constitutional arrangements with those in continental systems, such as France, which had a distinct system of public law administered in separate courts. "With us," Dicey opined, "every official, from the Prime Minister down to a constable or a collector of taxes, is under the same responsibility for every act done without legal justification as any other citizen."[71] Thirdly, the rule of law means that "with us the law of the constitution is not the source but the consequence of the rights of individuals, as defined and enforced by the courts."[72] The British constitution on this account was the product of the ordinary law, developed by the courts on a case by case basis, as distinct from (and, implicitly, superior to) a constitutional order superimposed in the manner of a written constitution. Individual rights were not conferred by a constitutional document, which might at any moment be torn up, but secured by the availability of ordinary legal remedies to those whose rights were, like Entick's, unlawfully infringed.

Each of these three senses of the rule of law may be criticised. In the first place, Dicey's equation of arbitrariness and discretion must be seen as misconceived. No workable scheme of social welfare or regulation can be cast in terms of rules alone: those charged with the scheme's implementation and administration must be entrusted with discretion in order to adapt and apply its general principles to the circumstances of specific cases. In recognition of this elementary truth, Parliament routinely confers wide discretionary powers on public authorities and officials. And such discretionary power is plainly compatible with the rule of law in its narrow sense (the principle of legality): having the imprimatur of the legislature, its legal pedigree is incontestable. If one wishes to deny its compatibility, that is because one attaches to the rule of law a further, and political, meaning. Thus for Jennings, this aspect of Dicey's rule of

---

[69] Dicey, *The Law of the Constitution, op.cit.*, p.202.
[70] *ibid.*
[71] *ibid.*, p.193.
[72] *ibid.*, p.203.

law was premised on a vision of an ideal state which concerned itself only with external relations and the maintenance of order and eschewed any role in combatting poverty, disease, pollution and "other incidents of nineteenth-century industrialism."[73] Dicey was not alone in harnessing his account of the rule of law to a particular worldview. But without falling into the same trap, we may concede that his vision is neither an accurate picture of the modern state nor (one would have thought) an especially attractive one. That granted, it might be accepted that discretionary power and the rule of law can coexist. But that is not to dismiss the first branch of Dicey's rule of law as manifestly ill founded. Arbitrariness (which may take many forms) is not readily reconciled with the idea of government under law. The question is, then, whether we have appropriate legal (and political) controls with which to regulate the exercise of discretionary power, and to ensure that it is not exercised arbitrarily.[74]

Dicey's second sense of the rule of law is also difficult to sustain. In point of fact, it is simply wrong to say that there is equality before the law in Britain.[75] Even in Dicey's time, the organs of the state enjoyed a whole host of special rights, privileges and immunities before the law, many of which persist to this day.[76] Moreover, the distinction Dicey drew between the ordinary courts in Britain and the administrative courts in France became less and less marked during the twentieth century as Parliament removed the resolution of disputes arising out of new welfare and regulatory legislation from the jurisdiction of the ordinary courts, entrusting it instead to specialist tribunals.[77]

---

[73] Which is of course a political viewpoint itself. But this begins to reveal a deeper deficiency with the rule of law as a concept: it attempts (or is amenable to attempts) to cast intrinsically political disputes in the supposedly neutral language of law.

[74] It should be noted that some accounts of the rule of law neglect the role that political controls play in checking and confining governmental power, often quite deliberately in so far as the whole thrust of their argument is that power not subject to *legal* control is power unfettered and, therefore, illegitimate.

[75] Before even entering into discussion of equality of access to the courts which, being largely a matter of wealth, we have yet to achieve.

[76] Thus, *e.g.* the Sovereign cannot be sued in her own courts; coercive legal remedies are unavailable against the Crown by virtue of the Crown Proceedings Act 1947; and, absent express terms or necessary implication to the contrary, the Crown is not bound by the burden of a statute: *Dumbarton DC v Lord Advocate* [1990] 2 A.C. 580.

[77] Not least for fear that the ordinary courts would drive a coach and four through the operation of this legislation if the prejudices of the judges, clothed in the language of the rule of law, were allowed free rein. But there was also an argument from expertise, which underpinned the French separation between public and private law: on this account, separation was necessary not to protect the executive but to ensure that *effective* control was applied.

Dicey's third meaning of the rule of law is perhaps the most curious. He clearly regarded individual rights and liberties as secured by the rule of law, but saw no inconsistency between this fundamental principle of the constitution and the other, parliamentary supremacy. The common law may insist, as in *Entick*, that when government officials infringe individual rights they show clear legal authority for doing so; but that is easily met by the provision of sweeping statutory powers whose validity the courts cannot question.[78] Individual freedom was not, at least until recently, a matter of *right* but of *residual liberty*: it occupied the space left after subtracting all the statutory (and common law) constraints imposed upon it. Thus the principle of legality alone provides no guarantee that fundamental freedoms will be respected.[79] The answer to this apparent inconsistency may lie in Dicey's perception that Parliament would not enact laws harmful to the interests of its electors: Dicey argued only for the absence of legal limitations on Parliament's legislative competence, not for the absence of political or moral constraints. But the objection to that is readily anticipated: Parliament's legislative supremacy is at the disposal of the government of the day through its command of a majority in the House of Commons; the government does force illiberal legislation through Parliament; and neither Parliament nor the courts[80] can do anything about it. More than anything else, it is this perception which has led many commentators to conclude that parliamentary supremacy and the rule of law are irreconcilable and that, if the values of the rule of law are to be respected, the supremacy of Parliament must be subjected to judicially enforceable restraints.[81]

These arguments are premised upon substantive conceptions of **2–12** the rule of law, which regard the rule of law as the source of rights and as justifying the rejection of legislative supremacy. There is no

---

[78] Although they may, and do, subject such powers to implied limitations.

[79] As Profs Ewing and Gearty suggest, however, once legal rights are cast in statutory form, they "may be removed or qualified only by law, and although this is always possible, the principle of legality at least clothes these rights with the protection of a legal process which must be complied with before any removal of qualification can be effective. In other words, the principle of legality offers an important measure of procedural protection to substantive rights.": K. D. Ewing and C. Gearty, *The Struggle for Civil Liberties* (Oxford University Press, Oxford, 2000), pp.12, 13.

[80] Subject now, of course, to the HRA 1998.

[81] See, *e.g.* Lord Woolf, "Droit Public: English style" [1995] P.L. 56; Sir John Laws, "Law and Democracy" [1995] P.L. 72 and "The Constitution: Morals and Rights" [1996] P.L. 622; T. R. S. Allan, *Law, Liberty and Justice: The legal foundations of British constitutionalism* (Oxford University Press, Oxford, 1993) and *Constitutional Justice: A liberal theory of the rule of law* (Oxford University Press, Oxford, 2001); P. Craig, "Constitutional Foundations, the Rule of Law and Supremacy" [2003] P.L. 92.

single substantive conception of the rule of law.[82] For the International Congress of Jurists meeting in New Delhi in 1959, the function of a legislature in a free society under the rule of law was "to create and maintain the conditions which will uphold the dignity of man as an individual. This dignity *requires* not only the recognition of his civil and political rights but also the establishment of the social, economic, educational and cultural conditions which are essential to the full development of his personality."[83] Other accounts follow Dworkin, holding that the rule of law requires that the moral and political rights of individuals be captured in positive legal rules (statutory and common law), so that they may be enforced through the courts.[84] The Kantian conception advanced by Sir John Laws is founded on individual autonomy: this rule of law "gives effect to the necessary minimum legal standards required by the imperative . . . of freedom."[85] On this analysis, the rule of law does not embrace positive rights, which require affirmative state action, but stipulates the legal entrenchment of negative rights, or rights not to be subjected (except on certain narrow grounds) to state interference. Allan, on the other hand, argues that the rule of law does not express any particular theory of rights or justice. His rule of law establishes a "floor" of basic requirements, over and above the components of formal conceptions of the rule of law: equality, rationality, proportionality and fairness, together with substantive rights of freedom of speech, conscience and association and access to information.[86] Beyond this, it is for particular legal orders to decide whether and to what extent to recognise other individual rights.

Thus, perhaps, the only thing advocates of a substantive conception of the rule of law are agreed upon is that some such conception is necessary, because formal conceptions do not go far enough to secure the protection of individual freedom. The response to that is that substantive theories overinflate the idea of

---

[82] Which may be why the differing conceptions carry greater force as a critique of existing constitutional doctrine and constitutional arrangements than as a blueprint for reform: see N. Walker, "Setting English Judges to Rights" (1999) 19 O.J.L.S. 133 at 149.

[83] *Report of Committee I of the International Congress of Jurists* (1959), cl.1 (emphasis added).

[84] R. Dworkin, *A Matter of Principle* (Fontana, London 1985), Ch.1. Craig, n.81, subscribes to this view. It has been argued, however, that Dworkinian jurisprudence does not "translate" to the Westminster constitution or systems modelled thereon: see R. Ekins, "Judicial Supremacy and the Rule of Law" (2003) 119 L.Q.R. 127.

[85] Sir John Laws, "The Constitution: Morals and rights" [1996] P.L. 622 at 629.

[86] Which substantive rights are necessary for the maintenance of a participative democracy and to preserve individual autonomy in the face of governmental authority: Allan, *Constitutional Justice*, n.81.

the rule of law, and in doing so weaken its claim to constitute a universal standard of criticism and social discourse.[87] Raz disparaged the account given by the International Congress of Jurists as a perversion of the doctrine of the rule of law, including within its scope "just about every political ideal which has found support in any part of the globe during the post-war years."[88] He continued:

> "If the rule of law is the rule of the good law, then to explain its nature is to propound a complete social philosophy. But if so the term lacks any useful function. We have no need to be converted to the rule of law just in order to discover that to believe in it is to believe that good should triumph. The rule of law is a political ideal which a legal system may lack or may possess to a greater or lesser degree. ... It is also to be insisted that the rule of law is just one of the virtues that a legal system may possess and by which it is to be judged. It is not to be confused with democracy, justice, equality (before the law or otherwise), human rights of any kind or respect for persons or for the dignity of man."[89]

For Raz, and others of the formal school, the meaning of the **2–13** rule of law is limited (if not as limited as the bare principle of legality). The core idea illuminating the formal theory is that the law must be capable of guiding the behaviour of those subject to it. To that end, conformity with the rule of law requires that laws should be prospective in operation,[90] open and clear. The law should be relatively stable. The making of particular laws or rules, whether legislative or administrative in nature, should be guided by open, stable, clear and general norms. None of this denies a role to the courts in securing the preservation of the rule of law; on the contrary, formal conceptions insist on the independence of the judiciary, observance of the principles of natural justice and the importance of access to the courts. Nor does it necessarily exclude judicial review of primary legislation,[91] or treat the rule of law as wholly unrelated to the protection of individual freedom. Rather

---

[87] R. S. Summers, "A Formal Theory of the Rule of Law" (1993) 6 *Ratio Juris* 127.

[88] J. Raz, "The Rule of Law and its Virtue" (1977) 93 L.Q.R. 195.

[89] *ibid.*, 196.

[90] The virtue of prospectivity is reflected in ECHR, Art.7, and the maxim, *nulla poena sine lege*, recognised in most legal systems. For the application of the presumption against retroactivity in civil law, see now reported: *Wilson v First County Trust Ltd (No.2)* [2003] 3 W.L.R. 568, at paras 186–202, *per* Lord Rodger.

[91] Raz, n.88, alludes, somewhat obliquely, to this possibility, but argues that it could only ever be very limited review, confined to ensuring conformity with the principles of prospectivity, legal certainty and due process.

than deriving all the virtues of a virtuous state from the rule of law, however, the formal theory makes the more modest claim that respect for the rule of law is a necessary, if not a sufficient, condition for respecting individual freedom and human dignity.

There is a further objection to the thrust of substantive visions of the rule of law, which has particular resonance in the context of the British constitution. Pressed to their logical conclusion, substantive conceptions require the imposition of legal limitations on the legislature: so much, indeed, is explicitly acknowledged by the academic and judicial exponents of "common law constitutionalism". On this view, the rule of law sets its face against arbitrary power; arbitrary power is power unconstrained by law; therefore, the legislative supremacy of Parliament is, in principle, arbitrary (or at least capable of being exercised arbitrarily) and must be made subject to judicial control (if only on particular and/or limited grounds). But since there "cannot be an infinite regress of lawmakers able to impose limits on the authority of each one in turn",[92] this necessarily involves the substitution of judicial for legislative supremacy: only one institution can have the last word on whether or not a law is valid. The idea that, as a matter of the rule of law, that institution should be the courts has been strenuously resisted on a number of grounds.

The most obvious criticism is that the whole idea is profoundly undemocratic.[93] In answer to the assertion that the limitation of democratic power is essential to the survival and flourishing of democracy,[94] the critics point out that fundamental rights said to be derived from the rule of law[95] do not provide self-executing criteria

---

[92] J. Goldsworthy, "Legislative Sovereignty and the Rule of Law" in *Sceptical Essays on Human Rights* (Campbell, Ewing and Tomkins eds, Oxford University Press, Oxford, 2001), Ch.4.

[93] See, *e.g.* J. A. G. Griffith, "The Brave New World of Sir John Laws" [2000] 63 M.L.R. 159; Ewing, "The Human Rights Act and Parliamentary Democracy" [1999] 62 M.L.R. 79; R. Ekins, n.84.

[94] See, *e.g.* Sir John Laws, "Law and Democracy" [1995] P.L. 72 at 81; Sir Stephen Sedley, "The Common Law and the Constitution" in *The Making and Remaking of the British Constitution* (Nolan and Sedley eds, London, 1997); Allan, *Constitutional Justice*, n.81, pp.261, 262.

[95] It may be noted in passing that the same critics ask why it is that only a particular package of rights, in the main the classic, negative, civil and political rights, are derived from the rule of law. As has been said of the rights enshrined in the ECHR and, now, HRA 1998, "they represent a particular political (indeed party political) vision of what it is a society should privilege and prioritise. We find the paradigmatic right of liberal political theory (freedom of expression) but not the core of republican philosophy or deliberative democracy (freedom of information, commitment to open government). Property is protected for those who possess it, but the homeless have no right to be housed. Religious freedom is protected, but not the right to an adequate standard of health care." See A. Tomkins, "On Being Sceptical about Human Rights" in *Sceptical Essays on Human Rights* (Campbell, Ewing and Tomkins eds, Oxford University Press, Oxford, 2001), Ch.1.

of legal validity. The minute it is accepted that few, if any, substantive rights are absolute, it must also be accepted that what such rights involve in any given situation is a matter of controversy. It is not made less controversial by reposing the ultimate choice with judges rather than an elected legislature; and although, to be sure, a constitutional system may choose (or end up with) judicial review of legislation, in the British constitutional tradition, moral and political controversy is the province of Parliament.[96] Nor is this objection confined to the fact that judges are unaccountable. There is the further point that the judicial process, typified by basically two-sided disputes, is ill suited to the performance of an essentially legislative function.[97] Law making in a legislature harnesses a wide range of influence, expertise and support, none (or little) of which is available to a judge charged with deciding, on "constitutional" grounds, whether a foetus has a right to life or a terminally ill adult a right to die.[98] Not only that, but it is also questionable how far rights-based review of legislation itself conforms to the formal values of the rule of law.[99]

The battle over the merits and threats of common law constitu- **2–14** tionalism may be said to have been overtaken by the enactment of the Human Rights Act 1998, which specifies with reasonable clarity the functions of the courts in rights adjudication under the Act and explicitly denies them any power to invalidate primary legislation. The courts, too, may be said to have accepted more limited parameters of intervention than those indicated by the substantive theorists by developing the concept of "judicial deference" in their scrutiny of legislative (and, if to a lesser degree, administrative) acts on human rights grounds.[1] But the Human Rights Act has

---

[96] Or indeed Parliaments. See J. A. G. Griffith, "The Political Constitution" (1979) 42 M.L.R. 1.

[97] L. Fuller, "The Forms and Limits of Adjudication" [1978] 92 Harvard L.R. 353.

[98] See Ekins, n.84, pp.144, 145; N. Barber, "Prelude to the Separation of Powers" (2001) 60 C.L.J. 59.

[99] Ekins notes that, as judicial law making is inherently retrospective, it is inconsistent with the rule of law's emphasis on prospectivity (although an answer to that might be to confer on the courts, or for the courts to develop, a means of limiting the retrospective effect of their decisions, as is provided by the SA 1998, s.102(2)). In terms of legal certainty, it has been argued that content-oriented standards of legality, such as moral principles or fundamental rights, generate greater uncertainty than source-oriented standards, such as the principle of parliamentary supremacy: see P. S. Atiyah and R. S. Summers, *Form and Substance in Anglo-American Law* (Clarendon Press, Oxford, 1987), p.53.

[1] The classic account of judicial deference is found in the speech of Lord Hope in *R. v DPP, ex p. Kebilene* [2000] 2 A.C. 326 at 380, 381. Note, however, that the concept is already under attack from some commentators, who insist that it is incompatible with the fundamental nature of the rights enshrined in the Human Rights Act: see, *e.g.* I. Leigh, "Taking Rights Proportionately: Judicial review, the Human Rights Act and Strasbourg" [2002] P.L. 265; R. A. Edwards, "Judicial Deference under the Human Rights Act" (2002) 65 M.L.R. 859.

been described as representing merely the democratic validation of a jurisdiction the courts were developing as a matter of the common law,[2] and one may wonder whether the ambitions of common law constitutionalism will be satisfied by the enactment of the Human Rights Act alone. In that regard, it is pertinent to recall that the origins of the present debate owe much to a widespread disenchantment with the democratic process in Britain and the diminished status of Parliament: since political institutions are effectively incapable of properly protecting individual freedom (so the reasoning runs) that role must fall to the courts. Certainly, the enactment and judicial enforcement of a bill of rights is one response to that malaise. But it is not the only, or even the most obvious, response. As much if not more might be achieved by reinvigorating the democratic process, by way of reform of the electoral process, the composition of the legislature and the procedures by which it makes laws, and indeed by the devolution of legislative competence to sub-state institutions.[3]

The view taken here, then, is that the rule of law is better and more usefully considered as a formal concept, embodying a relatively narrow range of neutral values bearing on the form of laws rather than their content. Substantive theories are inevitably shackled to a contingent package of political precepts, and involve implications which sit uncomfortably with a constitutional tradition founded on parliamentary democracy.[4] There are those who argue that common law constitutionalism (and the role of the courts thereunder) is in keeping with older traditions of the common law, which have been obscured by the post-Diceyan fixation with parliamentary sovereignty.[5] That view is contestable, at

---

[2] See Sir J. Laws, "Judicial Review and the Meaning of Law" in *Judicial Review and the Constitution* (Forsyth ed., Hart Publishing, Oxford, 2000), Ch.8: "the deep constitutional significance of the Human Rights Act is that it gives democratic validation to the concrete expression of constitutional rights."

[3] See, *e.g.* K. D. Ewing, "Human Rights, Social Democracy and Constitutional Reform" in *Understanding Human Rights* (Gearty and Tomkins eds, Continuum International Publishing, 1996); J. Goldsworthy, "Legislative Sovereignty and the Rule of Law" in *Sceptical Essays on Human Rights* (Campbell, Ewing and Tomkins eds, Oxford University Press, Oxford, 2001), Ch.4. For consideration of the potential tension between devolution to the Scottish Parliament and the limitation of its legislative competence by reference to the Convention rights, see C. M. G. Himsworth, "Rights versus Devolution" in *Sceptical Essays on Human Rights* (Campbell, Ewing and Tomkins eds, Oxford University Press, Oxford, 2001), Ch.8.

[4] Which is not to deny their force. Indeed, the arguments of the common law constitutionalists may be said to have contributed to, if not created, a legal and political climate in which the enactment of a bill of rights became practically inevitable.

[5] P. Craig, "Public Law, Political Theory and Legal Theory" [2000] P.L. 211.

least.[6] But whatever the arguments for and against sovereignty theory, it cannot be denied that "British constitutionalism has always relied on representation, together with 'checks and balances' internal to the legislative process, rather than substantive limits to legislative power enforced by an external agency."[7] *If legislative power is arbitrary, it can be—and is—controlled by structuring it rather than subjecting it to content-based limits enforceable, when ascertained, by the courts. And if the rule of law requires the subjection of "arbitrary" power to legal limits, the substantive theorists have yet to explain how it is that the power of Parliament is arbitrary and inconsistent with constitutionalism but a power conferred on or asserted by the courts, to invalidate legislation on grounds of incompatibility with rights of indeterminate content, is not.[8] In the hands of the substantive theorists, invocation of the rule of law has served to excuse a number of lapses in terms of justifying the legitimacy of the judicial role contended for.

SEPARATION OF POWERS

For supposedly fundamental doctrines of the constitution, the **2–15** meaning and force of both parliamentary supremacy and the rule of law turn out to be surprisingly contested questions. So too with the doctrine of the separation of powers, which Britain was once taken to exemplify, which was subsequently written off as irrelevant, but which seems withal to have clung on to its claim to be a central feature of the constitution.[9] Its claim will no doubt be all the stronger now that the New Labour axe has fallen on the Lord Chancellor, who rejoiced in membership of the legislature, executive and judiciary and who was generally regarded as something of an affront to constitutional propriety.

The classic statements of the separation of powers doctrine were made in the period following the Glorious Revolution, when British constitutional arrangements were assuming a recognisably

---

[6] J. Goldsworthy, *The Sovereignty of Parliament: History and Philosophy* (Clarendon Press, Oxford, 1999).
[7] J. Goldsworthy, n.3, p.77.
[8] On that score, see T. Poole, "Dogmatic Liberalism? T. R. S Allan and the Common Law Constitution" (2002) 65 M.L.R. 463.
[9] In defence of the separation of powers, see e.g. M. J. C. Vile, *Constitutionalism and the Separation of Powers* (1967); C. R. Munro, *Studies in Constitutional Law* (2nd ed., Butterworths, London, 1998), Ch.8; E. Barendt, "Separation of Powers and Constitutional Government" [1999] P.L. 599; N. Barber, "Prelude to the Separation of Powers" (2001) 60 C.L.J. 59.

modern form.[10] John Locke wrote: "It may be too great a
temptation to human frailty, apt to grasp at power, for the same
persons who have the power of making laws to have also the power
of executing them."[11] Lord Bolingbroke distinguished the legislative, executive and judicial functions of the state,[12] but is perhaps
less well remembered for his own contribution to separation of
powers thinking than for the influence he had on his friend, a
visiting French aristocrat named Montesquieu. In *The Spirit of the
Laws*, Montesquieu wrote:

> "In every government there are three sorts of power . . . that
> of making laws, that of executing public affairs and that of
> adjudicating on crimes and individual causes. . . . When the
> legislative and executive powers are united in the same person
> or in the same body of magistrates, there can be no liberty. . . .
> Again, there is no liberty if the power of judging is not
> separated from the legislature and executive. There would be
> an end to everything if the same man or the same body . . .
> were to exercise those powers."[13]

Thus the crucial evil which the separation of powers seeks to avoid
is the concentration of power in too few hands, with all that that
implies in terms of loss of liberty. This may be achieved by a rigid
separation of the legislative, executive and judicial functions, and
their allocation to three distinct agencies; more probably, it will be
achieved by structuring the institutions of the state in such a way
that no one institution has complete autonomy in the exercise of its
functions, but is subject to a degree of control by one or both of
the others.[14] On this account, it is less important correctly to
identify and distribute particular functions of the state than to
ensure that at no one time does one branch of the state have too
much power by comparison with the others: the "health" of a
constitution is a function of the efficacy of the "checks and
balances" whereby the different institutions may encroach upon
one another's territory.

2–16   *Prima facie*, our constitutional arrangements appear to conform
to this doctrine: we have legislatures, executive authorities and
judicial organs, each performing its respective role. Why then did it

---

[10] Although the ideas illuminating separation of powers thinking have a longer
historical pedigree than that implies, going back to the experiments with mixed
government in Ancient Greece and Rome.

[11] J. Locke, *Second Treatise on Civil Government* (1690).

[12] Visc. Bolingbroke, *Remarks on the History of England* (1743).

[13] Baron de Montesquieu, *The Spirit of the Laws* (1749).

[14] Although Montesquieu insisted that the judicial power be wholly independent of
the other two branches of government.

become so fashionable to dismiss the separation of powers as a "tiresome talking point"?[15] There are obvious institutional overlaps in terms of personnel: the Sovereign, for example, is part of the legislature, the executive and the judiciary, if only in a formal sense[16]; the government is drawn from Parliament; our senior judges (for now) sit in the House of Lords and may take part in its legislative business. Indeed, when they did not simply ignore it, the critics of the separation of powers would enumerate in exhaustive detail the instances of Parliament performing non-legislative functions, of the government making laws and (through the growth of the system of administrative tribunals) adjudicating on legal rights and obligations, and of the judiciary acting non-judicially.[17] There is some truth in these observations, though they rarely tell the whole story and, taken at face value, may give a distorted impression. Thus it is true that Parliament has a penal jurisdiction in the protection and enforcement of its privileges; but it has not been used for more than a century.[18] A great deal of legislative power is delegated by Parliament to ministers, local authorities and others; but primary legislation prescribes the scope and limits of these powers, subordinate legislation is (in theory) subject to parliamentary approval, and the courts can invalidate subordinate legislation which is found to be *ultra vires*. Certain judicial functions are performed by administrative tribunals or officials; but since the Franks Report on Administrative Tribunals and Inquiries, and the legislation to which it led,[19] such tribunals have been absorbed into the machinery of justice, and their determinations are subject either to appeal or review by the ordinary courts. So the British constitution fails to adhere to the pure theory of the separation of powers: the various functions of the state do stray across institutional boundaries to some extent. But Montesquieu himself did not insist on an absolute division of the functions of the state between separate institutions. It may be that the critics of the doctrine have perpetuated the pure theory which, in its lack of correspondence to actual constitutional arrangements, is easier to knock down.

---

[15] S. A. de Smith, "The Separation of Powers in New Dress" [1966] 12 McGill L.J. 491.
[16] As was the Lord Chancellor in a rather more practical sense.
[17] This led Sir Ivor Jennings to argue that there was no coherent distinction between the three functions of the state. In consequence, separation of powers doctrine could provide no real guide to the proper distribution of power, and so was ineffective to restrain tyranny: *The Law and the Constitution* (5th ed., 1959).
[18] It is almost inconceivable that it will ever be used again, certainly since the decision of the ECHR in *Demicoli v Malta* (1991) 14 E.H.R.R. 47. There, a journalist had been convicted of a breach of parliamentary privilege for criticising M.P.s by a tribunal numbering amongst its membership two of the M.P.s named in his article. The Court held that his rights to a fair trial under Art.6 had been violated.
[19] Now the Tribunals and Inquiries Act 1992.

2–17   There are numerous references in the case law to the separation of powers, and some of the dicta might usefully be considered in the context of the debate over common law constitutionalism, which seems sometimes to contemplate the extension of judicial authority unrestrained by considerations of practicality or relative expertise. This is not to say that invocation of the separation of powers doctrine necessarily involves judicial restraint, although that was its effect in *Duport Steels Ltd v Sirs*, where Lord Diplock held:

> "At a time when more and more cases involve the application of legislation which gives effect to policies that are the subject of bitter public and parliamentary controversy, it cannot be too strongly emphasised that the British constitution, though largely unwritten, is firmly based on the separation of powers: Parliament makes the laws, the judiciary interprets them."[20]

Again in *Secretary of State for the Home Department v Rehman*,[21] where the question was whether and to what extent the Special Immigration Appeals Committee could question the Home Secretary's decision that a person's deportation was "in the interests of national security", Lord Hoffmann held:

> "However broad the jurisdiction of a court or tribunal, whether at first instance or on appeal, it is exercising a judicial function and the exercise of that function must recognise the constitutional boundaries between judicial, executive and legislative power. Secondly, . . . limitations on the appellate process . . . arise from the need, in matters of judgment and evaluation of evidence, to show proper deference to the primary decision-maker."

---

[20] [1980] 1 W.L.R. 147 at 157.

[21] [2003] 1 A.C. 153, para.49. In a *general* sense, the development of judicial review may be justified in terms of the separation of powers: it was a necessary response to the enormous growth, largely unchecked by political or judicial controls, of governmental power during the 20th century. Equally, the articulation in more recent case law of a concept of judicial deference illustrates the limits separation of powers thinking places upon the judicial role. Even while asserting the competence (whether as a matter of the common law or, now, under the Human Rights Act) to control the legality of governmental acts, the courts require to be mindful of two things: first, the democratic credentials of Parliament, the source of much of the executive's power; and, secondly, the limits of judicial expertise.

By contrast, the Privy Council has on a number of occasions struck down retrospective criminal legislation or legislation transferring sentencing powers to the executive as unconstitutional usurpations of the judicial function,[22] and separation of powers thinking may be said to informs decision such as *Commissioners of Customs and Excise v Cure & Deeley Ltd*,[23] where the Court of Appeal declined to interpret a statute so as to permit an administrative authority to make the final decision on a person's liability to tax. More broadly, as Professor Munro observes, it is notable how often the separation of powers crops up as a tool of criticism of aspects of constitutional practice. The Franks Report in 1957, and the concerns that prompted the establishment of the Committee on Administrative Tribunals and Inquiries, may be seen as a powerful vindication of the continuing relevance of the reasoning underpinning the separation of powers doctrine.[24] To speak of one institution of the state "usurping" the functions of another is pejorative, and reflects a sense of offence to the proper order of things. As with the rule of law, then, it is possible to load too much weight on to the doctrine of the separation of powers. It contributes to our constitutional traditions not as a precise yardstick of quality, but as a political ideal that has far greater resonance than its twentieth century critics allowed.

Going forward, it may be argued that the tripartite division of **2–18** powers, and indeed the whole focus of the doctrine on the state, no longer provides an accurate or adequate picture of a constitution. This is not to abandon the doctrine, but to seek to strengthen it: the separation of powers in the modern age is as much concerned with the proper allocation of competence between national and supranational institutions, or between separate legislatures, as it is with the balance between legislature and executive, or legislature and the courts.[25] Barber argues that the separation of powers properly understood aims not only to safeguard individual liberty, but also to secure efficiency in government, in the sense that a given function should be allocated to the institution best fitted to

---

[22] See, *e.g. Liyanage v R.* [1967] 1 A.C. 259 and *Hinds v R.* [1977] A.C. 195. As a matter of UK constitutional law, of course, it was not open to the courts so to impugn the powers conferred on the Secretary of State in relation to sentencing, and it has required successive trips to the ECtHR to exclude the executive from this branch of criminal justice at least: see most recently *Stafford v United Kingdom* (2002) 35 E.H.R.R. 32.

[23] [1962] 1 Q.B. 340.

[24] As may the earlier report of the Donoughmore Committee on Ministers' Powers, which reported in 1929 and which was set up to consider whether the increasing use of delegated legislative power required to be checked. The committee concluded that it did not, subject to appropriate safeguards to prevent abuse.

[25] See Barber, n.9.

discharge it.[26] In that regard, the separation of powers doctrine may acquire added significance as the devolution settlement beds down and questions are raised about the balance of competences it presently enshrines.

---

[26] Under reference to John Locke, James Madison (*The Federalist Papers*, No. 47) and the decision of the Supreme Court in *Myers v United States* (1926) 272 US 52.

CHAPTER 3

ELECTIONS

Introduction

In a democratic society, a number of basic decisions must be **3–01** made about how the holders of elective office are chosen: on the franchise, or who is entitled to vote; on who is entitled to stand for election, and on what conditions; on the method by which, and the framework within which, votes are cast and counted; and on the conduct of elections and election campaigns. While there is general agreement about certain fundamental aspects of the electoral process, such as the secret ballot and universal suffrage, other elements of the system are more controversial.[1]

Within any particular elected institution, there is always likely to be resistance to reform of the electoral process: the desire of political parties "to improve the electoral system has tended to vary in inverse proportion to their ability to do anything about it."[2] Thus the electoral reform movement has made little headway at Westminster, although the rules on the conduct of elections and the funding of political parties have recently been revised.[3] With the establishment of the new devolved institutions, however, there has been a significant break from established practice in the use of more proportionate methods of voting.[4] The electoral law of the United Kingdom is therefore something of a patchwork at present. Where the differences between the various tiers of the state are significant, as with the actual electoral systems used, each tier is discussed separately. Where there is greater uniformity, the subject is explained on that footing, noting such differences as exist.

---

[1] European Convention on Human Rights, First Protocol, Art.3 binds state parties only "to hold free elections at reasonable intervals by secret ballot, under conditions which will ensure the free expression of the opinion of the people in the choice of the legislature."

[2] Report of the Independent Commission on the Voting System, Cm.4090–I (1998), para.23 ("the Jenkins Report").

[3] By the Political Parties, Elections and Referendums Act 2000, of which more presently. See generally K. D. Ewing, "Transparency, Accountability and Equality: the Political Parties, Elections and Referendums Act 2000" [2001] P.L. 542.

[4] Proportional representation has also been adopted for elections to the European Parliament, and is to be adopted in Scotland for local government elections.

It should be noted that electoral law is largely a matter reserved by the Scotland Act 1998 to the exclusive competence of the Westminster Parliament.[5] The key exception relates to local government elections in Scotland: here, only the franchise is a reserved matter, with others aspects of local government elections falling within the devolved competence of the Scottish Parliament.[6]

ELECTORAL SYSTEM

Westminster and voting reform

3–02   Briefly, during that period of limited Liberal Democrat involvement in government policy making following the 1997 Labour landslide, there was a sense that the British electoral system might be in for some serious reform. At that time, elections to the Westminster and European Parliaments[7] and to local councils were conducted in accordance with the simple plurality, or "first-past-the-post" (FPTP), system of voting. Under FPTP, the candidate receiving the largest number of votes in a constituency wins the seat, even if he receives only one vote more than the runner-up and his votes represent nothing like a majority of the votes cast overall. The Liberal Democrats, in particular, had long campaigned for reform, and there was (and is) much to be said against the system.[8] First, it tends to distort voter preferences. A party may win a substantial majority of seats in the House of Commons on significantly less than a majority of votes cast[9]; conversely, a party may win more votes than its opponents but lose the election because its votes do not translate into a majority of seats.[10] Secondly (and relatedly), FPTP discriminates against smaller parties or parties whose support is not concentrated. This matters, not least because disenchantment with a system which converts every election into, generally speaking, a two-horse race may have contributed to the decline in electoral turnouts; and this itself undermines the legitimacy of a government claiming a

---

[5] SA 1988, Sch.5, Head B3.
[6] Local government elections are discussed separately, in Ch.7.
[7] With one exception. Under the European Parliamentary Elections Act 1978, which was then in force, the three Northern Irish Members of the European Parliament were elected according to the single transferable vote system. This system continues to apply NI under the legislation now governing elections to the European Parliament, the European Parliamentary Elections Act 2002.
[8] The deficiencies of FPTP are discussed in detail in the Jenkins Report, paras 27–42
[9] The second Labour landslide in 2001 gave the party 63% of the seats in the House of Commons from only 41% of votes cast (and that on a turnout of only 59%).
[10] As happened to the Labour Party in 1951 and to the Conservative Party in Feb. 1974.

popular mandate. Voters may prefer to withhold their vote than waste it, or, if theirs is a constituency in which the election of their preferred candidate is assured, may find they have better things to do on election day than register their personal support.

Equally, there are advantages to FPTP. It is easily understood by voters. It is simple (and therefore relatively cheap) to operate. It creates a link between constituency M.P. and local electors, which in some cases matures into a bond transcending party preferences. It has tended to give one party an overall majority of seats in the House of Commons at election time, which avoids minority or coalition governments.[11] If it operates unfairly to smaller parties, it may at least be said to prevent the extreme and/or disagreeable from rising to any prominence. And as the Jenkins commission noted, there is no surging popular agitation for abandoning FPTP, however strongly electoral reformers might feel about it.

But, with constitutional reform very much the flavour of the **3–03** month in the summer of 1997, the new Labour government appointed an independent commission, chaired by the late Lord Jenkins of Hillhead, to examine the voting system and to recommend an appropriate alternative system to FPTP which might be put to the British people in a referendum. Any alternative the commission came up with was required to reflect the need for "broad proportionality", stable government, the extension of voter choice and the maintenance of a link between M.P.s and geographical constituencies. Striving to reconcile these not absolutely compatible objectives, the alternative to FPTP adopted by the Jenkins commission involved a two-vote mixed system, described in the final report of the commission as "limited AMS" or "AV top-up". Elucidation may be in order. "AMS" denotes the additional member system of voting.[12] As the name implies, it is not a system which operates alone; its object, rather, is to mitigate the unfairness involved in a strictly majoritarian system. In effect, at any election involving AMS, there are two types of candidate: the constituency candidates, elected by FPTP or some similar method, and the additional or top-up candidates, elected in accordance with proportional representation. The "AV" or alternative vote system works on the basis of single-member constituencies in the same way as FPTP. It differs from FPTP in that the voter does not simply cast his vote for his preferred candidate, but ranks the

---

[11] But there are risks in overstating this as a virtue for FPTP. The Jenkins Report notes that FPTP produced a single party government having the command of a reliable House of Commons majority in only 64 of the 150 years to 1998. In any case, coalition governments, at least, have worked perfectly well—indeed, are the norm—in other countries, and may well prove to be the norm in a devolved Scotland. Moreover, as noted, possession of a majority of seats in the House of Commons rarely denotes the mandate of a majority of voters.

[12] As used, in part, in elections to the Scottish Parliament.

candidates listed on his ballot paper in order of preference. If one candidate wins 50 per cent or more of the first-preference votes outright, that candidate is elected to represent the constituency. Failing that, the candidate receiving the lowest number of first preferences is eliminated and his supporters' second preferences are redistributed. The process of elimination and redistribution continues until one candidate secures an overall majority of votes by comparison to the others.[13] But this is to use the word "majority" in the loosest sense; research has shown that AV may produce results even more distortive of voter preferences than FPTP. The Jenkins commission itself recognised that AV unmitigated by a second, more proportionate method of voting, would not constitute an acceptable alternative to FPTP. Hence its recommendation for a combination of AV and AMS, whereby some four-fifths of M.P.s would be elected on the basis of single member constituencies, but using AV rather than FPTP, with the remaining top-up members being elected on a second vote based on regional lists.

At Westminster, the Jenkins recommendations met with the same lack of enthusiasm that has frustrated other reforming initiatives in that arena: as noted, the achievement of the electoral reformers—in advance of Jenkins—was to secure a departure from FPTP in the new arrangements for elections to the devolved assemblies and the revised arrangements for European elections. This is not especially surprising, even leaving aside the cynicism of political parties, whose disquiet about the electoral system evaporates when they do well out of it. The Jenkins Report does not discuss the matter directly (and it may be that, in recommending the election of a relatively small proportion of additional members, it was not perceived as a problem), but reform of the electoral system is not necessarily a stand-alone business. Its operation, and the operation of any alternative, must be considered in the context of the web of conventions that regulate matters such as the dissolution of Parliament and the timing of elections. At present, in normal circumstances, the timing of a general election is a matter within the discretion of the Prime Minister: subject to the requirement imposed by the Parliament Act 1911 that no Parliament shall last for more than five years, he is free to decide when to advise the Queen to dissolve Parliament and require that an election be held. Where circumstances are not normal, the conventional position is as follows. One of the key functions of Parliament is to provide a

---

[13] The AV system was recommended for use in county constituencies by an all-party Speaker's Conference in 1917; and in 1931, a bill providing for the adoption of the AV system was actually passed by the House of Commons. The bill was rejected by the House of Lords and nothing more was heard of it after the fall of the second Labour government later that year.

pool from which the government may be formed. By convention, the person invited by the Queen to form a government is the person who appears best able to command the confidence of the House of Commons—usually, if not invariably, the leader of the party having an overall majority of seats in the House. If the government should lose the confidence of the Commons, it is obliged by convention to resign so that an alternative administration, better able to harness the Commons' support, may be appointed. If this is not possible, however, or if the Parliament is from the outset "hung" (in the sense that no one party has or can count on a majority of seats in the Commons), it may be that the Parliament thus elected is simply incapable of sustaining any government in office. In that event, the only viable solution may be to dissolve the Parliament with a view to the election of a more stable mix of M.P.s. Regular elections are a virtue, and indeed a matter of international legal obligation, but few would argue for unduly frequent general elections at the behest of Prime Ministers unable to control a recalcitrant Commons.[14] In short, if the electoral system were to be reformed in such a way as to increase the likelihood of minority or coalitions governments, thought would also need to be given to translating the present conventional framework surrounding the calling of elections to legally-enforceable rules. That this can be done is amply illustrated by the provisions of the Scotland Act dealing with this situation.

Scottish Parliament

In the first place, the First Minister has no discretion in relation **3–04** to the timing of a Scottish general election. In terms of section 2(2) of the Scotland Act 1998, ordinary general elections are to be held every four years on the first Thursday in May.[15] In terms of section 3(1), extraordinary general elections are only to be held where the Parliament resolves that it should be dissolved (and only then where the number of members voting in favour of dissolution constitute two-thirds of the total number of MSPs) or where the Parliament fails to nominate a First Minister within the period (normally 28 days) provided for by section 46. In either event, it is

---

[14] Although it should not be assumed that the Queen is obliged by convention to accede to absolutely every request for a dissolution and election: see paras 1–06—1–08.
[15] Subject to SA 1998, s.2(5), which allows the Presiding Officer of the Scottish Parliament to propose an alternative date, within one month of the first Thursday in May, as the date for an ordinary general election, and provides for the Queen, in accordance with that proposal, to dissolve the Parliament, require the election to be held on the date proposed and require the Parliament to meet within a week of the poll. In the ordinary case, the Parliament will be dissolved by virtue of s.2(3) on a date prescribed by order, without the need for a royal proclamation.

for the Presiding Officer to propose a date for the election, and for the Queen to act on that proposal by proclamation dissolving the Parliament, requiring the extraordinary general election to be held on the date proposed and requiring the Parliament to meet within a week of the poll. Where an extraordinary election is held within six months of the first Thursday in May of a year in which an ordinary election is due to take place, the ordinary election will not be held, but the ordinary four year life-cycle of the Parliament will run from that date (*i.e.* May 1) rather than from the date of the extraordinary election.[16]

The applicable electoral system also differs from Westminster. The voter in a Scottish general election has two votes, one for a constituency member, and one for a regional or top-up member. Seventy-three constituency members are elected in the same way as Westminster M.P.s, on the basis of FPTP in the same single-member constituencies as are used in Westminster elections (except that the composite Westminster constituency of Orkney and Shetland is divided into two constituencies for Scottish elections). Where the seat of a constituency MSP falls vacant by reason of the death, disqualification or resignation of the incumbent, the Presiding Officer will appoint a date for a by-election to fill the vacancy unless such date would fall within three months of the date of the next ordinary general election. In that event, the seat will remain vacant until filled in the usual way.

The 56 regional members are elected on the basis of lists drawn up in each of the eight constituencies provided for by the European Parliamentary Constituencies (Scotland) Order 1996.[17] A person may be listed either as an individual candidate or as a member of a political party registered under the Political Parties, Elections and Referendums Act 2000. In the latter case, each party may nominate up to 12 of its members as regional candidates on the list, but the list is "closed" in the sense that the voter cannot express a preference for a candidate within a party list: which of its candidates win through is a matter for the party itself to decide.

3–05   The method of allocating the seven available regional seats in each region is complex and need only be outlined here. Once the regional votes have been counted, each party and each individual candidate is allotted a "regional figure" calculated in accordance with an arithmetic formula prescribed by section 7(2) of the Scotland Act. The first regional seat is awarded to the party or individual candidate having the highest regional figure. Where a seat is awarded to a party in this way, it is then necessary, in order to maintain proportionality in the distribution of seats, to recalculate that party's regional figure. Again the arithmetic is prescribed

---

[16] SA 1998, s.3(3) and (4).
[17] Although for European elections, these constituencies have now been supplanted by the European Parliamentary Elections Act 2002.

by the Act. Each successive seat is awarded to the party or candidate having, on that particular round, the highest regional figure, until all seven seats are filled. If at any stage of the process, that figure is shared between two parties or between a party and an individual candidate, the Act provides that a regional seat shall be allocated to each.

The use of party lists in the election of regional members obviates the need for by-elections should a regional seat fall vacant during the life of the Parliament: the regional returning officer will simply notify the Presiding Officer of the next-named nominee in the appropriate party's regional list (no doubt having first ascertained that he or she is willing to serve). On purely practical grounds, the Scotland Act makes no provision for regional by-elections in other situations, as where a party's regional list is exhausted, or where a regional seat held by an individual candidate falls vacant.

European Elections

Elections to the European Parliament are different again, **3–06** though here too a proportionate method of voting is now in place by virtue of the European Parliamentary Elections Act 2002. Under the 2002 Act, Northern Ireland's three MEPs are elected, as they have been since the first direct elections to the European Parliament in 1979, in accordance with the single transferable vote (STV) system.[18] The system is based on multi-member constituencies not unlike the regional constituencies utilised in Scottish elections. With STV, however, the voter does not merely vote for one party or candidate, but expresses his preferences for the candidates in numerical order. The first candidate whose "first preference votes" meet a pre-determined quota is awarded the first seat in the constituency. His second (and subsequent) preference votes are then redistributed to the appropriate candidates until someone else achieves the quota figure. If no candidate meets the quota on the first round of counting, the candidate receiving the lowest number of first preferences is eliminated, with second and subsequent preferences being redistributed to other candidates as appropriate. The process continues until enough candidates have met the quota to fill the seats available in the constituency. Complex it may be, but it was adopted in Northern Ireland with the acknowledged aim of reducing the risk of the electorate

---

[18] STV is also for elections to the NI Assembly under the Northern Ireland Act 1998, and has been proposed for local government elections in Scotland.

splitting along sectarian lines and in practice has worked well there.[19]

The system applicable in the rest of the United Kingdom is based on regional party lists. Like Northern Ireland, Scotland and Wales constitute a single region for the purposes of European elections; England is divided into nine regions. In Scotland, there are eight seats available. The voter casts his vote either for an individual candidate or registered political party named on his regional list. The first seat is awarded to the party (or first-named candidate on the party's list) or candidate having the highest number of votes. The voting figures are then adjusted. If the first seat has been taken by an individual candidate, he and all the votes cast for him drop out of the picture; where it has been taken by a party, the party's total number of votes is divided by two. The second seat is then awarded to the party or candidate having the highest number of votes after these adjustments. The figures are then recalculated again, in the same way, and so the process continues until all the available seats have been filled.[20]

CONSTITUENCIES

3–07 The number and distribution of parliamentary constituencies is governed by the Parliamentary Constituencies Act 1986 as amended.[21] At present there are 659 constituencies, each returning

---

[19] STV is also used for elections to the Dáil, the Parliament of the Rep. of Ireland. It was recommended for adoption in the UK's urban constituencies by the 1917 Speaker's Conference, and was actually used in a number of the old multi-member university seats until their abolition in 1948. The principal objection to its adoption for Westminster elections, at least, was identified by the Jenkins Report in the following terms (para.94): "In Britain, with a population of 58.5 million as against Ireland's 3.5 million, the multi-member STV constituencies (unless there were to be a massive increase in the number of MPs, which the Commission regards as unacceptable) would need to be approximately four or five times as large as the Irish constituencies. This would make them geographically far-flung in rural or semi-rural areas, and, even in concentrated urban areas, constituencies of about 350,000 electors would entail a very long ballot paper and a degree of choice which might be deemed oppressive rather than liberating".

[20] Provision was made by the Treaty of Nice to adjust the levels of national representation in the European Parliament with a view to the accession to the EU of former eastern bloc states. In order to accommodate those adjustments, Parliament enacted the European Parliament (Representation) Act 2003.

[21] Most recently by the Political Parties, Elections and Referendums Act 2000. Many of the amendments provided for by that Act have still to be brought into force, including those which provide for the transfer of the functions of the present boundary commissions to four new boundary committees to be established under the aegis of the Electoral Commission, itself a creation of the 2000 Act.

one M.P. to Westminster. The number was increased from 651 to 659 prior to the 1997 general election, following the last boundary commission review of constituency numbers in 1994. There are four boundary commissions, one each for England, Scotland, Wales and Northern Ireland, whose job it is to keep the size and distribution of constituencies under continuous review and to report periodically to the Secretary of State. The key considerations to be taken into account in any review are prescribed by Schedule 2 to the 1986 Act. So far as Scottish constituencies are concerned, this provides that regard must be had in setting constituency boundaries to the boundaries of Scottish local authority areas and to achieving in each constituency an electorate which is as near as possible in number to the "electoral quota".[22] It is permissible to depart from these touchstones if special geographical considerations, including in particular the size, shape and accessibility of a constituency, appear to require it. Furthermore, in proposing any alteration to constituency boundaries, the boundary commission must have regard to the inconvenience likely to flow from, and any local ties which would be broken by, such alteration.

Formerly, Schedule 2 provided that the number of Scottish constituencies should be no less than 71.[23] This requirement was deleted by section 86 of the Scotland Act. Section 86 also provided that for the purposes of the boundary commission's next review of Scottish constituency boundaries, the electoral quota for England rather than Scotland should be used. The object of both provisions was to free the boundary commission to recommend a reduction in the number of Scottish M.P.s if, following the establishment of the Scottish Parliament, it saw fit. While, quite clearly, devolution does not obviate altogether the need for Scottish representation in the UK Parliament, it does remove the justification for the over-representation of Scotland at Westminster.[24]

---

[22] This figure is arrived at by dividing the total number of persons registered to vote in existing Scottish constituencies on the "enumeration date" by the number of Scottish constituencies at that time. The enumeration date is the date on which the boundary commission publishes a notice under s.5 of the Act of its intention to conduct a statutory review. Note, however, the disapplication of this provision for the purposes of the boundary commission's most recent review of Scottish constituency boundaries.

[23] It is presently 72 for Westminster elections, 73 for Scottish elections: SA 1998, Sch.1, para.1 splits the Westminster constituency of Orkney and Shetland into two separate constituencies for the purposes of Scottish elections.

[24] The ratio of Scottish M.P.s to constituents is 1:55000; that of English M.P.s to constituents 1:70000. Historically, this situation was explained principally by reference to the extra work laid on Scottish M.P.s by the enactment of specifically Scottish legislation. The removal of that role raised in the minds of certain Westminster M.P.s the spectre of the "West Lothian question": underemployed Scottish members meddling with purely English legislation in which they had no direct interest as to which, see para.4–08.

In February 2002 the boundary commission published provisional recommendations for a reduction in the number of Scottish M.P.s from 72 to 59. This had repercussions for the Scottish Parliament as well as Westminster, because Schedule 1 to the Scotland Act currently provides that any reduction in the number of Scottish seats at Westminster will apply equally to the number of constituency seats available in the Scottish Parliament. Schedule 1 also requires the ratio between regional seats and constituency seats to be maintained, so far as reasonably practicable, at 56:73. Were the boundary commission's provisional recommendations to be adopted without amendment of the Scotland Act, the net result would be a Scottish Parliament significantly smaller than it is at present. Following consultation, however, the Secretary of State for Scotland announced in December 2002 that primary legislation would be introduced to amend the Scotland Act, so as to retain the present number of 129 MSPs. The Westminster constituencies will, in all probability, be changed to reflect the boundary commission's provisional recommendations in time for a general election by (at the latest) June 2006. In answer to the point that different parliamentary constituencies as between Westminster and Holyrood will prove confusing and difficult to operate, the Secretary of State said that an independent commission would be set up after the 2007 Scottish general election to examine any issues arising out of different constituency boundaries.

THE FRANCHISE

3–08 The franchise, or who is entitled to vote in any election held in the United Kingdom, is defined in the Representation of the People Acts 1983, 1985 and, now, 2000. The 2000 Act makes a number of significant amendments to the 1983 Act, including the replacement of sections 1 and 2 of the earlier Act with new provision relating to parliamentary electors and the local government franchise. Critical to one's entitlement to vote is being registered to vote in a constituency or local government electoral area, and entitlement to be registered depends (together with criteria relating to age, capacity and citizenship) on being resident in the constituency or electoral area on the "relevant date". Previously, the 1983 Act prescribed a single annual qualifying date[25] on which a person's residence fell to be tested. As amended by the 2000 Act, section 4 of the 1983 Act now defines the "relevant date" as the date on which an application for registration is made or, in the case of a person applying for registration pursuant to a declaration of local

---

[25] Oct. 10.

connection or a service declaration, the date on which the declaration was made. This "rolling system" allows a person to be entered on and removed from the electoral register at any time of year.

Sections 5 and 7 of the 1983 Act make provision as to the meaning of "residence" for the purposes of registration.[26] Patients resident in a mental hospital, whether on a voluntary or detained basis, are able either to register in respect of the hospital, if they are likely to be there some time; or to register at some other address (such as the address the patient would regard as his home address were he not in hospital). Alternatively, such patients may make a "declaration of local connection". Remand prisoners[27] may register at the establishment where they are being held, at some other address or by means of a declaration of local connection.[28] Homeless persons who would not otherwise be able to satisfy a residence-based test may also make declarations of local connection. Declarations of local connection must state the declarant's name, an address to which correspondence may be sent (or an undertaking to collect correspondence from the electoral registration office), the date of the declaration and a statement that the declarant falls into one of the categories permitted to make a declaration of local connection. They must also state that the declarant conforms to the nationality requirements and is 18 years of age or over (or, if not, his date of birth). Section 7 of the 2000 Act repeals and replaces section 12 of the 1983 Act, enabling service personnel to vote in the same way as other voters or as overseas electors as well as by way of a service declaration. Lastly, section 12 of and Schedule 4 to the 2000 Act makes significant changes to the rules relating to absent voting (voting by post or by proxy) at parliamentary or local government elections, including local elections in Scotland.

---

[26] Without prejudice to the case law which has accumulated on whether a person is resident in a constituency such as to be entitled to be registered to vote there, see, *e.g. Scott v Philp*, 1974 S.L.T. 32; *Hipperson v Newbury Electoral Registration Officer* [1985] Q.B. 1060.

[27] For whom provision is made in the new s.7A of the 1983 Act, inserted by the 2000 Act.

[28] Note that the position of remand prisoners differs from that of persons detained pursuant to a custodial sentence imposed by a court following conviction in respect of a criminal offence. The latter remain disenfranchised (and offenders detained in mental hospitals join their ranks pursuant to the 2000 Act). In *R. (Pearson and Martinez) v S of S for the Home Dept and Others*; *Hirst v Attorney-General* [2001] H.R.L.R. 31, the Divisional Court ruled that domestic law disqualifying prisoners from voting at parliamentary or local government elections was not incompatible with their rights under the European Convention on Human Rights, First Protocol, Art.3.

CONDUCT OF ELECTIONS

3–09 Previously, the controls on the conduct of elections focused on the constituency level of an election campaign: there were virtually no controls on the conduct of the national campaign or on the expenditure incurred by parties at that level, or indeed on the financing of political parties. The Political Parties, Elections and Referendums Act 2000 radically changed all of this,[29] making fresh provision for the registration and regulation of political parties[30]; for the financing and expenses of registered political parties; for the conduct of election and referendum campaigns; and for proceedings in connection with elections.[31] Nevertheless, the older controls on the conduct of campaigns at a constituency level, provided for by the Representation of the People Act 1983 remain in force. Before we go further, however, it is necessary first to say something about the Electoral Commission, the body charged with the major role in the supervision and enforcement of the regulatory regime prescribed by the 2000 Act.

Electoral Commission

3–10 The principal job[32] of the Electoral Commission is to report on the administration of parliamentary general elections, European parliamentary general elections, Scottish parliamentary general elections, National Assembly for Wales ordinary elections and Northern Ireland Assembly general elections; and on referendums held throughout the United Kingdom, throughout one or more of England, Scotland, Wales or Northern Ireland, or in any English region as specified in Schedule 1 to the Regional Development

---

[29] So radically that further legislation was needed to suspend its operation in relation to election publications when it became apparent that none of the main political parties would be able to comply with its requirements in time for the 2001 general election: see the Election Publications Act 2001.

[30] Re-enacting, with modifications, the provisions of the Registration of Political Parties Act 1998.

[31] It should however be noted that many of the amendments made to earlier legislation by the Political Parties, Elections and Referendums Act 2000 do not apply to Scottish local government elections (which are, with the exception of the franchise, a devolved matter).

[32] As noted above, the Electoral Commission is also required by the 2000 Act to establish four new boundary committees, one for each of England, Scotland, Wales and NI. In due course, the functions of the existing boundary commissions will be transferred to the Electoral Commission, which in practice will delegate their tasks to the appropriate boundary committee. So far only the English boundary committee has been established; it has absorbed the functions of the Local Government Commission for England, but English parliamentary boundaries continue to be subject to the Boundary Commission for England. When the Secretary of State is satisfied that the boundary commissions have no further functions to perform, he shall by order direct that they cease to exist.

Agencies Act 1998. In addition, it is charged with reviewing (on its own initiative) and reporting to the Secretary of State on matters relating to elections and referendums, including the distribution of seats at parliamentary elections, the conduct of local government elections, the registration and regulation of political parties and their funding. It may also act on a specific request from the Secretary of State. It should be noted, however, that the commission does *not* have power to review or report on (among other things) the funding of political parties under section 97 of the Scotland Act[33]; the conduct of referendums held pursuant to an Act of the Scottish Parliament; or the law relating to either of these. Nor does it have the power under section 6 to review or report on local elections in Scotland.[34]

In other respects, the commission is more in the nature of an advisory body. It must be consulted on changes to electoral law.[35] It may express views on party political broadcasting, to which independent broadcasters are required to have regard. It may provide advice and assistance on electoral matters to bodies including registered political parties, the Scottish Parliament, Scottish Executive and councils constituted under the Local Government etc (Scotland) Act 1994. More broadly, it has a general duty to promote public awareness of electoral systems, systems of local and national government in the United Kingdom (including the devolved administrations, but excluding Scottish local government unless the Scottish Ministers by order provide otherwise) and the institutions of the European Union.[36]

Registration of political parties

The whole regulatory regime contained in the Political Parties, **3–11** Elections and Referendums Act 2000 revolves around *registered* political parties. Unless registered a party cannot field candidates

---

[33] SA 1998, s.97 provides that Her Majesty may by Order in Council provide for the Scottish Parliamentary Corporate Body to make payments to "registered political parties" for the purpose of assisting MSPs who are connected with parties in the performance of their parliamentary duties. Such sums—the equivalent in Scotland to "Short money" in the House of Commons and "Cranborne money" in the House of Lords—are not payable to parties any of whose members are members of the Scottish Executive or junior Scottish Ministers unless otherwise specified in the enabling Order.

[34] However, by s.19 of the 2000 Act, the Scottish Ministers may by order make provision transferring to the Electoral Commission or to the boundary committee for Scotland any of the functions of the Local Government Boundary Commission for Scotland, terminating or modifying certain functions of the Scottish commission or the Scottish Ministers under the Local Government (Scotland) Act 1973, or preventing the Scottish Ministers from exercising such functions without first obtaining the advice of the Electoral Commission.

[35] Including changes to provision made by the Secretary of State pursuant to SA 1998, s.12 for the conduct of elections in Scotland.

[36] This being by way of the government's principal response to tumbling electoral turnouts and other symptoms of voter malaise.

at elections,[37] that is parliamentary elections, European parliamentary elections, Scottish parliamentary elections, elections to the National Assembly for Wales, elections to the Northern Ireland Assembly and local government elections.[38] This is without prejudice to the right of any person who does not purport to represent any party[39] to stand for election. The register of political parties previously maintained by the registrar of companies under the Registration of Political Parties Act 1998 is replaced under section 23 of the 2000 Act with two new registers maintained by the Electoral Commission. The Great Britain Register contains details of parties intending to contest elections in one or more of England, Scotland or Wales; the Northern Ireland Register contains details of parties intending to contest elections in Northern Ireland. An entry in the Great Britain Register must be marked to indicate the part or parts of Great Britain in respect of which the party in question is registered. A party can apply to be registered in both registers, but the party as registered in the Great Britain Register and the party as registered in the Northern Ireland Register are required to be constituted as two separate parties with separate financial affairs.

Each registered party must register a person as the party's leader, the party's nominating officer and the party's treasurer (although the same person may hold all three offices). The nominating officer has responsibility for the submission by representatives of the party of lists of candidates for elections; the issuing of certificates attesting that a candidate in an election is a representative of the party; and the approval of descriptions and emblems used on nomination and ballot papers at elections. The treasurer has responsibility for compliance on the part of the party with the provisions of Parts III and IV of the Act (concerning accounting requirements[40] and the control of donations) and, unless a different person is registered as the party's campaigns officer, with the provisions of Parts V to VII of the Act (concerning campaign expenditure, third party expenditure and referendums).

A party may not be registered unless it has adopted a scheme which sets out the arrangements for regulating the financial affairs

---

[37] Nor, in terms of s.37 of the Act, can broadcasters transmit party political broadcasts on behalf of a party which is nor registered.

[38] In other words, all elections in the UK other than parish and community elections.

[39] Which is to say, a person whose nomination paper describes him as "independent" or as "the Speaker seeking re-election", or gives no description at all.

[40] Unless the party has accounting units, in which case the treasurer is only responsible for compliance with the accounting requirements by the party's central organisation. Compliance with the requirements of Pts III and IV by each accounting unit is the responsibility of the person registered as treasurer of the unit.

of the party for the purposes of the 2000 Act and which has been approved in writing by the Electoral Commission. In particular, the scheme must specify whether the party is to be regarded as a single organisation with no division of responsibility for the financial affairs and transactions of the party for the purposes of the Act's accounting requirements, or as consisting of a central organisation and one or more separate accounting units (that is, constituent or affiliated organisations each of which is responsible for its own financial affairs). In the latter case, the scheme must identify the various accounting units within the party by name; and in every case, must include such other information as may be required by regulations made by the Electoral Commission. The commission may either approve a scheme as submitted, or give notice to a party requesting it to submit a revised scheme. The same process applies where a registered party wishes to replace an approved scheme with a revised scheme.

Applications for registration must be in the form prescribed by **3–12** the 2000 Act,[41] specifying a name to be the party's registered name[42]; the address of the party's headquarters, or an address to which communications to the party may be sent; the name and home address of each of the party's registered officers; a copy of the party's constitution and a draft of the accounting scheme submitted to the Electoral Commission; (where the party has accounting units) the name of each accounting unit, its address and the name of its treasurer; and such additional information as the Electoral Commission may prescribe in regulations. A party may also apply to register up to three emblems to be used by the party on ballot papers. The Electoral Commission is obliged to grant applications unless the application falls foul of the conditions prescribed in section 28(4).[43] Applications must be signed by the proposed registered leader or nominations officer, the treasurer and (where a party has one) by the campaigns officer, each of whom must declare that he is authorised to sign the application on the party's behalf. Thereafter, subject to applying to change registered particulars, the registered treasurer of a party must at the time of sending its annual statement of accounts to the Electoral Commission also give notification to the commission confirming that its registered particulars remain accurate.

---

[41] Political Parties, Elections and Referendums Act 2000, s.28 and Sch.4, Pt 1.
[42] Where the name is not in English, an English translation must be given.
[43] *e.g.* the party proposes to register a name which has already been registered by another party, which is likely to result in voters confusing the party with another registered party, which comprises more than six words, or which is obscene, offensive or includes words the publication of which might amount to the commission of an offence.

Donations to political parties

3–13 Party funding perennially excites controversy.[44] On the one hand, generous donors (if they back the right horse) are seen to obtain political favours or even appointment to high government office; on the other, the minnows of the system cannot compete with the big players for want of funds to promote themselves and their policies. State funding of the political and electoral processes is limited and indirect. Once a party has managed to secure a foothold in Parliament it is eligible for a contribution from public funds towards its parliamentary work (but not its election expenses).[45] At election time, candidates are entitled to such money-saving benefits as free postage (for one constituency mail-shot) and free use of public buildings for election meetings. If a party is sufficiently sizeable to register on the national scale, it is also entitled to at least one party election broadcast. Beyond that, the amount a party has to spend at election time on advertising and other forms of promotion depends on its membership income and, crucially, support from companies, trades unions, private individuals and others. The Labour and Conservative parties are not noticeably choosy about the sources of donations. Neither are they slow to accuse one another of all kinds of scandalous corruption in the acceptance of such money.

As the Committee on Standards in Public Life noted in its Fifth Report,[46] the decline in public confidence in the political system may not be unrelated to suspicion about the basic integrity of political parties. Yet the committee was not convinced by the arguments in favour of state funding of political parties. Its recommended solution involved limits on campaign expenditure coupled with new requirements of disclosure and registration. It is the committee's recommendations which provided the foundation for Part IV of the Political Parties, Elections and Referendums Act 2000 concerning donations to political parties.

"Donation" is defined by section 50 to include any gift to a party of money or other property[47]; any sponsorship provided in relation

---

[44] See K. D. Ewing, *The Funding of Political Parties* (Cambridge University Press, Cambridge, 1987); more recently, the Fifth Report of the Committee on Standards in Public Life, *The Funding of Political Parties in the United Kingdom*, Cm.4057-I (1998).

[45] Known as "Short money" in the House of Commons and "Cranborne money" in the House of Lords, this system of funding has a statutory foundation in relation to the Scottish Parliament in SA 1998, s.97. The sums involved could fairly be described as insignificant.

[46] See n.45.

[47] This includes the provision of property, services, facilities or other consideration of monetary value for payment of a sum less than the market value of the property transferred; and also includes bequests.

to the party[48]; any subscription or other fee paid for affiliation to, or membership of, the party; any money spent (otherwise than by or on behalf of the party) in paying any expenses incurred by the party; any money lent to the party otherwise than on commercial terms; and the provision otherwise than on commercial terms of any property, services or facilities for the use or benefit of the party, including the services of any person. Anything given or transferred to any officer, member, trustee or agent of a registered party in that capacity is also to be regarded as a donation to the party.

Section 52 then lists items which are *not* to be regarded as donations, including: "policy development grants" made to a party by the Electoral Commission[49]; grants made to cover security costs at party conferences[50]; payments made by or on behalf of the European Parliament for the purpose of assisting MEPs in the performance of their functions; the transmission by a broadcaster, free of charge, of a party political broadcast or referendum campaign broadcast; any other facilities provided in pursuance of any right conferred on candidates or a party at an election or a referendum by any enactment; the voluntary provision by any individual of his own services, in his own time and free of charge; payments made for the hire of a stand at a party conference (provided the payment does not exceed a maximum deemed by the Electoral Commission to be reasonable).

Part III of the 2000 Act, which lays down the accounting **3–14** requirements for registered parties, also makes provision in relation to donations. In compiling the party's accounts, the treasurer is entitled to disregard donations which fall to be included in a return as to election expenses in respect of a candidate at a particular election and small donations of less than £200.[51] Chapter II of Part III then sets out various restrictions on donations and donors. In essence, donations may only be accepted by a party if

---

[48] Defined in s.51 as money or other property transferred to the party or to any person for the benefit of the party for the purpose of helping the party to meet any defined expenses (*i.e.* expenses in connection with a conference, meeting or other event organised by or on behalf of the party; the preparation, production or dissemination of any publication by or on behalf of the party; or any study or research organised by or on behalf of the party) or to secure that to any extent such expenses are not incurred.

[49] 2000 Act, s.12, authorises the Commission to make such grants to registered political parties to assist with the development of their policies and manifestos.

[50] Under the Criminal Justice and Public Order Act 1994, s.170.

[51] Although s.68 of the Act provides that where a donor makes a number of small donations in the course of a calendar year which, taken together, exceed £5,000 in amount, the donor must submit a report to the Electoral Commission setting out the aggregate value of his donations and the year in which they were made, the name of the recipient party, and his full name and address (if an individual) or the details required by Sch.6, para.2 (if a company or other entity).

made by a "permissible donor" and/or a person whose identity is ascertainable. Permissible donors are defined in section 54(2) to include individuals registered in an electoral register; companies registered under the Companies Act 1985, incorporated within the United Kingdom or other Member State of the European Union and carrying on business in the United Kingdom[52]; registered political parties; limited liability partnerships; and any unincorporated association which carries on its business or activities wholly or mainly in the United Kingdom and whose main office is here. Where a party receives a donation and it is not immediately clear whether the party should refuse the donation, section 56 obliges the party to take all reasonable steps to verify or ascertain the identity of the donor and all such details about him as are required by Schedule 6 to the Act (concerning the preparation of donation reports). If a party receives a donation which it is prohibited from accepting or which it decides for other reasons to refuse, the donation or a payment of an equivalent amount must within 30 days of receipt be sent back to the donor or any person appearing to be acting on his behalf. If the party cannot ascertain the identity of the donor, it must follow the steps prescribed by section 57. This provides that if the donation was passed on by a person other than the donor, whose identity is known, the donation must be returned to that person. Failing that, if it is apparent that the donor has used any facility provided by an identifiable financial institution to make his donation—most obviously, a cheque—the donation must be returned to that institution. Failing *that*, the donation must be handed over to the Electoral Commission, which will pay it into the consolidated fund. If the party accepts a donation which it is not entitled to accept, the court (in Scotland, the sheriff, with a right of appeal to the Court of Session) may on an application from the Electoral Commission order the forfeiture by the party of a sum equal to the value of the donation, which sum will again be paid into the consolidated fund.

Party treasurers have a statutory duty[53] to prepare quarterly donation reports recording "relevant donations", that is, donations of more than £5,000 or a donation which, when added to any other relevant donations, comes to more than £5,000. These requirements apply separately in relation to the central organisation of a party and each of its accounting units where it has accounting units (subject to the substitution of £1,000 for £5,000 where donations are made to an accounting unit). During general election periods—the period beginning with the announcement of the

---

[52] This in response to disquiet about the receipt, particularly by the Conservative Party, of donations from foreign sources.
[53] Under s.62 of the Act.

Queen's intention to dissolve Parliament and ending with the date of the poll—party treasurers are required to compile weekly donation reports (unless the party intends to field no candidates at the election and has made an "exemption declaration" accordingly).[54] Donation reports are submitted to the Electoral Commission, together with a declaration by the party treasurer that to the best of his knowledge and belief all the donations recorded in the report as having been accepted by the party are from permissible donors and that no other donations requiring to be recorded have been accepted by the party during the reporting period. Where the treasurer records a nil return, he must state that to the best of his knowledge and belief that return is accurate. Section 71 together with Schedule 7 makes similar provision for controlling donations to individual members of registered parties, associations of such members and certain elected office holders.

The Electoral Commission is required by section 69 of the Act to maintain a public register of all donations reported to it under Part IV.

Constituency campaigns

The Representation of the People Act 1983 controls both the **3–15** amounts of expenditure that may be incurred by a candidate for election and/or his election agent and the manner in which it can lawfully be spent.[55] Section 75 provides that no expenditure shall be incurred other than by the candidate or his agent. The present limit on election expenses within a constituency at a parliamentary election is set out in section 76(2)(a).[56] Within 35 days of the date on which the result of a poll is declared, the election agent must submit to the returning officer a return in the prescribed form

---

[54] Under s.67 of the Act, the requirement to submit weekly donation reports may by order of the Secretary of State, following consultation with the Electoral Commission and all registered parties, be applied in relation to elections to the European Parliament, the Scottish Parliament, the National Assembly for Wales and the NI Assembly.

[55] See, generally, Pt II of the Act. Contravention of the provisions of Pt II may constitute a corrupt or illegal practice attracting liability to a fine and/or imprisonment, *e.g.* exceeding expenditure limits; bribery ("any money, gift, loan or valuable consideration, office, place or employment, in order to influence how an elector will cast his vote"); treating (where a candidate offers or gives food, drink or entertainment with a view to influencing how electors will vote); and undue influence. For the definition of "election expenses", see 1983 Act, s.90A.

[56] As amended by the Representation of the People (Variation of Limits on Candidates' Election Expenses) Order 2001 (SI 535/2001). Expenditure limits applicable to Scottish local government elections are provided for by the 1983 Act, s.76(2)(b)(ii), as inserted by the Representation of the People (Variation of Limits of Candidates' Local Government Election Expenses) (Scotland) Order 2003 (SSI 76/2003), art.2.

setting out all election expenses incurred by or on behalf of the candidate and all payments made by the agent together with all bills or receipts relating to the payments.[57] Returns and declarations received by returning officers must then be forwarded to the Electoral Commission, and arrangements made for their publication.[58]

Previously it was an offence for a third party—meaning a person other than a candidate or his agent—to incur expenditure in excess of £5 during an election period "with a view to promoting or procuring the election of a candidate" at that election, which might be contravened as much by denigrating a candidate (since his opponents stood to benefit) as by actively promoting him. In *Bowman v United Kingdom*,[59] the European Court of Human Rights held that this constituted a disproportionate restriction on freedom of expression contrary to Article 10 of the Convention, and provision is now made in relation to third-party expenditure by Part VI of the 2000 Act. A third party is permitted to incur expenditure on "election material" made available to the public or a section of the public with a view to promoting or procuring the election, or otherwise enhancing the standing, of one or more parties or candidates, provided the third party is registered as such with the Electoral Commission. Controlled expenditure in excess of £200 must be notified to the commission in a return under the Act, and it is an offence knowingly to make a false return.

Controls on campaign expenditure

3–16   Part V of the Political Parties, Election and Referendums Act 2000 makes provision, for the first time, to control expenditure incurred by or on behalf of a registered party for "election purposes", namely promoting or procuring electoral success for the party's candidates at any relevant election or otherwise enhancing the standing of the party or any such candidates with the electorate in connection with future relevant elections, whether or not imminent.[60] The law is complex and places a heavy burden of compliance on party officials.[61]

---

[57] Representation of the People Act 1983, s.81. Section 82 provides for declarations in relation to election expenses.

[58] *ibid.*, s.87A.

[59] (1998) 26 E.H.R.R. 1.

[60] Both categories of purpose include activity designed to prejudice the electoral prospects of other parties or candidates.

[61] The public interest in transparency may be felt to justify this, but the burden will not necessarily be an easy one to discharge, particularly for smaller parties without the resources to employ professional advisers.

Expenses deemed to be incurred for election purposes (and so qualifying as "campaign expenditure") are listed in paragraph 1 of Schedule 8[62] as expenses in respect of, *inter alia*, party political broadcasts (including all production costs); advertising of any nature, in any medium; any manifesto or other document setting out the party's policies; market research or canvassing; rallies and other events, including public meetings (but not annual or other party conferences) organised to obtain publicity in connection with an election campaign or for other purposes connected with an election campaign. Campaign expenditure does *not* include anything which falls to be included in a return as to election expenses in respect of a candidate or candidates at a particular election. Nor does it include such items as expenses in respect of newsletters issued by or on behalf of the party in order to inform the local electorate about a representative or candidate; the costs of employing party staff; or travelling expenses incurred by an individual from his own resources and not reimbursed. Responsibility in relation to campaign expenditure is vested in the treasurer of a party and such deputy treasurers (not exceeding 12) as he may appoint under section 74.

The restrictions on campaign expenditure are provided for in sections 75 to 84. Under section 75, it is an offence to incur campaign expenditure without the authority of a registered party's treasurer, deputy treasurer or other person authorised in writing by the treasurer or deputy treasurer. Under section 76, payments in respect of campaign expenditure may only be made by the treasurer, deputy treasurer or other authorised person.[63] Under section 77, a claim for payment in respect of campaign expenditure incurred by or on behalf of a registered party during a campaign period is not payable unless, within 21 days of the end of the period,[64] the claim is sent to the treasurer, deputy treasurer or other authorised person. Qualifying claims are then payable within 42 days of the end of the campaign.

The actual limits applicable to campaign expenditure are **3–17** imposed by section 79 and Schedule 9. For the purposes of Schedule 9, campaign expenditure incurred by or on behalf of a party registered in the Great Britain Register is to be attributed to each of England, Scotland and Wales in proportion to the number of parliamentary constituencies presently situated in that part of Great Britain unless the effects of the expenditure are confined

---

[62] Note also the provision for "notional campaign expenditure" in s.73 of the Act.
[63] And any such payment must be supported by an invoice or receipt, unless it is for a sum less than £200.
[64] Subject to special leave being granted by the court—in Scotland, the sheriff court or the Court of Session—for a claim to be paid even though submitted after the lapse of the 21-day period.

wholly or substantially to any particular part. In that event, the expenditure is attributable solely to that part. The provisions vary as between parliamentary general elections, European parliamentary elections and general elections (ordinary and extraordinary) to the devolved assemblies, and special provision is made for the situation in which elections to more than one body are held at the same time. At the end of the prescribed accounting period, the party treasurer must prepare a return in accordance with section 80 in respect of the campaign expenditure incurred by or on behalf of the party during that period in the relevant part or parts of the United Kingdom. The return must specify the poll or polls that took place in that time and must contain a statement of all payments made in respect of campaign expenditure incurred by or on behalf of the party during the relevant period in the relevant parts of the United Kingdom; a statement of all disputed claims for payment, if any; and a statement of all unpaid claims, if any, in respect of which an application is to be made to the court. The return must be accompanied by all invoices and receipts relating to the payments recorded in the return. Where the campaign expenditure incurred by the party exceeds £250,000, the return prepared by the party treasurer must be independently audited. Both return and auditor's report, if necessary, must then be submitted to the Electoral Commission within six months of the end of the campaign period. The commission in turn is obliged to make copies of the returns and reports available for public inspection.

ELECTION BROADCASTS

3–18 The media as a whole is replete with coverage of parliamentary and governmental business, but access to the broadcast media by political parties remains limited in the United Kingdom. The British Broadcasting Corporation (BBC) is prohibited by its Charter and Agreement with the Secretary of State from accepting payment in return for broadcasting, and the independent broadcasters may not transmit advertisements for organisations whose objects are of a political nature.[65] An exception to this rule is made for party political and party election broadcasts, both of which are transmitted free of charge.[66] The first election broadcast was made on the radio during the general election of 1924, with the first

---

[65] Communications Act 2003, ss.319–321.
[66] There is no intrinsic difference between the two other than the fact that the latter are made at election time, whereas the former are offered to the main political parties (*i.e.* the Labour, Conservative and Liberal Democrat parties, the Scottish National Party (in Scotland) and Plaid Cymru (in Wales) at key points of the political calendar, such as the occasion of the Queen's speech or the budget.

televised broadcast following in 1951. Section 333 of the Communications Act 2003 provides that any licence granted to an independent broadcaster by the Office of Communications (OFCOM) must contain conditions requiring the broadcaster to include party political and party election broadcasts in its services, and to observe rules adopted by the OFCOM in respect of such broadcasts.[67] The BBC is under no duty to screen political or election broadcasts, but does so as a matter of practice.

Broadcasts may only be made by registered political parties. Their allocation is a matter agreed between the BBC and the independent broadcasters, having regard to the views of the Electoral Commission and subject in a general sense to the public law principles of legality, rationality, fairness and, now, compatibility with the Convention rights. Thus at the 2001 general election, the Labour, Conservative and Liberal Democrat parties were offered a series of election broadcasts in each of the four nations of the United Kingdom, whilst smaller parties qualified for at least one broadcast in the territory of any nation in the United Kingdom if they were fielding candidates in at least one-sixth of its seats.[68] The editorial content is primarily a matter for the parties themselves, but the BBC is obliged by clause 5.1(d) of its Agreement with the Secretary of State to do all that it can to ensure that all broadcasts transmitted by it "do not include anything which offends against good taste or decency or is likely to encourage or incite crime or lead to disorder or to be offensive to public feeling." OFCOM is also under a duty to secure through the licences it grants to independent broadcasters that such material is not included in their programmes.[69] On this basis, the BBC and independent broadcasters refused to transmit a party election broadcast submitted to them by the ProLife Alliance prior to the

---

[67] In making such rules, the ITC and BBC alike are required to have regard to the views of the Electoral Commission (Political Parties, Elections and Referendums Act 2000, s.11); and must also comply with the general effect of any code adopted by the Office of Communications (OFCOM) under s.319 of the Communications Act 2003.

[68] In *R. v British Broadcasting Corp., ex p. Referendum Party* [1997] C.O.D. 459, the applicant complained that the basis for allocation of election broadcasts adopted prior to the 1997 election (in which it fielded 547 candidates) was irrational and unfair, since, being premised in part on a party's performance at the previous general election, it discriminated against new parties. Buckley J. agreed that past performance could not be the sole determining factor, but upheld the BBC's decision to offer the Referendum Party one broadcast in each of the four nations of the UK (against four each for the major parties) on the grounds that it had not attached undue weight to that factor.

[69] Communications Act 2003, s.211, Broadcasting Act 1990, s.6.

2001 general election.[70] In their application for judicial review of the BBC's decision,[71] the Alliance did not contend that the "taste and decency" requirement was *per se* incompatible with their right to freedom of expression under Article 10 of the Convention, but that the BBC had in giving effect to that requirement failed properly to balance their duty to avoid offence to members of the public with the Alliance's right to express its political message in its chosen form. Their application was dismissed at first instance, but the Court of Appeal held that the BBC had indeed acted unlawfully. By a majority, the House of Lords reversed the decision of the Court of Appeal. It was noted, first, that the right to freedom of expression under Article 10 is primarily a right "to receive and impart information and ideas without interference by public authority". That does not, as the European Court and Commission have held, imply a "general and unfettered right for any private citizen or organisation to have access to broadcasting time on radio or television in order to forward his opinion, save in exceptional circumstances, for instance if one political party is excluded from broadcasting facilities at election time while others are given broadcasting time."[72] As this implies, secondly, private citizens and organisations do have a right not to be denied access to the media on arbitrary or discriminatory grounds.[73] The error into which the Court of Appeal fell, in the opinion of the majority, was to treat this case as if the BBC had *prevented* the Alliance from expressing its views on the (inadequate) grounds of taste and decency. The question, rather, was whether the taste and decency requirement was neutral as between different viewpoints and, if not, whether any discrimination could be objectively justified. The majority found that the requirement was neutral in the sense that it applied to all political parties in the same way, and if it might be said to discriminate against those who considered it necessary to breach standards of taste and decency in order to get their message across, that was objectively justifiable: "the standards are part of the country's cultural life and have created expectations on the part of viewers as to what they will and will not be shown on the screens in their homes."[74]

---

[70] The party, which campaigns for "absolute respect for innocent human life, from fertilisation until natural death", fielded six candidates in Wales, thereby qualifying for one election broadcast in the principality. Its proposed broadcast consisted mainly of "prolonged and deeply disturbing images of aborted foetuses". The broadcast was eventually screened five days before the election with these images replaced by a blank screen bearing the word "censored".

[71] *R (ProLife Alliance) v British Broadcasting Corp.* [2003] U.K.H.L. 23.

[72] *Haider v Austria* (1995) 83 D.R. 66 at 74.

[73] As to which, see *Benjamin v Minister for Information and Broadcasting* [2001] 1 W.L.R. 1040.

[74] *ProLife Alliance*, above, para.70, *per* Lord Hoffmann.

The impact of the Convention on election broadcasts, political **3–19** advertising and other aspects of the electoral process remains to be fully worked out. As we have seen, in *Bowman v United Kingdom*,[75] the European Court held that the provisions of section 75 of the Representation of the People Act 1983 violated the rights of the applicant under Article 10 as being disproportionate to the legitimate aim of securing equality between candidates at election time.[76] Again in *VgT Verein Gegen Tierfabriken v Switzerland*,[77] the Court held that the applicant organisation's Article 10 rights had been violated by the Swiss ban on political advertising. The thrust of the argument for the applicant (an animal rights organisation) was that the broadcasting authorities refused to transmit their advertisement, arguing that commercial meat production and hence meat eating were cruel, even while they accepted advertisements from the meat industry. The Court agreed that this difference of treatment could not be objectively justified. For this reason, the government was unable to make a statement of compatibility in terms of section 19 of the Human Rights Act 1998 in respect of what is now section 319 of the Communications Act 2003, which continues the prohibition on political advertising.[78] The objective of this prohibition is clear, and plainly legitimate for the purposes of a human rights analysis: it is to achieve, so far as possible, a level playing field for political parties by preventing wealthy organisations buying airtime in order to promote their views. But this is not the only concern relevant to party political access to the media. Party political and party election broadcasts are transmitted free of charge, and, as the Electoral Commission has noted, "the estimated commercial value of free airtime far exceeds the cost of lost candidate deposits in one-sixth of the seats" within a given nation of the United Kingdom.[79] The point is that an organisation may register as a political party and field the number of candidates necessary to qualify for an election broadcast less for genuine electoral purposes than for publicity purposes, which publicity costs it little.[80] The Electoral Commission has also

---

[75] *Bowman v United Kingdom* (1998) 26 E.H.R.R. 1.
[76] Mrs Bowman, at her own expense, printed and distributed leaflets within a constituency setting out the candidates' views on abortion. Accordingly, she was prosecuted under the 1983 Act, s.75 for incurring expenditure in excess of the prescribed limit (£5) "with a view to promoting or procuring the election of a candidate" during an election period. Third-party expenditure of this sort is now regulated by the Political Parties, Elections and Referendums Act 2000, Pt VI: see para.3–15.
[77] (2002) 34 E.H.R.R. 159.
[78] Even though the ECHR held that "in certain circumstances" content-based discrimination between broadcasts might be objectively justifiable.
[79] Electoral Commission Discussion Paper (Dec. 2001).
[80] In that respect, it is pertinent to note that the ProLife Alliance's six candidates in Wales secured only 1,609 votes, 0.117% of the total cast.

stated its view that election broadcasts should be relevant to electors' voting intentions. Television and radio reach mass audiences, only a tiny proportion of which will have even the opportunity to vote for an independent candidate or such candidates as a smaller party may field. It therefore remains unpersuaded that the public interest requires greater opportunities to be extended to smaller parties in terms of access to the broadcast media.

CHAPTER 4

PARLIAMENTS

"Parliaments", not "Parliament", because there are of course two **4–01**
legislative bodies whose activities interest Scotland.[1] In the sphere
of devolved competence, the Scottish Parliament has since July 1,
1999 enacted legislation for Scotland; outwith that sphere, exclusive legislative competence remains with the Westminster Parliament (although, as section 29(8) of the Scotland Act 1998 makes
clear, nothing in the devolution settlement affects the competence
of the Westminster Parliament to enact legislation applicable to
Scotland on any matter).[2] There are significant differences between
the Westminster Parliament and the Scottish Parliament going
beyond the differences in their legislative competences, the one
legally unlimited, the other confined by reference to, among other
things, matters reserved to Westminster and compatibility with the
Convention rights and Community law. Westminster is a bicameral
legislature, the Scottish Parliament unicameral (although it was
thought that the checking and revising functions performed by the
House of Lords at Westminster would be fulfilled in Scotland
through the work of the parliamentary committees). There are
differences in the functions of such committees as between Westminster and the Scottish Parliament; perhaps most prominently,
the committees of the Scottish Parliament have a power to initiate
legislation, which the Westminster committees do not share. Yet
there are also many similarities and parallels between the two
institutions: it would indeed be strange if it were otherwise. Both
perform the same general functions of a representative,
law-making body in a "parliamentary system"[3]: the enactment of
legislation, the provision of a government and the sustaining of
that government in office, and the important function of holding
the government and other public authorities to account on behalf

---

[1] Indeed, more than two if we include the institutions of the EU.
[2] The extent to which Westminster may enact legislation for Scotland the subject
matter of which falls within the definition of devolved competence is regulated for
the present by the so-called "Sewel Convention", whereby Westminster will not
normally enact such legislation without first obtaining the consent of the Scottish
Parliament: see above, paras 1–10—1–11.
[3] As contrasted with a system such as that of the USA, which draws a rigid
distinction between its legislature and executive.

of the public as a whole. The rules and procedures governing both bodies have much in common, in so far as those applicable in Scotland often represent a statutory rendering of the conventions that have grown up at Westminster. The same is true in matters of privilege and standards, in that both bodies have jurisdiction to regulate their own procedures and the conduct of their members. It is thought, therefore, that it would be instructive to consider the two Parliaments side by side, highlighting the distinctions between them where such exist, but noting also what they have in common where that is the case.

LIFE OF PARLIAMENT

Westminster

4–02   The life of a Parliament at Westminster begins when the Sovereign exercises her prerogative to summon it to meet. By convention, the Queen exercises this prerogative following a general election. Parliament must meet in the subsequent years of its life to approve the appropriation of monies for the provision of public services and perform its other constitutional functions, but no Parliament may run for more than five years from the date first appointed for it to meet.[4] At the end of that time, if it does not happen sooner, the Queen will dissolve Parliament and cause writs to be issued for the election of a new Parliament. In practice, most Parliaments are dissolved rather sooner on the advice on the Prime Minister, at a date politically favourable for his party to contest an election.[5] Alternatively, a government may be obliged to advise a dissolution where it loses the support of the House of Commons on a motion of confidence or on an issue of confidence such as its programme for government as set out in the Queen's Speech.

The Queen's Speech takes place early on in a newly summoned Parliament, and at the commencement of subsequent parliamentary sessions within the Parliament. It marks the formal opening of each new session following the summoning or re-summoning of Parliament. Sessions usually run for about 12 months from November to November, although there is no legal requirement that they should. A session is brought to an end either by the dissolution of Parliament or by its prorogation. The significance of prorogation is that it suspends all parliamentary business until the next session (which may begin the following day). In particular, public bills

---

[4] Parliament Act 1911, s.7.
[5] Although a doomed government is likely to hang on for as long as possible, as with the Conservative administration of 1992–97.

which do not complete their parliamentary stages before the end of the session lapse and have to be started again from scratch in the session following (although there is now provision for the carrying over of government legislation from one session to the next with the agreement of the House of Commons).[6]

Holyrood

The First Minister does not enjoy the same freedom as his **4-03** Westminster counterpart in terms of being able to advise the Queen when to dissolve the Scottish Parliament. The life cycle of the Scottish Parliament is fixed by the Scotland Act. It begins on a date falling within the period of seven days beginning with the day immediately after that on which the poll at a general election was held.[7] Ordinarily, it will end with its dissolution with a view to a general election being held on the first Thursday in May of the fourth calendar year following that in which the previous ordinary general election was held.[8] Should the first Thursday in May be for some reason unsuitable, the Presiding Officer of the Scottish Parliament may propose an alternative date, no earlier than one month before and no later than one month after the first Thursday in May, to the Queen; and the Queen may[9] then by proclamation dissolve the Parliament, require the poll to be held on the date proposed and require the new Parliament to meet within the period of seven days beginning with the date of the poll.

Section 3 of the Scotland Act makes provision for extraordinary general elections. Where no fewer than two-thirds of the total number of MSPs vote in favour of a resolution that the Parliament be dissolved, the Presiding Officer must propose a date for the holding of an election and the Queen may, by proclamation, dissolve the Parliament, require an extraordinary general election to be held on the date proposed and enjoin the new Parliament to

---

[6] In Scotland, bills have the full remaining spread of the parliamentary cycle following their introduction in which to complete their parliamentary stages.

[7] SA 1998, s.2(3)(b). For the purposes of calculating the seven-day period, Saturday and Sunday, Christmas Eve and Christmas Day, Good Friday, a Scottish bank holiday or a "day appointed for public thanksgiving or mourning" are to be disregarded: s.4.

[8] SA 1998, ss 2, 3(a). If the election is to be held on the first Thursday in May, the Parliament must be dissolved at the beginning of the "minimum period" ending with the date of the poll. The "minimum period" is specified in accordance with orders made under s.12, which confers power on the Secretary of State to make provision about Scottish elections.

[9] Here, "may" not "shall" (*cf.* SA 1998, s.2(3)(a)). Presumably this is to preserve an element of discretion on the Queen's part as the ultimate safeguard against abuse (although it is significant that it is the Presiding Officer, not the First Minister, who is charged with proposing an alternative date), much as the convention requiring the Queen to act on the advice of her Ministers could yield at Westminster were the P.M. to request a dissolution inappropriately.

meet within seven days of the date of the poll.[10] An extraordinary general election may also be required where the Parliament fails to nominate one of its members for appointment as First Minister within 28 days of a general election, or of the resignation or death of an incumbent First Minister, or of the incumbent First Minister ceasing to be an MSP otherwise than by virtue of a dissolution of the Scottish Parliament.[11] In any of these situations, if the extraordinary election is held within the six-month period prior to the first Thursday in May, and an ordinary election was due to take place on the latter date, the ordinary election will not be held.[12]

COMPOSITION

The Sovereign

4–04   As we have seen, the Sovereign has an important, if formal, role to play in the dissolution and summoning of the Westminster and Scottish Parliaments (as a matter of royal prerogative in the case of Westminster, and as a matter of statute in the case of Holyrood). But the Sovereign is also a component part of the Westminster Parliament—"the King, Lords and Commons assembled"—in that Acts of Parliament are Acts of the Queen in Parliament, and must receive Royal Assent in order to become law.[13] The Queen is not part of the Scottish Parliament even in this formal sense, but Royal Assent is nonetheless necessary in order that a bill passed by the Parliament may become an Act of the Scottish Parliament.[14]

Westminster

House of Lords

4–05   "No one shall be a member of the House of Lords by virtue of a hereditary peerage." At a stroke (promptly qualified), section 1 of the House of Lords Act 1999 did away with what was widely accepted as an indefensibly undemocratic blemish on British constitutional arrangements. Perhaps the most that could be said for the historic right of hereditary peers to sit and vote in the House of Lords was that they happened to provide a form of counterweight to the "elective dictatorship"[15] flowing from the

---

[10] SA 1998, s.3(1)(a), (2)(b).

[11] SA 1998, s.3(1)b); and see also s.46.

[12] SA 1998, s.3(3). This does not affect the year in which the subsequent ordinary general election will be held: s.3(4).

[13] By convention, of course, the Sovereign never refuses Royal Assent. The last time this happened was in the reign of Queen Anne, and even then seems to have been on the advice of her Ministers.

[14] SA 1998, s.28(2)–(4).

[15] A term coined by Lord Hailsham, *The Dilemma of Democracy* (Collins, London, 1978).

command of a majority in the House of Commons. But it was not a particularly compelling argument for retention of the hereditary principle: if nothing else, there was a question about how even-handed a counterweight the hereditaries actually were.[16] The issue as yet unresolved, however, is what form a reformed House of Lords should take.

The House of Lords at present is in a transitional state, comprising 92 hereditary peers exempted from the effects of the 1999 Act, 542 life peers (including the Lords of Appeal in Ordinary) and 26 Lords Spiritual (bishops and archbishops of the Church of England). The Life Peerages Act 1958 provided for the conferment of life peerages on men and (for the first time) women[17] with the right to sit and vote in the Lords. This helped to mitigate, if not remove, the political imbalance in the upper house, and to the extent that life peerages are often conferred in recognition of outstanding public service and/or expertise in particular fields, has brought to the House of Lords a rather wider range of experience and specialism than tends to exist in the Commons. But as appointees, nominated by political parties, life peers have no obviously greater claim to democratic legitimacy than the hereditaries. Does it matter? The secondary, subordinate role of the House of Lords is enshrined in any case in the Parliament Acts of 1911 and 1949, which provide that a bill[18] approved by the Commons and rejected by the Lords in one parliamentary session may, if approved afresh by the Commons in the session following, proceed directly to Royal Assent without the consent of the Lords. It is questionable whether, if there were to be a move towards the election of members of the House of Lords, this position could continue to be justified; in that event, reform of

---

[16] Historically, the hereditary peers have provided the Conservative Party with an inbuilt majority. While a Conservative government was able to call out its "backwoods peers" if necessary to get one of its measures through the Lords, as it did with the poll tax legislation in 1989, the Labour government of 1997–2001 alone was twice required to invoke the Parliament Acts procedure to ensure the enactment of its legislation.

[17] The right of hereditary peeresses in their own right to sit and vote in the House of Lords was only established by the Peerage Act 1963, which also enabled hereditary peers wishing to seek election to the House of Commons to disclaim their peerages for life. Most of the provisions of the 1963 Act were repealed or amended by the House of Lords Act 1999, which in depriving (most) hereditary peers of their right to sit in the Lords also provides in s.3 for them to be elected as M.P.s.

[18] Other than a bill certified by the Speaker of the House of Commons to be a money bill, which may go forward for Royal Assent without the consent of the Lords if not passed without amendment within one month of being sent up from the Commons; and any bill to extend the life of Parliament, over which, together with private bills, the Lords retain a veto.

the Lords might trigger a more fundamental reappraisal of the constitutional relationship between Lords and Commons.[19]

The interim solution of the Labour government elected in 1997 was to abolish the right of hereditary peers to sit and vote, subject to a saving in respect of the Earl Marshal, Lord Great Chamberlain and 90 other hereditary peers elected by their fellows; to reform the system of appointments to life peerages in the "transitional House"[20]; and to establish a Royal Commission to consider and make recommendations on the changes needed to bring about a fully reformed and modernised second chamber.[21] But having managed to attain the transitional stage, Lords reform seems at present to be marooned there.

4–06 The Royal Commission, chaired by Lord Wakeham, reported in January 2000.[22] It recommended no substantial changes to the functions of the House of Lords or to the balance of power between the two Houses of Parliament, but dealt in detail with the question of the composition of a reformed upper house. In essence, the commission favoured a mixed membership of about 550, consisting of elected "regional members" and members appointed on the nomination of an independent statutory appointments commission charged with securing a "broadly representative" chamber. Some one-fifth of the members of a reformed House of Lords would sit on the cross-benches; the remaining, politically affiliated members would be required to reflect the voting preferences expressed at the most recent general election. In its 2001 election manifesto, the government pledged to implement the conclusions of the Wakeham commission "in the most effective way possible". Following its election victory, it published a further White Paper, emphatically endorsing Wakeham's conclusions concerning the maintenance of the pre-eminence of the Commons:

---

[19] Including, perhaps not least, a reconsideration of the names of our Houses of Parliament. 13% of respondents to the consultation on the government's 2001 White Paper on Lords' reform as to which, see para.4–06 dealt with the names question, and almost all favoured renaming.

[20] Pending legislation, the P.M. established an Appointments Commission in May 2000 to make recommendations on the appointment of non-party political peers and to vet all nominations for membership of the House of Lords. In an attempt to broaden the pool of potential life peers, the commission invited applications for appointment from members of the public, and in April 2001 the Queen duly appointed 15 "people's peers" on the commission's recommendation. They were rather less representative of the public than might have been anticipated, and the experiment—described by the then Leader of the House of Commons, Robin Cook M.P., as a "public relations disaster" (see Commons *Hansard*, HC Vol.399, col.157 (Feb. 4, 2003)—has not been repeated since.

[21] See the government White Paper, *Modernising Parliament: Reforming the House of Lords*, Cm.4183 (1999).

[22] Report of the Commission on Reform of the House of Lords, *A House for the Future*, Cm.4534 (2000) ("the Wakeham Report").

"Reform of the House of Lords must satisfy one key condition: it must not alter the respective roles and authority of the
two chambers and their members in a way that would obscure
the line of authority and accountability that flow between the
people and those they elect directly to form the government
and to act as their individual representatives. Decisions on
functions, on authority and on membership of the House of
Lords need to be consistent with these settled principles of our
democracy."[23]

Viewed through this lens, the House of Lords was, and should
remain, a "revising and deliberative" assembly with a membership
appropriate to that role, political in approach but not dominated
by any one party and representative both of independent expertise
and of the broader community in the United Kingdom. To that
end, the White Paper proposed to abrogate entirely privileged
rights of membership of hereditary peers. Henceforward, it was
proposed that the majority of members would be nominated by the
political parties in proportions intended to reflect the shares of the
national vote at the previous general election, with some 120
members directly elected to represent the nations and regions of
the United Kingdom, a similar number of appointees with no
political affiliations and a continuing role for the Law Lords and
Lords Spiritual.[24] In due course, membership would be capped at
600. Finally, an independent Appointments Commission would be
established by statute to appoint independent members and to
decide, within certain limits, how many members each major
political party would be entitled to at any time. These proposals
were then put out for consultation, and if the expectation were that
public reaction would be favourable then it was badly misjudged.

Over a thousand responses were received. Of these over 80 **4–07**
per cent supported either a wholly or predominantly elected
second chamber, and in other respects besides the majority of
respondents parted company with the government's line. The
government's response was to hand responsibility for the matter
over to Parliament: a joint committee of both Houses of
Parliament was established in May 2002 and charged with finding
a way through to the next stage of reform.[25] In its first report,[26] the

---

[23] *The House of Lords: Completing the reform*, Cm.5291 (2001), para.18.
[24] It now appears that serving Lords of Appeal in Ordinary at least will be removed
from the House of Lords and relocated to a new Supreme Court: see *Constitutional Reform: A Supreme Court for the United Kingdom* (Dept for Constitutional
Affairs, July 2003).
[25] Its terms of reference require it only to "have regard to" the Wakeham Report,
previous government White Papers and responses thereto, perhaps of necessity if
the Joint Committee is to have a chance of resolving the present stalemate.
[26] First Report of the Joint Committee on House of Lords Reform, HC 171
(2002–03).

committee identified seven options for the composition of a reformed second chamber: fully appointed; fully elected; 80 per cent elected, 20 per cent appointed; 80 per cent appointed, 20 per cent elected; 60 per cent appointed, 40 per cent elected; 60 per cent elected, 40 per cent appointed; and 50 per cent elected, 50 per cent appointed. These options were voted on in both the Commons and the Lords on February 4, 2003.[27] The only decisive vote in favour of any of them was the House of Lords' vote, 335 against 110, for a fully appointed House. The Lords decisively rejected the other six options. The Commons, to compound matters, rejected all seven.[28] The issue has therefore reverted to the joint committee, where for the time being it remains, stubbornly unresolved.[28a]

House of Commons

4–08   At present, 659 M.P.s sit in the House of Commons, of whom 72 represent Scottish constituencies. The number of Scottish M.P.s will be reduced at some point prior to the next general election (which must occur no later than June 2006), following the boundary commission review of Scottish representation at Westminster in light of devolution. This recommended a reduction in the number of Scottish M.P.s, from 72 down to 59, which the government has accepted.[29]

This constitutes the government's response to what is dubbed the "West Lothian question".[30] The problem the question addresses is whether it can be right that Scottish M.P.s should retain the ability to vote on legislation intended to apply only to England and

---

[27] In both Houses, members were allowed a free vote.

[28] Option Four, 80% elected and 20% appointed, came closest to securing a majority in the Commons, with 281 votes in favour and 284 against. Even if the ayes had had it, however, it would in no sense have constituted the "commanding majority" sought by the Leader of the House and arguably necessary to give legitimacy to the mode of reform approved.

[28a] For the government's latest foray, see *Constitutional Reform: Next Steps for the House of Lords*, published by the Department of Constitutional Affairs in September 2003. This proposes to bring the transitional arrangements contained in the House of Lords Act 1999 to an end, removing the remaining hereditary peers and placing the Appointments Commission on a statutory footing. It is acknowledged that this is not a complete solution to the stalemate.

[29] The government is also to introduce a bill to amend the provisions of the SA 1998 which provide that any reduction in the number of Scottish M.P.s at Westminster will automatically bring about a corresponding reduction in the membership of the Scottish Parliament. It was accepted, following consultation, that the membership of the Scottish Parliament should remain at its present level: see above, para.3–07.

[30] So-called because it was articulated in the debates on the earlier Scotland Bill in the 1970s by Tam Dalyell, then M.P. for West Lothian.

Wales[31] when English and Welsh M.P.s have forfeited that ability in relation to matters devolved to a Scottish Parliament. The reduction in Scottish representation at Westminster recommended by the boundary commission may mitigate, but does not go to the root of, the problem; arguably, only a shift to a federal model of constitutional organisation could achieve that,[32] and the present government has made clear that federalism is not on its agenda. Plainly, so long as Westminster continues to enact legislation for the whole of the United Kingdom, an appropriate level of Scottish representation must be maintained. It is not obvious, however, that the West Lothian question can be dismissed as an incidental, and ultimately minor, untidiness occasioned by devolution.[33]

Holyrood

The Scotland Act 1998 provides that there shall be 129 Members **4–09** of the Scottish Parliament.[34] Seventy-three of these are elected by the familiar "first past the post" or simple majority method used for electing members of the Westminster Parliament in each of the existing Westminster constituencies (with the exception of Orkney and Shetland, which constitute two constituencies for these purposes). The remaining 56 members are elected in accordance with the "additional member" system of proportional representation from each of the eight European parliamentary constituencies provided for by the European Parliamentary Constituencies (Scotland) Order 1996[35] (although for European elections these have now been supplanted by the electoral system provided for by the European Parliamentary Elections Act 2002, under which Scotland constitutes a single region for the purposes of electing its eight MEPs). Thus seven regional members are returned from each region.[36]

---

[31] Conceivably with decisive effect, as where a government's majority is secured by its Scottish M.P.s.

[32] A. Olowofoyeku, "Decentralising the United Kingdom: The federal argument" [1999] Edin. L.R. 57.

[33] Already a Commons vote on a matter falling with devolved competence has been secured by the government only with the support of its Scottish M.P.s. During the debates on the Scotland Bill in the late 1970s, an amendment was tabled which would have provided for the taking of a second vote in such circumstances (the idea being that, in the meantime, the Scottish M.P.s could be persuaded to abstain). The government of the day rejected the idea as a "constitutional imbecility", but something like it may in the longer run require to be adopted.

[34] SA 1998, s.1 and Sch.1.

[35] European Parliamentary Constituencies (Scotland) Order 1996 (SI 1996/1926).

[36] For an account of the process governing elections to the Scottish Parliament, see above, paras 3–04—3–05.

ELIGIBILITY AND DISQUALIFICATION

4–10   The conditions of eligibility to stand for election differ slightly as between the Westminster and Scottish Parliaments. Common grounds of disqualification are those contained in section 1(1)(a) to (e) of the House of Commons Disqualification Act 1975,[37] which cover judges, civil servants, members of the armed forces, members of police forces and members of foreign legislatures.[38] The 1975 Act also disqualifies from membership of the House of Commons all those office holders listed in Part II of Schedule 1 to the Act. Corresponding provision in relation to the Scottish Parliament is currently contained in the Scottish Parliament (Disqualification) Order 2003,[39] made under section 15 of the Scotland Act.

A number of categories of person are disqualified from membership of both the Westminster and Scottish Parliaments otherwise than by virtue of the 1975 Act,[40] namely aliens,[41] persons under the age of 21,[42] those suffering from a mental illness,[43] undischarged bankrupts,[44] convicted prisoners serving a custodial sentence of

---

[37] s.1(1)(za) (inserted by the House of Commons (Removal of Clergy Disqualification) Act 2001), does not apply to the Scottish Parliament. The provision disqualifies Lords Spiritual from membership of the House of Commons. The 2001 Act modified SA 1998, s.16, to provide that a Lord Spiritual is not disqualified from membership of the Scottish Parliament.

[38] Meaning the legislature of any country or territory outside the Commonwealth, other than Ireland. The provision in relation to Ireland was inserted by the Disqualifications Act 2000. The purpose of that Act, however, as set out in its long title, is to remove the disqualification of members of the Irish legislature from membership of the House of Commons and NI Assembly only. There is nothing in the Act to suggest that members of the Irish legislature were also to be made eligible for election to the Scottish Parliament.

[39] Scottish Parliament (Disqualification) Order 2003 (SI 2003/409). Office holders named in Pt I of the Schedule to the Order are absolutely disqualified from membership of the Parliament; those named in Pt II of the Sch.(namely the various Lieutenants in Scotland) are only disqualified from standing for election in a constituency or region falling within the area which they represent.

[40] SA 1998, s.15(1)(b).

[41] Commonwealth citizens and citizens of the Republic of Ireland are excluded from the definition of aliens contained in the British Nationality Act 1981 and so are eligible to stand for election. By virtue of SA 1998, s.16(2), EU citizens who are resident in the UK are eligible to stand for election to the Scottish Parliament.

[42] Parliamentary Elections Act 1695 (as extended to Scotland by the Acts of Union), specified 21 as the age at which a person becomes eligible for membership of the House of Commons. The provision survived the lowering of the age of majority to 18 by the Family Law Reform Act 1969 and the Age of Majority (Scotland) Act 1969.

[43] Mental Health Act 1983, s.141, as applied to Scotland by SA 1998, s.17(4).

[44] Insolvency Act 1986, s.427, as applied to Scotland by SA 1998, s.17(4).

more than one year,[45] and those convicted of corrupt or illegal election practices contrary to sections 60 or 61 of the Representation of the People Act 1983.[46]

From the outset, persons who had been ordained or who were ministers of any religious denomination, together with peers other than Lords of Appeal in Ordinary, were eligible to stand for election to the Scottish Parliament. Those hereditary peers who no longer have the right to sit and vote in the House of Lords now have the right to stand for election to the Commons by virtue of the House of Lords Act 1999, but life peers and Lords Spiritual remain disqualified from membership. The House of Commons (Removal of Clergy Disqualification) Act 2001 made it possible for ministers of religion to seek election to the House of Commons also.

The consequences of disqualification also differ somewhat as **4–11** between the Westminster and Scottish Parliaments. At Westminster, a person claiming that an individual disqualified by virtue of the 1975 Act has been elected to the House of Commons may apply to the Judicial Committee of the Privy Council for a declaration to that effect under section 7. The Judicial Committee may direct that the issue be tried in the High Court of England and Wales, the Court of Session or the High Court of Northern Ireland, depending on the location of the constituency in question; if so, the decision of that court is final. In Scotland, if a disqualified person is elected either as a constituency or a regional member, his election is void and his seat vacant.[47] Where a person becomes disqualified during the currency of his membership, he ceases to be an MSP and his seat falls vacant accordingly. Where an MSP becomes disqualified on grounds of mental illness or bankruptcy, his seat is not automatically vacated but he does become ineligible to participate in the proceedings of the Parliament and may lose other rights and privileges incidental to membership. In any of these situations, the Parliament may by resolution elect to disregard the member's disqualification under section 16(4) of the Scotland Act, if it considers that the ground of disqualification has

---

[45] Disqualified by virtue of the Representation of the People Act 1981, s.1. Note, also, that a person convicted of treason is disqualified from election to the House of Commons and hence also to the Scottish Parliament. If already elected, the member may not sit or vote until any sentence imposed on him has expired or unless he is pardoned: see Forfeiture Act 1870, ss 2 and 7.

[46] s.173 of the 1983 Act, provides that a person convicted of a corrupt or illegal practice shall, for a period of five years (if convicted of a corrupt practice) or three years (if convicted of an illegal practice), be incapable of being registered as an elector or voting at any parliamentary or local election and of holding or being elected to any elective office, including membership of the House of Commons and Scottish Parliament. If already elected, the person must vacate his seat (subject to any rights of appeal he may have against his conviction).

[47] SA 1998, s.17(1).

been removed or that it is proper to disregard any disqualification incurred by the member.[48] Any person who believes that a person is or has become disqualified from membership of the Scottish Parliament may apply to the Court of Session for a declarator to that effect.[49] It should be noted that the jurisdiction of the Court of Session in this respect extends to all possible grounds of disqualification, not merely, as with the Judicial Committee of the Privy Council, those arising from the House of Commons Disqualification Act 1975.

FUNCTIONS OF PARLIAMENTS

4–12 The Westminster and Scottish Parliaments alike have three essential functions: to provide and sustain a government in office; to make law; and to hold the executive to account.[50] The first of these we touched on in Chapter 1, in the context of the constitutional conventions (or, in Scotland, statutory rules) surrounding the appointment and resignation of governments; we revisit the matter in Chapter 5. Suffice to say here that the democratic legitimacy of a government in a parliamentary system depends upon its ability to command the continuing confidence of the House of Commons or Scottish Parliament as the case may be; that confidence withdrawn, the government must fall. That might or might not provoke an election. Certainly at Westminster, there is no reason why a Prime Minister defeated on a motion of confidence should request a dissolution of Parliament (or, if he did, why the Queen should necessarily accede to the request) if Parliament as currently composed is able to sustain an alternative administration in office. Likewise in Scotland, while the members of the Scottish Executive must in terms of sections 45(2) and 47(2)(c) of the Scotland Act resign if the Parliament resolves that the Executive no longer enjoys its confidence, the duty laid on the Presiding Officer by

---

[48] But no such resolution may be adopted where an election petition has been presented in respect of the member, or where the disqualification has been established in election petition proceedings or proceedings under SA 1998, s.18.

[49] SA 1998, s.18. The procedure provides an alternative mechanism for challenging a person's election to the election petition procedure laid down by the Representation of the People Act 1983, with the possible advantage that, whereas election petitions must be presented within 21 days of the contested election, there is no comparable time-limit on proceedings under s.18. However, the jurisdiction of the court under s.18 is excluded if an election petition has already been presented; it is also excluded if the Scottish Parliament has adopted a resolution under s.16(4) to disregard a member's disqualification.

[50] Plainly that is not an exhaustive account. There are other parliamentary functions, such as the regulation of internal procedures and the supervision of parliamentary standards; and as elected representatives M.P.s and MSPs have a variety of functions in relation to their constituents and constituencies.

section 3(1)(b) to recommend a date for the holding of an extraordinary general election only crystallises if the Parliament fails to nominate an alternative First Minister within 28 days of the incumbent's resignation.[51]

The primary legislative function of the Parliaments we examine later in this chapter. There is of course a salient difference between the UK and Scottish Parliaments in this respect, in that while the legislative competence of the former is subject to no legal limits, the legislative competence of the latter is restricted in terms of the Scotland Act 1998.[52] It should not necessarily be assumed, however, that the legislative sovereignty of the Westminster Parliament means that it is wholly unfettered. True it is that a government in command of a reliable Commons majority may secure the enactment of legislation that is in some sense disagreeable or offensive to popular (or élite) sentiments. Nonetheless, a process, more or less protracted, must be followed in order to obtain the seal of parliamentary approval, and if the process provides no guarantee as to the substance of the legislative outcomes, it offers a measure of procedural protection the importance of which, in structuring and confining the will of the executive, is often overlooked.[53]

The role of the Parliaments in holding the executive to account **4–13** is frequently disparaged. As we shall see in Chapter 5, there is certainly scope for doubting the adequacy of the convention of ministerial responsibility to Parliament as a mechanism for securing accountability for the exercise of political power. Much is made, for example, of the persistent failure of ministers to resign in response to departmental wrongdoing or error, as if this were a vital component of the concept. The emphasis on resignation flows from the fact that, as a matter of nineteenth century practice, before the emergence of the modern party system and the consolidation of government control over the legislature, Parliament

---

[51] SA 1998 makes no provision for the possibility that, for 28 days and the period leading up to and immediately following an extraordinary general election, there would be no Scottish Executive at all. It is open to the Parliament within that 28-day period to resolve that it should be dissolved, which would trigger the duty of the Presiding Officer under s.3(1)(a) to recommend to the Queen a date for an extraordinary election. But such a resolution requires the support of at least two-thirds of the total number of MSPs, and if the political complexion of the Parliament is such that it is unable within 28 days to nominate a replacement First Minister, it may be equally unfavourable to securing a resolution for dissolution. At Westminster, a government which loses a vote of confidence continues in office *de facto* on a caretaker basis during the currency of the election period, and arguably some such arrangement would require to be made in Scotland in the circumstances envisaged here; but there is no basis for it in the SA 1998.

[52] As we shall see, there are also significant differences between the two Parliaments in relation to legislative procedures.

[53] See K. D. Ewing and C. Gearty, *The Struggle for Civil Liberties* (Oxford University Press, Oxford, 2000), pp.12, 13.

could and sometimes did force the resignation of a minister or ministry in whose fitness for their offices it had lost confidence. Nowadays, such events are vanishingly rare.[54] But however ephemeral the sanction attaching to ministerial responsibility, the expectation that ministers should answer to Parliament, and account as fully and clearly as possible for their and their departments' actions and decisions, even to the extent of acknowledging errors where errors are made, remains very much alive. Not only that, but ministers do appear before Parliament and parliamentary committees, do subject themselves to questioning, and do not *routinely* mislead Parliament in the process (even if their answers may be evasive or at least less comprehensive than parliamentarians would like).[55] To be sure, difficulties remain in "investigating the facts, agreeing on the application of the convention [of ministerial responsibility] to the facts, and enforcement",[56] difficulties which are attributable, at least in part, to what has been justly described as "the *intense* inefficiency of our parliamentary system."[57] The tabling of parliamentary questions, for example, is not an especially efficient means of eliciting information; and parliamentary debates, even when they do not collapse completely into a political slanging match, are too often disfigured by the absence of any meaningful debate at all. But the convention of ministerial responsibility is not the only mechanism, nor even the only parliamentary mechanism, of accountability. Parliamentary committees both at Westminster and Holyrood provide a more exacting forum for the scrutiny of the executive than the parliamentary floor. Their fact-finding capacities may have been blunted in the past, and their effectiveness unduly dependent on ministerial co-operation, but the first of these at least may be enhanced by the enactment of freedom of information legislation, the utility of which is in no sense confined to pressure groups and busybodies.[58] Equally, the Parliamentary Commissioner for Administration has provided an important adjunct to parliamentary control of the executive at Westminster; in Scotland, there is no reason why the newly established Scottish Public Services Ombudsman should not do the same.[59]

---

[54] The last time the government lost a vote of confidence was in 1979.

[55] Both the Ministerial Code of Conduct and the Scottish Ministerial Code now spell out the duty of ministers to account fully to Parliament. The contents of the former were adopted in resolutions of both Houses of Parliament in 1997, the effect of which, on one view, is to codify the terms of ministers' responsibility to Parliament such that the government may no longer decide for itself how far its responsibility should extend.

[56] I. Leigh, "Secrets of the Political Constitution" [1999] 62 M.L.R. 298.

[57] D. Judge, "Parliament in the 1980s" (1989) 60 *Political Quarterly* 400.

[58] See Ch.9.

[59] See Ch.13.

LEGISLATIVE PROCESSES

Westminster

At Westminster, bills—proposals for legislation—are public, **4–14** private or hybrid.[60] Private bills provide for the conferment of special powers, benefits or exemptions on a person or body of persons in excess of or in conflict with the general law. Public bills relate to matters of general public interest and are of general application. All government legislation is enacted by means of public bills, sponsored by ministers and occupying the greater part of the parliamentary time devoted to the legislative process each session. Private members' bills (PMBs)—public bills too, despite their name—are introduced by backbench M.P.s and undergo the same procedure as government bills.

A government bill first comes to the formal notice of Parliament at first reading, although it contents may have been more or less extensively trailed in advance of that.[61] First reading is a purely formal stage, after which the bill is printed and published. At second reading, the Commons[62] considers the principles of the bill. If the bill is passed (and it is rare for a government bill to be denied a second reading), the bill proceeds to committee, usually one of the standing committees but occasionally a special standing committee or Committee of the Whole House. If, following line by line scrutiny, the bill is amended in committee, it is reprinted as amended and "reported" to the Commons. At third reading, the bill is debated in final form, and thereafter proceeds to the House of Lords. Procedure in the Lords is much the same as in the Commons, except that bills are normally considered by a Committee of the Whole House after second reading, amendments may

---

[60] *Erskine May's Parliamentary Practice* (22nd ed., Butterworths, London, 1997) describes hybrid bills as "public bills which affect a particular private interest in a manner different from the private interest of other persons or bodies of the same category or class." After second reading, a hybrid bill is sent to a select committee. If petitions objecting to the bill are received, the committee deals with it in much the same way as a private bill; if not, the bill is recommitted to a standing committee or Committee of the Whole House and dealt with as a public bill. An example is the Channel Tunnel Rail Link Act 1996.

[61] In addition to established forms of pre-legislative consultation, such as the publication of White Papers or royal commission reports, the government has since 1997 pledged to publish draft bills where possible in order to facilitate pre-legislative scrutiny by the appropriate select committee. The House of Commons Select Committee on Modernisation has recommended that where it is not possible to produce a draft bill, the government should instead submit detailed policy proposals for pre-legislative scrutiny: Second Report, *Modernisation of the House of Commons: A Reform Programme*, HC 1168–I (2001–02).

[62] Assuming the bill was introduced in the Commons. Government bills may be introduced in either House, with the exception of finance bills, which are always introduced in the Commons.

be made at third reading as well, in committee and at report, and there is no provision in the Lords for curtailing debate. In the Commons, by contrast, the minister responsible for a bill may move an allocation of time, or guillotine, motion to fix the time available for its remaining stages; and increasing use is also being made of programme motions, whereby by the whole progress of the bill through the Commons is timetabled in advance.[63]

If the Lords make no amendments to the bill, it may be sent forward at once for Royal Assent.[64] If amendments are made, the bill returns to the Commons, which may agree to the amendments, substitute amendments of its own or reject the amendments outright. In the latter two cases, the bill is sent back to the Lords with the Commons' reasons. As a rule, the Lords acquiesce in the wishes of the Commons; but from time to time, they stand their ground. The bill will then be batted back and forth between the two Houses until some form of compromise is reached, as usually happens. If, exceptionally, the two Houses fail to reach agreement within the parliamentary session, the bill will lapse.[65] Where such failure is attributable to insoluble differences between the two Houses, the Parliament Acts 1911 and 1949 provide for the will of the Commons to prevail over that of the Lords. The House of Lords may delay a public bill for one session (other than a bill certified by the Speaker of the House of Commons as a money bill, which may be sent forward for Royal Assent if at the end of one month the Lords have failed to pass it), but it is open to the Commons to revive the measure in the following session, bypass the Lords and proceed directly to Royal Assent.[66]

4–15 There are a number of procedures whereby an M.P. may introduce a PMB. Shortly after the start of each new parliamentary session, a ballot is held among backbench M.P.s to determine

---

[63] While sensible in principle, in practice programme motions often have the effect of seriously constraining the time available for proper scrutiny of the detail of a bill in committee.

[64] Even major bills—as witness, *e.g.* the Anti-Terrorism, Crime and Security Act 2001—may complete their parliamentary stages in a matter of days.

[65] Where the bill fails to complete within the space of a session not because of disagreement between the two Houses but on account of simple lack of time, it may be saved from lapse if the Commons resolve to carry it forward to the next session. The bill which became the Financial Services and Markets Act 2000 was carried forward in this way from the 1999–2000 session to the 2000–01 session. The House of Commons Select Committee on Modernisation has recommended the use of the carry-over only for an "experimental period": Second Report, *Modernisation of the House of Commons: A Reform Programme*, HC 1168-I (2001–02).

[66] The Parliament Acts procedure never actually required to be used until the enactment of the War Crimes Act 1991. The Labour government of 1997–2001 had to resort twice to the procedure, to secure the enactment of the European Parliamentary Elections Act 1999 and the Sexual Offences (Amendment) Act 2000.

priority in the use of the time set aside for private members' business; in practice, only the first 20 names in the ballot have a realistic chance of seeing their bills through to the statute books.[67] Ten-minute rule bills may be introduced on a motion under standing orders,[68] seeking leave to present a bill to the Commons; and "ordinary presentation" bills may be introduced by M.P.s under standing orders[69] in the same way as a government bill.[70] Similar procedures obtain in the House of Lords, although with this difference: a PMB from the Lords cannot be proceeded with, or even printed, in the Commons until an M.P. had indicated a willingness to take it up, whereas, when a Commons PMB is sent up to the Lords, it is deemed already to have had a first reading and is printed at once (although a peer must still be found to pilot it through its stages in the Lords).

Making it through to the statute books is not the only criterion of success for a PMB.[71] Some are introduced to publicise a cause, or to prompt the government to take action. But many are introduced with the aim and intention of changing the law, and have proved an important means of achieving this, particularly in areas of social or moral controversy which cross party lines and where governments are unwilling to risk their own hard-pressed legislative time. The abolition of the death penalty, and reform of the law on abortion and homosexuality, for example, were brought about by PMBs; another area where PMBs achieved some, if piecemeal, success, was in the area of freedom of information.

Private legislation, designed to obtain special rights or privileges over and above those provided by the general law, is introduced by parliamentary agents acting on behalf of the prospective beneficiary. Since the powers sought may interfere with the rights and interests of others, who might therefore wish to object, the promoters of a private bill must comply with requirements concerning publicity and notification. Subject to that, and provided the bill is otherwise competent and in proper form, private bills go through essentially the same stages as public bills. After second reading,[72] the bill will be sent either to an Opposed Bill Committee

---

[67] Assuming they have a bill. A common practice is for M.P.s to wait to see where they are placed in the ballot and then choose between the draft bills proffered them by interest groups or, indeed, the government, if it has been unable to find time for a measure in its own programme for the session.

[68] Standing Order 23.

[69] Standing Order 57.

[70] But such bills cannot be presented until the ballot bills have been presented and set down for second reading, which is likely to exhaust the time available for private members' business.

[71] The success rate in that sense is variable. In some sessions, only a handful of PMBs are enacted into law; in others, upward of 20.

[72] Whether a private bill commences in the Commons or the Lords is determined by the Commons' Chairman of Ways and Means and the Lord Chairman of Committees; as a rule, private bills promoted by local authorities or those raising complex issues commence in the Lords.

or Unopposed Bill Committee, depending on whether objections have been lodged. In either case, the committee sits in a quasi-judicial capacity to determine whether the case for having the provision sought by the bill is established; if it finds that it is not, the bill is effectively thrown out. If, however, the committee finds the bill to be acceptable, it reports accordingly (together with any amendments it may have made). The bill is then read for a third time, and if it is passed it proceeds to the other House where it undergoes much the same process once again.

4–16   A special procedure applies to the enactment of private legislation intended solely for application in Scotland which relates to matters reserved to Westminster by the Scotland Act 1998.[73] Under the Private Legislation Procedure (Scotland) Act 1936, the promoter lodges a petition for a provisional order with the Secretary of State, on or before November 27 or March 27 in any year. Petitions objecting to the order sought must be received by January 23 or May 24, whichever follows the date of submission of the petition for the order. The Secretary of State may grant or refuse the petition, or may order that an inquiry be held. The Commissioners of Inquiry sit in Scotland and follow the procedure of an Opposed Bill Committee; if they recommend that the order be granted, the Secretary of State may so grant it, with or without modifications. A provisional order granted by the Secretary of State, whether or not following an inquiry, then requires to be confirmed by Parliament.[74]

Holyrood

4–17   The Scottish Parliament is to a great extent the master of its own house in terms of procedure. The Scotland Act does require that the proceedings of the Parliament be regulated by standing orders,[75] and in places specifies the content of standing orders,[76] but much latitude is left to the Parliament to adopt such procedures as it chooses. The rules relating to legislative procedure are presently contained in Chapters 9 and 9A of the standing orders (relating respectively to public bills and private bills). In total, the standing orders provide for no fewer than 10 different

---

[73] Private legislation on devolved matters in Scotland naturally falls now to be enacted by the Scottish Parliament itself: see SA 1998, s.36(3)(c), Scottish Parliament Standing Orders, Ch.9A, and see also below, para.4–18.

[74] By virtue of SA 1998, s.94, where any pre-devolution enactment requires an order to be confirmed by Act of Parliament or approved by way of special procedure (as to which see the Statutory Orders (Special Procedure) Act 1945), and the order-making power is one which passed to the Scottish Ministers under s.53 on July 1, 1999, the power to confirm falls to be exercised by the Scottish Parliament.

[75] SA 1998, s.22.

[76] See SA 1998, Sch.3.

species of Scottish legislation.[77] Rules 9.2 to 9.13 of the standing orders lay down general rules applicable to all public bills introduced in the Parliament, except to the extent that the special rules set out in Rules 9.14 to 9.16 and 9.18 to 9.21 are inconsistent with the general rules in relation to particular types of bill. In that event, the special rules prevail to the extent of the inconsistency.

Executive bills are the most important type of bill in numerical terms, being bills introduced by a member of the Scottish Executive in order to carry forward the Executive's programme for government.[78] The rules make provision for the form and manner of introduction of executive bills, and for the lodging of various accompanying documents. These are: a written statement by the Scottish Minister in charge of the bill stating that in his view its provisions are within the competence of the Parliament[79]; a written statement signed by the Presiding Officer, indicating whether in his view the provisions of the bill would be within the competence of the Parliament and, if in his view they would not be, his reasons[80]; a financial memorandum and policy memorandum; explanatory notes summarising the purposes and effects of the bill; and (if the bill contains provisions charging expenditure on the Scottish consolidated fund) a report signed by the Auditor General for Scotland setting out his views on whether the charge is appropriate. Once the bill and its accompanying documents have been lodged with the Clerk to the Parliament, it is the job of the clerk to arrange for their printing and publication. The substantive part of the legislative process then gets underway.

At stage one, the Parliamentary Bureau[81] refers the bill to the committee within whose remit its subject-matter falls.[82] The committee considers the general principles of the bill, often taking evidence thereon from experts and interested parties, and, in the

---

[77] Namely, executive bills, members' bills, committee bills, budget bills, consolidation bills, codification bills, statute law repeals bills, statute law revision bills, emergency bills, and private bills.

[78] Since devolution, the Scottish Executive's programmes have not been the preserve of one party but have instead been settled post-election by the parties combining to form the coalition.

[79] SA 1998, s.31(1).

[80] SA 1998, s.31(2).

[81] The bureau is comprised of the Presiding Officer, a representative of each political party having five or more MSPs in the Parliament, and the representative of any group formed by MSPs representing parties with fewer than five MSPs in the Parliament (provided that the group itself numbers at least five MSPs). It has responsibility for organising the business of the Parliament: see Scottish Parliament Standing Orders, Ch.5.

[82] If the subject-matter of the bill falls within the remit of more than one committee, the Parliamentary Bureau will move that one be designated lead committee on the bill. The other committee(s) report to the lead committee, which must take its (or their) views into account in preparing its report for the Parliament.

case of an executive bill, the accompanying policy memorandum. Having done so, it reports to the Parliament on whether the general principles of the bill should be agreed. The Parliament is in no sense bound by the committee's recommendation.[83] If the Parliament does agree to the general principles, the bill proceeds to stage two, where it undergoes detailed scrutiny by the committee or lead committee in charge of it.[84] Bills may be amended at stage two, and any MSP may lodge amendments for the committee's consideration following the completion of stage one. If at the end of stage two the bill has been amended, it is reprinted in amended form. Further amendments may be lodged at stage three, at which the Parliament decides whether to pass or reject the bill.[85] If there is a division at stage three on whether the bill is passed, the result will be valid only if at least one-quarter of the total number of MSPs vote, whether for or against or to abstain. If the result of the division is not valid, the bill is deemed to be rejected.

4-18 Space precludes detailed consideration of all the other species of Scottish legislation, but it is worth noting the rules applicable to members' bills, committee bills, emergency bills and private bills.[86] Members' bills are the equivalent in Scotland of PMBs at Westminster, although again the applicable procedural rules differ considerably. Any MSP who is not a Scottish Minister may introduce up to two members' bills in any one session (bearing in mind that in the Scottish Parliament, the term "session" denotes the full four-year cycle of the Parliament, not each year within that cycle). The MSP proposing a member's bill must notify his proposal by lodging it with the clerk, setting out his name, the short title of the bill and a brief summary of its purposes. The notice is published in the Business Bulletin, and if within one month it attracts the support of at least 11 other MSPs, it is printed, published and thereafter subject to the same procedure as an executive bill.[87]

Committee bills are an important innovation: each of the Parliament's committees may make a proposal for a bill relating to a competent matter falling within its remit. A proposal for a committee bill consists of a report to the Parliament setting out the

---

[83] Thus in 2001, the Parliament voted to agree the general principles of the Protection of Wild Mammals (Scotland) Bill, despite the negative recommendation of the Rural Development Committee.

[84] Unless the Parliamentary Bureau successfully moves that Stage Two be taken by a different committee or by a Committee of the Whole Parliament.

[85] The standing orders make provision for the Scottish Minister in charge of an executive bill to refer no more than half of the total number of its clauses back to committee for further Stage Two consideration. This can only happen once.

[86] Note that the Scottish Parliament's tax-varying power, as provided for by SA 1998, Pt.IV, is exercisable by way of resolutions rather than primary legislation.

[87] In the 1999–2003 Parliament, 8 out of the 62 Acts of the Scottish Parliament enacted began life as members' bills.

committee's recommendations for legislation together with an account of why the legislation is needed. The committee may, but need not, append to its report a draft bill.[88] If the Parliament agrees to the proposal, the committee convenor may instruct that a bill be drafted (if necessary) and may subsequently introduce the bill in the Parliament. The subsequent stages of the bill are the same as those applicable to executive bills, except that at stage one (the committee, of course, having already committed itself to the general principles of the bill) it is referred directly to the Parliament for consideration of its general principles and a decision on whether these are agreed to.[89]

The very first Act of the Scottish Parliament[90] was an emergency bill. These are a species of executive bill in relation to which a member of the Scottish Executive or a junior Scottish Minister moves that it be treated as an emergency bill. If agreed, the bill is referred directly to the Parliament at stage one for consideration of its general principles and a decision on whether these are agreed; stage two is taken by a Committee of the Whole Parliament; and the final vote at stage three is taken immediately thereafter. Unless the Parliament decides otherwise, all of the stages of an emergency bill must be taken on the day on which the Parliament agrees to treat it as such.

As to private legislation, and as at Westminster, the role of the Parliament is not merely to legislate but also to arbitrate between the competing private interests of the promoter of the legislation and any objectors. The applicable procedures, which are contained in Chapter 9A of the standing orders, must therefore be both parliamentary and quasi-judicial in nature. The promoter must submit a text of the bill, together with a substantial amount of supporting documentation,[91] to the clerk at least three weeks before the proposed date of introduction.[92] The promoter must also comply with requirements for notification and advertisement of the bill in order to draw it to the attention of potential objectors. The bill is introduced when it is formally lodged with the clerk. Any person, body corporate or unincorporated association may

---

[88] The Parliament has established a Non-executive Bills Unit to assist MSPs, committees and the promoters of private legislation in the drafting and formatting of bills.

[89] In the 1999–2003 Parliament, three out of the 62 Acts of the Scottish Parliament enacted began life as committee bills.

[90] Mental Health (Public Safety and Appeals) (Scotland) Act 1999.

[91] This includes a statement by the Presiding Officer on legislative competence; explanatory notes; a promoter's statement and memorandum; and, where the bill seeks to authorise the construction or alteration of certain classes of works or the compulsory acquisition of land or buildings, various maps and plans, a book of reference and an environmental statement.

[92] This in order to allow the clerk to arrange for the distribution of copies of the bill and supporting documentation to "partner libraries" throughout Scotland.

lodge objections to the bill, within 60 days of its introduction, if it would adversely affect their private interests.[93] A Private Bill Committee is convened following introduction of the bill to consider its provisions and report to Parliament. It will have up to five members, and although the normal rules on party political balance do not apply to its composition, it may not include among its number any MSP who resides in, or represents a constituency falling wholly or party within, the area which would be affected by the bill. The bill is then subject to a three-stage process. At the preliminary stage, the committee considers the general principles of the bill and whether these should be agreed. It may take evidence from the promoter or his legal representatives, and should certainly do so if it minded to recommend that the bill be rejected. If following the committee's preliminary stage report the Parliament agrees to the general principles of the bill, it proceeds to the consideration stage, which falls into two parts. In the first, quasi-judicial, part, the committee hears evidence on the bill and the objections to it. On completion of this part, the committee prepares a report giving its decisions on the objections considered, with reasons where appropriate.[94] In the second part, the committee sits in a legislative capacity to consider and dispose of amendments to the bill.[95] At the final stage, at which further amendments are competent, the Parliament votes on whether or not to pass the bill.[96] As with other enactments of the Scottish Parliament, the Presiding Officer may not send the bill as passed forward for Royal Assent until after the expiry of the four-week period during which the Law Officers or Secretary of State may intervene in terms of sections 33 or 35 of the Scotland Act.

4–19   It is apparent, then, that legislative procedures at Holyrood differ markedly from legislative procedures at Westminster. How well do they work; and how do they compare? In raw numerical terms, the record of the first Scottish Parliament is impressive simply in that it got 62 Acts of the Scottish Parliament enacted, many of which are major measures by any standards. But in both arenas, there is concern about the capacity of existing procedures

---

[93] The Private Bill Committee charged with consideration of the bill has a discretion to admit late objections where reasonable cause is shown for the delay, but not beyond the expiry of the preliminary stage.

[94] Determinations of a Private Bill Committee made without sufficient reasons, or on grounds disclosing some other species of procedural impropriety or unreasonableness, might be susceptible to judicial review on that account.

[95] If substantial amendments are made, the promoter is expected to produce revised or supplementary explanatory notes.

[96] Only one private Act of the Scottish Parliament was enacted in the 1999–2003 Parliament.

to cope with the pressures placed on them.[97] It is arguable, as is implicit in many of the recommendations made by the Modernisation Committee of the House of Commons, that the only way of alleviating the strain on legislative procedures is to move much of the debate over the policies and principles of legislative proposals back to the pre-legislative stage, so that at least the main outstanding areas of disagreement are focused for the legislative process proper. In this respect, the greater willingness of government north and south of the border to engage in greater pre-legislative consultation is an important advance, although it is fair to say that the Scottish Parliament has made better efforts to institutionalise public participation in the legislative process, via the practice of committees of taking evidence on the general principles of bills at stage one.[98] But overload is a problem both at Westminster and Holyrood. At Holyrood, it may not yet have manifested itself with the same seriousness as at Westminster, but it is still noticeable that much the greater part of legislative time is spent on executive bills, contrary to an expectation in the early days that more legislation would emanate from committees or members.[99] At Westminster, there is widespread disquiet that the advance programming of major bills precludes proper scrutiny of their finer points; on more than one occasion in recent years, large numbers of amendments tabled for consideration in committee have had to be abandoned for simple lack of time. This matters, for to the extent that much of the parliamentary time devoted to legislation is (quite properly) spent on government bills, the legislative process provides as much an opportunity for holding the government to account as questions and debates.

---

[97] The Procedures Committee of the Scottish Parliament strongly recommended that its successor in the 2003–07 Parliament undertake a comprehensive review of legislative procedures, and made certain more specific suggestions geared towards extending the time between the stages of the legislative process and increasing the opportunities for MSPs to contribute to debates on bills: Third Report of the Procedures Committee, *The Founding Principles of the Scottish Parliament: The Application of Access and Participation, Equal Opportunities, Accountability and Power-Sharing in the Work of the Parliament*, S.P.P. 818 (Session 1, 2003).

[98] This is not to say that external perspectives will not influence the legislative process at Westminster, for M.P.s and peers alike draw on the views expressed to them by interested groups and parties in their contributions to legislative debate; the difference, however, is that in Scotland that participation is direct rather than filtered through the medium of elected members.

[99] This expectation was founded on the recommendations of the Consultative Steering Group on the Scottish Parliament, established in advance of devolution to consider parliamentary procedures, geared towards the achievement of (among other things) "power-sharing" in the new Parliament. This was felt to imply if not equality as between executive and non-executive bills, at least greater priority for the latter than they have in fact received.

LEGISLATIVE COMPETENCE

4–20 In relation to the legislative competence of the Westminster Parliament, there is little one can usefully add to the earlier discussion of the supremacy, or sovereignty, of Parliament.[1] If there are things Westminster would not do on moral or political grounds, there are nevertheless no legal limitations, ultimately, on its ability to enact whatever legislation it chooses.[2] The focus of this section is therefore on the legislative competence of the Scottish Parliament, which is limited in terms of section 29(2) of the Scotland Act. A number of mechanisms exist to ensure, so far as possible, that the Scottish Parliament does not stray outwith the bounds of its competence. Most of these operate at the pre-Assent stage, *i.e.* before a bill becomes an Act of the Scottish Parliament on the signifying of Royal Assent. However, it follows from the fact that an Act, or provision of an Act, "is not law"[3] if it is outside the legislative competence of the Parliament that its validity may be questioned after it has been enacted and entered into force. A question of this sort may be raised as a "devolution issue" in terms of section 98 and Schedule 6, and to date two Acts of the Scottish Parliament have been challenged on this ground.

It is worth noting the terms of section 29(2) in full:

"(2) A provision is outside [the legislative competence of the Scottish Parliament] so far as any of the following paragraphs apply—

(a) it would form part of the law of a country or territory other than Scotland, or confer or remove functions exercisable otherwise than in or as regards Scotland,

(b) it relates to reserved matters,

(c) it is in breach of the restrictions in Schedule 4,

(d) it is incompatible with any of the Convention rights or with Community law,

(e) it would remove the Lord Advocate from his position as head of the systems of criminal prosecution and investigation of deaths in Scotland."

---

[1] See paras 2–01—2–09.

[2] "Ultimately", because the courts may require Parliament to express its legislative intention in clear and explicit terms in particular circumstances, and because Acts of Parliament may be declared to be incompatible with Community law or the Convention rights. In the former case, the courts are enjoined by the European Communities Act 1972 to give effect to Community law over an inconsistent Act of Parliament, but it does not necessarily follow from that that the 1972 Act is itself sacrosanct. In the latter case, a declaration of incompatibility under HRA 1998, s.4, does not affect the validity or continuing operation or enforcement of the Act in respect of which it is granted, and although provision is made for remedial action to be taken, a minister is not obliged to take it.

[3] SA 1998, s.29(1).

The reference to extraterritorial effect in section 29(1)(a) must be understood in light of section 126(1), whereby the term "Scotland" includes "so much of the internal waters and territorial sea of the United Kingdom as are adjacent to Scotland."[4] The reservation in relation to the functions of the Lord Advocate in section 29(1)(e) reflects the perceived need to secure his independence as public prosecutor and head of the system of investigation of deaths in Scotland, even though he ceased on devolution to be a member of the UK government and became instead a member of the Scottish Executive. The principal restrictions on the competence of the Scottish Parliament, however, are those contained in section 29(1)(b) to (d): reserved matters, the protection of certain enactments from modification by the Scottish Parliament, and compatibility with the Convention rights and Community law.

Reserved matters

The list of matters reserved to the exclusive competence of the **4–21** Westminster Parliament is contained in Schedule 5 to the Scotland Act, which is arranged in three parts.[5] Part I sets out a number of "general reservations" under six headings.[6] Part II sets out a number of "specific reservations" grouped under eleven headings.[7] Part III contains five paragraphs of general provisions relating primarily to the reservation of certain public bodies.

A provision of an Act of the Scottish Parliament will fall foul of this restriction if it "relates to" one of the reserved matters specified in Schedule 5, and in that regard section 29(3) provides that "the question whether a provision of an Act of the Scottish Parliament relates to a reserved matter is to be determined, subject

---

[4] Her Majesty may by Order in Council determine or make provision for determining any boundary between waters which are to be treated as internal waters or territorial sea of the UK, or sea within British fishery limits, adjacent to Scotland and those which are not.

[5] Under SA 1998, s.30, the list may be modified by Order in Council as necessary or expedient.

[6] The constitution (including the Crown, but not Her Majesty's prerogative and other executive functions, or functions exercisable by any person acting on behalf of the Crown; the Union of the Kingdoms of Scotland and England; the UK Parliament; and the continued existence of the High Court of Justiciary and the Court of Session); the registration and funding of political parties; foreign affairs (with the important exception of "observing and implementing international obligations, obligations under the Human Rights Convention and obligations under Community law"); the civil service of the state; defence; and treason.

[7] Financial and economic matters; home affairs; trade and industry; energy; transport; social security; regulation of the professions (though not the legal profession); employment; health and medicines; media and culture; and miscellaneous matters including judicial remuneration and equal opportunities. It should be noted that few of these headings are comprehensive, and many of the reservations are subject to exceptions.

to subsection (4), by reference to the purpose of the provision, having regard (among other things) to its effect in all the circumstances."[8] Thus the *purpose* and *effects* of a provision are the critical factors in determining whether or not it relates to reserved matters.[9] It is clear, however, that some ancillary impact on reserved matters is not to be taken as fatal to the validity of the provision. This emerges from paragraph 3 of Schedule 4, which provides that modifications of the law on reserved matters are permissible so long as they are "(a) incidental to, or consequential on, provision made (whether by virtue of the Act in question or another enactment) which does not relate to reserved matters; and (b) do not have a greater effect on reserved matters than is necessary to give effect to the purpose of the provision." Moreover, section 101 provides that, where a provision of an Act of the Scottish Parliament[10] could be read in such a way as to be outside competence, that provision is to be read "as narrowly as is required for it to be within competence, if such a reading is possible, and is to have effect accordingly." As this implies, those acting under Acts of the Scottish Parliament will themselves need to consider whether its provisions require to be "read down" to avoid a conflict with reserved matters, for the legality of their own actings, if not the validity of the Act, may otherwise be vulnerable to challenge. Consider, for example, the Regulation of Care (Scotland) Act 2001. This confers various regulatory functions on the Scottish Ministers and the Scottish Commission for the Regulation of Care which require to be exercised in accordance with the general principle stated in section 59(2) of the Act, whereby the safety and welfare of all persons who use or are liable to use care services are to be protected and enhanced. Sections 2 and 3 of the Health and Safety at Work etc Act 1974—the subject-matter of which is reserved[11]—obliges employers to conduct their undertakings in such a way that, so far as reasonably practicable, their employees *and* persons not in their employment are not exposed to risks to

---

[8] SA 1998, s.29(4), provides that a provision which would not otherwise relate to reserved matters but which modifies Scots private law or Scots criminal law as either applies to reserved matters shall be treated as "relating to" reserved matters (and thus invalid) unless its purpose is to make the law in question "apply consistently to reserved matters and otherwise."

[9] In this we find echoes of the "pith and substance" and "colourability" doctrines developed by the Judicial Committee of the Privy Council in its heyday as the Empire's final court of appeal: see P. Craig and M. Walters, "The Courts, Devolution and Judicial Review" [1999] P.L. 274 at 297–302.

[10] Or of a bill before the Scottish Parliament, or of subordinate legislation made by a member of the Scottish Executive.

[11] See SA 1998, Sch.5, Pt II, Head 2. It is pertinent to note that as originally enacted, S.H2 excepted from this reservation "public safety in relation to matters which are not reserved." This exception was *deleted* by the Scotland Act 1998 (Modifications of Schedules 4 and 5) Order 1999 (SI 1999/1749), art.6.

their health and safety. The primary purpose of the 2000 Act is to improve the quality of care services in Scotland, which purpose is a devolved matter. But there is clearly scope here for the powers and functions conferred by the Act to be given effect so as to trespass on that which is reserved, namely health, safety and welfare in connection with work and risks to the public arising therefrom. It would therefore follow that the competence of the Care Commission and Scottish Ministers under the 2000 Act must be understood as excluding those matters if their actions are not to be impugned as falling outwith devolved competence, even though taken under a valid Act of the Scottish Parliament. The validity of the Act can be saved by a narrow reading; the actions taken under it, if outwith the scope of that reading, cannot.

There is a separate issue here, to which we shall have cause to **4–22** return. Some incidental or consequential impact on reserved matters is permitted, provided it does not have a *greater effect on reserved matters than is necessary* to give effect to the purpose of the provision. The question is: Who decides whether the effect on reserved matters is greater than necessary? Of course, the initial judgment is for the promoters of the legislation and the Scottish Parliament itself (and indeed for those who have a locus to initiate pre-assent challenges to the competence of a bill). But when the court comes to consider that judgment, what is the nature of its role? In the human rights context, a distinction has been drawn between primary and secondary judgments.[12] If the court's function is one of reviewing the reasonableness of the legislative choice, then it makes merely a secondary judgment. The court makes a primary judgment if it decides for itself whether the legislative choice is incompatible with human rights. It would appear that here, as in the human rights sphere, the court will be required to make a primary judgment. It must determine at what point the effect of a provision on reserved matters becomes "greater than necessary" and then ask whether the Scottish Parliament went beyond that point. In the human rights sphere, the courts grant a certain latitude to the legislature, identifying the area within which, consistently with human rights, it has a free choice. But in relation to the reserved/devolved boundary the issue seems sharper. Intuitively, one would have thought a particular legislative choice has greater than necessary effect on reserved matters or it does not; a line must be drawn, not points on a spectrum, and it is to be drawn by the courts.

---

[12] R. Clayton and H. Tomlinson, *The Law of Human Rights* (Oxford University Press, Oxford, 2000), paras 5.122–5.124 and 5.133.

Enactments protected from modification

4–23   Schedule 4 to the Scotland Act complements the reservation of specified matters to Westminster by section 29 and Schedule 5 and preserves certain existing legislation from modification by the Scottish Parliament,[13] including the Scotland Act itself so far as it prescribes the principal features of the devolution settlement. Exempted from this general prohibition are modifications to a number of specified sections of the Scotland Act, most of which relate to the statutory versions of the privileges enjoyed by the Houses of Parliament at Westminster and thus have to do with the Scottish Parliament's internal procedures.

Community law

4–24   The Scottish Parliament cannot make laws which are inconsistent with European Community law. Section 126(9) of the Scotland Act defines "Community law" to mean, or include, "(a) all those rights, powers, liabilities, obligations and restrictions from time to time created or arising by or under the Community Treaties, and (b) all those remedies and procedures from time to time provided for by or under the Community Treaties."

A Member State of the European Union must take all necessary steps to ensure the fulfilment of its obligations arising from the Community treaties or resulting from action taken by Community institutions. The United Kingdom is the entity recognised in international law as the entity bound by these obligations. But it is for the state to decided how to parcel out responsibility for securing observance of its international obligations as a matter of its internal domestic law. In that regard, it should be noted that that while Part I of Schedule 5 reserves "international relations, including relations with territories outside the United Kingdom, the European Communities (and their institutions) and other international organisations", it expressly exempts from the scope of that reservation "observing and implementing international obligations, obligations under the Human Rights Convention and obligations under Community law."[14] So far as Community obligations fall within the scope of devolved competence, therefore, they are to be fulfilled by the devolved institutions, and by the same token the devolved institutions will be liable for any breach of Community law within that sphere.

---

[13] The statutes or statutory provisions protected from modification include arts 4 and 6 of the Union with Scotland Act 1706 and of the Union with England Act 1707, so far as they relate to freedom of trade; Private Legislation Procedure (Scotland) Act 1936; European Communities Act 1972, s.1 and Sch.1; and HRA 1998.

[14] para.7(1), (2).

Convention rights

The Convention rights are those fundamental human rights **4–25** enshrined in the European Convention on Human Rights that have been incorporated into the legal orders of the United Kingdom by the Human Rights Act 1998.[15] The Human Rights Act did not enter fully into force until October 2, 2000. Section 129(2) of the Scotland Act therefore provided for the Human Rights Act to be treated as if it were in force for the purpose of certain provisions of the Scotland Act, namely those relating to the devolved competence of the Scottish Parliament and Scottish Executive, proceedings under the Act involving human rights questions and the definition of devolution issues.[16] The consequence of this was that the Scottish Parliament and Scottish Executive were bound by the Convention rights for over a year before they became binding on other Scottish public authorities and on governmental bodies and public authorities south of the border.[17]

Few of the Convention rights are absolute. Some infringement of protected rights by an Act of the Scottish Parliament may therefore be justifiable by reference to a countervailing public interest, provided the measure is a proportionate response to a pressing social need. More broadly, the European Court of Human Rights recognises that a fair balance must be struck between the interests of the individual and the general interest of the community, and has described the search for that balance as "inherent in the whole of the Convention".[18] Any question about the validity of an Act of the Scottish Parliament must be approached with this in mind. Moreover, even if the natural and ordinary meaning of a provision is incompatible with one or more Convention rights, it may be possible to "rescue" it from invalidity by reading it down in the manner prescribed by section 101 of the Scotland Act.[19]

As we have seen, when deciding whether a provision of an Act of **4–26** the Scottish Parliament is outwith the Parliament's legislative competence, whether on grounds of incompatibility with the Convention rights or otherwise, the court is making a primary judgment: the question is whether the provision at issue accords with that primary judgment. But where human rights, at least, are

---

[15] HRA 1998, s.1 and Sch.1.
[16] SA 1998, s.29(2)(d), 57(2) and (3), 100, 126(1) and Sch.6.
[17] The Convention rights became binding on the Lord Advocate on May 22, 1999, and on the Scottish Parliament and other members of the Scottish Executive on July 1, 1999.
[18] See, *e.g. Sporrong and Lönnroth v Sweden* (1982) 5 E.H.R.R. 35.
[19] Although Profs Himsworth and Munro make the point in their annotations to the SA 1998 that "from the perspective of human rights protection it is not necessarily an advantage to have a measure survive because narrowly construed rather than be struck down as invalid under a more balanced interpretation of the measure".

involved, the primary judgment of the court may not be a simple matter of identifying the "right" answer. The European Court accords a "margin of appreciation" to national authorities in deference to the fact that they are better placed than itself to assess whether there is a "pressing social need" to impose some restriction on fundamental rights. While the margin of appreciation doctrine is not available as such to the national courts when considering the compatibility of national legislation with the Convention rights, a similar latitude is allowed because, as Lord Hope put it in *R. v Director of Public Prosecutions, ex parte Kebilene*[20]:

> "[D]ifficult choices may need to be made by the executive or the legislature between the rights of the individual and the needs of society. In some circumstances it will be appropriate for the courts to recognise that there is an area of judgment within which the judiciary will defer, on democratic grounds, to the considered opinion of the elected body or person whose act or decision is said to be incompatible with the Convention. ... It will be easier for such an area of judgment to be recognised where the Convention itself requires a balance to be struck, much less so where the right is stated in terms which are unqualified. It will be easier for it to be recognised where the issues involve questions of social or economic policy, much less so where the rights are of high constitutional importance or are of a kind where the courts are especially well placed to assess the need for protection."

The extent to which it will be appropriate for the courts to defer to the legislative choice expressed in a given statutory provision will vary. In *International Transport Roth*,[21] Laws L.J. noted that there was greater scope for deference where, in addition to the factors enumerated by Lord Hope, the measure in question was an Act of Parliament rather than an executive decision or "subordinate measure". Now in that regard it must be noted that Acts of the Scottish Parliament are defined as "subordinate legislation" for the purposes of the Human Rights Act. It does not, however, follow that the courts should accord a lesser degree of latitude to the Scottish Parliament when reviewing its enactments on human rights grounds than they extend to the Westminster Parliament. It is true, as the Inner House stressed in *Whaley v Lord Watson of Invergowrie*,[22] that the Scottish Parliament is a body limited by law.

---

[20] [2000] 2 A.C. 326 at 380, 381. See to similar effect, *e.g.* Lord Steyn in *Brown v Stott*, 2001 S.C. (P.C.) 43 at 66.

[21] *International Transport Roth GmbH v S of S for the Home Dept* [2003] Q.B. 728, paras 82–87.

[22] 2000 S.C. 340 at 348, 349, *per* Lord Rodger, and 357, 358, *per* Lord Prosser.

If the Scottish Parliament is not sovereign, however, it is still, indubitably, a democratically elected legislature,[23] and if the democratic imperative compels deference, then:

"[A] decision on whether there is or not an incompatibility with the Convention rights will have to recognise that the only place in which democratic debate on devolved issues will take place will be in the Scottish Parliament. There is a popular view that sovereignty is being returned to and will now reside with the people of Scotland. So the will of the people as expressed through their elected representatives will, in the right context, have to be respected as a function of the principle of subsidiarity. Numerous decisions of the European Court of Human Rights have shown that, within limits, a free and democratic society has the right to choose for itself the human rights policies which best suit its own people and circumstances."[24]

CONTROLLING LEGISLATIVE COMPETENCE

Pre-assent checks

Even allowing for the power of the courts under section 102 of **4–27** the Scotland Act to limit the effects of a finding that a provision of an Act of the Scottish Parliament is outside the competence of the Parliament, it is obviously desirable, for a variety of reasons, that the Parliament endeavours to remain within the limits set by section 29. To that end, the Scotland Act provides for a number of devices designed to ensure, prior to the passage of a bill into law, that it is *intra vires*. In the case of executive bills, the member of the Scottish Executive in charge of the bill must, on or before its introduction in the Parliament, state that in his view the provisions of the bill would be within the competence of the Parliament.[25] In the case of all bills, the Presiding Officer must, on or before the introduction of a bill, decide whether or not in his view its provisions would be within the competence of the Parliament and state his decision.[26] Presumably both the Scottish Ministers and the

---

[23] With, in a sense, superior democratic credentials to those of the Westminster Parliament, given its absence of unelected members and the use of a proportionate electoral system. See also the remarks of Lord Nimmo-Smith in *Adams v Scottish Ministers*, 2003 S.C. 171, para.62.

[24] Lord Hope of Craighead, "The Human Rights Act 1998: The task of the judges" [1999] 20 Statute L.R. 185 at 188.

[25] SA 1998, s.31(1).

[26] SA 1998, s.31(2). A negative statement by the Presiding Officer would not, however, block the bill's further progress.

Presiding Officer take legal advice in forming their views on the competence of a measure.[27] The form of these statements of competence and the manner in which they are to be made are provided for in Rules 9.2 and 9.3 of the Standing Orders of the Scottish Parliament.

Naturally, the views of the Scottish Ministers and/or Presiding Officer are not conclusive of the issue of competence,[28] and the bill may yet have a variety of further hurdles to clear. If the bill is passed by the Scottish Parliament, it is for the Presiding Officer to send it forward for Royal Assent.[29] But section 32(2) of the Scotland Act provides that he may not so submit it at any time during which the Advocate General, Lord Advocate or Attorney-General is entitled to refer the bill to the Judicial Committee of the Privy Council under section 33[30]; where such a reference has been made but not disposed of; or where the Secretary of State has made an order under section 35 of the Act prohibiting the Presiding Officer from submitting the bill for Royal Assent.[31]

A reference may be made under section 33 at any time during the four-week period commencing with the passing of the bill by the Parliament, although the Law Officers may notify the Presiding Officer that they do not intend to make a reference. In that event (subject to a section 35 order) the Presiding Officer may send the bill for Royal Assent at once. If a reference is made in relation to a bill, the Scottish Parliament may choose simply to wait until the reference is disposed of one way or the other. If the Judicial Committee finds that the provisions of the bill are within the powers of the Parliament, then the Presiding Officer may submit it for Royal Assent without further ado. If it does not so find, the bill cannot be sent forward for Royal Assent in unamended form. The Parliament may in that event reconsider the bill in a form designed

---

[27] Although the nature of such advice is not disclosed. At Westminster, where the minister in charge of a bill must make a "statement of compatibility" under HRA 1998, s.19 (or state that, although he is unable to state that the provisions of the bill are compatible with the Convention rights, the government nevertheless wishes the bill to proceed), it is now the practice for the explanatory notes accompanying the bill to give an outline of the legal advice obtained by the government.

[28] See the speech of Lord Hope in *A v Scottish Ministers*, 2002 S.C. (P.C.) 63, para.7: "they are no more than statements of opinion, which do not bind the judiciary."

[29] SA 1998, s.32(1).

[30] The government has stated its intention to shift the jurisdiction of the Judicial Committee in relation to devolution issues and pre-Assent checks on competence to the new Supreme Court to be established.

[31] This latter is not a control over the competence of a bill, but is considered here since it is grouped with the controls on competence within the scheme of the SA 1998.

to rectify the problems of the earlier version.[32] A reference to the Judicial Committee may, of course, take some time to dispose of. This is particularly likely to be the case where the bill raises some question of compatibility with Community law. Although the Judicial Committee may competently deal with such a question itself, it may elect to refer the matter on to the European Court of Justice for a preliminary ruling under Article 234 of the EC Treaty. In that event, the Scottish Parliament has the right under section 34 to resolve that it wishes to reconsider the bill before the references (*i.e.* to the Judicial Committee and to the European Court of Justice) are decided. If it does so resolve, the Presiding Officer will notify the Law Officers accordingly and the person who made the reference must request its withdrawal. The Parliament may then consider and vote on an altered version of the bill which seeks to accommodate the concerns that gave rise to the original reference. Even if the bill is passed in its amended form, however, it may still be the subject of a second reference by a Law Officer, should one of them remain unsatisfied as to its *vires*.

The power of the Secretary of State to intervene under section **4–28** 35 is quite different from the reference power conferred on the Law Officers by section 33. In making a reference, the Law Officers are raising questions of legislative competence in relation to a bill—whether the Scottish Parliament can validly enact such legislation. An intervention by the Secretary of State has nothing to do with the legislative competence of the Scottish Parliament as such, despite the position of section 35 in the scheme of the Scotland Act. Thus even if a bill is within the competence of the Scottish Parliament, the Secretary of State may make a section 35 order preventing its submission for Royal Assent in two situations: where it contains provisions which he has reasonable grounds to believe would be incompatible with any international obligations of the United Kingdom or with the interests of defence or national security; or where it contains provisions which modify the law as it applies to reserved matters and which he has reasonable grounds to believe would have an adverse effect on the operation of the law as it applies to reserved matters. As with the Law Officers, the Secretary of State may not exercise this power if he has notified the Presiding Officer that he does not intend to make an order under section 35. Subject to that, he may make such an order at any time during the four-week period commencing with the passing of the bill by the Parliament; within four weeks of any subsequent approval of the bill in amended form; or within four weeks of a reference to the Judicial Committee being decided or otherwise disposed of. The order must be laid before both Houses of the Westminster Parliament and is subject to annulment by resolution of either House.

---

[32] SA 1998, s.36(4).

Devolution issues

4-29   It follows from the fact that a provision in an Act of the Scottish Parliament "is not law" if it is outwith the boundaries of legislative competence prescribed by section 29 of the Scotland Act that, even where a bill has survived pre-assent scrutiny, received Royal Assent and entered into force, its validity remains open to challenge. Such a challenge constitutes a devolution issue in terms of paragraph 1(a) of Schedule 6: "a question whether an Act of the Scottish Parliament or any provision of an Act of the Scottish Parliament is within the legislative competence of the Parliament." As such, it must be raised and resolved in accordance with the rules laid down by Schedule 6.

Under Part II of Schedule 6,[33] proceedings for the determination of a devolution issue may be instituted by the Advocate General or the Lord Advocate, but devolution issues may equally be raised, either by way of claim or defence, by any person. So, for example, a person might seek judicial review of an Act of the Scottish Parliament in the Court of Session on the grounds that it is outside the competence of the Parliament; or, when charged with a criminal offence, plead the invalidity of the legislation under which he is charged or the illegality of the decision to prosecute him.[34]

While only the Judicial Committee of the Privy Council has jurisdiction to pronounce on the competence of Scottish legislation prior to its receiving Royal Assent, a devolution issue in the sense defined by Schedule 6 may be raised in any proceedings before a court or tribunal. However, a tribunal from which there is no right of appeal must refer a devolution issue which arises before it to the Inner House of the Court of Session. Other tribunals, and any court other than the House of Lords or a court consisting of three or more judges of the Court of Session, may do so. In criminal matters, a court other than a court consisting of two or more

---

[33] SA 1998, Pt II, concerns proceedings in Scotland. Pt III makes corresponding provision for proceedings in England and Wales, and Pt IV for proceedings in NI.

[34] The great majority of devolution issues have been raised in criminal proceedings. All but one of the devolution issues to have reached the Judicial Committee of the Privy Council to date have involved questions of the compatibility of aspects of Scots criminal procedure with the right to a fair trial under Art.6 of the Convention: see *Montgomery and Coulter v H.M. Advocate*, 2001 S.C. (P.C.) 1; *Brown v Stott*, 2001 S.C. (P.C.) 43; *McIntosh v H.M. Advocate*, 2001 S.C. (P.C.) 89; *Buchanan v McLean*, 2002 S.C. (P.C.) 1; *Millar v Dickson*, 2002 S.C. (P.C.) 30; *Dyer v Watson*, 2002 S.C. (P.C.) 89; *Mills v H.M. Advocate (No.2)*, 2002 S.L.T. 939; *R. v H.M. Advocate*, 2003 S.L.T. 4; and *Clark v Kelly*, 2003 S.L.T. 308. In two further cases, *Hoekstra v H.M. Advocate (No.3)*, 2001 S.C. (P.C.) 37 and *Follen v H.M. Advocate*, 2001 S.C. (P.C.) 105, the Judicial Committee refused leave to appeal and declined to pass on the substantive issues the appellants sought to raise. The one civil exception to devolution case law of the Judicial Committee thus far is *A v Scottish Ministers*, 2002 S.C. (P.C.) 63.

judges of the High Court of Justiciary, may refer a devolution issue arising in proceedings before it to the High Court. Where a devolution issue is raised before either the Court of Session or the High Court (that is, where it does not come before them on a reference from an inferior court) they may choose to refer the issue to the Judicial Committee of the Privy Council for resolution. In any event, an appeal against a determination by the Inner House of the Court of Session of a devolution issue lies to the Judicial Committee. Similarly, there is a right of appeal to the Judicial Committee in respect of a determination of a devolution issue by a court consisting of two or more judges of the High Court of Justiciary or a court of three or more judges of the Court of Session from which there is no appeal to the House of Lords, but only with the leave of the court concerned or, failing that, with special leave from the Judicial Committee itself.[35] Paragraph 37 of Schedule 6 provides that any power to make provision for regulating the procedure before any court or tribunal shall include the power to make provision in relation to devolution issues.[36]

To date, the validity of an Act of the Scottish Parliament has **4–30** been challenged in two cases. In *A v Scottish Ministers*,[37] the Judicial Committee held that the Mental Health (Public Safety and Appeals) Scotland Act 1999 did not violate the rights of persons detained thereunder in the state hospital under Articles 5(1)(e) and 5(4) of the Convention on Human Rights.[38] In *Adams v Scottish Minister*,[39] Lord Nimmo Smith dismissed an application for judicial review of the Protection of Wild Mammals (Scotland) Act 2002. The petitioners argued that the provisions of the Act were incompatible with certain rights under the Convention, including

---

[35] Which is worthy of note, in that prior to the entry into force of the SA 1998, there was no right of appeal in Scots criminal cases beyond the High Court of Justiciary.

[36] Provision in relation to the handling of devolution issues is made in Judicial Committee (Devolution Issues) Rules Order 1999 (SI 1999/665), Judicial Committee (Powers in Devolution Cases) Order 1999 (SI 1999/1320), A.S. (Devolution Issues Rules) 1999 (SI 1999/1345), A.J. (Devolution Issues Rules) 1999 (SI 1999/1346) and A.S. (Proceedings for Determination of Devolution Issues Rules) 1999 (SI 1999/1347).

[37] 2002 S.C. (P.C.) 63.

[38] The 1999 Act was passed following the decision of the sheriff at Lanark in *Ruddle v S of S for Scotland*, 1999 G.W.D. 29–1395 (which itself followed the decision of the House of Lords in *R. v S of S for Scotland*, 1999 S.C. (H.L.) 17) to grant an absolute discharge to a restricted patient in the State Hospital on the grounds that the legislation then in force did not authorise the continued detention in hospital of a person whose mental condition was not "treatable". It was enacted as an emergency measure under the procedure prescribed by the Scottish Parliament Standing Orders, r.9.21, to prevent the release from the state hospital of other violent and/or sexual offenders whose continued detention was shown to be necessary on grounds of public safety.

[39] 2003 S.C. 171.

the right to respect for private life under Article 8 and the right to peaceful enjoyment of possessions under Article 1 of the First Protocol, and that in enacting it the Scottish Parliament had acted illegally, unfairly and irrationally, contrary to the established grounds for judicial review. As to the former, following the dicta of Lord Hope in *Kebilene* and Lord Bingham in *Brown v Stott* concerning judicial deference, Lord Nimmo Smith found that the legislative choices expressed in the 2002 Act fell within the appreciable "margin of discretion" to be accorded to the Scottish Parliament on a subject of such moral and political controversy as hunting with dogs. As to the latter, his Lordship held that the ordinary principles of judicial review did not apply to the actings of the Scottish Parliament. The basis of this argument for the petitioners was that the Scottish Parliament was a limited body, whose enactments had the character of subordinate legislation, and which was as such subject to the supervisory jurisdiction of the Court of Session in the same way as any other body acting under delegated powers. Lord Nimmo Smith held, however, that Acts of the Scottish Parliament, despite their inclusion within the definition of "subordinate legislation" in section 21 of the Human Rights Act, had "far more in common with public general statutes of the United Kingdom Parliament than with subordinate legislation as it is more commonly understood."[40] More importantly, it appeared from the construction of the Scotland Act itself that the scheme it prescribed for the regulation of the Parliament and for the relationship between the Parliament and the courts was intended to be exhaustive: "sections 28, 29, 100, 101, 102 and Schedule 6 are definitive of the extent of the court's jurisdiction and of the procedure to be followed when a devolution issue is raised."[41] It therefore followed that the common law grounds for judicial review were excluded when considering the legislative competence of the Parliament. Only if an Act of the Scottish Parliament (or any of its provisions) breached any one of the limits on legislative competence set out in section 29(2) could the court hold that it "is not law". His Lordship questioned, moreover, what the common law grounds could add to the grounds provided by the Scotland Act for challenging the validity of an Act of the Scottish Parliament. As he rightly noted, review for procedural impropriety is excluded as a ground for review by section 28(5) of the Act. In his Lordship's opinion, moreover, review for illegality and irrationality was covered by section 29 itself, illegality in the sense that section 29 defined the legal limits of the Scottish Parliament's powers and irrationality in so far as proportionality review was available in the context of a Convention-based challenge. So far as illegality review

---

[40] *ibid.*, para.62.
[41] *ibid.*, para.63.

is concerned, however, it goes beyond merely identifying and enforcing the prescribed limits of a body's powers. As we shall see, the courts construe legislation subject to various presumptions, to the effect, for example, that the powers delegated or conferred will not be exercised oppressively or gratuitously, inconsistently with fundamental rights or the policy and purposes of the enabling statute, or on the basis of irrelevant considerations and in ignorance of relevant ones. To be sure, appropriate deference would fall to be accorded to the decisions of the Scottish Parliament about the weight it attaches to the evidence on which it acts but, as counsel for the petitioners argued, so to concede does not exclude the general principle that bodies exercising delegated powers are subject to review. It is arguable that express provision required to be made to exclude review for procedural impropriety because those who drafted the Scotland Act *assumed* that review on the ordinary grounds, as well as review under the Act, would lie in respect of Acts of the Scottish Parliament. At all events, the decision of Lord Nimmo Smith has been reclaimed and at the time of writing the decision of the Inner House was awaited.[42]

PARLIAMENTARY COMMITTEES

In any institution, it is impracticable to expect all of its work to be **4–31** done by the institution *in plenum*. But delegation to committees is not merely necessary, it is also desirable, since committees charged with specific remits develop an expertise in their fields which enables the institution as a whole better to perform its functions. At Westminster, a distinction is drawn between standing and select committees; at Holyrood, the committees of the Scottish Parliament combine the functions of the two (and have other functions besides).

Westminster

Standing committees are not the permanent fixtures implied by **4–32** the name: they do not "stand" but are appointed afresh by the House of Commons Committee of Selection as and when required. They may consist of between 16 and 50 M.P.s—18 to 20 is

---

[42] Counsel for the petitioners also suggested that one effect of admitting the common law grounds for review would be to enable those other than "victims", within the meaning of SA 1998, s.100(1), to challenge the competence of an Act of the Scottish Parliament. Lord Nimmo Smith took the view, however, that the intention of Parliament as reflected in s.100(1) was to confine title and interest to sue in that regard to "victims" in the sense there defined, and not to permit vexatious challenges by busybodies who simply opposed the policy of the measure.

typical—and are always constructed so as to reflect party political balance in the House as a whole. They fall into four categories: committees appointed to consider public bills; those appointed to consider subordinate legislation; those appointed to consider EU documents; and the grand committees of Scotland, Wales and Northern Ireland. At any one time, there will be up to 10 standing committees up and running to take the committee stages of public bills, up to two of which are Scottish standing committees to which bills certified by the Speaker as relating wholly or predominantly to Scotland are allocated.

Select committees are appointed for the life of each Parliament, and fall into five categories: domestic committees[43]; scrutiny committees[44]; internal committees[45]; the departmental select committees; and the committees charged with supervision of the work of the main officers of Parliament.[46] Although select committees have been a feature of parliamentary life for many years, the present structure of departmental select committees dates back only to 1979. They are charged with examining the expenditure, administration and policy of "their" departments of state and associated public bodies; they are also routinely criticised for failing to alter the nature of the relationship between Parliament and government. Such criticism is not altogether fair. Unlike the congressional committees in the United States, they are neither constituted nor staffed so as to allow them to be systematic in their scrutiny, and though they have the power to "send for persons, papers and records", they cannot compel the attendance of witnesses or the production of documents.[47] Their investigations are

---

[43] These advise the House of Commons Commission on the provision of services to and within the House.
[44] Namely, the Regulatory Reform Committee and the Select Committee on European Legislation.
[45] These oversee aspects of the House's procedures and practices, and include the Liaison Committee, the Select Committee on Procedure, the Select Committee on Standards and Privileges and the Select Committee on Modernisation of the House of Commons.
[46] Namely, the Comptroller and Auditor General and the Parliamentary Commissioner for Administration, who report to the Public Accounts Committee and the Select Committee on Public Administration respectively.
[47] In any case, the power of congressional committees can be overstated. Among the limitations on their effectiveness: Congress must establish a legitimate *legislative* interest in a matter it wishes to investigate (*i.e.* it is not free simply to embark on an investigation purely in the interests of exposing executive wrongdoing); "executive privilege" shields the executive branch from scrutiny and is regularly claimed; and the constitutional rights of individual witnesses ("taking the Fifth") must be respected. For all of these reasons, as has been pointed out, Congress uncovered far less about the sale of arms and defence-related equipment to Iraq, in breach of export controls, than did the Scott Inquiry in the UK (which may be an argument for more inquiries, if not for

therefore dependent upon ministerial co-operation to a significant extent. Even so, as the Select Committee on Procedure concluded in 1990, the new select committees provided "a far more vigorous, systematic and comprehensive scrutiny of ministers' actions and policies than anything that went before."[48] Since the committees are constituted to reflect political balance in the House as a whole, voting can split along party lines; but it is not an invariable practice. Some committees if not others have shown willing to challenge the government (possibly at some cost to any ministerial aspirations their members may harbour).[49] Outwith the category of departmental select committees, the Select Committees on Procedure, Public Accounts and Public Administration have done much valuable work on constitutional fundamentals in an effort to improve Parliament's capacity to hold the executive to account.[50] In assessing the contribution made by select committees, moreover, there is a danger of viewing their work in isolation from other constitutional developments. In the past, they were one of the few mechanisms that existed for extracting information from the government. Now, via the Code of Practice on Access to Government Information and, in the fullness of time, under the Freedom of Information Act,[51] much governmental information is published as a matter of course and more is available on request, all of which strengthens the capacity of the select committees in the discharge of their functions.

Holyrood

The rules on the committees of the Scottish Parliament are **4–33** contained in Chapter 6 of the Standing Orders. These require the Parliament to establish and maintain a number of mandatory

---

the worth of select committees): see A. Tomkins, *The Constitution After Scott: Government Unwrapped* (Clarendon Press, Oxford, 1998).

[48] HC 19–I (1989–90).

[49] Perhaps by way of compensation, the Select Committee on Modernisation has recommended that committee chairmen be paid an increased salary in recognition of their services to Parliament.

[50] See, *e.g.* Third Report of the Select Committee on Procedure, *Parliamentary Questions*, HC 622 (2001–02); Third Report of the Select Committee on Public Administration, *Ombudsman Issues*, HC 448 (2002–03), which excoriates the government for failing to make good its pledge to introduce legislation to reform the ombudsman system and for obstructing the work of the Parliamentary Commissioner; and the series of reports from the same committee (three in the 1997–2001 Parliament, and two so far in the present Parliament) on ministerial accountability.

[51] See Ch.9.

committees.[52] The Parliament may also, on a motion from the Parliamentary Bureau, establish subject committees. Each committee, other than a private bill committee, is required to have between five and 15 members. The Parliamentary Bureau is charged with drawing up a provisional list of members for each committee, having regard to party political balance in the Commons and preferences expressed by MSPs, which must then be approved by the Parliament. The Parliament must also approve any changes to a committee's remit or membership.

The functions of the parliamentary committees are extensive. Each is empowered to examine such matters within its remit as it may deem appropriate, or as may be referred to it by the Parliament or another committee, and report to Parliament thereon. Each is charged, within its remit, with considering the policy and administration of the Scottish Administration (including financial proposals and administration), any proposal for legislation (whether before the Scottish Parliament or the Westminster Parliament), and any relevant European legislation or international convention. They may consider the need for reform of the law and to that end may initiate legislative proposals. In the latter respect, their impact has been slight: only three committee bills were enacted into law in the course of the first Parliament. But in general terms, it is fair to say that the greater part of the Parliament's work is done through its committees, and the verdict of civil society (if not of the often hostile Scottish media) on their performance to date has been broadly favourable.[53] The values identified by the Consultative Steering Group as underpinning the Parliament's work—public participation, accountability and power-sharing—may have an aspirational flavour, but the committees have to a significant extent succeeded in capturing them.

PARLIAMENTARY PRIVILEGE

Westminster

4–34   The privileges of the Westminster Parliament are rooted in the law and custom of Parliament. At the opening of each new Parliament, the Speaker formally claims from the Crown for the

---

[52] Namely, the Audit Committee, Equal Opportunities Committee, European and External Relations Committee, Finance Committee, Procedures Committee, Public Petitions Committee, Standards Committee and Subordinate Legislation Committee.

[53] Third Report of the Procedures Committee, *The Founding Principles of the Scottish Parliament: The Application of Access and Participation, Equal Opportunities, Accountability and Power-sharing in the Work of the Parliament*, S.P.P. 818 (Session 1, 2003,). Perhaps the main source of disquiet about the committees stemmed from the tendency to go into private session rather more routinely than the public interest in transparency might warrant.

Commons "their ancient rights and privileges", namely freedom of speech; freedom from arrest; the exclusive right to regulate their composition; and exclusive jurisdiction over their internal affairs. The Houses of Parliament also assert an exclusive jurisdiction over the existence and extent of their privileges and over breaches of privilege and contempts of Parliament, which has in the past provoked confrontation with the courts.

Article 9 of the Bill of Rights 1689 provides that "the freedom of speech and debates or proceedings in Parliament ought not to be impeached or questioned in any court or place out of Parliament." This confers on members of both Houses of Parliament an immunity from civil and criminal liability in respect of words spoken during debates or in the course of parliamentary proceedings (although members may expose themselves to the disciplinary jurisdiction of the House itself). The precise scope of the privilege is unclear owing to the inexact nature of the term "proceedings in Parliament". In 1938, the House of Commons asserted that the privilege extends to "everything said or done by a member in the exercise of his functions as a member in a committee in either House, as well as everything said or done in either House in the transaction of parliamentary business."[54] Physical location does not provide a conclusive answer. On the one hand, letters posted to M.P.s within the Palace of Westminster have been held not to be protected by the privilege.[55] On the other, a proceeding in Parliament may take place outside, or nowhere near, Parliament, as was established in 1968 after a meeting of a parliamentary sub-committee at Essex University was disrupted by protestors.[56] The Strauss case in 1958 illustrated the difficulties that can arise at the borderline. George Strauss M.P. wrote a letter to a minister, condemning certain practices of the London Electricity Board. The letter was passed to the board, which threatened to sue Mr Strauss for libel. The Committee of Privileges found that the letter fell within the definition of "proceedings in Parliament", but the House of Commons as a whole took the opposite view.[57]

The most significant effect of the privilege of freedom of speech **4–35** is the absolute immunity enjoyed by M.P.s in the law of defamation, which rests on the notion that M.P.s should be able to speak

---

[54] HC 101 (1938–39).

[55] *Rivlin v Bilainkin* [1953] 1 Q.B. 485.

[56] HC 308 (1968–69).

[57] Even had the board proceeded against Mr Strauss, which it did not, it seems that he would have been protected by qualified privilege, which is only lost if the statements complained of were actuated by malice: see *Beach v Freeson* [1972] 1 Q.B. 14. For the avoidance of doubt, it is sometimes expressly provided in legislation that M.P.s shall be protected by absolute privilege, as where the Parliamentary Commissioner Act 1967 conferred absolute privilege on communications between M.P.s and the Parliamentary Commissioner for Administration.

freely in Parliament without any fear that what they say might later be used against them in court. This is not to say that a Member of Parliament cannot be sued in defamation at all; in respect of his utterances outwith the meaning of "proceedings in Parliament", he is as liable to be sued as anybody else.[58] Neither does it man that *no* reference may be made in court to parliamentary proceedings. Since 1980, the House of Commons has permitted reference to be made in court to *Hansard* and published reports of parliamentary committees. In the case of *Pepper v Hart*,[59] the House of Lords (in its judicial capacity) held that, in interpreting ambiguous legislation, the courts might properly have regard to clear ministerial statements made during the passage of the legislation through Parliament. The courts have also established the practice of examining ministerial statements made in Parliament when considering applications for judicial review of the legality of ministerial decisions. And an important amendment to Article 9 was made by section 13 of the Defamation Act 1996, which enables M.P.s to waive their privilege in order to pursue an action in defamation. The section was utilised by Neil Hamilton, former Minister for Corporate Affairs, in his abortive libel action against *The Guardian* newspaper.

It is not only parliamentary proceedings which attract the protection of the privilege, but also the publication of parliamentary proceedings. This was established by the Parliamentary Papers Act 1840, the enactment of which followed one of the great confrontations between Parliament and the courts over the existence and extent of parliamentary privilege. In *Stockdale v Hansard*,[60] it was held that privilege did not extend to the publication by *Hansard* of a report by the Inspectors of Prisons, which referred to an indecent book, published by Stockdale, found circulating in Newgate Prison. By resolution, the House of Commons responded by asserting its "sole and exclusive jurisdiction to determine upon the existence and extent of its privileges."[61] It added that the institution or prosecution of any action bringing the privileges of Parliament into discussion or decision by a court outwith Parliament itself constituted a breach of privilege "and renders all parties concerned therein amenable . . . to the punishment consequent

---

[58] Although even here it is not possible to fortify one's case against an M.P. with reference to remarks he has made in Parliament, or rely on these to prove malice: see *Church of Scientology of California v Johnson-Smith* [1972] 1 Q.B. 522; *Prebble v T.V. New Zealand* [1995] 1 A.C. 321.

[59] [1993] A.C. 593.

[60] (1837) 2 Mood & R. 9.

[61] H.C.J. 418 (1837).

thereon."[62] The 1840 Act gave statutory force to the Commons' view of what the law was, making clear that the protection of absolute privilege from civil and criminal proceedings extended to papers published under the authority of Parliament as certified by an officer of either House. Qualified privilege applies to the publication of fair and accurate reports of parliamentary proceedings and papers, so that there will be no liability in defamation without proof of malice.[63]

The privilege of freedom from arrest protects members from **4–36** civil arrest, but not from arrest in connection with criminal offences. Since the abolition of imprisonment for debt in the nineteenth century, it has had little practical significance.[64] The importance of the exclusive right to regulate its own composition has also been attenuated by the transfer of the right of the Commons to determine the result of disputed parliamentary elections to the ordinary courts.[65] The Houses of Parliament do retain the right to determine whether a person is disqualified from membership of either House, as when, in 1960, the House of Commons declared vacant the seat of Tony Benn M.P. after he succeeded to a viscountcy on the death of his father and barred him from the House. This jurisdiction is not, however, exclusive, as a person claiming that an individual disqualified from membership of the House of Commons by virtue of the House of Commons Disqualification Act 1975 has been elected to the Commons may

---

[62] The matter descended even further into farce when subsequently Stockdale obtained judgment against Hansard and the two holders of the office of the Sheriff of Middlesex were imprisoned by order of the Commons for attempting to enforce the judgment. The court dismissed their application for *habeas corpus* on the basis that it could not go behind the Speaker's warrant to the effect that the two men were guilty of a breach of privilege and contempt of Parliament: *Case of the Sheriff of Middlesex* (1840) 11 Ad. & El. 273. They were later released by the Commons upon undertaking not to execute any orders of the court against Hansard, which in turn led to their being imprisoned by the courts for contempt of court.

[63] But while the 1840 Act resolved the differences between Parliament and the courts over this aspect of freedom of speech, it did not resolve the basic jurisdictional conflict over who it is—Parliament or the courts—that has the last word over the existence and extent of privileges when claimed. It is to be noted in this regard that Parliament, other than the House of Lords in its judicial capacity, is expressly excluded from the duty laid on public authorities by HRA 1998, s.6, to act in conformity with the Convention rights. While the domestic courts may not therefore hold any act of either House to be incompatible with the Convention rights, that does not exclude the potential liability of the state before the ECHR.

[64] However, collateral privileges flow from the basic principle underlying freedom from arrest, namely the right of Parliament to the uninterrupted attendance and services of its members, such as the exemption of M.P.s from jury service and from citation to attend court as witnesses.

[65] See now the Representation of the People Act 1983, Ch.2, Pt III.

apply under section 7 of the Act to the Judicial Committee of the Privy Council for a declaration to that effect.[66]

The privilege consisting of Parliament's exclusive right to control its own proceedings and to regulate its internal affairs without interference from the courts remains significant. It was on this basis that the ordinary courts declined to intervene in the celebrated case of *Bradlaugh v Gossett*.[67] Mr Bradlaugh, an atheist who had been refused the opportunity of taking the oath required before an M.P. may sit,[68] contested the legality of a resolution of the House of Commons to exclude him and sought an injunction to restrain the serjeant-at-arms from enforcing that resolution. The court held it had no jurisdiction to pronounce on the matter. It is also on the grounds of this privilege that the courts decline to investigate alleged procedural defects in the legislative process when the validity of an Act of Parliament is challenged. As we have seen,[69] the effect of the "enrolled bill rule" is that a court of law can do no more than look to the Parliamentary Roll: "if from that it should appear that a bill has passed both Houses and received the Royal Assent, no court can inquire into the mode in which it was introduced into Parliament, nor into what was done previous to its introduction, nor what passed in Parliament during its progress."[70] If the enactment of legislation, whether public or private, has been obtained by fraud or other impropriety, or in contravention of the standing orders of Parliament, only Parliament can rectify matters by repealing the measure in question.

4–37 The Houses of Parliament retain a jurisdiction to deal with breaches of privilege and contempts of Parliament. "Contempt of Parliament" is a generic term to cover any offences punishable by Parliament, namely conduct offensive to the authority and dignity of the Houses or, as Erskine May puts it[71]:

> "Any act or omission which obstructs or impedes either House in the performance of its functions, or which obstructs or impedes any member or officer of such House in the discharge of his duty, or which has a tendency, directly or indirectly, to produce such results."

---

[66] The Judicial Committee may direct that the issue be tried in the High Court of England and Wales, the Court of Session or the High Court of Northern Ireland, depending on the location of the constituency in question; if so, the decision of that court is final.

[67] (1884) 12 Q.B.D. 721.

[68] This in the days before provision was made allowing M.P.s to make a solemn affirmation: see now the Oaths Act 1978.

[69] Above, para.2–01.

[70] *Edinburgh and Dalkeith Ry v Wauchope* (1842) 8 Cl. & F. 710, *per* Lord Campbell. See also *Pickin v British Railways Board* [1974] A.C. 765, in which the House of Lords eschewed any jurisdiction to inquire into parliamentary procedures.

[71] *Parliamentary Practice* (22nd ed., Butterworths, London, 1997).

The term "contempts" therefore includes breaches of privilege, that is, the infringement of any of the specific privileges noted above. The distinction between the two may be important, however, for while the Houses of Parliament cannot extend the scope of their own privileges and questions of the existence and extent of privilege may be addressed by the courts, the list of possible contempts remains open and the courts cannot question the causes of committal for contempt. Established examples of contempt include disorderly conduct within the precincts of Parliament; the obstruction of members going to or coming from the Houses; bribery, corruption and other species of dishonesty; and refusal to give evidence before parliamentary committees.

The fact that certain conduct is found to constitute contempt does not mean that Parliament will take any further action against the contemnor. The House of Commons resolved in 1978 only to use its powers of punishment when "satisfied that to do so is essential to provide reasonable protection for the House, its members or its officers, from such improper obstruction or attempt or threat of obstruction as is causing or is liable to cause substantial interference with the performance of their respective functions." Nevertheless, the range of penalties at the theoretical disposal of the House is considerable. A member may be expelled or suspended; members or "strangers" may be admonished or reprimanded at the Bar of the House. Persons may be committed for contempt by the High Court of Parliament, without recourse to the ordinary courts; and the House retains a power, last used in 1880, of imprisonment (although curiously it has no power to impose fines).[72]

As to the House of Lords, Erskine May comments that "the Lords enjoy their privileges simply because of their immemorial role in Parliament as advisers of the Sovereign." Just as much as the House of Commons, the House of Lords claims the exclusive right to be the judge of its own privileges and the power to punish breaches of privilege and contempts, although issues of privilege arise less frequently in the Upper House. The privilege of peerage confers immunity from civil arrest.[73] Article 9 of the Bill of Rights 1689 applies equally to the Lords as to the Commons in protecting

---

[72] It is questionable now whether it would be consistent with the international obligations of the UK under the Convention for either House of Parliament to resort to its penal jurisdiction. It is not merely that the procedures of the Houses may lack compatibility with Art.6 (particularly the right to be tried before an independent and impartial tribunal) but also that, in so far as the categories of contempts are not closed, imposition of criminal liability could be regarded as contrary to Art.7, which prohibits the retrospective creation of criminal offences. See, generally, the decision of the ECHR in *Demicoli v Malta* (1991) 14 E.H.R.R. 47.

[73] See *Stourton v Stourton* [1963] 1 All E.R. 606.

freedom of speech. The House of Lords is master of its own affairs and decides, through the Committee for Privileges, the right of newly created peers to sit and vote and on claims to old peerages.[74] Lastly, the Lords have the power to commit a person for contempt and, unlike the Commons, also have a power to fine and to order security to be given for good conduct.[75]

4–38   Many of these privileges may appear archaic, but their underlying rationale remains broadly sound, as attested by the provision made in the Scotland Act to extend aspects of parliamentary privilege as developed at Westminster to the Scottish Parliament. Even so, as part of the general drive to modernise the workings of Parliament, a joint committee consisting of members of the House of Lords and of the House of Commons was established in July 1997 to review the law and practice of parliamentary privilege at Westminster and to make recommendations. The committee, chaired by Lord Nicholls of Birkenhead, published its First Report in April 1999.[76] The joint committee's approach to its task was informed by the following considerations:

> "The overall guiding principle is that the proper functioning of Parliament lies at the heart of a healthy parliamentary democracy. It is in the interests of the nation as a whole that the two Houses of Parliament should have the rights and immunities that they need in order to function properly. But the protection afforded by privilege should be no more than Parliament needs to carry out its functions effectively and safeguard its constitutional position. Appropriate procedures should exist to prevent abuse and ensure fairness. Thus the thread running through this report involves matching parliamentary privilege to the current requirements of Parliament and present-day standards of fairness and reasonableness."

In that light, the committee made a number of recommendations for change. It favoured abolition of existing privileges only in a few cases.[77] Otherwise, its proposals generally involved clothing existing

---

[74] In the *Wensleydale Peerage Case* (1856) 5 H.L. Cas. 958, the House of Lords decided that the life peerage created for the judge Sir James Parke did not entitle him to sit in Parliament. The Appellate Jurisdiction Act 1876 authorised the appointment of Lords of Appeal in Ordinary carrying with it a right to sit and vote in the Lords, while the Life Peerages Act 1958 provided for the conferment of life peerages on men and women with the right to sit and vote.

[75] Although here again, it seem unlikely that such power would ever now be used: see n.69.

[76] First Report of the Joint Committee on Parliamentary Privilege, HL 43-I and HC 214-I (1998–99).

[77] The Joint Committee recommended abolition of freedom from arrest in civil cases and of the collateral privilege exempting members from citation to attend court as witnesses (although it considered that citations should not be issued against members without the prior approval of a judge).

privileges in statutory form or removing more glaring anachronisms. Thus, it recommended the enactment of legislation confirming the traditional view of Article 9 of the Bill of Rights as a blanket prohibition on the examination of parliamentary proceedings in court, subject to specific and limited exceptions,[78] clarifying the meaning of the term "proceedings in Parliament",[79] and replacing the provisions of the Parliamentary Papers Act 1840 with legislation in modern form.[80] It also called for the replacement of section 13 of the Defamation Act 1996 with new provision enabling the House, rather than an individual member, to waive privilege in court proceedings (and not merely those involving defamation). It favoured the introduction of new statutory offences of bribery and corruption, but noted that, since the prosecution of such offences would inevitably impact upon Article 9, any prosecution should be subject to the consent of the Attorney-General or Lord Advocate.[81]

The right of each House to administer its internal affairs within **4–39** its precincts should be confined to activities directly and closely related to proceedings in Parliament and "Parliament should no longer be a statute-free zone in respect of Acts of Parliament relating to matters such as health and safety and data protection. In future, when Parliament is to be exempt, a reasoned case should be made out and debated as the legislation proceeds through Parliament." While each House should retain its disciplinary and penal jurisdiction over its own members, the disciplinary procedures of both Houses should be revised to bring them into line with contemporary standards of fairness, including rights guaranteed by the Convention. Parliament's jurisdiction over contempts committed by strangers should be transferred to the courts, although Parliament should retain a residual jurisdiction including a power to admonish in non-contentious cases. It has yet to be seen whether these proposals will bear fruit in a new Parliamentary Privilege Act.

---

[78] Such as that established by *Pepper v Hart* [1993] A.C. 539.

[79] The Joint Committee recommended in particular that members' constituency correspondence should be excluded from the statutory definition, whilst the registers of members' financial interests should form a part of "proceedings in Parliament".

[80] The Joint Committee being apparently unimpressed by the "impenetrable early Victorian style" of the 1840 Act.

[81] On this, see *The Draft Corruption Bill*, Cm.5777 (2003). The bill creates new offences for England and Wales; in its proposed application to Scotland (see cl.29) it would disapply parliamentary privilege rules in relation to the admissibility of evidence where a person is prosecuted at common law for bribery or accepting a bribe, an offence under the Public Bodies (Corrupt Practices) Act 1889, s.1, or the first two offences under the Prevention of Corruption Act 1906, s.1.

Holyrood

4–40   As the Joint Committee on Parliamentary Privilege noted in its
First Report:

> "Unlike earlier parliamentary institutions which the United
> Kingdom established by statute, the new devolved institutions
> do not derive their rights and powers by reference to privileges
> which exist at Westminster. Instead, in each case, they are set
> out in detail in the relevant legislation."

As this implies, the Scottish Parliament and its members do not
enjoy the same range of privileges as obtain at Westminster, and
such "privileges" as they have find their source in the Scotland Act
itself. The Act extends two aspects of the privilege of free speech
to the Scottish Parliament, its members and officers. First, by virtue
of section 41, any statement made in proceedings of the Parliament
and the publication under the authority of the Parliament of any
such statement is absolutely privileged in the law of defamation.
Even if an MSP makes a defamatory statement maliciously, or with
the intention of injuring the reputation of the object of the
statement, he cannot be held liable in respect of it (although, as at
Westminster, he may fall foul of the disciplinary jurisdiction of the
Parliament itself). Secondly, by virtue of section 42, certain proceedings of the Scottish Parliament—namely, parliamentary proceedings in relation to a bill or subordinate legislation—are
shielded from criminal liability for contempt of court. A fair and
accurate report of such proceedings, provided it is made in good
faith, is similarly protected. This immunity is narrower than that
which obtains at Westminster: it would appear, for example, that
contemptuous utterances made in the course of a general debate in
the Scottish Parliament could result in the prosecution of the
speaker. However, paragraph 1 of Schedule 3 requires standing
orders to make provision for the prevention of conduct constituting
contempt of court and to lay down a *sub judice* rule; in view of this,
it is unlikely that many instances of contemptuous behaviour will
arise from the proceedings of the Scottish Parliament. Like members of the Westminster Parliament, MSPs are exempt from jury
service, but by virtue of section 85 of the Scotland Act, rather than
freedom from arrest and its associated privileges. No immunity
from arrest, either criminal or civil, is extended to MSPs by the
Scotland Act.

The aspect of parliamentary privilege that finds the most echoes
in the Scotland Act is that of exclusive cognisance of internal
affairs. The underlying rationale for this privilege is not dissimilar
to that found in Article 9 of the Bill of Rights: namely, to prevent
outside interference, and specifically interference by the courts,
with the proceedings of the Parliament. Absent such privileges, the

ordinary work of the Parliament could be obstructed by the commencement of legal challenges to its activities. The Scotland Act, therefore, provides that the validity of any proceedings of the Scottish Parliament is unaffected by any vacancy in its membership[82] or by the participation of a member who is subject to disqualification.[83] The validity of any act of the Presiding Officer or either of his deputies is unaffected by any defect in his or their election,[84] and the validity of an Act of the Scottish Parliament is unaffected by any invalidity in the proceedings of the Parliament leading to its enactment.[85]

The courts have largely acquiesced in Westminster's assertion of **4–41** exclusive jurisdiction over its internal affairs, and that there are still good reasons for this is reflected in these provisions of the Scotland Act. It is important to note, however, that the jurisdiction of the ordinary courts is not wholly excluded in relation to the internal workings of the Scottish Parliament. Certain aspects of its internal affairs are governed by the Scotland Act itself, or by subordinate legislation made under it or Scottish legislation required to be enacted by the Scotland Act. The rules on members' interests are an example.[86] At first instance in *Whaley v Lord Watson of Invergowrie*,[87] Lord Johnston refused the petitioners' motion for interim interdict to restrain Mike Watson MSP from proceeding further with the Protection of Wild Mammals (Scotland) Bill on the grounds that he was in breach of the rules against paid advocacy contained in the 1999 Order.[88] His Lordship's decision was founded partly on his view that the grant of the remedy would intrude upon the exclusive competence of the Parliament to regulate its own affairs. But as the Inner House made clear on the petitioners' reclaiming motion, that competence is not exclusive. The 1999 Order, being a statutory instrument made under primary legislation, creates legal rules enforceable as such by the ordinary courts. The fact that the Standards Committee of the Scottish

---

[82] SA 1998, s.1(4).

[83] SA 1998, s.17(5).

[84] SA 1998, s.19(7).

[85] SA 1998, s.28(5). See also s.50, which provides that the validity of any act of a member of the Scottish Executive or of a junior Scottish Minister is unaffected by any defect in his nomination by the Parliament or, as the case may be, in the Parliament's agreement to his nomination; and s.69(3), which makes similar provision in respect of any procedural defects in the appointment of the Auditor General for Scotland.

[86] See for the time being the Scotland Act 1998 (Transitory and Transitional Provisions) (Members' Interests) Order 1999 (SI 1999/1350). This is provided to continue in force until such time as the Scottish Parliament makes the provision required by SA 1998, s.39: see further paras 4–45—4–46.

[87] 2000 S.C. 340.

[88] Scotland Act 1998 (Transitory and Transitional Provisions) (Members' Interests) Order 1999 (SI 1999/1350).

Parliament had a parallel jurisdiction to scrutinise alleged breaches of the Order did not affect the point, nor was the court in any way bound by the fact that the Standards Committee had rejected a complaint that Mr Watson had breached the rule against advocacy. The position *might* be different if a petition raised a question of compliance with the standing orders of the Scottish Parliament, which do not require to be cast in legislative form[89] and which are in fact contained in a resolution of the Parliament. But the Scotland Act requires that the rules on members' interests, when adopted by the Scottish Parliament, be adopted by way of legislation. The difference matters, for in the latter case the court will have the last word on the meaning and effect of the provision made.

A further issue raised by *Whaley* concerned the effect of section 40(3) and (4) of the Scotland Act. These provide that in any proceedings against the Scottish Parliament, the court shall not make an order for suspension, interdict, reduction or specific performance (or other like order) but may instead make a declarator. Similarly, in any proceedings against an MSP, the Presiding Officer or his deputies, any member of the staff of the Parliament or the Parliamentary corporation, the court may make no coercive order, but must confine itself to declarator, if the effect of making a coercive order would be to give relief against the Parliament which is prohibited by section 40(3). In *Whaley*, it was argued that the court could not grant interdict against Mike Watson MSP because the effect of doing so would be to interdict the Parliament from proceeding with the Protection of Wild Mammals (Scotland) Bill. As the Inner House held, however:

"Section 40(4) of the 1998 Act is designed to prevent parties from obtaining in substance remedies affecting the Parliament which they could not obtain in proceedings against the Parliament. It follows that subsection (4) applies where proceedings for some legal wrong could lie against the Parliament. In the present case . . . the petitioners seek to interdict the first respondent from breaching Article 6 of the members' interests order—a wrong which could be committed only by a member and which could never be committed by the Parliament itself. . . . In other words, any interdict against the first respondent could not have the effect of interdicting a wrong by the Parliament."[90]

So, for example, even if there were a compelling argument that the Scottish Parliament was proposing to enact legislation trespassing

[89] SA 1998, s.22.
[90] *per* Lord Rodger at 351.

upon reserved matters, the court could not restrain it from proceeding by way of interdict.[91] Nor could it interdict the printing and publication of the bill by the Clerk to the Parliament, because that would effectively amount to an interdict against the Parliament proper. But coercive remedies are competent against members and officers of the Scottish Parliament where section 40(3) is not implicated, even though their grant may involve some disruption to the Parliament's internal affairs.

Finally, there are certain parallels to be drawn between the **4–42** inherent jurisdiction enjoyed by the Houses of Parliament at Westminster as the High Court of Parliament and the conferment of specific powers on the Scottish Parliament in relation to witnesses, evidence and discipline. Section 22 of the Scotland Act provides for the regulation of parliamentary proceedings by standing order, and gives effect to Schedule 3 which specifies how certain matters are to be dealt with by standing orders. Among the matters that Schedule 3 requires standing orders to cover are the withdrawal from a member of the Parliament of his rights and privileges.[92] But while, as such, the Scottish Parliament has an independent disciplinary jurisdiction over its members, it does not, by contrast to Westminster, have an autonomous penal jurisdiction, either over members or strangers. Sections 22 and 23 provide for the power of the Parliament to compel the attendance of witnesses and the production of documents, the exceptions to and modalities surrounding that power, and for the creation of summary offences of refusing or failing without statutory justification or reasonable excuse to attend or co operate as required. The Houses of Parliament at Westminster, as the High Court of Parliament, have powers in relation to compelling attendance and the production of evidence similar to those of the ordinary courts, and have jurisdiction to deal with any breaches of privilege or contempts involved in non-compliance with their requirements. These provisions of the Scotland Act provide a statutory statement of the extent to which the Scottish Parliament is to have an equivalent jurisdiction, and it should in particular be noted that criminal offences under these provisions will be triable in the ordinary courts, but *not* before the Parliament itself. Similarly, an MSP who takes part in any parliamentary proceedings in contravention of the rules on the registration of financial interests or the rules against paid advocacy will be guilty of a criminal offence punishable by a fine, but again triable by the ordinary courts rather than the Parliament. Lastly, section

---

[91] Assuming the applicant had title and interest to seek such a remedy.
[92] This is provided for by the Standing Orders, r.1.7, in the following terms: "The Parliament may, on a motion of the Standards Committee, withdraw from a member his or her rights and privileges as a member to such extent and for such period as are specified in the motion."

43 provides that the Scottish Parliament is a "public body" for the purposes of the Prevention of Corruption Acts 1889 to 1916, with the consequence that the members (and staff) of the Scottish Parliament, unlike members of the Westminster Parliament, are subject to liability for offences involving the corrupt making or accepting of payments, in money or in kind, for activity or inactivity in connection with the public body's business.

STANDARDS

Westminster

4–43   On several occasions in the past century, the House of Commons has had cause to inquire into possible contempts of Parliament, breaches of privilege and other species of unparliamentary conduct connected with links between a member's parliamentary role and outside financial (or equivalent) interests. But not until 1975 was a public register of members' interests actually established. This followed an inquiry into the business network of one John Poulson, which was found to include three M.P.s, all of whom had used their position to promote Poulson's business without disclosing the benefits they received from him in return. Even so, the register as it then stood was insufficiently rigorous to prevent the growth of commercial political lobbying during the 1980s or, more to the point, to scotch the willingness of certain M.P.s to hire out their parliamentary services for reward. This became inescapably apparent as the many-faceted "cash for questions" affair began to unfold from 1993.[93] In October 1994, the Prime Minister responded to the torrent of sleaze allegations engulfing his government by announcing the appointment of a Committee on Standards in Public Life with the following remit[94]:

---

[93] First, two Conservative Parliamentary Private Secretaries were suspended from Parliament for accepting offers of money from journalists posing as businessmen in return for tabling parliamentary questions. The then Chief Secretary to the Treasury, Jonathan Aitken, resigned office to fight allegations that he had accepted gifts and hospitality which he had failed to declare—a fight which ended in his imprisonment for perjury and conspiracy to pervert the course of justice. Most notoriously of all, Neil Hamilton, former Minister for Corporate Affairs, took on—in neither case successfully—first *The Guardian* and then Mohamed Al Fayed, on whose behalf he was alleged to have taken money to ask parliamentary questions.

[94] In Nov. 1997, the P.M. added "issues in relation to the funding of political parties" to the committee's terms of reference. The committee was chaired initially by Lord Nolan, subsequently by Lord Neill of Bladen, and is now chaired by Sir Nigel Wicks.

"To examine current concerns about standards of conduct of all holders of public office, including arrangements relating to financial and commercial activities, and to make recommendations as to any changes in present arrangements which might be required to ensure the highest standards of probity in public life.

For these purposes, public life should include ministers, civil servants and advisers, members of Parliament and United Kingdom members of the European Parliament, members and senior officials of all non-departmental public bodies and of National Health Service bodies, non-ministerial office-holders, members and other senior officers of other bodies discharging publicly-funded functions, and elected members and senior officers of local authorities."

The Nolan Committee published its First Report, concerning the holding by M.P.s of paid outside interests, in May 1995. The Report acknowledged the widespread loss of public confidence in the probity of M.P.s, but found no evidence of "a growth in actual corruption." What it did find was that almost 70 per cent of M.P.s, not including the Speaker and ministers, had some form of financial relationship with outside bodies, ranging from company directorships and consultancies with lobbying firms and trade associations to sponsorship agreements with trade unions. The committee did not recommend the introduction of an outright ban on outside financial interests, taking the view that this would deter otherwise eligible and well-qualified people from seeking election to the House of Commons: "a Parliament composed entirely of full-time professional politicians would not serve the best interests of democracy." It did, however, recommend the establishment of a new Select Committee on Standards and Privileges and the appointment of a Parliamentary Commissioner for Standards, who would supervise compliance with a new Code of Conduct for M.P.s and report to the select committee on alleged breaches. It called for a specific prohibition on paid advocacy and the adoption of rules requiring members to deposit with the Commissioner for Standards, and thereby make available for public inspection, any agreements with bodies outside Parliament relating to the provision of services by them in their capacity as M.P.s, together with details of the remuneration received from any such employment. More generally, the committee set out seven general principles which were to be taken to govern all aspects of public life.[95] The House of Commons endorsed both the statement of principles and the specific recommendations of the committee in a free vote in

---

[95] Namely selflessness, integrity, objectivity, accountability, openness, honesty and leadership.

November 1995, at the same time approving a resolution banning paid advocacy. The House subsequently approved a new Code of Conduct for M.P.s in July 1996.

4–44   The code is contained in a resolution of the House, and as such is not legally binding in the sense of being enforceable by the courts.[96] It is policed and enforced, rather, by the House of Commons itself, through the machinery it has chosen to set up.[97] The code opens by re-stating the seven Nolan principles of conduct in public life. It then sets out eight rules dealing with matters such as general conduct, acceptance of gifts, lobbying and advocacy, and registration of interests. When in doubt as to the requirements of the code, members are exhorted to seek the advice of the Parliamentary Commissioner for Standards who, if necessary, will put the matter before the Select Committee on Standards and Privileges.

The Commissioner for Standards is also charged with the compilation and updating of the Register of Members' Interests. Registrable interests include any pecuniary interest or other material benefit which a member receives and which might reasonably be thought by others to influence his actions, speeches or votes in Parliament, or actions taken in his capacity as an M.P.[98] Members of Parliament must notify their registrable interests to the Commissioner for Standards within three months of taking their seats after a general election; and must thereafter notify any changes in their interests within four weeks of each change occurring. In addition to registering their interests, members are also required to disclose or declare any relevant interests verbally in the course of debate in the House of Commons and in other contexts.

Although the House of Lords did not come under the same sort of pressure as the House of Commons over standards of conduct, peers were nevertheless moved to adopt a resolution of their own in November 1995, albeit in less prescriptive terms, and a register

---

[96] But it could hardly have been otherwise without abrogating the privilege of exclusive cognisance.

[97] That is, the Select Committee on Standards and Privileges, whose remit and membership are prescribed in Standing Order 149 of the House of Commons; and the Parliamentary Commissioner for Standards, whose functions are defined in Standing Order 150.

[98] The code of conduct divides registrable interests into the following 10 categories: directorships; remunerated employment, office, profession, etc; the provision of services to clients where the services arise out of the member's position as an M.P.; sponsorships; gifts, benefits and hospitality in the UK exceeding a specified value; overseas visits; overseas benefits and gifts exceeding a specified value; land and property other than the member's personal residence(s) (or those of a spouse) which generate an income; shareholdings; and miscellaneous relevant interests not caught by any of the specific categories.

of interests, albeit less broad in its coverage.[99] In light of the seventh report of the Committee on Standards in Public Life,[1] however, the House of Lords adopted a code of conduct modelled on that applicable to M.P.s and containing the seven principles of public life, and a new Register of Lords' Interests requiring registration by peers of all relevant interests.[2]

Holyrood

The ground was laid for the establishment of the Scottish **4–45** Parliament at a time when public life was racked by allegations of sleaze and corruption. As has been seen, the response at Westminster was to set up the Committee on Standards in Public Life in an attempt to repair the damage caused to Parliament's reputation by the behaviour of some M.P.s and to restore public confidence in the probity of the political process. The advantage for the fledgling Scottish Parliament in this regard was that it was starting with a clean sheet, and much was made of the avowedly superior commitment of the Scottish Parliament to high standards of probity. One hesitates to cavil at the high-mindedness of the aim. It may nonetheless be said that local authorities and other public bodies in Scotland have felt the impact of ethical standards in a far more pronounced manner than MSPs.[3]

Certain provisions concerning the maintenance and enforcement of standards in the Scottish Parliament are contained in the Scotland Act itself. Section 39 deals with members' interests, and it should be noted that the reference to "members" includes the Lord Advocate and the Solicitor General for Scotland whether or not they are MSPs. It requires provision to be made for a register of members' interests to be published and made available for public inspection. Broadly speaking, the terms of section 39 mirror the rules laid down in the House of Commons following the First Report of the Nolan Committee in 1995, but there is one crucial difference: the Westminster rules, contained in resolutions of the House, are only enforceable by the House; the terms of section 39 and provision made pursuant to it have statutory force and as such may be adjudicated upon and enforced by the courts. Section 39

---

[99] Registration was mandatory only in the case of consultancies and financial interests in lobbying companies; that apart, it was for individual peers to decide whether they wished to register other "matters which they consider may affect the public perception of the way in which they discharge their parliamentary duties."

[1] Seventh Report of the Committee on Standards in Public Life, *Standards of Conduct in the House of Lords*, Cm.4057–I (2000).

[2] The code of conduct took effect on Mar. 31, 2002.

[3] See O. Gay, "The Regulation of Parliamentary Standards after Devolution" [2002] P.L. 422; D. Woodhouse, "Delivering Public Confidence: Codes of conduct, a step in the right direction" [2003] P.L. 511 (contrasting the regulatory regime adopted in Scotland favourably with that which obtains at Westminster).

also provides that any contravention of provisions made under it shall constitute criminal offences punishable on summary conviction by a fine not exceeding level 5 on the standard scale.[4] In addition, section 43 provides that the Scottish Parliament is a "public body" for the purposes of the Prevention of Corruption Acts 1889 and 1916. Thus members and staff of the Parliament may be subject to criminal liability for corruptly making or accepting payments, in money or in kind, for activity (or inactivity) in connection with the Parliament's business.

The provision required by section 39 was made on an interim basis by the Secretary of State under the Scotland Act 1998 (Transitory and Transitional Provisions) (Members' Interests) Order 1999.[5] At the time of writing it remained in force, although the Standards Committee of the Scottish Parliament brought forward a proposal for a committee bill to replace the 1999 Order in July 2002.[6] The Schedule to the Order sets out eight categories of registrable interests.[7] The maintenance of the Register is the responsibility of the Clerk to the Parliament. Within 30 days of taking the oath of allegiance or making a solemn affirmation, a member must lodge with the clerk a written statement giving details of his registrable interests or, as the case may be, declaring that he has none. It is for the Presiding Officer to specify the form of such statements, and the degree of detail required. Independently of the obligation to record registrable interests, members are also required to make an oral statement declaring the existence and nature of an interest before participating in proceedings of the Scottish Parliament on any matter if it is an interest which would prejudice or give the appearance of prejudicing the member's ability to participate in a disinterested way.[8]

The prohibition on advocacy is contained in Article 6 of the Order. This proscribes any action in an MSP's capacity as such, in

---

[4] Currently £5,000.

[5] Scotland Act 1998 (Transitory and Transitional Provisions) (Members' Interests) Order 1999 (SI 1999/1350).

[6] Standards Committee, *Seventh Report on Replacing the Members' Interests Order: Proposals for a committee bill*, S.P.P. 621 (2002).

[7] Namely, remuneration (defined as "any salary, wage, share of profits, fee, expenses, other monetary benefit or benefit in kind"); related undertakings (essentially, unremunerated directorships); election expenses; sponsorship; gifts exceeding a certain value; overseas visits; heritable property other than the member's residence exceeding a certain value; and interests in shares.

[8] It is worth noting that the standard prescribed here for the conduct of MSPs differs from that prescribed for councillors and other public officials in the Ethical Standards in Public Life (Scotland) Act 2000. That Act requires registration and declaration of non-pecuniary interests, if they could be seen as influencing the individual's judgment. The Standards Committee acknowledged in its Seventh Report for 2002 that the disparity could not be justified, but no steps have yet been taken to put an end to it.

any proceedings of the Parliament, which relate to the affairs of, or which seek to confer a benefit upon, a person from whom the member received or expects to receive remuneration.[9] It was this rule which was in issue in *Whaley v Lord Watson of Invergowrie*.[10] The nub of the petitioners' complaint was that, by accepting legal and administrative assistance from a group campaigning against field sports, and by agreeing to introduce and promote a bill outlawing hunting with dogs, Mike Watson MSP had breached the rule against advocacy in the sense that the assistance received constituted a "benefit in kind".[11] Both the Lord Ordinary and, by a majority, the Inner House dismissed the petition, but there were, as noted above, significant differences between the reasoning adopted at first instance and that adopted on the reclaiming motion.[12] The Inner House held that the legal nature of the Members' Interest Order (as distinct from the standing orders, which under section 22 of the Scotland Act might or might not take legislative form) made plain their jurisdiction to pronounce on the issue of breach of Article 6, and held further that in these circumstances there was nothing in section 40(4) to prevent the court awarding interdict. What did defeat the petitioners' claim, in the opinion of the majority, was that the Scotland Act properly construed did not confer on members of the public a "civil right" to secure compliance with the Members' Interests Order. It followed that no member of the public could prevent an apprehended breach of the order by bringing proceedings for interdict against the MSP concerned. In arriving at this conclusion, the majority had particular regard to the presence of alternative sanctions for breaches of the duty under Article 6, namely criminal prosecution or exclusion from the proceedings of the Parliament.

Apart from the rules on the registration and declaration of **4–46** financial and other interests and the prohibition on paid advocacy, MSPs are also constrained to abide by the terms of the Code of Conduct for Members of the Scottish Parliament. This was drafted by the Standards Committee of the Scottish Parliament, presented to the Parliament on February 24, 2000 and adopted by resolution on the same day.[13] The code begins by stating its own set of core principles.[14] It then makes provision in relation to the registration

---

[9] Or which relate to the affairs of, or seek to confer a benefit upon, a client or associate of that person.

[10] 2000 S.C. 340.

[11] The Standards Committee had upheld a complaint that Mr Watson had breached the rules on registration of interests by failing to register the assistance received as "sponsorship", but rejected the complaint that he had also breached the rule against advocacy.

[12] See para.4–41.

[13] Six Annexes are appended to the code of conduct.

[14] Namely, public duty, duty as a representative, selflessness, integrity, honesty, accountability and openness, and leadership.

and declaration of interests and the rule against advocacy,[15] general conduct and conduct in the Chamber, the regulation of cross-party groups and lobbying. Like the standing orders, but unlike the rules on members' interests, it represents a non-statutory form of self-regulation, alleged breaches of which will be investigated and dealt with primarily, if not exclusively, by the Parliament itself rather than by the courts.[16] It has yet to be determined whether breaches of the standing orders or code of conduct are justiciable or not. While distinguishing their legal form from that of the Members' Interests Order in *Whaley*, the Inner House was careful to avoid stating in terms that the court would have no jurisdiction over the Parliament's non-statutory regulatory devices. The standing orders, at least, are adopted under authority of section 22 of the Scotland Act, Schedule 3 of which requires that specified provision be made therein. In that sense at least, the standing orders could be seen as having the requisite legal pedigree. As to the code of conduct, while it is contained in a resolution, the machinery for its enforcement is now prescribed in part by the Scottish Parliamentary Standards Commissioner Act 2002.[17]

The principal duty of the Parliamentary Standards Commissioner is to investigate whether the conduct of a member[18] breaches one or more provisions of the standing orders of the Parliament, the code of conduct, the Members' Interests Order or any enactment adopted to replace the Members' Interests Order. The commissioner may not, however, investigate a complaint which is excluded from his jurisdiction by either the standing orders or

---

[15] Hence the overlap in jurisdiction between the Standards Committee and the courts.

[16] The code of conduct does reiterate and affirm the statutory, and therefore justiciable, provisions concerning the registration and declaration of interests and the ban on advocacy.

[17] The relevance of this is twofold. First, the Parliamentary Standards Commissioner at least, acting as he does under statutory powers, would be subject to judicial review in the exercise of his functions. Secondly, however, both the Commissioner and the Standards Committee would appear to constitute "public authorities" for the purposes of the HRA 1998. That Act does not bind members or officers of the Westminster Parliament, but there is no such exclusion in respect of the Scottish Parliament. Thus *even if* a decision of the Standards Committee could not be challenged on the ordinary grounds for judicial review (its jurisdiction not being founded in statute but in instruments adopted by resolution of the Parliament), it could be challenged on grounds of breach of a person's Convention rights; and the commissioner could be challenged on both fronts, even though his function is investigative rather than dispositive (although this latter might affect the intensity of judicial scrutiny).

[18] Defined by 2002 Act, s.20, to include the Scottish Law Officers, whether or not MSPs; and former MSPs and Law Officers (although the reach of this will be limited by the requirement in s.6(5)(c) that complaints be made within one year of the conduct in question.

the code of conduct.[19] The Parliament (meaning in practice the Standards Committee) may direct the commissioner to undertake an investigation into an excluded complaint in terms of section 12 of the Act, although it is not clear on what basis the committee might do so.[20] Nor may the commissioner investigate a complaint which he deems inadmissible; and the grounds of "admissibility in" are numerous. The complaint must first be shown to be "relevant", not only in the sense that it relates to the conduct of an MSP and is not excluded, but also in the sense that it discloses a *prima facie* case of breach.[21] Secondly, the complaint must be made within one year of the conduct in question, in writing and signed by an individual, who must state his name and address, name the MSP concerned, and set out the facts relevant to his complaint.[22] Thirdly, the commissioner must be satisfied, on an initial investigation, that the complaint warrants further investigation. If all of these conditions are met, the commissioner must proceed to the second stage of the process, notifying the complainant and MSP concerned, and the committee, of that fact accordingly.[23] At the second stage, the commissioner's task is to investigate the complaint in order to determine whether, on the balance of probabilities, the MSP concerned committed the conduct complained of and, if so, whether that conduct constitutes a breach of the relevant provisions.[24] His investigation is conducted in private and he has powers co-extensive with those of the Parliament itself under section 23 of the Scotland Act to require the attendance of witnesses to give evidence and the production of documents.[25] He

---

[19] 2002 Act, s.3(2). As the standing orders and code of conduct are contained in resolutions, this offers scope for the Parliament to limit the jurisdiction of the commissioner otherwise than by way of primary legislation.

[20] Presumably, if the commissioner rejected a complaint as being excluded but considered that it merited investigation, he might draw the matter to the committee's attention in the hope if not expectation of an order being made under s.12 of the 2002 Act. Equally, it would no doubt be open to a disappointed complainant to approach the committee directly.

[21] 2002 Act, s.6(4).

[22] 2002 Act, s.6(5). These requirements may be contrasted with the requirements in the Freedom of Information (Scotland) Act 2002, which are designed to ensure that a request for information under the Act is not rejected simply because the applicant is unable to submit a request in writing or specify with sufficient clarity exactly what he is looking for. The Standards Committee may however direct the commissioner to proceed with a complaint which fails to comply with the requirements in s.6(5) but which is otherwise admissible: 2002 Act, s.7(4), (7).

[23] 2002 Act, s.7(2). The commissioner is obliged to notify an MSP of the fact that a complaint has been made against him, and of the nature of the complaint and (unless he considers it inappropriate) the identity of the complainant, when the complaint is received.

[24] 2002 Act, s.8.

[25] 2002 Act, s.13(1), (2). A person cannot be compelled to give evidence or produce documents that he could not be compelled to give or produce in proceedings in a court in Scotland.

is expressly empowered to examine witnesses on oath, and a witness who refuses to take an oath when so required is guilty of a criminal offence.[26]

On completion of an investigation, the commissioner reports to the Standards Committee on his findings of fact and his decision whether there has been a breach of the relevant provision(s). There, in effect, his role ceases (unless the Standards Committee directs him to undertake further investigations). He may not express a view about the appropriate sanction, nor is the committee bound by his findings or conclusion. The subsequent stages in the process, if it goes any further, are the responsibility of the Standards Committee itself. If the committee accepts a finding of breach by the commissioner or, contrary to the commissioner's conclusion, finds a breach itself (whether or not following a further investigation of its own), it may recommend enforcement action to the Parliament.[27]

SCOTTISH AFFAIRS AT WESTMINSTER

4–47 It remains to consider the machinery provided at Westminster for the consideration of Scottish affairs. For many years prior to devolution, special arrangements were made for the handling of Scottish business in the House of Commons, through time set aside for Scottish questions, the establishment of the Scottish Grand Committee, Scottish standing committees and the Select Committee on Scottish Affairs. Unsurprisingly, devolution entailed some reassessment of these arrangements.[28] The Select Committee on Procedure recommended, and the House by resolution accepted, that the range of questions that might properly be put to ministers in the Scotland Office (or, now, Department of Constitutional Affairs) should be formally reduced to include only those matters for which they retained responsibility,[29] and that the time available for Scottish questions be reduced. The latter was given

---

[26] 2002 Act, s.13(6), (7). As David Cobb points out in his annotations to the 2002 Act, the penalties attaching to this offence—as much as a Level 5 fine (currently £5,000) or three months' imprisonment—are at the top end for a summary prosecution.

[27] Independently of sanctions which may be imposed by the courts where the member's misconduct also constitutes a criminal offence, the committee may recommend, and the Parliament agree to, the exclusion of an MSP from participation in parliamentary proceedings in which he has an interest; exclusion from all parliamentary proceedings; suspensions for a specified period; or forfeiture of certain rights and privileges.

[28] Select Committee on Procedure, *The Procedural Consequences of Devolution*, (1999).

[29] Corresponding provision is made in Scottish Parliament Standing Orders, r.13.3.3.

effect in November 1999, since when Scottish questions take place once every four weeks, lasting for 30 minutes.[30]

The Scottish Grand Committee, which consists of all 72 Scottish M.P.s, met for the last time prior to devolution in March 1999. The Select Committee on Procedure had recommended that its operation be suspended, but the government disagreed and a motion to retain it was approved by the House of Commons without a vote in October 1999. Certainly devolution has deprived it of much of its raison d'être—previously it functioned rather as a substitute for a Scottish Parliament in the proper sense of the term—but, as the government pointed out, "there will still be occasions after devolution where members representing constituencies in Scotland . . . will want to have debates on reserved matters for which time cannot be found on the floor of the House." On this footing, the Scottish Grand Committee continues in existence, meeting from time to time as required.

The role of the Select Committee on Scottish Affairs will also require reappraisal, not merely in light of devolution, but also in view of the winding-up of the Scotland Office and its absorption into the new Department for Constitutional Affairs. At present, a House of Commons standing order defines the purpose of the Select Committee as being to examine the expenditure, administration and policy of the Scotland Office and associated public bodies.[31] Up to 11 M.P.s may be appointed to serve on it (not all of whom need represent Scottish constituencies). While it will remain necessary for the House of Commons to have some vehicle for the scrutiny of ministers concerned with reserved matters, it seems probable that this will be provided not through a distinctively Scottish select committee, but instead through a new Select Committee on Constitutional Affairs.

---

[30] Naturally M.P.s remain free to table questions for written answers.
[31] Standing Order 152.

CHAPTER 5

GOVERNMENTS

5–01 As with Parliaments, so too with governments: within the sphere of devolved competence, the Scottish Executive is the government of Scotland[1]; outwith that sphere,[2] the UK government continues to exercise executive authority north of the border.

"Executive authority" is a concept of some complexity. Other than, perhaps, their width, there is no difficulty with the statutory powers of executive institutions—Ministers of the Crown, central government departments, the Scottish Administration, and the penumbra of executive agencies, local and other public authorities operating to greater or lesser degree at arm's length from central or devolved government. Subtler questions arise, however, in relation to the non-statutory powers of governmental institutions, often (if not wholly accurately) referred to as "the prerogative". Explaining the nature of the prerogative requires something of a historical inquiry into the nature of that entity in which (if not whom) the prerogative is vested, namely the Crown. As we shall see, there are differences as between Scots and English law in the understanding of the Crown, which differences continue to carry consequences to this day. Broader questions arise about the extent to which prerogative powers are, or should be, subject to judicial control. The scheme of this chapter is therefore as follows. We begin with a consideration of the sources of executive power in a general sense. We then move on to an account of the institutional structure of executive government as that relates to Scotland. At one time, such an account would have been relatively straightforward, in so far as it involved a reasonably clear demarcation between the executive powers of central and local government.[3] Now, however (and leaving local government to a later chapter),

---

[1] Although, as we shall see, the powers of the Scottish Ministers go beyond that sphere in various ways, particularly in that s.63 of the SA 1998 makes provision for the transfer of functions exercisable in or as regards Scotland by a Minister of the Crown to the Scottish Ministers. This goes beyond the provision made in s.53 for a general transfer to the Scottish Ministers of ministerial functions exercisable within devolved competence, which transfer occurred on July 1, 1999.

[2] Subject to the above.

[3] Although there has always been a Scottish dimension to the government of the UK, which may be said to cut across this distinction.

executive authority is exercised at a variety of levels and in a variety of institutional settings. This is not simply a consequence of devolution, but also of what might be termed the "marketising" of the state. Particularly in the last 20 years, efforts have been made to improve the efficiency of government[4] by repackaging or reallocating aspects of executive authority to entities better able (in theory) to capture the efficient practices of the private sector. In some respects, as with privatisation and contracting out, the reallocation is clear, and the question which remains is whether and to what extent we should, nevertheless, continue to regard the powers and functions thus reallocated as public functions. In others, as with executive agencies, the change is less obvious, being internal to the orthodox structure of government; but similar issues arise about the adequacy of political and legal controls over their powers.

THE CROWN AND PREROGATIVE

In one sense, the Crown is simply that "piece of jewelled headgear **5–02** under guard at the Tower of London."[5] In another, the term serves as a synonym for the central executive government of the United Kingdom, for it is in the name of the Crown that executive acts of government are carried out.[6] The attribution to the Crown of acts of ministers and officials might be "fictional", as Lord Diplock had it, where they exercise statutory powers conferred on them in their official capacity. But the fiction is perhaps less obvious where prerogative powers are concerned.[7] Prerogative powers are powers

---

[4] Some commentators detect ulterior motives in this process, and it is fair to say that marketisation, in its various guises, has tended to be at the expense of the powers of local authorities and at some cost too to accountability for the exercise of executive power.

[5] *Town Investments Ltd v Dept of the Environment* [1978] A.C. 359, *per* Lord Simon.

[6] *Town Investments*, above, *per* Lord Diplock.

[7] Nor can the equation between the Crown and the government be described as "fictional" where it involves the reach of the privileges of the Crown, such as the privilege whereby the Sovereign is immune from suit in her own courts. The (not obviously salutary) consequence of the identification of the Crown as Sovereign with the Crown as government in *Town Investments*, above, was that, since the lease to a government Dept there in issue was a lease to the Crown, the lessor could not enforce its terms against the lessee. See also, *e.g. Lord Advocate v Dumbarton DC* [1990] 2 A.C. 580, on the principle of statutory construction whereby the burden of a statute does not bind the Crown other than by way of express words or necessary implication. Absent any express or implied intent to the contrary in the Roads (Scotland) Act 1984, the local roads and planning authorities were unable to enforce the normal requirements for notification and consent against the Ministry of Defence when it undertook works on the perimeter fence at Faslane.

"which of necessity inhered in kings as governors of the realm,"[8] founded on custom rather than the common law itself. Before the constitutional upheavals of the seventeenth century—provoked to no small extent by the claims of the Stuart kings to rule by prerogative right—the prerogative was clearly an autonomous source of governmental power. But civil war and the settlements of 1688–89 secured (although not without certain ambiguities) the subjection of the prerogative, both to Parliament and to the common law.[9] The power of Parliament to alter or abolish prerogative powers was conclusively established by the provisions of the Bill of Rights and Claim of Right which did exactly that, and by the Act of Settlement 1700,[10] which regulated the succession to the Crown. To the courts fell the task of determining the existence and extent of prerogative powers when such were claimed, and, as has been held, it is now "350 years and a civil war too late for the Queen's courts to broaden the prerogative. The limits within which the executive government may impose obligations or restraints on citizens of the United Kingdom without any statutory authority are now well settled and incapable of extension."[11] Now, therefore, the prerogative is a remnant (though far from an insignificant remnant) consisting of those legal attributes of the Crown in the sense of the Sovereign, exercisable by Her Majesty either as she sees fit or, more commonly, on the advice of her ministers, or of the Crown in the sense of the central government.

It is sometimes said that it is on the basis of the prerogative that the government enters into contracts, employs its staff, holds and conveys property and so on. Certainly there is often no statutory authority for these functions. But in fact, these are less prerogative powers than the ordinary common law powers of any natural or

---

[8] C. R. Munro, *Studies in Constitutional Law* (2nd ed., Butterworths, London, 1999), Ch.8.

[9] Prior to that the position had not been clear, either in Scotland or England. In England, cases such as *Prohibitions del Roy* (1607) 12 Co. Rep. 63 (where the King was told that he must dispense justice only through his courts) and the *Case of Proclamations* (1611) 12 Co. Rep. 74 (where Coke C.J. held that the King had not the power to alter the general law of the land by way of royal proclamation) must be set against those cases which conceded the autonomy of the prerogative, such as *Darnel's Case* (1627) 3 *State Trials* 1 (where it was held sufficient answer to a writ of habeas corpus to state that the prisoner was detained by order of the King) and the *Case of Ship Money* (1637) 3 *State Trials* 826 (where a tax not authorised by Parliament was upheld as justifiable at a time of national emergency, of which the King alone was the judge). In Scotland, these questions figured less in case law and more in legal writings, but opinion was far from uniform. There is, however, evidence to suggest that Scots law treated the Crown and prerogative, both before and after the Revolution, with less deference than English law: see J. D. B. Mitchell, "The Royal Prerogative in Modern Scots Law" [1957] P.L. 304.

[10] As extended to Scotland pursuant to the Acts and Treaty of Union in 1707.

[11] *British Broadcasting Corporation v Johns* [1965] Ch.32 at 79, *per* Diplock L.J.

legal person.[12] That is not to suggest that they are unimportant. In a manner even less visible than the prerogative, the common law powers of the Crown, exercisable by its agents in government (central and devolved) enable a wealth of governmental activity without any need for parliamentary authority.[13] The constitutional legitimacy of this state of affairs is increasingly questionable.[14]

As to the personal prerogatives of the Sovereign, it appears that the Queen only acts solely on her own initiative in the conferment of certain honours, principally appointment to the Order of Merit, the Order of the Garter and the Order of the Thistle.[15] Beyond that, the role of the Sovereign in the actual government of the country is said to be dignified rather than effective: "in a constitutional monarchy such as ours, the Sovereign has three rights: the right to counsel, the right to encourage and the right to warn."[16] That is true, and by and large that is where it stops: she reigns, but she does not rule. Two points should not, however, be forgotten. First, in strict legal terms, the powers of assenting to legislation, dissolving Parliament, and appointing (or dismissing) the Prime Minister and his ministry are personal prerogatives of the Sovereign.[17] Secondly, the Sovereign is immune from suit in her own courts. Any issue arising about the Sovereign's exercise of these prerogatives, then, would not be one susceptible to resolution by legal processes. Some might object to that state of affairs on principle. But concrete questions about the exercise of the personal prerogatives arise only very exceptionally, because as a matter of constitutional convention the Sovereign may only act on the advice of her ministers, who are in turn answerable to Parliament (in

---

[12] It is generally said that the Crown is a corporation sole, and a legal person on that account.

[13] Not only that, but on current approaches, it is unlikely that the exercise of these powers would be amenable to judicial review either in Scotland or in England.

[14] See B. V. Harris, "The 'Third Source' of Authority for Government Action" (1992) 108 L.Q.R. 626; A. Lester and M. Weait, "The Use of Ministerial Powers without Parliamentary Authority" [2003] P.L. 415. At the time of writing, the House of Commons Select Committee on Public Administration was engaged upon an inquiry into the use and scrutiny of the prerogative, the consequences of which may have an impact in Scotland in so far as the prerogative powers of the Crown are, so far as exercisable within devolved competence, exercisable now by the Scottish Ministers by virtue of s.53 of the SA 1998.

[15] Although Prof. Mitchell suggests that, at least in relation to the Order of the Thistle, the Queen is likely to act on advice since the appointments "may well take on a political significance": J. D. B. Mitchell, *Constitutional Law*, (2nd ed., 1968), p.176.

[16] W. Bagehot, *The English Constitution* (1867). For discussion of the significance of these three rights, see, *e.g.* Mitchell, *op.cit.*; R. Brazier, *Constitutional Practice: The foundations of British government* (3rd ed., Oxford University Press, Oxford, 1999).

[17] Even under the SA 1998, the Scottish Ministers hold office at Her Majesty's pleasure: ss 45(1) and 47(3)(a).

theory) for the advice they tender.[18] The controls, then, are political and parliamentary, which need worry only those who would subject everything to control by the judges.

The far greater portion of surviving prerogative power has in practice been transferred to the Crown in the sense of the central government, and the association of these prerogatives with the uniquely governmental functions of the state is apparent when we note that they are mostly connected with foreign affairs (e.g. the despatch and receipt of ambassadors, recognition of foreign states, entering into international treaties), defence (e.g. declaring a state of war or national emergency, mobilising the armed forces) and the maintenance of the peace and order of the realm. This is not to say that these areas are governed solely by the prerogative. Since the precise extent of a given prerogative power may be uncertain, or since its extent, though certain, is insufficient to meet the ends of government, many "uniquely governmental" matters are in fact governed wholly or partly by statute. Where this is the case, the powers provided by Parliament override the prerogative, although the prerogative power only lapses *pro tanto* and will revive on repeal of the legislation unless expressly abrogated thereby.[19]

5–03   The common law interlocks with these prerogative functions in two main ways. First, as already noted, the courts have, at least since the Revolution of 1688–89, claimed jurisdiction to determine the existence and extent of prerogative power. But the courts did not, until recently, inquire into the manner of exercise of an admitted prerogative. Their jurisdiction to do so was authoritatively established by the decision of the House of Lords in the *GCHQ* case.[20] As Lord Scarman put it:

"If the subject matter in respect of which prerogative power is exercised is justiciable, that is to say if it is matter upon which

---

[18] For discussion of the operation of constitutional conventions, see paras 1–06—1–11.

[19] *Attorney-General v De Keyser's Royal Hotel* [1920] A.C. 508.

[20] *Council of Civil Service Unions v Minister for the Civil Service* [1985] A.C. 374. A power of judicial review had been asserted by some judges in earlier cases, notably by Lord Denning M.R. in *Laker Airways Ltd v Dept of Trade* [1977] Q.B. 643. See also *R. v Criminal Injuries Compensation Board, ex p. Lain* [1967] 2 Q.B. 864, often regarded as the first instance of judicial review of the prerogative. Certainly the Court of Appeal treated the scheme for compensating victims of violent crime as established "under the prerogative" (it is now statutory), but "anyone may set up a trust or other organisation to distribute money, and for the government to do so involves no unique prerogative power": H. W. R. Wade and C. Forsyth, *Administrative Law* (8th ed., Oxford University Press, Oxford, 2000), p. 223. The wider usage of the term "prerogative" may be traced to Dicey, who attributed to the prerogative "every act which the executive government can do without the authority of an Act of Parliament": *Introduction to the Law of the Constitution* (10th ed., Macmillan, London, 1959), p.425.

the courts can adjudicate, the exercise of the power is subject to review in accordance with the principles developed in respect of the review of the exercise of statutory power. The controlling factor in determining whether the exercise of prerogative power is subject to judicial review is not its source but its subject matter."

Professor Craig sees *GCHQ* as updating the heritage of the *Case of Proclamations*[21] and *Attorney-General v De Keyser's Royal Hotel*.[22] The first denied the Sovereign any autonomous legislative power, independent of Parliament; the second affirmed the priority of statute over prerogative when they touched the same ground; and *GCHQ* tells us that since the executive is subject to judicial control when acting pursuant to "the most legitimate discretionary power, that given by statute", it should in principle be subject to like control where its discretion is founded in the prerogative.[23] In practice, of course, the very subject-matter of prerogative powers may render them immune from review as being non-justiciable: whether it is "right" to declare war, or purchase nuclear weapons, or enter into a particular international treaty are questions better left (at the present stage of the common law's development) to the political arena.[24] But non-justiciability has not been allowed to deprive *GCHQ* of its effects. Thus in one case, the court held the Secretary of State's refusal to renew a passport to be reviewable, even though taken under the prerogative, as an "administrative decision affecting the rights of individuals and their freedom to travel" and of a wholly different order of magnitude to decisions of high policy on matters of defence or foreign affairs.[25] In another, the court took the same view of the prerogative of mercy, an important feature of the criminal justice system the exercise of which was of critical importance to the individual.[26]

But if we follow Craig and locate *GCHQ* within a continuum of gradual progress towards the proper subjection of governmental

---

[21] (1611) 12 Co. Rep. 74.
[22] [1920] A.C. 508.
[23] P. Craig, "Prerogative, Precedent and Power" in *The Golden Metwand and the Crooked Cord: Essays on Public law in honour of Sir William Wade QC* (Forsyth and Hare eds, Oxford University Press, Oxford, 1998), Ch.4.
[24] Although note that challenges were brought to the legality of government action in the sphere of treaty-making in *R. v H.M. Treasury, ex p. Smedley* [1985] Q.B. 657 and *R. v S of S for Foreign and Commonwealth Affairs, ex p. Rees-Mogg* [1994] Q.B. 552, and although both were unsuccessful neither was dismissed as raising questions inherently unsuitable for judicial resolution. In matters of national defence, by contrast, see *Chandler v DPP* [1964] A.C. 763; *Lord Advocate's Reference (No. 1 of 2000)*, 2001 S.C.C.R. 296.
[25] *R. v S of S for Foreign and Commonwealth Affairs, ex p. Everett* [1989] 1 All E.R. 655.
[26] *R. v S of S for the Home Dept, ex p. Bentley* [1993] 4 All E.R. 442.

authority to the rule of law, we must also concede that that progress has sometimes faltered. Indeed for Scotland, the assimilation of English doctrine on the Crown and prerogative after the Union appears positively harmful. In England, the notion that "the King can do no wrong", coupled with theories as to the indivisibility of the Crown, led lawyers not merely to refer to central government as "the Crown" but also to assimilate to central government the privileges and immunities enjoyed by the Crown as Sovereign. It was generally taken, for example, that as an entity having legal personality the Crown could like any other natural or legal person do anything that was not specifically prohibited by law—a position formally reconcilable with the result in *Entick v Carrington*, but scarcely reconcilable with its spirit.[27] At one time, the Crown's immunity from suit was of little practical importance, because English law made ministers and other officials personally liable for wrongs committed in the exercise of their official functions and for which they could produce no legal authority (meaning something more than the orders of the Crown).[28] But latterly even this distinction—between the Crown and its servants, the one immune from suit, the other not—came to be overlooked, so that in *Merricks v Heathcoat-Amory*,[29] for example, the court was able to hold that a minister enjoyed immunity in respect of all acts done in the name of the Crown.[30]

5–04   Scots law, by contrast, and perhaps because there was less of the "awe of majesty" Professor Mitchell detected in the writings of Blackstone, did not accept that the King could do no wrong and found no difficulty in the notion of the Crown whether as Sovereign or government answering to the courts.[31] Section 1 of the Crown Suits (Scotland) Act 1857 makes this abundantly clear

---

[27] (1765) 19 *State Trials* 1029. *Entick* is often cited as authority for the common law's embrace of the principle of legality, but effect of conceding to the Crown as government all the powers and attributes incidental to legal personality is that the government need not qualify positive legal authority for its actions unless its actions violate the common law rights of the citizen. For criticism of this position, see the articles cited at n.14.

[28] So, *e.g.* a person run over by an army lorry could sue the driver of the lorry, but not the Crown as employer of the driver. This position was amended by the Crown Proceedings Act 1947, as to which, see further below.

[29] [1955] Ch. 567, criticised by the Court of Appeal in *R. v S of S for the Home Dept, ex p. Herbage* [1987] Q.B. 872, expressly approved by the House of Lords in the first *Factortame* case, *R. v S of S for Transport, ex p. Factortame Ltd (No. 1)* [1990] 2 A.C. 85 and finally laid to rest in *M v Home Office* [1994] 1 A.C. 377.

[30] Which, to draw on the analogy of vicarious liability for the acts of an employee, amounts to saying that the minister is immune in respect of everything done "in the course of his employment".

[31] J. D. B. Mitchell, "The Royal Prerogative in Modern Scots Law" [1957] P.L. 304; for a more recent survey, see W. J. Wolffe, "Crown and Prerogative in Scots Law" in *Edinburgh Essays in Public Law* (Finnie, Himsworth and Walker eds, Edinburgh University Press, Edinburgh, 1991), pp.351–369.

in providing that "every action, suit or proceeding to be instituted in Scotland *on behalf of or against Her Majesty, or in the interest of the Crown (including the Scottish Administration)*, or on behalf of or against any public department" may be raised by or against the appropriate Law Officer.[32] Thus, historically there was no issue in Scotland about the liability of the Crown in contract or delict, nor its susceptibility to interdict. Only in more recent times did the influence of English law spread so that, for example, it came to be accepted that no action in reparation would lie against the Crown.[33] This was reversed by the Crown Proceedings Act 1947, which made the Crown liable in tort and delict in respect of acts committed by its servants or agents[34]; but the Crown Proceedings Act reserved the immunity from injunction and orders for specific performance enjoyed by the Crown in England and extended its application to Scotland, thereby depriving the Scots of remedies they had had against the Crown for generations.[35] The operative provision is section 21, and it merits close attention.

Section 21(1)(a) provides that in any civil proceedings against the Crown, the court cannot make an order for specific implement or grant interdict, but may "in lieu thereof make an order declaratory of the rights of the parties." Section 21(2) then provides that the court cannot in civil proceedings grant any interdict or make any order against an officer of the Crown if the effect of doing so would be to give relief against the Crown which could not have been obtained in proceedings against the Crown directly. North and south of the border, this was taken to mean (but for different reasons) that since neither interdict nor specific

---

[32] Emphasis added. Thus the distinction is made between the Crown *qua* Sovereign and the Crown *qua* government, but not so as to affect the liability of either to be proceeded against in the courts. For the rules that do affect that liability we must look elsewhere, see *infra*. Note that s.1 of the 1857 Act was amended by the SA 1998, Sch.8, para.2, to include reference to the Scottish Administration and to provide that, where an action is raised under s.1 on behalf of or against a member of the Scottish Administration, the appropriate Law Officer shall be the Lord Advocate, but in all other circumstances the Advocate General for Scotland.

[33] See *MacGregor v Lord Advocate*, 1921 S.C. 847. The spread was not uniform, and on occasion Scots law influenced the approach of the English courts, as where the House of Lords in *Glasgow Corp. v Central Land Board*, 1956 S.C. (H.L.) 1 declined to follow the earlier decision of the House in *Duncan v Cammell Laird & Co* [1942] A.C. 624 on the doctrine of Crown privilege (or public interest immunity), prompting a reappraisal of the doctrine in English law in *Conway v Rimmer* [1968] A.C. 910.

[34] In relation to actions in contract, the 1947 Act also abolished the English petition of right procedure, whereby a very determined litigant might obtain contractual damages from the Crown, and placed English law on the same footing as Scots law in this respect.

[35] See Mitchell, *op.cit.*, pp.304–314; Sir Stephen Sedley, "The Crown in its own Courts", in *The Golden Metwand and the Crooked Cord: Essays on Public Law in Honour of Sir William Wade Q.C.* (Forsyth and Hare eds, Oxford University Press, Oxford, 1998), pp.202–203.

implement could be awarded against the Crown (*qua* Sovereign), neither remedy could be awarded against an officer of the Crown, which term is defined to include ministers of the Crown and members of the Scottish Executive. In successive editions of his book, Professor Wade argued that as a matter of English law this was radically to misread section 21: "Correctly understood, [section 21(2)] applies only to protect the Crown's own immunity, and does not alter the personal liability of a minister or official who commits a wrong or who misuses a power conferred upon him in his own name."[36] That is persuasive as a matter of English law, which does distinguish between the Crown and its agents and servants. But Scots law does not, so it is difficult even at first blush to see how section 21 could have anything other than the effect it was given.

5–05   By force of Community law, the House of Lords were obliged in *Factortame* to extend injunctive relief against the Crown where necessary to protect Community law rights.[37] Subsequently, in *M v Home Office*,[38] the House of Lords held the Home Secretary in contempt of court for disregarding an injunction requiring the Home Secretary to arrange for the immediate return to the jurisdiction of M, a Zairean asylum-seeker. The injunction was granted as an emergency measure during the night, when it became apparent that, in breach of an undertaking to the court, the Home Secretary had countermanded arrangements to keep M in Britain. The following morning the judge discharged the injunction on the grounds that the authority of *Factortame* entitled him to grant injunctive relief against the Crown only where necessary to protect Community law rights, which were not here in issue. Nevertheless, during the currency of the injunction—a presumptively valid order of the court—the Home Secretary had ignored it. In concurring with the leading speech of Lord Woolf, Lord Templeman came closest to the nub of the case when he remarked that the argument for the Crown—effectively, that ministers comply with court orders as a matter of grace and not of legal obligation—would, if accepted, "reverse the result of the civil war." This is percipient, and a point to which we shall return.

---

[36] This passage is taken from H. W. R. Wade and C. Forsyth, *Administrative Law*, *op.cit.*, p.817. Sir Stephen Sedley makes the point that notes on the clauses of the Crown Proceedings Act, made by its draftsman and now available for inspection in the Public Record Office, reveal that Wade's analysis was correct all along: "The Crown in its own Courts" in *The Golden Metwand and the Crooked Cord*, *op.cit.*, Ch.12.

[37] *R. v S of S for Transport, ex p. Factortame Ltd (No.2)* [1991] 1 A.C. 603. Necessarily this involved recognition in Scotland that relief by way of interdict, interim or perpetual, would require to be granted against the Crown, despite s.21 of the 1947 Act, in like circumstances: see *Millar & Bryce Ltd v Keeper of the Registers of Scotland*, 1997 S.L.T. 1000.

[38] [1994] 1 A.C. 377.

Lord Woolf's approach was less direct. Much of the reasoning in support of his conclusion that the courts could grant injunctive relief against a minister, even in the absence of a Community law element, turned on the peculiarities of English civil procedure.[39] That apart, his Lordship reiterated the "theoretical" position that the Crown can do no wrong, with its consequence, that the Crown is not to be impleaded by name, but held that, nonetheless, a named minister might be impleaded in his official capacity. Shortly afterwards, the question was raised in Scotland whether, following *M v Home Office*, interdict was now to be regarded as available to restrain unlawful acts by the Secretary of State for Scotland or those acting on his behalf.[40] The Second Division frankly acknowledged that the enactment of the Crown Proceedings Act had changed the law in Scotland.[41] The Lord Justice-Clerk also held that, so far as the decision in *M v Home Office* had turned substantially on aspects of English law and procedure, it was not authoritative as to the meaning of section 21 of the 1947 Act in Scots law. Addressing that question, the Second Division made no secret of its difficulty in discerning how its provisions were supposed to fit into Scots law. In England, as Lord Woolf explained in *M*, section 21(2) is necessary to prevent litigants circumventing the bar on injunction and specific performance in proceedings against the Crown (who can do no wrong) by suing the Crown's officers (who can; and who now, after *M*, may be the subject of injunctive relief in their official capacity). But in Scots law, section 21(2) is redundant. So far as Scots law prior to 1947 was concerned, the King could do wrong, which is why the Crown Suits (Scotland) Act 1857 makes provision for suing him. There was no bar on interdict against either the Crown or its servants or agents. Here, the concept of the indivisibility of the Crown worked to ensure that the Crown in all its manifestations was subject to the jurisdiction of the courts, whereas in England it seemed to militate in the opposite direction.[42] None of which alters the plain effect of section 21(1)—interdict and specific implement are stated to be

---

[39] In particular, his Lordship's finding that judicial review in England does not constitute "civil proceedings" for the purposes of the 1947 Act, so that the jurisdiction to grant injunctive relief in the context of judicial review conferred by the Supreme Court Act 1981, is unimpaired by the 1947 Act.

[40] *McDonald v S of S for Scotland*, 1994 S.L.T. 692.

[41] Under reference to *Bell v S of S for Scotland*, 1933 S.L.T. 519 and *Russell v Magistrates of Hamilton* (1897) 25 R. 350, two instances in which interdict or interim interdict issued against the Crown. The Lord Justice-Clerk also cited an observation made in Fraser's *Constitutional Law* (2nd ed.), p.165, to the effect that interdict procedure is especially valuable to litigants, not least in its interim form. This may sit uneasily with the remarks made in *Davidson v Scottish Ministers*, 2002 S.L.T. 420, on the adequacy of declaratory relief under the HRA 1998.

[42] As to which, see *Smith v Lord Advocate*, 1980 S.C. 227 at 231, *per* Lord Avonside.

unavailable in proceedings against the Crown, from which, given the understanding in Scots law of the meaning of "the Crown", it follows that in proceedings against the Secretary of State or, now, the Scottish Ministers, or the Crown in any of its other guises, declarator is the only competent remedy. So the Second Division concluded in *McDonald v Secretary of State for Scotland*[43]; and *McDonald* was affirmed in *Davidson v Scottish Ministers*.[44] There it was argued that a coercive order might competently issue against the Scottish Ministers where, in light of the Human Rights Act, the applicant's Convention rights are in issue. The Extra Division was unimpressed, holding that the right to an effective remedy for breaches of Convention rights does not entitle a litigant to a remedy of his choice and that appeals to the rule of law as requiring coercive orders to be granted against the Crown were to no purpose unless means were shown of construing the plain language of section 21 in that way.

5–06 The upshot is that, despite its historic treatment of the Crown in litigation, Scots law is now in a worse position than English law, first because section 21 of the 1947 Act abrogated the right to claim coercive remedies in proceedings against the Crown, and secondly because the reasoning which has enabled the courts in England to outflank the immunity so far as it applies to ministers and other servants of the Crown does not translate into Scots law, which does not distinguish between the Crown and its servants in the same way. It is probably true, as Lord Weir concluded in *Davidson*, that the only cure for this discrepancy lies in the hands of Parliament. But as Sir Stephen Sedley has argued, the decision in *McDonald* (and hence also in *Davidson*) touches on a deeper point which the House of Lords in *M v Home Office* failed to confront. Describing the distinction between the Crown and its servants as unreal and unsound, Sir Stephen said this:

> "Whether the powers being exercised are allocated by statute to named ministers or to secretaries of state at large or are prerogative powers being exercised in the Crown's name by its ministers, and whether they are being exercised ministerially or departmentally, it is by the state acting in the name and in right of the Crown that they are being exercised; and when the courts call them to account for transgressions committed in office, it is the Crown that in a strict and proper constitutional sense answers for them."

What this implies for English law is that its reliance on the personal liability of officials is anachronistic, and the common law

---

[43] 1994 S.L.T. 692.
[44] 2002 S.L.T. 420.

requires now to move beyond *M v Home Office*, recognise governmental power for what it is, regardless of the particular form it
happens to come in, and control it accordingly.[45] What it implies
for Scots law is that it had it right all along, but has been disfigured
by the extension to Scotland of an immunity from coercive
remedies which only makes any constitutional sense—at least in a
country which is supposed to have subjected government by
prerogative to law—if a distinction is drawn, as Wade insisted,
between the Crown as Sovereign and the Crown as government.
Scots law did not need to draw that distinction, which is why
section 21 opened up a major lacuna in its system of remedies.

So much, then, for the legal control of the prerogative: it is **5–07**
limited in terms of the remedies available in respect of its exercise,
and limited more generally by considerations of justiciability, which
are apt to render many instances of alleged illegality in the exercise
of prerogative power unsuitable for judicial resolution.[46] That
being so, it is the more important that political and parliamentary
channels of accountability for the exercise of prerogative power are
adequate and effective. The extent to which that is the case is
questionable. In the course of the ongoing inquiry into ministerial
powers and the prerogative before the House of Commons Select
Committee on Public Administration, Sir Sydney Chapman M.P.
quoted the Prime Minister to the effect that, the exercise of
prerogative powers having grown up over many years, it would not
be possible to draw up an exhaustive list, and (perhaps more
worryingly) "records are not kept of the individual occasions on
which powers under the royal prerogative are exercised, nor would
it be practicable to do so." Mr Tony Benn would refute at least the
first of these statements: in 1999, before he stood down as an M.P.,
he introduced a private member's bill the aim of which was to
re-establish existing prerogative powers (as listed in his bill) on a
statutory footing.[47] Mr Benn argues that effective parliamentary

---

[45] If this requires English law to abandon the notion that the Crown can do no
wrong, then, says Sir Stephen, so be it: "in a constitutional monarchy, there seems
no reason why the sovereign should be—or should want to be—any freer than the
rest of us to break the speed limit." On that note, see also I. S. Dickinson,
"Crown Immunity Post-1998", 2003 S.L.T. (News) 107. The author suggests, in
light of the right of a fair trial under ECHR, Art.6, and of the collapse of the trial
of the late Diana Princess of Wales' butler, Paul Burrell, after the Queen
volunteered information to the prosecution, that the immunity of the Sovereign
may have to yield at least to the extent of rendering her compellable as a witness
in civil and criminal proceedings.

[46] It should not be assumed that considerations of justiciability do not influence the
intensity of judicial review of *statutory* powers. Where the subject-matter of such
powers touches on issues of high governmental policy, or questions of social,
economic or regulatory policy that the courts are ill-equipped to determine, only
manifest illegality is taken to justify judicial intervention.

[47] Crown Prerogatives (Parliamentary Control) Bill.

control of the prerogative at present is prevented by its invisibility. Up to a point, this seems correct. But certain exercises of the prerogative—the dissolution of Parliament and appointment of the Prime Minister not least amongst them—are highly visible, and it is rather difficult to see how Parliament could assert any meaningful control over them.[48] In other respects, as where decisions are taken about the deployment of armed forces and commencement of hostilities, the complaint may be less that these are prerogative decisions than that they require no *a priori* parliamentary authority.[49] Even if such powers were to be placed on a statutory footing, however, it is almost inconceivable that their exercise would be made subject to prior parliamentary approval. In some circumstances the government needs—and in no circumstances is it likely to surrender—the power to act of its own initiative. Any attempt to capture the prerogative in legislative form would have to capture the "flex" necessary to enable the government to respond, with appropriate speed, to contingencies foreseen and unforeseen. Nor should it be thought that placing the prerogative on a statutory footing would render it more susceptible to judicial control. The justiciability of the subject-matter of a power is not affected as such by its legal form. In sum, then, while there is force in the view that Parliament is insufficiently rigorous in its scrutiny of prerogative powers, it is not obvious that codification of the prerogative would improve the position.

UNITED KINGDOM GOVERNMENT

Prime Minister, Cabinet and Ministers of State

5–08   The appointment of the government is a prerogative act, and we have already noted the constitutional conventions surrounding this. The Queen is obliged by convention to appoint as Prime Minister the person who appears best able to command the confidence of

---

[48] Short, perhaps, of abolishing them altogether and placing the whole business of dissolving Parliament, calling elections and choosing a government on a statutory basis. Certainly the scope for discretion in these matters can be curtailed, as the SA 1998 shows. But it cannot, it is suggested, be excluded altogether; that being so, the question is whether one prefers the final say to rest with political institutions or the courts. The view taken here is that it is infinitely preferable to leave it where it is.

[49] Nor do they require parliamentary authority *ex post facto*. One doubts whether, supply guaranteed, the P.M. would have withdrawn British troops from Iraq had the division on the Iraq debate gone against him: see *Hansard*, HC Vol.401, cols 761–912 (Mar. 18, 2003).

the House of Commons—it is usually clear who this is, even in the event of a hung Parliament, but the possibility of the Queen requiring to exercise some personal discretion cannot be absolutely excluded—and the Prime Minister then advises the Queen whom to appoint to ministerial office in his government, which advice she must follow. For as long as he retains the confidence both of the Commons and of his party (or, at least, his Cabinet), the powers of the Prime Minister are considerable indeed, not only by virtue of being in charge but also because, for practical purposes, the principal prerogatives of the Crown vest in him. Perhaps curiously, the office of Prime Minister receives very little statutory recognition, and indeed received none at all prior to the enactment of the Chequers Act 1918. But he is very much a creature of constitutional convention, as also is the Cabinet. There are no legal rules in any Act of Parliament governing the composition, procedures and functions of the Cabinet.[50] As an institution, it emerged and developed in the late eighteenth century, and in the nineteenth century at least functioned very much as a collegiate body, likened by one former Prime Minister to a company board of directors. Yet by 1963, according to one Cabinet minister of the day, the Cabinet, like the Sovereign, had become a dignified rather than effective element of the constitution.[51] At first blush, that seems unsurprising. Government has grown immensely in volume, intensity and complexity, yet the Cabinet continues to meet weekly and is no larger now than it was a century ago. It is true that much of its work is now delegated to Cabinet committees, but this in itself may function to disperse power away from the Cabinet proper.[52] And for Crossman, as the power of Cabinet diminished, so the power of the Prime Minister increased. Not only that, but the institutional mechanisms and constitutional conventions which once served a genuinely collegiate body—the convention of

---

[50] Apart from the fact that the Ministerial and Other Salaries Act 1975 restricts the number of salaried Cabinet posts, the P.M. and (soon to be late) Lord Chancellor apart, to 20.

[51] R. Crossman, *British Government*. He is not the only Cabinet minister to hold this view. The former Chancellor of the Exchequer, Lord Lawson, observed in his memoirs that he always looked forward to Cabinet meetings, because they were the only break he got in what was otherwise a heavy job: N. Lawson, *The View From Number Eleven: Memoirs of a Tory Radical* (Bantam Press, London, 1992).

[52] The Ministerial Code states that matters which are solely the responsibility of an individual minister, or which do not significantly engage the collective responsibility of ministers, need not be taken either to Cabinet or even to committee. The job of committees is described in terms of settling issues brought before them at that level, or, if a decision of the full Cabinet is absolutely necessary, clarifying the issues and identifying the points of disagreement.

confidentiality of Cabinet discussions[53] and the convention of collective responsibility for government policy—had come to serve the Prime Minister instead.

The "presidential" style of leadership adopted by recent Prime Ministers has tended to lend support to the Crossman thesis, but it can be overstated. The extent of prime ministerial power seems very much a function of circumstances. If the premierships of Mr Blair and Mrs Thatcher might fairly be described as "presidential", the manner of Mrs Thatcher's fall from office, and the intervening premiership of Mr Major, indicate that there is more to central government than prime ministerial power alone. Moreover, as has been said, a focus on the Prime Minister obscures the point that "departments enjoy a greater degree of autonomy within the executive branch than is commonly acknowledged . . . by reason of the fact that their functions are vested directly in them."[54] This autonomy is reinforced by the convention of individual ministerial responsibility to Parliament, whereby the minister must answer for the actions of his department and associated public authorities.[55] The implication of this—and it may be to state the obvious—is that central government is a far more complex organism than it is sometimes depicted. One does not need to be an avid student of political economy to perceive that executive power is distributed far more widely than the inner circle of Prime Minister and Cabinet; in practice, much of it reposes with ministers, officials and the web of agencies and public bodies beyond that.

5–09   Ministers are appointed by the Queen on the advice of the Prime Minister and hold office at Her Majesty's pleasure. By convention, ministers must be members either of the House of Commons or of the House of Lords. Section 2 of the House of Commons Disqualification Act 1975 provides that no more than 95 ministers may sit and vote in the House of Commons, and Schedule 1 to the Ministerial and Other Salaries Act 1975 places limits on the total number of ministerial salaries that may be paid at any one time. These provisions are practical restrictions on the Prime Minister's powers of patronage, but there is no upper limit as such to the total number of ministers that may be appointed provided the excess are peers and/or unpaid. Peers as ministers are a necessary consequence of the statutory provisions and it is not at

---

[53] Which Crossman himself disregarded in authorising the publication, after his death, of his memoirs (on which see *Attorney-General v Jonathan Cape Ltd* [1976] 1 Q.B. 752), thus establishing a tradition of ex-ministerial memoir writing, some of which is interesting enough but most of which decidedly is not.

[54] T. Daintith and A. Page, *The Executive in the Constitution* (Oxford University Press, Oxford, 1999), pp.29, 30.

[55] It may also be reflected in the conclusions reached by the Cabinet Secretary, having conducted a review at the P.M.'s request in 1998, that cross-departmental issues were often not well-handled.

all uncommon for a political ally of the Prime Minister to be elevated to high ministerial office following the conferment of a life peerage.[56]

Some ministerial offices have a much longer historical pedigree than that of the Prime Minister. The office of the Lord Chancellor, although shortly to be consigned to history, can be traced back to the thirteenth century; the office of Secretary of State emerged in England during the Tudor period, and from the eighteenth century two or more Secretaries of State were customarily appointed, dividing responsibility for home affairs and the colonies on the one hand and foreign affairs on the other. A Secretary of State for War was first appointed in 1794, and since then further Secretaryships of State have been created, merged and abolished as needs arise and lapse. The oldest government departments, such as the Treasury and the Home Office, are creatures of the prerogative; more modern manifestations of governmental activity owe their origins to statute. Where new departments are created, the modern practice is to create by way of the prerogative a new Secretary of State, to whom functions are transferred by order made under the Ministers of the Crown Act 1975.[57] Once functions are vested in a Secretary of State, however, there is no need for further transfer orders when the distribution of functions between Secretaries is altered, for in law the office of Secretary of State is "in commission", one and indivisible, with the consequence that any one Secretary of State may act for or carry out the functions of any other.[58] Thus in *Agee v Secretary of State for Scotland*,[59] it was held that the validity of a deportation order made by the Home

---

[56] It is safe to say that by convention the P.M. requires to be a member of the House of Commons. The last peer to serve as P.M. was Lord Salisbury, who left office in 1902 (his nephew, Arthur Balfour, led the House of Commons and took the title of First Lord of the Treasury, which is normally held by the P.M. himself). It appears that, following the resignation of Neville Chamberlain in May 1940, the King's preference for his replacement was Lord Halifax, but it became clear that Labour M.P.s would refuse to serve under Halifax in a wartime coalition Cabinet. Since the House of Commons controls supply, the Chancellor of the Exchequer and the Treasury ministers also require to be M.P.s, but the position with regard to the other high offices of state may be more equivocal. Lord Carrington served as Foreign Secretary from 1979–82; and Lord Young as Secretary of State for Trade and Industry from 1987–89, so it probably cannot be said that there is any convention preventing the appointment of peers as senior non-Treasury ministers if political realities permit.

[57] It is also common practice, when creating a new department, to incorporate it, usually as a corporation sole, so that it may hold property, enter into contracts, sue and be sued in its own name rather than in the name of the Crown: see Daintith and Page, *The Executive in the Constitution, op.cit.*, pp.32, 33.

[58] This is reflected in statutory drafting practice, which refers simply to "the Secretary of State", meaning "any one of Her Majesty's Principal Secretaries of State."

[59] 1977 S.L.T. (Notes) 54.

Secretary in London and served on the deportee in Edinburgh
could not be impugned on the basis that it was not made by the
Secretary of State for Scotland. In practice, however, each Secretary of State will normally confine himself to the performance of
functions related to the workings of his department.

Ministers are defined by section 8(1) of the Ministers of the
Crown Act 1975 as the holders of "any office in Her Majesty's
Government in the United Kingdom", a definition plainly apt to
include the Secretaries of State, who head up government departments and sit in the Cabinet. Below Cabinet ministers in rank are
Ministers of State, who share in the administration of departments
and often have specific portfolios of their own. Their powers are
largely statutory,[60] but as agents of the Crown they "can do
anything an ordinary person can do provided that there is no
statute to the contrary and Parliament has voted the money."[61] The
Ministerial Code of Conduct puts matters in the following way:

> "38. The Minister in charge of a department is alone answer-
> able to Parliament for the exercise of the powers in which the
> administration of that department depends. The Minister's
> authority may, however, be delegated to a Minister of State, a
> Parliamentary Secretary or to an official; and it is desirable
> that Ministers should devolve on their junior Ministers
> responsibility for a defined range of departmental work,
> particularly in connection with Parliament. A Minister's pro-
> posal for the assignment of duties to junior Ministers together
> with any proposed "courtesy titles" descriptive of their duties,
> should be agreed in writing with the Prime Minister, copied to
> the Secretary of the Cabinet.
>
> 39. Ministers of State and Parliamentary Secretaries will be
> authorised to supervise the day to day administration of a
> defined range of subjects. This arrangement does not relieve
> the Permanent Secretary of general responsibilities for the
> organisation and discipline of the department or of the duty to
> advise on matters of policy. The authority of Ministers outside
> the Cabinet is delegated from the Minister in charge of the
> department; the Permanent Secretary is not subject to the
> directions of junior Ministers. Equally, junior Ministers are
> not subject to the directions of the Permanent Secretary. Any
> conflict of view between the two can be resolved only by
> reference to the Minister in charge of the department or, if
> the latter is absent and a decision cannot be postponed, by

---

[60] Again, drafting practice is to refer to "the Minister of the Crown" generically
rather than specifically.
[61] *Agency Chief Executives' Handbook* (Cabinet Office, 1996), para.16; and see
Daintith and Page, *The Executive in the Constitution, op.cit.*, pp.34, 35.

reference to the Prime Minister or to a Minister whom he has nominated for that purpose."

Parliamentary secretaries assist with the parliamentary work of a **5–10** department and may have some limited administrative responsibilities. They are appointed by their ministerial chiefs with the written approval of the Prime Minister rather than by the Queen, and, as this implies, they are neither ministers nor members of the government. Thus the Ministerial Code of Conduct:

> "44. They are private members and should therefore be afforded as great a liberty of action as possible; but their close and confidential association with Ministers imposes certain obligations on them. Official information given to them should generally be limited to what is necessary to the discharge of their parliamentary and political duties. This need not preclude them from being brought into departmental discussions or conferences where appropriate, but they should not have access to secret establishments, or to information graded secret or above, except on the personal authority of the Prime Minister. While, as private members, they need not adhere to the rules on private interests which apply to Ministers, they should, as a general rule, seek to avoid a real or potential conflict of interest between their role as a Parliamentary Private Secretary and their private interests."

Scottish dimension to the UK government

With the handover of powers from the UK government to the **5–11** Scottish Executive on July 1, 1999, the Scottish Office[62] was renamed the Scotland Office and the number of ministers working within it, including the Secretary of State for Scotland, reduced to two.[63] Following the ministerial reshuffle in June 2003, the Scotland Office was wound up and merged into the new Department of Constitutional Affairs, although a Cabinet minister[64] assumed the title of Secretary of State for Scotland and will for the time being speak on non-devolved Scottish affairs in Parliament as well as on matters falling within his principal portfolio. It is important to note that, as well as ensuring the continuing representation of Scottish interests within the UK government, the

---

[62] As established in 1885; the original Secretary for Scotland assumed the full status of Secretary of State in 1926 (although the office did not attract a salary commensurate with those of other Secretaries of State until 1937).

[63] Each had the assistance of a Parliamentary Secretary. The Advocate General for Scotland, and the Scotland Office's spokesman in the House of Lords were also attached to the department.

[64] Alistair Darling M.P., Secretary of State for Transport.

Secretary of State for Scotland has a number of powers under the
Scotland Act 1998[65] in relation to such reserved matters as the
conduct and funding of Scottish parliamentary elections,[66] the
payment of grants into the Scottish consolidated fund and other
financial transactions arising out of devolution,[67] and, perhaps most
significantly, in relation to Scottish legislation and acts of the
Scottish Executive. As to the first, section 35 confers on the
Secretary of State the power to make an order preventing the
Presiding Officer from sending a bill passed by the Scottish
Parliament for Royal Assent if the bill contains provisions which he
has reasonable grounds to believe would be incompatible with any
international obligations of the United Kingdom or with the
interests of defence or national security, or which modify the law as
it applies to reserved matters in a way which he has reasonable
grounds to believe would have an adverse effect on the operation
of the law in relation to reserved matters.[68] Such an order may be
made at any time within the four-week period commencing with
the passing of the bill, and must be laid before both Houses of the
Westminster Parliament. As to the second, the Secretary of State
may by order made under section 58 direct the Scottish Executive
not to take action where he has reasonable grounds to believe that
such action would be incompatible with any international obligations of the United Kingdom, or to act where he has reasonable
grounds to believe such action to be necessary to give effect to any
such obligations.[69] Section 58 also entitles the Secretary of State to
revoke subordinate legislation made by the Scottish Executive
where one or more of the conditions for the exercise of the power
under section 35 are met.

Since the Scotland Act devolved most of the issues falling within
the responsibility of the Lord Advocate and Solicitor General for
Scotland, it was considered appropriate that they should cease to
be Ministers of the Crown in the UK government and become
members of the Scottish Executive. But the UK government
continues to require advice from time to time on matters of Scots
law and devolution issues arising under the Scotland Act, as it may
also require to be represented in litigation arising out of the

---

[65] This is not of course to say that these powers could not be exercised by another
Secretary of State.

[66] SA 1998, s.12.

[67] SA 1998, Pt III.

[68] Note, therefore, that the exercise of the power in no sense turns on the *vires* of
the bill in question. As Lord Brodie observed in *Whaley v Lord Advocate*, June 20,
2003 (not yet reported), the provision appears to presuppose that the Scottish
Parliament was acting *intra vires*, but the effects of its enactment are such as to
necessitate intervention at the UK level.

[69] This may include a requirement that the Scottish Executive introduce a bill in the
Scottish Parliament.

devolution settlement.[70] With that in mind, the Scotland Act established the new ministerial office of Advocate General for Scotland.[71] Apart from her role in relation to litigation and legal advice, the Advocate General has the power under section 33, in common with the Lord Advocate and Attorney-General, to refer to the Judicial Committee of the Privy Council the question whether the provisions of a bill passed by the Scottish Parliament are within its competence. She is also entitled, by virtue of section 98 and Schedule 6, to institute proceedings for the determination of a devolution issue.

Reinventing government

An account of departmental government is hardly a complete depiction of the organisation of the modern executive. Much, even most, of the work of government is in fact conducted at some distance from the ministerial core, as the result of what has been termed a "quiet revolution" in public administration.[72] It is a revolution often associated with the Thatcher governments of the 1980s, and it is certainly true that much of its initial impetus stemmed from the Thatcherite drive to roll back the frontiers of a state perceived as being bloated and inefficient. But "new public management" in its various guises has become an international phenomenon, and in no sense is it (at least any longer) the preserve of the political right wing.

    5–12

The commitment of the Conservative governments to rolling back the state manifested itself most prominently in the privatisation of state-owned industries. Within the government machine itself, freezes were imposed on civil service pay and recruitment and businessmen were brought in to advise on improving efficiency and effectiveness in the public sector. But, despite the government's best efforts at reinventing government and the transfer of over half of the state trading sector to private ownership, the level of public expenditure at the end of the 1980s was not noticeably different from its level in 1979: a near-doubling in real terms of welfare expenditure during the period kept the state's toll on annual gross domestic product at between 35 per cent and 40 per cent, where it remains yet. As the eighties gave way to the nineties, and the Thatcher administration was replaced by that of John Major, the reinvention of government began to focus less on the simple, if crude, objective of making government smaller and more

---

[70] L. Clark, "Three Years On: The Rôle of the Advocate General for Scotland," 2002 S.L.T. (News) 139.

[71] SA 1998, s.87.

[72] M. Hunt, "Constitutionalism and the Contractualisation of Government in the United Kingdom" in *The Province of Administrative Law* (Taggart ed., Hart Publishing, Oxford, 1997), Ch.4.

on making what there was work better. This new approach was already in evidence by the close of the Thatcher years with the introduction of executive agencies and the emergence of private sector solutions to the perceived problems of government.

5–13   Executive agencies were spawned by the 1988 report *Improving Management in Government: The next steps*.[73] Having reviewed the organisation of the civil service and the way in which public services were provided, the authors of the report recommended that a complete separation be made between policy-making functions and service delivery functions. The latter, covering an estimated 95 per cent of civil service activity, should be devolved to executive agencies instead of being (inefficiently) undertaken within the traditional structure of Whitehall departments. The government accepted the recommendations, and required all departments to review their activities in order to assess their suitability for hiving off to agencies. The rigour of the procedure intensified in 1991 with the introduction of "market testing" or "prior options".[74] This required departments to scrutinise particular functions and ask themselves, first, whether a particular function could be abolished; if not, whether it could be privatised; if not, whether its performance could be contracted out to a private company; and if not, whether it could be hived off to an executive agency. Only if the answer to all of these questions was "no" might things stay as they were.

There are now well over 100 executive agencies in existence and, as the Next Steps Report predicted, some 90 per cent of civil servants now work for agencies.[75] Each agency operates within the terms of a "framework document" which establishes the respective responsibilities of the relevant minister and agency chief executive (who may be a civil servant but may equally be recruited from the private sector). The framework document also prescribes performance and financial targets, plus the operating arrangements for the agency. Initially, and in theory at least, the chief executive answered to the minister for his agency's operational efficiency and performance in implementing the policies settled by the minister; the minister, in turn, answered to Parliament for the agency's work and for the policies he had formulated. Now, the accountability of agencies to Parliament is more direct: written parliamentary questions are referred, where appropriate, to agency chief executives;

---

[73] (HMSO, 1988). The title of the report, drafted by Sir Robin Ibbs, a businessman appointed to head up the P.M.'s Efficiency Unit within the Cabinet Office, explains the term "next steps agencies", which is often used to describe its progeny.

[74] *Competing for Quality*, (Cabinet Office, 1991).

[75] *List of Ministerial Responsibilities* (Cabinet Office, 2001), Pt.IV, lists 90 executive agencies for which UK government ministers are responsible. Executive agencies falling within the competence of the devolved administrations are answerable now to those administrations.

agencies are subject to the jurisdiction of the Parliamentary Commissioner for Administration; and chief executives routinely appear before departmental select committees to answer for their operational effectiveness.

The framework agreements between minister and agency are not contracts, nor could they be: agencies have no identity or legal personality separate from that of their parent departments. But they are intended to work like contracts and, as the Next Steps Report envisaged, have brought about a fundamental shift in civil service thinking and working practices. The essence of that shift lies in the preference it represents for "marketised" solutions, modelled on the practices of the private sector, to public sector problems: "contract has replaced command and control as the paradigm of regulation."[76] Nor is this merely a matter of the "contract-like" arrangements that typify the executive agencies. Where possible, as *Competing for Quality*[77] made clear, the actual contracting out of government functions should be pursued.[78] But contrast to the establishment of executive agencies, which was essentially a managerial matter internal to the structure of government, the contracting out of statutory ministerial functions required primary legislation.[79] The necessary legislative framework was put in place by Part II of the Deregulation and Contracting Out Act 1994: in the result, the contracting out of public functions, some, such as cleaning and catering, inconsequential, others, such as the running of prisons, rather more governmental in character, is now commonplace. A variation on this theme is the Private Finance initiative and the adoption of public/private partnerships, whereby the government or other public authority enters into long-term contractual arrangements with private consortia for the provision of public infrastructure such as roads, hospitals and schools.

Nor have these reforms taken place only on the supply side. In a genuine market, consumers have a part to play: in particular, if they are dissatisfied with a product or service, they may take their custom elsewhere and the below-par producer or provider is driven out of business, leaving the field to the efficient and the effective.

---

[76] M. Hunt, "Constitutionalism and the Contractualisation of Government in the United Kingdom" in *The Province of Administrative Law, op.cit.*, p.12.

[77] *op.cit.*

[78] The slightly less prescriptive New Labour view is that contracting out should be used where it would offer "better quality services at optimal cost": *Better Quality Services: A handbook on creating Public/Private Partnerships through market testing and contracting out* (HMSO, 1998).

[79] It would otherwise have fallen foul of the *Carltona* principle, derived from the decision of the Court of Appeal in *Carltona Ltd v Commissioners of Works* [1943] 2 All E.R. 560, which holds that while an act of a civil servant may be treated as the act of the responsible minister, any wider delegation of functions by ministers will be unlawful absent express or implied statutory authority.

Consumer power may not be quite so extensive when it comes to "shopping" for one's public services. But the object of the so-called Citizen's Charter initiative, launched by the Prime Minister in 1991, was to enhance such consumer power as there is in the public sector by specifying clearly what its "customers" are entitled to expect from public services and providing mechanisms for redress should those expectations be disappointed. The charter idea originated in local government, and, supervised by the Cabinet Office, is still going strong.[80]

5–14   It is these changes rather than the better-advertised efforts to slim down the state, such as privatisation, which have had radical consequences for the nature of government in the United Kingdom. Old distinctions between the public and private spheres have been blurred if not dissolved.[81] Not surprisingly, such developments have met, and continue to meet, with suspicion and hostility in many quarters. Even those who concede that efficient service delivery is an important government objective have argued that efficiency cannot be measured in terms of cost-cutting alone. Concern has also been expressed that this "marketising" of the state has created insoluble tensions between old-fashioned administrative relationships based on an ethos of public service and contractual or quasi-contractual relationships based on the profit motive and the pursuit of efficiency and couched in thickets of management-speak. Yet, as noted above, the ideas underpinning the reinvention of the state are now mainstream, and any notion that a Labour government would halt or reverse these reforms was rapidly scotched after the 1997 election. On the contrary, the government has wholeheartedly embraced the "public choice" logic of the restructuring of government described here and has taken it further, partly by marrying it up with a wider programme of constitutional reform and partly by absorbing it into its wider drive to modernise the machinery of government. As asserted in the White Paper, *Modernising Government*:

> "Most of the old dogmas that haunted governments in the past have been swept away. . . . Better government is about much more than whether public spending should go up or

---

[80] As noted in Ch.9, the adoption by the Major government of the Code of Practice on Access to Government Information, the forerunner of today's freedom of information legislation, was in large part prompted by the notion that the provision of information about the standards of public services would support the improvements pursued by the charter initiative. For the current status of the Citizen's Charter initiative, see G. Drewry, "Whatever Happended to the Citizen's Charter?" [2002] P.L. 9.

[81] In a manner which has presented certain problems, discussed in other chapters of this book, in relation to the reach of human rights protection, judicial review and freedom of information regimes.

down, or whether organisations should be nationalised or privatised. Now that we are not hidebound by the old ways of government, we can find new and better ones."

In no sense did Scotland prior to devolution escape the effects of these changes.[82] Thus the new devolved institutions were superimposed upon a structure of older governmental bodies, characterised by the presence of elected representatives; and the newer, less easily definable web of non-departmental public bodies and agencies. Unsurprisingly, the well-rehearsed objections to the legitimacy and accountability of such bodies were aired afresh following devolution, and in the summer of 2001 the Scottish Executive published a review of the structure of public authorities in Scotland.[83] Against a statement of guiding principles concerning the establishment or retention of agencies and quangos,[84] the Executive announced its intention to abolish 52 public bodies and to place a further 61 under ongoing review. According to the latest edition of the annual government survey *Public Bodies*,[85] there are presently 149 appointed public bodies extant in Scotland.[86]

GOVERNMENT OF SCOTLAND

It is well, when speaking of the government of Scotland **5–15** post-devolution, to be careful with terminology. Just as at the United Kingdom level the functions of government are in no sense confined to the ministerial core, so too in Scotland executive

---

[82] Indeed, it has been suggested that "under the Conservative governments, quangos, and especially local public spending bodies, became an alternative territorial system to the local authorities, whose political affiliation in Scotland had moved completely away from the party": see R. Parry, "Quangos and the Structure of the Public Sector in Scotland" (1999–2000) *Scottish Affairs* 12 at 18.

[83] *Public Bodies: Proposals for change* (Scottish Executive, 2001)

[84] In short, an "arm's length body" may be established or retained if it has a distinct role to play that cannot be carried out at least as effectively by any other organisation; if it is clearly accountable to ministers and the people it serves; if it is able to work in a co-ordinated way with other organisations; and if it delivers value for money.

[85] Cabinet Office, 2003.

[86] As against 849 bodies sponsored by the UK government. It is worth noting, in passing, that the published figures cover only nationalised industries and public corporations, executive and advisory non-departmental public bodies and executive agencies. As such they exclude the significant number of "task forces" and the like, appointed for a limited period to consider and report on specific policy issues (and as such not subject to the rules on public appointments now contained, in Scotland, in the Public Appointments and Public Bodies etc (Scotland) Act 2003). As at April 2000, according to a survey by the House of Commons Select Committee on Public Administration, there were 303 such entities in operation, no fewer than 102 of which were Scottish.

authority does not repose in the Scottish Executive alone. The "Scottish Executive" refers to the nucleus of Scottish government, namely the First Minister, the Ministers appointed by him and the two Law Officers, collectively referred to as "the Scottish Ministers".[87] The Scottish Executive in this sense is the central component of the wider "Scottish Administration", which also includes junior Scottish Ministers, non-ministerial office holders and civil servants appointed to the staff of the Scottish Administration.[88] But the UK government as considered above, and indeed the supranational institutions of the European Union, remain relevant to the government of Scotland, whilst, at a lower level, there is the layer of (at least) 149 Scottish public authorities exercising executive authority at arm's length from the ministerial core.

Scottish Executive

5–16   The UK model of parliamentary government is replicated in Scotland, although the 1998 Act casts the conventions that surround the formation of governments at the UK level in statutory form. Like the Prime Minister, then, the First Minister is appointed by the Queen from among the members of the Scottish Parliament; like the Prime Minister, he holds office at Her Majesty's pleasure.[89] He may resign his office at any time, and must do so if the Parliament resolves that the Scottish Executive no longer enjoys the confidence of the Parliament.[90] Although the Queen carries out the formal task of appointment, she will act (the Scotland Act does not in terms require this, but it is plainly the intention) on the nomination of the Parliament as communicated to her by the Presiding Officer; and the Parliament must make its nomination with 28 days of a Scottish general election, the resignation of an incumbent First Minister, the office falling vacant for a reason other than resignation, or of the First Minister ceasing to be an MSP other than by virtue of a dissolution of the Parliament.[91] If the 28-day period expires without a nomination being made, section 3(1)(b) requires the Presiding Officer to

---

[87] SA 1998, s.44. A person appointed to ministerial office in the UK government may not be a member of the Scottish Executive, or *vice versa*.

[88] SA 1998, s.126(7). The non-ministerial office holders are defined by s.126(8) as the Registrar General for Births, Marriages and Deaths for Scotland, the Keeper of the Registers of Scotland and the Keeper of the Records of Scotland.

[89] SA 1998, s.45(1).

[90] SA 1998, s.45(2).

[91] SA 1998, s.46(2). Note that, whereas at Westminster an incumbent P.M. who wins a second general election simply continues in office without being reappointed, s.46(2)(a) seems clearly to envisage the renomination and reappointment of a victorious First Minister, even though he will in no sense have vacated the office. Provision is made in Chs 4 and 11 of the Standing Orders of the Scottish Parliament for the nomination of the First Minister.

propose to the Queen a date for the holding of an extraordinary general election, the result of which may produce a party balance in the Parliament more conducive to the nomination of one of its members to be First Minister.

Once the First Minister has been appointed, it falls to him under section 47 of the Scotland Act to appoint the other members of the Scottish Executive and the junior Scottish Ministers.[92] The Scottish Ministers, like the First Minister, must be members of the Scottish Parliament and their appointment must meet with the formal approval of the Queen. The First Minister may not, however, seek Her Majesty's approval for any ministerial appointment "without the agreement of the Parliament".[93] Once appointed, the Scottish Ministers hold office at Her Majesty's pleasure (that is, they are, in theory, dismissable at will by the Queen). They may in any case be removed from office at any time by the First Minister, with no requirement of parliamentary agreement. A minister who ceases to be an MSP (otherwise than by reason of a dissolution of the Parliament) ceases also to be a minister. Otherwise, a minister may resign at any time of his own choosing, and must do so if the Parliament resolves that the Scottish Executive no longer enjoys the confidence of the Parliament. Junior Scottish Ministers are appointed by the First Minister under section 49, again with the approval of the Queen and the agreement of the Parliament as signified in accordance with standing orders, in order to assist the Scottish Ministers in the exercise of their functions. The conditions of tenure of office for junior Scottish Ministers are the same as those for the Scottish Ministers proper.[94]

The position of the Law Officers differs in significant ways. The **5–17** offices of Lord Advocate and Solicitor General for Scotland are of some antiquity in Scottish government, the one dating back to the fourteenth century and the other to the sixteenth century. After the

---

[92] The Scottish Ministerial Code states that, where a coalition government is in office, the First Minister shall himself decide on the overall structure of the Executive, and decide on the allocation of ministerial posts to particular persons together with the Deputy First Minister.

[93] As to the means by which the Parliament's approval is to be signified, see r.4.6 of the Standing Orders. Note that there is nothing in the SA 1998 to dictate to the First Minister how many ministers he must appoint or what their portfolios should be (the only "named" members of the Scottish Executive, the First Minister apart, being the Lord Advocate and the Solicitor General for Scotland).

[94] Scottish Ministerial Code, para.4.6, also makes provision for the appointment, by the First Minister at the request of a member of his Cabinet, of a "ministerial parliamentary aide" (equivalent to parliamentary private secretaries at Westminster) to assist the Cabinet minister in the performance of his parliamentary tasks. They are not members of the Scottish Executive and retain many of the freedoms of any other backbencher, but, as para.4.9 of the code makes clear, " their close and confidential association with Ministers imposes certain obligations on them . . . [and] their position as Ministerial Parliamentary Aides means that they must support the Executive on key policy issues."

Anglo-Scottish union of 1707, the Lord Advocate became a
member of the new government of Great Britain, and from 1746
(in which year the office of Scottish Secretary was abolished, not to
be revived until the end of the nineteenth century) he assumed
general ministerial responsibility for the government of Scotland in
addition to his traditional legal duties. Members of the UK
government, the position of the Scottish Law Officers was yet
slightly anomalous. The normal constitutional convention to the
effect that Her Majesty's ministers be members either of the House
of Commons or of the House of Lords did not apply to them,
although it did become customary to confer on the Lord Advocate
a life peerage if he was not already a peer or an M.P.[95] But if they
were anomalous, their ministerial responsibilities, prior to devolution, were extensive. They represented the Crown before the
Scottish courts, advised the government on issues of Scots law,
controlled the system of public prosecutions in Scotland and were
in charge of the drafting of bills applying to Scotland. Many of the
functions relating to law reform and the machinery of justice which
for England and Wales were performed by the Lord Chancellor
were in Scotland vested in the Lord Advocate.

Matters relating to Scots criminal law and procedure, the
criminal justice system and the Scottish courts were prime candidates for devolution, and, as these encompassed most of the
responsibilities of the Scottish Law Officers, it was deemed appropriate that they should cease to be Ministers of the Crown in the
government of the United Kingdom and become instead members
of the Scottish Executive. This is provided for by the Scotland Act,
although, as noted, their position of the Law Officers remains
special and distinctive in a number of respects. Under section 48, it
is now for the First Minister to recommend to the Queen the
appointment of a person as Lord Advocate or Solicitor General
(formerly, the Queen made the appointments on the advice of the
Prime Minister). As with the Scottish Ministers and junior Scottish
Ministers, the First Minister must secure the agreement of the
Parliament before forwarding the names of his recommended
candidates for appointment to Her Majesty. It is to be noted,
however, that with the Law Officers it is the Queen who makes the
appointments; she does not, as with the Scottish Ministers, simply
approve the appointments made by the First Minister. Similarly,
the First Minister cannot remove either of the Law Officers from
office at his own discretion: only the Queen may do this when the
First Minister so recommends with the agreement of the Parliament. This greater security of tenure than is enjoyed by other

[95] No life peerage was conferred on the present Lord Advocate when he took over
the post from the transitional Lord Advocate, Lord Hardie; now that the Lord
Advocate is a member of the Scottish Executive it is probably deemed
unnecessary.

members of the Scottish Executive is a reflection of the greater constitutional significance of the Law Officers' role in the administration of justice in Scotland, with a correspondingly greater need for a degree of independence on the Law Officers' part. The independence of the Lord Advocate is further secured by a number of provisions scattered throughout the Scotland Act. Section 48(5), for example, states in terms that "any decision of the Lord Advocate in his capacity as head of the systems of criminal prosecution and investigation of deaths in Scotland shall continue to be taken by him independently of any other person." Section 29 limits the legislative competence of the Scottish Parliament so that it cannot remove the Lord Advocate from his position as head of the systems of criminal prosecution and investigation of deaths. Again, the general transfer of ministerial functions provided for by section 53 does not apply to the "retained functions" of the Lord Advocate (that is, those functions exercisable by him immediately before he ceased to be a Minister of the Crown and other statutory functions conferred on him alone after he ceased to be a Minister of the Crown). In all of these ways, then, the Scotland Act seeks to preserve the traditional autonomy enjoyed by the Law Officers in the discharge of their responsibilities.

Powers of the Scottish Executive

Section 52(1) of the Scotland Act provides that "statutory **5–18** functions may be conferred on the Scottish Ministers by that name." In the fullness of time, the greater part of the Scottish Executive's functions will find their source in Acts of the Scottish Parliament and Scottish statutory instruments: a number of their functions already do, under the legislation enacted in the Parliament's early years. Acts of the Westminster Parliament will in certain areas continue to confer functions on the Scottish Ministers. In the meantime, the majority of Scottish executive powers are founded on existing UK legislation, and to a lesser extent on executive powers rooted in the prerogative and the common law. The logic of devolution required not only that legislative competence over devolved matters be transferred from Westminster to the Scottish Parliament, but also that executive competence in these matters (and others) move from ministers in the UK government to the Scottish Ministers.

At one level, this was accomplished by a general transfer of ministerial functions (statutory or prerogative) exercisable within devolved competence, effected on July 1, 1999 by operation of section 53 of the Scotland Act without more.[96] To that extent,

---

[96] The concept of "devolved competence" for the purposes of s.53 is defined by reference to the definition of legislative competence contained in SA 1998, s.29.

therefore, the devolved competence of the Scottish Ministers is co-extensive, in principle, with the legislative competence of the Scottish Parliament.[97] But section 63 then provides for the transfer of *additional* functions "exercisable by a Minister of the Crown in or as regards Scotland." These are functions the subject-matter of which falls outside the legislative competence of the Scottish Parliament, which accordingly has no power to alter or abrogate them.[98] Section 63 provides, rather, for various forms of administrative or executive devolution.[99]

EU law and Convention rights

5–19   Compatibility with EU law is a condition of the validity of Acts of the Scottish Parliament by virtue of section 29 of the Scotland Act; and by virtue of section 54, as reinforced by section 57(2), a condition of the legality of acts of members of the Scottish Executive. But the relevance of Community law to Scottish legislation and executive decision-making goes further than this. While Schedule 5 of the Scotland Act reserves to Westminster competence over foreign affairs, including relations with the European Communities and European institutions, "observing and implementing . . . obligations under Community law" are expressly exempted from the scope of that reservation.[1] Thus the Scottish Parliament has a degree of positive competence in relation to the implementation in Scotland of Community obligations. Similarly, section 2(2) of the European Communities Act 1972 together with Schedule 2 of that Act empowers Ministers of the Crown to implement or give effect to the obligations of the United Kingdom arising under EU law. Now, by virtue of section 53 of the Scotland Act, so far as the section 2(2) power is exercisable within devolved competence, it is for Scottish purposes exercisable by the Scottish

---

[97] Under SA 1998, s.56, however, a number of statutory powers contained in pre-1998 enactments (mostly involving grant-making and funding powers) continue, despite the terms of s.53, to be exercisable by a Minister of the Crown concurrently with the Scottish Ministers. The list of jointly exercisable powers may be extended by subordinate legislation. Provision is also made for the joint exercise of powers in relation to bodies, offices or office-holders whose responsibilities touch on both reserved matters and devolved matters.

[98] The Scottish Ministers are, however, answerable to the Scottish Parliament for the way in which they exercise such transferred powers.

[99] A transfer under SA 1998, s.63, is effected by Her Majesty in Council, where the specified functions are to be exercised by the Scottish Ministers instead of by a Minister of the Crown; by the Scottish Ministers concurrently with a Minister of the Crown; or by a Minister of the Crown only with the agreement of, or after consultation with, the Scottish Ministers. Any such order must first be approved in draft by a resolution of both Houses of the Westminster Parliament and of the Scottish Parliament.

[1] A similar exception is made to the general reservation in respect of the UK's international obligations.

Ministers instead of by a Minister of the Crown. So, for example, if a Community directive were adopted requiring the Member States of the European Union to take some specified action in the field of animal welfare, the Scottish Ministers could make the necessary subordinate legislation to give effect to the directive in Scotland and, to the extent that such latitude is allowed by the directive, could conceivably impose higher (or lower) standards than the rest of the United Kingdom. This reflects the tenor of the 1997 White Paper on devolution which emphasised that the new Scottish institutions should and would be involved in the processes of European policy formation and negotiation and in the scrutiny and implementation of Community obligations. By the same token, liability for breaches of Community law for which the Scottish Executive was responsible would be laid at the Scottish Executive's door.

Yet the relatively straightforward division of labour in Community matters between London and Edinburgh as envisaged in the White Paper is complicated somewhat by the terms of section 57(1) of the Scotland Act. This provides that, despite the transfer to the Scottish Ministers by virtue of section 53 of functions in relation to observing and implementing obligations under EU law, any function of a Minister of the Crown in relation to any matter shall continue to be exercisable by him as regards Scotland for the purposes specified in section 2(2) of the European Communities Act 1972. A number of questions flow from this. First, what would happen if the Scottish Ministers adopted subordinate legislation to give effect to a Community obligation in Scotland, and then, pursuant to section 2(2), so too did a Minister of the Crown (and in a manner different from that of the Scottish Ministers)? The action of the Minister of the Crown could conceivably be raised before the courts as a "devolution issue" under section 98 and Schedule 6 of the Scotland Act. But in view of the wording of section 57(1), there seems to be little doubt that in this context such trenching on the devolved competence of the Scottish Ministers is entirely lawful (and probably not accurately described as "trenching" at all). If this is correct, however, and if for this reason competence in relation to the observance and implementation in Scotland of Community obligations is properly to be regarded as shared, it is questionable how far the Scottish Executive may properly be held liable for breaches of Community law. While the primary responsibility for the implementation of Community obligations falling within devolved competence may be that of the Scottish Ministers, there must on this reasoning always be a residual responsibility on the part of the UK government because of section 57(1) and, as such, a residual liability founded on its failure to act to rectify breaches occasioned by the Scottish Ministers.[2]

5–20   As provided for by section 29 in relation to the legislative competence of the Scottish Parliament, by section 54 in relation to the devolved competence of the Scottish Executive and as explicitly reinforced by section 57(2), "a member of the Scottish Executive has no power to make any subordinate legislation, or to do any other act, so far as the legislation or act is incompatible with any of the Convention rights". Section 57(3) then provides that subsection (2) does not apply to an act of the Lord Advocate in prosecuting any offence, or in his capacity as head of the systems of criminal prosecution and investigation of deaths in Scotland, "which, because of subsection (2) of section 6 of the Human Rights Act 1998, is not unlawful under subsection (1) of that section." Section 6 of the Human Rights Act makes it unlawful for a "public authority" to act in a manner inconsistent with Convention rights unless (subsection (2)) they are unable to act in any other way because of the terms of the primary or subordinate legislation pursuant to which they are acting. It is therefore incumbent upon public authorities to read and give effect to their statutory powers, so far as they are able, in a manner compatible with the Convention rights; and indeed the courts are required by section 3 of the Human Rights Act to do so. Only if a statutory provision is incapable of bearing a Convention-proofed meaning are the courts relieved of this strong interpretive duty. In that event, the offending legislation may, if it is an Act of the Scottish Parliament, be struck down; or, if it is an Act of the Westminster Parliament, be the subject of a "declaration of incompatibility" under section 4 of the Human Rights Act.

One could be forgiven for assuming that the Scottish Executive would qualify as a public authority for the purposes of the Human Rights Act not only so as to be bound by the duty to act in a manner compatible with the Convention rights but also so as to take the benefit, in appropriate cases, of the "defence" in section 6(2) of that Act. Yet the duty laid on members of the Scottish Executive by section 57(2) of the Scotland Act to act in conformity with the Convention rights is absolute in its terms. Not only that, but section 98 and Schedule 6 of the Scotland Act provide that a question whether, *inter alia*, a purported or proposed exercise of a function, or a failure to act, by a member of the Scottish Executive

---

[2] In practice, efforts would of course be made to avoid conflicts of this sort through the channels of co-operation and consultation established pursuant to the intergovernmental memorandum of understanding and supplementary concordats: as to which, see para.5–21.

is incompatible with the Convention rights shall be resolved in accordance with the procedure therein prescribed. It follows that only the Lord Advocate may take the benefit of section 6(2) of the Human Rights Act in the context of proceedings to determine a devolution issue, and only then because section 57(3) of the Scotland Act explicitly so provides.[3]

Intergovernmental relations

As the 1997 White Paper noted, following devolution arrange- **5–21** ments would require to be made to cover information exchanges, advance notification and joint working between the Scottish Executive and UK government. It envisaged the vast majority of matters being handled on a routine basis by officials, with an "appeal" to the Cabinet Office and its Scottish Executive counterpart and, if necessary, to the Scottish Executive and UK government proper. Agreement was reached on joint working arrangements in October 1999, and is embodied in a series of documents known collectively as the "concordats". The principal Memorandum of Understanding provides for the establishment of a Joint Ministerial Committee bringing together UK ministers and representatives of the devolved administrations.[4] There are then four supplementary agreements providing for "broadly uniform" treatment of government of matters with a EU dimension; matters concerning financial assistance to industry; international relations touching on the responsibilities of the devolved administrations; and statistical work across the United Kingdom. Since 1999, the memorandum and supplementary agreements have been supplemented further by bilateral departmental concordats between UK government departments and their Scottish counterparts.

These agreements are intended to guide and to structure intergovernmental relations, but it is important to note that they are not legally binding and therefore neither the Scottish Ministers nor their colleagues in London are obliged to abide by the terms of the concordats in their mutual dealings. There are, of course, good reasons why the two levels of government should strive to maintain harmonious working relationships. But ultimately, the establishment and maintenance of such relationships is a matter of political will rather than of legal duty.[5]

---

[3] See, generally, I. Jamieson, "The Relationship between the Scotland Act and the Human Rights Act", 2001 S.L.T. (News) 43.

[4] *Memorandum of Understanding and Supplementary Agreements between the United Kingdom Government, the Scottish Ministers and the Cabinet of the National Assembly for Wales*, Cm.4444 (1999).

[5] For discussion, see A. Scott, "The Rôle of Concordats in the New Britain: Taking Subsidiarity Seriously" [2001] Edin. L.R. 21.

GOVERNMENT ACCOUNTABILITY

5–22 Accountable government, like respect for the rule of law, is one of the hallmarks of a democratic society, and serves to distinguish it from a totalitarian state. It is often described as having two dimensions, explanatory and amendatory, the first implying an obligation to answer for and justify policies adopted and decisions taken, the second an obligation to acknowledge deficiency and error, where necessary, and to undertake to put things right (which may or may not involve a change in the responsible personnel).[6] The former is at least as important as the latter, although a tendency to focus on blame and sanction may obscure this. Plainly, in any democracy, the government will have the support of only a portion of the people to whom it is ultimately answerable via the ballot box. Not everyone will share its ideological persuasion, nor agree with its particular policies. But where a government accepts in good faith an obligation to explain itself and justify its actions (which implies at least that thought has been given to alternative means of pursuing its policy goals) it is easier to accept its choices; to that extent, accountable government is conducive to cohesion. In the same way, accountability reduces the risks of governmental fallibility. A government which feels obliged to account for its actions is the more likely to think things through properly in the first place, and although mistakes will inevitably be made—either because a policy is intrinsically flawed, or because it is poorly implemented—accountability is its amendatory form should ensure that they are rectified.

5–23 There is more than one way in which accountable government may be secured, and one may well obtain a better sense of the extent to which it is achieved in the United Kingdom by focusing less on the defects of particular mechanisms and more on the adequacy of all the mechanisms taken together. As noted, in the final analysis, a government is accountable to the people through periodic elections, and if this control is sporadic and, often, blunted by the vagaries of the electoral process, it is nonetheless occasionally effective.[7] That apart, ongoing political accountability is traditionally held to be secured by parliamentary scrutiny of the executive, which rests on the constitutional doctrines of collective and individual ministerial responsibility to Parliament. We have touched on these doctrines already.[8] Collective ministerial responsibility denotes the responsibility of all members of a government

---

[6] C. Turpin, "Ministerial Responsibility" in *The Changing Constitution* (4th ed., Jowell and Oliver eds, Oxford University Press, Oxford, 2000), Ch.5.

[7] As in the 1997 general election, the result of which was as much a verdict on the outgoing Conservative administration as a mandate for its New Labour successor.

[8] See para. 1–09.

for all of its policies. However those policies are arrived at, it is the duty of each government minister publicly to defend them, and if a particular minister cannot do then, by convention, he should resign.[9] Individual ministerial responsibility, by contrast, denotes the responsibility of each minister for everything that is done in his name by his department. In keeping with the traditional ideas of the anonymity and impartiality of the civil service, the minister takes the credit for departmental successes; the corollary is that he should take the blame for departmental failures, even—so the traditional theory has it—where he is not directly and personally implicated therein. Again, the sanction attaching to individual ministerial responsibility—that which gives the doctrine its teeth—is said to be resignation. In practice, of course, loss of office is not the automatic consequence either of a breach of collective ministerial responsibility or of departmental failure. In the former case, while the minister who is unable to support a particular aspect of government policy may step down, and while the Prime Minister or First Minister may simply dismiss him, political considerations may militate against dismissal if the recalcitrant minister is not otherwise minded to go. In the latter case, we have already seen that departmental wrongdoing is rarely attended by a ministerial resignation.[10] In neither case, in normal circumstances, is Parliament likely to be in a position to enforce the sanction by withdrawing its confidence, either from a particular minister or the ministry as a whole.

But the ephemeral (at best) nature of the sanction does not necessarily deprive the doctrine of ministerial responsibility of all its force. There are numerous mechanisms, at Westminster and Holyrood alike, designed to facilitate parliamentary scrutiny of the executive. Questions are tabled by M.P.s and MSPs for oral or written answer. Motions and debates provide a means of requiring a minister to appear and give an account. The parliamentary committees, moreover, furnish a specialised and systematic forum for control at various levels, through their pre-legislative and post-legislative scrutiny of executive measures and inquiries undertaken into matters falling within their respective remits. Considered in isolation, the adequacy of all of these devices is open to

---

[9] Both the Ministerial Code and Scottish Ministerial Code state upholding the principle of collective responsibility as the first duty of a minister. Indeed in Scotland, where coalition governments are likely to be the norm, the principle of collective responsibility may assume even greater importance than at Westminster: see B. Winetrobe, "Collective responsibility in devolved Scotland" [2003] P.L. 24.

[10] Both the Ministerial Code and Scottish Ministerial Code make clear, however, that an individual minister may only remain in office for so long as he retains the confidence of the P.M. or First Minister as the case may be. In other words, a minister who is (or is seen to be) a liability will be let go.

question. A key reason for this relates to the availability of information to Parliament. Political accountability cannot function unless information about the activities of governmental bodies is provided to Parliament and parliamentary committees. By and large, that information is in the hands of the government, which is therefore in a position to control its dissemination. Parliamentary questions, motions and debates may seek to elicit information, but are an inherently inefficient way of doing so, even assuming a basic willingness on the part of the executive to answer such questions as are put. Ministers may and do refuse to answer questions on a variety of grounds—the information sought is confidential; the cost of its retrieval would be excessive; the subject-matter does not fall within the particular minister's responsibility at all; and so on. As for parliamentary committees, while they provide a sharper focus on governmental activity, their efficacy too is limited by their reliance on ministerial co-operation, deficiencies in the provision of information, their inherently party political make-up and the restrictions placed on the candour of officials appearing before them. Specific inquiries may be illuminating on occasion, but committees are not well suited to the ongoing audit of the departments they monitor. In all of these ways, the ability of parliamentary institutions to secure accountability is diminished.[11]

5–24 The reinvention of government has also heightened concern about the reach of parliamentary control. That reinvention involved drawing a distinction between the functions of policy making and policy execution, the latter of which is increasingly performed, whether by executive agencies, non-departmental public bodies or external contractors, at some distance from the ministerial core. It has been said, in light of these developments, that while the minister remains accountable to Parliament for the delivery as well as the formation of government policy, he is only properly responsible for the latter.[12] On this reckoning, responsibility can only properly attach where a minister is himself culpable, either in the sense of being personally implicated in a serious departmental error or in the sense that he knew or should have known what was amiss, but "pure vicarious headrolling is not

---

[11] It may be noted, however, that the Parliamentary Commissioner for Administration (whose opposite number in Scotland, now, is the Scottish Public Services Ombudsman) has a number of strengths lacking in parliamentary committees, which enable him to supplement, in an important way, the limited fact-finding abilities of M.P.s and committees. The role and jurisdiction of both parliamentary ombudsmen is discussed in Ch.13.

[12] This distinction between the general accountability of ministers and their personal responsibility is not necessarily of recent provenance: something like it appears, for example, in the so-called Maxwell-Fyfe guidelines, laid down by the Home Secretary in his response to the findings of the public inquiry into the disposal of land at Crichel Down in 1954: see *Hansard*, HC Vol.241, cols 1290, 1291 (July 20, 1954).

required".[13] In principle, this seems unobjectionable: responsibility should be commensurate with the degree of power and control actually possessed. But in the reconfigured constitutional structure, it has led to the tactical employment by ministers of a distinction between policy and operational matters, which implies that the minister can be expected to know nothing about the latter.[14] What the distinction has allowed is the deflection of blame, away from the minister and on to officials; and constitutional accountability to Parliament is diminished, not enhanced, if the extent of the minister's duty to Parliament is to turn up and condemn the agency or quango charged with implementation.

The parliamentary and academic criticism of this reworking of ministerial responsibility was amply justified by the instrumental way in which ministers applied the policy/operational distinction. That distinction presupposes clarity and certainty in the division of roles where neither exists to any marked extent. It also led to major blind spots in parliamentary scrutiny, in so far as agency chief executives were no freer than other civil servants to attend select committees and give evidence unencumbered by ministerial directions. But it may be that what was (and is) needed is a conscious adjustment to the modern constitutional landscape. Professor Woodhouse[15] suggests that, within this environment, the political accountability of ministers would be better captured by focusing on their role responsibility rather than causal responsibility in a simplistic sense. On that view, there is no reason why the Home Secretary should fall on his sword because a prison warder leaves a cell door open. But his general *supervisory* responsibility for ensuring, so far as possible, that such things do not occur should be acknowledged explicitly:

> "Ministers are . . . responsible for seeing that mechanisms are in place to provide them with the necessary and correct information so that they can respond to problems, if appropriate by taking direct control, and account to Parliament and the public. They are also responsible for ensuring that their departments have adequate human and financial resources to implement government policies, that those appointed as heads of executive agencies are suitably qualified, and that there are systems or procedures in place which minimise the dangers of

[13] G. Marshall, *Ministerial Responsibility* (Oxford University Press, Oxford, 1989), p.11.
[14] D. Woodhouse, "The Reconstruction of Constitutional Accountability" [2002] P.L. 73 at 75. In fact, the evidence suggests that ministers concern themselves far more with operational matters than the distinction implies. Moreover, the flaws in a policy are likely to become apparent only when the policy is put into operation.
[15] "The Reconstruction of Constitutional Accountability" [2002] P.L. 73 at 75.

Public Law

errors being made. Such . . . 'positive' responsibilities . . . are supplemented by 'negative' responsibilities, so that the failure of ministers to intervene, when they should have done so, is not an appropriate excuse; neither is not knowing that something has happened when they should have known."[16]

5–25 Systemic operational failures should therefore be seen as engaging the responsibility (not merely the accountability) of the minister, either because he has failed to ensure that an agency is staffed and funded sufficiently to perform its allotted task,[17] or because he has failed to step in to arrest and correct maladministration.[18] According to Woodhouse, recent practice suggests that this lesson is being absorbed in governmental circles.[19] The duties of ministers to account to Parliament and be held to account have been committed to paper, both at the Scottish and UK levels,[20] in the latter case reflecting the terms of resolutions adopted by both Houses of Parliament. But at least as important as recognising (if recognition it be) that ministerial responsibility does not stop with settling on a policy and charging others with its implementation is the insistence on the provision to Parliament of information.[21] The Scott Inquiry[22] into the sale of defence equipment to Iraq rightly identified this as the key to improved lines of political accountability. At present, government departments, agencies and others

---

[16] *ibid.*, at 78.

[17] As was the case with the establishment of the Child Support Agency, in the view both of the Parliamentary Commissioner for Administration and the House of Commons Select Committee on Social Services.

[18] Thus the Enterprise and Lifelong Learning Committee of the Scottish Parliament, in its inquiry into the Scottish Qualifications Authority débâcle in the summer of 2000, located the principal causes of the incident at the managerial level within the organisation, but questioned whether the Education Minister's appointment of an inexperienced chief executive had been an appropriate one, and whether the Minister had had proper oversight of the work of the SQA: *Report on the Inquiry into the Governance of the Scottish Qualifications Authority*, S.P.P.225 (2000).

[19] Under reference to the inquiries into the sale of arms to Iraq (*Report of the Inquiry into the Export of Defence Equipment and Dual-Use Goods to Iraq and Related Prosecutions* (HC 115 (1995–96)), the failure to notify changes to the rules of entitlement to inherit a deceased spouse's State Earnings Related Pension (Select Committee on Public Administration, *Administrative Failure: Inherited SERPS*, HC 433 (1999–2000)) and the supply of military equipment to Sierra Leone; and to the ministerial response to Passport Agency crisis in the summer of 1999.

[20] *Scottish Ministerial Code* (Scottish Executive, Feb. 2002), at s.1.1(b); *Ministerial Code* (Cabinet Office, 1997), at s.1(ii). The latter but not the former refers expressly to ministers' responsibility for their executive agencies.

[21] Both ministerial codes stress that it is of "paramount importance that ministers give accurate and truthful information" to Parliament and require ministers to be as open as possible with Parliament and the public, refusing to disclose information only when it would be in the public interest to do so.

[22] *Report of the Inquiry into the Export of Defence Equipment and Dual-Use Goods in Iraq and Related Prosecutions, op.cit.,* n.22.

are obliged by the Code of Practice on Access to Government Information or, in Scotland, the Code of Practice on Access to Scottish Executive Information, to publish certain information as a matter of routine and to make available other information (subject to various categories of exemption) on request. Neither code is legally binding but there is a right to complain, in the event of alleged failure to comply, to the Parliamentary Commissioner for Administration or to the Scottish Information Commissioner as appropriate.[23] From 2005, when the Freedom of Information Act 2000 and the Freedom of Information (Scotland) Act 2002 enter fully into force, governmental and other public authorities will come under statutory duties of publication and disclosure, enforceable by the Information Commissioner and Scottish Information Commissioner respectively and, ultimately, by the courts. True it is that both statutory regimes contains exemptions for various categories of information. Both however will institutionalise transparency, and, by facilitating access to information by parliamentarians and parliamentary committees, will significantly improve their capacity to hold government in all its forms to account.

Nor should the legal accountability of ministers be neglected. The development of the law of judicial review may be seen in part as a response to the inadequacies of political channels of accountability. Even before the entry into force of the Human Rights Act 1998, the courts were able to insist that governmental powers were exercised lawfully, rationally and fairly, with appropriate regard to the fundamental rights of the citizen; now, all statutory powers fall to be read and given effect consistently with the Convention rights and may be the subject of declarations of incompatibility should this be impossible.[24] Finally, devolution itself has contributed in an important way to improving the accountability of government. By breaking government down into smaller parts and subjecting it to the control of separate parliaments or assemblies, devolution may well have made the attainment of political accountability more manageable and achievable.

---

[23] The Parliamentary Commissioner has noted an increasing tendency on the part of central government departments to delay responding to his requests for information following receipt of complaints under the code of practice. In his Fourth Report, HC 353 (2001–02), the commissioner also reported that, for the first time since the introduction of the code and, in his view, in breach of the convention of disclosure, the government had actually refused to comply with his finding that information requested should be released.

[24] Acts of the Scottish Parliament which cannot be read and given effect consistently with the Convention rights are of course invalid and may be struck down: see, generally, Ch.9.

CHAPTER 6

THE COURTS AND JUDICIARY

Introduction

6–01   Few parts of our constitutional structure have escaped at least a measure of reform in the recent past, and the judicial system has certainly had its fair share. Partly this has been the result of external pressure, as for example in relation to the system of judicial appointments. Partly however, it has been the result of a reappraisal by judges themselves of their role in society. We do not have to go back very far to the time when judges were perceived (and sought to be perceived) as the remote dispensers of disinterested justice, wholly insulated from political controversy.[1] More recently, there has been a far greater readiness on the part of senior judges, at least, to engage with controversial issues (albeit, as a rule, issues within the sphere of a lawyer's competence) and to muse openly on the merits of an expanded role for an activist judiciary. Nor is this expanded role a self-invented one: with the devolution legislation and the incorporation of the European Convention on Human Rights under the Human Rights Act 1998, the courts acquired a new and explicitly "constitutional" jurisdiction which must, of necessity, prompt a reassessment of their proper functions and their relationship with other organs of the state.[2]

At its simplest, the key function of the courts is to adjudicate on and determine disputes of fact and law, meaning the law as laid down in and under statutes and the common law as expounded and applied by the courts themselves. The performance of this function

---

[1] A perception which, as Prof. Griffith has convincingly argued, was seriously ill-founded: see J. A. G. Griffith, *The Politics of the Judiciary* (5th ed., Fontana, London, 1997).
[2] See S. Tierney, "Constitutionalising the Role of the Judge: Scotland and the new order" in *Human Rights and Scots Law* (Boyle *et al.* eds, Hart Publishing, Oxford, 2002), Ch.5.

is in no sense confined to professional judges sitting in the civil and criminal courts, but falls also to the many members (lay and legally qualified) of administrative tribunals and to senior public investigative officers such as the Parliamentary Commissioner for Administration. Similarly, lay justices of the peace exercise significant judicial powers in relation to summary criminal justice and other matters in the district courts. One of the more salutary lessons taught us by the incorporation of the Convention was quite how wide a range of bodies merited the description "judicial", in the sense that they determine (even if not in a final sense) the civil rights and obligations of others.[3] Article 6 of the Convention entitles every person, in the determination of his civil rights and obligations or of criminal charges against him, to a *fair* hearing, which is a function of, among other things, the independence and impartiality of the tribunal in question. The one denotes freedom from constraint—and the appearance of constraint—by other institutions of the state; the other denotes absence of bias—and the appearance of bias—on the part of the individual decision-maker.[4] Aspects of the Scottish judicial system have been found wanting in both respects.

SCOTTISH JUDICIARY

Though the legal system of Scotland is distinct from that of **6–02** England and Wales and that of Northern Ireland, the Scottish judiciary is not, at least in its upper echelons, exclusively Scottish. The Judicial Committee of the Privy Council is the final court of appeal on devolution issues raised under section 98 and Schedule 6 of the Scotland Act 1998, and also have jurisdiction in relation to "pre-assent references" made in respect of bills passed by the Scottish Parliament by one of the Law Officers.[5] The Judicial Committee was established by the Judicial Committee Act 1833,[6]

---

[3] Indeed the considerable delay between the signifying of Royal Assent to the HRA 1998 on Nov. 19, 1998 and its final entry into force throughout the UK on Oct. 2, 2000 was due to no small extent to the need to educate all of these decision-makers as to their new obligations under the Act.

[4] Although the difference between independence and impartiality may be less pronounced than this implies: see Lord Irvine, "Activism and Restraint: Human Rights and the Interpretative Process" [1999] E.H.R.L.R. 350 at 356 and Lord Bingham in *Millar v Dickson*, 2002 S.C. (P.C.) 30, para.18.

[5] SA 1998, s.33. No such references have yet been made.

[6] The Judicial Committee Act 1844 provided that the Queen may by Order in Council admit appeals from courts of British colonies or overseas territories and in its heyday the Judicial Committee served as the Supreme Court of the British Empire (not always, in the view of some, with wholly salutary results: see, *e.g.* K. D. Ewing, "A Bill of Rights: Lessons from the Privy Council" in *Edinburgh Essays*

and consists of all members of the Privy Council who hold or have held high judicial office under the Crown, including the Lord Chancellor (pending abolition), the Lords of Appeal in Ordinary (serving and retired), judges of the English Court of Appeal, the Lord President and Lord Justice-Clerk, members of the Inner House of the Court of Session,[7] and senior Commonwealth judges.[8] Technically it does not give judgments, but tenders advice to the Queen; yet it is clearly a judicial body, and its "advice" is treated as binding judgment.[9]

The House of Lords has exercised a judicial function for more than 600 years as part of the High Court of Parliament.[10] Immediately prior to the Union of 1707, there was likewise a right of appeal from the Court of Session to the Scots Parliament. The Union agreement of that year made no provision for appeals from the Scottish courts to the new Parliament of Great Britain, but such appeals were quickly taken, in civil cases at least.[11] At one time, any peer could participate in the judicial business of the House, but in the early nineteenth century this practice began to die out.[12] The procedures and composition of what is now known as the Appellate Committee of the House of Lords were placed on

---

in *Public Law* (Finnie, Himsworth and Walker eds, Edinburgh University Press, Edinburgh, 1991), p.231; but *cf*. R. Lane, "Alternative Approaches to Constitution Building: The Judicial Committee of the Privy Council" in D. Curtin and T. Hewkel (eds), *The Institutional Dynamics of European Integration*, Vol.II, Liber Amiconium Henry G. Schermein (Martinus Nijhoff, Dordrecht, 1994), p.30). With the dismantling of Empire, its territorial jurisdiction was pared away so that it is now confined to the Channel Islands, Isle of Man, the remaining British colonies and protectorates, and a few independent Commonwealth states such as New Zealand and Jamaica which have opted to retain a right (with or without leave) of appeal to the Committee. Until Apr. 2003, it also had jurisdiction in relation to appeals from such professional bodies as the General Medical Council and General Dental Council in disciplinary matters.

[7] The appointment of members of the Inner House to the Privy Council is a relatively recent innovation, intended to ensure that there will always be a sufficiency of Scottish judges to deal with devolution issues brought before the Judicial Committee.

[8] SA 1998, s.103(2) provides that, in hearing devolution issues, only British members of the Judicial Committee may sit.

[9] See generally Lord Hope, "The Judicial Committee of the Privy Council: Its practice and procedure" (1999) S.L.P.Q. 1.

[10] The House of Commons has exercised no judicial function, other than in respect to its privileges, since 1399.

[11] The first such appeal to the House of Lords was *Earl of Rosebery v Inglis* (1708) 18 HL Journals 464. The jurisdiction of the House was challenged in *Greenshields v Edinburgh Mags* (1710–11) Robert 12, HL; but the challenge failed and the jurisdiction of the House of Lords in relation to civil appeals is now clearly established. For reasons not altogether clear, criminal appeals were not taken to the House of Lords, and it is now equally well established that the final court of criminal appeal in Scotland (devolution issues excepted) is the High Court of Justiciary.

[12] R. Stevens, *Law and Politics: The House of Lords as a judicial body, 1800–1976*.

a statutory footing by the Appellate Jurisdiction Act 1876, which made provision also for the conferment of "judicial peerages" some 80 years in advance of the Life Peerages Act 1958. The last occasion on which a lay peer took part in the House's judicial work was in 1883, and it is now performed only by the Lord Chancellor (again, pending abolition) and the Lords of Appeal in Ordinary, of whom there are presently 12 (including two Scottish judges).[13] They are appointed by the Queen on the advice of the Prime Minister, usually from among the ranks of the senior appeal court judges in each jurisdiction of the United Kingdom.

It now appears that both the Judicial Committee and the **6–03** Appellate Committee of the House of Lords are to be replaced by a new Supreme Court of some description.[14] Support for such an initiative is widespread.[15] The major deficiency critics discern in current arrangements is the inconsistency between the doctrine of the separation of powers on the one hand and the presence of the judicial peers in the House of Lords as a legislative body, and in particular the very existence of the Lord Chancellor, on the other.[16] Now we have seen that the doctrine of the separation of powers does not necessitate an absolute and rigid division between the three branches of the state. But it is a rare account of the separation of powers that does not treat the independence of the judiciary as a, if not the, crucial element in the doctrine. We consider the independence of the judiciary more fully below; suffice to say here that is not merely a function of *actual* absence of constraint but also a matter of *appearances*. Instinctively one is disinclined to argue for the abolition of a system that works well, as the Judicial Committee and Appellate Committee do. It is often said that the House of Lords in its legislative capacity benefits from the participation of the judicial peers; the judicial peers, in return,

---

[13] "In Ordinary" denotes the fact that these Lords of Appeal work as full-time judges and receive a salary paid out of the consolidated fund. "Lords of Appeal" (retired Lords of Appeal in Ordinary and other senior judges who happen to be peers) may also participate in the judicial business of the House as and when necessary, provided they meet the criteria of the Appellate Jurisdiction Act 1876 and have not attained the age of 75.

[14] *Constitutional Reform: A supreme court for the United Kingdom* (Dept for Constitutional Affairs, July 2003).

[15] See, *e.g.* Lord Bingham, "The Highest Court in the Land" (Constitution Unit, 2002); Lord Steyn, "The Case for a Supreme Court" (2002) 118 L.Q.R. 382; A. Le Sueur and R. Cornes, "The Future of the United Kingdom's Highest Courts" (Constitution Unit, 2001). For a dissenting viewpoint, see Lord Cooke, "The Law Lords: An endangered heritage" (2003) 119 L.Q.R. 49.

[16] It has been suggested by one commentator that cases such as *Venables and Thompson v UK* (1999) 30 E.H.R.R. 121 and *McGonnell v UK* (2000) 8 B.H.R.C. 56 indicate a growing disquiet on the part of the ECHR about "the casualness of British attitudes to the separation of powers": see R. Stevens, "A Loss of Innocence? Judicial independence and the separation of powers" (1999) 19 O.J.L.S. 365.

have said that they benefit from the "wider perspective derived from [their] closer contact with the legislative process and also from their awareness of debates in the House on matters of current concern."[17] In practice, the judicial peers do not engage in legislative debates on matters of "strong party political controversy".[18] They are also mindful that they may render themselves ineligible to sit judicially if they were to express an opinion on a matter that later turned out to be relevant to an appeal before the House.[19] That being so, the greater part of the evidence appears to suggest that the contribution of the judicial peers is valuable and valued, and is made without compromising their independence.[20] Even so, given the culture of justification that, in matters constitutional, has supplanted the old culture of complacency,[21] it was probably inevitable that a reform such as the present would eventuate.

In one sense, the establishment of a new Supreme Court will make little difference from the Scottish perspective.[22] The government is not minded to alter the present practice, whereby only civil appeals may be taken from Scotland, devolution issues raising questions of criminal law or procedure apart. On that note, the government proposes to transfer the jurisdiction presently vested in the Judicial Committee in relation to devolution issues and pre-assent references under the Scotland Act to the new Supreme Court, as well as the jurisdiction of the House of Lords.[23] It is suggested that 12 full-time judges should sit on the court, as is

---

[17] Unpublished memorandum submitted by the Lords of Appeal in Ordinary in response to the Wakeham Commission on Reform of the House of Lords, 1999 (cited by Lord Cooke, "The Law Lords: An endangered heritage" (2003) 119 L.Q.R. 49).

[18] As Lord Bingham, speaking on behalf of the Lords of Appeal in Ordinary, put it in a statement to the House of Lords: *Hansard*, HL Vol.614, cols 419, 420 (June 22, 2000)

[19] *ibid.*

[20] As we shall presently see, the *cause célèbre* on this score—the participation of Lord Hoffmann in the first Pinochet case—had nothing to do with his Lordship's activities within the House of Lords, but related rather to the relationship of himself and his wife to an intervener in the case.

[21] See Lord Steyn, "The Case for a Supreme Court" (2002) 118 L.Q.R. 382.

[22] Lord Hope, however, has drawn attention to the fact that the Treaty of Union 1707 provides that no cases from Scotland can be heard by the "Courts of Chancery, Queen's Bench, Common Pleas or any other Court in Westminster Hall." (The House of Lords did not sit in Westminster Hall, nor was it a court "of the like nature" as those barred from hearing Scottish cases). For this reason, Lord Hope stresses that the new supreme court could not be part of the Royal Courts of Justice nor funded by the Courts Service: *The Times*, June 19, 2003. The government appears to concede as much in the consultation paper, emphasising that the new court will be a "United Kingdom" court and established as such.

[23] The Judicial Committee would however retain its appellate jurisdiction in respect of those Commonwealth states and dependencies which recognise it.

presently the case with the House of Lords, but that provision should be made enabling the court to supplement its numbers with part-time judges.[24] Members of the Supreme Court who are also peers will lose the right to sit and vote in the House of Lords for so long as they serve on the court. As to the manner of appointment of the members of the court, the government is conducting a parallel consultation on this question, with a view to establishing an independent judicial appointments commission charged with recommending candidates for appointment and possibly, in some cases, making appointments itself.[25]

Whatever it is that the government puts in place of the Judicial **6–04** and Appellate committees, there are no plans at present to reform the Scottish judicial hierarchy,[26] although even here the effects of the new constitutional climate have made themselves felt. Scotland's supreme civil court is the Court of Session. Its jurisdiction is both original and appellate and extends over the whole of Scotland, by contrast to that of the sheriff courts. It is composed of the Lord President and Lord Justice-Clerk, together with the Senators of the College of Justice or Lords of Session, as the Court of Session judges are collectively known,[27] and has the power both at common law and under statute to regulate its own procedure by way of Act of Sederunt. Scotland's supreme criminal court is the High Court of Justiciary, and it is perhaps supreme in a truer sense than the Court of Session, for there is no right of appeal beyond the High Court sitting as an appellate body[28] except, now, in respect of devolution issues, which carry a right of appeal to the Judicial Committee of the Privy Council. All judges of the High Court (the Lords Commissioners of Justiciary) have, since 1887, also been judges of the Court of Session. The head of the High Court is the Lord Justice-General, an office which since 1836 has been held by the Lord President of the Court of Session. It has exclusive jurisdiction to try the most serious crimes, known as the Pleas of the Crown, and concurrent jurisdiction with the sheriff court to try less serious crimes when a trial on indictment by

---

[24] The consultation paper recognises that the need for this will be particularly apparent in cases from Scotland and NI raising devolution issues.

[25] *Constitutional Reform: A New Way of Appointing Judges* (Dept of Constitutional Affairs, July 2003).

[26] Note that the Scottish Parliament has no power to legislate on "the continued existence of the High Court of Justiciary as a criminal court of first instance and of appeal [or] the continued existence of the Court of Session as a civil court of first instance and of appeal": SA 1998, s.29(2)(b) and Sch.5, Pt I, para.1(d) and (e).

[27] The maximum number of Court of Session judges that may now be appointed, including the Lord President and Lord Justice-Clerk, is 32: Court of Session Act 1988, s.1. Temporary judges may also be appointed to sit in the Court of Session in terms of the Law Reform (Miscellaneous Provisions) (Scotland) Act 1990, s.35.

[28] Criminal Procedure (Scotland) Act 1995, s.124.

solemn procedure (*i.e.* before a judge and jury of 15) is deemed appropriate by the prosecutor.[29] It was empowered to sit as an appellate court in 1926, the normal quorum being three,[30] and it too has power to regulate its own internal procedure by way of Acts of Adjournal.

The sheriff courts, which go back at least as far as the twelfth century, are presently regulated by the Sheriff Courts (Scotland) Acts 1907 and 1971. Scotland is divided into six sheriffdoms, each headed by a sheriff principal; each sheriffdom, bar one, is then sub-divided into sheriff court districts based on the principal towns within the sheriffdom. For each district, there is at least one sheriff, the total number depending on the level of work involved. Their jurisdiction, although confined in the main to their particular districts, is extensive, encompassing both civil and criminal matters.[31] More local still are the district courts, established of new by the District Courts (Scotland) Act 1975. A district court may consist of a stipendiary magistrate or of one of more lay justices of the peace.[32] The jurisdiction of justices of the peace is limited to minor offences and certain local administrative matters. They sit with a legally qualified clerk when hearing cases.

So much for the basic structure of the Scottish judicial hierarchy. The key questions with which we are now concerned are, first, how far the independence of the judiciary is secured in practice; and secondly, the extent to which the impartiality of the judiciary is maintained.

JUDICIAL INDEPENDENCE

Judicial Appointments

6–05   Judicial independence requires that an appropriate distance be maintained between the courts and other institutions of the state. It is well established in the jurisprudence of the European Court of

---

[29] A prosecution will be brought in the High Court if a sentence of more than three years' imprisonment is sought, since the sheriff courts may only imprison convicted persons for up to three years.

[30] Criminal Procedure (Scotland) Act 1995, ss.103 and 104.

[31] Broadly, the civil jurisdiction of the sheriff courts covers small claims, summary causes and ordinary causes, the distinction between the three depending on the value of the claim involved. In criminal matters, the sheriff has jurisdiction to try all crimes other than the Pleas of the Crown, and may conduct trials in accordance with summary or solemn procedure (*i.e.* in the latter case, with a jury).

[32] Only Glasgow has elected to appoint stipendiary magistrates (*i.e.* full-time, salaried and legally-qualified magistrates) in four of its district court areas. A stipendiary magistrate has powers in criminal matters approximating to those of the sheriff.

Human Rights that the way in which judges are appointed, their term of office and security of tenure, their mode of remuneration and the presence or absence of guarantees against outside pressure are all factors relevant to the question whether the tribunal presents a sufficient appearance of independence.

Judicial appointments in the United Kingdom are a matter for the executive, although in Scotland at least steps have been taken, within the limits imposed by the Scotland Act, to introduce a measure of independence and transparency into the process.[33] Lords of Appeal in Ordinary are appointed by the Queen on the advice of the Prime Minister. The Lord President of the Court of Session and the Lord Justice-Clerk are also appointed by the Queen on the advice of the Prime Minister, although section 95(2) of the Scotland Act provides that the Prime Minister shall not recommend to the Queen the appointment of any person who has not been nominated by the First Minister; and before making any nomination, the First Minister must consult the Lord President and Lord Justice-Clerk (unless, in either case, the office is vacant). Under section 95(4), judges of the Court of Session, sheriffs principal and sheriffs are appointed by the Queen on the recommendation of the First Minister. Again, the First Minister is obliged first to consult the Lord President. Moreover, section 95(5) provides that any nomination or recommendation the First Minister may make shall also "comply with any requirement . . . imposed by virtue of any enactment." Thus the Scottish Parliament may prescribe further statutory conditions in relation to such nominations or recommendations, and it is expected that a bill to constitute the Judicial Appointments Board for Scotland on a statutory footing will be enacted in the course of the 2003–2007 Parliament.[34] Finally, under section 9 of the District Courts (Scotland) Act 1975,[35] the Scottish Ministers themselves appoint justices of the peace, in accordance with such regulations as may be made by them and approved by resolution of the Scottish Parliament.

There are also certain statutory criteria of eligibility for appoint- **6–06** ment to judicial office. To be appointed a sheriff principal or sheriff, one must have been legally qualified as a solicitor or advocate for at least 10 years.[36] By virtue of section 7 of the Bail, Judicial Appointments etc (Scotland) Act 2000, which inserts a new

---

[33] See "Judicial Appointments Reform", 2001 S.L.T. (News) 101.

[34] The board was established on a non-statutory basis in May 2001. Chaired by a lay person, its role is to advertise for applicants for appointment to the Court of Session or shrieval benches, to interview candidates and make recommendations accordingly to the First Minister.

[35] As amended by the Scotland Act and by the Bail, Judicial Appointments etc (Scotland) Act 2000 (hereafter "BJA(S)A 2000").

[36] Sheriff Court (Scotland) Act 1971, s.5.

section 11A into the Sheriff Courts (Scotland) Act 1971, the same condition of eligibility applies to the appointment of a person as a part-time sheriff. This office is new, and was created in light of the abolition by the 2000 Act of the office of temporary sheriff following the decision of the High Court of Justiciary in *Starrs v Ruxton*.[37] Under Article 19 of the Treaty of Union of 1707, appointments to the Court of Session bench are governed by a requirement of at least five years' standing as a member of the Faculty of Advocates. In 1990, eligibility was extended to sheriffs principal or sheriffs who have held office as such for a continuous period of at least five years, and also to solicitors who have enjoyed rights of audience in both the Court of Session and High Court of Justiciary for at least five years.[38]

Such are the rules. In practice, of course, they have been supplemented by various conventions and practices that have developed over time. In that respect, it has been suggested that there are two traditional paths to the Court of Session bench: the professional route (election to the post of Dean of the Faculty of Advocates is generally taken to "qualify" the holder for appointment to the bench) and the political route (service as Lord Advocate or Solicitor General).[39] Critics argue that, either way, there is nothing to insulate the appointments process from preferment based on factors other than merit, and that the net result is a judiciary quite unrepresentative of the society it serves.[40] Hence the establishment of the Judicial Appointments Board for Scotland; but while this may place the business of selecting candidates for appointment on a footing more closely resembling normal job interviews, it remains to be seen whether it will go far enough to satisfy those who attack the present system as élitist and unfair.[41] However that may be, it seems right in principle that the transparency and independence of the judicial appointments process should be tested and, so far as possible, enhanced. For as one judge has held, "it is a basic premise of the Convention system that only an entirely neutral, impartial and independent judiciary can carry out the primary task of securing and enforcing Convention rights."[42] The same may be said of the judicial role in relation to the devolution settlement.

---

[37] 2000 S.L.T. 42.
[38] Law Reform (Miscellaneous Provisions) (Scotland) Act 1990, s.35(1).
[39] See S. Styles, "The Scottish Judiciary, 1919–1986," 1988 J.R. 41.
[40] It is questionable how much can be done, in practical terms, to address the latter problem, if the pool from which judges are drawn is itself unrepresentative of society.
[41] There may, for example, be issues about how members of the board are themselves appointed, and whether their selections may in any case be overridden by the First Minister after consultation with the Lord President. For parliamentary consideration of the matter, see the Scottish Parliament Official Report (Mar. 4, 2003), cols.2581–2594.
[42] *Brown v Stott*, 2001 S.C. (PC) 43 at 63G, *per* Lord Steyn.

Tenure and Pay

At common law, it was presumed that a judicial office was held **6–07** *ad vitam aut culpam* ("for life or until blame").[43] Tenure of judicial office is clearly a necessary adjunct of judicial independence, and although Parliament may (and does) override the presumption of the common law, any limitations on tenure must not be such as to undermine the appearance of a tribunal's independence.[44] Thus in *Starrs v Ruxton*,[45] the High Court of Justiciary held that, although the initial appointment of temporary sheriffs by the executive was not inherently objectionable, the brevity of their term of office (only one year), coupled with the power (albeit unused) under section 11 of the Sheriff Courts (Scotland) Act 1971 to recall a temporary sheriff's commission and the practice of appointing permanent sheriffs from the pool of temporary sheriffs,[46] was fatal to the compatibility of the system with the right to a fair hearing before an independent and impartial tribunal under Article 6 of the Convention. But fixed-term appointments are not necessarily inconsistent with the requirements of the Convention. As Lord Sutherland put it in *Clancy v Caird*,[47] dismissing an Article 6 challenge to the independence and impartiality of a temporary judge of the Court of Session: "There can be no objection per se to the appointment of judges for a fixed term, provided that during that period there is security of tenure which guarantees against interference by the executive in a discretionary or arbitrary manner."

Both as a matter of fact and law, temporary judges of the Court of Session do enjoy security of tenure during their term of office. Their independence and impartiality on that ground, at least, were therefore unimpeachable. The commissions of all temporary sheriffs, however, were revoked following *Starrs* and provision made in the Bail, Judicial Appointments etc (Scotland) Act 2000 for their replacement by a new body of part-time sheriffs.[48]

---

[43] *Mackay and Esslemont v Lord Advocate*, 1937 S.C. 860.

[44] For the approach of the ECHR to this question, see *Campbell and Fell v UK* (1984) 7 E.H.R.R. 165. The test is an objective one: whether there are grounds for reasonable apprehension that the tribunal is not independent. On that basis, the ECHR held a prison board of visitors to constitute an independent and impartial tribunal, even though its members were appointed for fixed terms of three years and were as a matter of law removable from office. The ECHR accepted, however, that as a matter of fact if not of law the government treated members as irremovable during their terms of office.

[45] 2000 S.L.T. 42.

[46] Which might raise the possibility of temporary sheriffs deciding their cases in such a way as to improve their chances of a permanent appointment.

[47] 2000 S.C. 441.

[48] Sheriff Courts (Scotland) Act 1971, s.11A (as inserted by BJA(S)A, s.7).

No judicial office is held for life any longer. For Court of Session judges, sheriffs principal and sheriffs, there is a statutory retirement age of 70 (with the possibility of extension to age 75 by way of appointment as a "retired judge"). Short of retirement, there are statutory procedures for the dismissal of judges on certain grounds. Section 95(6) of the Scotland Act provides that a Court of Session judge may be removed from office by the Queen on the recommendation of the First Minister.[49] The First Minister may only make such a recommendation if the Scottish Parliament, on a motion of the First Minister, resolves that it should be made. The First Minister may only move the Parliament so to resolve if he has received a reasoned report from a tribunal constituted under section 95(8) concluding that the judge in question is unfit for office by reason of inability, neglect of duty or misbehaviour. Where the judge in question is the Lord President or Lord Justice-Clerk, the First Minister must also consult the Prime Minister. The Scottish Parliament may impose upon him additional requirements to these if it so chooses. However, section 95(8) *requires* provision to be made by or under an Act of the Scottish Parliament for a tribunal of at least three persons, constituted by the First Minister, to investigate and report on a judge's fitness for office and for its reports to be laid before the Parliament. That provision must include provision for the constitution of the tribunal in such circumstances as the First Minister thinks fit or at the request of the Lord President, and for the appointment as chairman of a member of the Judicial Committee of the Privy Council. It may include provision enabling the suspension from office of the judge who is under investigation.

6–08   Clearly, this procedure has been designed to insulate, so far as possible, the removal of a judge from office on political grounds and to prevent its manipulation for political reasons. It borrows a number of the features of the procedure prescribed by section 12 of the Sheriff Courts (Scotland) Act 1971 for the dismissal of sheriffs principal or sheriffs. As amended by the Scotland Act, this provides that the Scottish Ministers may make an order removing a sheriff principal or sheriff from office if, after an inquiry by the Lord President and Lord Justice-Clerk, he or she is found to be unfit for office by reason of inability, neglect of duty or misbehaviour. The order of the Scottish Ministers is laid before the Scottish Parliament and is subject to annulment pursuant to a

---

[49] Prior to this, no procedure actually existed for dismissing a Court of Session judge. It was thought that, should the need ever have arisen, the procedure prescribed for the dismissal of judges of the Supreme Court of England and Wales, which also applies to Lords of Appeal in Ordinary in terms of the Appellate Jurisdiction Act 1876, s.6, would be used. According to this procedure, the Sovereign dismisses the errant judge from office following the presentation to her of an address of both Houses of Parliament.

resolution of the Parliament. The procedure for dismissing part-time sheriffs is prescribed by section 11C of the 1971 Act.[50] Responsibility for deciding whether a part-time sheriff should be removed from office (again, by reason of inability, neglect of duty or misbehaviour) is placed with a tribunal of three persons appointed by the Lord President. The tribunal must be chaired by a Court of Session judge or sheriff principal, and one of its members must be a solicitor or advocate of at least 10 years' standing. The Scottish Ministers may provide in regulations for the suspension of a part-time sheriff who is under investigation.

It is not only the security of a judge's tenure which underpins his independence. The terms of his remuneration are also relevant to the question. The Act of Settlement of 1700, which was incorporated into Scots law by the Treaty of Union, provides that judicial salaries must be "ascertained and established"—in other words, not subject to executive discretion. The remuneration of Court of Session judges, sheriffs principal, sheriffs, members of the Lands Tribunal for Scotland and the Chairman of the Scottish Land Court is reserved to Westminster by section L1 of Schedule 5 to the Scotland Act; but payment of the salaries thus fixed is charged on the Scottish consolidated fund. Parliamentary authority for the payment of judicial salaries is deemed to be permanent and does not require to be reviewed and renewed each year.[51]

JUDICIAL IMPARTIALITY

Impartiality is fundamental to the integrity of the judicial role. If a **6–09** judge has an interest of some kind in the outcome of proceedings before him, he must decline jurisdiction to decide the matter (or at least disclose his interest to the parties, so that they may decide whether he may properly sit). The great difficulty in this area, as recent case law amply illustrates, is identifying at what point beliefs and opinions personally held or expressed cross the line into disqualifying bias. Judges do not operate in a vacuum. They are human beings, with (no doubt) the same propensity for rational and irrational notions and viewpoints as the rest of us. That is not necessarily objectionable, but it undermines claims to moral and political neutrality on the part of the judiciary. Indeed some take the argument still further, contending that a judge, whether he realises it or not, will bring to bear on the performance of his

---

[50] As inserted by BJA(S)A, s.7.
[51] Note, however, that in terms of the Sheriff Courts (Scotland) Act 1971, s.11A (as inserted by BJA(S)A, s.7), part-time sheriffs are paid by the Scottish Ministers, at a rate determined by them, out of moneys earmarked for the Justice Dept of the Scottish Executive.

judicial role the values typically held by those of his class, his age, his racial, gender and educational background. And, so the reasoning runs, since judges are much of a muchness in those terms, the judiciary as a whole must be tainted by the biases of a relatively small social group.[52]

Without question, there is a certain amount of empirical truth in these observations, though the inferences drawn from them, and the solutions proposed, seem at times to part company with reality.[53] If we rightly reject as fiction the older conception of judges as oracular and remote, we ought not to stray too far in the other direction and depict them as the prejudiced defenders of an elitist social structure. As the very debate shows, however, we place a special value on the impartiality of the judiciary. It is for this reason that judges are disqualified from membership of the House of Commons and Scottish Parliament.[54] Similarly, convention requires a judge to dissociate himself from party political matters.[55]

6–10 As against that, however, it must be noted that a previous political career, whether as M.P., MSP or Law Officer, is no bar to judicial appointment, although there are likely to be situations in which a former Law Officer, at least, could not sit compatibly with Article 6 of the Convention. The Court of Session accepted as much in *Davidson v Scottish Ministers (No.2)*.[56] There, the petitioner had brought proceedings against the Scottish Ministers for an order requiring them to remove him to conditions of detention compatible with his rights under Article 3 of the Convention.[57] Central to his case was the argument that section 21 of the Crown Proceedings Act 1947[58] (which exempts the Scottish Ministers from

---

[52] Indeed it has been suggested that judicial independence is undermined by "the high degree of ideological congruence" that exists between ministers, legislators and judges, all of whom are "for the most part agreed on the fundamental features of the social order": see R. Miliband, *Socialism for a Sceptical Age* (W. W. Norton, 1995).

[53] That the judges themselves sometimes see the matter this way is suggested by the somewhat irritable tone of recent judgments dismissing challenges to the impartiality of the courts: see *e.g. Robbie the Pict v H.M. Advocate,* Appeal Court (HCJ), Mar. 13, 2003.

[54] See House of Commons Disqualification Act 1975, s.1(1)(a), and the SA 1998 s.15(1)(a). It should also be noted that senior judges, whose jobs attract life peerages, are entitled as such to sit in the House of Lords and contribute to its legislative debates. They sit on the cross benches and take no party whip.

[55] On this basis, a Court of Session judge felt obliged to resign from a committee set up by the Leader of the Opposition in 1968 to formulate Conservative policy on the constitutional future of Scotland. Subsequently, in 1977, a sheriff was dismissed from office after using his judicial office as a platform for the promotion of his political beliefs.

[56] 2002 S.L.T. 1231.

[57] The incompatibility with Article 3 of conditions at H.M. Prison Barlinnie had previously been recognised in *Napier v Scottish Ministers*, [2002] U.K.H.R.R. 308.

[58] As amended by the SA 1998, Sch.8.

the coercive jurisdiction of the court) had been overridden by the Human Rights Act.[59] His petition was dismissed at first instance, and the Extra Division subsequently dismissed his reclaiming motion and refused leave to appeal to the House of Lords. Mr Davidson thereupon petitioned the *nobile officium* of the court to set aside the interlocutors of the Extra Division as being vitiated by the participation in the decision of Lord Hardie. As Lord Advocate and principal government spokesman on the Scotland Bill in the House of Lords, Lord Hardie had moved the amendment which brought the Scottish Ministers within the scope of section 21 of the 1947 Act, and in doing so had expressed his opinion as to the legal effect of the amendment. According to the petitioner, this was sufficient to raise a legitimate doubt about Lord Hardie's objective impartiality in dealing with the arguments before the court. It was argued in response that Lord Hardie had expressed a ministerial rather than personal view, and that, in any case, his Lordship's judicial oath provided a sufficient guarantee of his impartiality in relation to the reclaiming motion. But the Second Division was unpersuaded, noting that in the jurisprudence of the European Court of Human Rights[60] the interpretation of legislation by a judge who had been involved in its enactment was viewed with disfavour. Neither was Lord Hardie's judicial oath in point. As the Lord Justice-Clerk put it:

"Lord Hardie's personal impartiality in this case is presumed; but, this being a question of public confidence in the administration of justice, we are concerned with the appearance of things. The question has to be decided from the standpoint of the onlooker rather than that of the judge."

The elevation of Law Officers to judicial office is not the only way in which judicial independence and impartiality may be compromised. Senior judges, whose jobs attract life peerages, are entitled as such to sit in the House of Lords and contribute to its legislative debates (although, as we have seen, this is set to change).[61] Concern has also been expressed that judicial independence is undermined by the regular appointment of serving judges to chair

---

[59] Or, specifically, by his right to an effective remedy for a breach of his rights. The petitioner's contention was that an order declaratory of his rights, the only remedy open to the court under the Crown Proceedings Act, was not an effective remedy for these purposes.

[60] Citing *Procola v Luxembourg* (1995) 22 E.H.R.R. 193 and *McGonnell v UK* (2000) 8 B.H.R.C. 56.

[61] See also the statement made on behalf of the judicial peers by Lord Bingham as to the proper extent of judicial participation in the legislative work of the House of Lords (n.18).

royal commissions, public inquiries and the like.[62] We have seen that judicial independence requires an appropriate degree of institutional distance to be maintained between the courts and executive. Now, it may be that the objective of appointing a judge to chair an inquiry is to "neutralise" the controversy of the matter.[63] But in some cases at least there are no politically neutral solutions.[64] For this reason, judges in other jurisdictions, including the United States and Australia, generally[65] refuse to serve on government-sponsored inquiries.

6–11   There is a broader question about the relationship between judicial impartiality and the expression of extra-judicial opinion in published writings, interviews and lectures. Since the lifting of the so-called Kilmuir Rules in 1987,[66] there has been a marked increase in activity of this sort. It reflects a sense of autonomous legitimacy not evident in the past: far from being bound to remain aloof from controversy, many if not all judges regard themselves as entitled, *as judges*, to engage in it.

But there are risks in doing so, particularly in the present, reconfigured constitutional environment. The devolution settlement and the incorporation of the Convention into national law have conferred on the judiciary a crucially important, and politically sensitive, jurisdiction that places a higher premium than ever

---

[62] Examples are legion. Among the inquiries ongoing or recently completed at the time of writing are the BSE inquiry chaired by Lord Phillips, the inquiry under Dame Janet Smith into the murders committed by Dr Harold Shipman, the Bloody Sunday inquiry under Lord Saville, and the inquiry under Lord Hutton into the circumstances surrounding the death, on July 18, 2003, of Dr David Kelly. The current Lord President, Lord Cullen, has made something of a speciality of this line of work, chairing the inquiries into the Ladbroke Grove rail disaster, the explosion of the Piper Alpha oil rig, and the Dunblane shootings.

[63] Certainly that is the thrust of Lord Phillips' argument in favour of judicial involvement in such work, to the effect that judges are the best-placed to undertake public inquiries and better able to generate public confidence in their procedures and findings.

[64] See in particular the report of Scott L.J. on the "Arms to Iraq" affair: *Report of the Inquiry into the Export of Defence Equipment and Dual-use Goods and Related Prosecutions* (HC 115 (1995–1996)).

[65] But not always. One of the most explosive inquiries of the 20th century, into the assassination of President Kennedy in 1963, was chaired by Earl Warren, the Chief Justice of the Supreme Court.

[66] The Kilmuir Rules derived from a letter sent in 1957 by the Lord Chancellor, Lord Kilmuir, to the Director General of the BBC. Their object was to discourage appearances by judges in any medium without prior clearance by the Lord Chancellor, in view of "the importance of keeping the judiciary insulated from the controversies of the day." They were widely flouted, even by Lord Kilmuir himself.

on judicial impartiality.[67] Lord Mackay adverted to this when, looking ahead to the adoption of a human rights charter in the United Kingdom and the consequent involvement of judges in "political" decision making, he remarked:

"The question which would then be asked, and to which an answer could not be postponed indefinitely, is whether the introduction of such a political element into the judicial function would require a change in the criteria for appointing judges, making the political stance of each candidate a matter of importance as much as his or her ability to decide cases on their individual facts and the law applicable to those facts. Following on from that is the question of how confidence in judicial independence and impartiality can be maintained, and whether their appointment should be subjected to political scrutiny of the sort seen in the United States."[68]

Given this, it is unsurprising that recent years should have witnessed renewed pressure for reform of the judicial appointments process. Relatedly, there has been a surge of cases involving allegations of judicial bias, which have obliged the judges to scrutinise their own conduct more closely than might have been the case in the past. The times demand what has been described as continual judicial self-definition, "whereby judges evaluate the extent to which they themselves satisfy the requirements of due process in terms of . . . independence and impartiality".[69] Consciousness of this is apparent in the case law, to which we now turn.

It is well established that where a judge has a direct pecuniary or proprietary interest, however small, in the outcome of a case before him, he is automatically disqualified from sitting.[70] Thus in *Dimes v Proprietors of the Grand Junction Canal*,[71] the Lord

---

[67] It has been argued that human rights protection, at least, does not draw the courts into matters of political controversy: the judicial role here is simply to define the sphere within which legislature and executive have a free hand. "[Rights] may not be submitted to the vote; they depend on the outcome of no elections", *per* Jackson J., *Virginia State Board of Education v Barnette* (1943) 319 US 624. But it is difficult to reconcile this view with the very real controversy ignited by the Supreme Court's own pronouncements on issues such as abortion (*Roe v Wade* (1973) 410 US 113), homosexuality (*Bowers v Hardwick* (1986) 478 US 186; *Lawrence v Texas*, Apr. 26, 2003) and affirmative action (*Califano v Goldfarb* (1977) 430 US 199; *Gratz v Bollinger*, June 23, 2003).

[68] Lord Mackay of Clashfern, quoted in R. Clayton and H. Tomlinson, *The Law of Human Rights* (Oxford University Press, Oxford, 2000), para.1.57.

[69] S. Tierney, "Constitutionalising the Role of the Judge: Scotland and the new order" in *Human Rights and Scots Law* (Boyle *et al.* eds, Hart Publishing, Oxford, 2002), p.58.

[70] See, *e.g. R. v Rand* (1866) L.R. 1 QB 230; *R. v Camborne Justices, ex p. Pearce* [1954] 1 Q.B. 41.

[71] (1852) 3 HL Cas. 759.

Chancellor was held to be disqualified from affirming a judgment of the Vice-Chancellor in favour of the canal company by virtue of his substantial shareholding in the company.

6–12   The categories of automatic disqualification were extended by the decision of the House of Lords in *R. v Bow Street Metropolitan Stipendiary Magistrate, ex parte Pinochet Ugarte (No. 2)*,[72] overturning the earlier decision of the House of Lords in which it was held by a 3:2 majority that Senator Pinochet, as a past Head of State, enjoyed no immunity from arrest and extradition in respect of alleged crimes against humanity. Lord Hoffmann (who agreed with the speeches of Lord Nicholls and Lord Steyn, but who gave no separate reasons for holding that Senator Pinochet was not entitled to immunity) turned out to be a director and chairman of Amnesty International Charity Ltd, while his wife had worked for Amnesty's International Secretariat since 1977. Amnesty International had sought, and been granted, leave to intervene in the first appeal to the House of Lords. In overturning that decision, Lord Browne-Wilkinson held:

> "[A]lthough the cases have all dealt with automatic disqualification on the grounds of pecuniary interest, there is no good reason in principle for so limiting automatic disqualification. The rationale of the whole rule is that a man cannot be judge in his own cause. In civil litigation the matters in issue will normally have an economic impact; therefore a judge is automatically disqualified if he stands to make a financial gain as a consequence of his own decision in the case. But if, as in the present case, the matter at issue does not relate to money or economic advantage but is concerned with the promotion of the cause, the rationale disqualifying a judge applies just as much if the judge's decision will lead to the promotion of a cause in which the judge is involved together with one of the parties."

In such cases, then, the maxim that justice must not only be done but must manifestly and undoubtedly be seen to be done[73] applies with its full force: disqualification is automatic and nothing more requires to be proved. If the judge proceeds to decide nevertheless, his decision cannot stand.

This rule against bias also comes into play, even though the judge is not financially interested in the outcome or otherwise acting as a judge of his own cause, where for some other reason there are grounds for suspicion about his impartiality. In *R. v Gough*,[74] the House of Lords held that in such cases there must be

---

[72] [2000] 1 A.C. 119.
[73] *R. v Sussex Justices, ex p. McCarthy* [1924] 1 K.B. 256.
[74] [1993] A.C. 646.

a "real danger" of bias. This denoted a possibility rather than a probability, and instances of it are legion. Family or other personal connections may give rise to an inference of bias,[75] as may evidence of predisposition for or against a party on the part of the judge.[76] As the Court of Appeal noted in *Locabail (UK) Ltd v Bayfield Properties Ltd*,[77] however, the "real danger" test did not command approval in other jurisdictions. The courts in Scotland[78] followed their counterparts in Australia[79] and South Africa[80] in applying a test of "reasonable suspicion" or "reasonable apprehension" of bias which, as the Court in *Locabail* conceded, "may be more closely in harmony with the jurisprudence of the European Court of Human Rights."[81] As the Human Rights Act was not in force at the time of the *Locabail* decision, the Court of Appeal were constrained to follow *Gough*. After the entry into force of the Act, however, the Court of Appeal revisited the matter and substituted for the *Gough* test the test of whether the circumstances were such as to give a fair-minded and informed observer a reasonable apprehension of a lack of impartiality on the part of the judge.[82]

Jurisdictional uniformity does not necessarily mean that cases of **6–13** alleged bias will be resolved more easily. The problem with such cases was succinctly identified by Mason J. in the High Court of Australia:

> "Although it is important that justice must be seen to be done, it is equally important that judicial officers discharge their duty to sit and do not, by acceding too readily to suggestions of appearance of bias, encourage parties to believe that by seeking the disqualification of a judge, they will have their case tried by someone thought to be more likely to decide the case in their favour."[83]

Moreover, as the Court of Appeal noted in *Locabail*, the subject of impartiality is uncommonly resistant to definition and classification.

---

[75] *Metropolitan Property Co Ltd v Lannon* [1969] 1 Q.B. 577.
[76] See, *e.g. Bradford v McLeod*, 1986 S.L.T. 244 and *R. v Inner West London Coroner, ex p. Dallaglio* [1996] 4 All E.R. 139.
[77] [2000] Q.B. 451. In fact the Court of Appeal heard four joined appeals in this case.
[78] *Doherty v McGlennan*, 1997 S.L.T. 444.
[79] *Webb v R* (1994) 181 C.L.R. 41.
[80] *Moch v Nedtravel (Pty) Ltd*, 1996 (3) S.A. 1.
[81] See, *e.g. Piersack v Belgium* (1982) 5 E.H.R.R. 169; *De Cubber v Belgium* (1984) 7 E.H.R.R. 236; *Hauschildt v Denmark* (1989) 12 E.H.R.R. 266; and *Kingsley v UK* (2002) 35 E.H.R.R. 10.
[82] *Director General of Fair Trading v Proprietary Association of Great Britain* [2001] H.R.L.R. 17, approved by the House of Lords in *Porter v Magill* [2002] 2 A.C. 357.
[83] *Re JRL, ex p. CJL* (1986) 161 C.L.R. 342.

While declining to list the factors which might give rise to an apprehension of bias, however, the court was at pains to stress that it could not:

> "conceive of circumstances in which an objection could be soundly based on the religion, ethnic or national origin, gender, age, class, means or sexual orientation of the judge. Nor, at any rate ordinarily, could an objection be soundly based on the judge's social or educational or service or employment background or history, nor that of any member of the judge's family; or previous political associations; or membership of social or sporting or charitable bodies; or Masonic associations; or previous judicial decisions; or extra-curricular utterances (whether in textbooks, lectures, speeches, articles, interviews, reports or responses to consultation papers); or previous receipt of instructions to act for or against any party, solicitor or advocate engaged in a case before him, or membership of the [professional body]."

Yet the tenor of this passage is not easily reconciled with a number of authorities on what constitutes disqualifying bias, among them one of the four *Locabail* appeals, *Timmins v Gormley*. There, the court allowed the appeal of the defendant in a personal injuries action against the judgment of Mr Recorder Braithwaite Q.C. The decision of the recorder, a personal injuries practitioner working primarily on behalf of claimants, was struck down and a retrial ordered on the basis of four articles written by him on issues of personal injury practice which were said to demonstrate a pre-disposition to claimants. Not without misgiving, the Court of Appeal agreed, although it expressly held that the articles were not couched in inappropriate language and did not exhibit such a lack of balance and proportion as to indicate a blinkered approach. However, "anyone writing in an area in which he sits judicially has to exercise considerable care not to express himself in terms which indicate that he has preconceived views which are so firmly held that it is not possible for him to try a case with an open mind."

6–14 This was a caution Lord McCluskey might have observed before publishing a newspaper article to mark his retirement from the Court of Session bench.[84] Following his retirement, Lord McCluskey had been appointed to sit as a retired judge, and was sitting in that capacity in the High Court of Justiciary when on January 28 it dismissed devolution issue minutes lodged by four persons convicted of offences under the Customs and Excise Management Act 1979. When the hearing before the High Court

---

[84] *Scotland on Sunday*, Feb. 6, 2000.

continued in March, the petitioners submitted that, in view of the tenor of the comments made in his article about the Convention,[85] Lord McCluskey could not be regarded as impartial in relation to issues of human rights and that both he and the other judges of the court of which he was a member were disqualified from hearing any further part of their appeal. The issue was passed to a differently constituted bench, which upheld the arguments of the petitioners, set aside the High Court's interlocutors of January 28 and ordered that any further proceedings in the appeal be heard by a new bench.[86]

---

[85] To the effect that the ECHR would provide "a field day for crackpots, a pain in the neck for judges and legislators, and a goldmine for lawyers." Lord McCluskey had expressed the same view when the Canadian Charter of Rights was adopted in 1986.

[86] *Hoekstra v H.M. Advocate (No.2)*, 2000 S.L.T. 605.

CHAPTER 7

LOCAL GOVERNMENT

Introduction

7–01   It is an unusual parliamentary session, at Westminster and Holyrood alike, that does not see the enactment of at least one measure of greater or lesser significance relating to local government. This rash of legislation reflects a process aptly described by Professor Loughlin as a "politicisation and juridification" of relations between central and local government.[1] If that relationship is less characterised, now, by antagonism on the one hand and resistance on the other, it is nevertheless profoundly different from the traditional model, wherein the essential autonomy of local government was taken not only as given but as necessary to the health of the constitution.[2] Loughlin identifies four key features of that traditional model. The first was multifunctionality: local authorities were charged with the performance of a diverse range of functions, allocated to them not necessarily because, on an abstract economic analysis, they were the institutions best placed efficiently to perform them, but because their role was shored up by the features of local accountability, via the election of local councillors, and a degree of financial independence through their ability to raise local taxes. In keeping with these features of multifunctionality, representation and financial autonomy was the fourth: the conferment of broad discretionary powers on local authorities, which left them largely "free to decide on the precise pattern on the services which they delivered and even to redefine the nature of the services they provided."[3] Local authorities were not, in this scenario, merely local agents for the implementation of

---

[1] M. Loughlin, "The Restructuring of Central-Local Government Relations" in *The Changing Constitution* (4th ed., Jowell and Oliver ed., Oxford University Press, Oxford, 2000), Ch.6.
[2] This viewpoint was captured by the *Report of the Royal Commission on Local Government in England*, Cmnd.4040 (1969) ("the Redcliffe-Maud Report") in the following terms: "It is only by the combination of local representative institutions with the central institutions of Parliament, Ministers and departments, that a genuine national democracy can be sustained."
[3] Loughlin, *op.cit.*, p.140.

central government policy. Within their accepted spheres of competence they enjoyed a substantial degree of freedom. Why then did this model break down?

At risk of oversimplification, the root cause was money. The share of national wealth consumed by local government increased five-fold in the period between 1890 and 1970. Over the same period, local authorities lost responsibility for income-generating trading activities, such as the local provision of utilities, whilst assuming responsibility for the delivery of welfare state services such as public housing and education. The costs associated with this, since they could not be met locally, required to be met by central government grants. As the financial dependency of the localities on the centre increased, so the latter could legitimately claim to take a closer interest in what local authorities were doing with the funds. For much of the post-war period, characterised by economic growth and a general political consensus on the virtues of the welfare state, the emerging tensions could be concealed. When, in the 1970s, economic growth faltered, the tensions became inescapably apparent. The Labour governments of the time sought to address the public expenditure crisis through the well-established methods of consensus and dialogue, with little if any success. The election of the Conservative government in 1979 marked the real watershed in central-local government relations, for this was a government committed not only to controlling public expenditure but also to a "rolling back" of the state in all its guises and a fundamental reappraisal of the assumptions which had underpinned the welfare state. The unwillingness of local government to co-operate with the centre in the pursuit of its objectives led central government to resort to what was, after all, always at its disposal: the sovereignty of Parliament. Disregarding the conventional restraints and understandings which had previously characterised central—local government relations, the Conservative administrations of the eighties and nineties progressively replaced the facilitative legislative framework within which local government was accustomed to working with a prescriptive, regulatory framework that radically altered the role of local authorities. Conflict was prevalent, but resolved less and less via administrative mechanisms and more and more through the courts.[4] If necessary, whole tiers of local government could simply be swept away.[5] Short of that, local

---

[4] As witness, among the more prominent examples, *Bromley LBC v Greater London Council* [1983] 1 A.C. 768; *Nottinghamshire C v S of S for the Environment* [1986] A.C. 240; and *Hazell v Hammersmith and Fulham LBC* [1991] 2 A.C. 1.

[5] As with the abolition of the Greater London Council and the metropolitan borough councils in England in 1986, and, in Scotland, with the replacement of the regional and district councils by a single tier of unitary local authorities pursuant to the Local Government etc (Scotland) Act 1994.

authorities could be, and were, subjected to a battery of new duties in the interests of efficiency, some of which required the wholesale transfer of local authority functions to the private sector,[6] others of which imposed on local government a range of "market-mimicking" disciplines.[7] The central government vision for local government involved "a formal separation between service specification and service provision, requiring service provision to be achieved through market competition, and altering the governmental function to the residual one of planning only for services that the market cannot provide."[8] It was an impoverished vision, and one understandably resented by local authorities of all political stripes.[9] As the House of Lords Select Committee on Relations between Central and Local Government noted in 1996, its pursuit had damaged if not destroyed the older idea of mutually tolerant partnership between the centre and the localities:

> "This we believe will severely impair the ability of local government to respond to changing economic and social circumstances. [The Conservative legislation] will seriously dilute the legitimacy of local authorities, their institutional, administrative and political capacity and their ability to offer effective local services. They will also seriously diminish the accountability and responsiveness of government to the community at a time of growing social and economic stress."

Not for nothing did the Select Committee entitle its report *Rebuilding Trust*.[10]

7–02　　Many of the recommendations made by the Select Committee were picked up by the Labour Party in advance of its election victory in 1997, and informed its first major White Paper on local government.[11] But Labour was in no sense bent on restoring the *status quo ante*. Explicitly or implicitly, its programme for local government accepts many of the elements of the Conservative reforms. It remains wedded to strict financial controls. Under the guide of "modernising" the management, performance and

---

[6] As with the compulsory competitive tendering regime, introduced, initially, by the Local Government, Planning and Act 1980 and subsequently, in fortified form, by the Local Government Act 1988.

[7] See, *e.g.* Local Government Act 1988, s.35, which required district auditors in Scotland to undertake "value for money" audits to ensure that local authorities had made "proper arrangements for securing economy, efficiency and effectiveness in [their] use of resources."

[8] Loughlin, *op.cit.*, p.157.

[9] For an account of this process, see S. Jenkins, *Accountable to None: The Tory Nationalisation of Britain* (Hamish Hamilton, London, 1995).

[10] HL 97 (1995–96).

[11] *Modern Local Government: In touch with the people*, Cm.4014 (1998).

accountability of local authorities, it has confined the discretion of local authorities in relation to their own internal organisation and has introduced new, overarching codes on ethical standards. It insists on local authorities working in partnership with a variety of other agencies, whether public, private or voluntary in character. In the latest round of legislative initiatives, then, there remains a strong sense that central government still cannot bring itself to trust local authorities.

Whatever the ills bedevilling local government in Scotland, however, it lies within the competence of the Scottish Parliament, now, to address them. All matters relating to local government, and most of the functions of local authorities, fall within the devolved competence of the Parliament as defined by Schedule 5 to the Scotland Act 1998, with the single exception of the franchise in local government elections. In anticipation of devolution, the Secretary of State for Scotland established a Commission on Local Government and the Scottish Parliament, charged with considering how to build the most effective relations between local government and the Scottish Parliament and Executive, and how local authorities might best make themselves responsive and democratically accountable to the communities they serve. The Commission, chaired by Sir Neil McIntosh, reported in June 1999.[12] Its recommendations ranged widely, including the establishment of formal working relationships between local authorities on the one hand and MSPs and the Scottish Executive on the other, the conferment on local authorities of a statutory power of general competence, the introduction of a four-year term for local authorities and a system of proportional representation for local elections, the establishment of an independent inquiry into local government finance, and various changes to the way in which local authority business is conducted. Many of these have been, or are to be, taken forward in some way, and are discussed further below. For the present, it suffices to note that the Scottish Parliament, in the exercise of its power to establish subject committees of its own choosing, elected to establish a Local Government (and Transport) Committee, and beyond that has enacted no fewer than six Acts of the Scottish Parliament directly relating to local government at the time of writing.[13] Perhaps inevitably, given that the devolved institutions are yet in their infancy, and given also the fact that the

---

[12] *Moving Forward: Local government and the Scottish Parliament* (1999) ("the McIntosh Report").

[13] Namely, Ethical Standards in Public Life etc (Scotland) Act 2000, Scottish Local Authorities (Tendering) Act 2001, Scottish Local Government (Elections) Act 2000, Housing (Scotland) Act 2001, Scottish Public Services Ombudsman Act 2002 and Local Government (Scotland) Act 2003. During the course of the 2003–07 Parliament, the Scottish Executive is to introduce legislation providing for a system of proportional representation in local government elections.

Scottish Executive is Labour-led, these initiatives have much in common with similar legislation enacted at Westminster (although there are significant differences of approach in some respects). It remains to be seen whether, in the future, central–local government relations in Scotland, and indeed models of local government, will develop along lines distinct from those which obtain south of the border.

STRUCTURE OF SCOTTISH LOCAL GOVERNMENT

7–03 The present structure of local government in Scotland is the product of the Local Government etc (Scotland) Act 1994, which took full effect on April 1, 1996. Prior to that, Scottish local government was organised on two basic levels, with nine regional councils and 53 district councils (together with three all-purpose islands councils representing Orkney, Shetland and the Western Isles). The regional/district split was founded in the recommendations of the Royal Commission chaired by Lord Wheatley, which was appointed to inquire into the structure of local government in Scotland and which reported in 1969.[14] The touchstones of the Wheatley Report were that the structure of local government should be such as to enable local authorities to play "a more important, responsible and positive part in the running of the country", equipping them to deliver public services effectively, ensuring proper accountability for the exercise of their powers to the local electorate and securing, so far as possible, the participation of local people in decision-making. With these objectives in mind, Wheatley rejected the idea of a single tier of all-purpose local authorities in favour of a two-tier system, wherein regional authorities would take responsibility for major strategic services[15] and district councils would take charge of more "local" services.[16] Little altered,[17] the Wheatley recommendations were enacted into law by the Local Government (Scotland) Act 1973, much of which remains in force, and took effect in May 1975.

In 1991, however, the Secretary of State for Scotland announced the government's intention to abolish this structure and replace it with a single-tier system of unitary authorities. In keeping with its

---

[14] Report of the Royal Commission on Local Government in Scotland, Cm.4150 (1969) ("the Wheatley Report").

[15] Identified by Wheatley to include structure planning, roads and transportation, water and sewerage, education, social work and housing.

[16] Identified to include building and development control, environmental health and some licensing functions.

[17] The principal changes made to the Wheatley recommendations involved increasing the proposed numbers of district and regional councils, and allocating housing to the district councils.

general approach to local government, the government indulged in only minimal consultation on its proposals: two consultation papers were published,[18] but represented less ideas for discussion than a statement of legislative intent. At all events, widespread opposition to the government's plans counted for nought, and the proposals were duly enacted in the 1994 Act.[19] The net result was the present, single layer of 32 unitary local authorities.[20] Certain functions were removed from local authority control altogether.[21] Arrangements were also put in place for the establishment of joint boards and other forms of joint arrangements between the new authorities. Such arrangements are not new—the 1973 Act makes provision for them, as amended by the 1994 Act—but the 1994 reorganisation brought about a significant expansion in their use, principally because many of the new authorities are too small in size to assume individual responsibility for particular functions in their areas. In some cases, joint arrangements are mandatory under the 1994 Act.[22] In others, it is for the local authorities to decide

---

[18] *The Structure of Local Government in Scotland: The case for change* (HMSO, June 1991) and *The Structure of Local Government in Scotland: Shaping the new councils* (HMSO, Oct. 1992), together with a parallel consultation (of sorts) on the establishment of new water and sewerage authorities, *Investing in our Future* (HMSO, Nov. 1992).

[19] As Jean McFadden notes, this had the effect, presumably unintended, of depriving the government of one of its main arguments against devolution, namely that Scotland would be over-governed. This was not merely an argument against the addition of a Scottish Parliament to the existing tiers of Westminster and European Parliaments and regional, district and community councils. It was also a matter of doubt whether a Scottish Parliament would be able to co-exist with Strathclyde RC, a body representing more than half of Scotland's population and having an annual budget in excess of £2 billion. At a stroke, the 1994 Act did away with this potential rival to a future Scottish Parliament: see J. McFadden, *Stair Memorial Encyclopaedia, Local Government* (6th Reissue), para.447.

[20] Which left Scotland "in terms of average population per elected council . . . about the most locally under-represented nation in Western Europe": see D. Wilson and C. Gane, *Local Government in the United Kingdom* (3rd ed., Macmillan, London, 1998).

[21] Water and sewerage functions were vested in three new water authorities pursuant to Pt II and Schs 7–11 of the Act (and see now the Water Industry (Scotland) Act 2002, which transferred the functions of the three water authorities to a single body, Scottish Water). Responsibility for the Children's Reporter system passed to the new Scottish Children's Reporter Administration pursuant to Pt III and Sch.12 of the Act; and responsibility for the promotion of tourism transferred to new area tourist boards established and appointed by the Secretary of State (or, now, the Scottish Ministers).

[22] The Scottish Ministers have the power under s.27 of the 1994 Act to establish joint boards to discharge the functions of two or more valuation authorities. Responsibility for structure planning under the Town and Country Planning (Scotland) Act 1997 is to be exercised in the context of "structure plan areas" designated by the Scottish Ministers, which may cover the area of more than one planning authority. In that event, the planning authorities concerned are to perform their function in accordance with such joint arrangements as they may

whether they wish to enter into joint arrangements, but it should be
noted that where the Scottish Ministers consider that any functions
should be discharged jointly by particular authorities, and that
those authorities have failed to make any, or satisfactory, arrangements for the joint discharge of those functions, they may by order
establish a joint board for those purposes after consulting the
authorities in question.[23] The provisions in relation to joint
arrangements are of interest, for they (or more accurately, the
inevitable and acknowledged extension in their use) sit oddly with
the rationale for abolishing the dual tiers of local government in
the first place. The government's case for shifting to a single tier of
unitary authorities rested on the claims that the two tiers created
confusion in the public mind about who was responsible for what,
encouraged duplication of functions and hence waste, and were apt
to generate friction between local authorities and hence delay and
inefficiency. It is not obvious how the institution of a single tier of
unitary authorities coupled with a proliferation of joint arrangements was supposed to address any of these problems, if problems
they were. On the contrary, one would have thought that, if
anything, the new structure would simply make matters worse. Not
only that but "smaller councils tend to feel dominated by their
larger colleagues, [joint arrangements] tend to be officer-led rather
than member-led, and since members are appointed by their
councils rather than directly elected, they lack democratic legitimacy and direct accountability to the electorate."[24]

LOCAL AUTHORITIES—MEMBERSHIP AND ELECTIONS

7–04   Unless disqualified by virtue of the Local Government (Scotland)
Act 1973 or any other enactment, a person is entitled to stand for
election as a member of a local authority if he has attained the age
of 21, is a British subject, citizen of the Irish Republic or a citizen
of the European Union, and is not subject to any legal incapacity,
provided (this in contrast to parliamentary elections) he can show a
relevant local connection. That is established where the person is a

adopt under ss.56–58 of the 1973 Act: see, generally, 1994 Act, s.33. S.34 of the
1994 Act makes provision for the amalgamation of new local authority areas into
new police areas, out of which joint police boards are formed to supervise the
functions of the eight Scottish police forces. Like provision is made by s.36 of the
1994 Act in relation to fire services.

[23] See s.20 of the 1994 Act, which inserts new ss.62A–62C into the 1973 Act for
these purposes.

[24] J. McFadden, *Stair Memorial Encyclopaedia, Local Government* (6th Reissue),
para.447. For some, this was interpreted simply as part of the government's
general strategy to undermine and diminish local government as much as
possible.

registered local government elector in the area of the authority, or the occupier (whether as owner or tenant) of any land or other premises in the area during the whole of the 12-month period preceding the election, or has his principal or only place of work in the area during that same period, or is resident in the area throughout that time.[25] This general entitlement to seek election is then subject to a number of grounds of disqualification. A person whose estate has been sequestrated by a court in Scotland or who has been adjudged bankrupt elsewhere than in Scotland is disqualified,[26] as is a person who has been convicted anywhere in the British Islands[27] of a criminal offence carrying a sentence of not less than three months' imprisonment at any time in the five years preceding his nomination or election,[28] and a person who is disqualified under Part III of the Representation of the People Act 1983.[29] More controversially, a person is disqualified if he or a commercial partner of his holds any paid office or employment with the authority, other than the office of convenor or depute convenor, or any other place of profit in the authority's gift or disposal.[30] The rule is intended to preserve the important distinction between members and officers of local authorities, but, as has been said, it has the effect of excluding from membership of their own local authority not only senior managers and policy advisers but also staff in technical or manual occupations.[31] More broadly still, a person who holds a "politically restricted post" in *any* local authority in Great Britain is disqualified from becoming a member of any other local authority.[32] Where it is claimed that a disqualified person is, or is seeking to become, a member of a local authority, proceedings may be brought before the sheriff principal

---

[25] Local Government (Scotland) Act 1973, s.29.

[26] 1973 Act, s.31(1)(b) and (2).

[27] That is, anywhere in the UK, the Republic of Ireland, the Channel Islands or the Isle of Man.

[28] 1973 Act, s.31(1)(c).

[29] s.31(1)(d). This includes disqualification following conviction in respect of corrupt or illegal election practices.

[30] s.31(1)(a). A like disqualification extends to those employed by a joint committee or joint board whose expenses are defrayed wholly or in part by the authority.

[31] See C. M. G. Himsworth, *Local Government Law in Scotland* (T. & T. Clark, Edinburgh, 1995), p.21.

[32] Local Government and Housing Act 1989, s.1. This provision is based on the recommendations of the Widdicombe Committee of Inquiry into Local Authority Business, Cm.9797 (1986) and survived a challenge to its compatibility with ECHR, Art.10, in *Ahmed v UK* (1995) 20 E.H.R.R. 278. See, generally, Himsworth, *Local Government Law in Scotland, op.cit.*, pp.76–82 and J. McFadden, *Stair Memorial Encyclopaedia, Local Government* (6th Reissue), paras 245, 256; for criticism, see G. Morris, "Local Government Workers and Rights of Political Participation: Time for a change" [1998] P.L. 25.

under section 32 of the 1973 Act. The participation of a disqualified person in any proceedings of the council or its committees does not, however, affect the validity of any decisions taken
therein.[33]

As to the timing of local government elections, the Scottish
Local Government (Elections) Act 2002 amends section 5(3) of the
1994 Act, substituting a four-year term for local councils for the
three-year term which previously obtained.[34] Not only that, but the
Act also provides for the synchronisation of local government and
Scottish parliamentary elections.[35] At present, the electoral system
used is the familiar first-past-the-post method, but the Scottish
Executive is to introduce legislation in the course of the 2003–07
Parliament providing for a proportional system in time for the next
tranche of elections in 2007.[36]

LOCAL GOVERNMENT POWERS

7–05 Local authorities have no inherent powers to undertake functions
of their own choosing. They are creatures of statute, and everything
that they do must find its source in law.[37] This is the *ultra vires* rule,
and the restraint that it imposes on local authorities should not be
lightly discounted. It is true that many local government powers
and functions are cast in broad discretionary terms, but even where
this is so the courts will insist that the powers are not exercised for
purposes ulterior to those envisaged by the statute,[38] or on the
basis of irrelevant considerations,[39] or in an unreasonable
manner.[40]

---

[33] 1973 Act, ss 33 and 43.
[34] In accordance with the recommendation of the McIntosh Report.
[35] Perhaps not unwisely, for the claims of local government to democratic legitimacy
can appear somewhat thin when local election turnouts habitually fail to rise
above 25% of the local electorate. It is hoped (and the evidence of the 2003
elections appears to bear it out, although even then turnout barely cleared 50%)
that synchronisation will induce a greater number of voters to vote in local
elections.
[36] Again in accordance with the recommendation of the McIntosh Report. A
member's bill providing for the introduction of proportional representation in
local government elections was rejected by the Scottish Parliament in 2003.
[37] And not merely in the words of a statute alone. The common law grounds for
judicial review—illegality, procedural impropriety and irrationality—provide a
further level of legal constraint, as do such other jurisprudential innovations as
the extension to local authorities of a fiduciary duty to local taxpayers in the use
and management of their funds: see *Bromley LBC v Greater London Council*
[1983] 1 A.C. 768, followed in Scotland by the Inner House in *Commission for
Local Authority Accounts in Scotland v Stirling DC*, 1984 S.L.T. 442.
[38] *McColl v Strathclyde RC*, 1983 S.C. 225.
[39] *Gerry Cottle's Circus Ltd v Edinburgh DC*, 1990 S.L.T. 235.
[40] *Kelly v Monklands DC*, 1986 S.L.T. 169.

An important aspect of local authorities' functions, which may be seen as distinct from their role in providing, or facilitating the provision of, public services, relates to their powers to make subordinate legislation for their areas.[41] The nature of these measures varies. At one end of the spectrum, there are rules that are primarily administrative in character, such as orders made for the regulation of public processions under section 63 of the Civic Government (Scotland) Act 1982, structure and development plans drawn up under the Town and Country Planning (Scotland) Act 1997 and local housing strategies adopted under section 89 of the Housing (Scotland) Act 2001. The adoption of such rules, plans and strategies may be authorised or required by statute, and statute (or regulations made thereunder) may similarly prescribe or guide their content. Even non-statutory guidance or statements of policy published by a local authority may have a rule-like effect in certain circumstances, as where, for example, it provides the foundation for a legitimate expectation in judicial review proceedings, or for a finding of maladministration by the Scottish Public Services Ombudsman where it is said that the local authority has failed to follow its own criteria. At the other end of the spectrum are the numerous statutory provisions authorising local authorities to make byelaws for their areas.[42] In addition to the more specific powers contained in such statutes as the Civic Government (Scotland) Act 1982 and the Local Government and Planning (Scotland) Act 1982, there is a general byelaw-making power in section 201 of the Local Government (Scotland) Act 1973, which provides that a local authority "may make byelaws for the good rule and government of the whole or any part of its area and for the prevention and suppression of nuisances therein." It should be noted, however, that quite apart from the limitations imposed on a local authority's byelaw-making power by the *ultra vires* rule, any byelaw adopted by the authority must first be confirmed by the Scottish Ministers (or such other confirming authority as the relevant legislation may specify). At least one month before the local authority applies to the Scottish Ministers for confirmation, it must give public notice of its intention to do so[43] and advise members of the public of their

---

[41] This power is distinct again from the power of local authorities to promote or oppose private legislation. By virtue of s.82(1) of the Act 1973 a local authority may promote or oppose any private legislation where it is satisfied that it is expedient to do so, and may defray the expenses incurred in so doing. The decision to promote or oppose must be authorised by resolution of the council adopted in accordance with s.82(2) of the 1973 Act. For private legislative procedures, see paras 4–15—4–18.

[42] See, generally, Himsworth, *Local Government Law in Scotland, op.cit.*, pp.46–51; J. McFadden, *Stair Memorial Encyclopaedia, Local Government* (6th Reissue), paras 276–301.

[43] Normally by depositing copies of the byelaw at local authority offices and advising the public of their location in a local newspaper.

right to object to the byelaw proposed.[44] The Scottish Ministers may, having considered any objections received, confirm the byelaw, with or without modifications, or refuse to confirm it.[45]

7–06 Where byelaws are duly adopted, the responsible local authority is obliged to review them at intervals not exceeding 10 years, to ensure that they are updated or revoked as necessary.[46] Where the authority proposes to revoke any byelaw, it must comply with the procedures as to advance publicity prescribed by section 202B of the 1973 Act. All local authorities are required to keep a register of byelaws, containing a description of each byelaw and any offences or penalties attaching to it, its dates of confirmation and coming into force and the date on which it was last renewed. The register is open to public inspection free of charge, although a reasonable charge may be made for providing certified copies of byelaws.[47]

The Civic Government (Scotland) Act 1982, as well as amending the rules and procedures relating to byelaws, also introduced a new form of subordinate legislation known as "management rules".[48] Unlike byelaws, management rules may be made by a local authority without the further approval of the Scottish Ministers, although the local authority must give public notice of its intention to adopt particular rules and accord to objectors the right to make representations before bringing the rule into effect (if this is what the authority decides to do). But management rules may only be made for the purpose of regulating the use of, and the conduct of persons on or in, "land or premises which are owned, occupied or managed by the authority or are otherwise under its control and to which the public have access, whether on payment or not."[49] Where an "authorised officer" of the local authority reasonably believes that a person is breaching or has breached the terms of a management rule, he may exclude or expel that person from the land or premises. The local authority may make exclusion orders effective for up to one year in the case of persistent offenders. Failure to comply with an exclusion order, or with an instruction to leave (or not to enter) land or premises, is a criminal offence.

7–07 Over and above their functionally specific powers and duties, local authorities have a variety of powers that may be described as ancillary or subsidiary.[50] Some of these are reasonably precise in their terms, such as the power conferred by section 83(3) of the

---

[44] Failure to follow these procedures would itself entitle the Court of Session to reduce the byelaw.
[45] See, generally, 1973 Act, s.202.
[46] 1973 Act, s.202A.
[47] 1973 Act, s.202C.
[48] Civic Government (Scotland) Act 1982, ss 112–118.
[49] 1982 Act, s.112(1).
[50] For a comprehensive survey, see J. McFadden, "Local Government" in *Stair Memorial Encyclopaedia*, (Butterworths, London, 6th Reissue), paras 315–356.

1973 Act to make contributions to charitable funds, appeals and the like. Others are (at least on their face) more permissive, though even the latest additions to the legislative corpus do not go so far as to confer on local authorities a power of general competence.[51] One such power is contained in section 69 of the 1973 Act.[52] This provides that "a local authority shall have the power to do anything (whether or not involving the expenditure, borrowing or lending of money or the acquisition or disposal of any property or rights) which is calculated to facilitate, or is conducive or incidental to, the discharge of any of their functions." It is, in fact, nothing more than a statutory statement of the common law position in relation to the *ultra vires* rule,[53] and was for a long time widely understood as a generous enabling power. That belief was exploded by the decision of the House of Lords in *Hazell v Hammersmith and Fulham London Borough Council*.[54] There, the local authority had entered into "interest rate swap" contracts with financial institutions.[55] It purported to do so on the basis of section 111 of the Local Government Act 1972, assuming that swaps could legitimately be entered into as being incidental to their borrowing powers. The House of Lords disagreed.[56] It was for a local authority, acting prudently in accordance with its fiduciary duty to local taxpayers,[57] to determine at the time of borrowing money whether it would be able to afford interest payments thereon.

---

[51] Such as was recommended not only by the McIntosh Report but also by the Wheatley Report before that.

[52] The corresponding provision in England and Wales, the Local Government Act 1972, s.111, is in identical terms.

[53] As Lord Selborne L.C. put it in *Attorney-General v Great Eastern Ry* (1880) 5 App. Cas. 473 at 478, the doctrine of *ultra vires* "ought to be reasonably, and not unreasonably, understood and applied, and whatever may fairly be regarded as incidental to, or consequential upon, those things which the legislature has authorised ought not (unless expressly prohibited) to be held by judicial construction to be *ultra vires*."

[54] [1992] 2 A.C. 1. In Scotland, see to similar effect *Morgan Guaranty Trust Co. of New York v Lothian RC*, 1995 S.C. 151.

[55] It was far from being alone in this. Following the decision of the House of Lords in *Hazell v Hammersmith and Fulham LBC*, [1992] 2 A.C. 1, over 200 actions were commenced, both by local authorities and banks, to recover sums paid under contracts held in *Hazell* to be *ultra vires* the local authorities.

[56] As Lord Templeman explained in *Hazell*, at 24, "the transactions in the swap market which are now impugned were not carried out in order to enable the council to borrow or to enable the council to choose to borrow at a fixed rate rather than at a variable rate or vice versa. The transactions were undertaken in the hope that the burden of interest payable in respect of borrowings [legally undertaken] by the council would be mitigated by profits from swap contracts whereby the council successfully forecast movements in interest rates. If the council swapped from a fixed interest to a variable interest rate, the council gained if, after the swap, interest rates went down. The council lost if, after the swap, interest rates rose."

[57] See n.37.

Speculating on the capital markets was neither conducive nor incidental to that function. Interest rate swap contracts were therefore *ultra vires* and void.[58]

If the message of *Hazell* were not clear enough, the House of Lords reinforced it in *R. v Richmond London Borough Council, ex p. McCarthy & Stone (Developments) Ltd.*[59] The local authority purported to charge the developer for responding to inquiries relating to speculative development or redevelopment proposals. The developer argued that the authority had no power, either under section 111 or any other provision, to levy the charge. The House of Lords agreed, holding that the giving of informal pre-development advice was not a "function" of the local authority to which the charge could be described as incidental.[60] This is not to say that the *ultra vires* rule always operated against the interests of local authorities. In the *Crédit Suisse* cases, the Court of Appeal held that agreements between the local authorities and the bank, whereby the authorities undertook to guarantee the borrowings of companies established by the authorities in purported performance of their functions, were *ultra vires* and unenforceable by the bank.[61] But the ramifications of these decisions went beyond the immediate financial consequences for local authorities and banks. Previously, local authorities had been generally regarded as pre-eminently low risk counterparties by financial and commercial institutions. That perception changed sharply for the worse, putting at risk the drive by central government—meaning the Conservative administrations of the time and their Labour successors—to encourage (if not force) the contracting-out of service delivery and other forms of public/private partnership.

7–08   The government has responded to this on a number of fronts. One of the first enactments of the new Labour government was the Local Government (Contracts) Act 1997 which, while it does not abrogate the *ultra vires* rule in its application to local government contracts, significantly mitigates the risks associated with it. Its aim, in the words of the minister responsible for piloting it through the House of Commons, was "to make explicit the power of a local authority to enter into contracts of the sort envisaged in public/private partnership schemes . . . and to provide a safe harbour, by protecting contractors and lenders, if an authority is later found to have entered into an arrangement which is invalid."

---

[58] For the consequences of this decision on the law of unjust enrichment, see *Morgan Guaranty Trust Co. of New York v Lothian RC*, 1995 S.C. 151 and (in England) *Kleinwort Benson Ltd v Lincoln CC* [1999] 2 A.C. 349.

[59] [1992] 2 A.C. 48.

[60] See in Scotland the decision, on similar facts and grounds, of Lord Clarke in *SPH Ltd v City of Edinburgh Council*, June 25, 2003 (not yet reported).

[61] *Crédit Suisse v Allerdale BC* [1997] Q.B. 306 and *Crédit Suisse v Waltham Forest LBC* [1997] Q.B. 362.

Section 1(1) makes clear the power of a local authority to enter into contracts with others for the provision of, or in order to make available, assets or services or both (whether or not together with goods) for the purposes of, or in connection with, the discharge of their functions. Where a local authority enters into such a contract, it has the power also to enter into a contract with a financial institution, where the latter makes a loan or provides any other form of finance to a party to the primary contract other than the local authority itself.[62] The Act then establishes a certification mechanism in respect of such contracts. Provided the certification requirements[63] are met by the local authority (and they are not especially rigorous), the validity of the certified contract cannot be questioned in any private law proceedings. It remains possible in public law proceedings—judicial or audit review—for the court to hold the contract unlawful, but the court may order that the unlawful contract continue to have effect. Even if the contract is set aside, agreed contractual "discharge terms" will apply to determine compensation due, unless these too are *ultra vires* (or none have been agreed). In that event, statutory damages terms apply. In the context of certified contracts, therefore, the risks of invalidity are placed firmly on the shoulders of local authorities.

But contract is only one means through which local authorities may perform their functions. While the incoming government was not, as noted above, of any mind to reverse all the Conservative reforms relating to public service delivery, it was prepared to think about the matter in less rigid terms. In Scotland, this found expression in the Local Government in Scotland Act 2003, which proclaims itself in its long title as an Act "to provide anew about the way in which local authorities discharge their functions."[64] The three main parts of the Act make provision for the achievement by local authorities of "best value" in their delivery of public services, the introduction of a duty of "community planning" and for a power to advance community well-being. The duty to secure best value is a duty to pursue "continuous improvement in the performance of [local authority] functions",[65] which in turn is defined in terms of maintaining an appropriate balance between the quality of performance and the costs of performance, both to the authority and to persons paying, fully or partly, for the services provided. In striking that balance, the authority must have regard to efficiency,

---

[62] Local Government (Contracts) Act 1997, s.1(2).

[63] 1997 Act, s.3(2)(a)–(g).

[64] The equivalent legislation south of the border is the Local Government Act 1999 and the Local Government Act 2000, Pt I. In many respects, the 1999 Act, 2000 Act and 2003 Act simply take forward, and give legislative force to, what was already taking place as a matter of local government or audit practice.

[65] 2003 Act, s.1(1) and (2).

economy, effectiveness and equal opportunities.[66] At the same time, Part 1 relaxes certain of the restrictions imposed on local authorities' contracting powers[67] and on their powers to enter into trading arrangements for the provision of goods and services.[68] Moreover, with the formal introduction of best value, the compulsory competitive tendering regime contained in the Local Government Act 1988 is abolished.[69] It is to be noted, however, that whereas the CCT regime only ever applied to around one-fifth of local authority functions, the duty to secure best value applies across the board. To that extent alone, its implications for local authorities are the more profound.

7–09   Monitoring compliance with section 1 falls to the Controller of Audit and the Accounts Commission for Scotland.[70] On receipt of a report from the controller alleging failure by a local authority to comply with its duties, the commission may direct the controller to carry out further investigations or state its findings, with or without a preliminary hearing. On receipt of the commission's findings, the authority concerned is obliged to consider those findings at a meeting of the council and to notify the commission of any remedial action it proposes to take.[71]

Part 2 makes provision in relation to community planning. It is the duty of each local authority to initiate, maintain and facilitate a "community planning process".[72] The object of this process is to institutionalise consultation between the local authority, all public bodies responsible for providing public services in its area, and such community bodies and other bodies or persons as appropriate, in planning for the provision of, and providing, those public services.[73] Apart from local authorities themselves, health boards,

---

[66] 2003 Act, s.1(3) and (4). Not only that, but the local authority must also perform its functions in relation to best value in such a way as to contribute to the achievement of sustainable development. What price Utopia?

[67] Namely, the restrictions contained in the Local Government Act 1988, s.17(5)(a), (b) and (d), which prohibit local authorities from taking into account specified "non-commercial considerations" when deciding whether and on what terms to enter into contracts. It should be noted that these restrictions are not abrogated entirely, as was contended for in some quarters, but only in the circumstances defined in s.7(2)(a)–(c) of the 2003 Act. The restrictions in respect of non-commercial considerations elsewhere in s.17(5) of the 1988 Act are unaffected.

[68] 2003 Act, ss 8 and 9. Note that in terms of the Local Authorities (Goods and Services) Act 1970, s.1M, a local authority is obliged, before entering into any trading arrangement thereunder, to consider whether the arrangement will be likely to improve or promote the well-being of either or both of its area and persons living in that area.

[69] 2003 Act, s.60(1)(e) and (f).

[70] 2003 Act, s.3.

[71] 2003 Act, s.5. For the further enforcement powers vested in the Scottish Ministers, see *infra*.

[72] 2003 Act, s.15(1).

[73] For definition of "public bodies" and "community bodies", see 2003 Act, s.15(4).

joint police boards, joint fire services boards, chief constables, Scottish Enterprise, Highlands and Islands Enterprise and Strathclyde Passenger Transport Executive are required to participate in community planning.[74] Under section 19, local authorities and their community planning partners may request the Scottish Ministers to establish by order corporate bodies to "co-ordinate and further" community planning.[75] Monitoring compliance with the duty of community planning is shared between the local authorities themselves,[76] the Scottish Ministers[77] and the Accounts Commission for Scotland.[78]

Part 3 concerns the power to advance well-being, the nearest the legislation comes to conferring a power of general competence.[79] Under section 20(1), a local authority has the power "to do anything which it considers is likely to promote or improve the well-being of (a) its area and persons within that area; or (b) either of those." The power includes power to incur expenditure; give financial assistance to any person; enter into agreements or arrangements with any person; co-operate with, facilitate or co-ordinate the activities of any person; exercise functions on behalf of any person; or to provide staff, goods, materials, facilities, services or property to any person.[80] On the face of this, there would seem to be few forms of innovation in service delivery that

---

[74] 2003 Act, s.16(1). This list may be amended by the Scottish Ministers. As Dr Kenneth Meechan notes in his annotations to the 2003 Act, the omission from the list of community councils is curious, although presumably they would qualify as "community bodies" for the purposes of s.15.

[75] It is not, as Dr Meechan says, obvious what such bodies are intended for. While s.19(4) of the 2003 Act exempts such bodies from the normal rule whereby statutory functions cannot be delegated in the absence of express statutory authority to do so, the responsible Scottish Minister did not envisage corporate bodies taking responsibility for the substantive delivery of services.

[76] Presumably the discharge of their duty to report from time to time under s.17(1) of the 2003 Act is intended to provide an opportunity for self-assessment.

[77] In addition to their power to issue guidance about community planning under s.18 of the 2003 Act and to adopt regulations governing the form, content and frequency of reports provided under s.17(1), the Scottish Ministers have the power under s.17(8) to call for reports and information from local authorities about the implementation by them of community planning, together with their wider enforcement powers under Pt IV: discussed *infra*.

[78] The Accounts Commission for Scotland has the power under s.1(1) of the Local Government Act 1992 to direct the publication of information about local authorities' standards of performance in such a way as to "facilitate the drawing of conclusions" about the discharge of their community planning functions.

[79] Pursuant to the enactment of the power to advance well-being, essentially obsolete powers, including aspects of the power contained in s.83 of the Local Government (Scotland) Act 1973 (the general power of local authorities to incur expenditure) and s.171A–171C of that Act (the power of local authorities to promote economic development in their areas) are repealed: see 2003 Act, s.60(1).

[80] 2003 Act, s.20(2).

would now fall foul of the *ultra vires* rule. But it is not quite that generous. First, section 22(1) provides that nothing in section 20 is to be taken as enabling a local authority to do anything which, by virtue of a "limiting provision", it is unable to do.[81] Secondly, a local authority may not by virtue of section 20 do anything which would "unreasonably duplicate" something which a person other than the local authority is obliged or empowered to do pursuant to its statutory functions. In short, then, Part 3 restates, albeit in relaxed form, the *ultra vires* doctrine. Perhaps for that reason, it is not attended by the usual raft of provision for ministerial monitoring and audit: whether a local authority has acted properly within the scope of its powers under section 20 will be, as ever, a question for the courts. Or so one would have thought; but there is a surprise in store in Part 4.

Part 4 makes overarching provision for enforcement of the duties created by Parts 1 to 3. Among other things, it confers on the Scottish Ministers the power to issue "preliminary notices" and, thereafter, "enforcement directions" where it appears to the Scottish Ministers that a local authority has "significantly exceeded its power under section 20."[82] As with the enforcement powers conferred on the Scottish Ministers in relation to best value, accounting and community planning by sections 23 and 24, this is open to the immediate objection that it allows the Executive to dictate to a democratically elected council what it must do and how it must do it. But the objection to the powers under sections 26 and 27 goes further. They purport to authorise the Scottish Ministers to issue binding determinations on questions of *vires*, which are questions of law, and a local authority to which an enforcement direction is given is under a duty to comply with it.[83] Now let us unwrap this a little. In issuing an enforcement direction, the Scottish Ministers may require the local authority to take such action as is specified in the direction "being action calculated to remedy or prevent the recurrence of its significant excess of power."[84] Suppose the action required were the cessation of a particular arrangement into which the authority had entered and

---

[81] "Limiting provision" is defined as a provision in any enactment which expressly prohibits or prevents a local authority from doing something or which limits its powers in that respect. Mere absence of positive authority is not to be taken as a prohibition in this sense: s.22(2) and (3).
[82] 2003 Act, ss 26 and 27.
[83] 2003 Act, s.27(7).
[84] 2003 Act, s.27(1).

the payment of compensation to its partners therein.[85] The response of the local authority, one would have thought and hoped, would be along the following lines: if our act or decision was *ultra vires*, it is void *ab initio* and nobody has any right to compensation in respect of it unless they can qualify a cause of action in delict[86] or have a remedy in the law of unjust enrichment; and if it was *intra vires*, there is no legal basis for your requirement at all. Presumably if a local authority were to resist an enforcement notice in this way, it would fall to the Scottish Ministers to bring proceedings for an order requiring the authority to comply with its duty. But the right of the Scottish Ministers must depend on the validity of their own direction, and the court could not decide that without inquiring into the nature of the local authority's alleged breach of section 20. In that regard, moreover, a court is not confined to finding a given act or decision to be *ultra vires* only when the excess of competence is "significant". Put bluntly, sections 26 and 27 are inexplicable.[87] They are an affront to the most elementary understanding of the separation of powers, and if they are not to be erased from the statute book it is at least to be hoped that they remain unused.

It becomes apparent that, if there is much in the 2003 Act that is **7–10** genuinely enabling, it falls a long way short of according autonomy to local authorities within the limits of the law. At all times, local authorities are required to have regard to guidance and regulations promulgated by the Scottish Ministers under the Act. The choices made by local authorities in the exercise of their functions in relation to best value, community planning and the promotion of well-being may exceptionally be subject to judicial oversight, but they are *routinely* subject to ministerial oversight and audit control, both of which are reinforced by the rigorous reporting requirements laid on local authorities by the Act. In significant respects, the regime contained in the 2003 Act is more prescriptive and interventionist than the regime contained in the Local Government Acts 1999 and 2000 south of the border. Is this acceptable because

---

[85] Dr Meechan, who appears to harbour similar doubts about the intent and effect of ss.26 and 27 of the 2003 Act, suggests that the purpose of the enforcement power might be to "rescue" the act of the local authority, if only to the extent of securing compensation for those who have relied to their detriment on its presumed validity, from the consequences of a judicial decision to the effect that the act is *ultra vires* and void *ab initio*. That may be its intent. But it does not resolve the issue that a given act is either *ultra vires* or it is not, and that is a question not for ministers but for a court.

[86] *e.g.* for negligent misstatement (see *Ministry of Housing and Local Government v Sharp* [1970] 2 Q.B. 223) or misfeasance in public office (see *Three Rivers DC v Bank of England (No. 3)* [1996] 3 All E.R. 558; *Micosta SA v Shetland Islands Council*, 1986 S.L.T. 193).

[87] Note that there is no comparable power vested in Ministers of the Crown under the Local Government Act 2000, Pt I.

the centre is now more local? No doubt, *via* the Scottish Executive and Accounts Commission and thence the Scottish Parliament, all of this may be said to enhance the accountability of local authorities for the performance of their functions to the public. But there is a strong sense here that this accountability is but a by-product of, and secondary to, the consolidation of central control and supervision over the activities of local government in Scotland.

ORGANISATION OF LOCAL AUTHORITY BUSINESS

7–11 Within the UK government and Scottish Executive, executive decisions are taken by ministers, who answer for their decisions to Westminster or the Scottish Parliament. The organisation of local authority business is quite different: "there is no source of executive authority other than the council itself."[88] But while the functions of local authorities are vested in the council for each local government area, it would obviously be impracticable for the full council to take every decision. Except where statute provides otherwise, therefore, the council may delegate its functions to committees, sub-committees, joint committees[89] or officers of the councils, though not to a single councillor.[90]

Local authorities are accorded a good deal of latitude as to how they carry out their business. They are required to hold a first meeting within 21 days of a local election, at which they must elect a convenor and, if they wish, a depute convenor.[91] Thereafter, it is

---

[88] Report of the Committee of Inquiry into the Conduct of Local Authority Business, Cm.9797 (1986). para.5.2. ("the Widdicombe Report").

[89] Bearing in mind that committees must reflect the political balance of the full council.

[90] See, generally, 1973 Act, s.56. Local authorities are not permitted to delegate major financial decisions, defined by s.56(6) as functions with respect to determining the level of council tax for their area and borrowing money. Note also s.82 of the 1973 Act, which requires the decision to promote or oppose private legislation to be taken by the full council. A number of statutory provisions also require certain reports to be considered by the full council, in the interests of publicity: see, *e.g.* Ethical Standards in Public Life etc (Scotland) Act 2000, s.18, which requires the written findings of the Standards Commission to be considered at a meeting of the full council; and Local Government in Scotland Act 2003, s.5, which requires a local authority, on receipt of a report by the Accounts Commission for Scotland on its compliance with the duty to secure best value, to consider the report at a meeting of the council and notify the commission of the remedial steps it proposes to take. Interestingly, like provision in the Local Government (Scotland) Act 1975, s.29, in relation to consideration of reports by the Commissioner for Local Administration in Scotland is repealed by the Scottish Public Services Ombudsman Act 2002 and replaced with a rather weaker mechanism for redressing maladministration.

[91] Local Government etc (Scotland) Act 1994, s.4. There is no statutory definition of the functions of a convenor or depute convenor, other than in para.3 of Sch.7 to the 1973 Act, which states that the convenor (or depute convenor) shall chair meetings of the council. At meetings where a vote is taken, the convenor or depute convenor has a casting vote in the event of a tie.

largely up to individual authorities how often they hold meetings.[92] It is also, subject to the restrictions already noted, for each authority to decide whether and to what extent it wishes to delegate functions to committees and officers, and on the particular model of delegation it wishes to adopt. There is no longer any requirement that particular committees be established. Again, it is for the council to provide for the conduct and procedures of committee meetings through standing orders of its own choosing.[93]

At various times, thought has been given to the adoption of different models of organising local authority business. The Maud Committee recommended that each local authority should appoint a management board of five to nine councillors, to which all other committees would be answerable.[94] The Widdicombe Committee considered three different models—the management board, the ministerial model and the separation of powers model based on an elected or appointed executive—but found none of them to be sufficiently advantageous to justify a departure from prevailing practice. The government revisited the issue again in its 1998 White Paper.[95] In England and Wales, this was followed by a further round of consultation on new forms of governance for local authorities,[96] which led in turn to the provision contained in Part II of the Local Government Act 2000.[97] This provides for the adoption by English and Welsh local authorities of "executive arrangements" under which certain functions of the local authority become the responsibility of the executive.[98]

Section 11 gives authorities a choice as to the form of their executive arrangements between three options: an elected mayor, acting with two or more councillors appointed to the executive by him (the "mayor and cabinet" model); a councillor elected as executive leader by the council, acting with two or more councillors

---

[92] Apart from the requirement to hold a first meeting within 21 days of the election, the only other requirement is that a local authority should hold as many meetings as it thinks necessary. Sch.7 to the 1973 Act makes provision in relation to the calling and conduct of meetings, but broadly it is for each council to regulate its own practice by way of standing orders. The usual pattern is for meetings of the full council to be held every four or six weeks, with a summer recess and Christmas break.

[93] 1973 Act, s.62. The Local Government and Housing Act 1989, s.20, confers on the Scottish Ministers the power to prescribe standing orders to be adopted by local authorities, but the power has never been used. For the legal effect of standing orders, see *R. v Hereford Corp., ex p. Harrower* [1970] 1 W.L.R. 1424.

[94] Report of the Committee of Inquiry into the Management of Local Government, Cm.4840 (1969) ("the Maud Report").

[95] *Modern Local Government: In touch with the people*, Cm.4014 (1998).

[96] *Local Leadership, Local Choice*, Cm.4298 (1999) and *A Stronger Voice for Local People* (Welsh Office, 1999).

[97] Separate provision was made in relation to London in the Greater London Authority Act 1999.

[98] Local Government Act 2000, s.10.

appointed by him or by the authority (the "leader and cabinet" model); or an elected mayor acting with an officer of the authority appointed by the council (the "mayor and council manager" model). Sections 13 to 17 then make provision for the denomination of executive functions. Consulting in Scotland, the McIntosh Commission found little support for any of these alternatives to the status quo.[99] As the commission noted, however, if Scottish local authorities do not have formal executives, majority groups constitute something very similar. In effect, many decisions of a local authority are in no sense thrashed out in public meetings, but agreed in private meetings of the controlling group on the council. The McIntosh Committee, therefore, recommended that councils should review their procedures with a view to ensuring that policy proposals and matters for decision are subject to open debate, and that the council is able to scrutinise the majority group and hold it properly to account for its decisions.[1] The Scottish Ministers have chosen to take this forward not by introducing legislation along the lines of Part II of the Local Government Act 2000, but by requiring councils to review their organisational structures and appointing an advisory panel to assist them in that task. The panel reported in 2001.[2] All but three of Scotland's 32 local authorities undertook reviews of their internal structures, and all but three of those made some changes, involving either a streamlining of their existing committee systems, the introduction of formal executives, or the adoption of devolved structures of decision-making.

7–12   So far as the organisation of local authority business in Scotland is concerned, then, statutory regulation is relatively light. Two areas into which statute does intrude, however, relate to public access to local authority meetings and to the policing of standards of conduct.[3] As to the first, statutory rights of access to council meetings were accorded initially only to the press.[4] Substantially extended rights of access, for press and public, were provided for by the Public Bodies (Admission to Meetings) Act 1960, which applied to meetings of the full council and to education committees; this was extended again by the Local Government (Scotland) Act 1973 to all committee (but not sub-committee) meetings. The current law is contained in the Local Government (Access to Information) Act 1985, which inserted into the 1973 Act a new Part IIIA and a new Schedule 7A. It requires, first, that public notice of the time and place of all meetings, including

---

[99] *Moving Forward: Local government and the Scottish Parliament* (1999).
[1] *ibid.*
[2] *Report of the Leadership Advisory Panel* (2001) ("the McNish Report").
[3] In both cases, the statutory regimes constitute further expression of the central desire to control and confine local authorities.
[4] Local Authorities (Admission of the Press to Meetings) Act 1908.

meetings of committees and sub-committees, be posted at the offices of a local authority at least three clear days in advance or, that failing, at the time the meeting is called. Secondly, it provides that meetings of the council and any committee and sub-committee shall be open to the public. This general rule is then qualified in a number of ways. The council (or committee) has the power to exclude where necessary to prevent or suppress disorderly conduct.[5] It may also, acting by formal resolution, exclude the public from a meeting during consideration of an item of business that is likely to involve disclosure of "exempt information".[6] There is no provision for challenging a resolution to exclude, although it is in principle subject to judicial review and in one case the Court of Appeal apparently assumed that the exclusion of the public pursuant to an unlawful resolution would render invalid the subsequent proceedings and any decision taken therein.[7] Section 50A(2) of the 1973 Act further provides that the public *must* be excluded from a meeting during consideration of an item of business that is likely to involve disclosure of confidential information.[8] The right of access to meetings is then reinforced by provision for access to documents relating to meetings. Before a meeting, copies of the agenda, the report for the meeting and any background papers must be made available for public inspection at the offices of the local authority.[9] A reasonable number of copies of the agenda and reports must be made available at the meeting itself for use by members of the public,[10] and after the meeting copies of the minutes, the agenda and any reports provided to members must be retained for six years and made available for public inspection.[11] All this accounted for, it should also be noted

---

[5] 1973 Act, s.50A(8).
[6] 1973 Act, s.50A(4). The categories of exempt information are defined in Sch.7A, and include information relating to individual employees, tenants, clients and other recipients of benefits from the authority; information concerning contracts of the authority; information relating to the prevention or investigation of crime; and legal advice given to the authority. "Information" is defined to include "an expression of opinion, any recommendations and any decision taken: s.50K(1).
[7] *R. v Liverpool CC, ex p. Liverpool Taxi Fleet Operators' Association* [1975] 1 All E.R. 379, a case involving the 1960 Act.
[8] "Confidential information" has a special meaning for these purposes, being confined by s.50A(3) of the 1973 Act to information provided by a government department on terms which forbid its disclosure to the public, and information the disclosure of which is prohibited by or under any enactment or by order of the court.
[9] 1973 Act, s.50D.
[10] 1973 Act, s.50B.
[11] 1973 Act, s.50D. Where the minutes fail to provide a fair and coherent record of the proceedings, on account of removal of any references to "exempt information", the authority is required instead to make available a summary version of the record of the meeting. Background documents must also be retained and made available for inspection, but only for a period of four years following the meeting.

that the Freedom of Information (Scotland) Act 2002 will, when it enters fully into force, impose on local authorities extensive new statutory duties in relation to the disclosure of information held by them, both as a matter of routine publication and on request.[12]

7–13 As to the probity of local councillors, the old patchwork of provision for controlling standards in public life has largely been replaced by the Ethical Standards in Public Life etc (Scotland) Act 2000.[13] The Prevention of Corruption Act 1906 extended (and extends) to local councillors, and certain other species of unethical behaviour constitute criminal offences under the Local Government (Scotland) Act 1973.[14] Beyond that, the 1973 Act together with the Local Government and Housing Act 1989 made provision for a register of interests, and section 31 of the 1989 Act authorised the Secretary of State (or, post-devolution, the Scottish Ministers) to adopt a code of conduct by which all councillors undertake to be bound. The regulatory gap is obvious: on the one hand, a number of criminal offences dependent on the criminal standard of proof; on the other, a code breach of which carries no formal sanction other than anything the member's party, the authority or the local electorate might happen to mete out. In its Third Report, the Nolan Committee on Standards in Public Life described the situation as wholly insufficient to secure public confidence in the probity of local government, and recommended the adoption of a national code of ethical standards to be enforced at local level.[15]

The matter being devolved, the Scottish Executive took over responsibility for consulting on these proposals, and came up with a framework for ethical standards differing from the Nolan recommendations in two important ways. First, it extended the scope of the code beyond local government to include also the plethora of "devolved public bodies". Secondly, it rejected the idea of local enforcement in favour of a national standards commission, charged with investigating complaints concerning breaches of the new codes of conduct. This framework is reflected in the 2000 Act.[16] The Scottish Ministers are charged with issuing a mandatory code of conduct for local councillors, including provision about the registration and declaration of their interests and their ineligibility to

---

[12] The Freedom of Information (Scotland) Act 2002 is considered in detail in Ch.9. It is an Act of some complexity and may have significant resource implications for local authorities (not least since the Scottish Ministers have already made clear that no further central funding will be made available to assist authorities in compliance with the Act).

[13] In England and Wales, less onerous provision is made in the Local Government Act 2000, Pt III.

[14] See, *e.g.* s.38(2), which makes it a criminal offence to fail to declare an interest in a contract.

[15] Third Report of the Committee on Standards in Public Life, *Standards of Conduct in Local Government in England, Scotland and Wales* (July 1997).

[16] See, generally, D. Cobb, "Shutting the Door or Cleaning the Stable? The Ethical Standards in Public Life etc (Scotland) Act 2000", 2001 S.L.T. (News) 205.

participate in council business affecting those interests,[17] together with a model code of conduct for members of devolved public bodies containing a mixture of mandatory and optional provisions so that individual public bodies have some scope for tailoring the model code to suit their particular circumstances.[18] Every local authority and devolved public body is required by section 7 to set up, maintain and make available for public inspection a register of members' interests. Section 8 and Schedule 1 then provide for the establishment of the Standards Commission for Scotland and the remainder of Part 2 is devoted to the conduct of investigations where breaches of the codes of conduct are alleged to have taken place.

Section 9 and Schedule 2 provide for the appointment of a Chief **7–14** Investigating Officer (CIO),[19] who takes responsibility for the initial investigation of complaints made to the commission. The commission may issue general directions to the CIO relating to the performance of his functions, but may not direct him as to how he conducts particular investigations.[20] Investigations must be carried out in confidence, so far as possible, and should normally be completed within three months.[21] The CIO has the same powers as the Court of Session to require the attendance and examination of witnesses and the production of documents,[22] although no one may be compelled to give evidence or produce documents that he could not be compelled to give or produce in civil proceedings in the Court of Session. Therefore it might be open for a witness to claim, say, confidentiality or privilege in relation to particular documents. Conceivably, the CIO could treat such a claim as obstruction, which entitles him to certify the matter to the Court of Session. The Court of Session may in turn treat the matter as a contempt of

---

[17] Ethical Standards in Public Life etc (Scotland) Act 2000, s.1. "Interests" are defined by s.1(8) to include "pecuniary and non-pecuniary interests", in which respect the regime contained in the 2000 Act is stricter than that which MSPs have seen fit to apply to themselves in terms of the Code of Conduct for Members of the Scottish Parliament, compliance with which now falls to be supervised in part by a statutory commissioner and in part by the Standards Committee of the Parliament and the Parliament itself: see the Scottish Parliamentary Standards Commissioner Act 2002 and above, paras 4–45—4–46.

[18] 2000 Act, s.2. Devolved public bodies are required to submit their individual codes of conduct for the approval of the Scottish Ministers within time-limits stipulated by order made under s.3.

[19] The CIO may not be a member of the commission itself, or of a local authority, joint board, joint committee or devolved public body.

[20] 2000 Act, s.10.

[21] Where it appears that the investigation will take longer to complete, the CIO must notify the commission, the individual subject to the investigation and the relevant authority or body of that fact: 2000 Act, s.12(5).

[22] "Documents" includes information held by means of a computer or in any other electronic form: 2000 Act, s.13(5).

court.[23] On conclusion of an investigation, it is for the CIO to decide whether or not to report to the Standards Commission.[24] If he is minded to report that the subject of the investigation has breached the applicable code of conduct, he must first give the subject a copy of his proposed report and accord him an opportunity to make representations thereon.[25] But it should also be noted—here again in marked contrast to the ethical regime MSPs have adopted as sufficient for themselves—that the CIO may or, if so directed by the commission, shall submit an interim report on an investigation in progress, and that the commission may on receipt of such a report suspend the member concerned from office for a period not exceeding three months (which may, however, be renewed).[26] The commission may only exercise the power of suspension where satisfied that the further conduct of the investigation is likely otherwise to be prejudiced or (more broadly) that it would be in the public interest to do so. The commission is not required to hold a hearing before imposing a suspension, although the subject of the interim report must be given an opportunity to make representations on its contents.[27]

---

[23] 2000 Act, s.13(3). Similar powers to certify non-compliance with directions are conferred on the Scottish Information Commissioner by the Freedom of Information (Scotland) Act 2002. In both cases, the difficulty for the individual concerned is that the primary judgment on the legal question of whether a claim to withhold evidence or documents is well-founded is made by commissioner or CIO, as the case may be, both of whom are in a very real sense party to the issue they are charged with deciding and neither of whom is a court, even though they are given certain powers of a court. Given the quasi-criminal nature of contempt of court, the Court of Session should not be quick to stigmatise as contemptuous an advised refusal to give evidence or produce documents. Seen in that light, it may be that the certification mechanism will serve rather as a means of securing an authoritative judicial decision on the question whether a claim to withhold evidence is made out than as a means of procuring the conviction and punishment of a person who asserts, rightly or wrongly, a legal right to withhold that evidence.

[24] 2000 Act, s.14.

[25] On the principle of procedural fairness recognised in, *e.g. Re Pergamon Press Ltd* [1971] Ch. 388 to the effect that, even though an investigator's report is not dispositive of an issue, its publication may nonetheless be harmful to the interests of the subject thereof, who should accordingly have the chance to see the report and make representations in advance of its release.

[26] 2000 Act, s.21.

[27] There is a right of appeal to the sheriff principal against, inter alia, a suspension following the submission by the CIO of an interim report, though not, it would appear, against subsequent decisions by the commission to renew a suspension. The latter would however be judicially reviewable, as indeed may an initial suspension, since the right of appeal in that respect is available only on the grounds that the commission has acted unreasonably (presumably in the *Wednesbury* sense). The fact that an alternative remedy is open to a petitioner may indeed exclude judicial review, but only where it is reasonable to expect the petitioner to have had recourse to the alternative remedy. If the individual

Where the CIO submits a final report under section 14 of the Act, the commission may decide to take no further action, direct him to conduct further investigations or hold a hearing. If a hearing is held, it must be conducted by at least three members of the commission, and the individual whose conduct is being considered is entitled to be heard, either in person or through a representative (legal or otherwise); but that apart, the procedure to be followed at the hearing is for the commission itself to determine.[28] The commission has the power to require the attendance of any person to give evidence and the production of documents, and is expressly authorised to examine witnesses on oath. Failure to attend a hearing, give evidence or produce documents, without reasonable excuse, is a criminal offence.[29] At the conclusion of a hearing, the members of the commission must state their findings in writing and provide copies to the subject of the inquiry, the council or body concerned, any other person the commission considers should receive a copy, and any other person who pays a "reasonable charge" for a copy.[30] The findings, adverse or otherwise, must be considered at a full meeting of the council.

Where the commission's verdict is that the applicable code of conduct has been breached, it has a number of possible sanctions at its disposal. It may censure the member concerned, but otherwise take no action; suspend that person, for a period not exceeding one year, from all or specified meetings of the council or body; or (in the case of a councillor) disqualify him from being, or

---

wishes to challenge his suspension on grounds other than unreasonableness (*e.g.* procedural impropriety or breach of his Convention rights), the right of appeal is effectively worthless.

[28] 2000 Act, s.17.

[29] 2000 Act, s.17(7). Again, however, a person cannot be compelled to give evidence or produce documents that he could not be compelled to give or produce in civil proceedings in the Court of Session. The legislation therefore places the individual in the same (indeed, in a worse) dilemma as alluded to above (n.24): if he refuses to give evidence or produce documents in the (presumably advised) belief that he is under no legal duty to do so, he places himself at risk of criminal prosecution and conviction. It may be that, if an issue of this sort arose in the course of a hearing before the commission, an application could be made to the Court of Session for a declarator as to whether the person concerned is entitled to withhold the evidence sought (here, the certification mechanism does not obtain). At all events, while there is no doubt something to be said for conferring on the commission the powers necessary to secure ethical standards in public life, it is not obvious that the objective justifies placing individuals (and not merely individuals who are the subject of an investigation) at risk of criminal liability.

[30] 2000 Act, s.18. The section makes no provision for releasing the report in confidence or in redacted form, eve though s.17 permits the commission to conduct hearings in private if it considers that this would be in the public interest.

being nominated for election as, or being elected as a councillor, for a period of up to five years.[31] A person who is found to have contravened a code of conduct and/or upon whom a sanction is imposed under section 19 may appeal to the sheriff principal within 21 days of the relevant decision.[32] The grounds for appeal, in the case of an appeal against a finding of breach of the code, are that the commission's finding was based on an error of law; that there was procedural impropriety in the conduct of the hearing; that the commission has acted unreasonably in the exercise of its discretion; or that the facts found to be proved by the commission do not support its decision. The grounds for appeal in the case of an appeal against the imposition of a sanction are narrower: that the sanction was excessive, or that the commission has acted unreasonably in the exercise of its discretion. In the first case, the sheriff principal may confirm or quash the verdict of the commission, or quash the decision and remit the matter to the commission for reconsideration. In the second case, he may confirm or quash the sanction, or quash it and either substitute a different sanction or remit the matter to the commission. There is a further right of appeal from the decision of the sheriff principal to the Court of Session.

7–15   This short survey of modern local government law in Scotland reveals one salient fact. Only in one respect (that is, in relation to the internal organisation of local authority business) have the Scottish Ministers, and indeed the Scottish Parliament, accorded any real choice and autonomy to local authorities. In every other respect, the "juridification" of local government, if not its "politicisation", has continued post-devolution and may even be said to have accelerated.[33] Not only that, but the new legislation suffers from a number of flaws. It is not merely the width of the ministerial and audit powers that is objectionable (actually or potentially). There is also evidence of a failure, in providing for the enforcement of the new legal regimes, to appreciate the differences between executive or regulatory powers and powers more properly described as judicial, the exercise of which should remain the province of the courts. Used sparingly, the battery of new controls need not provoke undue conflict between local government on the one hand and the Scottish Executive and its allies in the

---

[31] 2000 Act, s.19. It is worth noting that both disqualification and suspension under s.21 could present problems for a local authority in terms of securing the necessary political balance on its committees, and could even deprive a majority group of its overall control of the council.

[32] 2000 Act, s.22.

[33] As we have seen, south of the border the approach to such matters as ethical standards, best value and community planning at least has been less doctrinaire than that adopted in Scotland.

enforcement process on the other. The fact remains that the controls exist, and have been imposed at the behest of an Executive which in political terms may be said to be more broadly sympathetic to the position of local government. Such a happy congruence may not always obtain.

CHAPTER 8

EUROPE

EVOLUTION OF THE EUROPEAN UNION

8–01   What has evolved into the European Union today was originally a product of the post-war period of reconstruction and reconciliation. That found expression in a number of intergovernmental initiatives, such as the signing and ratification of the European Convention on Human Rights under the auspices of the Council of Europe in 1951 and the establishment of the Organisation for European Economic Co-operation.[1] But the initial steps towards European *integration* were taken with the establishment in 1952 of the European Coal and Steel Community (ECSC) pursuant to the Treaty of Paris.[2] The distinctive characteristic of the ECSC was that it was not merely an intergovernmental organisation, acting by the unanimous agreement of its six founder members,[3] but a supranational body with independent institutions having power to bind the member states.[4] Its purpose was to develop a common market in coal and steel in the six member states, to which end the Treaty of Paris established a High Authority, the main executive institution with decision-making power and responsibility for implementing the aims of the Treaty; an Assembly, made up of delegates from national parliaments, with supervisory powers; a Council, consisting of one representative from each member state; and a Court charged with the interpretation and application of the Treaty.

---

[1] From 1961, the Organisation for European Co-operation and Development (OECD).

[2] The ECSC was given a life span of 50 years in its founding Treaty, which expired in July 2002. In Sept. 2000, the Commission submitted a draft decision to the Council on the transfer of ECSC funds to the European Community, to be used for research in sectors related to the coal and steel industries. For reasons of legal certainty, it was deemed preferable to provide for this through a Protocol annexed to the Treaty of Nice in 2001.

[3] Namely, France, the Federal Republic of Germany, Italy, Belgium, the Netherlands and Luxembourg.

[4] For which very reason the UK declined to participate.

The next integrationist initiative, for a European Defence Community, foundered on French anxieties about German rearmament. This did not stifle the integrationist project, but merely deflected it towards the sphere of economic relations.[5] The six ECSC member states were able to agree on plans for the establishment of a European Atomic Energy Community (Euratom) and a European Economic Community (EEC), both as provided for by Treaties signed at Rome in 1957. The EEC Treaty adroitly avoided references to political integration (which had sunk the EDC Treaty) in favour of an explicitly economic focus: its aims included the establishment of a common market and common customs tariff, the progressive approximation of the economic policies of the member states, increasing stability and raising living standards, the abolition of internal barriers to trade and the attainment of undistorted competition.[6] It provided for the establishment of a Council of Ministers and an executive institution named the European Commission, although the EEC was to share the Assembly and the Court of Justice set up under the ECSC Treaty.[7]

The European Communities were a conspicuous success, a fact not lost on the United Kingdom, which joined the European Free Trade Area in 1959, twice applied to join the Communities only to meet with a French veto, and which finally acceded to the Treaties on January 1, 1973.[8] As the Communities grew and matured, however, their more or less exclusively economic objectives came in for increasing criticism. Despite certain tentative steps towards the creation of social and other dimensions to the Community in the seventies—including the first direct elections to the European Parliament in 1979—it was to be some years before a "federalising logic"[9] was to win through. It should not however be forgotten that in a very real sense, European integration provided the inspiration

---

[5] S. Weatherill and P. Beaumont, *EU Law* (3rd ed., Penguin, London, 1999), p.3.

[6] The EEC Treaty also provided for the progressive harmonisation of member states' fiscal and social policies and the gradual co-ordination of national economic and monetary policies. Granting the relevance of all of these to the functioning of a common market, they are nonetheless closer to what many would regard as an irreducible core of "sovereign" powers, the attributes of nation states; here as elsewhere, the seeds of future tension between (in broad terms) integration and intergovernmentalism were sown.

[7] The 1965 Merger Treaty rationalised the institutional structure of the three Communities, so that with effect from 1967 the same institutions administered each of the Communities, although they continued in existence as distinct entities. The Merger Treaty was repealed and replaced, substantially unchanged, by the Treaty of Amsterdam in 1997.

[8] Ireland and Denmark joined that same year; Greece in 1981; Spain and Portugal in 1986; and Austria, Finland and Sweden in 1995. As we shall see, the EU is now poised for a major expansion into central and eastern Europe, which will almost double the present number of member states.

[9] Detected, and deplored, by the French President, General De Gaulle, in the 1960s.

and rationale for the Community, and even while progress on political integration stalled the "federalist" project was advanced in other ways, perhaps most importantly through the jurisprudence of the European Court of Justice.[10]

8–02   From the mid-1980s, however, integration through political processes began to accelerate. The Single European Act 1986, which embodied the first significant revision of the founding Treaties and committed the member states to a strict timetable for completion of the "single European market" by the end of 1992, was crucial to the revival of integrationist momentum. It introduced new legislative procedures designed to enhance the role of the European Parliament, gave the Parliament a power of veto over the accession of new member states, and provided for the establishment of a new Court of First Instance to assist the European Court of Justice. It provided for qualified majority voting in the Council of Ministers in areas which had previously required unanimity, and extended the competence of the Community to such areas as economic and monetary union, social policy, social and economic cohesion and the environment.[11]

The adoption of the Single European Act and an unashamedly integrationist Commission under the presidency, from 1985, of Jacques Delors, ushered in a period of genuine dynamism for the Community.[12] The direct consequences of this new momentum were an agreement on the achievement of economic and monetary union (EMU)[13] and a decision to couple discussion of EMU with discussion of political union at an intergovernmental conference. The product of that conference was the Treaty on European Union signed at Maastricht in 1992.[14] Laying the foundations of the European Union involved both amendment of the existing Treaties and provision for new Union competences; and the Treaty that emerged from the intergovernmental conference was not to everybody's taste. It established a "three pillar" structure for the European Union, with the Communities[15] forming the first pillar, a

---

[10] See P. Pescatore, "Direct Effect: An infant disease of Community law" (1983) 8 E.L.Rev. 155.

[11] In fact, areas in which the Community institutions had already asserted a competence, but without a compelling legal base in the Treaties for doing so.

[12] So much so that Margaret Thatcher was prompted to attempt to recall the Community to what she saw as its market-based credentials in her famous Bruges speech in 1988.

[13] A process from which, thus far, the UK (in common with Denmark and Sweden) has held aloof. The third stage of EMU was completed with the introduction of Euro notes and coins on Jan. 1, 2002.

[14] The Maastricht Treaty entered into force in 1993, having survived initial rejection by the people of Denmark in a national referendum, troubled progress through the British Houses of Parliament, and a challenge before the German Federal Constitutional Court to the constitutionality of its ratification.

[15] That is, the EEC (officially renamed the European Community), Euratom and the ECSC.

common foreign and security policy forming the second and co-operation on justice and home affairs forming the third. This unwieldy edifice embodies the tension at the heart of the European Union between integration and intergovernmentalism. The first, Community pillar is, as ever, genuinely supranational, a "new legal order of international law"[16] which binds the member states in ever-widening areas. The second and third pillars, on the other hand, are "more like the familiar creations of international law, not sharing the institutional structure, law-making processes or legal instruments of the Community pillar, largely beyond the jurisdiction of the European Court of Justice and lacking the key Community law characteristics of supremacy and direct effect."[17] Not only that, but Maastricht also endorsed the concept of "variable geometry" or differentiated integration, exemplified by the United Kingdom's "opt out" from the Protocol and Agreement on Social Policy.[18] The logic of variable geometry is that the member states can move towards integration at different speeds in different contexts. For its proponents, its flexibility is a virtue; for its detractors, it is a deeply retrograde step: "the potential victims [of Maastricht] are the cohesiveness and the unity and the concomitant power of a legal system painstakingly constructed over the course of some 30 odd years. . . . The whole future and credibility of the Communities as a cohesive legal unit, which confers rights on individuals and which enters into their national legal systems as an integral part of those systems, is at stake."[19] The difficulties with this multi-faceted conception of the European Union were reflected in the provision made in the Maastricht Treaty for a further intergovernmental conference in 1996 to consider "to what extent the policies and forms of co-operation introduced by this Treaty may need to be revised." It was this conference which led to the negotiation and signing of the Treaty of Amsterdam in 1997.[20]

---

[16] *Van Gend en Loos v Nederlandse Administratie der Belastingen* [1963] E.C.R. 1 at 12.

[17] See P. Craig and G. de Bùrca, *EU Law: Texts, Cases and Materials* (3rd ed., Oxford University Press, Oxford, 2002), Ch.1.

[18] Following the most recent institutional rethink at Nice in 2000, what is now termed "enhanced co-operation" is available under each of the three pillars of the EU, subject to compliance with the conditions prescribed in the relevant Treaties. See generally S. Weatherill, "The Provisions on Closer Co-operation" in *The Legal Issues of the Amsterdam Treaty* (D. O'Keeffe and P. Twomey eds, Hart Publishing, Oxford, 1999), Ch.2.

[19] D. Curtin, "The Constitutional Structure of the European Union: A Europe of bits and pieces" [1993] 30 C.M.L.Rev. 17 at 67.

[20] The Treaty itself is in three parts but, following a pattern established at Maastricht, concludes with 13 Protocols, 51 declarations adopted by the conference and annexed to the Final Act, and a further eight declarations of which the conference took note. It was notable mainly for renumbering the EC Treaty to take account of the amendments made to it over the years, and for replacing the letter headings adopted in the EU Treaty with numbers.

The three-pillar structure of the European Union was retained in modified form, the principal change effected by Amsterdam being the progressive transfer of a number of matters formerly contained within the third pillar on justice and home affairs to the first, Community pillar. The legislative role of the European Parliament was enhanced with the extension of the "co-decision" legislative procedure[21] to new areas, and provision was made for greater use of qualified majority voting in the Council of Ministers. As with each successive Treaty, Community competences were adjusted, extended or enhanced.[22] On the whole, however, Amsterdam met with a rather muted reception, perhaps because, unlike the Single European Act (geared towards completion of the internal market) and Maastricht (geared in large measure towards economic and monetary union), it lacked an identifiable grand design.[23] It was criticised for failing to address the deep-seated ideological tensions already alluded to, and, perhaps more importantly, it failed to grasp the nettle of constitutional and institutional reform in anticipation of enlargement, relegating the matter to a Protocol and leaving it for future decision. The triennial pattern of intergovernmental conferences established by Maastricht and Amsterdam was therefore followed with the convening of a conference in Nice towards the end of 2000, the principal object of which was to reach agreement on institutional issues left unresolved by Amsterdam and which had to be settled before the accession of new member states could proceed.[24]

8–03 The Treaty of Nice was signed on February 26, 2001. It required to be in force by the end of 2002 if the European Union were to be in a position to admit the candidate states of central and eastern Europe deemed ready to accede to the Treaties, a timetable which took a somewhat unexpected knock when, in June 2001, the people of Ireland rejected the Treaty of Nice in a national referendum. As the Danes had to be asked twice about Maastricht, so too were the Irish asked twice about Nice, and in a second referendum in October 2002 the original vote was reversed, removing the single

---

[21] The legislative processes of the European institutions are discussed below, paras 8–18—8–24.

[22] Matters brought within the first pillar, and thus subject to the general jurisdiction of the ECJ, included "fundamental principles of the European Union"; closer co-operation between member states; non-discrimination; visas, asylum, immigration and other policies related to the free movement of persons. The Community's competences in relation to matters such as citizenship of the EU and social policy were widened (and, following the election of the New Labour government on May 1, 1997, the Maastricht Protocol and Agreement on Social Policy—the British "opt-out"—was repealed).

[23] Weatherill and Beaumont, *EU Law, op.cit.*, p.19.

[24] Although certain other issues, not directly connected with enlargement, were also dealt with and included in the final Treaty.

remaining obstacle to ratification of the Nice Treaty.[25] The Treaty is arranged in two parts, together with the usual clutter of protocols (four) and declarations (24).[26] It also adopted, by way of a solemn proclamation, the Charter of Fundamental Rights drafted at the request of the European Council meeting in Cologne in July 1999.[27] Some of the rights set out in the Charter have already received some form of recognition in the Treaties or (more commonly) in the jurisprudence of the European Court of Justice; some are of the family of classic civil and political rights in relation to which there exists a well-established and mutually-reinforcing body of jurisprudence culled from jurisdictions the world over. Other Charter rights, such as the positive social and economic rights contained in Chapter IV, most decidedly do not fall into that bracket.[28] It does not yet have legally binding force, although it may be said to represent a codification or at least clarification of the general principle of Community law requiring respect for fundamental rights, which already binds the institutions and indeed member states when acting in the context of Community law.[29] To that extent alone it may be said to bind the institutions of the European Union and the member states when acting in the sphere of EU law.[30] The Convention on the Future of Europe included

---

[25] Consequent upon this, the European Council meeting in Copenhagen in December 2002 concluded accession negotiations with Cyprus, the Czech Republic, Estonia, Hungary, Latvia, Lithuania, Malta, Poland, Slovakia and Slovenia. The accession of these 10 states is now expected to take place in 2004. The same European Council approved the Commission's "road maps" for Bulgaria and Romania, confirming the intention to accept both states as full members of the EU in 2007 subject to satisfactory progress being made on the accession criteria. The position of Turkey remains unresolved pending the meeting of the European Council in Dec. 2004.

[26] The importance of certain of these protocols and declarations should not however be overlooked (see in particular the Protocol annexed to the EU Treaty and the EC Treaty on the Enlargement of the European Union and the Protocol annexed to the EU Treaty, the EC Treaty and the Euratom Treaty on the Statute of the ECJ. Five of the declarations were also directed to the ECJ and Court of First Instance. A further declaration called for the institution of a deeper and wider debate on the future of Europe, which debate has now borne fruit with the publication in July 2003 of a draft Treaty establishing a Constitution for Europe).

[27] The Charter of Fundamental Rights is incorporated as Pt II of the draft Treaty establishing a Constitution for Europe.

[28] Nonetheless, the Charter makes common provision in respect of all the substantive rights it contains: see Arts 51 and 52.

[29] See, *e.g. Stauder v Ulm* [1969] E.C.R. 419; *Nold v Commission* [1974] E.C.R. 491; *Wachauf v Germany* [1989] E.C.R. 2609. In *Philip Morris International Inc. v Commission*, Jan. 15, 2003, the Court of First Instance held that, while the Charter is not of itself a source of enforceable rights, it *affirms* the importance of the rights it sets out in the Community legal order (para.122).

[30] In terms of Art.51 of the Charter.

the Charter, in its entirety, as Part II of its draft Treaty establishing a Constitution for Europe.[31]

The enlargement of the European Union made possible by the institutional reforms effected at Nice is viewed with dismay by many advocates for European integration, who regard (and not without reason) the widening and deepening of the European Union as mutually incompatible goals. For exactly the same reason, enlargement is often welcomed by those who consider that the integrationists' "federalising logic" has gone far enough. With enlargement imminent, the question remains: in what direction is the European Union to be taken in the years ahead? There are those, who might loosely be described as federalists, who clearly aspire to the creation of a European state having all the usual trappings of statehood, including a constitution and bill of rights, an army and the power to tax its citizens. Others view this vision with unfeigned alarm, and contend that a more durable and workable European Union will be one that respects the heterogeneity and indeed the sovereignty of its members.

8–04 The elevation at Maastricht of the principles of proportionality and subsidiarity to the status of general principles of Community law may be seen as a response to the anxieties of the latter camp. Proportionality obliges the Community institutions to go no further than necessary to achieve the objectives of the Treaties; subsidiarity involves identifying the "best level"—national (or regional) or Community—for legislative or administrative action to be taken (which is not necessarily to say that decisions should be taken at the level closest to the citizens who will be affected by them).[32]

---

[31] Views on the merits of the Charter, inevitably, vary widely. For some, the expansion in the powers of the EU institutions into such "rights sensitive" areas as asylum, immigration and criminal justice necessities a limitation on its powers by reference to a justiciable charter of individual rights. Others deplore the Charter, partly on the basis of the package of rights it happens to enshrine and partly as a further milestone on the road to the creation of a federal Europe. The Council of Europe has also expressed disquiet about the adoption by the EU of a legally enforceable Charter of rights, in view of the possibility of conflict between two distinct European human rights regimes (although the Convention on the Future of Europe has recommended that legal personality be conferred on the EU in terms of Art.6 of the draft Treaty establishing a Constitution for Europe; were this to eventuate, it would be possible for the EU itself to accede to the ECHR). See generally K. Lenaerts and E. de Smijter, "A Bill of Rights for the European Union?" [2001] 38 C.M.L.Rev. 273.

[32] See L. Brittan, "The Institutional Development of the European Community" [1992] P.L. 567 at 574. Agreement was reached on the application of the principle of subsidiarity at the European Council meeting in Edinburgh in Dec. 1992, and in 1993 the European Parliament, Council and Commission adopted an inter-institutional Agreement on Procedures for Implementing the Principle of Subsidiarity. The contents of both texts are consolidated in the Protocol on the Application of the Principles of Subsidiarity and Proportionality annexed to the Treaty of Amsterdam.

Steps have also been taken to encourage the participation of national parliaments in European policy-making processes,[33] and some efforts have been made (not before time) to improve the quality and transparency of European governance.[34] The Commission has expressly recognised that improvement in governance is necessary not only to enable the European Union to cope with the challenges of economic and monetary union, enlargement and the evolution of a common foreign and security policy, but also to reconnect the European Union to European citizens: "the legitimacy needed for any extension of shared sovereignty depends on the citizens' ability to relate to the European Union."[35] But that is to presume a consensus on whether such extensions of shared sovereignty should occur at all.

Hence the declaration adopted by the European Council meeting in Laeken in December 2001, convening a European Convention on the Future of Europe charged with addressing four discrete issues: how to establish and monitor a more precise delimitation of powers between the European Union and the member states, reflecting the principle of subsidiarity; the status of the Charter of Fundamental Rights; the simplification of the Treaties, with a view to making them clearer and better understood; and the proper role of national parliaments in the European architecture.[36] The proposals of the convention, which presented its conclusions in the form of a draft Treaty establishing a Constitution for Europe to the President of the European Council on July 18, 2003, are intended to inform the discussion at the next intergovernmental conference. Certain of the recommendations embodied in the Articles of this instrument we have noted already. Whether and to what extent the draft Treaty proves acceptable to the member states remains to be seen.[37] Some will require to submit it for the approval of their

---

[33] The Ninth Protocol to the Treaty of Amsterdam, annexed to the EC Treaty and EU Treaty, makes provision in relation to the role of national parliaments in the EU.

[34] Including the establishment of a European Ombudsman and the adoption of Regulation 1049/2001 of the European Parliament and the Council regarding public access to European Parliament, Council and Commission documents.

[35] *Enhancing Democracy: A White Paper on governance in the European Union* (European Commission, 2001).

[36] Curiously, by the time the convention submitted its draft Treaty on establishing a Constitution for Europe, these four issues had become three, and quite different at that: how to bring citizens closer to the European design and European institutions; how to organise politics and the European political arena in an enlarged Union; and how to develop the Union into a stabilising factor and a model in the new world order.

[37] The President of the Convention on the Future of Europe, Valery Giscard d'Estaing, has already called upon member states to refrain from tinkering with the draft Treaty, which represents the settled conclusions of the convention, in which all existing member states, and, if to a lesser extent, the accession states were represented.

people in referendums. The UK government need not, but will be conscious of the difficulty of selling the draft Treaty to a generally eurosceptical press and public. That difficulty is not lessened by the fact that the draft Treaty resolves none of the issues that go to render the European Union such an "essentially contested concept".[38] It does not greatly simplify the existing Treaties. It will do little to bring the citizens of the member states closer to the European Union. It represents a compromise between the federalist and supranationalist wings of the European debate only in the worst possible sense of leaving both dissatisfied. Should the draft Treaty be adopted as it stands, therefore, the evolution of Europe will continue in much the same way as it has to date, by a process of "competence creep" and consolidation that owes much to the demands of greater governmental efficiency (viewed from the perspective of bureaucrats) and little to the values of democratic accountability, public participation and transparency.

EUROPEAN INSTITUTIONS

Introduction

8–05　　The five principal European institutions are enumerated in Article 7 of the EC Treaty: the Council (of Ministers); the Commission; the European Parliament; the Court of Justice and the Court of Auditors.[39]

Council

8–06　　The Council of Ministers is composed of "a representative of each member state at ministerial level, authorised to commit the government of that member state."[40] The Presidency of the Council rotates amongst the member states on a six-monthly basis. The Council meets in one form or another about 100 times a year, when convened by the President of the Council or at the request of the Commission or of one of the member states. Council meetings are generally arranged according to subject-matter, with different

---

[38] Z. Bankowski and E. Christodoulidis, "The European Union as an Essentially Contested Concept" (1998) 4 E.L.J. 341.

[39] There are a number of other Community bodies of greater or lesser importance, such as the Committee of the Regions and Economic and Social Committee, the European Central Bank and the European Investment Bank. These will not be addressed here (but see, *e.g.* Weatherill and Beaumont, *EU Law*, *op.cit.*, pp.169; 376, 377; 775–779). It is however necessary to refer to the European Council (not to be confused with the Council of Ministers), an institution of the EU rather than of the Community, but one which has come to play an increasingly important role in the Community's development.

[40] EC Treaty, Art.203.

ministers attending from the member states as appropriate. Thus the General Affairs Council, dealing with external relations and other issues of general Community policy, is attended by the Foreign Ministers of the member states; the Economic and Finance Council, dealing with such issues as the single market and EMU, is attended by the Finance Ministers of the member states. In addition, there are some 20 technical councils dealing with sectoral issues such as the environment, transport, energy, agriculture and fisheries and attended by the minister responsible for those matters within each member state.

Save as otherwise provided for by the Treaty, the Council acts by a simple majority of its members. However, unanimity is required under many Articles of the Treaty, among them those providing for the adoption of measures of a constitutional nature such as changes to the number of Commissioners or judges of the Court of Justice, decisions regarding the Community's "own resources" and the conclusion of association agreements with third states. Where unanimity is required, it may be achieved by only one vote in favour provided all the other member states abstain, since abstentions do not have a blocking effect in measures requiring unanimity. Where the Council is required by the Treaty to act by *qualified* majority, the votes of the member states are weighted by reference to their population sizes.[41]

Article 202 of the EC Treaty defines the powers of the Council: to ensure co-ordination of the general economic policies of the member states; to take decisions; to confer on the Commission powers for the implementation of rules adopted by acts of the Council, all in accordance with the provisions of the Treaty in order to ensure that the objectives set out in the Treaty are attained. Thus the most important function of the Council is its legislative function, which takes the following forms. In accordance with the maxim "the Commission proposes, the Council disposes", the Council may vote its approval of legislative initiatives emanating from the Commission[42] (which may have been prompted by a request from the Council to submit proposals under Article 208). In addition, the Council may delegate legislative powers to the Commission, authorising it to adopt further legislative measures in

---

[41] The weighting of the votes of each member state will change on the entry into force of the Treaty of Nice on Jan. 1, 2005. Note, however, that the amendments made to qualified majority thresholds in EC Treaty, Art.205, are in a sense academic, since the EU will have more than the present 15 member states when the new weightings take effect. It is envisaged that the thresholds will be adjusted as necessary, in terms of the Declaration on Enlargement of the Union annexed to the Nice Treaty and subject to a maximum threshold of 73.4% of qualified majority votes, as the accession of the new member states proceeds.

[42] Acting unanimously, by qualified majority or simple majority, depending on the requirements of the Treaty Article that provides the legal base for the measure.

particular fields. It also has significant powers in the context of the intergovernmental second and third pillars of the European Union concerning common foreign and security policy and police and judicial co-operation in criminal matters.[43] The Council is assisted in its work by a General Secretariat, which provides direct administrative support, and by the Committee of Permanent Representatives (COREPER).[44]

Commission

8–07   The Commission consists of 20 Commissioners (although this number may be increased by the Council of Ministers acting unanimously).[45] Each member state has at least one of its nationals serving on the Commission at any one time, and the larger member states—France, Germany, Italy, Spain and the United Kingdom—have, for the time being, two. The Commissioners are servants of the Community, whose "independence is beyond doubt" and who "neither seek nor take instructions from any government or other body." Their term of office is five years and may be renewed. The President of the Commission is nominated by common accord of the governments of the member states, which nomination must be approved by the European Parliament. The remaining Commissioners are nominated by common accord of the member states and the nominee for the presidency. The President and the Commissioners thus nominated must then be approved as a body by the Parliament. That approval signified, the President and Commissioners are then formally appointed by common accord of the member states.[46]

---

[43] Mention should be made of the power of the Council under EU Treaty, Art.7, acting by qualified majority, to suspend certain rights of a member state, including the voting rights of its representative on the Council, where the European Council (*i.e.* the heads of state or government), acting unanimously, determines that state is guilty of a "serious and persistent breach" of the principles of liberty, democracy, respect for human rights and fundamental freedoms and the rule of law as enshrined in Art.6(1).

[44] EC Treaty, Art.207. COREPER is organised on two levels. The lower level is composed of deputy permanent representatives and takes responsibility for such matters as the internal market, social affairs, transport and the environment. The upper level consists of permanent representatives having ambassadorial rank. It liaises with national governments and takes responsibility for the more thorny aspects of Community policy, such as external relations and economic and financial affairs.

[45] EC Treaty, Art.213.

[46] EC Treaty, Art.214(2). This procedure will change following the entry into force in 2005 of the amendments made to Art.214(2) by the Treaty of Nice, which amendment provides as follows: "The Council, meeting in the composition of Heads of State or Government and acting by a qualified majority, shall nominate the person it intends to appoint as President of the Commission; the nomination shall be approved by the European Parliament. The Council, acting by a qualified

The requirement of parliamentary approval is of relatively recent provenance, and exists alongside the Parliament's long-established power under Article 201 of the EC Treaty to dismiss the entire Commission on a motion of censure. It is possible that both powers are too blunt an instrument to be truly effective as a means of ensuring democratic control of the Commission: powers to reject individual nominees for appointment to the Commission or to censure and dismiss individual Commissioners from office might be preferable in this regard.[47] As it is, the power to dismiss the entire Commission has never been used and it remains to be seen how vigorous the Parliament will be in the use of its powers in relation to the appointment of the President and of the Commission as a whole. But it is certainly possible that the Parliament will show itself to be more exacting in its scrutiny of the Commission than it has been in the past, not least with the example of its part in bringing about the resignation of the Commission on March 15, 1999 behind it.[48]

The Commission is organised into 26 directorates-general, sup- **8–08** ported by an additional layer of specialist services. Each directorate-general is headed by a Director-General reporting to the Commissioner, who takes overall political and operational responsibility for the work of the directorate-general. As there are more directorates-general than there are Commissioners, an individual Commissioner's portfolio may well cover the work of more than one directorate-general. The allocation of portfolios to individual Commissioners is decided collectively, although initial proposals are made by the President. The Commissioners meet

majority and by common accord with the nominee for President, shall adopt the list of the other persons whom it intends to appoint as Members of the Commission, drawn up in accordance with the proposals made by each member state. The President and the other members of the Commission thus nominated shall be subject as a body to a vote of approval by the European Parliament. After approval by the Parliament, the President and the other members of the Commission shall be appointed by the Council, acting by a qualified majority."

[47] Individual commissioners may be dismissed during their term of office, but only by the ECJ on an application by the Council or the Commission where the commissioner no longer fulfils the conditions required for the performance of his duties or is guilty of serious misconduct, as provided for by EC Treaty, Arts 213(2) and 216. These powers have been used only once, in 1976. Art.217, as amended by the Treaty of Nice, empowers the President of the Commission to require the resignation of a commissioner, with the approval of the College of Commissioners.

[48] That crisis prompted the publication in March 2000 of a White Paper making proposals for the reform of the Commission, including improved procedures in relation to audit, financial management and control, whistle-blowing and discipline, and the establishment via an inter-institutional agreement of a European Committee on Standards in Public Life. At the same time, the Commission adopted a new Code of Conduct for Commissioners and a Code of Good Administrative Behaviour applicable to the staff and other servants of the Community. See generally V. Mehde, "Responsibility and Accountability in the European Commission" [2003] 40 C.M.L.Rev. 423.

collectively as the College of Commissioners once a week, act by majority and operate under the political guidance of the President.

The powers of the Commission, as provided for by Article 211 of the EC Treaty, are extensive. In order to secure the proper functioning and development of the common market, it is charged with ensuring that the provisions of the Treaty and measures taken pursuant thereto are observed; formulating recommendations or delivering opinions on matters dealt with in the Treaty, where the Treaty so provides or the Commission considers it necessary; taking decisions and participating in the shaping of measures taken by the Council and by the European Parliament in the manner provided for in the Treaty; and exercising the delegated legislative powers conferred on it by the Council. The European institutions do not observe the doctrine of the separation of powers as national constitutions, in their different ways, do; and the functions of the Commission in particular cross the board. It is not simply an executive body, although its executive and administrative responsibilities are extensive. It possesses broad rule-making powers delegated from the Council in addition to a range of autonomous legislative powers under the Treaties, but its principal role in this regard is in setting the general policy agenda for the European Union and in its right of legislative initiative. Even though most European legislation is formally adopted by the Council or, increasingly, by the Council and the Parliament, in most cases these institutions may act only on legislative proposals from the Commission itself. The Commission also has important investigative, enforcement and quasi-judicial functions, among them the power to bring enforcement actions under Article 226 against member states believed to be in breach of Community law; and powers in relation to the supervision and enforcement of the Community's rules on competition and state aids.

European Parliament

8–09   The European Parliament has 626 members directly elected from the 15 member states. Article 189 of the EC Treaty provides that the total number of MEPs is not to exceed 700. The number of members returned by each member state is determined by reference to its population size, and so, for the time being, the United Kingdom returns 87 members.[49]

---

[49] With a view to enlargement of the EU, the Treaty of Nice changes the maximum number of MEPs to 732. It also introduces a new distribution of seats in the European Parliament, looking ahead to a Union of 27 member states, which will be applicable as from the next European elections in 2004. Under that distribution, the number of seats held by the existing member states will fall from 626 to 535, with only Germany and Luxembourg retaining their present quota of MEPs.

Members of the European Parliament sit in the European Parliament not as national delegates but, in most cases, as members of "political groupings".[50] The Parliament elects its own President, together with 14 vice-presidents, for two and a half-year terms of office. President and vice-presidents together constitute the Bureau of Parliament; and the Bureau of Parliament together with the leaders of the political groups represented in the Parliament constitute the Conference of Presidents. The Parliament adopts its own Rules of Procedure pursuant to Article 199 of the EC Treaty, and is required by Article 190(5) to lay down regulations and general conditions governing the performance of MEPs' duties. It organises itself into a large number of specialist committees (some with sub-committees) on all matters falling with the competence of the Community and, in a wider sense, of the Union. In their work, the Parliament and its committees are provided with legal and administrative assistance by a large Secretariat.

As we shall see, the European Parliament has gradually assumed a more prominent role in the adoption of Community legislation as the member states, in successive revisions of the Treaties, have sought to respond to complaints about the "democratic deficit" under which the European Union labours.[51] In addition to the part it plays in Community legislation, the Parliament has important powers in relation to the Community budget, being able ultimately to reject the entire budget and require the Commission to present a revised draft budget.[52] It also has a role to play in providing a

---

The UK's membership will fall to 72 (and provision has been made for this by the European Parliament (Representation) Act 2003). These reductions will only be fully applicable, however, to the Parliament elected in 2009. Since the Union will not, by the 2004 elections, have garnered all 12 of its new members, the decision was taken to increase the number of MEPs to be elected in the current member states and those states which have acceded by Jan. 1, 2004 on a *pro rata* basis to bring the total up to 732 (although the number of MEPs elected in each member state cannot exceed the present allocations). In the course of the 2004–09 Parliament, the number of MEPs will climb above the 732 limit as new member states accede to the Treaties and contribute their elected representatives. The national quotas set out in the Declaration on Enlargement annexed to the Treaty of Nice will therefore take final effect in the European elections of 2009.

[50] There are presently eight political groups. Only a handful of MEPs refrain from aligning themselves to a political group, since considerable financial and practical advantages flow from membership.

[51] A. Maurer, "The Legislative Powers and Impact of the European Parliament" [2003] 41 J.C.M.S. 274.

[52] Any such vote requires the support of a majority of MEPs and two-thirds of the votes actually cast: EC Treaty, Art.272.

degree of democratic oversight and supervision of other Community institutions.[53]

European Council

8–10   Not to be confused with the Council of Ministers, the European Council is the product of summit meetings held between the heads of state or government of the member states and the President of the Commission from the early 1970s. It finally received institutional recognition of sorts in the Single European Act of 1986, and its role is now provided for by Article 4 of the Treaty on European Union. Essentially, its task is to "provide the Union with the necessary impetus for its development and [to] define the general political guidelines thereof." To that end, the heads of state or government, together with the President of the Commission, national foreign ministers and Commissioners as appropriate meet twice a year under the chairmanship of the head of state or government of the member state that holds the Presidency of the Council for the time being. In point of fact, the Treaties make few references to the European Council. This in no sense means that the role of the European Council within the institutional machinery of the European Union is only marginal. No important political or constitutional initiative has a chance of getting off the ground without the imprimatur of the heads of state or government meeting in the European Council.[54]

Court of Justice

8–11   The composition of the Court of Justice is governed by Articles 221 to 225 of the EC Treaty. Matters concerning the organisation and procedure of the Court are covered by the Protocol annexed to

---

[53] EC Treaty, Art.197 requires the Commission to reply orally or in writing to questions put to it by the European Parliament or its members. The Treaty also makes provision for the appointment by the Parliament of temporary Committees of Inquiry to investigate allegations of maladministration and for a right of public petition of the Parliament exercisable by any natural or legal person residing or having a registered office in any member state. In its supervisory role, the Parliament now has the assistance of an Ombudsman, whose appointment was originally provided for at Maastricht and whose functions are now governed by EC Treaty, Art.195(1).

[54] Not only that, but its role is still evolving. There was some discussion at the Nice intergovernmental conference about the extension of qualified majority voting to proceedings of the European Council, although, in the event, this was not adopted in the Nice Treaty. Art.20 of the draft Treaty establishing a Constitution for Europe makes provision for quarterly meetings of the European Council and for decisions to be taken by consensus "except where the Constitution provides otherwise". Art.21 provides for the election by the member states, acting by qualified majority, of a President of the European Council, who may not hold a national mandate and who is charged with chairing the meetings of the Council and driving forward its work.

the EC Treaty on the Statute of the Court of Justice. On the basis of the provisions of the Statute and as provided for by Article 245 of the EC Treaty, the Court adopts Rules of Procedure. These require the unanimous approval of the Council.

The Treaty of Nice, when it enters into force, will bring about major reforms in the structure of the European Union's legal system.[55] In the meantime, the Court of Justice consists of 15 judges, one from each member state, assisted by eight Advocates-General whose job it is to make reasoned submissions on the cases brought before the Court of Justice in advance of the Court handing down its final decision. Both judges and Advocates-General are required to be chosen from persons whose independence is beyond doubt and who possess the qualifications required for appointment to the highest judicial offices in their respective countries or who are jurisconsults of recognised competence. They are appointed by common accord of the member states for a term of six years, which may be renewed.[56] The overarching task of the Court of Justice, as set out in Article 220 of the EC Treaty, is to ensure that in the interpretation and application of the EC Treaty, the law is observed. Such questions may come before the Court in diverse ways. The Court is not a court of general jurisdiction, but may only be seised of disputes falling into defined categories, namely enforcement actions under Articles 226 and 227[57]; actions for the annulment of a Community act (effectively, applications for judicial review) under Article 230; actions in respect of a failure to act under Article 232; and preliminary rulings.

In the light of changes introduced by the Treaty of Amsterdam in 1997, there are now three distinct types of preliminary ruling procedure. The first, and most familiar, is provided for by Article 234 of the EC Treaty. This confers on the Court of Justice jurisdiction to give preliminary rulings, on a reference from a national court or tribunal, concerning, *inter alia*, the interpretation of the EC Treaty and the validity and interpretation of acts of the

---

[55] Briefly, the existing Arts 220–225 will be repealed and replaced; new Articles will be inserted providing for the creation of "judicial panels" and the conferment of jurisdiction on the ECJ in disputes relating to "the application of acts adopted on the basis of this [EC] Treaty which create Community industrial property rights"; the jurisdiction of the ECJ in actions for annulment of a Community act is extended; and the existing Protocols on the Statute of the ECJ, together with the 1988 Council decision establishing the Court of First Instance are repealed and replaced by the Protocol on the Statute of the ECJ annexed by the Treaty of Nice to the EU Treaty, the EC Treaty and the Euratom Treaty.

[56] Under the amendments made to Art.221 by the Treaty of Nice, the ECJ will continue to consist of one judge per member state.

[57] Enforcement actions are brought against a member state said to be in breach of the Treaties at the instance either of the Commission or of another member state.

institutions of the Community and of the European Central Bank. This procedure has been of enormous significance for the shaping of Community law. It is the vehicle through which the Court of Justice has expounded and developed some of the central doctrines of Community law, such as the principle of primacy and the concept of direct effect. It has also been critical to the development of the (generally harmonious) working relationship between the Court of Justice and the national courts of the member states. The other procedures for seeking preliminary rulings were provided of new at Amsterdam. The first applies under the new Title IV of the EC Treaty on visas, asylum, immigration and other policies concerning the free movement of persons, subjects shifted by the Amsterdam Treaty from the old third pillar on justice and home affairs into the first, Community, pillar of the European Union.[58] The second is contained in Article 35 of the consolidated Treaty on European Union, dealing with police and judicial co-operation in criminal matters (the new third pillar). This provides that the Court of Justice shall have jurisdiction to give preliminary rulings on the interpretation and validity of certain measures adopted in this field *provided that* the member state has accepted the jurisdiction of the Court of Justice by making a declaration to that effect. The Court also has jurisdiction in disputes relating to compensation for damage caused by the Community institutions or by servants of the Community in the course of their duties in terms of Articles 235 and 288(2) of the EC Treaty, together with special jurisdiction in terms of Articles 236 to 238 and 240 of the Treaty.[59]

Under Article 221 of the EC Treaty, the Court of Justice may sit in chambers of three or five judges as well as in plenary session, a vital facility given the ever-increasing caseload of the Court and one that is extensively used. Only when a member state or Community institution which is a party to proceedings before the Court so requests is the Court obliged to sit in plenary session. Overload, and consequent backlogs and delay, remains a problem for the Court, notwithstanding the establishment of the Court of First Instance in 1989. Imminent enlargement made reform of the judicial architecture of the EU imperative, hence the provision made by the Treaty of Nice and related instruments intended to bring about greater flexibility in the management of judicial business.[60]

---

[58] Only national courts from whose decisions there is no right of appeal in national law may seek preliminary rulings in accordance with this procedure.

[59] These relate to staff cases (Art.236), disputes concerning the European Investment Bank (Art.237), arbitration (Art.238), and certain disputes between member states relating to the subject-matter of the Treaty if submitted to the ECJ under a special agreement between the parties (Art.240).

[60] See H. Rasmussen, "Remedying the Crumbling EC Judicial System" [2000] 37 C.M.L.Rev. 1071; A. Johnston, "Judicial Reform and the Treaty of Nice" [2001] 38 C.M.L.Rev. 499.

Court of Auditors

The Court of Auditors was established in 1975, came into **8–12** operation in 1977 and was elevated to the status of the fifth Community institution by Article 7 of the EC Treaty in 1992. It has 15 members, appointed by the Council (acting unanimously after consulting the European Parliament) for renewable terms of six years.[61] Each member state selects for appointment a person who belongs or has belonged to an external audit body in that state or who is otherwise "especially qualified" for the office. Members of the Court are servants of the Community and must be wholly independent in the performance of their duties, neither seeking nor taking instructions from any government or other body.

The Court of Auditors is not in fact a court at all. It is charged with auditing the accounts of all revenue and expenditure of the Community and bodies set up by the Community; ascertaining whether all revenue has been received and all expenditure incurred in a "lawful and regular" manner and the soundness of financial management; assisting the European Parliament and the Council in exercising their powers of control over the implementation of the budget; and reporting on all of this at the close of each financial year.[62] Its workload is heavy. The financial operations of the European Union, including its borrowing and lending activities, now exceed 100 billion Euros in value each year. All institutions and bodies which have access to EU funds, including national, regional and local administrations which manage Community funds, are subject to the scrutiny of the Court of Auditors and are required to provide the Court of Auditors with the information and documentation it needs to carry out its tasks.

EUROPEAN LEGISLATION

We have seen that one of the distinctive features of the European **8–13** Union as an international organisation is the autonomous legislative power entrusted to its institutions by the member states. Article 249 of the EC Treaty provides:

"In order to carry out their task and in accordance with the provisions of this Treaty, the European Parliament acting jointly with the Council, the Council and the Commission shall

---

[61] The Treaty of Nice amends Art.247 to provide that the Court of Auditors shall consist of one national from each member state, and that the Council, acting by qualified majority after consulting the European Parliament, shall adopt the list of members drawn up in accordance with the proposals made by each member state.

[62] EC Treaty, Art.248.

make regulations and issue directives, take decisions, make recommendations or deliver opinions."

Of these legislative instruments, regulations, directives and decisions have legal force; recommendations and opinions are a species of "soft law" and have no binding force as such, although they may have an indirect impact or influence on the interpretation of the law.[63]

Community legislation must comply with certain general requirements of the Treaty. First, all legislative measures must have a legal basis in the Treaty and this should as a rule be stated in the preamble to the measure. The choice of legal base (where a measure could be founded on more than one provision of the Treaty) may make a difference as to the type of legislative procedure which requires to be followed and for that reason must be based on objective factors which are amenable to judicial review. It would not, for instance, be acceptable to select one legal base over another purely because the former allowed a lesser role to the European Parliament. It should also be noted in this regard that, aside from the specific legislative bases in different areas of the Treaty, Article 308 lays down a general legislative power in the following terms:

"If action by the Community should prove necessary to attain, in the course of the operation of the common market, one of the objectives of the Community and this Treaty has not provided the necessary powers, the Council shall, acting unanimously on a proposal from the Commission and after consulting the European Parliament, take the appropriate measures."

A further prerequisite for Community legislation, as laid down in Article 253 of the EC Treaty, is that it states the reasons on which it is based—that is, a statement of the facts and law which led to its adoption—and that it refers to any proposals or opinions which were required to be obtained pursuant to the Treaty. Failure to provide any, or adequate, reasons constitutes one of the grounds upon which the legality of a Community measure may be challenged before the Court of Justice.

Regulations

8–14   A regulation is a measure of general application, binding in its entirety and directly applicable in all the member states. The direct applicability of regulations means, first, that their entry into force

---

[63] In terms of Arts 32–36 of the draft Treaty establishing a Constitution for Europe, the names of these measures are changed.

and application within the national legal orders of the member states are wholly independent of any measure of reception into national law: they become part of the member states' national legal systems without any intervention on the part of the national governments. Secondly, it means that regulations are capable of conferring rights on individuals that can be enforced directly by them before the national courts, a characteristic the concept of direct applicability shares with the concept of direct effect.

Generally, the Treaty leaves open to the Community institutions the choice of whether to proceed by way of regulation, directive or decision.[64] Power to make regulations may be conferred on the Commission by the Council. Once adopted, regulations must be published in the Official Journal of the European Union. They come into force on the date specified in the notice or, if no date is specified, on the twentieth day following publication of the notice.

Directives

Article 249(3) of the EC Treaty provides: "A directive shall be **8–15** binding, as to the result to be achieved, upon each member state to which it is addressed, but shall leave to the national authorities the choice of form and methods." In other words, a directive will prescribe the policy objectives to be secured, but leaves it up to the member states to determine how best to accomplish this in the context of their differing political, administrative and legal structures and traditions. Directives are a particularly useful device when harmonisation is required rather than uniformity, and the signs are in the evolving Community that greater emphasis will be placed in future on directives than on regulations in order to accommodate the pressures of enlargement.

While the Treaty tends to leave open the choice of form of legislation, it is rather more prescriptive as to when directives only may be used. Directives applying to all member states must be published in the Official Journal and take effect in the same way as regulations, that is on the date specified in the official notice or, in the absence thereof, on the twentieth day following publication. In most cases, directives allow the member states a specified period of time in which to transpose the measures into national law. Failure on the part of a member state to implement a directive, at all or correctly, within that period may expose the state to enforcement action by the Community and to liability in damages for breach of Community law, and may result in individuals being able to reply

---

[64] Regulations are only required in the fields of workers' rights (Art.39(2)), state aids (Art.89), budgetary procedures and Community accounts (Art.279) and in relation to Community staff. The choice of form may be informed by considerations of proportionality and subsidiarity.

directly on the provisions of the directive in proceedings before the national courts where the measure satisfies the conditions for direct effect.

Decisions

8–16   Under Article 249(4), decisions are binding in their entirety upon those to whom they are addressed. As this implies, they are not intended to be measures of general application in the manner of regulations. Aside from the situations in which choice of form is permitted, the Treaty provides for the use of decisions in a number of cases, perhaps most notably in the context of notifying breaches of the competition rules or determinations that a state aid is incompatible with the common market. It is open to the Council to delegate power to the Commission to take decisions that are within the competence of the Council itself. Decisions must be notified to the addressee and take effect when notified to those to whom they are addressed. Decisions adopted under Article 251 of the EC Treaty (the co-decision legislative procedure) must be, and others may be, published in the Official Journal.

Recommendations and opinions

8–17   The EC Treaty specifically provides for the making of recommendations and opinions in a number of situations, and under Article 211 confers a general power on the Commission to adopt recommendations and opinions wherever it considers it necessary. The Treaty is clear that neither measure can have binding force; thus they are incapable of having direct effect within the legal orders of the member states. It is however competent for a national court to make a reference to the Court of Justice concerning the interpretation or validity of a recommendation or opinion. In recent years, greater use has been made of these measures as vehicles for the development of Community policy, together with other forms of "soft law" such as inter-institutional agreements, as the old stress on uniformity has given place to a new emphasis on flexibility. Consequently, it is a trend that may be expected to continue.

LEGISLATIVE PROCEDURES

Introduction

8–18   The Community legislative process—or processes, for there are several—is a complex business, chiefly because there is no one Community institution identifiable as the legislature. The various procedures for adopting Community legislation are distinguishable from one another principally by reference to the differing roles played in each by the European Parliament. Which procedure requires to be used in any given context is a question of the legal base chosen, for the Treaty will specify what must be done. Since the entry into force of the Treaty of Amsterdam on May 1, 1999, the greater part of important Community legislation requires to be adopted in accordance with the "co-decision" procedure under Article 251 of the EC Treaty. The trend towards greater use of the co-decision procedure, which gives the European Parliament a key role in the legislative process, is taken further by the Treaty of Nice.[65]

Another trend in Community legislation worth remarking is the progressive extension that has taken place, in the successive revisions of the Treaties, of qualified majority voting. The Treaty of Nice makes provision for a switch from unanimity to qualified majority voting in the Council in relation to 27 Articles of the Treaties. Most of the legislative measures which, following the entry into force of the Treaty of Nice, will require a decision from the Council acting by qualified majority will also be subject to the co-decision procedure.

Consultation

In the early days of the European Community, being consulted on **8–19** a legislative proposal was about as much as the European Parliament (or Assembly, as it was then called) could expect, and there are still a number of areas under the Treaty where this is the extent of the Parliament's involvement. In essence, the Commission proposes legislation and sends it to the Council of Ministers, which in turn refers the proposal to the Parliament (where it is considered by a standing committee) for its opinion. Once the Council has received the Parliament's views, and not before, it may pass the measure in question in accordance with the voting requirements prescribed in the provision founded upon as the legal basis for the proposal. Where substantial changes are made to the proposal prior to its adoption, the Parliament should be re-consulted. But its opinion is binding on neither the Commission nor the Council.[66]

---

[65] The draft Treaty establishing a Constitution for Europe provides that co-decision will be the normal means of enacting Community legislation.

[66] The consultation procedure currently applies, *inter alia*, to EC Treaty, Art.13 (measures to combat discrimination), Art.19 (rights to vote and stand in municipal elections), Art.22 (reinforcing rights of citizenship), Art.67(1) (visas, asylum and immigration), Art.89 (state aids), Art.93 (harmonisation of indirect taxation), Art.94 (approximation of laws affecting the functioning of the common market); EU Treaty, Art.21 (concerning the general direction of the Common Foreign and Security Policy) and Art.39 (concerning police and judicial co-operation in criminal matters). It should be also noted that certain Articles of the Treaties require the Economic and Social Committee or the Committee of the Regions to be consulted prior to the adoption of a Community act, again on a non-binding basis.

Co-operation

8–20   A limited legislative role for the European Parliament was more easily justified in the past for, until 1979, the Parliament was not directly elected. But even after the introduction of direct elections, it was some time before a more prominent role than that of bare consultation was accorded to the Parliament. The co-operation procedure was introduced by the Single European Act of 1986 and is now contained in Article 252 of the EC Treaty. The Council, acting by a qualified majority and after obtaining the opinion of the European Parliament, adopts a common position on a proposal from the Commission. That common position is communicated, with reasons, to the European Parliament. If the Parliament fails within three months to approve or otherwise take a decision in relation to the common position, the Council must adopt the act in question in accordance with the common position. But the Parliament may, within that three-month period and acting by an absolute majority of its members, either reject or propose amendments to the common position. In that event, the Commission must re-examine its original proposal within one month. If it accepts the amendments, the Council may adopt the amended proposal by qualified majority. If the Commission rejects the amendments, the Council may nonetheless adopt them by unanimous vote. It may also adopt its own amendments in relation to a proposal re-examined by the Commission and adopt such amendments acting unanimously. If the Council fails to act on a re-examined proposal within three months, the proposal is deemed not to have been adopted.[67]

This procedure must be followed wherever the Treaty provides that the adoption of an act is to be in accordance with Article 252. When originally introduced, the co-operation procedure was used chiefly for the adoption of measures relating to the implementation of the "single market" programme. Most such measures are now subject to the co-decision procedure, leaving co-operation applicable mainly in areas concerned with economic and monetary union.

Co-decision

8–21   The co-decision procedure, which further enhanced the role of the European Parliament in the adoption of Community legislation, was introduced by the Maastricht Treaty on European Union. In essence, the approval of both the Council and the Parliament is a prerequisite for the adoption of a measure under this procedure, for which reason such measures are referred to as "acts of the

---

[67] Subject to the possibility of extending the period by up to one month by common accord of the Council and Parliament.

European Parliament and the Council". The co-decision procedure is now contained in Article 251 of the EC Treaty. Again, the Commission has the initiative, submitting a proposal to the Parliament and the Council. The Council, acting by a qualified majority after obtaining the opinion of the European Parliament, may adopt the act as amended in terms of the Parliament's opinion (or, if the Parliament makes no amendments, as it stands). Otherwise, the Council must adopt a common position and communicate this to the Parliament with reasons. If, within three months of such communication, the European Parliament approves the common position or fails to take a decision, the act in question is deemed to be adopted in accordance with the common position. If, by an absolute majority of its members, the Parliament rejects the common position, the proposed measure is deemed not to be adopted. If, acting again by an absolute majority of its members, the Parliament proposes amendments to the common position, the amended text is sent to the Council and Commission, which must produce an opinion on those amendments. The Council may adopt the act as amended by the Parliament, acting by qualified majority except where the Commission has disapproved the amendments; in that event, unanimity is required. If the Council does not approve all the amendments, the President of the Council, in agreement with the President of the European Parliament, must within six weeks convene a meeting of the Conciliation Committee composed of the members of the Council, their representatives and an equal number of representatives of the European Parliament. The task of the Committee is to reach agreement on a joint text, by a qualified majority of the members of the Council or their representatives and by a majority of the representatives of the European Parliament. The Commission takes part in the Committee's proceedings and must do all that is necessary in an effort to reconcile the positions of the Parliament and the Council. If, within six weeks of its being convened, the Committee approves a joint text, the European Parliament, acting by an absolute majority of the votes cast, and the Council, acting by a qualified majority, shall each have a period of six weeks from that approval in which to adopt the act in question in accordance with the joint text. If either of the two institutions fails to approve the proposed act within that period, it is deemed not to be adopted. Likewise, the proposed act is deemed not to be adopted where the Committee fails to approve a joint text.

This procedure must be followed whenever the Treaty provides that the adoption of an act is to be in accordance with Article 251. The range of situations in which this is the case was considerably extended by the Treaty of Amsterdam and again by the Treaty of Nice, such that, at last, the European Parliament is beginning to approach a role in the legislative process more nearly co-extensive with that of the Council.

Assent

8–22 The assent procedure was introduced by the Single European Act in 1986 for such fundamental constitutional matters as enlargement of the Community and the concluding of association agreements between the Community and third states. It also governs such areas as the regulation of the European central banking system (Articles 105 and 107 of the EC Treaty).

The assent procedure, as its name suggests, means that the Council can only act after obtaining the assent of the European Parliament. The power of the Parliament in this regard rests on the fact that, although there is no formal way in which it may amend a proposal, it can simply reject it outright and is under no such constraints of time as apply under the co-decision procedure.

Legislation adopted by the Commission or by the Commission and Council

8–23 In a small number of cases, the Commission has autonomous authority under the Treaty to adopt legislation, as under Article 86(3) which provides that the Commission may adopt directives or decisions concerning enforcement of the rules to be observed by the member states in relation to public undertakings. There are also certain areas in which the Council and Commission may take action without reference to the European Parliament, among them aspects of the Treaty relating to the free movement of workers and capital and the common commercial policy, although the Council may consult the European Parliament if it wishes to do so.

Delegated legislation

8–24 The Council may, and does, adopt regulations authorising the Commission to adopt more specific measures in a given area, such as agriculture or competition, and in doing so considerably enhances the flexibility and speed with which the Community can respond to events. Such delegated legislation is now governed by Article 202(3) of the EC Treaty, which provides that, to ensure that the objectives set out in the Treaty are attained, the Council shall:

> "confer on the Commission, in the acts which the Council adopts, powers for the implementation of the rules which the Council lays down. The Council may impose certain requirements in respect of the exercise of these powers. The Council may also reserve the right in specific cases to exercise directly implementing powers itself. The procedures referred to above must be consonant with principles and rules to be laid down in advance by the Council, acting unanimously on a proposal from the Commission and after obtaining the Opinion of the European Parliament."

LEGAL EFFECTS OF EU LAW IN NATIONAL LEGAL SYSTEMS

Primacy of Community law

It was abundantly clear, well before the accession of the United **8–25** Kingdom to the European Treaties, that Community law was, to put it mildly, a highly distinctive species of international law. The Court of Justice made that much clear in *Van Gend en Loos v Nederlandse Administratie der Belastingen*, holding that "the Community constitutes a new legal order of international law, for the benefit of which states have limited their sovereign rights."[68] As it explained in *Costa v ENEL*[69]:

> "[T]he transfer by the states from their domestic legal systems to the Community legal system of the rights and obligations arising under the Treaty carries with it a permanent limitation of their sovereign rights against which a subsequent unilateral act incompatible with the concept of the Community cannot prevail."

Subsequently, the Court confirmed that Community law in all its forms prevails over all conflicting provisions of national law, even provisions of a national constitution.[70] It also prevails whether the conflicting national law was made before or after the relevant provisions of Community law. In either case, it is the duty of all national courts to "disapply" offending national rules to the extent necessary to resolve such conflicts.[71]

As we have seen, these statements of the primacy of Community law are not easily reconciled with traditional notions about the supremacy of the UK Parliament.[72] If the latter theory holds good—if the Westminster Parliament does have unlimited legislative competence and no court is competent to set aside or question the validity of an Act of Parliament—it would follow that any conflict between Community law and a UK statute should be resolved in favour of the latter. Now it is true that, without the European Communities Act 1972, Community law would never have become part of the law of the United Kingdom in the first place. It was that Act which made Community law binding and enforceable in the United Kingdom rather than some magical attribute of Community law itself. And, the defenders of Westminster's sovereignty argued, the very fact that an Act of Parliament was necessary to achieve this would seem to leave

---

[68] [1963] E.C.R. 1.
[69] [1964] E.C.R. 585.
[70] *Internationale Handelsgesellschaft v Einfuhr und Vorratsstelle für Getreide und Futtermittel* [1970] E.C.R. 1125.
[71] *Amministrazione delle Finanze dello Stato v Simmenthal* [1978] E.C.R. 629.
[72] See paras 2–05—2–08.

Community law vulnerable to a subsequent Act of Parliament which contradicted it: the role of national courts as traditionally understood is to give effect to the latest expression of the sovereign will of Parliament and, it may be said, that remains the case even though the 1972 Act itself directs the British courts to give effect to any measures of Community law which create enforceable individual rights. Not surprisingly, the Community-minded disagree.

8–26   For practical purposes, the national courts of the United Kingdom effected a reconciliation between the conflicting principles of the primacy of Community law and the legal supremacy of Acts of Parliament by adopting a special principle of statutory construction in this field.[73] The *Factortame* litigation[74] made clear that this principle of construction applies even in relation to an Act of Parliament enacted after the relevant Community norm or the 1972 Act. It is presumed that any inconsistency with Community law contained in a UK statute was unintended and accidental, so that the courts are doing no more than fulfilling Parliament's true intention—to comply with Community law—by disapplying the domestic provision. This approach seems necessarily to entail the conclusion that the 1972 Act cannot be impliedly repealed by a later Act of Parliament incompatible with Community law, for the only other basis upon which the overriding force of Community law could be founded is the special quality of Community law itself, derived from the transfer of sovereignty involved in membership. In *Thoburn v Sunderland City Council*, Laws L.J. made clear his view that the supremacy of Community law in the legal orders of the United Kingdom was the result of the will of Parliament as expressed in the 1972 Act.[75] A subsequent, incompatible statute did not override the 1972 Act merely by virtue of its incompatibility, however, for the 1972 Act was a "constitutional statute" amenable to repeal only by express words or irresistible implication. The Community-minded would have it that even an attempt by Parliament expressly to repeal or override the 1972 Act would be ineffective for so long as the United Kingdom remains a member of the European Union, for the duty of the courts to disapply legislation inconsistent with Community law continues unimpaired. Confirming the view expressed by Lord Denning M.R. in *Macarthys Ltd v Smith*, Laws L.J. insisted that in such circumstances, on the

---

[73] See, *e.g. Macarthys Ltd v Smith* [1979] I.C.R. 785.
[74] *R. v S of S for Transport, ex p. Factortame Ltd (No.2)* [1991] 1 A.C. 603.
[75] [2002] 3 W.L.R. 247.

contrary, the national courts' duty of fidelity is owed to the national legislature, and not to the European Union.[76]

The constitutional consequences of membership of the Community may have been the most pronounced in the accommodation of primacy, but this far from exhausts the domestic effects of Community law. Whereas the domestic effects of an international treaty are ordinarily a matter to be determined in accordance with the constitutional law of each of the states party to that treaty, the jurisprudence of the Court of Justice attributed to Community law special characteristics besides primacy which it considered necessary to secure the effectiveness of Community law on the one hand and, on the other, to foster and promote European integration to the extent that political processes seemed incapable of doing so. As with primacy, there was rarely any basis in the text of the founding treaties for this jurisprudence, and in that sense it has justly been described as "highly political . . . drawn from a perception of the constitutional system of the Community."[77] Its genius lay in its identification of the Community as an organisation not merely of states but also of peoples and persons, who could not only be made liable to burdens and obligations but could also acquire rights under Community law calling for effective legal protection. This "enfranchisement" of the individual, and the harnessing of the

---

[76] [1979] I.C.R. 785. It is not only the courts of the UK that have had to struggle with the constitutional consequences of EU membership and the primacy of Community law. In France, the Conseil d'Etat at one time refused to question the validity of French legislation on the ground that it conflicted with Community law and declined to accept the doctrine of direct effect of directives (see, *e.g. Syndicat Général de Fabricants de Semoules de France* [1970] C.M.L.R. 395; *Minister of the Interior v Cohn-Bendit* [1980] 1 C.M.L.R. 543) and has only relatively recently signalled its acceptance of the supremacy of Community law: J. Roseren, "The Application of Community Law by the French Courts" [1994] 31 C.M.L.Rev. 315. The German constitution permits the transfer of sovereign powers to intergovernmental institutions, so to that extent the reception of the supremacy of Community law caused little difficulty. Less straightforward was the question whether Community law could take priority over the inalienable fundamental rights enshrined in the Basic law. Following the decision of the ECJ in *Internationale Handelsgesellschaft*, the German Constitutional Court refused to renounce its right to uphold fundamental rights in German law even in the face of conflict with Community law (although it found on the facts of that case that no such conflict existed): *Internationale Handelsgesellschaft v Einfuhr- und Vorratsstelle für Getreide und Futtermittel* [1974] C.M.L.R. 540. Subsequently the German courts departed from this position, but in *Brunner v Treaty on European Union* [1994] 1 C.M.L.R. 57, the Constitutional Court, while confirming the legality of ratification of the Maastricht Treaty and acknowledging the primary responsibility of the ECJ for the protection of fundamental rights, suggested that it retained the competence to perform this task if the ECJ failed to do so adequately, and also asserted a right to review the legal instruments of the European institutions to ascertain whether they remained within the limits of the sovereign rights transferred to them.

[77] P. Pescatore, "The Doctrine of Direct Effect: An infant disease of Community law" [1983] E.L. Rev. 155 at 159.

national courts to the task of securing the observance of rights derived from Community law, has been absolutely central to the achievement of the uniform application of Community law throughout the member states.[78]

Direct applicability

8–27   Direct applicability is an attribute of Community regulations which, unusually, does have an explicit textual basis in the wording of Article 249(2) of the EC Treaty. Its meaning is two-fold: first, the entry into force and application of a regulation within the national legal orders of the member states are independent of any intervention or implementation on the part of national authorities; secondly, regulations are capable of conferring rights on individuals which can be enforced directly by them before the national courts. In this latter sense, regulations could be, and sometimes were, described as being directly effective or capable of having direct effects.

Direct effect

8–28   The notion of direct effect has not, however, been confined to its application to regulations. In *Van Gend en Loos v Nederlandse Administratie der Belastingen*,[79] a reference for a preliminary ruling from a Dutch tax tribunal, the Court of Justice addressed the question of the effect, as a matter of Dutch domestic law, of Article 12 of the EC Treaty. The Court held that, unlike most international treaties, which only create mutual obligations between the states party to them, Community law imposed obligations and conferred legal rights on individuals as well. These rights would arise "not only when an explicit grant is made by the Treaty, but also through obligations imposed, in a clearly defined manner, by the Treaty on individuals as well as on member states and the Community institutions." For a Treaty Article to have this direct effect of creating an enforceable individual right, the Court held that the provision in question required to be clear, negative, unconditional, containing no reservation on the part of the member state and independent of any national implementing measure. Since Article 12 satisfied these criteria, the applicants in the *Van Gend en Loos* case were able to invoke the protection of Community law in the proceedings before their national court.

Since then the doctrine of direct effect has expanded considerably, partly as a consequence of the Court of Justice being willing to apply the supposed criteria for direct effect in a generous

---

[78] See P. Craig, "Once Upon a Time in the West: Direct Effect and the Federalisation of EC Law" [1992] 12 O.J.L.S. 453.
[79] [1963] E.C.R. 1.

manner[80] and partly through the extension of the doctrine to other measures of Community law besides Treaty Articles and regulations. Decisions were first held to be capable of having direct effect in 1970,[81] and in 1974 it was held that directives too could have direct effect and create enforceable individual rights.[82] There are however two important riders to note in relation to the direct effect of directives. First, it is only after the expiry of the time period allowed for implementation of the directive that its capacity for direct effect crystallises. The reason for this is often explained in the following way. A key feature of directives is that they leave some discretion to national authorities as to the modalities of implementation. That discretion would be meaningless if individuals could, at any time, rely directly on the terms of a directive in proceedings before national courts. However, it is equally important that, where the directive requires enforceable rights to be conferred on individuals, the member states should not be able to defeat that intention by implementing the directive erroneously or not implementing it at all within the time allowed. In other words, once the time limit for implementation has elapsed, the individual *may* found directly on the provisions of the directive in legal proceedings (provided that the conditions for direct effect are satisfied) and the national authorities cannot plead their own mistake, tardiness or other shortcomings in their defence.

Secondly, the Court of Justice has consistently held that directives cannot produce *horizontal* direct effects, that is legal rights enforceable as between private parties.[83] Since the justification for according direct effect to directives at all is largely rooted in the desire to bind member states to the proper discharge of their Community obligations—by making non-implementation or mis-implementation of directives a profitless business—it stands to reason that the institutions of the state should be caught by the direct effect of a directive. So they are, because directives are capable of producing *vertical* direct effects, or effects binding on the state. But this does not provide convincing justification for horizontal direct effect: private persons are not responsible for the proper implementation of directives into national law; thus it would be unfair to expect them to suffer the consequences of the government's failings. There is force in this reasoning. But another species of unfairness flows from distinguishing between the horizontal and vertical direct effect of directives in this way. By virtue of the vertical direct effect of directives, public employees obtain

8–29

---

[80] See, *e.g. Defrenne v SABENA* [1976] E.C.R. 455.
[81] *Grad v Finanzamt Traunstein* [1970] E.C.R. 825.
[82] *Van Duyn v Home Office* [1974] E.C.R. 1337.
[83] *Marshall v Southampton Area Health Authority* [1986] E.C.R. 723; *Faccini Dori v Recreb Srl* [1994] E.C.R. I-3325.

rights against their employer the benefit of which is denied to the
employees of private sector organisations. The Court of Justice has
acknowledged that this state of affairs is less than ideal, but (with
reason) points out that it is easily avoided provided the member
states properly implement directives into national law. In any case,
the Court has sought to mitigate the consequences of distinguishing between horizontal and vertical direct effect by developing
complementary doctrines of Community law, namely the concept
of indirect effect and the principle of state liability in damages for
breaches of Community law.

Indirect effect

8–30   One way around the fact that European directives lack horizontal direct effect, which means that an aggrieved individual in
proceedings against a private person or company may only rely on
such rights as he has under national legislation, is to require the
national courts to read and give effect to national law in such a way
as to achieve conformity with Community law. This is the doctrine
of indirect effect, and it applies whether or not the provisions of
national law in question were enacted prior or subsequent to the
relevant provisions of Community law.[84]

The central deficiency of the concept of indirect effect, however,
is that where a provision of national law cannot be read and given
effect in a way that protects the rights Community law intended the
individual to acquire, he has no option but to fall back on the lesser
protection (if any) conferred by national law and, in effect, the
intentions of the Community are defeated by the mistakes or
inaction of the member state. The further consequence of this is
that it disrupts the uniformity of the conferment and judicial
protection of Community law rights throughout the member states.
For these reasons, Community law needed to develop further
doctrines to enable the individual to bring home to the national
authorities the consequences of their wrongdoing. This was
achieved in the articulation of the doctrine of state liability in
damages for breach of Community law.

State liability in damages

8–31   The decision of the Court of Justice in *Francovich v Italy*[85]
greatly stepped up the pressure on member states to give effect to
directives on time and properly. Individuals who had suffered loss
due to the persistent non-implementation of a directive by the
Italian authorities sued the Italian government to make good the

---

[84] *Von Colson and Kamann v Land Nordrhein-Westfalen* [1984] E.C.R. 1891.
[85] [1991] E.C.R. I-5357.

damage caused to them. The Italian court referred to the Court of Justice the question whether Community law recognised any principle of member state liability in damages for failure to implement a directive. The Court of Justice held that it did, provided that the directive was intended to confer rights on individuals (whether or not those rights also satisfy the criteria of direct effect); provided also that the content of the rights is capable of being identified from the provisions of the directive; and provided there was a causal link between the member state's failure to fulfil its obligations and the loss sustained by the complainant. Subsequently, it was held that the *Francovich* doctrine was applicable to any breach by a member state of Community law provided that the breach was "sufficiently serious".[86] The decisive criterion for proving a sufficiently serious breach of Community law is whether the member state in question has "manifestly and gravely disregarded the limits on its discretion" imposed by Community law.[87]

In all of these ways—sometimes, admittedly, on slender textual foundations—the Court of Justice has built up a body of law designed to be effective in securing uniform judicial protection between the member states in areas falling within Community competence. In this regard, the Court has been as powerful, if not more powerful, an engine of European integration than the Commission. Community law, and thus the Court of Justice, will remain strong centripetal forces for cohesion and uniformity within the European Union, although it may be that this unifying force is somewhat diluted in the future by the development of the second and third pillars of the European Union, which (so far) fall largely outside the jurisdiction of the Court.

SCOTLAND IN EUROPE

Schedule 5 to the Scotland Act 1998 reserves to Westminster **8–32** "international relations, including relations with . . . the European Communities (and their institutions)."[88] This is unsurprising: the entity which is recognised in international law and which undertakes to be bound by EU law is the United Kingdom, not one or more of its constituent nations. But if the obligations flowing from

---

[86] *Brasserie du Pêcheur SA v Germany*; *R. v S of S for Transport, ex p. Factortame Ltd (No. 5)* [1996] E.C.R. I-1029.

[87] See P. Craig, "Once More unto the Breach: The Community, the state and damages liability" (1997) 113 L.Q.R. 67; W. Van Gerven, "Bridging the Unbridgeable: Community and National Tort Laws after *Francovich* and *Brasserie*" [1996] 45 I.C.L.Q. 507; T. Tridimas, "Liability for Breach of Community Law: Growing Up and Mellowing Down?" [2001] 38 C.M.L.Rev. 301.

[88] para.7(1).

membership of the European Union are obligations incumbent in the first instance on the state, it is for the state to decide how as a matter of its internal constitutional law the performance of those obligations will be achieved. Thus the general reservation contained in Schedule 5 to the Scotland Act is then qualified, to exclude from its scope the observance and implementation of obligations under Community law.[89] It follows from this that in matters of Community law falling within the scope of devolved competence, it is for the Scottish Parliament or Scottish Ministers, as appropriate, to take whatever action is deemed necessary to comply with Community law (which may be different from the action taken in the rest of the United Kingdom). Even outwith the sphere of devolved competence, the impact of Community law on Scottish interests will often make it appropriate for the Scottish Parliament and/or Scottish Ministers to be consulted on legislative proposals, to assist in the formulation of the UK's policies in relation to Europe and even to represent the United Kingdom in meetings of the Council of Ministers. All of this was foreshadowed by the devolution White Paper, *Scotland's Parliament*, and broadly speaking is what has come to pass.[90] While relations with the European Union remain the primary responsibility of the UK government, the roles of the Scottish Parliament and Scottish Executive in meeting that responsibility are recognised.[91] Yet the formal "enfranchisement" of sub-state regions in the institutional structure of the European Union remains limited. This has led to mounting calls for change, to which Scotland has lent its voice.

The debate on the constitutional future of the European Union prompted by enlargement provided regional authorities with their opportunity. The government of Flanders organised a meeting of seven principal regions having autonomous legislative power in the autumn of 2000.[92] The meeting adopted a common position on the reinforcement of the EU's regional dimension, calling for formal

---

[89] In relation to the devolved competence of the Scottish Ministers, see also SA 1998, ss 53 and 57(1).

[90] It should be noted that even prior to devolution, Scotland had some distinct representation in Europe through its MEPs and Scottish members of the Committee of the Regions and Economic and Social Committee. Since devolution, the Scottish Executive has opened an office in Brussels, alongside but distinct from Scotland Europa, a wholly-owned subsidiary of Scottish Enterprise established in 1992 which represents a variety of organisations from the public, private and voluntary sectors.

[91] The European and External Affairs Committee provides the focus for the Scottish Parliament's European activity. So far as the role of the Scottish Executive is concerned, one of the intergovernmental agreements supplementing the Memorandum of Understanding between the UK government and devolved administrations deals with joint working on European issues.

[92] These were Bavaria, Catalonia, Flanders, North Rhine Westphalia, Salzburg, Scotland and Wallonia.

recognition in the Treaties of the status of the "constitutional regions".[93] This was presented for consideration at the Nice intergovernmental conference, where it fell, by and large, on deaf ears. Undeterred, the constitutional regions issued a political declaration in May 2001, asserting their specific interest in the debate initiated at Nice on the future of Europe and demanding the right to participate directly in the preparatory work for the intergovernmental conference of 2004. The declaration contended that the EU's institutional architecture, with its focus on the European Union and the member states, had become outdated and required adaptation if it were to reflect a changing political landscape characterised by, on the one hand, globalisation, and, on the other, the trend within member states in favour of regionalisation or devolution. Meeting in Laeken in December 2001, the European Council adopted a declaration conceding the force of the constitutional regions' arguments; subsequently, both the European Parliament and Commission adopted formal resolutions to similar effect.

The latest product of the European regional movement is the **8–33** resolution adopted by the regions with legislative power (now forty in number, including Wales) in Florence in November 2002. This makes the point that in eight of the 15 member states there are 74 regions, together accounting for over half of the total EU population, having autonomous legislative power and responsibility, within their areas of legislative competence, for implementing European legislation. It then calls (among many other things) for specific recognition of member states' internal rules regarding division of competences, the inclusion of subsidiarity and proportionality as binding obligations rather than political principles, the establishment of a mechanism designed to identify the need for direct involvement by the regions in the European legislative process, and the conferment of special rights on constitutional regions, as listed in the Treaty. It is perhaps unsurprising that the draft Treaty establishing a constitution for Europe goes nowhere near this far (and in fact does not go much further than making certain vague references to respect for diversity and the constitutional traditions of the member states). There are risks in extending special rights and status to entities less than states on the basis of the happenstance of internal constitutional organisation.[94]

---

[93] Defined as those sub-state entities accorded a package of powers by the constitutions of their parent states, which have their own government and parliament and which are competent to promulgate laws autonomously and sometimes even at the same level as the sovereign states

[94] Depending on the nature of the rights and status claimed, it is not inconceivable that by adroit constitutional reorganisation, a member state could substantially increase its influence in the legislative process. Arguably, that process is sufficiently complex already without incorporating further disputants.

While it is true that the constitutional regions have some telling points to make, and while greater connectivity between the institutions of the European Union and the regions might support the efforts of the former to enhance their legitimacy and accountability, the fact remains that the constitutional regions are larger, richer and more popular, in many cases, than some of the member states (and member states soon-to-be) strictly so-called. The bargaining position of such member states is already relatively weak. They will be resistant to moves to weaken it further; and that would indubitably be the effect of conferring some form of formal status on the regions, constitutional or otherwise.

CHAPTER 9

ACCESS TO INFORMATION

Introduction

One of the complaints of human rights sceptics is that a focus on **9–01** rights fosters a belief that social ills can be cured through litigation rather than political processes. As we have seen, those who dispute this view accept that political processes are deficient in many respects, but contend that the remedy for such deficiencies lies in revivifying those processes, and not in subjecting political power to ever-increasing legal controls. Freedom of information is seen as one of the key methods by which this may be achieved. On this analysis, freedom of information is necessary if the electorate are to make informed choices: it conduces to a genuinely participative democratic culture. This is not to say that the proponents of a "rights culture" are opposed to freedom of information. On the contrary, access to information, particularly personal information, may be a corollary of fundamental rights in certain circumstances.[1] Equally, freedom of information may be seen as necessary to enable effective criticism of governmental (and other) bodies, to detect them in wrongdoing, and thus to enhance existing avenues of accountability for the exercise of public power.

So the rationales for freedom of expression differ. But whatever the rationale, campaigners for freedom of information had for a long time to contend with the "British disease", a culture of secrecy which found its most perfect expression in the provisions of the Official Secrets Act 1911, under which virtually any unauthorised disclosure of official information constituted a criminal offence.[2] In this context, any public interest in hearing what is disclosed is irrelevant; official information is a species of property over which its owner—the state—must have control. Reform was gradual and grudging, driven in part by a need to comply with international

---

[1] See, *e.g. Gaskin v UK* (1989) 12 E.H.R.R. 36 and the Health Records Act 1990.
[2] See, *e.g.* K. G. Robertson, *Public Secrets* (Macmillan, London, 1982); D. Hooper, *Official Secrets: The Use and Abuse of the Act* (Secker and Warburg, 1987); and, now, the Official Secrets Act 1989.

obligations,[3] in part by less salutary motives.[4] The government took its first steps towards a comprehensive freedom of information regime in 1993, publishing a White Paper[5] in which it proposed the establishment of an informal Code of Practice on Government Information. The White Paper itself recognised that open government could be a means to more than one end, envisaging the dissemination of information in such a way as "to promote informed policy making and debate, and efficient service delivery"[6] and to provide "timely and accessible information to the citizen to explain the government's policies, actions and decisions."[7] The code brought much official information into the public domain at once.[8] Beyond that, although the code did not create *rights* to information as such, it entitled individuals to *request* its provision, and backed up that entitlement by adding compliance with the code to the jurisdiction of the Parliamentary Commissioner for Administration.[9]

---

[3] Thus, *e.g.* the Data Protection Act 1998 and Environmental Protection Regulations both originate in EU directives.

[4] The enactment of freedom of information legislation applicable to local authorities, such as the Local Government (Access to Information) Act 1985, is instructive here. As Birkinshaw has remarked of this Act, "there is an immediate irony in the fact that it was passed with the approval of a government which had steadfastly refused such legislation for itself" but which recognised its controlling potential as applied to others: see P. Birkinshaw, *Freedom of Information: The Law, the Practice and the Ideal* (3rd ed., Butterworths, London, 2001).

[5] *Open Government*, Cm 2290 (1993). It has been suggested that the timing of this initiative was no accident: "the Major government, with a small majority in the House of Commons, with the prospect of renewed attempts by the Freedom of Information Campaign to introduce Private Members' Bills creating statutory rights of access to official information, and with the near-certainty of a significant number of Conservative back-bench rebels willing to support such measures, calculated in 1993 that it was better to concede defeat on its own terms than to be forced into unconditional surrender" (R. Austin, "Freedom of Information: The constitutional impact" in *The Changing Constitution* (4th Jowell and Oliver ed., Oxford University Press, Oxford, 2000), p.356). Others have been more charitable, seeing the code's introduction as a sign that the climate of secrecy was slowly receding: see, *e.g.* C. Harlow and R. Rawlings, *Law and Administration* (2nd ed., Butterworths, London, 1997), pp.449–452.

[6] In the latter respect, the code of practice was of a piece with the Major government's Citizens' Charter Initiative, which required the publication of performance indicators and encouraged the giving of reasoned decisions.

[7] *Open Government*, at para.1.7.

[8] In so far as it required the publication of information relating to the running of public services; explanatory materials (including rules, procedures and internal guidance) on departments' dealings with the public; and "the facts and analysis which the government considers relevant and important in framing major policy proposals and decisions".

[9] Even critics of this arrangement have conceded that the PCA has approached this jurisdiction "in spirited fashion": see P. Birkinshaw, "I only ask for information" [1993] P.L. 557. The PCA deems every refusal to provide information to constitute *prima facie* "injustice", placing the burden of justification firmly on the shoulders of the department or agency concerned.

The code, supplemented since May 1999 by the Code of Practice **9–02** on Access to Scottish Executive Information, continues in force for the time being. But the Labour government elected in 1997 came to power with a clear manifesto commitment to introduce fully-fledged freedom of information legislation as an aspect of its wider programme of constitutional reform, the fruit of which commitment is the Freedom of Information Act 2000 and (less directly) the Freedom of Information (Scotland) Act 2002. Neither will enter fully into force until 2005. If nothing else, this delay will provide us with the opportunity, some years hence, of comparing the existing, non-statutory regime as enforced by the ombudsmen, with the new, statutory regimes as enforced by specialist commissioners and, ultimately, the courts.

As originally drafted, the Scotland Act 1998 did not reserve freedom of information to Westminster. Subsequently, Schedule 5 of the Act was amended[10] to exclude freedom of information from the scope of devolved competence except so far as it applied to purely Scottish public authorities. The effect of this is that cross-border public authorities,[11] together with UK departments and agencies, are subject only to the regime contained in the 2000 Act, even where a request for information concerns only its functions in relation to Scottish and/or devolved matters.

FREEDOM OF INFORMATION (SCOTLAND) ACT 2002

Like its Westminster counterpart, the Freedom of Information **9–03** (Scotland) Act 2002 was preceded by widespread consultation, initially on the basis of the Scottish Executive's consultation document *An Open Scotland*, and latterly on the basis of a draft bill published in March 2001. The Act provides a general right of access to information held by listed or designated "Scottish public authorities" (or companies wholly owned by such authorities) subject to a variety of exceptions, some absolute, others based on a test of "substantial prejudice to the public interest". It establishes the office of the Scottish Information Commissioner, to whom a dissatisfied applicant may appeal against a decision not to disclose. The applicant or authority may appeal against a determination of the commissioner to the Court of Session.

---

[10] By the Scotland Act 1998 (Modifications of Schedules 4 and 5) Order 1999 (SI 1999/1749).
[11] As provided for by SA 1988, ss 88–90.

The access right

9–04   Where a person ("the applicant") requests information from a
Scottish public authority which holds that information, he is
entitled to be given it by the authority.[12] If the authority reasonably
requires further information from the applicant in order to identify
and locate the requested information, it is not obliged to release
the requested information until it has that further information.[13]
The information to be given by the authority is that which it holds
at the time the request is received, except that any amendment or
deletion which it would have made regardless of the request may
be made before the information is released.[14] Nor is the requested
information to be destroyed before it can be given, unless the
circumstances are such that it is not reasonably practicable to
prevent its destruction.[15] A request must be made in writing or
such other form "which by reason of its having some permanency is
capable of being used for subsequent reference",[16] must state the
name of the applicant and an address for correspondence, and
describe the information sought.[17] An authority receiving a request
with which it is required by section 1 to comply *may*, within the
time allowed by section 10 for so complying, notify the applicant in
writing that a fee of the amount specified in the notice is payable,
and is not obliged to give the requested information until the fee is
duly paid.[18] Normally, where an authority is required to give the
information requested, it must do so "promptly, and in any event
not later than the twentieth working day after" its receipt of the
request or of the further information reasonably required by it in
order to locate the information requested.[19] It would appear that

---

[12] Freedom of Information (Scotland) Act 2002, s.1(1).

[13] 2002 Act, s.1(3).

[14] 2002 Act, s.1(4).

[15] In her excellent annotations to the 2002 Act, Rosalind McInnes suggests that
"reasonably practicable" as used here tends to denote not so much what is
feasible as what is administratively convenient.

[16] 2002 Act, s.8(1)(a). Electronic requests are acceptable. The section gives recordings made on audio or video tape as examples of alternative forms of request.

[17] 2002 Act, s.8(1)(b), (c).

[18] 2002 Act, s.9(1), (3). A fee is duly paid within the period of three months
beginning on the day on which the fee notice is given. Fees chargeable under
s.9(1) are to be determined by the authority in accordance with regulations made
by the Scottish Ministers after consultation with the Scottish Information
Commissioner. No such regulations have yet been made.

[19] 2002 Act, s.10(1). Section 10(2) allows a period of thirty working days for
compliance by the Keeper of the Records of Scotland where the information
sought is information to which s.22(2)–(5) applies, *i.e.* information contained in
records transferred to the Keeper by a Scottish public authority which has not
been designated by the authority as "open information" for the purposes of that
section. Where the authority has issued a fees notice to the applicant, the periods
of 20 or 30 working days are to be calculated disregarding the period between the

"promptly" means exactly that, and a public authority would not be entitled to delay until the end of the allowable period for compliance if the information could have been given sooner. Although the relative brevity of the allowable periods may mean that delay is of little consequence in most cases, it is conceivable that a public authority would attract censure from the Scottish Information Commissioner where, for example, information is requested by a journalist in connection with an issue of pressing topicality and the authority is seen to have dragged its feet.

Section 11 of the Act sets out the differing means whereby an authority may comply with its duty under section 1. It may, first, provide the applicant with a copy of the information requested, in permanent form or other form acceptable to the applicant; or provide a digest or summary of the information requested; or offer the applicant a reasonable opportunity to inspect a record containing the information.[20] Where the applicant expresses a preference for one or other of these means, the authority must give effect to that preference so far as reasonably practicable.[21]

Exceptions and exemptions

So much for when the authority is obliged to comply with a **9–05** request for information. But the general right of access under section 1 is qualified in a number of ways. Some of these qualifications are not related as such to the nature of the information sought: thus, the authority is not obliged to comply with a request for information where it estimates that the cost of compliance would exceed an amount prescribed by the Scottish Ministers in regulations[22]; nor is it obliged to comply with "vexatious"

---

date of issue of the notice and the date of receipt of payment: s.10(4). The Scottish Ministers may vary either period for compliance, whether generally or in relation to specific cases, but may not extend it beyond 60 working days.

[20] 2002 Act, s.11(2).

[21] 2002 Act, s.11(1). Section 11(3) provides that, in determining what is reasonably practicable, the authority may have regard to all the circumstances, including cost (although this is not to be taken as reducing the scope of any duties owed by the authority under the Disability Discrimination Act 1995). Where the authority concludes that it is not reasonably practicable to give effect to the applicant's preference, it must notify the applicant of its reasons.

[22] 2002 Act, s.12(1). In this respect, regulations may provide for the aggregation of costs associated with two or more requests from the same person, or requests from different persons "who appear to be acting in concert or whose requests appear to have been instigated wholly or mainly for a purpose other than the obtaining of the information itself": s.12(2)(a), (b). The latter provision in particular was contentious, being viewed as capable of frustrating legitimate campaigning activities (although the Justice Minister stated before the Justice 1 Committee at Stage One of the Bill that this was not its purpose, and that, together with a number of other statements by the Minister, may prove useful in the *Pepper v Hart* sense when, in the fullness of time, provisions of the Act fall for judicial interpretation). Note also s.12(2)(c), which permits authorities to elect to make information requested by different applicants available to the public at large by way of fulfilment of its s.1 duty.

requests or repeated requests for the same information from the same person.[23] These apart, the qualifications to the duty to disclose are based on the nature or contents of the information sought.

Absolute exemptions

9–06   Section 2(1) provides that, where information is exempt information by virtue of any provision in Part 2 of the Act, the section 1 duty applies only to the extent that "(a) the provision does not confer absolute exemption; and (b) in all the circumstances of the case, the public interest in disclosing the information is not outweighed by that in maintaining the exemption."[24] Absolute exemptions are created by sections 25, 26, 36(2), 37 and 38(1).[25] Let us deal with the more straightforward of these first. Section 25 provides that information which the applicant can reasonably obtain other than by requesting it under section 1 is exempt information, and for these purposes information *may* be reasonably obtainable even if a charge is made for access to it,[26] and is to be taken to be reasonably obtainable if the authority which holds it (or any other person) is obliged by or under any enactment to communicate it or if it is held and made available for inspection and copying by the Keeper of the Records of Scotland. Information which is not thus placed in the public domain is not to be regarded as reasonably obtainable, even though it is available on request, unless it is made available in accordance with the relevant authority's publication scheme.[27] Section 26 confers absolute exemption from disclosure on information the disclosure of which is prohibited by or under an enactment other than the 2002 Act itself, or which is incompatible with a Community obligation, or

---

[23] 2002 Act, s.14. The concept of vexatious requests also caused disquiet during the parliamentary stages of the Bill, inviting as it does inquiry into the motives of an applicant for information. Note, however, that the courts have a comparable power under the Vexatious Actions (Scotland) Act 1898, which may be felt to raise more serious questions so far as it impinges on the fundamental right of access to the courts. It may be that, in applying the criterion in s.14, public authorities and the Scottish Information Commissioner will obtain guidance from the approach of the courts to the question: see *H.M. Advocate v Bell*, 2002 S.L.T. 527.

[24] The drafting is inexplicable. The plain intention of the bill's sponsors, and the understanding of MSPs, is that absolute exemptions apply notwithstanding any public interest in the disclosure of the information, but the use of the word "and" to link paras (a), (b) indicates that, even where an absolute exemption applies, the information may be disclosed if the public interest in disclosure is greater than the public interest in withholding it.

[25] In the latter case, subject to qualifications.

[26] 2002 Act, s.25(2)(a).

[27] 2002 Act, s.25(3). For publication schemes, see s.23.

which would constitute, or be punishable as, a contempt of court.[28] Section 37 confers a like exemption, subject to the 30-year rule,[29] on court records and similar material.

The two remaining absolute exemptions raise broader questions, dealing as they do with confidential information and information subject to the regime contained in the Data Protection Act 1998. Section 36(2) confers absolute exemption from disclosure on confidential information if such was "(a) obtained by a Scottish public authority from another person (including another such authority); and (b) its disclosure by the authority so obtaining it to the public (otherwise than under this Act) would constitute a breach of confidence actionable by that person or any other person."[30] This is an exemption of considerable significance and scope, notwithstanding the Justice Minister's attempts to downplay it, and not merely because of recent developments in the law of confidentiality.[31] A duty of confidence may be imposed by an express or implied term of a contract, or it may arise from the receipt of information in circumstances importing such a duty. In the latter case at least, the information must have the necessary quality of confidentiality, *i.e.* it must not be merely trivial, and must not be already in the public domain.[32] It is recognised that a duty of confidence may be qualified or overridden by a countervailing

---

[28] Note, however, that s.64 of the 2002 Act confers on the Scottish Ministers power by order to repeal or amend extant statutory prohibitions on the disclosure of information, so far as they apply to Scottish public authorities.

[29] As to which, see ss.57 and 58 of the 2002 Act. Under s.57, a record benefits from exemption until such time as it becomes a "historical record", which is usually at the end of the 30th year following the year of creation of the record.

[30] The reference to disclosure "under this Act"—which again seems at first glance to sit ill with the concept of absolute exemption—here denotes the provision made in ss.57 and 58 of the 2002 Act for the lifting of the exemption once the record in which the information is contained becomes a "historical record", *i.e.* (subject to variations prescribed in regulations made under s.59) at the end of the period of 30 years commencing with the beginning of the calendar year following that in which the record is created.

[31] These developments have been driven primarily by the duty of the courts as "public authorities" for the purposes of s.6 of the HRA 1998 to provide an effective remedy for invasions of privacy, a right protected by ECHR, Art.8, in the absence of a domestic cause of action therefor: see, *e.g. Douglas v Hello! Ltd (No.6)* [2003] 3 All E.R. 996; *Peck v UK* (2003) 36 E.H.R.R. 41.

[32] Limited prior disclosure will not necessarily deprive information of its confidential character: see *Attorney-General v Guardian Newspapers Ltd (No. 2)* [1990] 1 A.C. 109 at 282, *per* Lord Goff ("the *Spycatcher* case"). It is implicit in Lord Goff's speech in this case that contractual obligations of confidence protect only truly confidential information, but dicta in other cases (see, *e.g. Coco v A. N. Clark (Engineers) Ltd* [1969] R.P.C. 41 at 47) suggest otherwise. Whether the claimed duty of confidence arises contractually or extra-contractually, it should be noted that information which is, or which comes into, the public domain might in any case be exempted from disclosure under s.25 of the 2002 Act on the basis that it is reasonably obtainable otherwise than by way of a request under s.1.

public interest in disclosure.[33] In some situations, the disclosure of confidential information is required by law despite its confidential character, as where a court compels production of confidential documents, other than those subject to legal professional privilege, in litigation. Here the focus is different: disclosure is only required under the 2002 Act where the information is shown *not* to be subject to duties of confidence. Whether or not that is the case is for the holder of the information, in the first place, to determine. Thereafter,[34] an applicant has a right of recourse to the Scottish Information Commissioner and the commissioner, if his view of things differs from that of the authority, may (among other things) issue an enforcement notice requiring the authority to disclose that which it believes to be confidential.

9–07 At this point it is worth pausing to observe that, predictably enough, the concerns of MSPs in relation to the confidentiality exemption focused almost wholly on the spectre of private contractors requiring public authorities to accept wide-ranging "gagging clauses" when contracting with them. In evidence to the Justice 1 Committee of the Scottish Parliament, the Justice Minister sought to reassure: "the Commissioner will have a broad supervisory role in ensuring that authorities do not accept unnecessary obligations of confidence . . . [and] will have a role in determining whether the exemption has been claimed properly."[35] So too he may.[36] But there is nothing in the 2002 Act which affects the contractual capacity of public authorities as such; and if the policy of the Act is to make as much information held by public authorities available for disclosure as possible, that policy does not override or alter the nature of confidential obligations. If information is placed in the hands of a public authority, whether by a private contractor or anybody else, in circumstances importing a duty of confidence, or subject to a valid contractual term prohibiting its disclosure, the authority has a legal duty, actionable not only at the instance of the confider but also, possibly, of third parties, to refrain from disclosing that information unless and until a court of law holds that some

---

[33] See R. G. Toulson and C. M. Phipps, *Confidentiality* (Sweet and Maxwell, London, 1996), paras 6.05–6.24. The authors suggest at para.6.11 that "the true principle is not (as *dicta* in some cases suggest) that the court will permit a breach of confidence whenever it considers that disclosure would serve the public interest more than non-disclosure, but rather that no obligation of confidence exists in contract or [otherwise] in so far as the subject-matter concerns a serious risk of public harm (including but not limited to cases of 'iniquity') and the alleged obligation would prevent disclosure appropriate to prevent such harm."

[34] For the enforcement powers of the Scottish Information Commissioner, see para.9–13.

[35] Official Report, Justice 1 Committee (Feb. 26, 2002), cols 3274, 3275.

[36] As may the Scottish Ministers, who have a duty under s.60 of the 2002 Act to issue guidance to public authorities in relation to, *inter alia*, "the inclusion in contracts entered into by public authorities of terms relating to the disclosure of information."

exception to the duty is established.[37] The Scottish Information Commissioner is not a court, and as such cannot issue legally conclusive determinations of the question whether a duty of confidence is properly claimed. If he should take enforcement action to compel disclosure, the authority could, to be sure, appeal to the Court of Session against that decision. Equally, it is suggested, it would be within its rights to do nothing. The Scottish Information Commissioner may certify a failure to comply with an enforcement order in writing to the Court of Session, and the Court of Session *may*, *if* it decides to inquire into the matter and having heard both sides, treat that failure as a contempt of court. Absent some element of bad faith on the part of the authority, however, the power to characterise compliance with a pre-sumptively valid legal duty of confidence should not be lightly stigmatised as contempt. Some of the statements made in the course of the Act's parliamentary passage do not accurately capture the limits of the commissioner's jurisdiction in this respect.

The fifth and final absolute exemption provided by the Act concerns personal information.[38] Information is exempt informa-tion under this section if it constitutes personal data of which the applicant is the "data subject"[39]; personal census information; a deceased person's health record[40]; or personal data the disclosure of which would contravene any of the "data protection principles" prescribed by the Data Protection Act 1998 or which would be likely to cause damage or distress contrary to section 10 of the 1998 Act.[41] The Data Protection Act and the freedom of information legislation are alike concerned with access to information. But while the latter approaches the matter from a "disclosure on request" perspective, the former is equally concerned with the protection of the privacy of data subjects. The general strategy of the freedom of information legislation north and south of the border is to ensure that applications for access to personal information are routed through the data protection regime. Achievable in principle this may be, but the potential practical difficulties are readily apparent.[42] Data protection is a reserved matter, so a single, UK regime applies in that field. The Data Protection Act was amended in various respects by the Freedom of

---

[37] Or, of course, unless the confider consents to the disclosure.
[38] 2002 Act, s.38.
[39] For a definition of "data subject", see the Data Protection Act 1998, s.10.
[40] In the case of personal census information and a deceased person's health records, the exemption lapses after 100 years in accordance with the provisions of ss.57 and 58 of the 2002 Act.
[41] Personal data to which the data subject would not have a right of access under the Data Protection Act 1998 is also exempt from disclosure under the 2002 Act.
[42] See K. Meechan, "Freedom of Information—North and South of the Tweed" [2001] J.L.G.L. 111 at 114, 115.

Information Act 2000, in a manner which took account of the needs of that Act but not of the parallel Scottish legislation. It is far from improbable, therefore, that a Scottish public authority could find itself facing enforcement action by the Scottish Information Commissioner under the 2002 Act if it does not disclose, and enforcement action by the Information Commissioner under the 1998 Act if it does.

Class and content exemptions

9–08 In keeping with the nonchalant indifference to logical order that marks the arrangement of the absolute exemptions, so too are the class- and content-based exemptions scattered more or less at random throughout Part 2 of the Act. Class-based exemptions protect documents falling within the classes specified from disclosure so long as it can be shown that the harm to the public interest that would flow from disclosure outweighs the public interest in disclosure. There are eight categories of protected documents prescribed by the Act, as follows.

Section 27(1) deals with information that is to be published in the near future. The exemption applies if, at the time a request is received, it is intended to publish the information within 12 weeks of that date, and it is reasonable in all the circumstances to withhold it from disclosure until then.[43] Section 29 applies to information held by the Scottish Administration[44] that relates to the formulation or development of government policy, ministerial communications, the provision of advice by any of the Law Officers or a request for such advice, or to the operation of any ministerial private office.[45] The exemption lapses in respect of information contained in a historical record over 30 years old. The justification for this exemption is, in essence, the need for candour in discussions between ministers and officials although, as a number of objectors pointed out, the "participation" rationale for freedom of information would normally require the disclosure of information relating to policy formation in order that those with an interest in doing so may contribute thereto on an informed footing. Section 31 provides a class exemption for information required for the purpose of safeguarding national security, and a certificate signed

---

[43] An amendment which would have removed the exemption were publication to be postponed beyond the twelfth week was rejected on the basis that, if publication were to be delayed repeatedly, the Scottish Information Commissioner would be entitled to conclude that it was no longer reasonable to rely on s.27(1) of the 2002 Act.

[44] As defined by the SA 1998 s.126.

[45] This does not include statistical information used to provide an informed background to the taking of policy decisions, once those decisions have been taken: 2002 Act, s.29(2).

by a member of the Scottish Executive that information falls within the scope of the exemption will be conclusive evidence of that fact.[46] Section 32(1)(b) provides a class exemption in respect of confidential information obtained from a state other than the United Kingdom, an international organisation or international court. Section 33(1)(a) confers a class exemption on information that constitutes a "trade secret". MSPs voiced much the same concerns here as in relation to the confidentiality exemption under section 36(2), to the effect that the exemption might be exploited by commercial undertakings dealing with public authorities. However, even if there is no universal formula for determining what constitutes a trade secret, the case law does provide substantial guidance.[47] Moreover, as these authorities imply, the presumptive exemption for trade secrets may often prove redundant, since the communication of information constituting a trade secret is likely to be regarded as covered by a duty of confidence, even absent a contractual term to that effect. Section 34 provides a class exemption for information that has at any time been held by a public authority for the purposes of investigations conducted by it or proceedings arising out of such investigations. Section 36(1) provides a class exemption for information "in respect of which a claim of confidentiality could be maintained in legal proceedings". This is intended to cover not only information in respect of which a claim of legal professional privilege could be maintained, but also, for example, communications protected from disclosure by section 10 of the Contempt of Court Act 1981. In relation to legal professional privilege at least, difficulties similar to those alluded to in the discussion of the confidentiality exemption exist. Put simply, an enforcement notice issued by the Scottish Information Commissioner requiring the disclosure of information for which privilege is claimed will not and cannot determine the validity of the claim. That must be a decision for the courts. Again, therefore, an

---

[46] It is the intention of the Scottish Executive to make arrangements under SA 1998, s.104, for a right of appeal against such certificates to a special national security panel of the Information Tribunal established by the 2000 Act, but no such arrangements are yet in place. While in principle the decision to issue a certificate would be susceptible to judicial review, the tendency of the courts has been to treat "conclusive evidence certificates" as exactly that, even outwith the context of national security: see, *e.g. R. v Registrar of Companies, ex p. Central Bank of India* [1986] Q.B. 1114.

[47] In *Faccenda Chicken Ltd v Fowler* [1987] 1 Ch. 117 at 137–138, Neill L.J. referred to "secret processes of manufacture" and "innumerable other pieces of information which, while not properly to be described as a trade secret, are in all the circumstances of such a high degree of confidentiality as to require the same protection." In *Lansing Linde Ltd v Kerr* [1991] 1 W.L.R. 251, Staughton L.J. held the term to cover information used in a trade or business which was restricted in its dissemination and the disclosure of which would be liable to cause real or significant harm to the party claiming confidentiality.

authority would be entitled to resist the enforcement notice (whether by way of appeal or by way of ignoring it) pending resolution of the privilege question.[48] Finally, section 41 confers a class exemption on information relating to communications with the Queen, other members of the Royal Family or the royal household, or to the exercise by the Queen of her prerogative of honour.[49]

9–09 The third species of exemption created by the Act is content-based, and may be claimed only where the disclosure of information would, or would be likely to, cause substantial prejudice to the public interest. There are 11 such categories, as follows.

Section 27(2) applies to information obtained in the course of, or derived from, a programme of research being undertaken with a view to publication by a Scottish public authority or any other person, provided its disclosure in advance of publication would, or would be likely to, prejudice substantially the interests of the programme or any person participating in it, or the interests of a public authority (whether or not the authority which holds the information).[50] Information the disclosure of which would or might substantially prejudice relations between the administrations of the United Kingdom[51] is exempted by section 28, although the exemption lapses after 30 years. Subject to the same long-stop, section 30 exempts from disclosure information the disclosure of which would or might prejudice substantially the "maintenance of the convention of the collective responsibility of the Scottish Ministers",[52] or which would or might inhibit substantially the free and frank provision of advice or exchange of views, or which would otherwise risk substantial harm to the effective conduct of public affairs.[53] Section 31(4) exempts information the disclosure of which risks substantial prejudice to the defence of the British islands or of any colony, or to the capability, effectiveness or security of any of the

---

[48] For a recent consideration of the scope of legal professional privilege, see *Three Rivers DC v Governor and Company of the Bank of England (No. 4)* [2002] 4 All E.R. 881.

[49] The former exemption lapses after thirty years, the latter after 60: 2002 Act, ss.57 and 58(1), (2)(b).

[50] This would include, but is not limited to, research having a potential commercial value.

[51] Namely, the UK Government, the Scottish Administration, the Executive Committee of the NI Assembly and the National Assembly for Wales.

[52] Nothing more is said about this by way of definition, but it presumably refers to disclosures apt to detract from the appearance of Cabinet solidarity on key issues of Executive policy. In practice, of course, such disclosures are routinely made (without the intervention of freedom of information legislation) in the form of leaks.

[53] This is the candour argument again, which in the context of s.29 of the 2002 Act justifies the application of the public interest test *simpliciter*. The line between the two, and thus the point at which it becomes necessary to demonstrate substantial harm to the public interest in order to resist disclosure, is not absolutely clear.

armed forces of the Crown or forces co-operating with those forces.[54] Under section 32(1)(a), information the disclosure of which risks substantial prejudice to the interests of the United Kingdom abroad or to relations between the United Kingdom and any other state, international organisation or international court is exempt. Section 33(1)(b) exempts information the disclosure of which would, or would be likely to, prejudice substantially the commercial interests of any person, whether or not a Scottish public authority[55]; and section 33(2) exempts information the disclosure of which risks substantial prejudice to the economic interests of the whole or part of the United Kingdom or the financial interests of an administration in the United Kingdom.[56] Section 35 exempts information the disclosure of which risks substantial prejudice to law enforcement activities, including the prevention and detection of crime, the administration of justice, the operation of immigration controls and the maintenance of security and good order in prisons.[57] Section 40 exempts information the disclosure of which risks substantial prejudice to the exercise of any Scottish public authority's functions in relation to the audit of the accounts of other Scottish public authorities, or the examination of the economy, efficiency and effectiveness with which such authorities use their resources in discharging their functions. Lastly, section 39 makes slightly differently worded provision in relation to health, safety and the environment. Section 39(1) provides that information is exempt from disclosure if its disclosure would, or would be likely to, endanger the physical or mental health or safety of an individual. Section 39(2) provides that information which an authority would be obliged to make available to the public under the Environmental Information Regulations is exempt from disclosure under the 2002 Act (which is to say that such information will be covered by the specific regime applicable to it, in a manner comparable to disclosures covered by the Data Protection Act). Power to adopt regulations in implementation of the 1998 Aarhus Convention on Access to Information, Public

---

[54] Again, the distinction between national security, which benefits from a class exemption and the added protection (if used) of ministerial certification under s.31(1), (2) of the 2002 Act, and the defence of the realm, which is subject to the substantial harm test, may prove a delicate one to draw in practice.

[55] Which information by definition cannot be information protected by a duty of confidence, since such would benefit from the absolute exemption under s.36(2) of the 2002 Act.

[56] This exemption may have a significant role to play in relation to the trading and commercial activities of public authorities and the activities of economic development agencies such as Scottish Enterprise. And what price disclosure of information relating to the Holyrood project?

[57] This exemption lapses only on the expiry of a 100-year period: 2002 Act, s.58(2)(b).

Participation in Decision Making and Access to Justice in Environmental Matters is conferred on the Scottish Ministers by section 62
of the Act.

9–10   The overall picture, then, is one of onerous complexity. In
respect of some categories of information, there is potential for
conflict between different statutory regimes. Within the scheme of
the 2002 Act itself (as with its Westminster counterpart) there are
significant overlaps between the different categories of exempt
information, and it remains to be seen how the Scottish Information Commissioner and, ultimately, the courts will approach claims
to a higher degree of protection (whether by way of an absolute or
class exemption) where the information in question also falls within
a category of exemption subject to the "substantial prejudice" test.
It is unfortunate that at neither the UK nor the Scottish levels was
a greater effort made to reconcile the competing regimes or to
introduce some degree of rhyme and reason into the various
categories of exemption. As it is, public authorities themselves, in
the front line of dealing with requests for information, will have to
address some difficult questions in responding, mindful not only of
their duties under the 2002 Act (and their susceptibility to censure
thereunder) but also their other legal duties.[58] It is to these
entities—the Scottish public authorities charged with giving effect
to the access right under section 1—that we now turn.

Scottish public authorities

9–11   As we have seen, the Human Rights Act 1998 generally eschews
a prescriptive approach to the definition of "public authorities" for
the purposes of that Act. Apart from courts and tribunals[59] and
"standard" public authorities—those whose status as such is too
obvious to merit further elucidation—a given entity is a public
authority under the Human Rights Act if and to the extent that it
exercises a "public function". The 2002 Act, like the 2000 Act, does
not follow this approach, preferring instead to limit the term
"Scottish public authority" by reference to the list of bodies
contained in Schedule 1, publicly-owned companies as defined by
section 6 and any other bodies designated by order under section
5(1). So far as this lends itself to greater clarity, it is to be
welcomed, particularly given the obscurity elsewhere in the Act.
But there are, and were, arguments the other way. A general
"public function" test comparable to that contained in the Human
Rights Act would place the onus on the recipient of a request for

---

[58] Most notably, their duty under s.6 of the HRA 1998 to act in conformity with the
Convention rights, in particular the right of third parties to respect for their
privacy.

[59] Which are *not* public authorities for the purposes either of the Freedom of
Information Act 2000 or of the Freedom of Information (Scotland) Act 2002.

information to demonstrate that it is not (either generally or in this particular respect) a public authority. As it is, something akin to that test will fall to be applied by the Scottish Ministers in considering whether to designate a body as a Scottish public authority under section 5(1),[60] but whether that body is in fact subject to the freedom of information regime prescribed by the Act will depend on the rigour with which the Scottish Ministers approach the business of designation. In that regard, the difficulty (even assuming the Scottish Ministers are appropriately assiduous) is that public functions fall to be performed in all manner of ways, through an ever-increasing (and frequently changing) variety of public/private partnerships, contracting out and other "arm's length" mechanisms. In this scenario, existing listings and designations are apt to become, if not redundant, then inaccurate and incomplete in their depiction of the way in which public functions are performed.

So too with the definition of publicly-owned companies in section 6 of the Act. Such a company, to be caught by the Act, must be wholly owned by either the Scottish Ministers or any other listed public authority.[61] It is only wholly owned if all its members are the Scottish Ministers or relevant public authority, or other companies wholly owned by the Scottish Ministers or authority, or persons acting on behalf of the Scottish Ministers or authority. A proposed amendment to extend the definition to companies in which the Scottish Ministers or authority had a controlling interest was rejected since, as the Justice Minister rightly observed, such a definition would easily be evaded by taking a less than controlling interest in the company concerned. But the same objection may be levelled at the definition as it stands: the introduction of one "independent" member would suffice to remove the company from the scope of section 6. Of course, such a company—or indeed any company engaging in the provision of public services or the performance of public functions—might be designated under section 5 of the Act. But that merely takes us back to where we started. Thus the coverage of the Act will depend to no small extent on the approach taken by the Scottish Ministers to designation. That in turn depends on effecting some kind of reconciliation between, on the one hand, the policy of the Act in facilitating disclosure and, on the other, the real practical and conceptual problems that arise at the margins.

It is not, it seems, the way of MSPs to extend the slightest sympathy to private sector organisations involved in public service

---

[60] See the test prescribed by s.5(2)(a), (b) of the 2002 Act. Note also that under s.7, the Scottish Ministers may limit the scope of a listing in Sch.1, which again may be necessary to reflect the fact that a body combines public and private functions.
[61] Other than one whose listing is restricted in terms of s.7 of the 2002 Act.

delivery, despite the fact that it is the explicit policy of the Scottish Executive to encourage innovative and imaginative approaches to that task.[62] But even if large commercial undertakings may fairly be expected to shoulder the legal, administrative and compliance costs involved in fulfilling the battery of duties laid on public authorities by the Act, small and medium-sized companies and voluntary organisations may be less fitted to cope. If we wish to improve the performance of public services, and if we recognise that improvement may best be achieved by new models of service delivery, to what extent is it appropriate, or indeed consistent, to inhibit the involvement of the private and voluntary sector by subjecting their involvement to the rigours of freedom of information? To raise this question is not to contradict the argument offered above, that private or voluntary sector bodies performing public functions on a contracted-out or like basis should be regarded, to that extent, as public authorities for the purposes of the Human Rights Act.[63] In that context, the burden placed on the service provider will typically extend no further than properly justifying its choices, when challenged, within the parameters permitted by the Convention rights.[64] The freedom of information regime, by contrast, entails ongoing compliance with a number of more or less onerous duties and controls, and it is at least arguable that any incidental advantage to the common weal flowing from the inclusion of such bodies within that regime would be outweighed by the harm done to developing approaches to service delivery.[65]

9–12   Let us turn now to the duties incumbent on Scottish public authorities under the Act, over and above their duty to satisfy requests for information where no exemption may properly be claimed. They have, first, a duty to provide advice and assistance, so far as is reasonable, to a person who proposes to make, or who has made, a request for information.[66] They are obliged, when issuing fees notices, refusal notices or notices that the information requested is not held,[67] to provide the applicant with such information as he may require to take matters forward, including details of

---

[62] As witness the powers of community planning and the duty to secure "best value" in the Local Government (Scotland) Act 2003.

[63] See paras 9–10—9–15.

[64] If no justification is possible, as where, *e.g.* there is a well-founded complaint of degrading treatment in a privately-run care home, then the importance of the right should be allowed to outweigh any incidental disadvantage to the provider.

[65] To the extent that such bodies hold personal data, they would in any event be subject to the Data Protection Act regime, which may add force to the suggestion that their inclusion within the freedom of information regime may involve only marginal advantage at best.

[66] 2002 Act, s.15(1). Under s.15(2), a Scottish public authority which acts in conformity with a code of practice issued by the Scottish Ministers under s.60 will be taken to have complied with this duty.

[67] Under 2002 Act, ss.9, 16 and 17 respectively.

their own internal complaints procedures and the applicant's right to seek a review by the authority of its decision and/or to apply to the Scottish Information Commissioner.[68] Where an applicant is dissatisfied with an authority's handling of a request for information, he may require the authority to review its actions and decisions in relation to that request.[69] Where required, a review must be conducted "promptly, and in any event by not later than the twentieth working day after receipt by it of the requirement."[70] If it undertakes a review, the authority may confirm its original decision, with or without modifications; substitute for the original decision a different decision; or (where the complaint is that no decision was reached) reach a decision.[71]

More broadly, each Scottish public authority is charged by section 23 of the Act with adopting and maintaining "publication schemes" relating to the publication by the authority of information held by it. Such schemes must be approved by the Scottish Information Commissioner.[72] The scheme must specify classes of information which the authority publishes or intends to publish (that is, on a proactive basis rather than in response to requests under section 1), the manner in which such publication is to be effected, and whether the published information will be available free of charge or on payment.[73] The authority is thereafter obliged to publish in accordance with its scheme, and to review the scheme from time to time. In adopting or reviewing its scheme, the authority must have regard to the public interest in allowing public access to information held by it, in particular information relating to "the provision of services by it, the cost to it of providing them

---

[68] 2002 Act, s.19.
[69] 2002 Act, s.20. As McInnes notes, the right to insist on a review covers not only the obvious causes of grievance, such as refusing or ignoring a request for information, but a whole host of other perceived sins, such as partial production of information, the production of information in redacted or unsuitable form, overproduction of information (with the object of swamping the applicant), defects in the provision of advice and assistance and so on.
[70] 2002 Act, s.21. A 30-day period applies where the requirement for review is received by the Keeper of the Records of Scotland and the Keeper is holding information transferred by another Scottish public authority which is not yet in the public domain. The authority may decline to review a decision if it considers that the requirement is vexatious, or relates to a vexatious or repeated request.
[71] 2002 Act, s.21(4).
[72] The commissioner also has power, under s.24 of the 2002 Act, to develop model publication schemes which might be then be adopted "off the peg" by individual authorities. Note that according to the timetable for implementation contained in the commissioner's *Report to the Scottish Parliament on Progress on Implementation of the Freedom of Information (Scotland) Act 2002* (SE/2003/94), all public authorities listed in Pts 1, 2, 3 and 6 of Sch.1 are to have submitted publication schemes for approval by Feb. 28, 2004 (with approvals to follow by June 1, 2004), with the authorities listed in Pts 4 and 5 of Sch.1 submitting by May 31, 2004 (with approvals to follow by Sept. 1, 2004).
[73] 2002 Act, s.23(2).

or the standards attained by services so provided", "facts, or analyses, on the basis of which decisions of importance to the public have been made by it", and the reasons for its decisions.[74] Presumably the acid test of such schemes will be whether they forestall requests under section 1 or, at least, enable them to be met with a claim to exemption under section 25.[75]

Under sections 60 and 61 of the Act, the Scottish Ministers are obliged to adopt codes of practice containing guidance for public authorities on, respectively, the discharge of their functions under the Act and the keeping, management and destruction if records held by them. Before either code is issued or revised, the Scottish Ministers must consult the Scottish Information Commissioner. The commissioner then has the power under section 44 of the Act to issue "practice recommendations" to a public authority which, in his view, is failing to conform to the codes of practice, specifying the steps which he considers it ought to take to rectify matters. Failure to follow the commissioner's recommendations will not attract enforcement action itself—here, we are deep in a thicket of soft law—but the commissioner must report annually to the Scottish Parliament (and may report to it at other times). An authority's non-compliance with recommendations, as well as any failures to comply with formal enforcement procedures, will presumably be matters the commissioner would wish to make known.

Scottish Information Commissioner

9–13   Part 3 of the Act makes provision for the appointment of the Scottish Information Commissioner by the Queen on the nomination of the Scottish Parliament.[76] The commissioner's general functions are defined in section 43: promoting the observance by Scottish public authorities of the provisions of the Act and codes of practice adopted under sections 60 and 61; advising the public generally and persons individually as to the operation of the Act and good practice under it; and making proposals to the Scottish Ministers for the exercise by them of their functions under sections

---

[74] 2002 Act, s.23(3). There is an echo here of the Citizens' Charter programme, which viewed freedom of information primarily as a mechanism for quality control.

[75] 2002 Act, s.25 confers an absolute exemption from disclosure under the Act on information which the applicant can reasonably obtain otherwise than by way of a s.1 request.

[76] 2002 Act, s.42(1). The manner of appointment differs from that prescribed by the 2000 Act for the appointment of the Information Commissioner (by the Queen on ministerial advice: s.6). The Scottish approach was proclaimed as underlining the independence of the commissioner from the Executive, but, given that the Parliament will almost invariably nominate whomsoever the Executive puts to them, it is not obvious that this is such an occasion for self-congratulation.

4 and 5. His more specific functions in connection with enforcement of the Act are provided for by Part 4.[77] Under section 47, any person who is dissatisfied with an authority's review of his request may apply to the commissioner for a decision whether the request was properly dealt with in accordance with Part 1. Applications must be made within six months of receipt of the authority's decision or of the last date by which the authority should have responded.[78] No application may be made under section 47 in respect of reviews conducted by a procurator fiscal, the Lord Advocate or the commissioner himself,[79] and the commissioner may reject applications which he finds to be frivolous or vexatious or which appear to have been abandoned or withdrawn.[80] Those qualifications apart, where the commissioner receives an application under section 47, he must notify the relevant authority and invite its comments, and thereafter reach a decision within four months of receipt of the complaint or such other period as is reasonable in the circumstances.[81] Under section 50, the commissioner may order the authority to provide him with such information as he reasonably requires (excepting only information protected by legal professional privilege) to determine an application under section 47.[82] Both applicant and the authority have a right of appeal against the decision of the commissioner, on a point of law only, to the Court of Session.[83]

Apart from his power to adjudicate on complaints, the commissioner has also an independent enforcement power under section 51, exercisable where he is satisfied that a Scottish public authority has failed to comply with any provision of Part 1.[84] An enforcement notice must identify the provision said to be breached, specify the steps the commissioner requires to be taken to secure compliance, and advise the authority of its right of appeal under section 56. It is important to note, however, that decisions under section 47 and enforcement notices under section 51 are alike subject to the power vested in the First Minister by section 52 to override the commissioner's findings. The power is exercisable only after consultation with the other members of the Scottish Executive, only in

---

[77] The commissioner also has power, under s.44 of the 2002 Act, to issue "practice recommendations" where it appears to him that a Scottish public authority is failing to comply with either of the codes of practice.

[78] Although the commissioner has a discretion to consider late applications.

[79] 2002 Act s.48.

[80] 2002 Act s.49.

[81] Unless he elects to mediate between the applicant and the authority and manages thereby to effect an settlement: 2002 Act, s.49(3), (4).

[82] The commissioner may also exercise this power to issue an "information notice" where he is considering whether a public authority has acted in breach of the codes of practice.

[83] 2002 Act, s.56(a), (b).

[84] In this regard, see 2002 Act, s.54 and Sch.3, which make provision for powers to enter and inspect, exercisable in accordance with warrants granted by the sheriff.

respect of decision or enforcement notices issued against the Scottish Administration,[85] and only where the notice relates to a failure to provide information falling within the exemptions for policy formulation, national security, confidential information provided by a foreign government, international organisation or international court, information relating to or derived from investigations conducted by a Scottish public authority, information covered by legal professional privilege, and information relating to the prerogative of honour—and only then when the information is of "exceptional sensitivity".[86] The First Minister's certificate must be issued within 30 working days of receipt of the commissioner's notice or, where an appeal is brought under section 56, of the date on which the appeal is determined, and the First Minister must lay a copy of the certificate before the Parliament within 10 working days of its issue. Clearly, then, the ministerial veto is not there to be used lightly.[87]

Absent any certificate under section 52, the authority against whom a decision notice, information notice or enforcement notice is issued must comply with it. Failure to comply entitles the commissioner to certify that fact to the Court of Session, which may inquire into the matter and, after hearing the parties, deal with the authority as if it had committed a contempt of court.[88]

Freedom of Information Act 2000

9–14   There are a number of differences between the freedom of information regime prescribed by the 2002 Act and that contained in the Freedom of Information Act 2000.[89] The latter contains a greater number of exemptions, and uses a test of simple "prejudice" rather than "substantial prejudice" in relation to those exemptions based on the subject-matter of information. Whereas in Scotland, a public authority which holds requested information is obliged (subject to the effect of any exemptions) to disclose it,

---

[85] Which, in terms of the SA 1998, s.44, comprises the First Minister, Ministers appointed by the First Minister under s.47, the Lord Advocate and the Solicitor General for Scotland.

[86] 2002 Act, s.52(2)(b).

[87] Note, however, the study cited by Rosalind McInnes of the practice in New Zealand, where a similar ministerial veto was used far more frequently than had been anticipated.

[88] In this regard, see also above at para.9–07. Here again, there can be no justification for treating as a contempt a mere failure to comply with a notice; the Court of Session will be required, in effect, to review the commissioner's decision and decide whether it was validly taken. If the authority refused to comply on the basis that the notice was *ultra vires* the commissioner, it does not follow that it should be treated as being in contempt of court even if the Court of Session finds in the commissioner's favour.

[89] Although fewer than are needed to justify some of the more grandiose claims for the 2002 Act, and the correspondingly scathing criticisms of the 2000 Act.

there is under the UK regime a preliminary duty to "confirm or deny" whether the information requested is held; only if it is must the authority disclose it.[90] More categories of exempt information are susceptible to ministerial certification (overriding a determination in favour of disclosure by the Information Commissioner) under the UK regime than under its Scottish equivalent. There are differences also in the arrangements for review of and appeal against decisions by public authorities and, subsequently, the commissioner. In Scotland, there is a right to insist on an internal review, followed by a right of appeal to the Scottish Information Commissioner and thence to the Court of Session on a point of law. The 2000 Act contains an intermediate stage, with appeals from the Information Commissioner lying in the first instance to the Information Tribunal.

The 2000 Act differs not only from its Scottish counterpart, but also, and in significant respects, from the draft bill published by the Home Office in 1999. In general terms, its legislative history was somewhat troubled. The original White Paper, published in 1997,[91] was widely applauded for the generosity of its proposals. In 1998, however, responsibility for the legislation was transferred from the Cabinet Office to the Home Office,[92] and only in May 1999 did the Home Office come forward with a further consultation document and draft bill.[93] Both represented a considerable dilution of the 1997 proposals, and although the Act which finally emerged from Parliament claws much back, its provisions still do not go so far as was originally anticipated. The two general duties created by section 1(1) of the Act—the duty, first, to confirm or deny whether information requested is held and, if the information is held, the duty to disclose it—have effect subject to sections 2, 9, 12 and 14. The latter three contain content-neutral qualifications to the right of access comparable to those found in the 2002 Act. Section 9 provides for the charging of fees, and entitles a public authority to withhold information from disclosure unless and until a free properly charged is paid; section 12 entitles it to refuse a request where the cost of compliance would exceed limits specified in regulations; and section 14 entitles it to reject vexatious or repeated requests. Section 2 introduces the substantive exemptions as provided for in Part II of the Act. The various exemptions may apply only to the section 1(1)(b) duty (the duty to communicate information) or to both the section 1(1)(b) duty and the duty to confirm or deny in section 1(1)(a), and may be absolute or subject

[90] Freedom of Information Act 2000, s.1(1)(a), (b).
[91] *Your Right to Know*, Cm.3818 (1997).
[92] Not, as Birkinshaw wryly observes, a department noted for its taste for constitutional innovation.
[93] Cm.4355 (1999).

to a public interest test cast, in some cases, in terms of prejudice. In the same way as the 2002 Act, section 2(3) then lists the provisions of Part II which are to be regarded as conferring absolute exemption.[94] As with the Scottish legislation, an absolute exemption may confer immunity from disclosure only in respect of the 2000 Act itself. Some categories of information will be available for disclosure other under regimes, and the object of the absolute exemption in this Act is to ensure, so far as possible, that the integrity of existing regimes, for example in the context of data protection, is secured. The remaining exemptions are divisible into two categories, class-based[95] and content-based.[96] Information falling into a protected class may still be disclosed if the public interest in disclosure outweighs that in withholding it; information protected by reference to its subject-matter must be disclosed unless its disclosure would actually cause prejudice to a specified aspect of the public interest. In any case, the burden of justifying the refusal of a request for information falls on the public authority concerned.

Similar provision to that contained in the Scottish legislation is made for the more general aspects of ongoing compliance with the freedom of information regime. Public authorities subject to the

---

[94] These are: s.21 (information accessible to the applicant by other means), s.23 (information supplied by, or relating to, bodies dealing with security matters), s.32 (court records), s.34 (information the disclosure of which would violate parliamentary privilege), s.36 (information the disclosure of which would be prejudicial to the effective conduct of public affairs, so far as held by the House of Commons or House of Lords), s.40 (personal information subject to the regime contained in the Data Protection Act 1998), s.41 (confidential information) and s.44 (information the disclosure of which is prohibited by any enactment, would be incompatible with a Community obligation, or which would constitute a contempt of court).

[95] The categories of information protected by a class-based exemption are contained in s.22 (information which the public authority intends to publish. Note that, whereas in Scotland, the public authority must intend to publish within 12 weeks of the request, there is no such time-limit here), s.30 (information connected with investigations and proceedings conducted by a public authority), s.35 (information relation to the formulation of government policy), s.37 (communications with the Queen and information relating to the prerogative of honour), s.39 (environmental information which will fall to be disclosed pursuant to regulations made under s.74 of the Act in implementation of the Aarhus Convention), s.42 (information subject to legal professional privilege), and s.43(1) (trade secrets. These are covered by an absolute exemption in the Scottish legislation).

[96] Content-based exemptions apply where disclosure would cause prejudice to national security (ss.24 and 25), defence (s.26), international relations (s.27), relations between the administrations in the UK (s.28), the economy (s.29), the conduct of law enforcement activities (s.31), the conduct of audit functions (s.33), the health and safety of any individual (s.38) or the commercial interests of any person (s.43(2)). It should be noted that class and content-based exemptions may lapse in accordance with the provision made by Pt VI of the 2000 Act in relation to historical records.

2000 Act will require to adopt publication schemes for the proactive release of information held by them, either on a bespoke basis or by adapting model schemes promulgated by the Information Commissioner.[97] The Secretary of State is charged with issuing codes of practice to public authorities containing guidance as to the discharge of their functions under Part I of the Act[98]; and a like duty is laid on the Lord Chancellor in relation to the proper keeping, management and destruction of records held by public authorities.[99] Monitoring compliance with these codes falls to the Information Commissioner, in addition to his other functions in relation to publication schemes and enforcement. In the latter respect, any person who considers that a public authority has failed to comply with its duties under Part I may bring a complaint before the commissioner. The commissioner is obliged to take a decision on the complaint unless the complainant has failed to exhaust any available complaints procedures, there has been undue delay in making the complaint, the complaint is frivolous or vexatious, or unless the complaint is withdrawn or abandoned.[1] The commissioner also has the power under section 52 to take independent enforcement action where it appears that a public authority is in breach of any of its duties under Part I. Where a decision notice or enforcement notice in relation to breaches of section 1(1)(a) or (b) is served on a government department, the National Assembly for Wales or any public authority designated for these purposes, however, the "accountable person"[2] for the recipient may, within 20 working days of receipt of the notice, certify to the commissioner that he has on reasonable grounds formed the opinion that there was no failure in duty.[3] The effect of such a certificate is to disapply the normal duty to comply with notices issued by the commissioner.[4] This scenario apart, there is a right of appeal against notices issued by the commissioner, at the instance either of the original applicant or of the public authority, to the Information Tribunal,[5] with a further right of appeal, but only on a point of

---

[97] 2000 Act, ss 19 and 20.

[98] 2000 Act, s.45.

[99] 2000 Act, s.46. Who will perform this function in future is presumably a matter to be addressed in the promised consultation to follow the effective abolition of the office of Lord Chancellor in the ministerial reshuffle of June 2003 and the establishment of a Dept of Constitutional Affairs.

[1] 2000 Act, s.50.

[2] As defined by 2000 Act, s.53(8).

[3] See, generally, 2000 Act, s.53.

[4] 2000 Act, s.54.

[5] 2000 Act, s.57. The Information Tribunal, together with the office of Information Commissioner, is established by s.18 and Sch.2. Neither is altogether new; rather, they assume the functions, as amended and extended by this Act, of the former Data Protection Tribunal and Data Protection Commissioner respectively.

law, to the Court of Session, where the public authority concerned is based in Scotland, and otherwise to the High Court of England and Wales or the High Court in Northern Ireland, as appropriate.

9–15	As to the central issue of who is subject to this regime, the approach of the 2000 Act, like that of the 2002 Act, is predicated upon listed public authorities, designated public authorities and publicly-owned companies.[6] Listed authorities fall into two categories. Those listed in Parts I to V of Schedule 1 are "core" public authorities, which cannot be removed from Schedule 1 other than by way of primary legislation.[7] Those listed in Parts VI to VII of Schedule 1 are public authorities so long as they continue to satisfy the criteria set out in section 4(2) and (3) (in essence, that they are established by the government and that their members are appointed by the government). If either condition ceases to be satisfied, the body in question ceases to be a listed public authority.[8] It should be noted that, in terms of section 7, a body may be listed only in relation to information of a specified description. Bodies may be designated as public authorities by order of the Secretary of State under section 5 if they appear to exercise public functions or are providing a service on behalf of a public authority under a contract with that authority.[9] In terms of section 6, a company is a wholly-owned public company and therefore subject to the Act without more if it is wholly owned by the Crown[10] or by any public authority listed in Schedule 1 other than a government department or authority listed only in respect of specified information. As to enforcement, where an applicant is dissatisfied with the decision of a public authority, he may (having first exhausted the authority's own internal complaints procedure) apply to the Information Commissioner under section 50, with a further, full right of appeal to the Information Tribunal and thereafter a right of appeal on a point of law to the High Court. As with the Scottish legislation, certain senior ministers[11] have the power under section

---

[6] 2002 Act, 3(1)(a), (b).

[7] New listings may be added by order made under s.4(1) of the 2002 Act.

[8] 2002 Act, s.4(4). Presumably this would not prevent the Secretary of State from designating the body as a public authority.

[9] Note that in terms of s.80 of the 2000 Act, the Secretary of State may make no order under s.4(1) or s.5 in respect of the Scottish Parliament, any part of the Scottish Administration, the Scottish Parliamentary Corporate Body or any Scottish public authority with mixed functions or no reserved functions as defined by or under the SA 1998.

[10] Which is to say that it has no members other than Ministers of the Crown, government departments, companies wholly owned by the Crown or persons acting on behalf of any of these: 2000 Act, s.6(2)(a).

[11] Namely (depending on the decision to be overridden) the First Minister and Deputy First Minister in NI, acting jointly; the First Secretary of the National Assembly for Wales; a Cabinet minister; or the Attorney-General, Advocate General or Attorney-General for NI: 2000 Act, s.53(8).

53 of the Act to override decisions of the commissioner or tribunal in limited circumstances; as in Scotland, the provision attracted controversy, but its potential for diluting the effects of the Act should not, in view of the procedural and political constraints to which it is subject, be overstated.

The value of freedom of information

By the time of the enactment of the freedom of information **9–16** legislation, the subject in general had acquired that aura of impregnable virtue against which counter-arguments appear eccentric at best and reactionary at worst. Like a bill of rights, freedom of information was seen as one of those essential accessories of a developed democracy, something that was vital to establishing the relationship between citizen and state on a proper footing. Most countries which have perceived the need to eradicate unnecessary governmental secrecy have adopted freedom of information legislation, creating legally enforceable rights of public access to all official information subject to limited and specific exceptions. It might also be said that, since the arguments for freedom of information were effectively conceded by the adoption of the Code of Practice in 1993, there was no tenable reason for not taking the further, final step of putting access on a statutory footing. At all events, we now have it. But it remains to be seen whether it will have the wholly salutary effects predicted by its supporters.

The costs of freedom of information, both in terms of adverse effects on public services and in raw financial terms, do not provide strong arguments against a statutory regime. The former in particular invites scepticism: one would instinctively have thought that low morale is less likely to be a product of freedom of information than of the working practices and conditions that obtain within an organisation, and in that respect heightened scrutiny flowing from freedom of information may be beneficial by encouraging improvements in working practices, record keeping and administrative efficiency. As to the latter, it is true that the enactment of freedom of information legislation has caused some disquiet amongst public authorities, which will require to finance their new statutory duties within existing, and already overstretched, budgets.[12] But studies in the United States have shown that the costs of administering freedom of information there are not only relatively low but considerably lower—less than 10 per cent—than the sums spent each year on government advertising and public relations. In the United Kingdom, there is a dearth as yet of readily comparable figures. In evidence to the Select Committee on Procedure, the

---

[12] The Scottish Executive has already told local authorities that no extra funding will be made available to assist them in complying with the 2002 Act.

government has stated that the cost per parliamentary session of answering parliamentary questions is £6 million. This does not strike one as an especially large sum, but provides only limited guidance as to the costs that will fall on local and other public authorities. At best it may be said that advance estimates, both of the number of freedom of information requests and of the costs involved in responding, tend to be over-inflated.[13]

Less easy still to quantify at this stage are the benefits likely to flow from statutory freedom of information regimes. Generally, though by no means exclusively, the sort of official information to which individuals want access is personal information, and access to that is governed by the Data Protection Act. In the United States, more than half of all freedom of information requests are submitted by commercial organisations seeking information on their business competitors. Members of the public account for between a fifth and a quarter of requests and (perhaps most surprisingly) the press only accounts for about five per cent. Freedom of information may enhance the participative capacity of the "empire of pressure groups" (indeed, there may be some evidence of this already in the increasing tendency of governments to deal directly with sectional interests affected by their policies); it may also strengthen parliamentary scrutiny and control over governmental bodies.[14] But perhaps its most profound effect will be internal. If a public authority is obliged to publish and disclose information relating to its activities, it is reasonable to suppose that it will have closer regard to the quality of its decisions and the justifications therefor. That is explanatory accountability at its most straightforward, and anything that improves our constitutional structures of accountability (even if only marginally) is to be welcomed. Much of course will depend on the willingness of public authorities to comply with their duties under the legislation, and on the attitude of the Information Commissioners to enforcement. Plainly, quick resort to exemptions, condoned by the Information

---

[13] As witness the 1993 White Paper, which estimated that between 50,000 and 100,000 requests would be made annually under the Code of Practice. In the code's first full year of operation, only 2,600 "Code requests" were made; in its second, only 1,353 (although it should be noted that "Code requests" include only those requests which identify the code, those for which a fee is levied, and those in respect of which information is refused under one of the exemptions). In 2000–01, the Scottish Executive received only 44 "Code requests" pursuant to the Code of Practice on Access to Scottish Executive Information, although this must be seen in the context of the proactive publication of information ordained by the code and the hundreds of thousands of items of non-code correspondence emanating from the Scottish Executive and other Scottish public authorities each year.

[14] R. Austin, "Freedom of Information: The constitutional impact" in *The Changing Constitution* (4th ed. Jowell and Oliver ed., Oxford University Press, Oxford, 2000), p.438.

Commissioner, will diminish the effectiveness of the new regimes in promoting openness. But no channel of accountability can be solely a matter of force. There must also be an institutional preparedness to accept accountability, and on this the success of freedom of information will turn.

CHAPTER 10

HUMAN RIGHTS

Introduction

10–01   Our constitutional tradition fondly depicts Britain as the cradle of civil liberty, and, in fairness, there is something to be said for this. But if respect for individual freedom was born here, it did not necessarily flourish.[1] To understand why this was, it is necessary to reflect briefly on the conception of civil liberty embraced by the British constitution, a conception which only now is losing its force. Founded in the revolution settlement of 1689, it was a conception of "liberty according to law", wherein any person was free to do whatever he chose except to the extent that he was forbidden to do so by some legal norm. Thus, the courts would restrain an interference with individual rights of property or personal liberty for which there existed no valid legal authority.[2] This was the rule of law as Dicey understood it, and fell to be contrasted with the constitutional guarantees of civil rights accorded in other jurisdictions.[3]

But there were two critical defects in the traditional account. The first was that legal authority was not required for all governmental acts, but only those which the common law would otherwise have treated as legal wrongs. The second rests in the subordination of the common law to the law of the sovereign legislature. Statutory authority to interfere with individual freedom was

---

[1] Rabinder Singh perhaps puts it best: "[Britain] has played an enviable role over the centuries in devising and exporting the idea of human rights. This is, after all, the land where Tom Paine was born. It is not, however, surprising that lawyers have found that the language of rights does not come readily to them. This is also the land from which Tom Paine was banished." See R. Singh, *The Future of Human Rights in the United Kingdom* (Hart Publishing, Oxford, 1997), p.1.

[2] *Entick v Carrington* (1765) 19 *State Trials* 1029 is the classic example.

[3] Which guarantees were generally regarded with scepticism and condescension. Witness, for example, Jeremy Bentham's condemnation of "natural" rights as "nonsense upon stilts". More recently, note the remarks of Lord Denning M.R. on the ECHR in *R v Chief Immigration Officer, Heathrow Airport, ex p. Salamat Bibi* [1976] 1 W.L.R 979 at 985: "It contains wide statements of principle. They are apt to lead to much difficulty in application, because they give rise to much uncertainty. They are not the sort of thing which we can easily digest. . . . So it is much better to stick to our principles".

granted with abandon as the balance between legislature and executive shifted in the latter's favour, and absent any recognition of "higher order" norms or values restraining the legislative competence of Parliament the courts could do nothing about it. We have seen that the growth of state power is not to be condemned out of hand.[4] But power must be coupled with appropriate controls. Liberty according to law came increasingly to be seen as an anaemic substitute for the formal protection of individual rights, going beyond the limited protection offered by the developing law of judicial review.

There was no shortage of templates for reform. It has been said that if the twentieth century had a "big idea" at all, it was the idea of human rights.[5] The post-war period was characterised by the emergence of a new international order in which, in response to the atrocities perpetrated during the war and (in some cases) with a view to securing social and economic advancement, human rights featured prominently. The European Convention on Human Rights was a product of these times, adopted under the auspices of the Council of Europe and signed and ratified by the United Kingdom in 1951.[6] Unlike many other international treaties, the Convention provided a mechanism for its own enforcement in the European Court of Human Rights, which was established in 1958 following the acceptance by the requisite eight signatory states of its compulsory jurisdiction. The United Kingdom accepted the compulsory jurisdiction of the Court in 1966, and granted its citizens the right of individual petition to the Court the same year.[7]

The first British case to be decided by the Court was *Golder v United Kingdom*,[8] in which the United Kingdom was held to have violated the applicant prisoner's implied right of access to the courts under Article 6(1) of the Convention in refusing him permission to write to his solicitor in connection with a proposed action in defamation against a prison officer. Since then, the United Kingdom has been found in breach of the Convention on approaching 100 occasions. It is a rather dismal record. But it prompted two not unrelated developments, both of which have carried enormous consequences for our constitutional law.

On the one hand, pressure grew for the adoption of a domestic bill of rights, whether by incorporation of the Convention into

---

[4] See paras 2–10—2–14.
[5] Singh, *Human Rights, op.cit.*, p.1.
[6] British lawyers played a prominent role in the drafting of the ECHR and (despite a measure of recalcitrance in some quarters of the government of the day) the UK was the first member state of the Council of Europe to sign and ratify: see G. Marston, "The United Kingdom's Part in the Preparation of the European Convention on Human Rights" (1993) 43 I.C.L.Q. 819.
[7] See A. Lester, "UK Acceptance of the Strasbourg Jurisdiction: What really went on in Whitehall in 1965" [1998] P.L. 237.
[8] (1975) 1 E.H.R.R. 524.

national law or otherwise.[9] On the other, perhaps stung by the European Court's exposure of the deficiencies of the common law in defending individual freedom, the courts themselves began to develop, in various ways, a domestic human rights jurisprudence.[10] In order to understand the constitutional climate in which the Human Rights Act was eventually enacted in 1998, it is necessary to consider the nature and foundation of that jurisprudence, for it signals a wider reappraisal of our constitutional traditions as a whole.

PRE-INCORPORATION STATUS OF HUMAN RIGHTS

10–02 As we have seen, the United Kingdom adopts a "dualist" view of the relationship between international treaties and domestic law.[11] On this view, a treaty does not form part of national law unless and until incorporated into the law by legislation. That failing, the treaty cannot create rights or duties enforceable before the national courts.[12] The rationale for this is that the making of a treaty is an executive, not a legislative, act, and the government should not be permitted to burden citizens with obligations unsanctioned by Parliament.[13]

This is not to say that the Convention was altogether without legal effect in the domestic laws of the United Kingdom. In England at least,[14] the courts would have regard to the Convention rights as an aid to the construction of *ambiguous* statutory provisions, on the presumption that Parliament would not have intended to legislate inconsistently with the UK's treaty obligations.[15] Further, where legislation was enacted specifically to comply with the UK's obligations under the Convention, the court

---

[9] Lord Scarman is generally credited with launching this movement: see Sir Leslie Scarman, *English Law: The New Dimension* (Stevens, London, 1974). In R. Clayton and H. Tomlinson, *The Law of Human Rights* (Oxford University Press, Oxford, 2000), the authors relate the history of the parliamentary campaign for a bill of rights (paras 1.43–1.49), including a Conservative amendment to the Scotland Bill in 1977 which would have incorporated the ECHR in Scotland in the event of devolution; the amendment was defeated by only 24 votes.

[10] It must be said that the initiative here was almost exclusively taken by the English courts. In Scotland, it was held in *Surjit Kaur v Lord Advocate*, 1980 S.C. 319, that the courts were not entitled to have regard to the ECHR, whether as an aid to statutory construction or otherwise. This remained the position until the decision of the Inner House in *T, Petr*, 1997 S.L.T. 724.

[11] See paras 1–12—1–13.

[12] *J. H. Rayner (Mincing Lane) v Dept of Trade and Industry* [1990] 2 A.C. 418.

[13] For criticism of this doctrine in relation to human rights treaties, see Lord Steyn, "Democracy Through Law" [2002] E.H.R.L.R. 723.

[14] See n.10.

[15] See, *e.g. Waddington v Miah* [1974] 1 W.L.R 683.

would strive to read and give effect to it consistently with the Convention rights.[16] By the same token, the Convention provided a guide to the development of the common law.[17]

More broadly, the courts began to recognise fundamental rights as factors material to the lawful and rational exercise of discretion by administrative officials. In so doing, they fashioned a domestic human rights jurisprudence offering, by the time of incorporation of the Convention, a level of protection comparable to, if not absolutely coextensive with, that accorded under the Convention proper.[18] This manifested itself in different ways. One technique was to develop (or rediscover) a robust principle of statutory construction, whereby, in the absence of clear and express provision to the contrary, Parliament was taken to authorise no interference with fundamental rights.[19] In other cases, an apparent failure to take cognisance of a "rights dimension" to a decision was treated as a failure to have regard to a relevant consideration, and the decision fell to be reduced on that well-established ground. In others still, the human rights dimension influenced the court's view as to the reasonableness of the decision. In *R. v Secretary of State for the Home Department, ex p. Bugdaycay*,[20] where the applicant, an asylum seeker, sought judicial review of the Home Secretary's decision to deport him, Lord Bridge held:

"The most fundamental of all human rights is the individual's right to life, and when an administrative decision under challenge is said to be one which may put the applicant's life

---

[16] See, *e.g.* the consideration by the House of Lords of the provisions of the Contempt of Court Act 1981 in *Re Lonrho plc* [1990] 2 A.C. 154 at 208, 209. The Contempt of Court Act was enacted to bring national law into conformity with the judgment of the ECtHR in *Sunday Times v United Kingdom* (1979) 2 E.H.R.R. 245.

[17] See in particular *Derbyshire C v Times Newspapers Ltd* [1993] A.C. 534. The Court of Appeal held, relying in part of the right to freedom of expression enshrined in ECHR, Art.10, that as a matter of the common law a local authority had no right to sue for defamation. The decision was upheld by the House of Lords without reliance on the ECHR, but without disapproval of the approach of the Court of Appeal.

[18] See J. Munro, "Judicial Review, *Locus Standi* and Remedies: The impact of the Human Rights Act 1998" in *Human Rights and Scots Law* (Boyle *et al.* eds, Hart Publishing, Oxford, 2002), Ch.6.

[19] Lord Browne Wilkinson made the case for this approach in "The Infiltration of a Bill of Rights" [1992] P.L. 397. The technique was applied, by Lord Browne Wilkinson and others, in a number of important decisions, including *R. v S of S for the Home Dept, ex p. Leech (No. 2)* [1994] Q.B. 198 (*cf.*, in Scotland, *Leech v S of S for Scotland*, 1993 S.L.T. 365); *R. v S of S for Social Security, ex p. Joint Council for the Welfare of Immigrants* [1996] 4 All E.R. 385; *R. v Lord Chancellor, ex p. Witham* [1997] 2 All E.R. 779; and *R. v S of S for the Home Dept, ex p. Pierson* [1998] A.C. 539. For more venerable authority, see *Pyx Granite Co Ltd v Ministry of Housing and Local Government* [1960] A.C. 260.

[20] *R. v S of S for the Home Dept, ex p. Bugdaycay* [1987] A.C. 514.

at risk, the basis of the decision must surely call for the most anxious scrutiny."[21]

The effect of *Bugdaycay* was to prepare the way for the reception of the principle of proportionality as a head of review apart from the orthodox test of *Wednesbury* unreasonableness. There were false starts,[22] but by 1996, in appropriate cases, the courts were prepared to hold that "the more substantial the interference with human rights, the more the court will require by way of justification before it is satisfied that the decision is reasonable."[23]

10–03   All of these developments—the recognition and application of new principles of statutory construction, and of new standards of relevancy, rationality and proportionality—took place against the backdrop of a wider debate on common law tools of human rights protection.[24] As this debate has evolved, some of its participants have grasped the nettle of parliamentary supremacy and contended that the courts might now, as the common law has developed, be justified in refusing to give effect to primary legislation which violates fundamental rights. The basis for this view is, broadly, as follows. If the doctrine of the sovereignty of Parliament is a common law doctrine, whose continuing truth lies in the keeping of the courts, then it follows that the content of the common law is "logically prior" to the content of legislation. If we accept that the common law may itself be the source of certain fundamental constitutional rights—the right to life and liberty, the right to

---

[21] *ibid.*, at 531. The "anxious scrutiny" doctrine, which essentially involves the substitution of orthodox *Wednesbury* review for a level of control approaching review for proportionality, was subsequently adopted in cases involving freedom of expression (see *R. v S of S for the Home Dept, ex p. Brind* [1991] 1 A.C. 696) and the right to respect for private life (see *R. v Ministry of Defence, ex p. Smith* [1996] Q.B. 517), although in neither case to the advantage of the applicant.

[22] Including *R. v S of S for the Home Dept, ex p. Brind*, above, although even there the majority, at least, did not dispute the proposition that stricter scrutiny of an administrative decision was called for when the decision interfered with human rights.

[23] *R. v Ministry of Defence, ex p. Smith*, above, at 554, *per* Lord Bingham M.R. See in Scotland *Abdadou v S of S for the Home Dept*, 1998 S.C. 504. Conversely, the orthodox *Wednesbury* standard continued to apply in areas not impinging upon fundamental rights, particularly where the decision challenged involves questions of high economic or social policy: see, *e.g. R. v S of S for the Environment, ex p. Hammersmith and Fulham LBC* [1991] 1 A.C. 521; *East Kilbride DC v S of S for Scotland*, 1995 S.L.T. 1238.

[24] The literature is vast, but see, *e.g.* Lord Browne Wilkinson, "The Infiltration of a Bill of Rights" [1992] P.L. 397; Sir John Laws, "Is the High Court the Guardian of Fundamental Constitutional Rights?" [1993] P.L. 59, "Law and Democracy" [1995] P.L. 72 and "Judicial Review and the Meaning of Law" in *Judicial Review and the Constitution* (C. Forsyth ed., Hart Publishing, Oxford, 2000), Ch.8; Sir Stephen Sedley, "Human Rights: A 21st century agenda" [1995] P.L. 386; J. Jowell, "Beyond the Rule of Law: Towards constitutional judicial review" [2000] P.L. 671.

freedom of expression and association, and so on—then those rights must, being prior to statute, impose limitations which a statute cannot lawfully transgress. The significance of the Human Rights Act, on this reckoning, is not so much that it confers a wholly new jurisdiction on the courts but that it gives democratic legitimacy to a jurisdiction already asserted as a matter of the common law.

It should not, however, be thought that these views are shared by all those who have entered the fray over human rights protection in the United Kingdom. As Lord Chancellor, Lord Irvine might not have been expected to accept the case for recognition of pre-legislative common law rights; but others besides have taken issue with the "judicial supremacism" latent in the above arguments, and contend that the assertion by judges of a power to controvert the will of Parliament as expressed in statute is altogether at odds with the established constitutional order.[25] As one judge has put it:

> "[The European Convention] does not require that the court should be able to substitute its decision for that of the administrative authority. Such a requirement would in my opinion not only be contrary to the jurisprudence of the European Court of Human Rights but would also be profoundly undemocratic. The [Human Rights Act] was no doubt intended to strengthen the rule of law but not to inaugurate the rule of judges."[26]

Whatever one's views on the merits of these competing positions, there remained the practical case for incorporation of the Convention into national law. As the White Paper, *Rights Brought Home: The Human Rights Bill*, pointed out, absent a domestic forum in which to vindicate their Convention rights, British citizens were obliged to resort to the European Court in Strasbourg, after having exhausted all available domestic remedies. The whole process took, on average, five years to complete at an average cost of £30,000 per case. One searches in vain for any reason why, if we are to have human rights at all (and it would be taking constitutional singularity to extremes to eschew them), we should not be able to defend them before our own courts.

---

[25] Lord Irvine, "Judges and Decision-Makers: The theory and practice of *Wednesbury* review" [1996] P.L. 59; see also, *e.g.* M. Elliott, "The Demise of Parliamentary Sovereignty? The Implications for Justifying Judicial Review" (1999) 115 L.Q.R. 119; K. D. Ewing, "The Human Rights Act and Parliamentary Democracy" (1999) 62 M.L.R. 79.

[26] *R. v S of S for the Environment, Transport and the Regions, ex p. Alconbury Ltd* [2001] 2 All E.R. 929, para.60, *per* Lord Hoffmann. If this is true of review of administrative decisions on human rights grounds, the point must apply with still greater force to the review of legislation.

HUMAN RIGHTS ACT 1998

10–04 Over the years, debates about the merits and demerits of enacting
a bill of rights have been bedevilled by the problem of parliamentary supremacy. Put shortly, the statute passed to establish a bill of
rights would (according to the Diceyan tradition) have no greater
status than any other statute. A subsequent statute inconsistent
with the provisions of the bill of rights would therefore override, or
impliedly repeal, the earlier enactment. Much ink was then spilt on
the question whether, to avoid this, it would be possible to
"entrench" a bill of rights against subsequent amendment (the
Diceyan answer is an emphatic negative: any attempt to curb the
legislative competence of a later Parliament is futile). Related to
this is the question whether the courts should be given power to
strike down subsequent legislation which conflicts with the bill of
rights, if so whether this power should apply in all cases of conflict
or only some,[27] or whether their jurisdiction should be merely
declaratory. The difficulty faced by proponents of entrenchment in
the past was that there was no real chink in the Diceyan armour,[28]
and no escape from its rigorous logic. By the time of the
publication of *Rights Brought Home* in 1997, however, the pressures
of conformity with EU law had forced a re-appraisal of the
traditional position.[29] As we have seen, EU law itself claims
primacy over the national laws, even national constitutions, of the
member states. In the *Factortame* case,[30] the House of Lords
accepted that EU law prevails over incompatible provisions of an
Act of Parliament, whether enacted prior or subsequent to the
European Communities Act 1972 (which provides for the application of EU law in UK courts) or the relevant Community
provisions. In the event of a conflict between an Act of Parliament
and EU law, the court, consistently with its duty to provide
effective protection for Community law rights, is entitled to declare
the statute to be incompatible with Community law. But it is

---

[27] The Canadian Charter of Rights and Freedoms gives the courts competence to
strike federal or provincial legislation down (among other things) where it is held
to be incompatible with protected rights, but qualifies this entrenchment by
enabling federal or provincial parliaments to state expressly that a statutory
provision shall have effect notwithstanding its inconsistency with the Charter: see
J. Black-Branch, "Entrenching Human Rights under Constitutional Law: The
Canadian Charter of Rights and Freedoms" [1998] E.H.R.L.R. 312.

[28] Certainly so far as judicial decisions were concerned; the only exceptions to
Diceyan orthodoxy in these islands in the pre-*Factortame* era were found in
MacCormick v Lord Advocate, 1953 S.C. 396 and *Gibson v Lord Advocate* [1975] 1
C.M.L.R. 563.

[29] For the clearest statement of the current constitutional lie of the land, see the
judgment of Laws L.J. in *Thoburn v Sunderland CC* [2003] Q.B. 151, especially
paras 62, 63.

[30] *R. v S of S for Transport, ex p. Factortame Ltd (No. 2)* [1991] 1 A.C. 603.

important to recall that such a declaration has no effect on the validity of the enactment in question. The enactment continues in force until Parliament is prompted to rectify the problem identified by the court.[31] In effect, then, *Factortame* provided the United Kingdom with judicial review of primary legislation (on grounds of inconsistency with EU law) but preserved a veneer of legal truth in the notion of parliamentary supremacy by confining the remedial jurisdiction of the courts.

Appropriately adapted, the "EU model" served as the template for the Labour government's proposals to incorporate the ECHR. Devices familiar to students of the application of EU law in the United Kingdom appear also in the Human Rights Act, including the interpretive obligation and the power to make declarations of incompatibility. And as with EU law, the Human Rights Act generates a number of compelling questions about its precise scope and extent.

The structure of the Act is simple and elegant. It begins by defining the Convention rights being incorporated.[32] Section 2(1) then provides that any court or tribunal determining a question relating to a Convention right must take into account[33] any relevant "(a) judgment, decision, declaration or advisory opinion of the European Court of Human Rights; (b) opinion of the Commission . . . ; (c) decision of the Commission . . . ; or (d) decision of the Committee of Ministers of the Council of Europe" whenever made or given. This is a vast amount of material, and to say that much of it was a closed book, even to many professional judges, prior to the enactment of the Human Rights Act implies no criticism.[34] By requiring courts and tribunals only to take into account Convention case law, section 2(1) leaves open the option of preferring to follow the human rights jurisprudence of other jurisdictions in appropriate cases, and already the case law under the Human Rights Act indicates that domestic human rights law will draw on a far wider range of sources than the Convention alone.

---

[31] Although it may be possible to interdict the *application* of an enactment which is *prima facie* incompatible with EU law.

[32] HRA 1998, s.1 and Sch.1. Section 1(2) provides that the Convention rights duly defined shall have effect subject to any designated derogation or reservation, and s.1(4) provides that the Secretary of State may amend the Act as necessary to reflect any Protocol to the ECHR signed and ratified by the UK.

[33] *cf.* European Communities Act 1972, s.3(1), whereby the jurisprudence of the ECJ is *binding* on UK courts and tribunals.

[34] The two-year delay between Royal Assent and entry into force of the HRA 1998 is partly explained by the intensive training programmes required to ready professional and lay judges and tribunal members for the impact of the Act.

INTERPRETIVE OBLIGATION

10–05 Section 3, which imposes the interpretive obligation, is one of the key provisions of the Act. It provides: "(1) So far as it is possible to do so, primary legislation and subordinate legislation must be read and given effect in a way which is compatible with the Convention rights."[35]

As has been said, the duty under section 3(1) only arises where an application of the "ordinary and natural meaning" of a statutory provision would involve a breach of Convention rights.[36] Thus for example in *R. v Lambert*,[37] the House of Lords accepted that the language of section 28(3) of the Misuse of Drugs Act 1971, in imposing on the accused a legal or persuasive burden of proof of his innocence, conflicted with the presumption of innocence enshrined in Article 6(2) of the Convention. It was possible to "rescue" the provision, however, by resorting to the interpretive obligation in section 3(1) taking the word "proves" to mean "gives sufficient evidence".[38] As to the options available to the court in the exercise of its function under section 3(1), opinion differs.[39] Lord Cooke has described section 3(1) as a "strong adjuration",[40] requiring the courts to depart from the natural and ordinary meaning of statutory language in appropriate cases. Likewise Lord Steyn regards section 3(1) as permitting the adoption of strained or distorted interpretations of the relevant statutory language, "reading down" to narrow the scope of a provision or "reading in"

---

[35] It has been persuasively argued that this wording owes much to the approach prescribed by the ECJ for the interpretation of domestic measures by reference to European directive: see *Marleasing SA v La Comercial Internacionale de Alimentación SA* [1990] E.C.R. I-4135, discussed by M. Beloff, "What Does It All Mean? Interpreting the Human Rights Act 1998" in *The Human Rights Act 1998: What It Means* (L. Betten ed., Nijhoff, 1999). Note also Lord Irvine, "The Development of Human Rights in Britain Under an Incorporated Convention on Human Rights" [1998] P.L. 221, in which his Lordship identifies the interpretive techniques employed in EU cases as providing useful guidance on the proper role of the courts under HRA 1998, s.3(1).

[36] See *Poplar Housing and Regeneration Community Ass. Ltd v Donoghue* [2002] Q.B. 48, para.75, *per* Lord Woolf C.J.

[37] [2002] 2 A.C. 545.

[38] In other words, by converting the legal burden laid on the accused to an evidential burden. For the attitude of the ECHR to presumptions of fact and law in relation to the right to a fair trial, see *Salabiaku v France* (1988) 13 E.H.R.R. 379.

[39] See, *e.g.* Lord Lester of Herne Hill Q.C., "The Art of the Possible: Interpreting Statutes Under the Human Rights Act 1998" [1998] E.H.R.L.R. 665; G. Marshall, "Interpreting Interpretation in the Human Rights Act" [1998] P.L. 167; F. Bennion, "What Interpretation is 'Possible' Under Section 3(1) of the Human Rights Act 1998?" [2000] P.L. 77; H. Fenwick, "The Interpretive Obligation under Section 3 of the Human Rights Act 1998" [2001] S.L. Rev. 8; R. Clayton, "The Limits of What is Possible: Statutory Construction under the Human Rights Act" [2002] EHRLR 559.

[40] *R. v DPP, ex p. Kebilene* [2000] 2 A.C. 326, at 373.

supplementary words or phrases if necessary to secure compatibility with the Convention.[41] For Lord Steyn, resort to the power to make declarations of incompatibility should only be had in exceptional circumstances, where it is *impossible* to construe the legislation consistently with the Convention rights.[42] Others have expressed rather more tentative views. While the interpretive obligation under section 3(1) is in no sense dependent on the existence of absurdity or ambiguity in the relevant legislation, and to that extent goes beyond the approach to statutory construction taken by the courts in the past, it remains a rule of construction and no more. It does not, in particular, entitle the courts to act as legislators. As Lord Nicholls put it in *Re S (Care Order: Implementation of Care Plan)*,[43] while section 3(1) is cast in "forthright, uncompromising language", its reach is not unlimited and the courts must be ever mindful of its limitations:

"The Human Rights Act reserves the amendment of primary legislation to Parliament. By this means the Act seeks to preserve parliamentary sovereignty. The Act maintains the constitutional boundary. Interpretation of statutes is a matter for the courts; the enactment of statutes, and the amendment of statutes, are matters for Parliament.

For present purposes it is sufficient to say that a meaning which departs substantially from a fundamental feature of an Act of Parliament is likely to have crossed the boundary between interpretation and amendment. This is especially so where the departure has important practical repercussions which the court is not equipped to evaluate. In such a case the overall contextual setting may leave no scope for rendering the statutory provision Convention compliant by legitimate use of the process of interpretation."

---

[41] *R. v A (No. 2)* [2002] 1 A.C. 45, paras 45–45; see also in *R. v Lambert* [2002] 2 A.C. 545.

[42] On this point, see the speech of Lord Hoffmann in *R. v S of S for the Home Dept, ex p. Simms* [2000] 2 A.C. 115, at pages 131–132. Lord Hoffmann describes the rule of construction in HRA 1998, s.3(1), as the express enactment of the principle of legality whereby, pre-incorporation, it was presumed that a statute authorised no infringement of fundamental rights absent express provision or necessary implication to the contrary. For his Lordship, the power to make declarations of incompatibility will obtain only in those "unusual cases in which the legislative infringement of fundamental human rights is so clearly expressed as not to yield to principle of legality."

[43] [2002] 2 A.C. 291, paras 37–40. See also, *e.g.* Lord Woolf C.J. in *Poplar Housing and Regeneration Community Ass. Ltd v Donoghue* [2002] Q.B. 48; Lord Hope of Craighead in *R. v A (No.2)* [2002] 1 A.C. 45, para. 108; and again in *R. v Lambert* [2002] 2 A.C. 545, paras 79–81.

His Lordship added that Lord Steyn's remarks in *R. v A*[44] were not to be taken to mean that insoluble incompatibility might arise only where a statutory provision contained a *clear* limitation on the Convention rights.

10–06   There is, with respect, much to commend this more cautious approach. First of all, there is a very real practical issue surrounding section 3(1) in that an interpretation rendered for the purposes and in the context of one particular case might have unforeseen consequences in others.[45] Furthermore, as was pointed out in *R v A*, it may be difficult to determine whether it is even necessary to resort to section 3(1). In that case, the accused was charged with rape. He claimed that he and the complainer were in a sexual relationship at the time of the incident and that this had a bearing on the issues of her consent and his belief in her consent. Accordingly he sought leave to adduce evidence to this effect. The trial judge ruled that such evidence was inadmissible under the "rape shield" provisions of section 41 of the Youth Justice and Criminal Evidence Act 1989.[46] The accused claimed that section 41 was incompatible with his right to a fair trial under Article 6. By varying routes, the House of Lords held that section 41 would require to be read and given effect subject to an implied provision that evidence and questioning necessary to ensure a fair trial conform to Article 6 should not be held inadmissible. But as Lord Clyde noted, deciding on issues of compatibility in the abstract, in advance of the actual trial, may leave the court with little option but to deal with the issue in an equally abstract manner.[47] In such cases it might be preferable to see whether *as applied at the trial* the statutory provisions in question resulted in a breach of the accused's rights under Article 6; if so, that would provide grounds for appeal against conviction.[48]

Thirdly, undue freedom with the interpretive obligation could pose a threat to the clarity and accessibility of the law. As Lord Clyde pointed out in *De Freitas v Permanent Secretary of the Ministry of Agriculture, Fisheries, Lands and Housing*,[49] a legislative

---

[44] [2002] 1 A.C. 45

[45] See the remarks of Lord Hope in *R. v A (No.2)*, above, para.105.

[46] For the corresponding (though not identical) Scottish provisions, see the Criminal Procedure (Scotland) Act 1995, ss 274, 275.

[47] *R. v A (No.2)*, above, para.120.

[48] Lord Clyde noted, however, that there might be practical advantages in disposing of compatibility issues as a preliminary matter, as was done in *Brown v Stott*, 2001 S.C. (P.C.) 43. In *R. v A (No. 2)*, above, itself, it was said that the same issue had arisen in 13 other pending prosecutions; as a matter of effective use of judicial resources, then, it will sometimes make little sense to require doomed cases to proceed, only to be overturned on appeal.

[49] [1998] 1 A.C. 69 at 79.

provision of general application could, by means of interpretive devices such as reading down or reading in, be rendered contingent, case-dependent and "altogether different . . . from that which Parliament enacted." On the basis that sometimes it will be better to scratch it than save it in mutilated form, Lord Clyde held that if reading down or reading in would leave a provision bearing little or no resemblance to the original, but the original is likely to conflict with fundamental rights in the majority of its applications, the court should leave it to the legislature to decide how the provision should be redrafted.[50] It must also be remembered that the Human Rights Act did not abrogate the traditional rule of construction, whereby the essential role of the courts in interpreting statutes is to discern the intention of the legislature. Section 3(1) may be taken to express a parliamentary intention that pre-incorporation enactments be construed consistently with the Convention rights, so far as possible, but it does not go so far as authorising the courts to attribute to the legislature an "intention" it plainly never had.[51] Thus in *Quilter v Attorney-General of New Zealand*,[52] for example, the New Zealand Court of Appeal rejected the argument that the prohibition on discrimination in the Bill of Rights Act 1990 required the court to reinterpret the provisions of the Marriage Act in such a way as to extend its scope to same-sex couples. *Re S* is also in point.[53] Under the Children Act 1990, once the court has made a care order in respect of a child, its responsibilities in relation to that child cease. The child's care thereafter is entrusted to the appropriate local authority. As Lord Nicholls explained, this "represents the assessment made by Parliament of the division of responsibility which would best promote the interests of children within the overall care system." But, his Lordship added, the system does not always work well, in the interest either of children or their parents. This prompted the Court of Appeal, relying on section 3(1) of the Human Rights Act, to read into the Children Act a power on the part of the court to call for reports from the local authority if there were a failure to

---

[50] Citing Sopinka J. in *Osborne v Canada (Treasury Board)* [1991] 82 D.L.R. (4th) 321. In other words, the court should make a declaration of incompatibility rather than attempt to recast the provision itself. This is desirable not only in deference to democratic principle and because it avoids the impracticability of deciding on the compatibility of a provision on a case by case basis but also because, as Sopinka J. noted, the legislature will have at its disposal information and expertise not available to the court.
[51] The position may differ, if only slightly, in relation to post-incorporation enactments, on which see further below.
[52] [1998] 1 N.Z.L.R. 523.
[53] [2002] 2 A.C. 291.

meet "starred milestones" in the child's care plan. Unanimously,[54] the House of Lords reversed the Court of Appeal decision. Lord Nicholls readily acknowledged the force of section 3(1). But he refuted the idea that its force extends to "[introducing] into the working of [an Act of Parliament] a range of rights and liabilities not sanctioned by Parliament."

10–07   There is evidence, also, of a more restrictive approach still to the use of section 3(1) in particular contexts. The courts may be more willing to render a provision compatible with the Convention rights, even at the cost of straining the ordinary meaning of the statutory language, where the subject matter of the legislation is felt to fall particularly within their sphere of constitutional competence, as with cases in the field of criminal justice.[55] They may be less willing to do so where the legislation prescribes a scheme of social welfare or economic regulation. Thus in *Hooper v Secretary of State for Work and Pensions*,[56] Moses J. found that discrimination between widows and widowers under the Social Security Contributions and Benefits Act 1992 could not be objectively justified and so constituted a breach of Article 14 of the Convention read together with Article 8 and Article 1 of the First Protocol. On the question whether the provisions could be saved by resort to section 3(1), his Lordship held:

> "That question directly engages questions of social and economic policy with which the court is ill equipped to deal. It concerns the appropriate allocation of resources. I cannot substitute my view for that of the government in relation to alternative solutions. . . . There is a significant difference between cases concerning the requirements of a fair criminal trial such as *R. v A*[57] and *Lambert*,[58] where the courts might be regarded as authoritative experts, and cases concerning social and economic policy in respect of which the courts are by no

---

[54] It is worth noting, in passing, that unanimity has been wanting in a surprising number of recent House of Lords decisions on the HRA 1998.

[55] Hence, among others, *Kebilene, R. v A (No.2)* and *Lambert*, above; but contrast, e.g. *R. v Daniel* [2002] EWCA Crim 959. In that challenge to a ruling on the burden of proof in an offence under the Insolvency Act 1986, Auld L.J. accepted that the courts could read down overbroad legislation, and read in necessary safeguards, but was not prepared to accept that "the plain meaning of statutory language could be ignored or simply changed in the cause of securing compatibility." The Court of Appeal therefore declined to follow the House of Lords' view in *Lambert* that "proves" could be read as "gives sufficient evidence" so as to convert a legal burden into a merely evidential one.

[56] [2002] U.K.H.R.R. 785.

[57] *R. v A (No.2)* [2002] 1 A.C. 45.

[58] *R. v Lambert* [2002] 2 A.C. 545.

means expert. . . . Such cases require the decision-maker, in considering the effect of adapting legislation, to be in a position to foresee the effects of such adaptation. Parliament is clearly in a better position to do that than the court. Such adaptation requires the reallocation of public funds, a field in which the courts are far less equipped to tread."[59]

Moses J., therefore, made a declaration of incompatibility in respect of the provisions in question.[60] This is not to say that statutory provisions representing legislative choices in the field of social and economic policy are by definition less apt to be resolved by application of the interpretative device, where they are found to breach Convention rights.[61] In *Mendoza v Ghaidan*,[62] for example, the Court of Appeal were prepared to read provisions of the Rent Act 1977 so as to allow the same-sex partner of a deceased tenant to succeed to the statutory tenancy of the property in which both had lived.[63] The essential issue in the case was not a legislative choice in the matter of housing policy, but discrimination, and "issues of discrimination . . . have high constitutional importance, and are issues that the courts should not shrink from. In such cases, [judicial] deference has only a minor role to play."[64] That is a valuable statement of principle,[65] but does not, it is suggested, controvert the basic point made here, which is that in certain areas, social and economic policy among them, where there is more than one method of securing compliance with the Convention rights, the choice of method is properly regarded as a legislative rather than

---

[59] [2002] U.K.H.R.R. 785, paras 107, 160.

[60] The declaration of incompatibility was subsequently recalled by the Court of Appeal: *R (Hooper) v S of S for Work and Pensions* [2003] 2 F.C.R. 504. The Court of Appeal accepted that the margin of discretion enjoyed by the S of S in such matters was broad, but held that, since the discrimination complained of could not be objectively justified, the Secretary of State came under a duty by virtue of HRA 1998, s.6 (on the entry into force of that section), to make extra-statutory payments to widowers in order to eradicate the discriminatory effects of the principal legislative provisions there in issue.

[61] Whether they involve such a breach remains the first issue, and in considering that the courts are likely to accord to the legislature a wider margin of discretion in fields of social and economic policy, and indeed other areas more suitable for democratic supervision and control: see Lord Woolf C.J. in *Poplar Housing and Regeneration Community Ass. Ltd v Donoghue* [2002] Q.B. 48, para.69.

[62] [2002] 4 All E.R. 1162.

[63] Thereby departing from the earlier decision of the House of Lords in *Fitzpatrick v Sterling Housing Ass.* [2001] 1 A.C. 27, that a same-sex partner could only succeed to the less secure assured tenancy.

[64] *Mendoza v Ghaidan* [2002] 4 All E.R. 1162, para.19, *per* Buxton LJ.

[65] See N. Bamforth, "A Constitutional Basis for Anti-Discrimination Protection?" (2003) 119 L.Q.R. 215.

judicial choice.[66] In such circumstances, therefore, a declaration of incompatibility will normally be the preferable disposal.

10–08   One point remains. Since November 24, 1998, a minister sponsoring a bill in either House of Parliament must, prior to its second reading, make a statement to the effect that the provisions of the bill are compatible with the Convention rights or that, although he is unable to make a statement of compatibility, the government nevertheless wishes the bill to proceed.[67] A statement of compatibility is clear evidence, appearing on the face of an enactment, that it was not the intention of the legislature to violate Convention rights, and may to that extent provide a strong incentive to the courts (whatever the subject matter of the legislation) to find means of construing the legislation consistently with the Convention.[68] Since January 1, 2002, the explanatory notes issued to accompany Westminster bills have given an outline of the government's views on compatibility, although falling short of the disclosure of its legal advice sought by some.[69] As to pre-incorporation enactments, there have been indications of a tendency to examine parliamentary materials, on a rather broader basis than was countenanced by *Pepper v Hart*,[70] in order to ascertain the mischief against which the legislation was aimed and the legislature's reasons for adopting the enactment in the chosen form.[71] In *Wilson v First County Trust Ltd (No.2)* [2003] 3 W.L.R. 568 (HL),[72] the Speaker of the House of Commons and the Clerk

---

[66] In *Mendoza*, above, Buxton L.J. considered that, "since Parliament has swallowed the camel of including unmarried [opposite-sex] partners within the protection given to married couples, it is not for this court to strain at the gnat of including such partners who are of the same sex as each other" (para.35). In the circumstances of that case, this seems an unobjectionable conclusion to draw. But as a general point, it may be said that in principle discrimination can be eradicated by levelling down rather than levelling up, withdrawing a benefit previously accorded to some group or groups but denied to another similarly situated.

[67] HRA 1998, s.19. In the Scottish Parliament, the Presiding Officer must make a statement confirming whether or not in his view the provisions of any bill introduced in the Parliament would be within the competence of the Parliament, which competence depends inter alia on compatibility with the Convention rights; and the Scottish Minister in charge of an Executive bill must make a similar statement in respect of that bill: Scottish Parliament Standing Orders, rr.9.1, 9.3(a).

[68] See Lord Irvine, "The Development of Human Rights in Britain under an Incorporated Convention" [1998] P.L. 221.

[69] Lord Lester, "Parliamentary Scrutiny of Legislation" [2002] E.H.R.L.R. 432.

[70] [1993] 1 A.C. 593.

[71] See, *e.g.* the Court of Appeal decision in *Wilson v First County Trust Ltd (No. 2)* [2002] Q.B. 74. Having examined the legislative history of the Consumer Credit Act 1974, the Court of Appeal remarked that the parliamentary debates "tended to confuse rather than to illuminate" (para.36), shedding no light on why Parliament thought it necessary to enact the provisions there in issue.

[72] See above.

of the Parliament intervened to object to this use of *Hansard* as an encroachment upon Article 9 of the Bill of Rights.[73] The House of Lords accepted that the Court of Appeal in *Wilson v First County Trust Ltd (No. 2)*[74] had made inappropriate use of parliamentary material. Nevertheless, it was held that where the courts are assessing the compatibility of legislation with the Convention rights, it is necessary to identify the rationale for the legislation, an exercise that may involve reference to "additional background material". Such material may be found in published documents, such as government white papers; or in statements made by ministers or members in either House of Parliament during debate on a bill. In either case, if relevant, the courts are entitled to take it into account without "questioning" proceedings in Parliament, intruding into the legislative process or ascribing to Parliament the views expressed by a minister: "The court would merely be placing itself in a better position to understand the legislation."[75]

DECLARATIONS OF INCOMPATIBILITY

If it is not possible to read and give effect to a statutory provision **10–09** consistently with the Convention rights, then certain higher courts[76] may make a declaration of incompatibility in respect of the provision.[77] In relation to a provision of subordinate legislation, the same courts may make a declaration of incompatibility if satisfied that the provision is incompatible with a Convention right and that the parent statute (disregarding any possibility of revocation) prevents removal of the incompatibility.[78] For the purposes of the Human Rights Act, Acts of the Scottish Parliament constitute

---

[73] Which provides that the proceedings of Parliament shall not be impeached or questioned in any court or place outside Parliament.

[74] [2002] Q.B. 74.

[75] *Wilson v First County Trust Ltd (No.2)* [2003] 3 W.L.R. 568, para.64, *per* Lord Nicholls. His Lordship added that in most cases, reference to *Hansard* was unlikely to prove useful. The same was said of the doctrine established in *Pepper v Hart* [1993] 1 A.C. 593, but lawyers nonetheless feel obliged to trawl through *Hansard* in search of ministerial statements or other material that may shed some favourable light on the meaning of statutory provisions (thereby increasing the costs of litigation). Lord Steyn has argued that the only defensible application of *Pepper v Hart* arises in situations where the government states in Parliament that a statutory provision means one thing and subsequently contends for a different meaning in litigation: *"Pepper v Hart*: A re-examination" [2001] 21 O.J.L.S. 59.

[76] For Scottish purposes, the House of Lords, the Judicial Committee of the Privy Council, the Courts-Martial Appeal Court, the Court of Session and the High Court of Justiciary sitting otherwise than as a trial court: HRA 1998, s.4(5)(a), (d).

[77] HRA 1998, s.4(2).

[78] HRA 1998, s.4(4).

subordinate legislation.[79] It should be noted, however, that in terms of the Scotland Act 1998, neither the Scottish Parliament nor members of the Scottish Executive[80] have any power to enact legislation, make subordinate legislation or do any other act so far as to do so is incompatible with any of the Convention rights,[81] and in terms of Schedule 6 any question whether an Act, or provision of an Act, of the Scottish Parliament, or any act or failure to act by a member of the Scottish Executive is incompatible with one or more Convention rights constitutes a devolution issue to be determined in accordance with the provisions of the Schedule. It follows, therefore, that a declaration of incompatibility will never be apposite in respect of an Act of the Scottish Parliament or an act of the Scottish Ministers: to the extent that the Act, or act, is inconsistent with the Convention rights, it is *ultra vires* and void and liable to be struck down accordingly.[82]

Where a court is considering whether to make a declaration of incompatibility, the Crown is entitled to notice of the proceedings and thereafter to be joined as a party to the proceedings.[83] The Crown in this sense is defined to include a Minister of the Crown (or any person nominated by him) and a member of the Scottish Executive.[84] If a declaration of incompatibility is granted, however, it has no effect on "the validity, continuing operation or enforcement of the provision in respect of which it is given; and . . . is not binding on the parties to the proceedings in which it is made."[85] Rather, it triggers the power in section 10 to take remedial action—and it is important to note that it is only a power. The minister is not obliged to make a remedial order, nor need Parliament enact amending legislation, although any failure to do so in response to a declaration of incompatibility will provide the

---

[79] HRA 1998, s.21. So too does "any order, rules, regulations, scheme, warrant, byelaw or other instrument made by a member of the Scottish Executive . . . in exercise of prerogative or other executive functions of Her Majesty which are exercisable by such a person on behalf of Her Majesty."

[80] With the exception of the Lord Advocate in terms of SA 1998, s.57(3).

[81] SA 1998, ss.29(2)(d), 57(2).

[82] See I. Jamieson, "The Relationship between the Scotland Act and the Human Rights Act" 2001 S.L.T. (News) 43.

[83] HRA 1998, s.5(1) and (2). By the same token, where a devolution issue arises in any proceedings in Scotland, it requires to be intimated to the Lord Advocate and the Advocate General for Scotland.

[84] Thus it might be appropriate for a member of the Scottish Executive to be joined as a party to proceedings relating to a pre-commencement enactment (as defined in SA 1998, s.53(3)) where that enactment confers functions exercisable post-devolution by the Scottish Ministers, either by way of the general transfer of functions provided for by s.53 or by way of a transfer of functions pursuant to s.63.

[85] HRA 1998, s.4(6)(a), (b).

aggrieved individual with a strong case to take to Strasbourg.[86] A remedial order may be made by Her Majesty in Council[87] or in accordance with the procedures prescribed by Schedule 2. The ordinary procedure[88] requires the relevant Minister of the Crown[89] to lay a draft of the remedial order before both Houses of Parliament after the expiry of a 60-day period commencing with the laying before both Houses of a document containing a draft of the proposed order and the "required information".[90] If during the 60-day period representations (including any parliamentary report or resolution) are made to the minister in relation to the proposed order, the minister must accompany the draft order laid under paragraph 2(a) with a statement summarising the representations received and giving details of any changes made to the proposed order as a result thereof.[91] The draft order must then be approved by affirmative resolution of both Houses of Parliament within 60 days of its being laid in its final form.[92] Schedule 2 also provides for an urgent procedure, applicable in cases where the incompatible provision is contained in subordinate legislation which has been quashed, or declared invalid, by reason of its incompatibility with the Convention rights.[93] In such cases, the minister may make a remedial order with immediate effect, but then lay the order before Parliament and declare that, because of the urgency of the matter, it was necessary to proceed without the order first being approved in draft by both Houses. Representations may be made to the minister in relation to the order during the period of 60 days following its laying before Parliament, at the end of which period the minister must lay before Parliament a statement summarising

---

[86] This power is also exercisable where, following an adverse decision of the ECHR in proceedings against the UK, it appears that a provision of legislation is incompatible with an obligation of the UK arising under the ECHR: HRA 1998, s.10(1)(b). In neither case *need* the power in s.10 be used; it may be preferable to remedy the defect identified by the ECHR or a declaration of incompatibility by way of primary legislation enacted in the normal way.

[87] By way of an Order in Council: HRA 1998, s.10(5).

[88] HRA 1998, Sch.2, para.2(a).

[89] That is, "the holder of an office in Her Majesty's Government in the United Kingdom": Ministers of the Crown Act 1975, s.8.

[90] HRA 1998, Sch.2, para.3(1). The "required information" is defined by para.5 as an explanation of the incompatibility which the proposed order seeks to remove, including particulars of the relevant declaration of incompatibility, funding or order; and a statement of the minister's reasons for proceeding under s.10 and for making an order in the terms proposed. It should be noted that the minister may only proceed under s.10 if he considers that there are "compelling reasons" for doing so (although it is inconceivable that his judgment in that matter could be challenged by way of judicial review).

[91] HRA 1998, Sch.2, para.3(2).

[92] In calculating the 60-day periods, no account is to be taken of any time during which Parliament is prorogued or dissolved, or both Houses are adjourned for more than four days: HRA 1998, Sch.2, para.6.

[93] HRA 1998, s.10(4) and Sch.2, para.2(b).

the representations and giving details of any changes he considers it appropriate to make to the original order in light thereof. If any changes are made, the minister must make a further remedial order replacing the original order. The order (original or replacement) ceases to have effect at the end of a 120-day period following the laying of the original order unless, during that time, both Houses of Parliament adopt resolutions approving it.[94]

HUMAN RIGHTS AND PUBLIC AUTHORITIES

10–10 Section 6 is pivotal to the scheme of incorporation adopted by the Human Rights Act. It makes it unlawful for a public authority to act in a way that is incompatible with a Convention right.[95] Two points are immediately apparent. First, it is critically important to identify who or what falls within the meaning of the term "public authority" because, secondly, the Human Rights Act does not, at least directly, regulate relations between private parties.[96]

"Standard" and "Functional" public authorities

10–11 Section 6 has this to say about public authorities:

"(3) In this section 'public authority' includes—

    (a) a court or tribunal, and
    (b) any person certain of whose functions are functions of a public nature

but does not include either House of Parliament or a person exercising functions in connection with proceedings in Parliament.

    (4) In subsection (3) 'Parliament' does not include the House of Lords in its judicialcapacity.
    (5) In relation to a particular act, a person is not a public authority by virtue only of subsection 3(b) if the nature of the act is private."

---

[94] But such lapse of the order will not affect the validity of anything previously done under it, or affect the power of the minister to make a fresh remedial order: HRA 1998, Sch.2, para.4(4).

[95] HRA 1998, s.6(1). The term "act" is defined in s.6(6) to include a failure to act, but does not include a failure to introduce in, or lay before Parliament, a proposal for legislation, or a failure to make any primary legislation or remedial order.

[96] As we shall see, however, there is considerable scope for the Act to apply *indirectly* in litigation between private parties, and the extent to which it may do so has been one of the most vexed questions raised by the Act.

This definition is not exhaustive: it was not thought necessary to define expressly bodies which are "obviously" public authorities, but only to make clear that the term included bodies which might otherwise be thought to fall outwith its scope.[97] It follows that obvious, or standard, public authorities, such as local authorities and government departments, are bound by the duty to act in conformity with the Convention rights in respect of all their activities, whereas "functional public authorities"—bodies exercising some "functions of a public nature"—are bound only in the performance of those functions and not, by virtue of section 6(5), in respect of their private acts.[98] None of which makes it any easier to demarcate precisely between the standard and functional public authorities or, in respect of the latter, to distinguish clearly between their private and public functions.

Here at least resort to parliamentary and pre-legislative material may be helpful. The White Paper, *Rights Brought Home*,[99] stated that:

> "Examples of persons or organisations whose acts or omissions it is intended should be able to be challenged include central government (including executive agencies); local government; the police; immigration officers; prisons; courts and tribunals themselves; and, to the extent that they are exercising public functions, companies responsible for the areas of activity which were previously within the public sector, such as privatised utilities."

The definition, in both its limbs, is intended to be broad, as both the White Paper and ministers made clear. On the second reading of the Bill in the House of Lords, Lord Williams of Mostyn said:

> "[W]e would anticipate the BBC being a public authority and that Channel 4 might well be a public authority, but other commercial organisations, such as private television stations, might well not be public authorities. . . . [A] newspaper is not a public authority."[1]

As to functional public authorities, the Home Secretary stated that the Jockey Club carried out public functions and so would fall

---

[97] See R. Clayton and H. Tomlinson, *The Law of Human Rights* (Oxford University Press, Oxford, 2000), paras 5.05–5.08.
[98] This distinction between standard and functional public authorities was drawn by Clayton and Tomlinson, and was approved by the Court of Appeal in *Poplar Housing and Regeneration Community Ass. Ltd v Donoghue* [2002] Q.B. 48.
[99] *Rights Brought Home: The Human Rights Bill*, Cm.3782 (1997), para.2.2.
[1] *Hansard*, HL Vol.582, cols 1309, 1310 (Nov. 3, 1997).

within section 6 in relation to those functions.[2] The Lord Chancellor said:

> "Railtrack would fall into that category [of functional public authorities] because it exercises public functions in its role as a safety regulator, but it is acting privately in its role as a property developer.[3] A private security company would be exercising public functions in relation to the management of a contracted-out prison but would be acting privately when, for example, guarding commercial premises. Doctors in general practice would be public authorities in relation to their National Health Service functions, but not in relation to their private patients."[4]

However, the Home Secretary observed that, "as we are dealing with an evolving situation, we believe that the test must relate to the *nature and substance of the act, not to the form and legal personality*."[5] Perhaps most tellingly, the Home Secretary made the point that: "One of the things with which we have had to wrestle was the fact that many bodies, especially over the last twenty years, have performed public functions which are private, partly as a result of privatisation and partly as a result of contracting out."[6] Ministers were at pains, however, to stress that the exact parameters of the definitions of standard and functional public authorities were for the courts to work out. In that regard, the Home Secretary suggested:

> "[T]here is much guidance to be gained from the way in which British courts have developed the concept of judicial review. . . . We wanted to ensure that, when courts were already saying that a body's activities in a particular respect were a public function for the purposes of judicial review, other things being equal, that would be the basis for action under the Bill."[7]

---

[2] *Hansard*, HC Vol.312, col.1018 (May 20, 1998).
[3] Railtrack plc was acquired by Network Rail Ltd, a not-for-profit company limited by guarantee in October 2002. Its functions as safety regulator on the national rail network had in any case been transferred to a separate industry body before it was put into administration by the Secretary of State for Transport in October 2001. *Quaere* to what extent Network Rail is to be regarded as a public authority.
[4] *Hansard*, HL Vol.583, col.811 (Nov. 24, 1997).
[5] *Hansard*, HC Vol.314, col.433 (June 17, 1998) (emphasis added).
[6] *Hansard*, HC Vol.314, col.410 (June 17, 1998).
[7] *Hansard*, HC Vol.314, cols 408, 409 (June 17, 1998).

It seems reasonably clear that, in referring to the jurisprudence on **10–12** the scope of judicial review, the Home Secretary had in mind the *English* jurisprudence which, like section 6, turns on a distinction between public and private functions.[8] If his intention was that this jurisprudence should serve only as a guide then it is unexceptionable; but there are a number of reasons why the test of what constitutes a public authority for the purposes of section 6 should not be regarded as the *same* as the English test for the scope of judicial review. First, section 2 enjoins the courts to take account of the principles developed by the European Court of Human Rights, and the Court has its own approach to what constitutes a public authority.[9] Secondly, the approach of Scots law to the scope of judicial review differs from that taken by the English courts. Whether an act is "public" or "private" in character is not determinative of its susceptibility to review in Scotland; rather, the test is whether there is "a tripartite relationship between the person or body to whom the jurisdiction, power or authority has been delegated or entrusted, the person or body by whom it has been delegated or entrusted and the person or persons in respect of or for whose benefit that jurisdiction, power or authority is to be exercised."[10] Now the Scottish approach to the scope of review cannot in all respects be treated as providing definitive guidance either, if only because section 6 itself requires a distinction to be drawn between public and private functions. But there is no reason why the Scottish courts (or indeed the English courts) should mechanically follow the English jurisprudence on the scope of judicial review, not least because that jurisprudence is unsatisfactory in a number of ways.[11] Further, as Kate Markus has argued:

---

[8] English Civil Procedure Rules, r.54.2, defines a judicial review claim as a claim to review the lawfulness of any enactment or "a decision, action or failure to act in relation to the exercise of a public function."

[9] See *Chassagnou v France* (1999) 29 E.H.R.R. 615, para.100.

[10] *West v S of S for Scotland*, 1992 S.C. 385 at 413, *per* Lord President Hope. See also Lord Clyde, "The Nature of the Supervisory Jurisdiction and the Public/Private Divide in Scots Administrative Law" in *Edinburgh Essays in Public Law* (Finnie, Himsworth and Walker eds, Edinburgh University Press, Edinburgh, 1991), p.281.

[11] In *R. v Panel on Takeovers and Mergers, ex p. Datafin plc* [1987] Q.B. 815, BSir John Donaldson M.R. held that the source of a body's power was not conclusive: "possibly the only essential element . . . [is] what can be described as a public element, which can take many forms." That element is almost invariably excluded by the presence of some contractual nexus between the parties, or by what is termed a "voluntary submission to the jurisdiction" of the body in question. Thus, for example, sporting bodies such as the Football Association and Amateur Athletics Association are not subject to judicial review in England although, in comparable circumstances, they are in Scotland. Other factors taken into account in the English cases include a "but for" test—whether the state would be obliged to regulate a given activity but for the existence of the body in question—and whether that body's functions are recognised in statute or have "statutory underpinning". For a brief overview, see D. Pannick, "Who is Subject to Judicial Review and in Respect of What?" [1992] P.L.

"It is only by ensuring that Convention rights are respected throughout our legal system and at all levels of society that the state can avoid liability in Strasbourg for permitting such violations [of the Convention rights]. This is the purpose of the Human Rights Act and it explains the non-incorporation of Article 13.[12] Unlike judicial review, the purpose is not limited to protecting individuals against abuses of power by the state and governmental bodies. While the presence of a governmental feature is probably conclusive of a body being a public authority within section 6, then, its absence should not be conclusive against it."[13]

The courts should, therefore, be eclectic in their reference to sources of guidance as to the meaning of the term "public authority" in section 6.[14] This is to acknowledge, not to disguise, the fact that difficult issues require to be addressed at the boundaries. If the nature of a function and not its form is crucial, are private schools and hospitals to be treated as public authorities, at least to the extent that they provide education and health care? Are charities, because of the nature of charitable objects and the state support they enjoy in terms of the tax advantages flowing from charitable status?[15] Are commercial organisations which contract to perform or provide services on behalf of a standard public authority? Are trade unions and professional bodies, because their functions relate to freedom of association (and may raise other significant questions, as in relation to the conformity of their procedures to due process guarantees)? Are religious organisations, because their functions relate to freedom of conscience

---

[12] Art.13 enshrines the right to an effective remedy for breaches of the Convention rights. It is not a Convention right in terms of the HRA 1998 because (according to the government) it need not be: the fact of incorporation of the other Convention rights is sufficient to secure their effective protection in domestic law. But that is only true if the definition of public authorities under s.6 accurately reflects the scope of state responsibility in the Strasbourg Court for breaches by the state of its duty under ECHR, Art.1, to secure the Convention rights and freedoms to all within its jurisdiction, and in that regard "the state cannot absolve itself from responsibility by delegating its obligations to private bodies or individuals": *Costello-Roberts v United Kingdom* [1993] 19 E.H.R.R. 112, para.27).

[13] K. Markus, *"Leonard Cheshire Foundation*: What is a Public Function?" [2003] E.H.R.L.R. 92 at 96.

[14] Lester and Pannick suggest that guidance might be had from the case law relating to the coverage of the Prevention of Corruption Act 1916 and the (now repealed) Public Authorities Protection Act 1893, as well as from the lists of public authorities covered by the provisions of the Freedom of Information Act 2000 and the Freedom of Information (Scotland) Act 2002: Lord Lester and D. Pannick, *Human Rights: Law and practice* (Butterworths, London, 1999), p.33.

[15] See *RSPCA v Attorney-General* [2001] 3 All E.R. 530.

and expression?[16] These are the questions with which the courts have had to grapple since the full entry into force of the Human Rights Act, and, perhaps predictably, differing answers have been given.

There has been little difficulty over the status of privatised **10–13** utilities. In *Marcic v Thames Water Utilities Ltd*, no point was even taken about whether or not the company was a public authority for the purposes of section 6.[17] That is consistent with the stated aims of the government in promoting the Human Rights Bill.[18] So too, on its face, is the decision in *R (A) v Partnerships in Care Ltd*,[19] which held that a private psychiatric hospital, registered as a mental nursing home under the Registered Homes Act 1984 and licensed to receive patients detained under the Mental Health Act 1983, was a public authority for the purposes of section 6. A, an NHS patient, had been placed in the hospital for treatment for a personality disorder. The hospital managers decided to cease offering such treatment. Keith J. held that the relevant statutory duties were laid directly upon the hospital as a registered facility and that the hospital managers were a body upon whom important statutory functions relating to the provision of appropriate care and treatment had been devolved. There was a strong public interest in securing the proper discharge of such functions. For those reasons, it was appropriate to place the hospital within the scope of section 6. This seems at one with the government's indications that privatised or contracted out methods of delivering public services should not exclude the provider from the coverage of the Human Rights Act. But the approach of Keith J. is in fact very close to the English law test of the scope of judicial review: the

---

[16] See *Aston Cantlow and Wilmcote with Billesley Parochial Church Council v Wallbank* [2003] 3 W.L.R. 283.

[17] *Marcic v Thames Water Utilities Ltd* [2002] Q.B. 949. The company was held to have violated Mr Marcic's rights under Art.8 and Art.1 of the First Protocol in failing to provide a proper drainage system, which failure exposed Mr Marcic's home to persistent flooding.

[18] It is also consistent with the jurisprudence of the ECJ on direct effect. EU directives have direct effect (*i.e.* confer enforceable individual rights) only as against the state or an "emanation of the state", namely "a body, whatever its legal form, which has been made responsible, pursuant to a measure adopted by the state, for providing a public service under the control of the state and [which] has for that purpose special powers beyond those which result from the normal rules applicable in relations between individuals": *Foster v British Gas plc* [1991] 1 Q.B. 405 at 427. Clayton and Tomlinson suggest, however, that an "emanation of the state" may be a broader category than that of standard public authorities, so that employees of an entity which qualifies as an emanation of the state will have the benefit of directly effective EU law rights as against their employer but will not, if the entity is only a functional public authority, have the benefit of the Convention rights, since employment will generally be regarded as a private function (para.5.12).

[19] [2002] 1 W.L.R 2610.

"statutory underpinning" of the hospital's role was central to his decision. Nor is this surprising, for Keith J. followed the approach of the Court of Appeal in *Poplar Housing and Regeneration Community Association Ltd v Donoghue*,[20] which starts from the premise that the tests for the scope of review and the scope of section 6 are the same. Contrary to the stated aims of the Human Rights Act, that approach reasserts the significance of legal form over function and may lead to indefensible unpredictability in the protection afforded by the Act.

In *Poplar Housing*, the defendant was granted a non-secure weekly tenancy of a flat by the local authority, pending its decision on whether she was intentionally homeless. The property was subsequently transferred to the claimant housing association, a registered social landlord under the Housing Act 1996 which had been established by the council for the purpose of transferring to it a substantial proportion of the council's housing stock. Almost a year later, the council decided that the defendant had become homeless intentionally, and the housing association moved for possession of her flat. The defendant claimed that the housing association was a public authority within the meaning of section 6 of the Human Rights Act, and that it was contravening her rights under Article 8 of the Convention. The Court of Appeal held that there was no breach of Article 8. It did, however, find the housing association to be a public authority. Lord Woolf C.J. said:

> "The fact that a body performs an activity which otherwise a public body would be under a duty to perform cannot mean that such a performance is necessarily a public function. A public body in order to perform its public duties can use the services of a private body. Section 6 should not be applied so that if a private body provides such services, the nature of the functions are inevitably public. . . . If this were to be the position, then when a small hotel provides bed and breakfast accommodation, as a temporary measure, at the request of a housing authority that is under a duty to provide that accommodation, the small hotel would be performing public functions and required to comply with the Human Rights Act. That is not what the Human Rights Act intended. . . . Section 6(3) means that hybrid bodies, who have functions of a public and private nature, are public authorities but not in relation to acts which are of a private nature. The fact that through the act of renting by a private body a public authority may be fulfilling its public duty, does not automatically change into a public act what would otherwise be a private act."

---

[20] [2002] Q.B. 48.

The factors relevant to determining whether a function which **10–14** would otherwise be regarded as private should be treated as a public function included: the existence of statutory authority for what was being done; the extent of control exercised by a public authority over the performance of the function; and the degree of intermingling of the function with the activities of a public authority. The list was not exhaustive, and no one factor conclusive. Here, the most significant factor was the closeness of the relationship between the housing association and local authority: the former was the creation of the latter, local councillors sat on the board of the housing association, and the association was subject to guidance by the council. The Court of Appeal also noted that the transfer of the council's housing stock had taken place during the currency of the defendant's tenancy, and that it was not intended that she should be any better or worse off as a result of the transfer.

The Court of Appeal returned to the question in *R (Heather) v Leonard Cheshire Foundation*.[21] The foundation ran a nursing home for the disabled. Residents were placed in the home by social services and health authorities pursuant to their statutory duties to provide accommodation to those in need of care and attention by reason of age, illness or disability, and to their power to make arrangements for such accommodation to be provided by third parties. The foundation decided to close the home and the residents applied for judicial review, arguing that the foundation was a public authority and that its decision was in breach of Article 8. The Court of Appeal held that "the role that [the foundation] was performing manifestly did not involve the performance of public functions."[22] Its reasons for so holding were (a) there was no material difference between the services provided by the foundation to privately funded and publicly funded residents, yet it was only in respect of the latter that it was said to be performing public functions; (b) the degree of public funding, while relevant, was not conclusive; (c) the foundation was not standing in the shoes of the local authorities or exercising any statutory powers; and (d) none of the criteria which decided the matter in *Poplar Housing* were met here (save for an element of regulation by a statutory body, the care commission).

Given the prevalence of contracting-out and other forms of **10–15** public/private partnership as a means of public service delivery,[23] the approach taken in *Poplar Housing*, *Partnerships in Care* and

---

[21] [2002] 2 All E.R. 936.
[22] *ibid.*, para.35.
[23] See above, paras 5–12—5–15, 7–07—7–11.

Leonard Cheshire ("the *Poplar* approach") matters.[24] Whether the recipient of public services will be able to rely on his Convention rights is made to turn on the happenstance of the identity of the service provider. This is indefensible on a number of grounds, not least its inconsistency with section 6(3) itself, which places the focus on the function not on the entity performing it. First, it is wrong in principle that the application of the Convention rights should depend upon a choice over which the individual has no control. He does not contract out of the Human Rights Act, but may (on the *Poplar* approach) be excluded from its protection merely by the administrative choice of a public authority. Secondly, even if there is any truth in the assumptions implicit in these cases—that burdening private organisations with duties under the Human Rights Act will increase their business risks and drive up the price a public authority must pay for their services—the *Poplar* approach hardly mitigates matters.[25] It involves such a minute focus on the specific details of particular situations that it will often be difficult for a public authority and its contracted out provider to predict how, given *this* statutory backdrop and *this* institutional relationship, the private provider will be categorised.

There are a number of inconsistencies, apparently unnoticed, between the *Poplar* approach and other aspects of the developing jurisprudence. For one thing, the Court of Appeal's analysis seems to presuppose that the Human Rights Act will have no effect on relations between private parties. But as the next section demonstrates, that is plainly not the case. For another, although disinclined to adopt a purposive and generous approach to the construction of section 6,[26] Lord Woolf had no problem with the possibility that a resident might "require[27] the local authority to enter into a contract with its provider which fully protected the residents' Article 8 rights. If this were done then not only could the local authority rely on the contract, but possibly the resident could do so as a person for whose benefit the contract was made."[28] Leaving to one side the intriguing questions this raises as a matter

---

[24] *Poplar Housing and Regeneration Community Ass. Ltd v Donoghue* [2002] Q.B. 48: *R (A) v Partnerships in Care Ltd* [2002] 1 W.L.R 2610; *R (Heather) v Leonard Cheshire Foundation* [2002] 2 All E.R. 936.

[25] In any case the assumption is questionable. It will normally be possible for a private provider to account for its decisions—to reallocate resources, close a facility or whatever—as being necessary and proportionate responses to a legitimate aim. The only burden this seems to impose is one of justification, which may have a marginal impact on administrative and/or legal costs, but which seems intuitively unlikely to make the provision of the service altogether uneconomic.

[26] Despite his avowed intention of doing so: see *Poplar*, above, para.58.

[27] *How* a resident might "require" the local authority to do anything is unexplained.

[28] *Leonard Cheshire*, above, para.34.

of contract law, it must be asked why, if the Court of Appeal can countenance the imposition of the section 6 duty on private providers under a contract, it is unwilling to achieve the same end by the simpler route, of construing section 6 to include private providers when they are performing public functions.[29] The key flaw in the reasoning of the Court of Appeal here stems from its failure to let go of the principles governing the scope of judicial review in England when analysing section 6. Those principles inevitably shift the focus away from the function being performed to the nature of the entity performing it, which explains why Lord Woolf had no difficulty in treating the provision of residential accommodation as public one minute (when undertaken in-house) and private the next (when contracted-out). But as Craig says, that is simply counter intuitive.[30] The *function* is the same. All contracting-out does is change the identity of the body performing it, but that is neither here nor there for the purposes of section 6 since, provided the function is a function of a public nature, the body is bound to act compatibly with the Convention rights, if only to that extent. The "judicial reviewability" factors—statutory recognition or underpinning, absorption into a scheme of statutory regulation, degree of supervision by a public authority, extent of public funding and so on—might have a role to play in deciding whether a function performed directly by a private body—non-statutory regulator, sporting body, private school, private hospital or whatever—should be treated as a public function for the purposes of the Human Rights Act,[31] but it is difficult indeed to see how they can deprive a function of its public character merely because it happens to be performed by a commercial or voluntary organisation on a contracted out basis. If there is any case for the Scottish courts developing an autonomous approach to the meaning and effect of the Human Rights Act, in short, this must be a prime candidate.

---

[29] Not least since that is what the plain wording of HRA 1998, s.6(3), seems to require.

[30] P. Craig, "Contracting Out, the Human Rights Act and the Scope of Judicial Review" (2002) 118 L.Q.R. 551, at 556.

[31] Although even in this context, reliance on these factors may blur the focus on the substance of a function rather than its form, as Murray Hunt has recognised. In a passage extra-judicially approved by Lord Steyn ("Law and Democracy" [2002] E.H.R.L.R. 723), he argues that the factors relevant to judicial reviewability should instead include "the nature of the interests affected by the body's decision, the seriousness of the impact of those decisions on those interests, whether the affected interests had any real choice but to submit to the body's jurisdiction, and the nature of the context in which the body operates.": M. Hunt, "Constitutionalism and the Contractualisation of Government in the United Kingdom" in *The Province of Administrative Law* (M. Taggart ed., Hart Publishing, Oxford, 1997), Ch.2.

Courts as public authorities

10–16 As noted above, the Human Rights Act is drafted to have *vertical* effect: it applies directly only to the organs of the state and other bodies falling within the definition of public authorities. But its potential *horizontal* effect—its application to purely private relationships—is considerable. This comes about in two ways. First, the interpretative obligation laid on the courts by section 3 applies to all legislation in any proceedings, not merely in proceedings involving a public authority.[32] Through the medium of existing statutory provisions, read and given effect in a manner compatible with the Convention rights, those rights may become binding as between private parties; and if it is not possible to read and give effect to a provision consistently with the Convention rights, a declaration of incompatibility may be made.[33] Secondly, the fact that courts and tribunals are themselves "public authorities" for the purposes of the Act means that it is unlawful for them to act incompatibly with the Convention rights. Views differ on the effect of this. Sir William Wade argued that both the spirit of the Act and a literal construction of section 6 mean that, if a Convention right is relevant to proceedings before it, the court must decide in accordance with it, no less in a case between private parties than in a case against a public authority.[34] Sir Richard Buxton, on the other hand, insisted that the Convention creates rights only against the state (in its various manifestations) and that incorporation of the Convention rights did not change their content so as to render them enforceable against private parties.[35] Murray Hunt offers an intermediate position, in which the Convention rights will "pervade the law" but will fall short of creating wholly new private law causes of action.[36] In fact, the question of horizontal effect may be

---

[32] Subject, however, to the presumption against retrospectivity, as explained by the House of Lords in *Wilson v First County Trust Ltd (No.2)* [2003] 3 W.L.R. 568 (see especially the speech of Lord Rodger, paras 186–214).

[33] The first declaration of incompatibility to be granted following the full entry into force of the HRA 1998 was made in respect of provisions of the Consumer Credit Act 1974 in proceedings between private parties: *Wilson v First County Trust Ltd (No. 2)* [2002] Q.B. 74 (although it was subsequently recalled, as being "a work of supererogation and improper": *Wilson v First County Trust Ltd (No.2)* [2003] 3 W.L.R. 568, para.127, *per* Lord Hobhouse).

[34] H. W. R. Wade, "Horizons of Horizontality" (2000) 116 L.Q.R. 217. See also, *e.g.* Lord Lester and D. Pannick, *Human Rights: Law and Practice* (Butterworths, London, 1999), pp.31, 32.

[35] R. Buxton, "The Human Rights Act and Private Law" (2000) 116 L.Q.R. 48. Both Wade and Buxton cite statements made by the Lord Chancellor during the parliamentary passage of the Human Rights Bill in support of their views. Given the inherent conflict between these statements, one of which cheerfully countenances horizontal effect and the other of which plainly does not, this would not seem to be a question amenable to resolution under the *Pepper v Hart* doctrine: see A. Bowen, "Fundamental Rights in Private Law" 2000 S.L.T. (News) 157.

[36] M. Hunt, "The Horizontal Effect of the Human Rights Act" [1998] P.L. 423.

a subtler one than any of these accounts acknowledge.[37] Consider first the influence the Convention rights have on the development of the common law. Since that influence was making itself felt even prior to the enactment of the Human Rights Act, it verges on the absurd to suggest that the process should not continue. "Statutory horizontality"—bringing the Convention rights into play by means of the interpretative obligation—is plainly justified by the terms of section 3; to argue otherwise would be to deprive section 3 of a good deal of its meaning. In so far as public authorities may have powers to prevent breaches of the Convention rights, and may be liable under the Act for failures to act as much as for their positive actions, a form of "intermediate horizontality" is created: if a private individual is not himself bound to respect another's Convention rights, a public authority may be obliged to prevent him from actually violating them.[38] There is also authority for the proposition that a court must, in order to comply with section 6(1), conform its own procedures to the requirements of the Convention rights.[39] This would extend to what is termed "remedial horizontality", which we see where the court's decision to grant or withhold a remedy is determined by reference to the effect on the parties' Convention rights. Thus in *Karl Construction Ltd v Palisade Properties Ltd*,[40] Lord Drummond Young recalled an inhibition granted on the dependence of the action between the parties on the grounds that its grant was incompatible with the defender's rights under Article 1 of the First Protocol to the Convention. Previously the remedy was granted as of right in actions for payment of a sum or for damages, where the pursuer had included a warrant for inhibition in his summons. The Rules of the Court of Session[41] required only that the summons be intimated to the defender. But the effect of an inhibition, once granted, is draconian: it freezes the whole of the defender's heritable assets, so that

---

[37] See I. Leigh, "Horizontal Rights, the Human Rights Act and Privacy: Lessons from the Commonwealth" (1999) 48 I.C.L.Q. 57.

[38] The analogy here is with the ECHR's treatment of "positive obligations" arising under the ECHR, *i.e.* those which require affirmative action by the state. Thus in *A v United Kingdom* [1998] 27 E.H.R.R. 611, the state was liable for failing to protect a child from punishment at the hands of his stepfather which was held to amount inhuman and degrading treatment contrary to Art.3 (the stepfather was acquitted by a jury, which accepted his defence of "reasonable chastisement" in his prosecution for assault).

[39] Thus, in *R (A) v Lord Saville of Newdigate (No. 2)* [2002] 1 W.L.R 1249, the Court of Appeal held that the Bloody Sunday Inquiry had breached the Art.2 rights (right to life) of former soldiers called to give evidence by requiring them to attend the tribunal in Londonderry to do so. For an unequivocal acceptance of procedural and remedial horizontality in Scotland, see the judgment of Sh. Prin. MacPhail Q.C. in *Newman Shopfitters Ltd v M. J. Gleeson Group plc*, Mar. 4, 2003 (unreported), para.40.

[40] 2002 S.L.T. 312.

[41] Rules of the Court of Session (S.I. 1994 No. 1443).

he is unable to use or dispose of them; the grounds for recall are (or were) limited; and the defender has no right to be compensated for wrongful use of the diligence. While Lord Drummond Young accepted that inhibition pursued a legitimate aim (namely, furthering the administration of justice by ensuring that assets are available to satisfy any decree granted in the pursuer's favour), he did not find that it struck the requisite "fair balance" between the general interests of the public and the rights of individuals to the use and enjoyment of their property.[42]

10–17   In fact, the Human Rights Act appears to have horizontal effect in every respect bar one: private individuals cannot sue one another for breaches of their Convention rights as such. Thus in *Douglas v Hello! Ltd*,[43] in which horizontality in the sense of "interpreting and developing the common law consistently with the Convention rights" was not taken to raise any difficulty, Keene L.J. noted:

> "[W]hether [horizontality] extends to creating a new cause of action between private persons and bodies is more controversial, since to do so would appear to circumvent the restrictions on proceedings contained in section 7(1) of the Act and on remedies in section 8(1)."

Likewise in *Venables and Thompson v News Group Newspapers Ltd*,[44] Dame Elizabeth Butler-Sloss P. held that although the Convention rights could not found *free-standing* causes of action in private law proceedings, the court was obliged to act consistently with the Convention rights in adjudicating on common law causes of action.[45] In *Douglas v Hello! Ltd (No. 2)*,[46] Lindsay J. drew on these cases and others[47] in holding the defendants liable to the

---

[42] *Karl Construction* was followed in *Fab-Tek Engineering Ltd v Carillion Construction Ltd*, 2002 S.L.T. (Sh.Ct) 113, in relation to the analogous diligence of arrestment on the dependence. The effect on the practice of the Court of Session and the sheriff courts has been dramatic: as Lord McEwan observed in his note to the Inner House *in causa Inland Revenue Commissioners v M. T.*, June 24, 2002 (unreported), what was once given almost as of right now requires a hearing, which has occupied a great deal of already scarce judicial, court and administrative time (with all that that implies in terms of costs).

[43] [2001] Q.B. 967.

[44] [2001] Fam. 430.

[45] Unsurprisingly, since it had felt the effects of the ECHR to no small extent prior to incorporation, the cause of action most prone to the influence of the Convention rights so far is defamation. See for example *Berezovsky v Forbes* [1999] E.M.L.R. 278 (on the defence of justification); *O' Shea v Mirror Group Newspapers Ltd* [2001] E.M.L.R. 943 (on liability for unintentional defamation); *Loutchansky v Times Newspapers Ltd* [2001] 3 W.L.R 104 (on the defence of qualified privilege); and *Branson v Bower* [2002] 2 W.L.R 452 (on the defence of fair comment).

[46] [2003] All E.R. (D) 209 (Apr).

[47] Principally *Campbell v Mirror Group Newspapers Ltd* [2003] Q.B. 633 and *A v B* [2002] 3 W.L.R 542.

claimants for breach of confidence but denying that there was any right of privacy under which Michael Douglas and Catherine Zeta-Jones were entitled independently to relief. In relation to breach of confidence, his Lordship held that the recent cases represented a fusion between older case law and the rights and duties arising under the Human Rights Act:

"Breach of confidence is an established cause of action but its scope now needs to be evaluated in the light of obligations falling upon the court under section 6(1) of the Human Rights Act. That can be achieved by regarding the often opposed rights conferred respectively by Articles 8 and 10 of the European Convention as absorbed into the action for breach of confidence and as thereby to some extent giving it new strength and breadth. The European Convention thus comes into play even in private law cases. It will be necessary for the courts to identify, on a case by case basis, the principles by which the law of confidentiality must accommodate Articles 8 and 10. The weaker the claim for privacy, the more likely it will be outweighed by a claim based on freedom of expression [but] a balance between the conflicting interests has to be struck."[48]

Lindsay J. did not, however, rule out the possibility that the Human Rights Act might have to be accorded direct horizontal effect if such were necessary to secure compliance by a court with its duties under section 6(1). In *Douglas (No. 2)*, denying the claimants a cause of action for invasion of privacy involved no conflict with the judge's section 6(1) duty because their privacy interests were sufficiently safeguarded by the cause of action for breach of confidence. In an ideal world, the privacy question would fall to be dealt with by Parliament, which is in a better position to consider the ramifications and can "consult interests far more widely than is possible in the course of ordinary *inter partes* litigation." On the other hand, the law of confidence does not cover every possible invasion of privacy interests, as the decision of the European Court of Human Rights in *Peck v United Kingdom* made plain.[49] As Lindsay J. put it:

"That inadequacy will have to be made good, and if Parliament does not step in then the courts will be obliged to. Further development by the courts may merely be awaiting the

---

[48] para.186.
[49] (2003) 36 E.H.R.R. 41. In that case, it was held that the applicant's right to privacy had been violated by the publication of images of him, captured on CCTV cameras in a public place, attempting to commit suicide.

first post-Human Rights Act case where neither the law of confidence nor any other domestic law protects an individual who deserves protection."[50]

Section 6(2) "defence"

10–18 Section 6(2) of the Human Rights Act disapplies section 6(1) in two situations: first, where a public authority could not, as the result of one or more provisions of primary legislation, have acted in any other way; or, secondly, where it was acting to give effect to or enforce statutory provisions which cannot be read and given effect in a manner compatible with the Convention rights. The first of these envisages a situation in which the public authority had no discretion at all, the second a situation in which such discretion as it had could not be exercised in conformity with the Convention. If that is the case then, assuming the act in question did breach a Convention right,[51] the only remedy open to the litigant will be a declaration of incompatibility.[52] But it will normally, if not invariably, be possible to argue that the public authority has in fact failed to read and give effect to its statutory powers consistently with the Convention rights—which is to say that, even if a public authority has always regarded a given statutory provision as unequivocal in its meaning, it must now ask itself whether that meaning remains sustainable, and, if not, whether it is possible to adopt a meaning compatible with the Convention rights. Only if this is not so should a public authority be able to take the benefit of the section 6(2) "defence". Moreover, when seeking to rely on section 6(2), a public authority should be in a position to demonstrate that it has had regard to the human rights dimension of its actions. As the White Paper *Rights Brought Home* pointed out, the attainment of a "culture of rights" is as much a matter of promoting changes in the practice and procedures of public authorities than of decided cases. That being so, public authorities (particularly the standard public authorities, which are bound in every respect to act in conformity with the Convention rights) must keep their powers and functions under continuous review, because mere invocation of section 6(2) should rarely, if ever, relieve them of liability for breach of a

---

[50] *Douglas v Hello! Ltd (No.2)* [2003] All E.R. (D) 209 (Apr), para.229.

[51] This must always be the first question to resolve, for there is no need to press the interpretative obligation into service, or consider whether the HRA 1998, s.6(2), defence is satisfied, or whether it is necessary to grant a declaration of incompatibility unless there is actually a breach of the Convention rights.

[52] The obvious drawback of which is that it has no effect on the validity, continuing operation or enforcement of the provision in respect of which it is made, and is not binding on the parties to the proceedings: see HRA 1998, s.4(6), and above, para.10–09.

Convention right. Where discretion exists, and is capable of bearing a meaning conform to the Convention rights, it is in the first instance the duty of the public authority to identify that meaning and act accordingly.[53]

PROCEEDINGS UNDER THE HUMAN RIGHTS ACT

Section 7(1) provides as follows: **10–19**

"A person who claims that a public authority has acted (or proposes to act) in a way which is made unlawful by section 6(1) may—
(a) bring proceedings against the authority under this Act in the appropriate court or tribunal, or
(b) rely on the Convention right or rights concerned in any legal proceedings

but only if he is (or would be) a victim of the unlawful act."

Title and interest

Plainly, judicial review will provide an appropriate forum for **10–20** raising a human rights issue under section 7(1)(a), if not section 7(1)(b)[54]; so much is envisaged by section 7(3) and (4), which modify the normal tests of standing to apply for judicial review in England and Scotland respectively.[55] The test of standing now (indeed the test of entitlement to rely on the Convention rights in any proceedings) is the "victim test" prescribed by Article 34 of the Convention. This caused almost unanimous consternation amongst the English commentators on the Human Rights Act.[56] Article 34

---

[53] See, *e.g. Marcic v Thames Water Utilities Ltd* [2002] Q.B. 949, para.66; also, *R (Hooper) v S of S for Work and Pensions* [2003] 2 F.C.R. 504, in which the Court of Appeal held that it became incumbent on the Secretary of State to eradicate discrimination in the extant statutory schemes for payment of bereavement pensions by paying such pensions to widowers on an *ex gratia* or extra-statutory basis following the entry into force of the HRA 1998.

[54] In Scotland, to date, the majority of human rights points raised in the cases have been of the HRA 1998, s.7(1)(b) type, albeit that they are almost invariably raised as devolution issues under SA 1998, Sch.6, being raised by the accused in the context of criminal proceedings. Indeed it is in the field of criminal law and procedure rather than public law that human rights have had their greatest impact in Scotland.

[55] Note also that proceedings under the HRA 1998 are subject to a time-limit of one year. In Scots law, there is no time-limit as such on raising a petition for judicial review, but the usual rules of *mora*, taciturnity and acquiescence (as to which, see para.12–07) apply.

[56] See, *e.g.* J. Marriott and D. Nicol, "The Human Rights Act, Representative Standing and the Victim Culture" [1998] E.H.R.L.R. 730; J. Miles, "Standing under the Human Rights Act: Theories of rights enforcement and the nature of Public law adjudication" (2000) 59 C.L.J. 133; Clayton and Tomlinson, *The Law of Human Rights* (Oxford University Press, Oxford, 2000), paras 3.84–3.87.

provides that the European Court of Human Rights may receive applications from any person, non-governmental organisation or group of individuals claiming to be a victim of a violation of one or more of the Convention rights. Local authorities and other organs of the state cannot institute proceedings. But legal persons and other bodies—for example, companies, newspapers, churches, trade unions and political parties—may be able to rely directly on at least some of the Convention rights. Neither are pressure groups necessarily excluded, provided that, in common with individual applicants, they can demonstrate a reasonable likelihood that the national measure complained of will be or was applied to them or their members, and provided they have authority to act on behalf of their members, who must be identified.[57] So the concept of victimhood is not absolutely coterminous with the concept of a directly affected individual.[58] But it is plainly narrower than the "sufficient interest" test in England which, since its inception, has been interpreted liberally so as to permit "representative challenges" to the legality of administrative decisions by groups not directly affected by the decision in question. Already a number of ways of outflanking the victim test have been mooted.[59] But it should be noted that the Scots law test of standing to seek judicial review—the ordinary principles of title and interest to sue—has more in common with the Court's approach under Article 34.[60] It is less receptive to representative challenges,[61] not least because it is not regarded as the job of the courts to pronounce on academic questions: "no person is entitled to put another to the trouble and expense of a litigation unless he has some real interest to enforce or protect."[62]

Thus the victim test sits more easily with Scots law than with English law where human rights points are raised by way of judicial review. But it should not be supposed that an active role for pressure groups in human rights litigation is excluded by the Human Rights Act.[63] In either jurisdiction it is open to them to fund, if not front, test cases in the human rights arena. More

---

[57] See *Norris v Ireland* (1985) 44 D.R. 132; and contrast *Open Door Counselling Ltd and Dublin Well Woman Centre Ltd v Ireland* [1992] 15 E.H.R.R. 244.

[58] See generally D.J. Harris, M. O'Boyle and C. Warbrick, *The Law of the European Convention on Human Rights* (Butterworths, London, 1995), p.633.

[59] See, *e.g.* S. Grosz, J. Beatson and P. Duffy, *Human Rights: The 1998 Act and the European Convention* (Sweet & Maxwell, London, 2000), paras 4.42–4.45; M. Elliott, "The Standard of Substantive Review after the Human Rights Act" (2001) 60 C.L.J. 301.

[60] Paras 12–05—12–06.

[61] See, *e.g.* *Scottish Old People's Welfare Council, Petrs*, 1987 S.L.T. 179; *Glasgow Rape Crisis Centre v S of S for the Home Dept*, 2000 S.C. 527.

[62] *Swanson v Manson*, 1907 S.C. 426 at 429, *per* Lord Ardwell.

[63] Nor should it necessarily be supposed that the litigation strategies of pressure groups is an unqualified good thing.

importantly, changes have been made to the rules of court north and south of the border to facilitate third party interventions in judicial review proceedings, whether or not involving human rights.[64] Act of Sederunt (Rules of the Court of Session Amendment No 5) (Public Interest Intervention in Judicial Review) 2000[65] inserts a new rule 58.8A into Chapter 58 of the Rules of the Court of Session,[66] providing that a person who is not directly affected by any issue raised in a petition for judicial review may nevertheless apply to the court for leave to intervene in the petition on in an appeal connected therewith. Where leave is granted, an intervention will normally take the form of a written submission, lodged with the court and copied to the parties, not exceeding 5,000 words in length, but the court may exceptionally allow longer written submissions to be made and may direct that it wishes to hear oral submissions from the intervener.[67]

In one situation, however, it is suggested that a reasonable case **10–21** may be made for permitting purely representative proceedings under the Human Rights Act. That is where the only remedy sought is a declaration of incompatibility under section 4. Because a declaration of incompatibility is not a concrete remedy, in the sense that it has no effect on the validity or continuing operation of the provision in respect of which it is made and is not binding on the parties to the proceedings in which it is given, it has little to commend it to an individual litigant. Campaigning organisations, however, may have no interest beyond securing a declaration that statutory provisions are incompatible with the Convention rights, if only because such a declaration would give them powerful leverage in political arenas for obtaining changes in the law. If one of the aims of the Human Rights Act is to nourish a culture of rights, and if it is accepted that campaigning groups have a role to play in that project, the Act is deficient in excluding them altogether from direct participation in human rights litigation.

Standard of review in human rights cases

We have seen that, even prior to the entry into force of the **10–22** Human Rights Act, the courts had begun to craft the tools of a domestic human rights jurisprudence which accorded a substantial,

---

[64] The rules of the ECHR make comparable provision for public interest interventions.

[65] A.S. (Rules of the Court of Session Amendment No 5) (Public Interest Intervention in Judicial Review) 2000 (SI 2000/317).

[66] Rules of the Court of Session (SI 1994/1443).

[67] For the merits and demerits of "public interest" interventions, see S. Fredman, "Scepticism under Scrutiny: Labour, Law and the Human Rights" in *Sceptical Essays on Human Rights* (Campbell, Ewing and Tomkins eds, Oxford University Press, Oxford, 2001), Ch.11; R. Charteris, "Intervention—in the Public Interest?" 2000 S.L.T. (News) 87.

if not equivalent, degree of protection on fundamental rights as a matter of the common law. By varying the intensity of judicial review, the courts were able to apply stricter standards of scrutiny where appropriate, whilst recognising that certain subjects were less amenable to judicial control, either because they involved choices to be accounted for through democratic channels, absent some manifest legal flaw, or because they involved exercises of specialist judgment that the court was ill equipped to second-guess.

In some circumstances, even where the Convention rights are engaged, it will remain appropriate for the courts to defer to the judgment of legislative or executive authorities. The challenge for the courts is to identify, in particular cases, the proper balance between undue restraint and unwarranted activism:

> "If the court adopts an excessively deferential approach to the views of the public authority, this could undermine the purpose of the Human Rights Act in the first place . . . [but] an extreme form of judicial activism would involve the courts in making decisions which are outside their area of expertise and which would breach the constitutional doctrine of the separation of powers."[68]

The jurisprudential tools through which the appropriate levels of deference fall to be calibrated are the principle of proportionality and the concept of a "discretionary area of judgment". The latter is the domestic rendering of the "margin of appreciation" doctrine developed in the case law of the European Court. That doctrine is premised on the fact that the machinery of protection established by the Convention is subsidiary to the national systems safeguarding human rights.[69] National authorities, by reason of "their direct and continuous contact with the vital forces of their countries . . . are in principle better placed than an international court to evaluate local needs and conditions."[70] The margin of appreciation accorded to national authorities therefore represents the natural deferential reflex of a supranational court, and will be more or less extensive depending on such factors as the nature of the Convention right in issue (for example, whether it is qualified in its terms or absolute), the nature of the justification advanced by the national authorities for the conduct complained of, and the presence or absence of consensus between states party to the Convention on matters of social or moral judgment. It recognises that "the convention, as a living system, does not need to be applied uniformly by all states but may vary in its application according to

---

[68] Clayton and Tomlinson, *The Law of Human Rights*, *op.cit.*, para.5.125.
[69] *Handyside v UK* (1976) 1 E.H.R.R. 737, para.48.
[70] *Buckley v UK* (1996) 23 E.H.R.R. 101, para.75.

local needs and conditions."[71] For that very reason, the doctrine is not available as such to the national courts when adjudicating under the Human Rights Act. Nonetheless, the Convention rights typically involve questions of balance between competing interests and the proportionality of state action, and in addressing such issues the considerations which influenced the variable intensity of judicial review prior to the entry into force of the Human Rights Act remain relevant. As Lord Hope put it in *Kebeline*[72]:

> "Difficult choices may have to be made by the executive or the legislature between the rights of the individual and the needs of society. In some circumstances it will be appropriate for the courts to recognise that there is an area of judgment within which the judiciary will defer, on democratic grounds, to the considered opinion of the elected body or person whose act or decision is said to be incompatible with the convention. . . . It will be easier for such an area of judgment to be recognised where the convention itself requires a balance to be struck, much less so where the right is stated in terms which are unqualified. It will be easier for it to be recognised where the issues involve questions of social or economic policy, much less so where the rights are of high constitutional importance or are of a kind where the courts are especially well placed to assess the need for protection."[73]

The concept of the discretionary area of judgment is distinct from **10–23** the principle of proportionality, although the two are related.[74] As to the latter, Lord Clyde has held that when determining whether a given act or decision offends against the principle of proportionality, the court should ask whether "(i) the legislative objective is sufficiently important to justify limiting a fundamental right; (ii) the measures designed to meet the legislative objective are rationally connected to it; and (iii) the means used to impair the right or freedom are no more than is necessary to accomplish the

---

[71] *R. v DPP, ex p. Kebilene* [2000] 2 A.C. 326 at 380, *per* Lord Hope.

[72] *Kebeline*, above, at 381 citing Lester and Pannick, *Human Rights Law and Practice, op.cit.*, para.3.21.

[73] Lord Hope added that even where a Convention right was stated in unqualified terms, special considerations (such as the need to protect society from terrorist crime) might justify infringements of the right. *Kebeline* itself illustrates the point, but see also *Brown v Stott*, 2001 S.C. (P.C.) 43, where prevention of the social ills associated with drink-driving was regarded as outweighing the individual's right not to be compelled to incriminate himself.

[74] Clayton and Tomlinson, *The Law of Human Rights, op.cit.*, criticise the tendency of the ECHR to run the concepts of proportionality and the margin of appreciation together, so that a decision is disproportionate if it exceeds the margin of discretion to be accorded to the decision-maker in any particular case (paras 6.49–6.53).

objective."[75] This approach may require the reviewing court "to assess the balance which the decision maker has struck, not merely whether it is within the range of rational or reasonable decisions" and may go further than traditional *Wednesbury* review "inasmuch as it may require attention to be directed to the relative weight accorded to interests and considerations."[76] The notion of the "discretionary area of judgment" provides guidance as to the rigour with which the court should question the legislative or executive assessment of the necessity for an infringement of protected rights. That exercise is itself multi-faceted, involving (at least) the identification of conduct or a state of affairs as calling for regulation or restriction (or, indeed, positive action on the part of public authorities),[77] an assessment of the gravity of the mischief against which a measure or decision or course of action is directed, and a judgment as to the means required to combat that mischief in view of the wider public interest.[78] Some of those questions may not be susceptible to absolutely objective resolution. Where the Convention right in question is one which requires a balance to be struck, or which requires consideration of social, economic or political factors, or which raises a question on which there is little or no consensus, the discretionary area of judgment to be accorded to the decision-maker in assessing the necessity of intervention (or justifiability of inaction) will be greater than where the Convention right is stated in absolute terms, or relates to matters of high constitutional importance in respect of which the courts claim particular expertise.[79]

The approach of the courts to the discretionary area of judgment and the proportionality of interferences with protected rights—often referred to in terms of "judicial deference"—has already been criticised by some commentators as unprincipled and insufficiently rigorous to secure appropriate protection for fundamental rights.[80] There may indeed be cause to question the *degree*

---

[75] *De Freitas v Permanent Secretary of Ministry of Agriculture, Fisheries, Lands and Housing* [1999] 1 A.C. 69 at 80.

[76] *R (Daly) v S of S for the Home Dept* [2001] 2 A.C. 532, at 547, 548, *per* Lord Steyn.

[77] In the language of the ECHR, the "pressing social need" to which the legislative or executive authorities of the state are compelled to respond.

[78] It may be said that in some cases, it has been possible to find a public authority to have breached one or more of the Convention rights without even inquiring into the justifiability or otherwise of its actions, because its actions betray no consciousness (at least prior to the commencement of legal proceedings) of the human rights dimension to its activities: see, *e.g. Marcic v Thames Water Utilities Ltd* [2002] Q.B. 949; *Hatton v UK* (2002) 34 E.H.R.R. 1.

[79] See Lester and Pannick, *Human Rights, op.cit.*, para.3.26, citing *Libman v Attorney-General of Quebec* [1998] 3 B.H.R.C. 269.

[80] See, *e.g.* I. Leigh, "Taking Rights Proportionately: Judicial review, the Human Rights Act and Strasbourg" [2002] P.L. 265; R. A. Edwards, "Judicial Deference under the Human Rights Act" [2002] 65 M.L.R. 859.

of latitude accorded by the courts to the legislative and executive authorities of the state. But to attack the very exercise is misconceived. Before the enactment of the Human Rights Act and since, the task of the courts has been to strike a constitutional balance between their own role in the identification and application of the law and the role within the state of the legislature and executive authorities. The difficulties involved in striking that balance were briskly identified by Lord Hoffmann, in the following discussion of the principle of equality of treatment, in *Matadeen v Pointu*[81]:

> "[Treating] like cases alike and unlike cases differently is a general axiom of rational behaviour. . . . But the very banality of the principle must suggest a doubt as to whether merely to state it can provide an answer to the kind of problem which arises in this case. Of course persons should be uniformly treated, unless there is some valid reason to treat them differently. But what counts as a valid reason for treating them differently? And, perhaps more important, who is to decide whether the reason is valid or not? Must it always be the courts? The reasons for not treating people uniformly often involve, as they do in this case, questions of social policy on which views may differ. These are questions which the elected representatives of the people have some claim to decide for themselves. The fact that equality of treatment is a general principle of rational behaviour does not entail that it should necessarily be a justiciable principle—that it should always be the judges who have the last word on whether the principle has been observed. In this, as in other areas of constitutional law, sonorous judicial statements of uncontroversial principle often conceal the real problem, which is to mark out the boundary between the powers of the judiciary, the legislature and the executive in deciding how that principle is to be applied."

As Lord Hoffmann further explained in *R (ProLife Alliance) v British Broadcasting Corporation*, the term "deference", with its "overtones of servility, or perhaps gracious concession", was somewhat inappropriate to describe the function of the courts in their approach to human rights adjudication[82]:

> "In a society based upon the rule of law and the separation of powers, it is necessary to decide which branch of government has in any particular instance the decision-making power and

---

[81] [1999] 1 A.C. 98 at 109.
[82] [2003] 2 W.L.R. 1403, paras 75, 76 (emphasis added).

what the legal limits of that power are. That is a question of law and must therefore be decided by the courts. *This means that the courts themselves often have to decide the limits of their own decision-making power.* That is inevitable. But it does not mean that their allocation of decision-making power to the other branches of government is a matter of courtesy or deference. The principles upon which decision-making powers are allocated are principles of law. The courts are the independent branch of government and the legislature and executive are, directly and indirectly respectively, the elected branches of government. Independence makes the courts more suited to deciding some kinds of questions and being elected makes the legislature or executive more suited to deciding others. The allocation of these decision-making responsibilities is based upon recognised principles. The principle that the independence of the courts is necessary for a proper decision of disputed legal rights or claims of violation of human rights is a legal principle. It is reflected in art 6 of the Convention. On the other hand, the principle that majority approval is necessary for a proper decision on policy or allocation of resources is also a legal principle. Likewise, when a court decides that a decision is within the proper competence of the legislature or executive, it is not showing deference. It is deciding the law."[83]

Remedies for breaches of Convention rights

10–24 Where, in proceedings under section 7(1)(a) or (b) of the Human Rights Act, the court find that the public authority respondent is acting, or proposes to act, in a manner made unlawful by section 6(1), it may grant "such relief or remedy, or make such order, within its powers as it considers just and appropriate."[84] In the context of judicial review, the Court of Session may "make any order that could be made if sought in any action or petition, including an order for reduction, declarator, suspension, interdict, implement, restitution, payment (whether of damages or otherwise) and any interim order."[85]

There are restrictions on the court's remedial discretion, most prominently the exclusion of the coercive remedies of interdict and implement in "civil proceedings" against the Crown under section 21 of the Crown Proceedings Act 1947.[86] That exclusion was

---

[83] There is perhaps an irony here in that, while the courts have been at pains to defer to the proper role and function of the legislative and executive authorities of the state, the same courtesy is not always extended to the courts: see A. W. Bradley, "Judicial Independence Under Attack" [2003] P.L. 397.

[84] HRA 1998, s.8(1).

[85] Rules of the Court of Session, r.58.4.

[86] Scottish Ministers are brought within the definition of the Crown for the purposes of the 1947 Act by SA 1998, Sch.8.

partially disapplied, both in Scotland and England, following the decision of the European Court of Justice in *Factortame (No 2)*,[87] in order to ensure the effective protection of Community law rights. In judicial review proceedings in England, the exclusion was wholly removed by the decision of the House of Lords in *M v Home Office*.[88] There, on the basis that judicial review is the modern incarnation of "proceedings on the Crown side of the King's Bench"—which the 1947 Act excludes from its definition of "civil proceedings"—it was held that the remedy of injunction was competent against a Minister of the Crown "acting in his official capacity" in the context of a claim for judicial review. The Second Division declined to follow this reasoning in *McDonald v Secretary of State for Scotland*.[89] In light of the Human Rights Act, however, a prisoner at H.M. Prison Barlinnie sought, *inter alia*, declarator that an order ordaining the Scottish Ministers to transfer him to conditions of detention compatible with Article 3 of the Convention could competently be made in judicial review proceedings, section 21 of the 1947 Act notwithstanding.[90] An Extra Division affirmed *McDonald*, holding, first, that the reasoning in *M*, turning as it did on the peculiarities of English procedural history, simply did not translate into Scottish terms. There was nothing in the 1947 Act to suggest that judicial review in Scotland did not constitute "civil proceedings". Secondly, the Extra Division accepted that, the non-incorporation of Article 13 of the Convention notwithstanding, an individual was entitled to an effective remedy in respect of breaches of his Convention rights; but denied that he was entitled to a remedy of his choice. The 1947 Act allows declaratory relief to be granted against the Crown, and "to suggest that a declarator, coupled with an undertaking from the Scottish Ministers, is not an effective remedy because it is not coercive is plainly wrong."[91] Declarator may indeed constitute an effective remedy in most circumstances. But it is not obvious that it will always do so, particularly where an interim interdict is sought as a matter of urgency.[92]

---

[87] *R. v S of S for Transport, ex p. Factortame Ltd* [1991] 1 A.C. 603.

[88] [1994] 1 A.C. 377.

[89] 1994 S.L.T. 692.

[90] *Davidson v Scottish Ministers (No.1)*, 2002 S.C. 205.

[91] *ibid., per* Lord Hardie, para.11. Lord Marnoch added that "it serves absolutely no purpose to assert that the 'rule of law' requires coercive orders to be granted against the Crown unless there can be shown a means of construing the [1947 Act] to that end" (para.16).

[92] At the time of writing, this litigation remained unresolved. It is suggested that an arguable case may be made for recognising that in some situations interdict may be the best (if not the only) remedy capable of satisfying the requirement of an effective remedy. Even so, the interpretive approach ordained by s.3(1) only applies where one of the Convention rights is in issue (and the Art.13 right is not

10–25   Section 8(2) of the Human Rights Act provides that damages
may be awarded by a court having power to award damages or
order the payment of compensation where a breach of the Convention rights is established. But damages may only be awarded where
such an award would be "just and appropriate": violation of one's
Convention rights alone will not necessarily be sufficient.[93] Moreover, in deciding whether an award of damages is necessary to
afford just satisfaction to the applicant, the court is required by
section 8(3)(b) to consider the consequences of the award, which is
likely to be regarded as calling attention to the risks of opening the
floodgates to hundreds of other potential claims. Here as
elsewhere, the court must take into account the principles applied
by the European Court of Human Rights in deciding whether to
award damages and, if so, in what amount. But the jurisprudence
of the Court in this respect has been justly criticised as inconsistent, opaque and premised upon unarticulated assumptions
about the "value" of different types of application.[94] In their joint
report on damages under the Human Rights Act, the Law Commission and Scottish Law Commission accepted that when the
Court awards damages, it seeks to restore the applicant to the
position he would have been in but for the breach complained of.[95]
But they were driven to remark upon the lack of principle in the
case law of the Court on the question of monetary redress. The
report concluded that the entry into force of the Human Rights
Act would involve little change to the law of damages in either
jurisdiction, in that "where the courts . . . have established appropriate levels of compensation for particular types of loss in relation
to claims in tort or delict, it would seem appropriate for the same
rules to be used in relation to a claim under the Human Rights
Act."[96]

---

a "Convention right" for those purposes). By the same token, a declaration of
incompatibility could not be made in respect of s.21 of the 1947 Act even if its
bar on interdict were found to breach the right to an effective remedy. That
being so, it would seem that Lord Weir was correct to conclude in *Davidson*,
above, at para.18 that the only solution to the present state of affairs lies in the
hands of Parliament.

[93] M. Amos, "Damages for Breach of the Human Rights Act 1998" [1999]
E.H.R.L.R. 178.

[94] A. Mowbray, "The European Court of Human Rights' Approach to Just
Satisfaction" [1997] P.L. 647.

[95] *Damages under the Human Rights Act 1998* (Law Com, No. 266 (Cm.4853); Scot
Law Com, No. 180 (SE/2000/182)). See to like effect the judgment of the Court
of Appeal in *R (Hooper) v S of S for Work and Pensions* [2003] 2 F.C.R. 504,
para.147 (in that case, it was held that "just satisfaction" required the payment
of compensation to only one of the applicants, and only then in the sum of
£1,000).

[96] For an outline of the prevailing approach to the delictual liability of public
authorities, see paras 12–38—12–39.

CHAPTER 11

POLICE POWERS AND PUBLIC ORDER

A person's human rights may matter for a number of reasons and **11–01** in a number of contexts, but for many concepts of fundamental rights and freedoms have the most direct resonance in their dealings with the police and criminal justice system. The vital functions of the police in the prevention and investigation of crime and the maintenance of public order all involve, to greater or lesser extents, invasions of the individual's liberty and fall to be justified, not only by reference to a common law or statutory source, but also, now, by reference to the additional standards imposed by the Convention jurisprudence.

SURVEILLANCE

In successive cases, the European Court of Human Rights has **11–02** made clear that an interference with protected rights will never be justifiable if it lacks a legal base. The traditional premise of the common law, however, is that all is allowed except that which is specifically *prohibited* by law. The police as much as anybody else have had the benefit of this. What it meant in practice was that the police required no positive legal authority for their actions provided their actions did not amount to an actual legal wrong. Hence in *Malone v United Kingdom*,[1] the claimant had no remedy before the domestic court because the tapping of his telephone by the police was not unlawful; but he had a remedy before the European Court because there was no positive legal basis for what the police had done.[2] Again in *R. v Khan*,[3] the entirety of the evidence against the accused consisted in tape-recorded conversations obtained via a listening device installed by the police in the house of a suspect. Since the installation of the device was not unlawful, the trial judge ruled the evidence admissible and the accused was obliged to plead

---

[1] [1984] 7 E.H.R.R. 14.
[2] Telephone tapping was placed on a statutory footing by the Interception of Communications Act 1985, which was repealed and replaced by the Regulation of Investigatory Powers Act 2000.
[3] [1997] A.C. 558.

guilty. Again, the European Court found that the individual's right to respect for his private life under Art.8 had been breached.[4]

The European Court of Human Rights first accepted surveillance techniques as constituting an interference with the rights protected by Article 8 in *Klass v Germany*.[5] As noted, any interference must be, among other things, prescribed by law, which is to say that the act in question must have some basis in domestic law (not necessarily statutory) and be "accompanied by adequate and effective safeguards . . . to protect against arbitrary interference."[6] In addition, the law must be sufficiently accessible and foreseeable, in the sense of being formulated with sufficient precision to enable one to foresee, with reasonable certainty, the consequences a given action may entail. This does not of course mean that potential subjects of surveillance require to be given advance warning of it, but the law must be sufficiently clear to give citizens "an adequate indication of the circumstances in which and the conditions on which public authorities are empowered to resort to this secret and potentially dangerous interference with the right to respect for private life and correspondence."[7] A statutory code which confers discretion on police officers is not necessarily inconsistent with the requirement of foreseeability, provided that the scope of the discretion and the manner of its exercise are prescribed with adequate clarity and provided that some form of *ex post facto* control is available.[8]

---

[4] *Khan v UK* (2000) 8 B.H.R.C. 310. Covert entry upon and interference with property by the police, Customs and Excise, the National Crime Squad and the National Criminal Intelligence Service was placed on a statutory footing by Pt III of the Police Act 1997. See also *Hewitt and Harman v UK* (1989) 67 D.R. 88, which exposed the absence of legal basis for secret surveillance activities and prompted the enactment of the Security Services Act 1989 and the Intelligence Services Act 1994; and *Govell v UK* (1999) E.H.R.L.R. 191, which exposed the absence of legal basis for intrusive surveillance activities and led to the enactment of the Regulation of Investigatory Powers Act 2000.

[5] [1978] 2 E.H.R.R. 214.

[6] *Malone v UK* [1984] 7 E.H.R.R. 14, paras 67, 68.

[7] *ibid.*, para.67. See also *Valenzuela Contreras v Spain* (1998) 28 E.H.R.R. 483, para.46, where the ECHR sets out the minimum conditions to be met by a statutory code on telephone-tapping: "a definition of the categories of people liable to have their telephones tapped by judicial order, the nature of the offences which may give rise to such an order, a limit on the duration of telephone-tapping, the procedure for drawing up the summary reports containing intercepted communications, the precautions to be taken in order to communicate the recordings intact in their entirety for possible inspection by the judge and by the defence, and the circumstances in which recordings may or must be erased or the tapes destroyed, in particular where the accused has been discharged by an investigating judge or acquitted by a court."

[8] See *Silver v UK* (1983) 5 E.H.R.R. 347, where the ECHR held that it was acceptable to limit the scope of discretionary powers, if not in the parent enactment itself, then in secondary legislation or guidance adopted under it.

If surveillance activities are shown to have a legal basis in this sense, they then fall to be justified by reference to the countervailing public interests specified in Article 8(2). Justification premised on the protection of national security or public safety is readily established in the jurisprudence of the Court.[9] When considering whether surveillance (and other aspects of police activity) are necessary for the prevention of disorder and crime, the Court looks to the seriousness of the interference with the protected right, the nature of the crime involved, and the presence or absence of a judicial warrant for the activity in question. Thus an interference with privacy which could not be justified by reference to the public interest in preventing petty crime may well be justifiable where the relevant criminal activity is serious.[10] By the same token, where the extent of the interference is slight, the absence of prior judicial authorisation is unlikely to be fatal.

The Regulation of Investigatory Powers Act 2000[11] and its sister **11–03** legislation in Scotland represent the latest, and most comprehensive, attempt to place police intelligence on a proper statutory basis conform to the requirements of the Convention. The UK Act extends to Scotland,[12] but in relation to the authorisation of surveillance activity, section 46 provides that no person may grant an authorisation if it appears that the proposed surveillance will take in place in Scotland.[13] In that case, the authorisation must be sought and granted under the Regulation of Investigatory Powers (Scotland) Act 2000 instead.[14]

---

[9] See, *e.g. Leander v Sweden* (1987) 9 E.H.R.R. 433, where the ECHR found that internal terrorist activity amounted to a serious threat to national security, ample to justify the collection of information and maintenance of secret files on candidates for sensitive employment positions.

[10] *cf. McLeod v UK* (1998) 27 E.H.R.R. 493 and *Murray v UK* (1994) 19 E.H.R.R. 193. In *McLeod*, police officers accompanied the applicant's ex-husband to her house in order to recover property said (by him) to be his. The ECHR found that the police power to enter upon private premises where a breach of the peace is occurring or is reasonably anticipated was not *per se* contrary to Art.8, but that the manner of its exercise here was disproportionate: the applicant, who might have objected to her ex-husband's behaviour, was not even in the house at the time. In *Murray*, however, the ECHR held that entry and search of the Murray family home by military authorities in NI was not disproportionate to the aim of arresting Mrs Murray, who was reasonably suspected of terrorist-linked crime.

[11] Hereafter RIPA.

[12] See para.11–05 for discussion of its provisions in relation to the interception of communications and the investigation of encrypted data.

[13] Subject to RIPA, s.46(2), which specifies the purposes for which an authorisation extending to Scotland may be granted under the UK Act. Such authorisations may be granted where necessary in the interests of national security or of the economic well-being of the UK, or on the application of, or to authorise conduct by, a member of either of the intelligence services (MI5 and MI6), Her Majesty's forces, the Ministry of Defence, the Ministry of Defence Police, the Commissioners of Customs and Excise, and the British Transport Police.

[14] Hereafter RIP(S)A.

The Scottish Act is concerned only with covert surveillance,[15] of which there are three categories: directed surveillance, intrusive surveillance and the conduct and use of covert human intelligence sources.[16] Directed surveillance is non-intrusive covert surveillance undertaken for the purposes of a specific investigation or operation, in a manner likely to result in obtaining private information about any person, whether or not he is the subject of the operation.[17] The term "private information" includes any information relating to the person's private and family life.[18] Intrusive surveillance is covert surveillance carried out in relation to anything taking place on residential premises or in any private vehicle,[19] which involves the presence of someone in the premises or vehicle, or which is carried out by means of a surveillance device.[20] Covert human intelligence sources are defined as persons who establish or maintain a personal or other relationship with another person for the covert purpose of facilitating the covert use of that relationship to obtain information or to provide access to information to another person.[21]

---

[15] "Surveillance" includes monitoring, observing or listening to persons, their movements, conversations or other activities or communications; recording anything so monitored, observed or listened to; and surveillance by or with the aid of surveillance devices: RIP(S)A, s.31(2). It does not include, among other things, any entry on or interference with property or wireless telegraphy, which would be unlawful unless authorised under Pt III of the Police Act 1997. Such surveillance is "covert" if it is carried out in a manner calculated to ensure that the subjects are unaware that it is or may be taking place: RIP(S)A, s.1(8).

[16] RIP(S)A, s.1(1).

[17] RIP(S)A, s.1(2). Note the saving in s.1(2)(c), for unauthorised surveillance of the sort which occurs when a police officer, observing a person acting suspiciously, follows the person to find out whether he is engaged in some criminal activity.

[18] RIP(S)A, s.1(9). Since this definition is expressly non-exhaustive, it would presumably extend to other species of private information, such as information about a person's business affairs.

[19] RIP(S)A, s.31(1) defines "residential premises" as "so much of any premises as is for the time being occupied or used by any person, however temporarily, for residential purposes or otherwise as living accommodation (including hotel or prison accommodation that is so occupied or used)" (but excluding any common parts of a building). "Private vehicle" is defined as any vehicle "used primarily for the private purposes of the person who owns it or of a person otherwise having the right to use it" (but excluding vehicles rented for a particular journey). In his annotations to the Act, Dr Alastair Brown makes the point that the confinement of intrusive surveillance to residential premises and private vehicles must presumably be deliberate, since authorisations under Pt III of the Police Act 1997 may be sought in relation to business premises, and the zone of privacy under ECHR, Art.8, has been held to extend to offices: *Niemietz v Germany* (1992) 16 E.H.R.R. 523.

[20] RIP(S)A, s.1(3) and (4).

[21] RIP(S)A, s.1(7). A purpose is covert if and only if the relationship is conducted in a manner calculated to ensure that one of the parties is unaware of the purpose; and a relationship is used covertly, and information disclosed covertly, if and only if it is used or disclosed in a manner calculated to ensure that one of the parties is unaware of the use or disclosure: RIP(S)A, s.1(8).

The key provision in the Regulation of Investigatory Powers (Scotland) Act—the source of legal basis for these activities—is section 5. This provides that surveillance in any of the senses defined above shall be lawful for all purposes if it is conducted by a person in accordance with the terms of an authorisation granted under the Act. Authorisations should normally be in writing, but may be granted or renewed orally in any urgent case.[22] An authorisation will normally cease to have to effect three months after its grant or latest renewal, unless it is an authorisation for the use of a covert human intelligence source, in which case the period is 12 months. Oral authorisations, or authorisations granted by a person entitled to grant them only in urgent cases, lapse after 72 hours.[23] An authorisation may be renewed by any person who would have been entitled to grant it as new at any time before it ceases to have effect, except where the application for renewal relates to the conduct and use of a covert human intelligence source.[24] An authorisation must be cancelled by the person who granted or last renewed it, if he is satisfied that the authorised conduct no longer satisfies the requirements of the Act.[25]

The controls applicable to directed surveillance and the use of **11-04** covert human intelligence sources are broadly similar. Either may be authorised by an officer having the rank of superintendent or above, or, in cases of urgency, inspector or above.[26] A person designated by reference to his rank in any police force as having power to grant authorisations may exercise that power only on the application of an officer in the same force.[27] In either case, an authorisation may only be granted if the granter is satisfied that surveillance of the type specified in the application is both necessary for certain specific purposes and a proportionate method of achieving the applicant's objectives. The specified purposes are the prevention and detection of crime, the prevention of disorder, the protection of public safety and the protection of public health.[28] In relation to an authorisation of the use of a covert human intelligence source, the granter must also be satisfied that arrangements

---

[22] RIP(S)A, s.19(1).
[23] RIP(S)A, s.19(3).
[24] In that case, the authorisation may only be renewed by a person who is satisfied that a review has been carried out of the use made of the source and the tasks given to and information obtained from the source since the authorisation was granted or renewed, and who has considered that review: RIP(S)A, s.19(6), (7).
[25] RIP(S)A, s.20.
[26] RIP(S)A, ss.6(1), 7(1), 8(1); and see also the Regulation of Investigatory Powers (Prescription of Officers, Ranks and Positions) (Scotland) Order 2000 (SSI 2000/343).
[27] RIP(S)A, s.11(1). Officers designated by reference to their rank in the Scottish Crime Squad may grant authorisations only on the application of a constable seconded to the squad: RIP(S)A, s.9(4).
[28] RIP(S)A, ss 6(3), 7(3).

exist for ensuring that an appropriate police officer is charged with day to day responsibility for dealing with the source and for the source's security and welfare, and that there will at all times be another officer of the same force charged with general oversight of the use made of the source and the maintenance of proper records.[29] Only conduct of the description specified in the authorisation, which is carried on in the circumstances and for the purposes of the investigation or operation therein identified, is clothed with legality by the authorisation.[30]

Intrusive surveillance is subject to stricter controls, representing as it does a greater invasion of individual privacy. It may be authorised only by a chief constable,[31] and only then if he is satisfied that it is both necessary for the purpose of preventing or detecting *serious* crime[32] and a proportionate method of achieving that end.[33] The chief constable may only grant authorisations on the application of a member of the police force of which he is head,[34] and, where the authorisation is sought in relation to residential premises, only where the premises fall within the area of operation of that force.[35]

The grant or cancellation of an authorisation for intrusive surveillance must be notified to a Surveillance Commissioner[36] as

---

[29] RIP(S)A, ss 7(2)(c), 7(6).

[30] RIP(S)A, ss 6(4), 7(4). It does not necessarily follow, however, that conduct falling outwith the scope of the authorisation is, by definition, unlawful (at least as a matter of domestic law), or that evidence thereby obtained would be inadmissible. While the ECHR takes a dim view of interferences with individual rights which lack a positive legal base, it has also held that evidence gathered in breach of a protected Convention right may be admitted provided the overall fairness of the trial is not thereby impaired : see *Schenk v Switzerland* (1988) 13 E.H.R.R. 242.

[31] Subject to RIP(S)A, s.12, which provides that, if it is not reasonably practicable for the application to be considered by the chief constable or a "designated deputy" in terms of s.5(4) of the Police (Scotland) Act 1967, the authorisation may be granted by an assistant chief constable.

[32] "Serious crime" is defined as conduct constituting one or more offences for which an adult with no previous convictions could reasonably be expected to be sentenced to at least three years' imprisonment, conduct involving the use of violence, conduct resulting in substantial financial gain, or conduct by a large group of persons in pursuit of a common purpose: RIP(S)A, s.31(6), (7).

[33] RIP(S)A, s.10(1), (2). Section 10(3) expressly requires the chief constable to consider whether the information sought could reasonably be obtained by means other than intrusive surveillance.

[34] See RIP(S)A, s.11(3) in relation to applications from officers seconded to the Scottish Crime Squad.

[35] RIP(S)A, s.11(2).

[36] Provision is made for the appointment of a Chief Surveillance Commissioner and other Surveillance Commissioners by RIP(S)A, s.2. They require to be persons who hold or have held high judicial office in terms of the Appellate Jurisdiction Act 1876, *i.e.* a judge of the Court of Session or High Court of Justiciary at least. Sheriffs, judges of the Crown or circuit courts of England and Wales, and judges of the county court of NI, may be appointed Assistant Surveillance Commissioners under s.3.

soon as reasonably practicable, specifying such matters as may be prescribed by order of the Scottish Ministers.[37] A notice of the grant of an authorisation must state either that the approval of a commissioner is required before the authorisation can take effect, or that the case is one of urgency (giving reasons for this belief).[38] An urgent authorisation so notified takes effect from the time of its grant; in other cases, the authorisation takes effect only once the granter receives written notice of a commissioner's approval.[39] Where a commissioner is satisfied that, at the time an authorisation was granted, there were no reasonable grounds to believe that its grant was either necessary or proportionate, he may quash it with effect from the time of its grant or any renewal thereof; and if he is satisfied that there were no reasonable grounds for treating the case as urgent, he may likewise quash the authorisation as granted.[40] The chief constable may appeal to the Chief Surveillance Commissioner.[41] The incorporation of Surveillance Commissioners into this machinery reflects the jurisprudence of the European Court of Human Rights, and specifically its requirements that the powers of the state be subjected to a measure of judicial control.[42] In addition to this, section 23 confers on persons aggrieved by any form of surveillance activity falling with its scope a right to complain to the tribunal established by section 65 of the UK Act, provided that the conduct in question is believed to have taken place in relation to that person or any of his property, and to have taken place in "challengeable circumstances"[43] or circumstances in which authorisation should have been sought.

The UK legislation applies in Scotland without qualification in **11–05** relation to the interception of communications and the investigation of electronic data protected by encryption, and a little needs to be said about these. As to the first, it is an offence for a person to intercept, intentionally and without lawful authority, any communications in the course of its transmission by a public postal service, a public telecommunications system or a private telecommunications system (except that, in the latter case only, no offence is committed by a person who intercepts a communication where that person has the right to control the operation or use of the system, or who has

---

[37] As to which, see the Regulation of Investigatory Powers (Notification of Authorisations) (Scotland) Order 2000 (SSI 2000/340).

[38] RIP(S)A, s.13(3).

[39] RIP(S)A, s.14.

[40] RIP(S)A, s.15.

[41] RIP(S)A, ss 16 and 17.

[42] See, *e.g. Klass v Germany* [1978] 2 E.H.R.R. 214; *Funke v France* (1993) 16 E.H.R.R. 297.

[43] RIP(S)A, s.23(2). Surveillance takes place in challengeable circumstances if it is conducted, or purports to be conducted, pursuant to an authorisation issued under the RIP(S)A or under s.93 of the Police Act 1997 (authorisations to interfere with property or wireless telegraphy).

the express or implied consent of such a person to the interception).[44] An interception has lawful authority if it is carried out under section 3 or 4 of the Regulation of Investigatory Powers Act, or takes place in accordance with an "interception warrant" granted under section 5. Section 3 provides authority for interception of communications which are (or which are reasonably believed to be) sent by and to persons who have consented to the interception[45]; interceptions authorised under Part II[46]; interceptions by the provider of a postal or telecommunications service; and interceptions carried out under section 5 of the Wireless Telegraphy Act 1949. Section 4 makes provision in relation to interceptions carried out in respect of a person outside, and using a public telecommunications service provided outside, the United Kingdom. The power to grant a warrant under section 5 is conferred on the Secretary of State, and he must exercise the power personally except in the limited circumstances in which section 7(2) permits a senior official to issue a warrant in the Secretary of State's stead. The power may be exercised only where the Secretary of State believes the interception to be necessary on grounds falling within section 5(3) and proportionate to what is sought to be achieved.[47] The grounds specified in section 5(3) are the protection of national security, the prevention or detection of serious crime[48] and the protection of the economic well-being of the United Kingdom. Only a limited number of persons may apply for interception warrants, among them the chief constables of the Scottish police forces.[49]

---

[44] RIPA, s.1. The inclusion of private telecommunications systems extends the ambit of the original offence contained in s.1 of the Interception of Communications Act 1985, and fills the gap in the law identified by the House of Lords in *R. v Effik* [1995] 1 A.C. 309 (to the effect that a conversation on a cordless phone, picked up by a radio receiver operated by police officers in the flat next door to that of the suspect, was not comprised in a public telecommunications system for the purposes of the 1985 Act) and *Halford v UK* (1997) 24 E.H.R.R. 523 (to the effect that the internal telephone network of Merseyside Police was not comprised in a public telecommunications system). It should perhaps be noted, in fairness, that at the time of the enactment of the 1985 Act—only one year after the privatisation of British Telecom—there was only one telecommunications system in the UK; the revolution in communications technology still lay in the future.

[45] RIPA, s.3(2). Such consent might be inferred from, for example, the fact that a person sends an email on a system carrying a clear warning that messages might be intercepted.

[46] RIPA, s.3(3). Pt II deals with surveillance, and is qualified in its application to Scotland: see *infra*.

[47] RIPA, s.5(2).

[48] Including where necessary to give effect to an international mutual assistance agreement.

[49] RIPA, s.6(2)(g).

The treatment of encrypted data is dealt with by Part III. Where "protected information"[50] comes into the possession of a person, such as a police officer, by virtue of a statutory power to seize, detain, inspect, search or otherwise interfere with documents or other property, or of a statutory power to intercept communications, or by other lawful means not involving the exercise of a statutory power,[51] that person may, subject to conditions, require a person whom he reasonably believes to possess the key to the information to disclose that key. A person wishing to impose such a disclosure requirement must first obtain written permission from a sheriff.[52] The sheriff must be satisfied that disclosure is necessary for the purposes, *inter alia*, of protecting national security, preventing or detecting crime or protecting the economic well-being of the United Kingdom, and that it is proportionate to those ends.[53] The effect of a disclosure notice duly issued under section 49 is to oblige its subject, on pain of criminal penalty, to hand over the key to the information or otherwise to translate it into intelligible form.[54] A duty to make arrangements to ensure that keys disclosed pursuant to a section 49 notice, and information thereby obtained, are not used improperly, is laid on certain officials, including the chief constables of the Scottish police forces.[55]

ARREST AND DETENTION

Where surveillance is concerned, the individual may never be **11–06** aware that his privacy has been invaded, or may become aware only after the interference has ceased. But there is no ignoring the deprivation of liberty involved in arrest or detention,[56] which is why Article 5 of the Convention provides as follows:

---

[50] Namely, electronic information which cannot, or cannot readily, be accessed or put into intelligible form without a "key" such as a password: RIPA, s.56(1).

[51] See, generally, RIPA, s.49(1).

[52] RIPA, s.49(2) and Sch.2.

[53] Specifically, the applicant for permission to issue a disclosure notice must show that it would not be reasonably practicable to access the encrypted information, or render it into an intelligible form, by means other than a disclosure notice: RIPA, s.49(2)(d).

[54] The government rejected suggestions that this provision might breach the right to a fair trial in ECHR, Art.6, in so far as it might require a person to incriminate himself, citing the decision of the ECHR in *Saunders v UK* (1997) 23 E.H.R.R. 313 to the effect that "the right against self-incrimination does not extend to the use in criminal proceedings of material that may be obtained from the accused by the use of compulsory powers, but which has an existence independent of the will of the suspect, for example, documents recovered under a warrant."

[55] RIPA, ss.55 and 56(1)(a).

[56] Except perhaps in situations where, through intoxication or other incapacity, the detainee is unaware of what is happening to him.

"No-one shall be deprived of his liberty save in the following cases and in accordance with a procedure prescribed by law: ... (c) the lawful arrest or detention of a person effected for the purpose of bringing him before the competent legal authority on reasonable suspicion of having committed an offence or when it is reasonably considered necessary to prevent his committing an offence or fleeing after having done so."

The right to liberty carries with it a number of ancillary rights, as set out in Article 5(2) to (5): the right to be informed promptly and in a language one understands of the reasons for one's arrest and of any charge against one; the right to be brought promptly before a judge where arrested or detained in connection with a criminal matter; the right to be brought to trial within a reasonable time or to be released pending trial[57]; and the right to compensation where arrested or detained in a manner incompatible with Article 5. The Court has described the right to liberty as being at the heart of any political system that purports to abide by the rule of law.[58] Whether a person has been deprived of his liberty in any particular case is treated by the Court as a function not merely of the duration of the period in which the person was subject to restraint but also of the type, manner and effects of that restraint. It is the substance of the act and not its form that is crucial.[59]

We have already noted the approach of the Court to the question whether a given interference with fundamental rights is prescribed by, or in accordance with, the law. In addition, any arrest or detention must conform to the substantive standards prescribed by Article 5(1)(c). So, for example, an arrest not founded on a reasonable suspicion would not constitute a lawful arrest. What is "reasonable" turns very much on what is known to

---

[57] Hence the Bail, Judicial Appointments etc (Scotland) Act 2000, Pt 1 of which made provision for bail to be granted even in serious cases, where previously it had been unavailable.

[58] *Winterwerp v Netherlands* (1979) 2 E.H.R.R. 387, para.37. Note that ECHR, Art.5, relates only to the fact of detention, not to the conditions thereof. The treatment of persons held in detention is covered by Art.3, which prohibits torture and inhuman or degrading treatment or punishment: see in that regard, *e.g. Napier v Scottish Ministers* [2002] U.K.H.R.R. 308.

[59] Difficulties of definition can arise at the margins, as seen in *Goodson v Higson*, 2002 S.L.T. 202. The accused was requested to stop his car in a car park by an off duty police officer, who perceived him to be drunk. Unknown to the accused, the police officer had asked the car park cashier to prevent his car from leaving the car park until the police arrived. The off-duty officer informed the accused that she had summoned the police and advised him to wait, which he did. The High Court held that there was no arrest (but added that the circumstances were such that the officer would have been entitled to make a citizen's arrest had she chosen to do so).

the arresting officer at the material time, but the test is an objective one.[60] Police practice in relation to arrest and detention may require to be reconsidered in light of this requirement if not of others.

An arrest may be effected with or without a warrant, under **11–07** statutory powers or at common law, but almost always arrests are made by police officers. The power of ordinary people to effect a "citizen's arrest" is strictly circumscribed in Scots law:

> "A private citizen is entitled to arrest without warrant for a serious crime he has witnessed, or where he has a moral certainty that the person he arrests has just committed a crime or perhaps where, being the victim of the crime, he has information equivalent to personal observation, as where the fleeing criminal is pointed out to him by an eyewitness. He has no power to arrest someone who has committed only a breach of the peace, although he may intervene to prevent the occurrence of such a breach. . . . Arrests by private citizens are not encouraged, especially where they involve the use of any force, and the limitations on this right of arrest are strictly enforced by the court."[61]

Beyond this, in other words, the private citizen who purports to arrest a person may render himself liable to conviction for assault.

For an arrest to be lawful, the High Court has stressed that the arresting officer should make it clear to the arrestee that he is under legal compulsion and should tell him the (correct) reason for his arrest.[62] It is preferable to use the word "arrest" here, but "any form of words will suffice to inform the person that he is being arrested if they bring to his notice the fact that he is under

---

[60] Thus there was a breach of Art.5 in *Fox, Campbell and Hartley v UK* (1990) 13 E.H.R.R. 157, where the applicants had been arrested under s.11(1) of the Northern Ireland (Emergency Provisions) Act 1978. S.11(1) conferred a power of arrest on a constable in respect of "any person whom he suspects of being a terrorist". In *McKie v Chief Constable for Northern Ireland* [1985] 1 All E.R. 1, this was held by the House of Lords to involve a subjective test: whether the officer had such a suspicion, and whether it was honestly held. The issue before the ECHR was not whether s.11(1) itself breached Art.5 but whether there was, in the circumstances, sufficient evidence to give rise to a reasonable suspicion. The ECHR found there was not, from which it follows that any power of arrest, common law or statutory, may only be exercised lawfully, in light of the HRA 1998, where there are "facts or information that would satisfy an objective observer that the person concerned may have committed the offence" (*Fox*, above, para.32).

[61] *Renton and Brown's Criminal Procedure* (6th ed., W. Green, Edinburgh), para.7–03 (R.7), cited with approval by the High Court of Justiciary in *Codona v Cardle*, 1989 J.C. 99; *Bryans v Guild*, 1990 J.C. 51; and *Wightman v Lees*, 2000 S.L.T. 111.

[62] *Forbes v H.M. Advocate*, 1990 J.C. 215.

compulsion and the person thereafter submits to that compulsion."[63] Reasonable physical force may be used to effect an arrest, and it is an offence under section 41 of the Police (Scotland) Act 1967 to resist a lawful arrest or to escape from lawful custody.

A person who has been arrested and is in custody has the right under section 15(1) of the Criminal Procedure (Scotland) Act 1995 to have the fact of his custody and the place where he is being held intimated to a third party without delay, or with no more delay than is necessary in the interest of the investigation or prevention of crime or the apprehension of offenders. He must be informed of this entitlement on arrival at the police station. Under section 17(1) of the 1995 Act, he is also entitled to request the attendance of a solicitor at the place where he is being held; again, he must be informed of this right. These rights apply regardless of whether the individual was arrested with a warrant or without.

11–08   Arrest with a warrant is perhaps the ideal mode of arrest, being predicated upon prior judicial authorisation. When an arrest is deemed necessary (because there is sufficient evidence to bring charges), the procurator fiscal applies to the appropriate sheriff or district court for a warrant to arrest the suspect.[64] The warrant must be signed by the sheriff, stipendiary magistrate or justice granting it, although execution may proceed, if not on the warrant itself, then on an extract copy signed by the clerk of court.[65] Arrest warrants normally also include warrant to search the arrestee and his property, including lockfast premises and places,[66] to remove any items likely to afford evidence of guilt, and to bring the accused before the court issuing the warrant or any other court competent to deal with him,[67] and in the meantime to detain him as appropriate.[68]

A great many statutes confer powers of arrest without warrant on police officers (usually "in uniform") where certain specified conditions are satisfied. In keeping with the normal presumption whereby statutes authorising invasions of the liberty of the individual fall to be construed narrowly, the court generally insist on strict

---

[63] *Alderson v Booth* [1969] 2 Q.B. 216, *per* Lord Parker C.J.
[64] See Criminal Procedure (Scotland) Act 1995, s.34, in relation to warrants on petition (*i.e.* in the context of solemn proceedings) and s.135 in relation to summary warrants.
[65] 1995 Act, s.296.
[66] See, *e.g.* 1995 Act, s.135(1).
[67] Note that justices of the peace may grant warrants to arrest persons in respect of offences the district courts are not competent to try.
[68] 1995 Act, s.135(2). The power to detain the suspect pending trial must be read subject to s.22, which provides for liberation of a person arrested and charged with an offence that may be tried summarily upon that person's undertaking to appear in court; and to ss 22A–25, which make provision in relation to bail. The bail provisions of the 1995 Act as originally enacted were amended by the Bail, Judicial Appointments etc (Scotland) Act 2000 to comply with the requirements of ECHR, Art.5.

compliance by the police with the terms of statutory powers of arrest. Failure so to comply renders the purported arrest an unlawful assault, which the individual is entitled to resist. Thus in *Wither v Reid*,[69] the accused was arrested under section 24(1) of the Misuse of Drugs Act 1971. She resisted a clothing and body search for drugs, and, no drugs being found, was charged with resisting a lawful search contrary to section 41 of the Police (Scotland) Act 1967. Section 24 of the 1971 Act provides that a constable may arrest without warrant a person whom he reasonably suspects of having committed an offence under the Act, if he has reasonable cause to believe that the person will abscond unless arrested, if he does not know and cannot ascertain the name and address of the person, or if he believes that the name and address given are false. The accused was arrested at Elgin station by police officers who had been informed by her estranged ex-fiancé that she had been to Aberdeen to buy drugs. The sheriff acquitted the accused, holding that there was nothing to justify her arrest under any of the provisions of section 24 and that, as her arrest was illegal, she was entitled to resist the consequently unlawful search. The High Court, by a majority, dismissed the procurator fiscal's appeal.

The state of mind of an arresting officer is a matter which may require to be approached with greater rigour in light of the Human Rights Act. As we have seen, Article 5 of the Convention only allows a person to be arrested on suspicion of having committed a criminal offence where there are reasonable grounds, objectively judged, for that suspicion. The domestic courts have not, in the past, tended to inquire too closely into the objective strength or weakness of the suspicion an arresting officer claims to have harboured at the relevant time; rather, provided it is shown that the suspicion was honestly held, it is for the accused to prove that the suspicion was unreasonable.[70] It is suggested that even where a statute confers a power of arrest which is worded in subjective terms, a court of review will require to satisfy itself that there was sufficient evidence to give rise to a reasonable suspicion (making such allowance as may be necessary for the urgency of the situation, and the need for the police officer to make a speedy decision) such as to justify the arrest.

The same may be said of the common law power to arrest without a warrant. This power may be exercised where the arresting officer reasonably believes the arrestee to have committed an offence, but only so far as necessary "to prevent justice from being defeated."[71] Thus the power might properly fall to be exercised where there is a risk that a person will abscond unless

---

[69] 1980 J.C. 7.
[70] See, *e.g. McLeod v Shaw*, 1981 S.L.T. (Notes) 93.
[71] *Peggie v Clark* (1868) 7 M. 89, *per* Lord Deas.

arrested, or will commit further crimes, or interfere with the course of justice by, for example, disposing of stolen goods. Urgency may justify an arrest in the interests of justice; by the same token, the longer the lapse of time since the commission of an offence, the less obvious will be the necessity of arresting without warrant. Similarly, the more serious the offence the arrestee is suspected of having committed, the easier it will be to justify arrest without warrant.[72] Generally, whether a given arrest is wrongful depends on whether it was reasonable for the arresting officer to believe it was justified. Here again, however, if it is shown that the belief was honestly held, it is for the arrestee to show that there were no reasonable grounds for it[73]; and again, it is questionable whether this approach is compatible with Article 5.

11–09 Short of arrest, the police have powers to detain persons suspected of crime and indeed potential witnesses to a crime. These are now contained in sections 13 and 14 of the Criminal Procedure (Scotland) Act 1995. Section 13 is best regarded as a power of "quasi-detention". Where a constable has reasonable grounds for suspecting that a person has committed or is committing an offence at any place, he may require that person to give his name and address and may ask him for an explanation of the circumstances which have given rise to the constable's suspicion. The constable may require that person to remain with him while he verifies the name and address and/or notes the explanation offered, provided that this can be done quickly, and may use reasonable force to ensure that the person remains with him. The constable must inform the person of his suspicion and of the general nature of the offence which he suspects the person has committed or is committing; and if necessary must inform the person why he is being required to remain with him. He must also inform the person that failure to comply with his requirements may constitute an offence for which he may be arrested without warrant.[74] Where the constable believes any other person to have information relating to the offence in question, he may require that person to give his name and address. He must inform that person of the general nature of the offence that he suspects has been or is being committed, and that the reason for the requirement is that he believes the person has relevant information. A person who fails to give his name and address without reasonable excuse is guilty of an offence.[75] Resort to the powers under section 13 is permissible only

---

[72] Although note that a constable may arrest without warrant a person who is committing, or who leads the constable reasonably to apprehend, a breach of the peace: see, *e.g. Montgomery v McLeod*, 1977 S.L.T. (Notes) 77.

[73] See, *e.g. Cardle v Murray*, 1993 S.L.T. 525.

[74] 1995 Act, s.13(1)(a).

[75] 1995 Act, s.13(1)(b). A police officer cannot, however, require a person detained under this provision to remain with him while he verifies the particulars given.

where the constable has reasonable grounds to suspect an offence has been or is being committed. As to what might constitute reasonable cause, the editors of *Renton and Brown's Criminal Procedure* note that it need not "rest upon personal ocular observation by the officer; [his suspicions] may stem from the observations of other persons, from 'information received' or from prior knowledge of the suspect's habits and background, as well as general knowledge of the area being policed."[76]

The status of a person required to "remain" under section 13 while a constable checks his name and address and/or notes his explanation is unclear. While the section must mean something less than detention (otherwise there would be no need for section 13 at all), note that a person can not only be required to remain but can be physically constrained to do so. Moreover, while the constable has the power to require an explanation of the circumstances which have given rise to his suspicion, he is not enjoined to administer a caution at this stage. Presumably if the circumstances were such that a constable felt a caution to be appropriate, the section 14 power to detain should be used instead (although this is not to say that anything volunteered by the person asked to remain would be inadmissible for want of a caution).

Section 14(1) provides that where a constable has reasonable grounds for suspecting that a person has committed or is committing an offence punishable by imprisonment,[77] he may, in order to facilitate the carrying out of investigations into the offence and as to whether criminal proceedings should be instigated against the person, detain that person. Reasonable force may be used. Where a person is detained, the constable may exercise the same powers of search as are available following arrest; again, reasonable force may be used.[78] The detainee must be taken as quickly as is reasonably practicable to a police station or other premises, and may thereafter be taken elsewhere.[79] Detention must be terminated

---

[76] (6th ed., W. Green, Edinburgh), para.A4.27. In *Dryburgh v Galt*, 1981 S.C.C.R. 27, Lord Wheatley held that even an ill-founded suspicion might constitute reasonable cause to suspect: "the fact that the information on which the police officer formed his suspicion turns out to be ill-founded does not in itself necessarily establish that the police officer's suspicion was unfounded. The circumstances known to the police officer at the time he formed his suspicion constitute the criterion, not the facts as subsequently ascertained."

[77] See *Houston v Carnegie*, 2000 S.L.T. 333.

[78] For police powers of search, see paras 11–11—11–12.

[79] In *Menzies v H.M. Advocate*, 1995 J.C. 166, the accused was detained near Airdrie and taken to Dunfermline police station, since the interviewing facilities at Airdrie were busy and all the documentation relating to the office with which the accused was subsequently charged was in Dunfermline. The High Court held that the "as quickly as reasonably practicable" requirement did not mean that a detainee required to be taken to the nearest police station. Rather, it was conditional upon what was reasonably practicable in the circumstances as they appeared to the constable by whom the person was detained.

at the end of six hours, and sooner if it appears that there are no longer grounds for detention or if the detainee is arrested or detained pursuant to another statutory provision. Where a person is released at the termination of a period of detention under section 14(1) he cannot be redetained under the subsection on the same grounds or on any grounds arising out of the same circumstances.[80] Where a person has previously been detained pursuant to another statutory provision, and is then detained under section 14(1) on the same grounds or on any grounds arising from the same circumstances, the six-hour detention period must be reduced by the length of his earlier detention.[81] A constable who detains a person under section 14 must inform the person at that time of his suspicion, of the general nature of the offence that he suspects has been or is being committed and of the reason for the detention.[82]

Detention is not to be used as a means of delaying arrest and charge. If sufficient evidence emerges to justify arrest of a detainee, detention must be terminated and must in any event be terminated after six hours.[83] A statutory caution must be administered to the detainee, both at the time of detention and again on arrival at the place of detention. Section 14(7)(a) provides that the power to question a detainee is without prejudice to any relevant rule of law regarding the admissibility in evidence of any answer given. The common law applies a test of fairness to determine issues of

---

[80] See *H.M. Advocate v Mowat*, 2001 S.L.T. 738.

[81] 1995 Act, s.14(2)–(4).

[82] 1995 Act, s.14(6). The subsection also requires the following matters to be recorded: the place where detention begins and the police station or other premises to which the detainee is taken; the general nature of the suspected offence; the time when detention begins and the time of the detainee's arrival at the police station or other premises; the time of the detainee's release from detention or, as the case may be, the time of his arrest; the fact that the detainee has been informed of his right, both at the moment of detention and again on arrival at the police station, to refuse to answer any question other than to give his name and address (this is the statutory caution); the fact that the detainee has been informed of his rights under s.15(1)(b), namely the right to have intimation of his detention and of the place where he is being held sent to a solicitor and to one other person reasonably named by him (*e.g.* a friend or relative) without delay, or with no more delay than is necessary in the interest of the investigation or prevention of crime or the apprehension of offenders; (where the detainee exercises his rights under s.15(1)(b)) the time at which his request is made and the time at which it is complied with; and the identity of the constable who informs the detainee of these rights. Failure to record a particular detail will not necessarily render the detention unlawful, however: see, *e.g. Cummings v H.M. Advocate*, 1982 S.L.T. 487.

[83] In *Grant v H.M. Advocate*, 1990 S.L.T. 402, the accused was not arrested until some twenty minutes after the expiry of the six-hour period, and objection was taken at his trial to the admissibility in evidence of statements he had made while detained. The High Court held that such lapses in compliance with the strict formalities did not of themselves vitiate what had taken place during the currency of the detention.

admissibility, and it was held in *Tonge, Grey and Jack v H.M. Advocate*[84] that a full common law caution should also be administered to a detainee prior to questioning to obviate the risk of evidence thereby obtained being held inadmissible. Failure to administer the statutory caution is less likely to be fatal to a subsequent prosecution.[85]

Provision is made in relation to the rights of persons arrested or **11–10** detained by sections 15 and 17. Section 15(1)(a) provides that a person[86] who has been arrested and is in custody is entitled to have the fact of his custody and the place where he is being held intimated to a person reasonably named by him without delay, or with no greater delay than is necessary in the interest of the investigation or the prevention of crime or the apprehension of offenders. Section 15(1)(b) provides that a person detained under section 14 is entitled to have the fact of his detention and the place where he is being detained intimated to a solicitor and to one other person reasonably named by him, again without delay or with no greater delay than necessary. A person arrested or detained must be informed of his right under section 15(1), whichever applies, on his arrival at the police station (or other place of detention).[87] These rights are without prejudice to the right of a person arrested on any criminal charge to have intimation sent to a solicitor that his professional assistance is required and informing the solicitor of the place where the person is being held, whether or not he is to be liberated and, if not, the court to which he is to be taken and the date of his first appearance in court.[88] The arrestee is must be informed of this right immediately upon his arrest, and if he chooses to exercise it, intimation must be made to the solicitor

---

[84] 1982 S.L.T. 506.

[85] See, *e.g. Scott v Howie*, 1993 S.C.C.R. 81. The statutory caution was not administered at the moment of detention, but at the commencement of questioning at the police station both the statutory and common law cautions were given. The accused then made a statement, upon which the Crown founded at his trial. The High Court held that what had occurred was a procedural defect that did not vitiate the admissibility in evidence of the accused's statement (although it noted, *obiter*, that any statement made by the accused between the moment of his detention and the commencement of questioning would have been inadmissible).

[86] Other than a person falling within 1995 Act, s.15(4), namely a person who appears to be a child, *i.e.* a person under 16 years of age. In that case the police officer must without delay intimate the fact of the child's arrest or detention to the child's parent, if known. The parent must be allowed access to the child, unless there is reasonable cause to suspect that the parent has been involved in the alleged offence in respect of which the child was arrested or detained. In that event, the parent may be allowed access to the child. The nature and extent of any access under s.15(4) is subject to any restriction "essential for the furtherance of the investigation or the well-being of the [child]": s.15(5).

[87] Or on his arrest or detention, if he is arrested or detained at the police station itself.

[88] 1995 Act, s.17(1).

immediately. At the same time, the arrestee must be informed of his right to have a private interview before his judicial examination[89] or first appearance in court. As this implies, there is no right to have one's solicitor actually present during the currency of police questioning, whether following arrest or detention. In *Paton v Ritchie*,[90] it was argued that this was inconsistent with the right of an accused under Article 6(3)(c) of the Convention to "defend himself in person or through legal assistance of his own choosing". The High Court accepted that the right to a fair trial in its various elements was engaged even at the stage of preliminary investigations into a criminal offence,[91] and that the right of an accused to communicate with his lawyer as a fundamental part of the preparation of his defence was implicit in Article 6(3)(c).[92] It noted, however, that the right was not immune from restriction, and that where an accused had been questioned without his solicitor being present, the question was whether in all the circumstances this was inconsistent with the general principle of fairness in Article 6(1). As the Court put it in *Imbrioscia v Switzerland*[93]:

> "[T]he manner in which Article 6(1) and (3)(c) is to be applied during the preliminary investigation depends on the special features of the proceedings involved and on the circumstances of the case, and in order to determine whether the aim of Article 6—a fair trial—has been achieved, regard must be had to the entirety of the domestic proceedings conducted in the case."

In many cases, whether the admission of evidence of statements made by an accused outwith the presence of his solicitor would render his trial unfair will only be determinable in the course of, if not after, the trial itself.

SEARCH

11–11   At common law, the police are entitled to search without warrant the person of anyone they have lawfully arrested or detained under section 14 of the Criminal Procedure (Scotland) Act 1995, and this right of search extends to fingerprinting and

---

[89] As to which see 1995 Act, s.35.
[90] 2000 S.L.T. 239.
[91] Under reference to *Murray v UK* (1996) 22 E.H.R.R. 29 and *Imbrioscia v Switzerland* (1993) 17 E.H.R.R. 441.
[92] See *Windsor v UK*, App. No. 13081/87.
[93] (1993) 17 E.H.R.R. 441, para.38.

photographing the suspect.[94] Section 18(2) provides, more specifically, that a constable may take from a person arrested or detained fingerprints, palm prints and other such prints and impressions of an external part of the body as the constable reasonably considers it appropriate to take, having regard to the circumstances of the suspected offence in respect of which the person has been arrested or detained. Section 18(6) provides that the constable may also take, with the authority of an officer of a rank no lower than inspector, a sample of hair; a sample of fingernail or toenail (or of material under the nails); a sample of blood or other body fluid, body tissue or other material from an external part of the body by means of swabbing or rubbing; or a sample of saliva. Reasonable force may be used. Section 58 of the Criminal Justice (Scotland) Act 1995 further provides that swabs may be taken from the mouth for the purpose of DNA fingerprinting. Before arrest, however, a person may not be searched at common law.[95] Search before arrest must be justified by reference to some statutory provision,[96] or must be founded on a warrant. It has been held that warrants to search a person prior to arrest "will not be lightly granted, and will only be granted where the circumstances are special and where the granting of the warrant will not disturb the delicate balance that must be maintained between the public interest on the one hand and the interest of the accused on the other."[97] But as the editors of *Renton and Brown's Criminal Procedure* observe, the requirement of "special circumstances" seems to be met by any intelligible explanation of the need for a warrant.[98] Provided the procurator fiscal applying for the warrant is able to satisfy the court that it is likely to turn up some useful evidence, it will normally be granted: the unusual cases will be those in which the warrant is refused.

In relation to the search of premises, again the ideal form of search is that which is authorised by a warrant. Arrest warrants

---

[94] *Adair v McGarry*, 1933 J.C. 72; and see 1995 Act, s.14(7)(b).

[95] Unless he consents to what would otherwise be an assault: see, *e.g. Devlin v Normand*, 1992 S.C.C.R. 875. Searches carried out before arrest in situations of urgency may also be excused in the interests of justice, and the evidence thereby obtained admitted at trial, subject to the overarching test of fairness: see, *e.g. Bell v Hogg*, 1967 J.C. 49.

[96] *e.g.* Misuse of Drugs Act 1971, s.23(2), which entitles a constable to detain and search a person whom he has reasonable grounds to believe is in possession of a controlled drug; Civic Government (Scotland) Act 1982, s.60(1)(a), which entitles a constable to search a person whom he has reasonable grounds to suspect is in possession of any stolen property; and Criminal Law (Consolidation) (Scotland) Act 1995, ss 48–50 conferring powers to search for offensive weapons and knives a person is reasonably believed to have about him.

[97] *Morris v MacNeill*, 1991 S.L.T. 607 at 609, *per* LJC Ross. See, *e.g. Hay v H.M. Advocate*, 1968 J.C. 40, where a warrant was granted for the taking of dental impressions.

[98] (6th ed., W. Green), para.5.08.

normally include warrant to search the arrestee's premises and vehicles for evidence,[99] but warrants to search may be granted in the absence of arrest or charge, either under the numerous statutory provisions which authorise this[1] or at common law. Where the grant of a warrant is conditional, on a constable giving information on oath that he has reasonable cause to suspect, for example, the presence of drugs on particular premises, the justice of the peace must inquire into the grounds for that suspicion and satisfy himself of its reasonableness,[2] and it would seem, in light of the Human Rights Act, that a justice should always so satisfy himself before granting any warrant to search.

A general warrant to search any premises for any article is incompetent.[3] A search warrant must be specific in its terms and the police must keep within its limits when conducting a search under it. As this implies, "law enforcement officers cannot be treated as acting under and in terms of legal powers of which they are at the time in question ignorant and heedless."[4] Any search conducted in ignorance of the terms of the warrant will, therefore, be a random search and unlawful on that account. The manner of execution of a search warrant may also be relevant to its legality and hence to the admissibility in evidence of items recovered under it. Certainly where a search warrant restricts the class or number of persons who may execute it, any breach of those restrictions will render the search unlawful unless the irregularity is excusable.[5] It may also be the case that the unduly oppressive execution of a search warrant—for example, in the middle of the night, or by an unnecessarily large number of officers—may render the search unlawful as being a disproportionate invasion of the subject's privacy.[6]

It often happens, however, that police officers engaged on a lawful search of premises stumble across articles not covered by the warrant. Can such articles lawfully be removed, and will they be admissible in evidence? In *H.M. Advocate v Hepper*,[7] Lord Guthrie held that "the police officers were not prevented from taking possession of other articles of a plainly incriminatory character which they happened to come across in the course of their search." Again, in *Drummond v H.M. Advocate*,[8] the accused was charged

---

[99] See, *e.g.* 1995 Act, s.135.

[1] See, *e.g.* Civic Government (Scotland) Act 1982, s.60(1)(b)–(d).

[2] *Birse v H.M. Advocate*, 2000 J.C. 503; *H.M. Advocate v Dickson*, 2001 S.C. 203.

[3] *Bell v Black and Morrison* (1865) 5 Irv. 57.

[4] *Hoekstra v H.M. Advocate*, 2002 S.L.T. 599, para.55, *per* LJG Cullen; see also *Leckie v Miln*, 1982 S.L.T. 177.

[5] See *Singh v H.M. Advocate*, 2001 S.L.T. 812; but *cf. Hepburn v Vannet*, 1998 J.C. 63 and *Lord Advocate's Reference (No.1 of 2002)*, 2002 S.L.T. 1017.

[6] See *Chappell v UK* (1990) 12 E.H.R.R. 1.

[7] 1958 S.L.T. 160. See also *Pringle v Bremner and Stirling*, 5 M. (H.L.) 55.

[8] 1992 J.C. 88.

with the theft of clothes. Some of the clothes had been found in a wardrobe at his home as it was searched by two police officers executing a warrant relating to stolen furniture. When the first constable was asked what he was looking for in the wardrobe, he admitted that he was looking for "stuff" from the clothing theft. The sheriff ruled his evidence inadmissible. The second constable, however, said that he had a list of the stolen furniture that included small items such as lamps, and that he was looking for these items in the wardrobe when the stolen clothing attracted his attention. The sheriff allowed the evidence of the second constable to go to the jury, which convicted the accused.

There are a number of statutory provisions authorising the **11–12** search without warrant of premises or vehicles,[9] but at common law the power of the police to enter and search private premises is limited. As a starting point, it may be said that the right of a police officer to enter private premises for any purpose without a warrant and without the occupier's consent is no greater than that of any other member of the public; and if the police do so enter, they must be prepared to justify their conduct by reference to special circumstances before any evidence thus obtained may be held admissible.[10] As the Lord Justice-General put it in *Lawrie v Muir*[11]:

> "Irregularities require to be excused, and infringements of the formalities of the law in relation to these matters are not lightly to be condoned. Whether any given irregularity ought to be excused depends upon the nature of the irregularity and the circumstances under which it was committed."

An urgent need to obtain evidence, particularly in relation to serious offences, may justify a search without warrant of private property.[12] Other circumstances that may excuse an irregular search are the authority and good faith of those who obtained the evidence. In *Lawrie v Muir*, one ground upon which the High Court quashed the conviction was that the evidence had been obtained from the accused's dairy not by police officers but by two inspectors who should have known "the precise limits of their authority and

---

[9] See, *e.g.* Civic Government (Scotland) Act 1982, s.60(1), where a constable has reasonable grounds to suspect that a person is in possession of stolen goods.
[10] *Cairns v Keane*, 1983 S.C.C.R. 277.
[11] 1950 S.L.T. 37 at 42.
[12] *H.M. Advocate v McGuigan*, 1936 S.L.T. 161.

should be held to exceed these limits at their peril."[13] Even where evidence is illegally obtained, it does not necessarily follow, either as a matter of domestic law or under the Convention, that it is by definition inadmissible in subsequent criminal proceedings.[14] In that light, the Convention-proofing of police powers of entry, search and seizure is less a matter for the police themselves, under reference to Article 8 of the Convention, but rather a matter for the court in considering the admissibility of evidence under reference to Article 6.

QUESTIONING

11–13 There are forms of questioning which, whatever the worth of the information they elicit, must be regarded as so offensive to the values of the Convention as to render the information inadmissible (or its admission a breach of Article 6) and the questioning itself a breach of some other Convention right.[15] Beyond that, the Court has derived a right to silence from the presumption of innocence enshrined in Article 6(2) of the Convention, such that a suspect cannot be obliged to answer questions[16] (although this is not to say that adverse inferences cannot be drawn from a suspect's silence).[17] Different issues are raised by compulsory powers of questioning, where the suspect is obliged to answer the questions put by a police officer or other investigative authority on pain of criminal penalty. In *Saunders v UK*,[18] it was held that the extensive use made by the prosecution at the applicant's trial of answers he had been compelled to give under sections 432 and 442 of the Companies Act

---

[13] See also, *e.g. Wilson v Brown*, 1996 S.L.T. 686, where it was held that while nightclub stewards might legitimately have detained the accused until the police arrived, they had no authority whatsoever to search him (finding 78 temazepam capsules in the process) and that the circumstances were not such as to excuse the irregularity of the search; and *Webley v Ritchie*, 1997 S.L.T. 1241, where the accused was convicted of the theft of three squash racquets found in the boot of his car, which the police had forced open while he was in detention in connection with the theft. The racquets were held to be admissible, despite the irregularity, since the police had acted reasonably and in good faith, and since there was a real risk that the six-hour period of detention would expire before a search warrant could be obtained (but the offence can hardly be described as serious).

[14] *Schenk v Switzerland* (1988) 13 E.H.R.R. 242; *Khan v UK* (2000) 8 B.H.R.C. 310.

[15] See, *e.g. Ireland v UK* (1978) 2 E.H.R.R. 25, where the ECHR found the "five techniques" employed in the interrogation of terrorist suspects to constitute inhuman and degrading treatment contrary to ECHR, Art.3.

[16] *Funke v France* (1993) 16 E.H.R.R. 297, para.44.

[17] See *Murray v UK* (1996) 22 E.H.R.R. 313, although the ECHR noted that it would be incompatible with ECHR, Art.6(2), to base a conviction wholly or mainly on an accused's silence or failure to answer questions or give evidence.

[18] (1997) 23 E.H.R.R. 313

1985 violated the presumption of innocence and rendered his trial unfair. Even so, it does not follow that all compulsory questioning, and any evidence gleaned thereby, is contrary to Article 6. As the Judicial Committee of the Privy Council held in *Brown* v *Stott*,[19] if the right in question is not absolute—and plainly the presumption of innocence is not—the question is whether the restriction or modification of the right pursued a legitimate aim, and whether there is a reasonable relationship of proportionality between the means employed and the aim sought to be realised.[20] In *Brown*, the accused was arrested at an all-night supermarket on suspicion of theft. The arresting officer perceived her to be drunk and required her to tell him who had been driving the car in which she had arrived at the supermarket. The power in question[21] applies only to more serious road traffic offences, including drink driving. The Judicial Committee was satisfied that the public interest in the prevention of such offences was sufficiently compelling to render the use of this compulsory power, and of the evidence elicited, proportionate to the aim pursued. The overarching question is always whether the trial viewed as a whole is fair.[22]

As a matter of Scots law, a person cannot be questioned further, once he has been formally charged, about the offence with which he is charged.[23] But there is no general rule that the police cannot question a person after he has been arrested, provided the questioning is not unfair,[24] and of course questioning is often the very point of detention under section 14 of the Criminal Procedure (Scotland) Act 1995. An important aspect of the fairness of questioning, and hence of the admissibility in evidence of statements made in response, is cautioning the person being questioned. We have seen, in the context of detention, that the police should administer a statutory caution to the detainee both at the moment of detention and again on arrival at the police station; and that a full common law caution should also be given prior to any questioning.[25] To avoid any risk of rendering statements inadmissible, the common law caution should be re-administered as often as necessary during a long period of questioning, and administered

---

[19] 2001 S.C. (P.C.) 43.
[20] *ibid*., at 74, 75, *per* Lord Hope.
[21] Road Traffic Act 1988, s.172
[22] Which is not, of course, merely a matter of the fairness of admitting particular items of evidence, but encompasses all the other incidents of a fair trial, such as the right to be tried within a reasonable time (see *Dyer* v *Watson*, 2002 S.C. (P.C.) 89), the right to an independent and impartial tribunal (see *Starrs* v *Ruxton*, 2000 S.C. 208) and the right to equality of arms, one aspect of which may be the presence, absence or adequacy of the accused's legal representation (see *Buchanan* v *McLean* , 2002 S.C. (P.C.) 1).
[23] *Carmichael* v *Boyd*, 1993 J.C. 219.
[24] *Johnston* v *H.M. Advocate*, 1993 J.C. 187.
[25] *Tonge, Grey and Jack* v *H.M. Advocate*, 1982 S.L.T. 506.

afresh after any break in questioning: the suspect should be told that he is not obliged to say anything, but that anything he does say will be taken down (and tape-recorded) and may be used in evidence. But failure to caution is not necessarily fatal:

> "There is . . . no rule of law which requires that a suspect must always be cautioned before any question can be put to him by the police or by anyone else by whom the inquiries are being conducted. The question in each case is whether what was done was unfair to the accused. . . . [I]t is important to note that there is no suggestion in [this] case that any undue pressure, deception or other device was used to obtain the admissions."[26]

11–14 A trial judge will normally be justified in withholding the evidence of statements from the jury only if he is satisfied that no reasonable jury could hold that the evidence had not been extracted from the suspect by unfair or improper means, only if, in other words, "it is abundantly clear that the rules of fairness and fair dealing have been flagrantly transgressed."[27] The stringency of these rules has varied over time. In *Chalmers v H.M. Advocate*,[28] the Lord Justice-General observed that, in Scots law:

> "[S]elf-incriminating statements when tendered in evidence at a criminal trial are always jealously examined from the standpoint of being assured as to their spontaneity; and if, on a review of all the proved circumstances, that test is not satisfied, evidence of such statements will usually be excluded altogether."

The emphasis shifted in *Miln v Cullen*,[29] where it was held that a self-incriminating statement might properly be admitted in evidence provided:

> "[T]here was no interrogation in the proper sense of that word, no extraction of a confession by cross-examination, no taint of undue pressure, cajoling or trapping, no bullying and nothing in the nature of third degree, and it is not suggested that the respondent, by reason of low intelligence, immaturity or drink, was incapable of appreciating what was going on."

---

[26] *Pennycuick v Lees*, 1992 S.L.T. 763 at 765, 766, *per* LJG Hope. See also, *e.g.* *Young v Friel*, 1992 S.C.C.R. 567; *H.M. Advocate v Graham*, 1991 S.L.T. 416.
[27] *H.M. Advocate v Whitelaw*, 1980 S.L.T. (Notes) 25 at 26, *per* Lord Cameron. See also *Lord Advocate's Reference (No.1 of 1983)*, 1984 S.L.T. 337.
[28] 1954 S.L.T. 177 at 181.
[29] 1967 S.L.T. 35 at 37, *per* LJG Grant.

In effect, this requires the accused to demonstrate why a statement should not be admitted, rather than requiring the Crown to show why it should. It is perhaps fortunate, therefore, that even in advance of the Human Rights Act the High Court chose to change tack:

> "If the question of impropriety is raised, it lies with the Crown to establish that any statement was in fact voluntarily made and that there was no unfairness in the extraction of that statement. It is not a matter of the accused having to establish that there was sufficient impropriety to justify the extraction of the statement made by him."[30]

Again in *Codona v H.M. Advocate*,[31] the Lord Justice-General held as follows:

> "In order that a statement made by an accused person to the police may be available as evidence against him, it must be truly spontaneous and voluntary. The police may question a suspect, but when they move into the field of cross-examination or interrogation, they move into an area of great difficulty. If the questioning is carried too far, by means of leading or repetitive questioning or by pressure in other ways in an effort to obtain from the suspect what they are seeking to obtain from him, the statement is likely to be excluded on the ground that it was extracted by unfair means. Lord Justice-General Emslie's definition of the words 'interrogation' and 'cross-examination' in *Lord Advocate's Reference (No. 1 of 1983)*, as referring only to improper forms of questioning tainted with an element of bullying or pressure designed to break the will of the suspect or to force from him a confession against his will, should not be understood as implying any weakening of these important principles."

Plainly, the stricter the test of fairness then the easier it is for a trial judge to justify withholding evidence from the jury on the basis that no reasonable jury could conclude that it had been fairly obtained. Equally plainly, the stricter approach is less likely to require reassessment in the light of the entry into force of the Human Rights Act.

PUBLIC ORDER

11–15 The police are charged not only with the prevention and investigation of crime, but also with the maintenance of public order.[32] Public peace and order may be disturbed in any number of ways,

---

[30] *Black v Annan*, 1995 S.C.C.R. 273 at 277, *per* Lord Sutherland.
[31] *Codona v H.M. Advocate*, 1996 S.L.T. 1100 at 1105.
[32] Police (Scotland) Act 1967, s.17(1)(a)(ii).

some of which are wholly devoid of merit, others of which are not (or not so obviously). It was noted in *Lord Advocate's Reference (No. 1 of 2000)*[33] that "demonstration and protest and civil disobedience have a long and indeed proud history"[34] in the United Kingdom. But this "important freedom"[35] is not exercisable at will. Up to a point, it may be conceded that the state has a legitimate interest in regulating protest activities in order to ensure that they do not unduly intrude upon the interests of others in going about their ordinary business. The question is whether the state strikes an appropriate balance between control on the one hand and the interests of public protest on the other. In Britain, neither the legislature nor the courts have viewed the claims of the latter with especial favour, even if more recent cases indicate an emergent recognition of the constitutional status of freedom of assembly.[36]

The Convention approaches the matter from a different perspective. The right of freedom of expression is enshrined in Article 10, and is expressed as including the right "to hold opinions and to receive and impart information and ideas without interference by public authority". Under Article 11, "everyone has the right to freedom of peaceful assembly and to freedom of association with others". Both Articles 10 and 11 admit of some restriction on the rights therein defined, provided such restrictions are prescribed by law and necessary in a democratic society in the interests of, among other things, national security, public safety, the prevention of disorder or crime, or the protection of the rights and freedoms of others. These restrictions fall to be construed narrowly, in accordance with the general principle of effectiveness in Convention jurisprudence, which insists that the purpose of the Convention is to guarantee rights that are "not theoretical or illusory but practical and effective."[37] But even where the law pursues a legitimate aim in restricting freedom of expression or assembly, it must still be shown that the restriction represents no greater an interference with protected rights than is necessary to achieve that aim.

The concept of "expression" in Article 10 has been held by the Court to extend to acts of protest, even where they involve physical interference with the activity protested against,[38] and even where the content of the expression is such as to "offend, shock or

---

[33] *Lord Advocate's Reference (No.1 of 2000)*, 2001 S.L.T. 507.
[34] *ibid.*, para.17.
[35] *Hubbard v Pitt* [1976] QB 142 at 179, *per* Lord Denning M.R. (dissenting).
[36] See in particular *DPP v Jones* [1999] 2 A.C. 240; but note that the decision was less a ringing endorsement of freedom of assembly than it could have been.
[37] *Artico v Italy* (1980) 3 E.H.R.R. 1, para.33.
[38] *Steel v UK* (1999) 28 E.H.R.R. 603, where the applicants were arrested while engaging in "direct action" against fox-hunting and road-building.

disturb."[39] The Court has consistently emphasised the importance of freedom of *political* expression in democratic societies,[40] and takes a broad view of what falls within the meaning of political speech.[41] Prior restraints, while not *per se* incompatible with Article 10, attract particularly strict scrutiny, since they prevent the communication of information and ideas; but the Court will also consider carefully the justifications advanced for subsequent sanctions in recognition of the "chilling effect" these may have on participation in political debate. In some circumstances, Article 10 may even impose positive obligations on the state, requiring it not merely to refrain from interfering with freedom of expression but also to take steps to protect and facilitate its exercise.[42]

Any restriction on protected expression must be prescribed by law, which means not only that the restriction must have some domestic legal base, but also that the law in question must be formulated with sufficient precision to enable the citizen to foresee with reasonable certainty the consequences of his conduct.[43] If the restriction passes this test, it must still be shown that it is proportionate; but where the relevant expression takes the form of political protest, the approach of the Court to the proportionality of the restriction is not exacting.[44] In regulating the expression of political opinion, then, the state is accorded a generous margin of appreciation, at least outwith the orthodox political and media channels for its exercise.

The same is true of the approach of the Court to Article 11. **11–16** Freedom of assembly has been described as "a fundamental right in a democracy and . . . one of the foundations of such a society."[45]

---

[39] See, *e.g. Handyside v UK* (1978) 1 E.H.R.R. 137; *Lehideux and Isornia v France* (1998) 5 B.H.R.C. 540. The ECHR is likely to apply only a low standard of review where restrictions are aimed at such forms of expression.

[40] Although its jurisprudence in this regard has been most extensively developed in the context of media freedom rather than that of public protest: see H. Fenwick and G. Phillipson, "Public Protest, the Human Rights Act and Judicial Responses to Political Expression" [2000] P.L. 627.

[41] See, e.g. *Barthold v Germany* (1985) 7 E.H.R.R. 383 and *Thorgeison v Iceland* (1992) 14 E.H.R.R. 843.

[42] See *Ozgür Gündem v Turkey* (2001) 31 E.H.R.R. 1083.

[43] In *Steel v UK* (1999) 28 E.H.R.R. 603, the ECHR accepted that the concept of breach of the peace in English law passed this test, but held in *Hashman and Harrup v UK* (2000) 8 B.H.R.C. 104 that the imposition of an order binding the applicants over to be of good behaviour on the basis that their conduct was *contra bonos mores* breached their rights under ECHR, Art.10, the test being insufficiently precise. As to breach of the peace in Scots law, see *Smith v Donnelly*, 2001 S.L.T. 1007.

[44] See R. Clayton and H. Tomlinson, *The Law of Human Rights* (Oxford University Press, Oxford, 2000), para.15.193, under reference to *Arrowsmith v UK* (1980) 19 D.R. 5 (E Comm HR) and *Choherr v Austria* (1993) 17 E.H.R.R. 358.

[45] *Rassemblement Jurassien Unité Jurassienne v Switzerland* (1979) 17 DR 93 at 119 (E Comm HR).

"Assembly" is construed widely, including public and private meetings, marches, public processions and sit-ins. The right is confined to peaceful assemblies, but an assembly does not lose that character merely because it is marred by "incidental" violence or because it attracts a violent response from others: "the possibility of violent counter-demonstrations, or the possibility of extremists with violent intentions, not members of the organising association, joining the demonstration cannot as such take away that right."[46] In appropriate circumstances, therefore, and having regard to the fair balance that must be struck between the general interests of the community and the interests of the individual, the police may come under a positive obligation to protect the right of peaceful assembly by restraining the violent attempts of others to prevent a demonstration taking place.[47]

Any restriction on peaceful assemblies falls to be justified as being prescribed by law and necessary in a democratic society in the interests of one or more of the legitimate aims listed in Article 11(2). Naturally, the ground for restricting freedom of assembly most commonly advanced is that it is necessary for the regulation of public order, and if a risk of public disorder is reasonably apprehended, the authorities are, again, accorded a wide margin of appreciation in deciding how to deal with it. On this basis, bans on particular assemblies and on all assemblies within a given area and period of time have been upheld.[48] Requirements of prior notification and permission have been held not to constitute, in themselves, interferences with freedom of assembly.[49] Penalties for participating in a prohibited assembly will be justified provided the prohibition was itself justified,[50] but penalties for participating in a lawful assembly may constitute a breach of Article 11.[51]

11–17 Before we consider the domestic law on the regulation of public order, one thing remains to be said. Powerful groups in society—mainstream political parties and pressure groups, and organised private interests—have no pressing need to resort to public protest because they are already secure in their access to established structures of political power, perhaps not the least of

---

[46] *Christians Against Racism and Fascism v UK* (1980) 21 D.R. 138, para.4.
[47] *Plattform 'Ärtze für das Leben' v Austria* (1988) 13 E.H.R.R. 209.
[48] See *Friedl v Austria* (1995) 21 E.H.R.R. 83; *Christians Against Racism and Fascism*, above.
[49] *Rassemblement Jurassien Unité Jurassienne*, above.
[50] *X v Norway* (1984) 6 E.H.R.R. 357.
[51] As in *Ezelin v France* (1991) 14 E.H.R.R. 362, where the applicant, a lawyer and trade union official, was disciplined by his professional body for "failing to dissociate" himself from a demonstration which turned violent, even though he was not himself involved in the violence. More difficult questions may be raised where a criminal penalty is imposed on a person for failing to comply with, say, a police instruction to disperse or otherwise behave in a way intended to avert a risk of disorder.

which is the media. The disadvantaged and/or marginalised, on the other hand, need a public forum for the expression of their views for without it, in effect, they have no forum.[52] Through public protest, the invisible—or barely visible, or at least uninfluential—gain access to the media (even if the media is too often wont to depict their activities in a negative light) and may persuade their immediate audience to sympathise with their position or cause.[53] These are considerations which, despite the lip service paid to the importance of public protest in democratic societies, hardly register in the jurisprudence of the domestic courts and even of the European Court and Commission of Human Rights. The task of the national courts, now that the Human Rights Act is in force, is to ensure that practical effect is given to the rights of free expression and assembly in domestic law. That is not simply a matter of assessing the compatibility in principle of statutory restraints on freedom of assembly with the Convention rights. Public authorities on whom statutory powers to maintain public order are conferred are required by section 6 of the Human Rights Act to act in conformity with the Convention rights, and this may involve a narrower (or at least more closely structured) application of those powers than has obtained in the past. The same is true of the common law: how far do common law limitations on free expression and assembly, both in principle and as applied, conform to the Convention rights? More broadly, given the potential of the Convention rights for horizontal application,[54] the courts will require to consider the extent to which rights of free expression and assembly fall to be respected in the private sphere.[55] In particular, the courts as public authorities may be constrained by section 6 of the Human Rights Act to refuse a remedy to a private party where its grant would constitute a disproportionate infringement of the Convention rights of others.[56] In their approach to all of these issues, the courts may find the European case law[57] of less assistance than the more sophisticated jurisprudence developed in other jurisdictions, perhaps most notably by the US Supreme Court under the First Amendment to the US Constitution.

---

[52] See D.G. Barnum, "The Constitutional Status of Public Protest Activity in Britain and the United States" [1977] P.L. 310; G. Clayton, "Reclaiming Public Ground: The Right to Peaceful Assembly" [2000] 63 M.L.R. 252.

[53] H. Fenwick, "The Right to Protest, the Human Rights Act and the Margin of Appreciation" [1999] 62 M.L.R. 491.

[54] As to what, see paras 9–16—9–17.

[55] See, *e.g. CIN Properties Ltd v Rawlins* [1995] 2 E.G.L.R. 130 and K. Gray and S. F. Gray, "Civil Rights, Civil Wrongs and Quasi-public Space" [1999] E.H.R.L.R. 46.

[56] *cf. Huntingdon Life Sciences Ltd v Stop Huntingdon Animal Cruelty* [2003] All E.R. (D) 280.

[57] To which they are required to have regard, though not to follow, by s.2 of the 1998 Act.

PUBLIC PROCESSIONS AND ASSEMBLIES

11–18 As a general rule, public processions must be notified at least seven days in advance to the relevant local authority and chief constable.[58] The local authority may, after consulting the chief constable, issue an order either prohibiting the procession or imposing upon it conditions as to its date, time, duration and route.[59] The order must be issued in writing at least two days before the procession is intended to be held. However, under section 64 of the 1982 Act, there is a right of appeal to the sheriff against an order made under section 63, exercisable within 14 days of the order's receipt. The sheriff may only uphold an appeal if he finds that the local authority made an error of law or material error of fact, exercised its discretion unreasonably (in the *Wednesbury* sense) or otherwise acted beyond its powers.[60] It is an offence to hold a procession without giving notice as required by section 62 or in contravention of the terms of an order under section 63,[61] and to refuse to desist from taking part in such a procession when required to do so by a uniformed police officer.[62]

Section 12 of the Public Order Act 1986 confers supplementary powers on the police to impose additional (or different) conditions on a public procession should this prove necessary. The power is exercisable only where the senior police officer present at the procession reasonably believes that it may lead to serious public disorder, serious damage to property or serious disruption of the life of the community; or that the purpose of the organisers is to intimidate others with a view to preventing them doing what they have a right to do or compelling them to do something that they have no right to do.[63] The conditions imposed must be those that the police officer believes to be necessary to prevent serious disorder, damage to property, disruption or intimidation. It is an offence knowingly to fail to comply with conditions imposed under section 12, although it is a defence to prove that the failure arose

---

[58] Civic Government (Scotland) Act 1982, s.62. Advance notification is not required for processions which are "customarily or commonly held" (although a local authority may disapply this exemption in respect of certain customary processions), and the full notice period may be waived in respect of processions which are spontaneous or organised urgently.

[59] 1982 Act, s.63. These conditions may include a prohibition on the entry by the procession into any public place specified in the order.

[60] 1982 Act, s.64(4). Note that in *DPP v Jones* [2002] EWHC Admin 110, it was held that the imposition of *ultra vires* conditions (there, on a public assembly pursuant to the Public Order Act 1986, s.14) did not render the order as a whole invalid, since the unlawful conditions could simply be severed from the notice.

[61] 1982 Act, s.65(1).

[62] 1982 Act, s.65(2).

[63] The power is exercisable in advance of the procession, but only where people are assembling with a view to taking part in it.

from circumstances beyond one's control[64]; or to incite others to commit an offence contrary to section 12.[65]

Powers to regulate and control public assemblies are conferred **11–19** directly upon the police by section 14. If the senior police officer, having regard to the time, place and circumstances in which any public assembly is being or is intended to be held, reasonably believes that it may lead to serious public disorder, serious damage to property or serious disruption of the life of the community, or that the purpose of the organisers is intimidatory in the sense described above, he may give directions imposing on the organisers and participants such conditions as to the venue, duration and maximum number of persons who may take part as appear necessary to prevent such serious disorder, damage or disruption. These powers apply only to a *public* assembly, defined by section 16 as meaning "an assembly of twenty or more persons in a public place which is wholly or partly open to the air".[66] A person who organises or takes part in such an assembly, and who knowingly fails to comply with such directions, is guilty of an offence,[67] although it is a defence in either case to prove that failure to comply was due to circumstances beyond one's control. It is also an offence to incite others to commit an offence contrary to section 14.[68]

The powers of the police in relation to assemblies were augmented by the Criminal Justice and Public Order Act 1994, which inserted new sections 14A–14C into the 1986 Act. Section 14A[69] prohibits "trespassory assemblies", meaning an assembly of 20 or more persons on land wholly in the open air to which the public has no or only limited right of access. If at any time the chief officer of police reasonably believes that a trespassory assembly is intended to be held and that it is likely to cause serious disruption to the life of the community or significant damage to the land or a building or monument on it (where the land, building or monument are of historical, architectural, archaeological or scientific importance), he may apply to the local authority for an order prohibiting for a specified period not exceeding four days all trespassory assemblies in an area not exceeding the area represented by a circle with a radius of five miles from a specified centre. Section 14B prescribes the offences in connection with trespassory

---

[64] Public Order Act 1986, s.12(4), (5).
[65] 1986 Act, s.12(6).
[66] "Public place" means "any road within the meaning of the Roads (Scotland) Act 1984" and "any place to which at the material time the public or any section of the public has access, on payment or otherwise, as of right or by virtue of express or implied permission".
[67] 1986 Act, s.14(4), (5).
[68] 1986 Act, s.14(6).
[69] 1994 Act, s.70.

assemblies. Thus, a person who organises or takes part in an assembly which he knows to be prohibited by an order made under section 14A is guilty of an offence, as is a person who incites others to take part in a prohibited assembly. Under section 14C, a uniformed police officer may stop a person whom he reasonably believes to be on his way to an assembly prohibited by an order made under section 14A and direct that person not to proceed in the direction of the assembly. This power is only exercisable within the area covered by the order. Failure to comply with the police officer's direction is an offence.

These provisions were considered by the House of Lords in *DPP v Jones*.[70] The defendants were arrested while participating in a peaceful, unobstructive assembly at a roadside near Stonehenge. At the material time, an order made under section 14A prohibiting trespassory assemblies in the vicinity of Stonehenge was in force. The defendants were convicted of offences under section 14B. By a bare majority, the House of Lords quashed the convictions. The critical element in the reasoning of the majority was the finding of fact by the justices of the peace that the defendants' presence at the scene involved no obstruction of the highway. That being so, it fell within the scope of what Lord Irvine L.C. at least was prepared to recognise as a common law right to use the highway for any reasonable purpose, provided that the activity in question did not amount to a public or private nuisance and did not unreasonably impede the public's primary right to pass and repass.[71] But this was the narrowest of victories for the claims of public protest. Only the Lord Chancellor's speech bore any relation to the analytical pattern established in other cases from the pre-Human Rights Act era involving fundamental rights, in that it identified the scope of the common law right and then insisted that this right was not to be whittled down in the absence of clear statutory words.[72] This apart, one could be forgiven for thinking that the House of Lords discerned no constitutional issue in *Jones* at all, which does not obviously augur well for the approach of the courts to the

---

[70] [1999] 2 A.C. 240.

[71] The other members of the majority were rather more equivocal on this point: Lord Hutton, for instance, went no further than saying that the common law right of assembly "is unduly restricted unless it can be exercised in some circumstances on the public highway." For Lord Slynn (dissenting), the common law recognised no common law right to use the highway other than for passage, and "reasonable incidental uses associated with passage."

[72] Fenwick and Phillipson (n.53), pertinently contrast the decision in *DPP v Jones* with those in the near-contemporaneous cases of *Reynolds v Times Newspapers Ltd* [2001] 2 A.C. 127 and *R. v S of S for the Home Dept, ex p. Simms* [2000] 2 A.C. 115. In both of these, freedom of expression, both as a common law "constitutional right" and as embodied in ECHR, Art.10, and the values underpinning that freedom, were articulated and formed the starting point for their Lordships' reasoning.

legitimacy and proportionality of statutory restraints on free expression and assembly in the post-Human Rights Act era.

The statutory provisions so far considered do not provide a **11–20** complete account of the regulation of public protest. As a matter of the civil law, interdict may lie to restrain an actual or anticipated demonstration at the instance of persons whose private rights or interests are or may be threatened thereby.[73] Equally, a gathering in a public place or even, conceivably, the presence of a single protestor, may constitute a breach of the criminal law.[74] More broadly, many rallies and assemblies will escape the reach of the 1986 Act altogether because they are held indoors.[75] Even here, however, the duty of the police under section 17 of the Police (Scotland) Act 1967, coupled with their common law power to prevent or restrain breaches of the peace, whether actual or apprehended, provides extensive scope for intruding upon freedom of expression and assembly. This might involve, in the first place, uninvited entry onto private premises, as in *Thomas v Sawkins*.[76] There, police officers attended a meeting, anticipating that breaches of the peace might occur. The organiser of the meeting, Mr Thomas, asked the police officers to leave, and when they refused made as if to remove an officer by force. Another officer, P.C. Sawkins, physically restrained Mr Thomas, who then prosecuted P.C. Sawkins for assault. The court held that the police had been lawfully on the premises and that, therefore, P.C. Sawkins had not assaulted Mr Thomas:

"[I]t is part of the preventative power, and, therefore, part of the preventative duty of the police, in cases where there are

---

[73] See, *e.g. Hubbard v Pitt* [1976] Q.B. 142; *McIntyre v Sheridan*, 1993 S.L.T. 412; *Huntingdon Life Sciences Ltd v Stop Huntingdon Animal Cruelty* [2003] All E.R. (D) 280.

[74] See, *e.g.* Civic Government (Scotland) Act 1982, s.53, which provides that any person who "being on foot in a public place—(a) obstructs, along with another or others, the lawful passage of any other person and fails to desist on being required to do so by a constable in uniform; or (b) wilfully obstructs the lawful passage of any other person" is guilty of an offence. "Obstruct" does not mean to block the street completely.

[75] In that respect, the owner of the premises in which meetings are held may exercise a measure of control over the assembly, even to the extent of denying access to facilities otherwise made available for public use. But this discretion is not unlimited: the decisions of a public authority as to the management of its property may be subject to control by way of judicial review (see, *e.g. Wheeler v Leicester CC* [1985] A.C. 1054; *R. v Somerset C, ex p. Fewings* [1995] 1 W.L.R. 1037) or for that matter by way of ordinary principles of the law of contract (*Verrall v Great Yarmouth BC* [1981] Q.B. 202); and the freedom of public and private sector organisations to deny access to their property by certain sections of the community is restricted in some circumstances by statute (see, *e.g.* of the Race Relations Act 1976, s.20).

[76] [1935] 2 K.B. 249.

> . . . reasonable grounds of apprehension [of a breach of the peace] to enter and remain on private premises."[77]

In other words, neither express statutory authority nor a warrant is necessary for the police to enter private premises uninvited where a breach of the peace is occurring or is reasonably anticipated. For England and Wales, this common law power was captured in section 17(6) of the Police and Criminal Evidence Act 1984, the exercise of which was considered by the European Court of Human Rights in *McLeod v UK*.[78] There it was held that the applicant's right to respect for her private life and home under Article 8 of the Convention was infringed by two police officers who entered her home and who failed to prevent the entry of her ex-husband when he arrived uninvited to recover property said (by him) to be his. The Court did not find the power under section 17(6) was *per se* incompatible with Article 8, but found that the manner of its exercise in the circumstances of this case—the applicant, who might have objected to her ex-husband's behaviour, was not even in the house at the material time—was disproportionate to the aim of preventing disorder. It would therefore seem that the police would now need to be able to point to a real and immediate threat to public order before entering private premises if they are to avoid censure under the Human Rights Act.

11–21   Prevention of breaches of the peace might also involve, secondly, the imposition of conditions on public meetings otherwise than on a statutory basis. In *Humphries v Connor*,[79] a police officer requested Mrs Humphries to remove an orange lily from her jacket to prevent a breach of the peace amongst an antagonistic crowd. When she refused, he removed it himself. Mrs Humphries brought an action for assault, but the court, by a majority, accepted the need to prevent a breach of the peace as a good defence.[80] A step further was taken in *Duncan v Jones*.[81] Mrs Duncan was preparing to address a crowd outside an unemployment training centre. She had spoken at the same place 14 months before and a disturbance had ensued. To avert the risk of further disturbance, a police

---

[77] at 253, *per* Lord Hewart C.J.
[78] (1999) 27 E.H.R.R. 493.
[79] (1864) 17 Ir.C.L.R. 1.
[80] The wearing of uniforms or other items or emblems intended to signify support for political objects is regulated by various statutory provisions (see Public Order Act 1936, s.1, and *O'Moran v DPP* [1975] Q.B. 864 on the wearing of uniforms; and Terrorism Act 2000, s.13, on the wearing of any item signifying support for an organisation proscribed under that Act), but these provisions are without prejudice to the broader power of the police to require the removal of an item the exhibition of which threatens, as in *Humphries v Connor* (1864) 17 Ir.C.L.R. 1, to provoke disorder.
[81] [1936] 1 K.B. 218.

officer asked her to move away from the training centre and deliver her speech in a nearby street. She refused, and was charged with and convicted of obstructing a police officer in the execution of his duty.[82] The court observed that once the police officer had formed a reasonable apprehension of a breach of the peace, "it then became his duty to prevent anything which in his view would cause that breach of the peace. While he was taking steps so to do, he was wilfully obstructed by [Mrs Duncan]."[83] Again, in *Piddington v Bates*,[84] the Court of Appeal upheld a conviction for obstruction of a police officer in the execution of his duty where the appellant had refused to comply with the instruction of a police officer, in attendance at a trade dispute at a factory, to move on, two pickets being sufficient. As all of these cases vividly demonstrate, then, the police have the power at common law to impose time, place and manner conditions on assemblies independently of their statutory powers under section 14 of the Public Order Act 1986. Nor are these common law powers subject to the limitations contained in section 14: they would apply to assemblies of less than 20 persons, indoors or outdoors. Similarly, a reasonable apprehension of a breach of the peace would seem to involve something less than the risk of "serious public disorder, serious damage to property or serious disruption of the life of the community" needed to trigger section 14. This is not to say that the common law powers of the police are by definition incompatible with the Convention. Plainly, however, their exercise involves an infringement of rights to freedom of expression and assembly requiring to be justified. In so far as they are premised upon the apprehension or prevention of a breach of the peace, that concept in turn must be scrutinised for compatibility with the Convention rights in all the circumstances in which it comes into play.

The power to order an assembly to disperse, if necessary to prevent a breach of the peace, is but an aspect of the power to impose conditions already considered.[85] Here, however, a specific

---

[82] In Scotland, this offence is contained in s.41 of the Police (Scotland) Act 1967, and is committed by any person who "assaults, resists, obstructs, molests or hinders a constable in the execution of his duty." At least in the past, it had to be shown that the obstruction had some "physical aspect" (*Curlett v McKechnie*, 1939 S.L.T. 11, *per* Lord Fleming), but in *Skeen v Shaw*, 1979 S.L.T. (Notes) 58, it was suggested that "hinders" may not require more than a minimal physical element, even if "assaults" or "obstructs" clearly do.

[83] *Duncan v Jones* [1936] 1 K.B. 218 at 223, *per* Humphreys J.

[84] [1961] 1 W.L.R. 162.

[85] Indeed the power may go further still, to the extent of preventing an assembly from taking place at all. Certainly during the miners' strike of 1984–85, the police power to prevent breaches of the peace was relied on to turn miners back from picket lines, and even to stop miners at roadblocks set up to prevent them from travelling to picket lines in other counties. Likened to "the Soviet internal

issue of compatibility with the Convention rights is raised: whether it is lawful for the police to order a peaceable assembly to disperse, where it attracts the attentions of a "hostile audience", rather than dealing with the hecklers.[86] In *Deakin v Milne*,[87] Salvation Army marches in Arbroath had attracted the aggressive opposition, as Salvation Army marches throughout Britain were apt to do at the time, of the so-called Skeleton Army. To preserve the peace, Arbroath magistrates banned Salvation Army marches. The Salvationists defied the ban and were convicted of breaching the ban and breach of the peace. The High Court of Justiciary affirmed the validity of the ban and the convictions. By contrast, in the analogous English case of *Beatty v Gilbanks*,[88] it was held that the Salvationists had been wrongly convicted. Their marches had caused no disturbance of the peace; rather:

"[O]n the contrary . . . the disturbance that did take place was caused entirely by the unlawful and unjustifiable interference of the Skeleton Army . . . and . . . but for the opposition and molestation offered to the Salvationists by these other persons, no disturbance of any kind would have taken place."[89]

Beatty v Gilbanks, powerful though it is as an expression of civil liberty, is sometimes made to bear more weight than it can carry, given the stance of the courts as exhibited in cases such as *Duncan v Jones*.[90] But the entry into force of the Human Rights Act may and should cause the courts to revisit the decision. If consistency with the Convention rights involves their effective and practical enforcement, then it is arguable that the first duty of the police as a public authority in a *Beatty v Gilbanks* situation would be to separate the opposing sides or to move a counter-demonstration on. Simply to order all persons to disperse would seem disproportionate, unless the threat of disorder is imminent and grave.

---

passport system or South African pass laws", the legality of these devices (and hence of the convictions which followed when miners, on refusing to comply, were charged with such offences as obstructing a police officer in the execution of his duty) was upheld in *Moss v McLachlan* [1985] I.R.L.R. 76.

[86] As noted above, the ECHR has held that, in appropriate circumstances, both ECHR, Arts 10 and 11, may involve the imposition of a positive obligation on public authorities such as the police to ensure that citizens are not prevented from exercising their rights of free expression and assembly.

[87] (1882) 10 R. (J.) 22.

[88] (1882) 9 Q.B.D. 308.

[89] *ibid.* at 311, *per* Field J.

[90] For a withering assessment of the record of the courts in the protection of freedom of expression and assembly, see K. D. Ewing and C. Gearty, *The Struggle for Civil Liberties* (Oxford University Press, Oxford, 2000).

What then of the compatibility of the concept of breach of the **11–22** peace with the Convention? In *McLeod v UK*[91] and *Steel v UK*,[92] the European Court of Human Rights accepted that the concept as it is understood in English law was sufficiently clear in its meaning to satisfy the "prescribed by law" requirement: "it is now established that a breach of the peace is committed only when an individual causes harm to persons or property, or acts in a manner the natural consequences of which would be to provoke violence in others." But the concept of breach of the peace in Scots law is accorded a wider meaning than this. As the Lord Justice-Clerk held in *Raffaelli v Heatley*[93]:

> "[W]here something is done in breach of public order or decorum which might reasonably be expected to lead to the lieges being alarmed or upset or tempted to make reprisals at their own hand, the circumstances are such as to amount to a breach of the peace."

But the offence is not confined to disorderly or aggressive conduct[94]; nor, it appears, is "positive evidence of actual harm, upset, annoyance or disturbance created by reprisal . . . a prerequisite of conviction."[95] Put shortly, then, conduct of a relatively inoffensive kind, which as a matter of fact upset or alarmed nobody, has sufficed in the past to constitute a breach of the peace, and it is on this basis that the power of the police to infringe upon freedom of expression and assembly is premised.

In *Smith v Donnelly*,[96] the appellant took objection to being charged with and convicted of breach of the peace[97] on the basis that, since the offence as understood in Scots law did not define with sufficient clarity the forms of behaviour it proscribed, her prosecution contravened the prohibition in Article 7 of the Convention on retrospective criminal penalties.[98] Lord Coulsfield,

---

[91] (1999) 27 E.H.R.R. 493.

[92] (1999) 28 E.H.R.R. 603.

[93] 1949 J.C. 101.

[94] On the contrary, it was held in *Montgomery v McLeod*, 1977 S.L.T. (Notes) 77 that "there is no limit to the kind of conduct which may give rise to a charge of breach of the peace. All that is required is that there must be some conduct such as to excite the reasonable apprehension to which we have drawn attention (*i.e.* that mischief may ensue) or such as to create alarm or disturbance to the lieges in fact."

[95] *Wilson v Brown*, 1982 S.L.T. 361 at 363, *per* Lord Dunpark.

[96] 2001 S.L.T. 507.

[97] Having taken part in a demonstration outside a naval base in which, according to the procurator fiscal's complaint, she conducted herself in a disorderly manner, lay down in the road, disrupted the free flow of traffic and refused to desist when required to do so.

[98] As to which, see *SW v UK* (1995) 21 E.H.R.R. 363, para.35.

giving the opinion of the High Court, acknowledged that the English requirement, that there should be harm or a threat of harm to persons or property, was not part of the law of Scotland. His Lordship also accepted that there were cases in which a breach of the peace had been held established "on grounds which might charitably be described as tenuous."[99] Having reviewed the leading authorities, it was held that the core meaning of the offence, at least, was sufficiently clear to meet the requirements of the Convention. Lord Coulsfield observed, however, that "there will be cases in which the courts will require to bear in mind the importance of freedom of expression, an issue which now involves reference to Article 10 of the Convention."[1] Neither Article 10 nor Article 11 was argued before the High Court in *Smith*. It is unlikely that, had they been, it would have made any difference in the circumstances of that case. Nonetheless, both Articles introduce considerations into the exercise of police powers to maintain public order that have not, hitherto, been accorded significant, if any, weight in determining the legality of particular controls.

---

[99] Smith v Donnelly, 2001 S.L.T. 507, para.19.
[1] *ibid.*, para.20.

CHAPTER 12

JUDICIAL REVIEW

Introduction

An application for judicial review invokes the supervisory juris- **12–01** diction of the Court of Session, meaning that "super-eminent" power of a supreme court to ensure that all those vested with a legal authority exercise that authority in accordance with the law.[1] As Clyde and Edwards note, while the supervisory jurisdiction has a long history, it is only relatively recently that the term "judicial review" has fallen into normal usage as a way of referring to it.[2] For present purposes, judicial review is sought by way of petition brought in accordance with Chapter 58 of the Rules of the Court of Session.[3]

CONSTITUTIONAL CONTEXT OF JUDICIAL REVIEW

Many, even most, applications for judicial review involve matters **12–02** which, however important to the individual applicants, are difficult to characterise as constitutionally significant. Others are not. Cases challenging the validity of the government's decision to ratify an international treaty, or the right of the Secretary of State to determine the length of a life prisoner's sentence, or the exclusion

---

[1] See Lord Clyde and D. J. Edwards, *Judicial Review* (W. Green, Edinburgh, 2000), para.1.01; also A. O'Neill, *Judicial Review in Scotland* (Butterworths, Edinburgh, 1999), paras 1.03–1.05; A. W. Bradley and C. M. G. Himsworth, "Administrative Law", *Stair Memorial Encyclopaedia* (Butterworths, Scotland, 1995).

[2] Clyde and Edwards, *Judicial Review, op.cit.*

[3] SI 1994/1443, which replaced r.260B as introduced by the A.S. (Rules of Court Amendment No. 2) (Judicial Review) 1985 (SI 1985/500). R.260B implemented the recommendations of the Dunpark Working Party on Procedure for Judicial Review of Administrative Action, which was appointed by the Lord President in light of remarks made by Lord Fraser of Tullybelton in *Brown v Hamilton DC*, 1983 S.C. (H.L.) 1 and *Stevenson v Midlothian DC*, 1983 S.C. (H.L.) 50, regretting the lack, in Scotland, of an expedited procedure for judicial review comparable to that established in England by reform of the rules of the court in 1977; see, now, for England, Supreme Court Act 1981, s.31, and Civil Procedure Rules 1998, r.54 (as inserted by the Civil Procedure (Amendment No.4) Rules 2000 (SI 2000/2092)).

from the armed services of homosexuals—and these are but examples—go to the heart of what is sometimes described as a "legitimacy problem" for judicial review. Simply put, judicial review commonly involves unelected, unaccountable judges in pronouncing upon the exercise of powers having a democratic source. That difficulty, if it is seen as such, is in fact present in most applications for review, however apparently mundane.

It is, therefore, vital to understand the constitutional context, and justifications, for judicial review. First, an exercise of the supervisory jurisdiction does not involve the substitution of a judge's decision for an administrative decision he finds to be wrong. Judicial review is not an appellate process, and the substantive grounds on which it may be sought are limited (if elastic, and, with or without human rights, increasing). The issue is not whether the "right" or "wrong" decision was made, or whether a better decision could have been taken, but whether the decision was taken in accordance with the law. That implies, at least in cases involving the review of statutory powers, that the decision-maker acted within the four corners of the power granted to him, and this basic principle of legality, otherwise known as the *ultra vires* doctrine, provides a compelling constitutional justification for what the courts do in the context of review. Is it, however, enough? In recent years, a lively, if perhaps slightly anglocentric, debate on this question has been taking place.[4] On the one hand, those who insist on the *ultra vires* doctrine as the orthodox justification for review contend that all judicial intervention in the decisions of public authorities, however bold, must be connected to the legal powers of those authorities.[5] Exponents of *ultra vires* orthodoxy contend that the doctrine refers not only to the limitations on a power spelled out in the statutory grant, but includes also those limitations which are implied; and in this respect it is presumed that Parliament does not, in conferring power, intend that it be used in a manner contrary to those constitutional values bound up in the rule of law which inform the well-established grounds of review, namely illegality, procedural impropriety and irrationality. Thus in performing judicial review, the courts are doing no more than ensuring that the will of the legislature is respected: democratic legitimacy is thereby enhanced, not undermined.

12–03   This analysis, to be sure, extends the reach of the *ultra vires* doctrine, but it is still felt by many to be too thin to explain the advances that have been made in the rigour and intensity of

---

[4] Both sides of the debate are nicely presented, in one volume, in *Judicial Review and the Constitution* (C. F. Forsyth ed., Hart Publishing, Oxford, 2000).

[5] See, *e,g,* C. F. Forsyth, "Of Fig Leaves and Fairytales: The *ultra vires* doctrine, the sovereignty of Parliament and judicial review" (1996) 55 C.L.J. 122; M. Elliott, "The *Ultra Vires* Doctrine in a Constitutional Setting: Still the central principle of judicial review" (1998) 57 C.L.J. 129. Both articles appear also in Forsyth, *Judicial Review and the Constitution, op.cit.*

judicial review. On the one hand, connected as it is to the will of Parliament as expressed in legislation, it may account for the review of statutory powers, but does not provide a constitutional justification for the review of other powers, not necessarily "public" in character, by the courts.[6] On the other, "the sovereignty of Parliament and the rule of law cover only a limited range of constitutional principle",[7] and flexible though the rule of law is, it cannot accommodate substantive principles such as the right to life, freedom of expression and assembly, respect for human dignity and autonomy, which the courts had already begun, even in advance of the Human Rights Act 1998, to take as a basis for their reasoning.[8] Hence the alternative account of the constitutional foundation of judicial review: that the common law itself provides the justification for what the courts do on review.[9] This is not (we are told) anti-democratic, or (as the defenders of the *ultra vires* doctrine have argued) a challenge to the sovereignty of Parliament, because the "higher order" rights endorsed by the courts in their recent jurisprudence are woven into the very structure of constitutional democracy within which Parliament operates. As Sir John Laws puts it, such rights "are not a consequence of the democratic process, but logically prior to it."[10] On that reckoning, the Human Rights Act may be seen as signifying legislative approval of something that was happening already in the courts.[11] Those of this persuasion are, generally speaking, careful not to suggest that, in the final analysis, Parliament is not supreme, or that the rule of

---

[6] As we shall see, the scope of review in Scotland does not depend, as it does in England, on a distinction between public law matters, which are reviewable, and private law matters, which are not. Even in England, however, the adequacy of the *ultra vires* doctrine as the organising principle of judicial review has been contested, not least on the basis that it fails to explain the review of non-statutory powers: see D. Oliver, "Is the *Ultra Vires* Rules the Basis of Judicial Review?" [1987] P.L. 543.

[7] J. Jowell, "Beyond the Rule of Law: Towards constitutional judicial review" [2000] P.L. 671.

[8] As we saw in Ch.2, there are those who would argue that such principles *may* be derived from an expanded, "substantive" conception of the rule of law. One of the difficulties with such conceptions is the lack of consensus over precisely what it is the rule of law does include or require, which is why critics of substantive theories prefer a formal conception not contingent upon a particular political theory.

[9] The reception of this approach into administrative jurisprudence has been more apparent in the English than the Scottish courts. Even in England, it is especially associated with a number of "activist" judges, whose activism was not always greeted with enthusiasm: see, *e.g.* Lord Irvine, "Judges and Decision Makers: The theory and practice of *Wednesbury* review" [1996] P.L. 59; J. A. G. Griffith, "The Brave New World of Sir John Laws" [2000] 63 M.L.R. 159.

[10] Sir J. Laws, "Law and Democracy" [1995] P.L. 72.

[11] See, Sir J. Laws, "Judicial Review and the Meaning of Law" in Forsyth, *Judicial Review and the Constitution, op.cit.*, Ch.8: "the deep constitutional significance of the Human Rights Act is that it gives democratic validation to the concrete expression of constitutional rights."

judges has been substituted for the rule of the legislature. Their arguments are presented, rather, as a response to a crude majoritarianism that would insist on judicial deference to anything bearing the loosely democratic imprimatur of having been propelled through Parliament by the executive. If Parliament wishes to contravene or override these fundamental rights, it may do so[12] provided it makes its intention clear.[13] Even after the Human Rights Act, it may do so: the courts are able to declare the incompatibility of the statute with Convention rights, but cannot annul it.

For practical purposes, the intricacies of these arguments may not appear especially pertinent, but the shift towards "constitutional judicial review" (however we justify it) does and will have an impact on litigators, judges and decision makers in so far as it requires "a more intense and disciplined review of administrative action than traditional administrative law allowed."[14]

Preliminary Issues

12–04 We have noted the procedural form of judicial review. In the context of that procedure, normally at the stage of the first hearing, certain preliminary matters may be raised which do not touch on the relevancy of the petitioner's claims but which may, if resolved against him, suffice to cause his application to be dismissed.

Title and interest

12–05 The first of these is whether the petitioner has title and interest to sue.[15] The classic definition of title to sue is contained in *D. & J. Nicol v Dundee Harbour Trustees*,[16] where it was held that the petitioner must be "a party (using the word in its widest sense) to some legal relationship which gives him some right which the person against whom he raises the action either infringes or denies." There, the pursuers were held to have title to sue as harbour ratepayers: "members of a constituency erected by Act of Parliament . . . and persons for whose benefit the harbour is kept up." Thus, title may be derived from the relationship created

---

[12] Subject to the possibility of international sanction before the ECHR.

[13] See *e.g. R. v S of S for the Home Department, ex p. Leech* [1994] Q.B. 198; *R. v S of S for the Home Dept, ex p. Pierson* [1998] A.C. 539; *R. v Lord Chancellor, ex p. Witham* [1998] Q.B. 575.

[14] J. Jowell, "Beyond the Rule of Law: Towards constitutional judicial review" [2000] P.L. 671.

[15] Clyde and Edwards, *Judicial Review, op.cit.*, Ch.10; O'Neill, *Judicial Review, op.cit.*, paras 6.04–6.11.

[16] 1915 S.C. (HL) 7.

between the parties by statute. In the absence of a direct statutory relationship, title to sue may be founded on a statutory function owed to the public as a whole or to a section of the public of which the petitioner is a member.[17] However, where a statutory function is drawn more narrowly, those falling outwith its ambit will be denied title to sue even in the presence of a demonstrable interest to do so. This was the case in *Paisley Taxi Owners' Association v Renfrew District Council*,[18] which concerned a challenge to an alteration in the council's taxi licensing policy. Similarly, petitions brought by business competitors indirectly affected by planning or licensing decisions have been dismissed for lack of title on the basis that, since the petitioners did not fall within the list of permitted objectors set out in the relevant legislation, they had no rights capable of being infringed by those decisions.[19] Again, in *Glasgow Rape Crisis Centre v Secretary of State for the Home Department*,[20] Lord Clarke dismissed the petition for judicial review of the Home Secretary's decision under the Immigration Act 1971 and the Immigration Rules to admit Mike Tyson into the United Kingdom in order to fight a boxing match in Glasgow, since the Act and Rules created no legal nexus between the petitioners and Home Secretary capable of founding title to sue.

The concept of interest was explained by Lord Ardwell in *Swanson v Manson*[21]:

> "The grounds for this rule are (1) that the law courts of this country are not instituted for the purpose of deciding academic questions of law, but for settling disputes where any of the lieges has a real interest to have a question determined which involves his pecuniary rights or his status; and (2) that no person is entitled to subject another to the trouble and expense of a litigation unless he has some real interest to enforce and protect."

In *Scottish Old People's Welfare Council, Petr*,[22] Lord Clyde commented that the phrase "pecuniary rights or status" should not be regarded as "an exhaustive or complete description of what may comprise an interest" (although in that case, the petitioners' interest was insufficient because they sued "not as a body of

---

[17] See, *e.g. Wilson v Independent Broadcasting Authority*, 1979 S.C. 351; *Scottish Old People's Welfare Council, Petr*, 1987 S.L.T. 179.

[18] *Paisley Taxi Owners' Ass. v Renfrew DC*, 1997 S.L.T. 1112; *cf. City Cabs (Edinburgh) Ltd v Edinburgh DC*, 1988 S.L.T. 184.

[19] See, e.g. *Matchett v Dunfermline DC*, 1993 S.L.T. 537; *Hollywood Bowl (Scotland) Ltd v Horsburgh*, 1993 S.L.T. 241.

[20] 2000 S.L.T. 389.

[21] (1907) S.C. 426.

[22] 1987 S.L.T. 179.

potential claimants . . . but as a body working to advance and protect the interests of the aged"). On the other hand, in *Glasgow Rape Crisis Centre*, Lord Clarke stated that he would have held the petitioners to have sufficient interest to sue, had they had title, and suggested that "in the field of administrative law and judicial review . . . there must be few cases where there is title but no interest, though such cases may arise, for example, where the issue is academic." This remark may have been prompted by the criticism often levelled at judicial review in Scotland, to the effect that the rules on title and interest, unlike the test of "sufficient interest" in England,[23] do not countenance an especially active role in the supervision of administrative legality for pressure groups and genuinely concerned, if not directly affected, members of the public.[24] In fact, there are cases which hint at a more liberal approach to the question of standing, and it has been argued that there is "no reason to suppose that the Scottish court would not recognise the title of a responsible pressure group to pursue an application for judicial review where the statute giving the power, the exercise of which has given rise to the challenge, can be seen to give, expressly or impliedly, a real interest to the group to complain of an alleged unlawfulness."[25] But this argument appears to conflate the two distinct issues of title and interest, and sits uneasily with the general trend of the case law. It is safer to conclude, with Lord Hope, that "the present position has still not got that far."[26]

12–06   Certain additional points should, however, be noted. First, as was pointed out in the light of *Scottish Old People's Welfare Council*,[27] it is always open to pressure groups to fund, if not front, applications for judicial review, provided they are able to locate a suitably qualified individual applicant. Secondly, and relatedly, the test for standing to bring (or defend) an action under section 7(1) of the Human Rights Act 1998—whether the applicant is, or would be, a "victim" of the breach of Convention rights, as that term is used in Article 34 of the Convention—is significantly narrower than the English test of sufficient interest, but is not wholly unlike

---

[23] Since the leading decision in *R. v Inland Revenue Commissioners, ex p. National Federation of Self-employed and Small Businesses Ltd* [1982] A.C. 617, the "sufficient interest" test has been interpreted liberally so as to "enfranchise" a whole host of pressure groups and representative bodies: see, *e.g. R. v S of S for Social Services, ex p. Child Poverty Action Group* [1990] 2 Q.B. 540; *R. v S of S for Foreign Affairs, ex p. World Development Movement Ltd* [1995] 1 All E.R. 611.

[24] See, C. R. Munro, "Standing in Judicial Review", 1995 S.L.T. (News) 279.

[25] Clyde and Edwards, *Judicial Review, op.cit.*, para.10–28; see also A. D. Murray, "Standing up for the Scottish Public", 1997 J.R. 250.

[26] Lord Hope of Craighead, "Mike Tyson Comes to Glasgow: A question of standing" [2000] P.L. 294 at 307.

[27] See A. W. Bradley, "Applications for Judicial Review: The Scottish model" [1987] P.L. 313.

that of title and interest in Scotland. Many were concerned that the effect of this would be to exclude pressure groups from an active role in human rights litigation.[28] But, thirdly, changes have been made to the rules of court north and south of the border to facilitate third party interventions in judicial review proceedings (whether or not involving human rights). Rule 58.8A of the Rules of the Court of Session[29] provides that a person who is not directly affected by an issue raised in a petition for judicial review may nonetheless apply to the court for leave to intervene in the petition or in an appeal in connection therewith. The court may grant leave if satisfied that the proceedings raise, and the issue which the applicant wishes to address raises, a matter of public interest; that the propositions to be advanced by the applicant are relevant to the proceedings and likely to assist the court; and that the intervention will not unduly delay or otherwise prejudice the rights of the parties. Where leave is granted, an intervention will normally take the form of written submissions; exceptionally, the court may direct that it wishes to hear oral submissions as well.

Delay

In England, applications for judicial review must be raised **12–07** "promptly, and in any event within three months", although the Administrative Court has a discretion to extend time in exceptional circumstances.[30] In Scotland, there is no specified time limit on applying for judicial review.[31] However, the common law principles of delay (*mora*), acquiescence and personal bar apply as much to judicial review proceedings as to ordinary actions,[32] and it has been said:

> "[I]n the field of administrative law, where a challenge is made against some decision or action the effects of which may be limited in time, the court will be more quick to infer from silence and inactivity that a person is acquiescing in a changed state of affairs . . . . Judicial review is a process designed to give speedy consideration to problems which arise, and where time is of materiality. In such a situation, potential litigants should lose no time in raising proceedings."[33]

---

[28] See, *e.g.* J. Marriott and D. Nicol, "The Human Rights Act, Representative Standing and the Victim Culture" [1998] E.H.R.L.R. 731.

[29] Inserted by the A.S. (Rules of the Court of Session Amendment No.5) (Public Interest Intervention in Judicial Review) 2000 (SSI 2000/317).

[30] See *R. v Hammersmith and Fulham London BC, ex p. Burkett*, [2002] 1 W.L.R. 1593 on when the three-month time-limit begins to run against an applicant.

[31] Except that, where an action under the HRA 1998, s.7, is brought by way of an application for judicial review, a time-limit of one year, commencing with the relevant breach of Convention rights, applies: see, s.7(5).

[32] See Clyde and Edwards, *Judicial Review, op.cit.*, paras 13.20–13.26; O'Neill, *Judicial Review, op.cit.*, paras 6.25–6.28.

[33] *Watt v S of S for Scotland* [1991] 3 C.M.L.R. 429 at 440, *per* Lord Weir.

Touching on the Scottish position in *R. v Hammersmith and Fulham London BC, ex p. Burkett*,[34] Lord Hope noted that "there is no Scottish authority which supports the proposition that *mere delay* (or . . . a mere failure to apply 'promptly') . . . is sufficient to bar proceedings for judicial review in the absence of circumstances pointing to acquiescence or prejudice."[35] There is acquiescence where inaction on the part of the petitioner amounts to implied consent to the changed state of affairs.[36] It is an aspect of personal bar, which Clyde and Edwards describe in terms of a representation by the petitioner:

> "[W]here A has by his words or conduct justified B in believing that a certain state of facts exists, and B has acted on such belief to his prejudice, A is not permitted to affirm against B that a different state of facts existed at the same time."[37]

The inquiry, then, when a plea of *mora*, taciturnity and acquiescence is taken, involves consideration of all the surrounding circumstances as well as the simple fact of the passage of time. So, for instance, in *Uprichard v Fife Council and St Andrews Bay Development Ltd*,[38] Lord Bonomy sustained the plea where the petitioner had allowed 19 weeks to elapse after the granting of planning permission for a golf-related development in St Andrew before lodging her petition. This was because the petitioner had apparently acquiesced in the grant; the developers, who had incurred expenditure in the order of £1 million since the grant, would suffer undue prejudice; and the lateness of the challenge would have "a disruptive effect on good administration."[39]

Prematurity

12–08   Equally, a petition may suffer from prematurity: being brought too soon rather than too late. This may arise where there is an exchange of correspondence on an issue between the putative applicant for review and the decision maker, out of which the applicant attempts to construct a "decision" which has not in fact

---

[34] [2002] 1 W.L.R. 1593.
[35] para.63 (emphasis added).
[36] In *Hanlon v Traffic Commissioner*, 1988 S.L.T. 802 at 805, Lord Prosser noted that "the length of any delay before implications of acquiescence arise will be almost infinitely variable depending on the circumstances." See also, *e.g. Atherton v Strathclyde RC*, 1995 S.L.T. 557; *McIntosh v Aberdeenshire Council*, 1998 S.L.T. 93.
[37] *op.cit.*, para.13.20.
[38] 2000 G.W.D. 14–514.
[39] See also, *e.g. Singh v S of S for the Home Dept*, 2000 S.L.T. 533; *Bett Properties Ltd v Scottish Ministers*, 2001 S.L.T. 1131.

yet been taken. Alternatively, there may be a complaint of prematurity where the applicant has failed to resort to an available statutory remedy.[40] Also, where there is real uncertainty whether the alleged unlawfulness is going to occur, an application may be dismissed as premature. Thus in *Scottish National Party v Scottish Television plc and Grampian Television plc*,[41] Lord Eassie remarked that the subject-matter of the application (allocation by the companies of broadcasting time for the SNP's party political broadcasts prior to the 1997 general election) was premature since neither company had at that point actually taken a decision on the question.[42]

Exhaustion of alternative remedies

As a general rule, a petitioner who has open to him alternative **12–09** remedies, such as a statutory appeal, must exhaust those remedies before he may competently apply for judicial review.[43] The rule reflects the underlying character of the supervisory jurisdiction, which exists to correct those wrongs for which no other remedy is provided; but it is not absolute,[44] and in "exceptional circumstances" a failure to exhaust will not bar a petition for review.[45]

Where the petitioner has failed to resort to his statutory remedy because of some mistake or procedural irregularity on the part of the respondent[46] recourse to judicial review will be permitted.[47] Other material factors include the adequacy of the alternative remedy[48]; the nature of the petitioner's complaint[49]; and, sometimes, considerations of pure practicality.[50]

---

[40] Clyde and Edwards, *Judicial Review, op.cit.*, para.13.09.
[41] Outer House, May 15, 1997 (unreported).
[42] See, generally, J. Beatson, "The Need to Develop Principles of Prematurity and Ripeness for Review" in *The Golden Metwand and the Crooked Cord: Essays in honour of Sir William Wade* (C. Forsyth and I. Hare eds, Clarendon, London, 1998), Ch.4.
[43] See Clyde and Edwards, *Judicial Review, op.cit.*, Ch.12; O'Neill, *Judicial* Review, *op.cit.*, paras 6.12–6.22; and see also the Rules of the Court of Session, r.58.3(2).
[44] See, *e.g. Leech v Deputy Governor of Parkhurst Prison* [1988] A.C. 533 at 581, where Lord Oliver doubted that the existence of an alternative remedy ever had the effect of ousting the court's jurisdiction.
[45] *British Railways Board v Glasgow Corp.*, 1976 S.C. 224.
[46] As in *Moss' Empires v Assessor for Glasgow*, 1917 S.C. (H.L.) 1 where the assessor omitted to inform the petitioner of its right of appeal.
[47] Where it is the petitioner's agent who fails to advise of a right of appeal, a like leniency is not shown: see, *e.g. Al-Mehdawi v S of S for the Home Dept* [1990] 1 A.C. 876; *Sangha v S of S for Scotland*, 1997 S.L.T. 544.
[48] See, *e.g. Accountant in Bankruptcy v Allans of Gillock Ltd*, 1991 S.L.T. 765.
[49] In *British Railways Board v Glasgow Corp.*, 1976 S.C. 224, Lord Wheatley held that averments of *ultra vires* or fraud would constitute "exceptional circumstances" justifying recourse to the supervisory jurisdiction.
[50] As in, *e.g. City Cabs (Edinburgh) Ltd v City of Edinburgh DC*, 1988 S.L.T. 184, where the decision challenged was of general application and one application for judicial review was thought to be a more expeditious way of dealing with the matter than via a large number of statutory appeals.

Ouster of judicial review

12–10   While factors such as prematurity, delay and exhaustion of alternative remedies may have the effect of excluding or limiting the availability of judicial review, preclusive or ouster clauses have that explicit objective. The courts have effectively declined to give effect to certain forms of ouster clause,[51] holding that, at most, all they are capable of doing is excluding the possibility of appeal as distinct from review, or that an ouster is effective only to protect *intra vires* determinations.[52] In principle, any such clause now falls to be tested against the common law canon of statutory interpretation to the effect that the subject's right of access to the court is not to be eroded other than by clear statutory language[53] and the parallel right of access to the courts under Article 6 of the Convention.[54]

A distinction must however be drawn between attempts to oust the jurisdiction of the courts outright, and those that limit it in some way. One example of this is to provide that a certificate or statement by the responsible authority stating the existence of a fact shall be "conclusive evidence" thereof, so that it is not open to the aggrieved individual to adduce evidence tending to show that the facts are not as so stated.[55] Another commonplace technique is for statutes conferring a right of appeal on a point of law to provide that the appeal must be taken within a specified, and usually short, period of time. The object of the statutory scheme is to oust the supervisory jurisdiction in favour of an exclusive, and time-limited, statutory remedy. In *Smith v East Elloe Rural District Council*,[56] the House of Lords held that the applicant was indeed confined to her statutory remedy, and although the speeches in *Anisminic Ltd v Foreign Compensation Commission*[57] appeared to

---

[51] Such as "finality clauses", which provide that the decision of a body shall be final; or "shall not be questioned" clauses, which provide that the decision shall not be questioned in any court of law whatever.

[52] *Anisminic Ltd v Foreign Compensation Commission* [1969] 2 A.C. 147.

[53] *Raymond v Honey* [1983] 1 A.C. 1; *R. v Lord Chancellor, ex p. Witham* [1998] Q.B. 575.

[54] First recognised as implicit in Art.6 in *Golder v UK* (1975) 1 E.H.R.R. 524.

[55] In *R. v Registrar of Companies, ex p. Central Bank of India* [1986] Q.B. 1114, Dillon L.J. noted that a computer search had unearthed over 300 instances of "conclusive evidence" clauses. For a home-grown example, see the Freedom of Information (Scotland) Act 2002, s.31(2), which provides that a certificate signed by a member of the Scottish Executive stating that information is exempt from the freedom of information regime on national security grounds shall be conclusive of that fact.

[56] [1956] A.C. 736.

[57] [1969] 2 A.C. 147.

cast doubt on *East Elloe*, its authority has been confirmed on a number of occasions since.[58]

SCOPE OF REVIEW

As is suggested by certain of the features of the application for **12–11** judicial review in Scotland, such as the absence of set time-limits and the reliance on the ordinary rules of title and interest, there is nothing inherently "public" about the supervisory jurisdiction. Naturally the nature of that jurisdiction was apt to include many actings by public authorities: as Lord Kinnear held in *Moss' Empires Ltd* v *Assessor for Glasgow*[59]:

> "Wherever any inferior tribunal or administrative body has exceeded the powers conferred on it by statute to the prejudice of the subject, the jurisdiction of the Court to set aside such excess of power as incompetent and illegal is not in doubt."

But the supervisory jurisdiction was invoked in many other cases where the decision making power in question was derived not from statute but from some other instrument such as a contract.[60]

The procedural changes introduced in 1985 did not (and could not) affect the jurisdiction of the Court of Session. But the advantages of the new application for judicial review in terms of expedition and, consequently, economy, were such as to prompt consideration of its proper scope. That exercise was greatly influenced, for a time, by developments in England as to the scope of judicial review there.[61] The principle of "procedural exclusivity", established by the House of Lords in *O'Reilly v Mackman*,[62] meant that in England, a person wishing to complain of an infringement

---

[58] See, *e.g. R. v S of S for the Environment, ex p. Ostler* [1977] Q.B. 122; *R. v Cornwall C, ex p. Huntington* [1994] 1 All E.R. 694. As Simon Brown L.J. put it in the latter case, "the intention of Parliament when it uses an *Anisminic* clause is that questions as to validity are not excluded. When paragraphs such as those in *ex p. Ostler* are used, then the legislative intention is that questions as to invalidity may be raised on the specified grounds in the prescribed time and in the prescribed manner, but that otherwise the jurisdiction of the court is excluded in the interests of certainty."

[59] 1917 S.C. (H.L.) 1 at 6.

[60] Hence, *e.g.* the susceptibility of arbiters to judicial review: see *Forbes v Underwood* (1886) 13 R. 465 and, more recently, *Shanks & McEwan (Contractors) Ltd v Mifflin Construction Ltd*, 1993 S.L.T. 1124.

[61] See, *e.g. Connor v Strathclyde RC*, 1986 S.L.T. 530; *Tehrani v Argyll and Clyde Health Board*, 1989 S.C. 342; *Safeway Food Stores Ltd v Scottish Provident Institution*, 1989 S.L.T. 131.

[62] [1983] 2 A.C. 237.

of "public law rights" was obliged to proceed by way of judicial review. This made it imperative to identify correctly the nature of one's claim, for a public law claim brought by way of ordinary action risked being struck out, without any inquiry into the merits, as an abuse of the process of the courts.[63] But reliance on this approach in Scotland was criticised as introducing unnecessary technicality at variance with the historical foundations of the supervisory jurisdiction in Scots law.[64] An authoritative statement of the scope of judicial review was finally provided in *West v Secretary of State for Scotland*, where Lord President Hope held as follows[65]:

> "The Court of Session has power, in the exercise of its supervisory jurisdiction, to regulate the process by which decisions are taken by any person or body to whom a jurisdiction, power or authority has been delegated or entrusted by statute, agreement or any other instrument. . . . The cases in which the supervisory jurisdiction is appropriate involve a tripartite relationship between the person or body to whom the jurisdiction, power or authority has been delegated or entrusted, the person or body by whom it has been delegated or entrusted and the person or persons in respect of or for whose benefit that jurisdiction, power or authority is to be exercised."

12–12   Plainly, therefore, judicial review is not confined to the statutory or prerogative powers of public authorities alone. Provided a reviewable jurisdiction exists, the supervisory jurisdiction may also extend to the acts and decisions of bodies which are not obviously "public" at all.[66] By the same token, however, just because a body is a public authority does not mean that all its acts and decisions will be subject to judicial review. In *West* itself, review was

---

[63] In time the English courts were able to mitigate the rigours of unbridled procedural exclusivity: see, *e.g. Roy v Kensington and Chelsea Family Practitioner Committee* [1992] 1 A.C. 624; *Trs of the Dennis Rye Pension Fund v Sheffield CC* [1998] 1 W.L.R. 840. Note, however, that the Civil Procedure Rules, r.54.1(2), still defines a claim for judicial review in England as (emphasis added) "a claim to review the lawfulness of—(i) an enactment; or (ii) a decision, action or failure to act in relation to the exercise of a *public function*."

[64] Lord Clyde, "The Nature of the Supervisory Jurisdiction and the Public/Private Distinction in Scots Administrative Law" in *Edinburgh Essays in Public Law* (Finnie, Himsworth and Walker eds, Edinburgh University Press, Edinburgh, 1991), p.281.

[65] 1992 S.C. 385 at 413.

[66] In addition to the cases on arbiters cited at n.60, see also *St Johnstone Football Club v Scottish Football Ass.*, 1965 S.L.T. 171 and *Gunstone v Scottish Women's Amateur Athletic Ass.*, 1987 S.L.T. 61 (sporting bodies); *McDonald v Burns*, 1940 S.C. 376 (religious bodies).

incompetent because the dispute between Mr West and the Secretary of State was essentially contractual, relating to the terms and conditions of Mr West's employment as a prison officer.[67] But while there is certainty at the core, uncertainty at the margins remains, and it may be that the Inner House will require at some point to revisit the test prescribed in *West*.[68] As it is, it is possible that, where the court finds difficulty in applying the tripartite relationship criterion to the facts before it,[69] the test collapses into something akin to the public/private divide used to determine the scope of review in England.[70]

GROUNDS FOR JUDICIAL REVIEW

In the *GCHQ* case,[71] Lord Diplock summarised the grounds on **12–13** which judicial review may be sought as follows:

> "Judicial review has I think developed to a stage today when one can conveniently classify under three heads the grounds on which administrative action is subject to control by judicial review. The first ground I would call 'illegality', the second 'irrationality' and the third 'procedural impropriety'."

These three headings, illegality, irrationality and procedural impropriety, each comprise a number of more specific principles of review, many of which interact or overlap. They are also elastic, in that the courts have progressively extended their scope and meaning, and do not necessarily exhaust the field. Lord Diplock himself anticipated the future reception into domestic administrative law of review on grounds of proportionality, which, if not explicitly by name, came to be applied by the courts even in advance of the Human Rights Act.

---

[67] But employment matters may in certain circumstances be reviewable, see, *e.g. Malloch v Aberdeen Corp.*, 1971 S.C. (H.L.) 85; *Rooney v Chief Constable of Strathclyde Police*, 1997 S.L.T. 1261; *Maclean v Glasgow CC*, 1997 S.C.L.R. 1049.

[68] For discussion of *West*, see W. J. Wolffe, "The Scope of Judicial Review in Scots Law" [1992] P.L. 625; C. M. G. Himsworth, "Judicial Review in Scotland" in *Judicial Review: A thematic approach* (Hadfield ed., Macmillan, London, 1995).

[69] As witness the differing outcomes in *Naik v University of Stirling*, 1994 S.L.T. 449 and *Joobeen v University of Stirling*, 1995 S.L.T. 120.

[70] It should be noted that the competency of an application for judicial review of an alleged breach of the HRA 1998, s.6 (*i.e.* the duty laid on public authorities, including bodies exercising "public functions"), will depend upon a distinction between public and private functions.

[71] *Council of Civil Service Unions v Minister for the Civil Service* [1985] A.C. 374 at 410. Lord Diplock's classification was adopted in Scotland *in City of Edinburgh Council v S of S for Scotland*, 1985 S.C. 261.

ILLEGALITY

12–14 In one sense, a decision could be said to be illegal whatever the reason for the court's intervention. But as a discrete head of review, illegality means something narrower than this. Judicial review involves the control of powers, and at the most basic level this means ensuring that a given power is only exercised in the circumstances envisaged and on the conditions imposed by the donor, whether Parliament or some other body. Where the decision-maker misinterprets or fails to apply the conditions of the grant of his power, or jurisdiction, he confers on himself an authority it was never intended that he should have.[72] Thus the court on review will as a matter of principle ascertain whether the conditions for an exercise of jurisdiction were met, and if it finds that they were not will[73] reduce the decision as being *ultra vires*. Review on this ground is often discussed in terms of error, whether of law or of fact, on the part of the decision-maker. But review for illegality goes further than this. A grant of power may be more or less prescriptive in the conditions it imposes on the power's exercise. But even where it apparently imposes no conditions[74] the courts presume that powers are granted subject to certain implied limitations. Although this is explained in terms of assumed legislative intent, these limitations are very much the product of judicial innovation, and have greatly extended the scope of review for illegality.

Jurisdiction and error

12–15   We have seen that the supervisory jurisdiction is to be distinguished from appellate procedures. One of the consequences of this distinction was that, since the supervisory jurisdiction is concerned only with the legal validity of decisions and not with their rightness or wrongness, errors were not reviewable and the only possibility of correcting these depended on the availability of a right of appeal. This was never an absolute rule. An error, whether of law or of fact, which vitiated the power of a body to act or decide might be reviewed because in making such an error the decision maker stepped outside the four corners of his jurisdiction, conferring on himself an authority he did not have. Such errors

---

[72] Thus, in *McColl v Strathclyde RC*, 1983 S.L.T. 616, it was held that the local authority's statutory duty to provide "wholesome water" did not entitle it to fluoridate the water in the interests of dental health.

[73] On when is appropriate for the court to decline to reduce a decision which has been held to be flawed, see *e.g. Anderson v S of S for Work and Pensions*, 2002 S.L.T. 68.

[74] *e.g.* where a statute confers "subjective discretion" on a minister or official to act "if he thinks fit".

were (and are) described as "jurisdictional" errors, and the scope
of review on this basis depended upon where the courts drew the
line between such errors and non-jurisdictional errors that the body
was at liberty (subject to any appeal) to make. The decision of the
House of Lords in *Anisminic Ltd v Foreign Compensation Commission*[75] is often said to have done away with the distinction between
jurisdictional and non-jurisdictional errors of *law*.[76] But that is true
neither of Scots law[77] nor even, strictly speaking, of English law.
Certainly in *R. v Hull University Visitor, ex p. Page*[78] the House of
Lords unanimously held that Parliament was to be presumed to
confer statutory powers only on the footing that they were
exercised on a correct legal basis, with the consequence that any
misdirection in law in making the decision would render it *ultra
vires*. But the majority also held that the decision in *Page* was not
susceptible to reduction[79] because his jurisdiction was not governed
by statute or the general law of the land, but by a peculiar,
domestic system of law founded in the rules of the institution.
Likewise in Scotland, where a "special jurisdiction" is being
exercised, the Court of Session will intervene on review to correct a
jurisdictional error, which causes the decision-maker to embark
upon an inquiry and take a decision where he should not, but will
decline to pronounce upon the proper interpretation and application of the rules within the exercise of that jurisdiction. As Lord
Eassie put it in *Codona v Appeal Tribunal of the Showmen's Guild
of Great Britain*[80]:

> "Perhaps in some contrast to the exercise by a public official
> or body of an administrative power, where parties have by

---

[75] [1969] 2 A.C. 147.

[76] See, *e.g. O'Reilly v Mackman* [1983] 2 A.C. 237 at 278, *per* Lord Diplock; *R. v Hull
University Visitor, ex p. Page* [1993] A.C. 682 at 702, *per* Lord Browne-Wilkinson.

[77] See, *Watt v Lord Advocate*, 179 S.C. 120, which followed *Anisminic*, above, but
which made clear that not every error of law made by a tribunal or other inferior
body would cause that body to exceed its jurisdiction.

[78] [1993] A.C. 682.

[79] In England, *certiorari* or, now, a "quashing order".

[80] 2002 S.L.T. 299. See also, *e.g. McDonald v Burns*, 1940 S.C. 376, where it was held
that ecclesiastical tribunals were "protected from review in the same degree as
the proceedings of arbiters are protected." An arbiter's decision is not reviewable
on grounds on non-jurisdictional error of law: *Shanks & McEwan (Contractors)
Ltd v Mifflin Construction Ltd*, 1993 S.L.T. 1124; nor is the decision of a domestic
tribunal exercising similar, arbitral functions: *O'Neill v Scottish Joint Negotiating
Committee*, 1987 S.L.T. 648. See, generally, P. Gilmour, "Judicial Review of
Errors of Law" 1993 S.L.T. 371. It may be said that, by different routes, Scots and
English law achieve similar results, Scots law by extending the scope of review to
bodies which are not public but by limiting the grounds on which, in respect of
certain bodies, review may be sought; English law by restricting review to public
authorities but applying certain principles derived from public law, notably in
relation to the observance of natural justice, in private law proceedings: see, *e.g.
Nagle v Feilden* [1966] 2 Q.B. 633, *Edwards v SOGAT* [1971] Ch. 354.

agreement conferred on a body the power of interpretation of the law and its application to their dispute and have agreed to accept the determination as final, that agreement on finality is a matter to be respected and provides reason for the court's not interfering with an intra-jurisdictional error of law."

There are other caveats to the proposition that all errors of law are reviewable, beyond this important qualification. In *Wordie Property Ltd v Secretary of State for Scotland*,[81] Lord President Emslie held that a decision of the Secretary of State acting within his statutory remit would be *ultra vires* if he improperly exercised a discretion confided to him, in particular "if [his decision] is based upon a *material error* of law going to the root of the question for determination."[82] More broadly, the language of "error" suggests that legal questions are susceptible only of one, objectively verifiable, answer. That is not (or not always) the case, as is apparent in the decision of the House of Lords in *R. v Monopolies and Mergers Commission, ex p. South Yorkshire Transport Ltd*.[83] There, the commission had power to take action where it was satisfied that a monopoly situation existed in "a substantial part of the United Kingdom". The commission purported to exercise this power on the basis of a monopoly situation found to exist in an area amounting to only 1.65 per cent of the total area of the United Kingdom. The company argued that in treating so small an area as "substantial", the commission had erred in law and its decision was accordingly *ultra vires*. The House of Lords disagreed:

> "The courts have repeatedly warned against the dangers of taking an inherently imprecise word and by redefining it thrusting on it a spurious degree of precision. . . . The question is whether the Commission has placed the phrase broadly in the right part of the spectrum of possible meanings [and] within the permissible field of judgment. . . . The statutory criterion of jurisdiction might itself be so imprecise that different decision makers, each acting rationally, might reach differing conclusions when applying it to the facts of a given case. In such a case, the court is entitled to substitute its

---

[81] 1984 S.L.T. 345.

[82] *ibid.*, at 347. See also *R. v Hull University Visitor, ex p. Page* [1993] A.C. 682 at 701, where Lord Browne-Wilkinson held that in order to justify intervention the error complained of required to be "relevant and material".

[83] [1993] 1 W.L.R. 23, followed in Scotland in *Stagecoach Holdings Ltd v S of S for Trade and Industry*, 1997 S.L.T. 940. See also, *e.g. R. v Broadcasting Complaints Commission, ex p. Granada Television Ltd* [1995] E.M.L.R. 163; *R. v Radio Authority, ex p. Bull* [1998] Q.B. 294; *R. v Broadcasting Standards Commission, ex p. British Broadcasting Corp.* [2000] 3 W.L.R. 1327.

own opinion for that of the person to whom the decision has been entrusted only if the decision is so aberrant that it cannot be classed as rational."[84]

This is not to say that the courts will always accord a generous margin of interpretation to the primary decision-maker.[85] In appropriate cases, particularly those involving fundamental rights, they may confine the "spectrum of possible meanings" so closely as to leave only one answer to a given question of statutory interpretation, such that the decision-maker falls into error if he fails to answer that question correctly.[86]

What then of errors of fact? As with errors of law, "jurisdic- **12–16** tional" errors of fact have always been reviewable.[87] Where material findings of fact are reached on the basis of no evidence, again the courts will intervene.[88] But "outside those categories, we do not accept that a decision can be flawed in this court, which is not an appellate tribunal, upon the ground of mistake of fact."[89] Such an approach is not without justification. While a court on review may fairly regard itself as best placed to provide an authoritative interpretation on questions of law (subject to the qualifications noted above), it does not follow that it is best placed to determine questions of fact. The primary decision-maker may have arrived at his findings of fact after a lengthy process of evaluation, possibly hearing witnesses or considering representations, and his function may involve the application of specialist expertise or experience. For a court on review to denominate such findings as erroneous, other than where the error is manifest, involves a substitution of judgment that is far less easy to justify or explain. It seems clear,

---

[84] *South Yorkshire Transport, op.cit., per* Lord Mustill.

[85] All the authorities noted above involved the exercise of regulatory functions, where the reasons for judicial deference (expertise of the decision maker and corresponding lack of judicial familiarity with the policy and other issues bound up in the decision) are perhaps especially pronounced.

[86] See, *e.g. R. v S of S for the Home Dept, ex p. Adan* [2001] 2 A.C. 477.

[87] *R. v S of S for the Home Dept, ex p. Khawaja* [1984] A.C. 74; *Tan Te Lam v Superintendent of Tai A Chau Detention Centre* [1997] A.C. 97.

[88] *Colleen Properties Ltd v Minister of Housing* [1971] 1 W.L.R. 433; *R. v Hillingdon London BC, ex p. Islam* [1981] 3 W.L.R. 942.

[89] *R. v London Residuary Body, ex p. Inner London Education Authority, The Times,* July 24, 1987, *per* Watkins L.J. After consideration of the "difficult and elusive issue" of whether error of fact qualified as an independent ground of review, the Court of Appeal in *Wandsworth London BC v A* [2000] 1 W.L.R. 1246, adopted this analysis, citing also the observation of Lord Brightman in *R. v Hillingdon London BC, ex p. Puhlhofer* [1986] A.C. 484 at 518 that "it is the duty of the court to leave the decision [as to the existence of a fact] to the public body to whom Parliament has entrusted the decision-making power, save in a case where it is obvious that the public body, consciously or unconsciously, was acting perversely."

however, that the courts are increasingly willing to intervene on the basis of errors of fact, even where the finding of fact is not a condition precedent to the exercise of jurisdiction. In *R. v Parliamentary Commissioner for Administration, ex p. Balchin*,[90] for example, where the question was whether the Parliamentary Ombudsman had asked himself the wrong question in deciding whether or not there was maladministration, Sedley J. held that "if there is such an error, it does not have to be defined as one of law or of fact (*the latter too being reviewable if crucial to the decision*)."[91] In particular, it may be that the courts now require to take a more exacting approach to the review of the factual basis of decisions in order to comply with their duties under the Human Rights Act, principally because judicial review might otherwise fail to satisfy the requirements of Article 6 of the Convention. European and domestic case law recognise that breaches of Article 6 by a primary decision-maker may be "cured" where there is recourse to a higher court or tribunal having "full jurisdiction" and which does meet the guarantees of Article 6. This need not in all circumstances involve a full right of appeal,[92] but in certain contexts the restriction of the supervisory jurisdiction to questions of legal validity may deprive it of the fullness of jurisdiction necessary to secure compliance with the fair hearing guarantees.[93] Thus in *R (Javed) v Secretary of State for the Home Department*.[94] The Court of Appeal held that, although historically reluctant to evaluate evidence when reviewing the decisions of the executive,[95] the courts have had a positive duty since the entry into force of the Human Rights Act to give effect to the Convention and to ensure that there is an effective remedy in cases of suspected breaches of the Convention rights. Therefore, where an executive decision requires to be reviewed on its facts, the court is competent to carry out the evaluative exercise once the relevant material is placed before it.[96] In that case, the applicants successfully claimed judicial review of the Home Secretary's decision to include and retain Pakistan on the so-called "white list" of countries in which it appeared to him that there was in general no

---

[90] [1998] 1 P.L.R. 1.
[91] *R. v Parliamentary Commissioner for Administration, ex p. Balchin* [1998] 1 P.L.R. 1 at (emphasis added) See also *Anderson v S of S for Work and Pensions*, 2002 S.L.T. 68.
[92] See, *e.g. Bryan v UK* (1995) 21 E.H.R.R. 342; *ISKCON v UK* (1994) 76-A D.R. 90.
[93] See, *e.g. Kingsley v UK* [2001] 33 E.H.R.R. 13.
[94] [2002] 3 Q.B. 129.
[95] For an emphatic expression of that reluctance, see the speech of Lord Templeman in *R. v Independent Television Commission, ex p. TSW Broadcasting Ltd* [1996] J.R. 185.
[96] See also *R. v S of S for the Home Dept, ex p. Turqut* [2001] 1 All E.R. 719 at 729, *per* Simon Brown L.J.

serious risk of persecution, on the grounds that such a conclusion simply was not justified by Pakistan's human rights record.[98]

Illegality and general principles of statutory construction

In construing legislation, the overriding aim of the court is to **12–17** give effect to the intention of the legislature as expressed in the words used. In identifying the intention of the legislature, the courts are guided by established and accepted principles of statutory construction.[99] For example, in the absence of express words or necessary implication, it is presumed that the legislature does not intend to authorise interference with the liberty of the individual; or the retrospective operation of its enactments so as to upset vested rights and interests; or the deprivation of property without payment of compensation. Prior to the entry into force of the Human Rights Act, the courts took this further, adopting a presumption that the legislature did not intend to authorise any violation of the rights protected by the Convention absent express words or necessary implication to the contrary.[99] This common law presumption has now been supplanted by section 3(1) of the Human Rights Act 1998, which requires all courts and tribunals to read and give effect to legislation, whenever enacted, in a manner compatible with the Convention rights.[1] But this far from exhausts

---

[97] In *Javed*, it may be that on the (extensive) evidence placed before the court, the Home Secretary's "error" had the qualities of materiality and obviousness that serve to excuse judicial intervention. Even in cases engaging the Convention rights, however, it may be appropriate, on grounds of relative institutional competence, for the court on review to accord a fairly generous margin of discretion to the primary decision maker when scrutinising the factual bases of his decision. The strict scrutiny of the decision maker's evaluation of the evidence available to him (leaving aside the question whether he had regard to all relevant considerations) that is apposite in cases engaging, *e.g.* the right to life or freedom from inhuman and degrading treatment, may be less apposite, and indeed offensive to the separation of powers, where the decision relates to complex issues of social or economic policy, and the determination to be reached is not simply an objective issue of fact but rather a question of "fact and degree": see, *e.g. Edwards v Bairstow* [1956] A.C. 14, and above, para. 12–15.

[98] See, *e.g. R. v S of S for the Environment, ex p. Spath Holme Ltd* [2001] 2 A.C. 349 at 397–398, *per* Lord Nicholls; *Wilson v First County Trust Ltd (No.2)* (2003) 3 W.L.R. 568 (HL), para.54, *per* Lord Nicholls.

[99] Among the leading cases, see *R. v S of S for the Home Dept, ex p. Leech (No. 2)* [1994] Q.B. 198; *R. v S of S for the Home Dept, ex p. McQuillan* [1995] 4 All E.R. 400; *R. v S of S for Social Security, ex p. Joint Council for the Welfare of Immigrants* [1996] 4 All E.R. 385; *R. v Lord Chancellor, ex p. Witham* [1997] 2 All E.R. 779; *R. v S of S for the Home Dept, ex p. Pierson* [1998] A.C. 539.

[1] Although HRA 1998, s.3(1), applies to legislation whether enacted prior or subsequent to the 1998 Act, the interpretive duty it prescribes does not operate retrospectively so as to render unlawful decisions and transactions which took place prior to the entry into force of the Act: *Wilson v First County Trust Ltd (No.2)* [2003] 3 W.L.R. 568. That case concerned a loan agreement entered into

the field of principles of statutory construction. The courts have always taken the view that a grant of power is subject to certain inherent, if implied, limitations of a general rather than specific nature.[2] Even where the legislature confers "subjective" discretionary power[3] there is no such thing as an unfettered discretion, as the House of Lords made clear in *Padfield v Minister of Agriculture*.[4] There, the minister had refused to exercise his statutory power to appoint a committee to investigate complaints that the Milk Marketing Board had fixed milk prices in a manner unduly unfavourable to the complainants. The House of Lords held that the reasons the minister had given for his refusal showed that he had acted *ultra vires*, in taking account of legally irrelevant considerations and using his power in such a way as to thwart the policy and purposes of the enabling Act read as a whole. Even if the minister had given no reasons, the court would still have been competent to infer that he had acted unlawfully, provided a *prima face* case of misuse of power was made out.

The extent to which the courts will intervene at this level varies according to the statutory wording itself, the subject-matter of the statute, its impact on the rights or interests of those affected, and to more general considerations of justiciability.[5] Irrelevant considerations as a ground of review shade into the pursuit of improper or extraneous purposes, simply because both issues have to be addressed by reference to the policy and purposes of the statute

---

by Mrs Wilson with a finance company, to whom the debtor pawned her car as security. The loan agreement was regulated by the Consumer Credit Act 1974, and, since it failed to comply with certain formalities required by that Act, was held unenforceable by the creditor. Thus the debtor, who failed to repay the loan timeously, was able to keep the sum of the loan and recover possession of her car. On the company's appeal to the Court of Appeal, which was heard after the entry into force of the HRA 1998, the Vice-Chancellor expressed the view that this outcome was inconsistent with the creditor's Convention rights and, following a hearing on that issue, made a declaration of incompatibility in respect of the relevant provisions of the 1974 Act: *Wilson v First County Trust Ltd (No.2)* [2002] Q.B. 74. The House of Lords held unanimously that this was, in the words of Lord Hobhouse (para.127), "a work of supererogation and improper." The transaction between the parties was concluded prior to the entry into force of the 1998 Act, and it was not open to a court to treat the Convention rights as if they were in force prior to that event. The declaration of incompatibility was therefore set aside on the basis that the Court of Appeal had had no jurisdiction to make it (and their Lordships also held, *obiter*, that in any case the provisions of the 1974 Act were not incompatible with the Convention rights).

[2] See, *e.g. Kruse v Johnson* [1898] 2 Q.B. 91 at 100, *per* Lord Russell of Killowen C.J.; *Associated Provincial Picture Houses Ltd v Wednesbury Corp.* [1948] 1 K.B. 223 at 229, 230, *per* Lord Greene M.R.

[3] Entitling a minister to act "if he thinks fit" or some similar formula.

[4] [1968] A.C. 997.

[5] See, *e.g. S of S for Education v Tameside Metropolitan BC* [1977] A.C. 1014 at 1047–1048, *per* Lord Wilberforce.

read as a whole. The difficulty is that most statutes do not make explicit which considerations are "relevant" and which purposes "proper".[6] Given the open-textured nature of the exercise, majority decisions are commonplace and the distinctions between the cases often appear rather fine.

Particularly vexed is the question whether a public authority may properly rely on financial or resource considerations in taking discretionary decisions. In *R. v Cambridge and Huntingdon Area Health Authority, ex p. B*,[7] the authority refused to provide treatment to a child suffering from leukaemia on the grounds that its cost could not be justified by reference to its likelihood of success. At first instance, Laws J. held that this was *ultra vires*: cost-benefit analyses had no part to play where a life was at stake. Reversing this decision, the Court of Appeal held that resource issues were a relevant consideration, properly taken into account, with other factors, by the authority. In such circumstances, the court should intervene only where bad faith or irrationality was apparent. Again, in *R. v Gloucester County Council, ex p. Barry*,[8] the House of Lords held (by a majority of three to two) that the local authority could have regard to resource constraints in assessing needs under the Chronically Sick and Disabled Persons Act 1970, provided that it had regard to other relevant consideration (currently acceptable living standards and the nature and extent of the individual's disability) and did not attach undue importance to resource considerations in this calculation. However, in *R. v Sefton Metropolitan Borough Council, ex p. Help the Aged*,[9] the Court of Appeal held that, while a local authority was entitled to have regard to its scarce financial resources in deciding whether a person was in need of care and attention, once it had so decided, it was obliged to fulfil its statutory duty to make arrangements for accommodation for that person and lack of resources was no excuse for failure. In a different context, the House of Lords held in *R. v East Sussex County Council, ex p. Tandy*[10] (reversing the decision of Court of Appeal) that a resource-driven decision to reduce the number of home tuition hours provided to a child unable for health reasons to attend school was *ultra vires*: the duty of the local authority was to provide "suitable education", which was to be determined solely by

---

[6] That is not invariably the case. Legislation and related instruments in fields such as planning or economic regulation often prescribe relevant considerations or relevant objectives to which the decision-maker must have regard. Such statements of objectives should *not*, however, be treated as exhaustive: see, *e.g. R. v Leicester C, ex p. Blackfordby and Boothorpe Action Group Ltd*, Mar. 15, 2000 (unreported); *R. v Derbyshire C, ex p. Murray, The Times*, Nov. 8, 2000.

[7] [1995] 2 All E.R. 129 ("the *Child B* case").

[8] [1997] A.C. 584.

[9] [1997] 4 All E.R. 532.

[10] [1998] A.C. 714.

reference to educational considerations. Only if there was more than one way of providing suitable education would the authority be entitled to have regard to its resources in choosing which method to adopt.

12–18   The cases are rather less opaque where the complaint is that a decision has been taken in order to promote particular moral or political objectives. Thus in *Gerry Cottle's Circus Ltd v City of Edinburgh District Council*,[11] the local authority acted *ultra vires* in refusing to licence a circus on the basis of a policy premised on the view that "the whole concept of animals performing in circuses is wrong". Again, in *R. v Somerset County Council, ex p. Fewings*,[12] the local authority resolved to ban deer hunting with dogs on council-owned land. The land had been acquired under a statute generally authorising acquisition of land for "the benefit, improvement or development of their area", which purpose was interpreted as allowing the pursuit of objects which would conduce to the better management of the estate. In founding solely on moral repugnance to hunting, the council had pursued a purpose ulterior to those allowed by the statute.

But where the very substance of a discretionary power pertains to wider moral, ethical or social choices, the courts may be less willing to intervene. In *Gillick v West Norfolk and Wisbech Area Health Authority*,[13] for example, Lord Bridge held that the supervisory jurisdiction should be exercised with "the utmost restraint in cases involving questions of social and ethical controversy." The legislature is the proper forum for the resolution of such questions (subject now to the constraints imposed on legislative competence by human rights considerations). Similar restraint is observable where the decision under attack involves questions of economic or regulatory policy, for the more complex and polycentric a question, the less suited are the courts to its resolution.[14]

These considerations are related to the broader question of justiciability, or the amenability of a decision to the judicial process.[15] Non-justiciability accounted for the near-immunity from review accorded in the past to exercises of prerogative power. In light of the *GCHQ* case,[16] it is now clear that the subject-matter of a power rather than its source is the crucial factor conditioning the

---

[11] 1990 S.L.T. 235.

[12] [1995] 3 All E.R. 20.

[13] [1986] 1 A.C. 112.

[14] *Nottinghamshire C v S of S for the Environment* [1986] A.C. 240; *R. v S of S for the Environment, ex p. Hammersmith and Fulham London BC* [1991] 1 A.C. 521; *East Kilbride DC v S of S for Scotland*, 1995 S.L.T. 1238.

[15] *Council of Civil Service Unions v Minister for the Civil Service* [1985] A.C. 374 at 418, *per* Lord Roskill.

[16] *Council of Civil Service Unions v Minister for the Civil Service* [1985] A.C. 374.

reach of judicial review.[17] But many prerogative powers do concern matters of high governmental policy, and will continue to be treated as non-justiciable on that account.

Wrongful delegation

Review at the level of illegality may also involve the question of **12–19** wrongful delegation, where it is argued that the decision-maker lacked competence to arrive at the decision complained of as the power to take such decisions was conferred on another. Thus, for example, in *Vine v National Dock Labour Board*,[18] the House of Lords granted a declaration that the dismissal of a registered dock worker was invalid because the Board, instead of deciding the matter itself, had improperly entrusted the decision to its disciplinary committee. But, although the maxim *delegatus non potest delegare* has been applied at the cost of official convenience,[19] it is not to be regarded as an absolute rule. Rather, it reflects a special canon of statutory construction, which may be displaced by indications of a contrary legislative intent.

The principle applies to powers of all kinds, but is likely to apply with greater rigour to powers classified as "legislative"' or "judicial" (bearing in mind that such classifications should be approached with caution).[20] While administrative processes are subject to the rule against wrongful delegation, greater tolerance tends to be shown to large or busy or multi-functional organisations.[21] On occasion, the application of the rule shades explicitly into procedural impropriety, as where decisions have been struck down because of delegation to an outside body or because of participation by non-members in the taking of decisions.[22] Similarly, arrangements characterised as "acting under dictation" have been held to fall foul of the rule,[23] although this might be better described as a species of wrongful fettering of discretion.

A special rule, the *Carltona* principle, applies to central government, whereby officials are treated as the Minister's *alter ego*.[24]

---

[17] For post-*GCHQ* examples of review of the prerogative, see *R. v S of S for Foreign and Commonwealth Affairs, ex p. Everett* [1989] Q.B. 811 and *R. v S of S for the Home Dept, ex p. Bentley* [1994] Q.B. 349.

[18] *Vine v National Dock Labour Board* [1957] A.C. 488.

[19] See, *e.g. R. v Gateshead Justices, ex p. Tesco Stores Ltd* [1981] 1 All E.R. 1027.

[20] See, *e.g. R. v Croydon Justices, ex p. W. H. Smith Ltd*, Nov. 6, 2000 (unreported), in which it was held that the power of a health and safety inspector to institute criminal proceedings under s.38 of the Health and Safety at Work Act 1974 could not be delegated.

[21] *Selvarajan v Race Relations Board* [1976] 1 All E.R. 12; *R. v Independent Broadcasting Authority, ex p. Whitehouse*, The Times, Apr. 4, 1985

[22] As in *Leary v National Union of Vehicle Builders* [1971] Ch. 34.

[23] As in *Lavender v Minister of Housing and Local Government* [1970] 1 W.L.R. 1231.

[24] *Carltona Ltd v Commissioner of Works* [1943] 2 All E.R. 560.

Exceptionally, statutes may exclude the *Carltona* principle, but it was held in *R. v Secretary of State for the Home Department, ex p. Oladehinde*[25] that the implication of exclusion is not easily to be drawn.

The rule against fettering

12–20 The whole point of discretionary powers is to allow the latitude for reaching decisions in accordance with the public interest and with the circumstances and merits of particular cases. Thus a public authority entrusted with discretionary powers cannot validly disable its decision-making freedom, whether by entering into contracts, making representations or adhering to over-rigid rules or policies. Again, the rule against fettering is not absolute. It should also be noted that the promises, representations and assurances given by a public authority may generate legitimate expectations on the part of citizens, which may be protected by a court on review.

Public authorities enter into contracts as a matter of routine, but as most contracts fetter freedom of action in some way there may be difficult questions of degree in determining exactly how far the authority may validly bind itself as to the future. In a number of cases, the courts have held contracts entered into by public authorities as being *ultra vires* and void because incompatible with the authority's wider statutory functions.[26] This is not to say that a public authority should in all circumstances be freed from its private law obligations, or that an authority is never competent to limit its discretion by entering into contracts. As Lord Blackburn held in *Attorney-General v Great Eastern Ry*[27]:

> "The doctrine of *ultra vires* ought to be reasonably, and not unreasonably, understood and applied, and whatever may fairly be regarded as incidental to, or consequential upon, those things which the legislature has authorised ought not (unless expressly prohibited) be held by judicial construction to be *ultra vires*."

As Viscount Simonds explained in *British Transport Commission v Westmorland County Council*,[28] a public authority cannot by contract sterilise or renounce "part of its statutory birthright". There will require to be a fairly manifest incompatibility between the contract and the authority's statutory functions in order to satisfy this test.[29]

---

[25] [1991] 1 A.C. 254.
[26] See, *e.g. Ayr Harbour Trs v Oswald* (1883) 8 App Cas 623; *Birkdale District Electricity Supply Co v Southport Corp.* [1926] A.C. 355.
[27] *Attorney-General v Great Eastern Ry* (1880) 5 App. Cas. 473.
[28] *British Transport Commission v Westmorland CC* [1958] A.C. 126.
[29] See, *e.g. R. v Hammersmith and Fulham London BC, ex p. Beddowes* [1987] 1 Q.B. 1050.

Short of contract, a public authority may make representations or give assurances to members of the public, from which it seeks subsequently to resile. May it do so? Unquestionably, where there has been reliance on a representation or assurance, substantial injustice may be done where the public authority goes back on its word. Equally, however, an *ultra vires* representation or assurance, if enforced, could have the effect of enlarging the scope of a public authority's powers beyond the limits prescribed by the legislature. In some cases, the courts drew an analogy between the representations of public authorities and common law doctrines of estoppel or personal bar in order to hold that an authority could not, adversely to the interests of the citizen, resile from a representation relied on by him.[30] The House of Lords recently conceded the similarity between the private law concepts of estoppel/personal bar and the public law concept of legitimate expectations, but added that "public law has already absorbed whatever is useful from the moral values which underlie the private law concept of estoppel and the time has come for it to stand upon its own two feet."[31] The key moral value underpinning the doctrine of estoppel is that it would be unconscionable for a person to deny what he has represented or agreed. But in the field of public law, this principle cannot be given its full force because there may be wider public interests at stake which justify departing from the representation or assurance in question.[32]

A complaint of unlawful fettering may also arise in circum- **12–21** stances where the over-rigid application of a rule or policy is said to have precluded proper consideration of an individual's claim or case.[33] In one sense, there is much to be said for the adoption of rules and policies. They may speed up decision-making processes, and conduce to greater consistency and certainty. But responsiveness is an equally important virtue of administrative decision

---

[30] This approach is especially associated with Lord Denning: see *Robertson v Minister of Pensions* [1949] 1 K.B. 227; *Wells v Minister of Housing and Local Government* [1967] 1 W.L.R. 1000; *Lever Finance Ltd v Westminster London BC* [1971] Q.B. 222. Lord Denning's reasoning in *Robertson* was disapproved by the House of Lords in *Howell v Falmouth Boat Construction Co Ltd* [1951] A.C. 837. Nor did arguments of personal bar avail the applicant in *Western Fish Products Ltd v Penwith DC* [1981] 2 All E.R. 204.

[31] *R. v East Sussex C, ex p. Reprotech (Pebsham) Ltd* [2003] 1 W.L.R. 348, para.35, *per* Lord Hoffmann.

[32] For the doctrine of legitimate expectations, see paras 12–30—12–32. Note also that in circumstances where an individual has suffered loss through reliance on a representation or assurance by a public authority, a remedy in damages might lie on the basis of negligent misstatement, as in *Minister for Housing and Local Government v Sharp* [1970] 2 Q.B. 223.

[33] As with representations and assurances, the adoption of rules and policies may also generate legitimate expectations which the courts will protect as a matter of procedural fairness.

making—indeed, it is in the interests of responsiveness that discretionary powers are conferred—and the task of the court in this regard is to reconcile the competing objectives. It is clear that an authority charged with a discretionary power may develop and apply a policy as to the approach he will adopt in the generality of cases.[34] But as Lord Browne-Wilkinson held in *R. v Secretary of State for the Home Department, ex p. Venables and Thompson*,[35] "the position is different if the policy adopted is such as to preclude the person on whom the power is conferred from departing from the policy or from taking into account circumstances which are relevant to the particular case in relation to which the discretion is being exercised. If such an inflexible and invariable policy is adopted both the policy and the decisions taken pursuant to it will be unlawful."[36]

PROCEDURAL IMPROPRIETY

12–22 As with review for illegality, procedural impropriety covers a variety of more specific grounds of attack. At one level, it may involve nothing more than ensuring that prescribed procedural standards have been observed; but the application for common law standards of natural justice and fairness goes much further than this, even to the extent of "supplying the omission of the legislature"[37] where necessary to ensure that decision-makers act fairly in their dealings with the citizen.

Compliance with prescribed procedural requirements

12–23 Statutes conferring power on public authorities commonly impose procedural conditions, such as the serving of notice, a duty to consult, or a requirement to give reasons for a decision once taken. A distinction is sometimes made in this regard between mandatory and directory procedural requirements: non-compliance with the former, but not the latter, is said to be fatal to the validity of a decision. The utility of the distinction, other than as a very general guide, may be questioned. It has been held, for example, that a condition may be both mandatory and directory: mandatory as to substantial compliance, but directory as to precise compliance.[38] Equally, like many of the distinctions drawn in

---

[34] See, *e.g. R. v Port of London Authority, ex p. Kynoch* [1919] 1 K.B. 176; *British Oxygen Co Ltd v Board of Trade* [1970] A.C. 610.

[35] [1998] A.C. 407.

[36] Instances of over-rigid application of policies contrary to this principle include *R. v Warwickshire C, ex p. Collymore* [1995] E.L.R. 217; *R. v Lambeth London BC, ex p. Njomo* [1996] 28 H.L.R. 737; and *R. v North West Lancashire Health Authority, ex p. A* [2000] 1 W.L.R. 977.

[37] *Cooper v Wandsworth Board of Works* (1863) 14 C.B. (NS) 180.

[38] *R. v Chief Constable of Merseyside Police, ex p. Calveley* [1986] Q.B. 424, CA.

administrative law, it is far from self-executing. Statutes rarely make clear what the effect of non-compliance with a prescribed procedural requirement is to be, so that it falls to the courts to determine the issue. This is a question of construction to be decided by reference to the whole scheme and purpose of the measure, weighing the importance of the condition, the prejudice to private rights and interests flowing from non-compliance and the claims of the wider public interest.[39] Seen in that light, as Lord Hailsham L.C. remarked in *London & Clydeside Estates v Aberdeen District Council,*[40] the mandatory/directory distinction presents "not so much a stark choice of alternatives as a spectrum of possibilities in which one compartment or description fades gradually into another." Again in *R. v Immigration Appeal Tribunal, ex p. Jeyeanthan,*[41] Lord Woolf M.R. held that "it is much more import-ant to focus on the consequences of the non-compliance" than to seek to force procedural requirements into rigid categories.

Even where a statutory procedural code is comprehensive in its coverage, the courts may be called upon to decide whether it has been properly fulfilled. A statutory duty to consult is unlikely to stipulate that the consultation be "genuine" and conducted in a manner which allows interested parties a reasonable opportunity to respond. A duty to give reasons will not insist in terms that the reasons are adequate, intelligible and properly connected to the facts. But the courts will add these glosses to the statutory language as a matter of necessary implication, to ensure that that the express requirements operate effectively. A wider question is whether a statutory procedural code is exhaustive or whether the courts may supplement it with further procedural conditions. In the past, the tendency was restrictive.[42] Now, as Lord Bridge held in *Lloyd v McMahon,*[43] it is clear that the courts will "not only require the procedure prescribed by the statute to be followed, but will readily imply so much and no more to be introduced by way of additional procedural safeguards as will ensure the attainment of fairness." A striking instance of this occurred in *R. v Secretary of State for the*

---

[39] Instances where non-compliance with a prescribed requirement has been held to render a decision *ultra vires* include *Moss' Empires Ltd v Glasgow Assessor,* 1917 S.C. (H.L.) 1 and *London & Clydeside Estates Ltd v Aberdeen DC,* 1980 S.C. (H.L.) 1 (failure to notify a party of a right of appeal); *Perfect Swivel Ltd v City of Dundee District Licensing Board (No. 1),* 1993 S.L.T. 109 (failure to notify right of appeal to a sheriff); *Stakis plc v Boyd,* 1989 S.L.T. 333 (commencement without sworn information of proceedings to condemn unfit food).

[40] 1980 S.C.(HL) 1.

[41] [2000] 1 W.L.R. 354.

[42] See, e.g. *Wiseman v Borneman* [1971] A.C. 297, in which Lord Reid held that the courts could only properly extend statutory procedures where "it is clear that the statutory procedure is insufficient to achieve justice and to require additional steps would not frustrate the apparent purpose of the legislation."

[43] [1987] A.C. 625 at 703.

Home Department, ex p. Fayed.[44] The Fayed brothers had applied
for naturalisation as British citizens under sections 6(1) and 6(2)
respectively of the British Nationality Act 1981. Without reasons,
their applications were refused. Prior to giving his decision,
however, the Home Secretary had indicated in a press release that
the applications were regarded as especially difficult and sensitive.
The brothers were not told why this was so. The Court of Appeal
therefore held that, even though section 44(2) provides that the
Home Secretary is "not required to assign any reason for the grant
or refusal of any application", the Home Secretary was nonetheless
obliged to act fairly in arriving at his decision. He was therefore
required to give the applicants sufficient information as to the
nature of his concern so that they would be able to make
representations. The refusal was quashed.

Natural justice

Introduction

12–24   The twin principles of natural justice—*nemo iudex in sua causa*
and *audi alteram partem*—state, first, that no-one may be a judge of
his own cause (the rule against bias) and, secondly, that everyone
has the right to be fairly heard. Both principles are derived from
and rooted in judicial decision making processes, but have been
extended by the courts in the exercise of their supervisory jurisdiction to the proceedings of inferior tribunals, whether statutory or
domestic, and to more strictly administrative decision making
procedures.[45] Judicial and administrative decision making processes do, however, differ considerably. To that extent, subjecting
administrative officials to standards of procedural fairness crafted
for a judicial context may not always be appropriate, for if the right
to a fair hearing in an administrative setting meant what it means
in a judicial setting, the administrative process would grind to a
halt. On the other hand, it is recognised that administrative
decisions may affect individuals' rights and interests as much as, if
not more than, judicial decisions in the modern administrative
state. For that reason, and also because intervention on procedural
grounds is perceived as less likely to intrude upon the substance
and merits of administrative decisions, the most vigorous development of administrative law has occurred in the context of natural
justice.

---

[44] [1998] 1 W.L.R. 763.
[45] The scope for their application to legislative decision making processes appears,
however, to be limited: see, *e.g. Bates v Lord Hailsham* [1972] 1 W.L.R. 1373.

Rule against bias

We have already examined the application of this rule to judges **12–25** and judicial decision-makers in the context of judicial independence and impartiality in chapter 6, to which reference is made. There it was seen that where a decision-maker has a direct pecuniary or proprietary interest in the outcome of proceedings before him, the consequence is automatic disqualification.[46] The categories of automatic disqualification were extended by the House of Lords in the *Pinochet* case, to include interest in the sense of the promotion of a cause in which the judge is involved together with one of the parties.[47] In either case, the maxim that justice must not only be done but must manifestly and undoubtedly be seen to be done[48] applies with its full force: disqualification is automatic and nothing more than the fact of the interest requires to be proved. If the disqualified judge proceeds nonetheless to decide, his decision cannot stand.[49] The rule against bias also comes into play, even though the judge is not financially interested in the outcome or otherwise acting as a judge of his own cause, where in some other sense his conduct or behaviour gives rise to doubt about his impartiality. Here the test is whether the circumstances were such as to give a fair-minded and informed observer a reasonable apprehension of partiality or bias on the judge's part.[50]

These rules have been applied readily to the decisions of disciplinary bodies,[51] administrative tribunals[52] and other bodies performing judicial and quasi-judicial functions,[53] but at one time it appeared different criteria applied in relation to administrative authorities. In some cases, for example, it was held that the test for bias could not apply to policy-based decisions, such as those of planning authorities, since these were "radically different" from the decisions of tribunals, which arrive at objective decisions according to rules.[54] In these cases, the local planning authorities had entered into contracts with developers for the exploitation of

---

[46] *Dimes v Proprietors of the Grand Junction Canal* (1852) 3 H.L. Cas. 759; *Wildridge v Anderson* (1897) 25 R. (J.) 27 at 34, *per* Lord Moncreiff.

[47] *R. v Bow Street Metropolitan Stipendiary Magistrate, ex p. Pinochet Ugarte (No.2)* [2000] 1 A.C. 119.

[48] *R. v Sussex Justices, ex p. McCarthy* [1924] 1 K.B. 256 at 262, *per* Lord Hewart C.J.

[49] Even where the disqualified judge sits as a member of a panel, his participation will suffice to vitiate the decision of the panel as a whole: see *Davidson v Scottish Ministers (No.2)*, 2003 S.C. 103.

[50] *Doherty v McGlennan*, 1997 S.L.T. 444; *Porter v Magill* [2002] 2 A.C. 357.

[51] See, *e.g. Palmer v Inverness Hospitals Board of Management*, 1963 S.C. 111.

[52] See, *e.g. Barrs v British Wool Marketing Board*, 1957 S.C. 72.

[53] See, *e.g. Brown v Executive Committee of the Edinburgh District Labour Party*, 1995 S.L.T. 985.

[54] *R. v Amber Valley DC, ex p. Jackson* [1985] 1 W.L.R. 298; *R. v St Edmundsbury DC, ex p. Investors in Industry Commercial Properties Ltd* [1985] 1 W.L.R. 1168.

land owned by the authorities, and had undertaken to do their best to procure planning permission (to be granted by themselves). In *R. v St Edmundsbury District Council, ex p. Investors in Industry Commercial Properties Ltd*,[55] Stocker L.J. considered that the disapplication of the rule against bias in such circumstances was justified because, were it otherwise, "an administrative impasse would occur in any case where a planning authority had, quite properly, become involved in some development within its area."[56]

However, as Sedley J. pointed out in *R. v Secretary of State for the Environment, ex p. Kirkstall Valley Campaign Ltd*,[57] this kind of pigeonholing—distinguishing between administrative and judicial functions for the purposes of determining the application of the rules of natural justice—was supposedly done to death by the House of Lords in *Ridge v Baldwin*.[58] In *Kirkstall Valley Campaign*, an urban development corporation as local planning authority had granted outline planning permission for a retail development on part of a rugby club's property. The applicant complained that this decision was vitiated by the participation of three members and an officer of the corporation, each of whom had disqualifying pecuniary or personal interests in the development such as to constitute a real danger of bias. Although the application failed on the merits, Sedley J. accepted the applicant's argument that the test for bias was a uniform test applicable to all bodies, judicial or administrative, which are subject to control by judicial review. His Lordship explained the *St Edmundsbury* line of cases[59] as being concerned not with bias[60] but with a different principle:

> "[T]he decision of a body, albeit composed of disinterested individuals, will be struck down if its outcome has been predetermined whether by the adoption of an inflexible policy or by the effective surrender of the body's independent judgment."[61]

---

[55] [1985] 1 W.L.R. 1168.

[56] See to similar effect the licensing decisions in *R. v Reading BC, ex p. Quietlynn Ltd* (1986) 85 L.G.R. 387 and *R. v Chesterfield BC, ex p. Darker Enterprises Ltd* [1992] C.O.D. 466.

[57] [1996] 3 All E.R. 304.

[58] [1964] A.C. 40, as to which see paras 12–27—12–28 below.

[59] Which were regarded as "plainly correct."

[60] "[T]he necessary involvement of local elected councillors in matters of public controversy, and the probability that they will have taken a public stand on many of them, limits the range of attack which can properly be made upon any decision in which even a highly opinionated councillor has taken part": *Kirkstall Valley Campaign*, above, at 325.

[61] *Kirkstall Valley Campaign*, above, at 321. On over-rigid policies, see para.12–21.

It may therefore be said that the distinction between judicial and administrative functions no longer determines the *application* of the application of the rule against bias, although it may continue to influence to rigour of the rule in any particular case. As Sedley J. observed[62]:

> "[W]hat will differ from case to case is the significance of the interest and its degree of proximity or remoteness to the issue to be decided and whether, if it is not so insignificant or remote as to be discounted, the disqualified member has violated his disqualification by participating in the decision."

Planning and licensing cases illustrate a particular problem with **12–26** the application of the rule against bias to administrative decisions. What might be described as "structural bias" is often built into particular statutory schemes, as where a minister or local authority is charged with responsibility both for promoting development or adopting policies and for determining appeals.[63] Viewed from the perspective of the right to a fair hearing in the determination of civil rights and obligations under Article 6 of the Convention, none of this is necessarily objectionable, provided the decision-maker is subject to subsequent judicial control by a court or tribunal having sufficiently full jurisdiction to secure compliance with Article 6.[64] In practice, such decisions are generally subject, if not to judicial review, then to a statutory right of appeal on a point of law to the Court of Session.[65] Following the entry into force of the Human Rights Act 1998, it was held north and south of the border that neither judicial review nor statutory appeals on a point of law was sufficient to "cure" the structural bias there complained of.[66] *R. v Secretary of State for the Environment, Transport and the Regions, ex p. Alconbury Developments Ltd*[67] was appealed to the House of Lords, where it was held that the availability of judicial review and/or statutory appeal on a point of law was sufficient to ensure compliance with Article 6, with the consequence that the relevant statutory provisions were compatible with the Convention.[68] It

---

[62] *Kirkstall Valley Campaign*, above, at 325.
[63] See, *e.g. Franklin v Minister of Town and Country Planning* [1948] A.C. 87; *City of Glasgow DC v S of S for Scotland (No.1)*, 1993 S.L.T. 198.
[64] *Bryan v UK* (1995) 21 E.H.R.R. 342.
[65] See, *e.g.* Town and Country Planning (Scotland) Act 1997, s.58.
[66] *County Properties Ltd v The Scottish Ministers*, 2000 S.L.T. 965; *R. v S of S for the Environment, Transport and the Regions, ex p. Alconbury Developments Ltd*, [2001] U.K.H.R.R. 270.
[67] [2001] U.K.H.R.R. 270.
[68] *R. v S of S for the Environment, Transport and the Regions, ex p. Alconbury Developments Ltd* [2001] U.K.H.R.R. 728. Following this decision, the Inner House reversed the first instance decision of Lord Macfadyen in *County Properties*: see *County Properties Ltd v Scottish Ministers*, 2002 S.C. 79.

should, however, be noted that this will not invariably be the case. Thus in *Kingsley v UK*,[69] the European Court held that judicial review proceedings were insufficient to cure the possibility of bias on the part of the Gaming Board of Great Britain in deciding to revoke the applicant's certificate of approval, because all that the court on review could do was quash the revocation and order the decision to be taken afresh by a differently constituted panel. In some circumstances, therefore, only a full rehearing by an appellate body will satisfy the requirements of Article 6.

Right to a fair hearing

12–27   In *Board of Education v Rice*,[70] Lord Loreburn remarked that the duty to afford a fair hearing is "a duty lying upon anyone who decides anything." This was in keeping with older authorities,[71] which insisted on the observance of fair procedures by public authorities and private or domestic bodies alike.[72] But in the first half of the twentieth century, during what has been termed the "long sleep" of public law,[73] there was a tendency, perhaps most marked in the English courts,[74] to restrict the application of principles of natural justice to circumstances in which the decision maker acted judicially or the decision affected actual legal rights or privileges.[75] It is for this reason that the decision of the House of Lords in *Ridge v Baldwin*[76] is so often credited with reawakening public law and establishing the foundations of modern administrative jurisprudence. There, a chief constable who had lately been acquitted of criminal charges was dismissed from office by the local watch committee. He was not invited to attend the committee's meeting but later learned of the resolutions adopted at the meeting, upon which the committee had based their decision. He sought a declaration that the purported termination of his appointment was illegal, *ultra vires* and void as being in breach of natural justice. By a majority, the House of Lords held that an official such as the chief constable, who was dismissable only for cause, was

---

[69] *Kingsley v UK* [2001] 33 E.H.R.R. 13.

[70] [1911] A.C. 179 at 182.

[71] Perhaps most notably *Cooper v Wandsworth Board of Works* (1863) 14 C.B. (NS) 180.

[72] In the latter case, often on the basis of implied terms: see, *e.g. Edwards v SOGAT* [1971] Ch. 591.

[73] Sir Stephen Sedley, "The Sound of Silence: Constitutional Law without a Constitution" (1994) 110 L.Q.R. 270.

[74] *cf.* A. W. Bradley and C. M. G. Himsworth, "Administrative Law" in *Stair Memorial Encyclopaedia* (Butterworths, Scotland, 1995), para.10.

[75] See, *e.g. Local Government Board v Arlidge* [1915] A.C. 120; *Franklin v Minister of Town and Country Planning* [1948] A.C. 97; *Nakkuda Ali v Jayaratne* [1951] A.C. 66.

[76] [1964] A.C. 40.

entitled to notice of the charge against him and to an opportunity to be heard before being dismissed, and quashed the decision of the committee. In doing so, the majority based themselves firmly on the nineteenth century case law and disapproved the impediments to the application of natural justice that had been imported by the more recent decisions.

Ridge v Baldwin[77] notwithstanding, the right to a fair hearing cannot mean the same thing in all contexts. In some situations, as was implicitly acknowledged in Re H.K. (An Infant)[78] by the adoption of the terminology of "fairness" or "a duty to act fairly", it may not involve a hearing as such at all. At its fullest, as seen in the proceedings of the ordinary courts, the right to a fair hearing requires notice of the case one has to answer, an oral hearing in public, conducted in accordance with the rules of evidence, legal representation, the right to cross-examine, a reasoned decision, and a right of appeal. Plainly, this is not what obtains in the context of much administrative decision-making, nor is there any reason why it should. Thus while the *application* of the duty to act fairly does not turn on whether the decision-maker acted judicially or otherwise, the *content* of the duty will depend on "the character of the decision making body, the kind of decision it has to make and the statutory or other framework in which it operates."[79]

It follows, then, that functional distinctions are not deprived of **12–28** all vitality: the more nearly "judicial" a decision-making process, then, all other things being equal, the stricter will be the demands for fairness.[80] Clearly, however, this is not the only factor material to determining the scope of the duty to act fairly. In so far as it pertained to the threatened destruction of the pursuer's property, *Errington v Wilson*[81] may be said to illustrate also the relevance of the nature of the right or interest affected by the decision under attack.[82] Another factor relates to the stage that a given decision-making process has reached. Often, a decision is arrived at only on completion of a number of procedural steps, such as a preliminary investigation or a public inquiry or consultation. On occasion, statutory procedural codes applicable to the preliminary stages of a process have been held to be exhaustive of the duty to act fairly.[83] On the other hand, it was held in *Re Pergamon Press*

---

[77] [1964] A.C. 40.
[78] [1967] 2 Q.B. 617.
[79] *Lloyd v McMahon* [1987] A.C. 625 at 702, *per* Lord Bridge.
[80] See, *e.g. Errington v Wilson*, 1995 S.L.T. 1193.
[81] 1995 S.L.T. 1193.
[82] See also *McInnes v Onslow-Fane* [1978] 1 W.L.R. 1520, where Sir Robert Megarry V.-C. distinguished between the levels of procedural protection to which an initial applicant for a benefit, an applicant for renewal of a benefit and the holder of a subsisting benefit, which benefit is revoked, would be entitled.
[83] *Wiseman v Borneman* [1971] A.C. 297; *Pearlberg v Varty* [1972] 1 W.L.R. 534; *Bushell v S of S for the Environment* [1981] A.C. 75.

Ltd[84] that a Department of Trade and Industry inspector conducting an inquiry into the company's affairs under the Companies Acts was obliged, before publishing a highly critical report, to communicate the gist of his findings to the persons concerned and accord them an opportunity to respond.[85] But that was the extent of the super-added duty to act fairly.[86] The extent to which the duty to act fairly applies to preliminary or interim stages of a decision-making process will therefore depend on a combination of factors: the terms of the statutory procedural code itself, the impact of the preliminary inquiry upon the individual, the proximity of the challenged decision to the final outcome, and, perhaps also, the nature of the inquiry undertaken. The more "investigative" an inquiry, the less likely are the courts to impose additional procedural safeguards over and above those prescribed by Parliament, in order to avoid hindering what may already be a difficult and delicate task.

Lastly, the duty to act fairly may be limited, even excluded, in situations where it would normally otherwise apply by reference to overriding public interests. A clear instance of this is the *GCHQ* case,[87] where the House of Lords held that the applicants' legitimate expectation of consultation prior to changes being made to the terms and conditions of staff at GCHQ was defeated by the interests of national security. Again in *R. v Gaming Board for Great Britain, ex p. Benaim and Khaida*,[88] the Court of Appeal held that the board was "under a duty to act fairly, but not very fairly" in rejecting applications for gaming licences on the basis of undisclosed information passed to them by the police. The public interest in maintaining the confidentiality of information leading to the detection of crime or wrongdoing outweighed the applicants' claim to be entitled to know the charges against them and to make representations in their own defence.[89]

---

[84] [1971] Ch. 388.

[85] The "nature of the interest" rationale is material here: even though the Secretary of State was not bound by the inspector's report in arriving at his decision, the report was a public document and could impact adversely on the applicant's reputation and creditworthiness.

[86] In *Maxwell v Dept of Trade and Industry* [1974] Q.B. 523, it was held that fairness did not oblige the inspector to allow cross-examination of witnesses by the subject of a report.

[87] *Council of Civil Service Unions v Minister for the Civil Service* [1985] A.C. 374.

[88] [1970] 2 All E.R. 528.

[89] This should be taken as illustrative only. It may be, now, that in such circumstances the courts would hold the applicants entitled at least to know the gist of what had been said against them, bearing in mind the possibility that the information might be false or malicious: see, *R. v Secretary of State for the Home Department, ex parte Fayed* [1998] 1 W.L.R. 763 and *Kingsley v UK* [2002] 33 E.H.R.R. 13.

Unfairness as an abuse of power

It is not always possible to categorise unfairness on the part of a **12–29** public authority as bias, or failure to give a hearing, or breach of a legitimate expectation, or any other specific head of procedural impropriety. Nevertheless, the unfairness complained of may be of such a degree as to call for redress. In *R. v Inland Revenue Commissioners, ex p. Preston*, the House of Lords held that such would be appropriate where unfairness in the exercise of statutory powers amounted to an excess or abuse of power.[90] The principle recognised in *Preston* was applied by the Court of Appeal in *R. v Inland Revenue Commissioners, ex p. Unilever plc*.[91] There, departing from a well-established practice, the revenue relied on a statutory time—limit as defeating claims for loss relief. The Court of Appeal accepted that there had been no such "clear, unambiguous and unqualified representation"[92] as to generate a legitimate expectation on Unilever's part that the former practice would continue to be followed. Even so, Sir Thomas Bingham M.R. noted that the categories of unfairness were not closed and that, in all the circumstances, "to reject Unilever's claims in reliance on the time limit, without clear and general advance notice, [was] so unfair as to amount to an abuse of power by the Revenue." Again in *R. v National Lottery Commission, ex p. Camelot Group plc*,[93] Richards J. quashed the decision of the commission to reject two rival bids to run the national lottery but to reopen the bidding process to one of the bidders. It was accepted that the enabling legislation accorded a wide discretion to the commission as to how it would perform its functions, but:

---

[90] [1985] A.C. 835 at 851, *per* Lord Scarman, and 866–867, *per* Lord Templeman. In that case, the unfairness complained of involved the commissioners' reopening an inquiry into the applicant's tax affairs after undertaking to close the inquiry if he withdraw certain claims, which he did. Although conceding the general principle, however, their Lordships held it inapplicable in this case: as Lord Templeman put it, "the commissioners may decide to abstain from exercising their powers and performing their duties on grounds of unfairness, but the commissioners themselves must bear in mind that their primary duty is to collect, not to forgive, taxes. And if the commissioners decide to proceed, the court cannot in the absence of exceptional circumstances decide to be unfair that which the commissioners by taking action against the taxpayer have determined to be fair".

[91] [1996] S.T.C. 681.

[92] As required by the decision of the Court of Appeal in *R. v Inland Revenue Commissioners, ex p. MFK Underwriting Agencies Ltd* [1990] 1 W.L.R. 1545.

[93] *R. v National Lottery Commission, ex p. Camelot Group plc*, [2001] E.M.L.R. 3.

"[S]uch a marked lack of even-handedness between the rival bidders calls for the most compelling justification, which I cannot find in the reasons advanced by the Commission in support of its decision. ... The Commission's decision to negotiate exclusively with The People's Lottery was, in all the circumstances, so unfair as to amount to an abuse of power."[94]

Legitimate expectations

12–30   The concept of legitimate expectations may be seen as furnishing a ground for judicial review in itself or, "which seems preferable, as a concept which helps to inform those grounds for judicial review which are concerned with procedural and substantive fairness."[95] In some situations, invocation of a legitimate expectation is essentially superfluous, since the circumstances of the case would call for the imposition of a duty to act fairly in any event, as where the decision maker is required to reach a quasi-judicial decision or where a decision deprives a person of a subsisting right or benefit.[96] But in some situations, the existence of a legitimate expectation may entitle a person to a level of protection, procedural or substantive, which, in the absence of the expectation, he would not have received.

A legitimate expectation may be derived from an express promise, assurance or representation, or from an implied representation based on the past practice or conduct of the decision-maker. Whether express or implied, however, a representation must be "clear, unambiguous and devoid of relevant

---

[94] This developing case law of unfairness as abuse of power provided the basis for the decision in *R. v North and East Devon Health Authority, ex p. Coughlan* [2001] Q.B. 213 that the courts could in appropriate cases enforce the substance of a legitimate expectation, as to which see para. 12–32.

[95] M. Fordham, *Judicial Review Handbook* (3rd ed., Hart Publishing, Oxford, 2001), para.41.1.

[96] See, *e.g. Stannifer Developments Ltd v Glasgow Development Agency*, 1999 S.C. 156 at 160; *R. v Devon C, ex p. Baker* [1995] 1 All E.R. 73 at 89, *per* Simon Brown L.J.; *Attorney-General for New South Wales v Quin* [1990] 93 A.L.R. 1 at 39, *per* Dawson J. Thus in *R. v S of S for Health, ex p. United States Tobacco International Inc.* [1992] 1 All E.R. 212, the Court of Appeal rejected the applicant's claim to a legitimate expectation that, having provided it with substantial funding for the construction of a factory manufacturing oral snuff, the government would not change its policy in relation to that product (by banning its sale in the UK). The Court of Appeal quashed the Secretary of State's decision on the separate ground that, the effects of the change of policy being so catastrophic for the applicant's business, and given the history of the dealings between the applicant and the government, fairness required the Secretary of State to consult the applicant prior to making his decision.

qualification."[97] Instances of express representations include *R. v Liverpool Corporation, ex p. Liverpool Taxi Fleet Operators Association*[98] and *Attorney-General of Hong Kong v Ng Yuen Shiu*.[99] In *Ng Yuen Shiu*, the Hong Kong authorities had announced that illegal immigrants would be interviewed, each case being dealt with on its merits, before any decision was taken to expel them from the territory. The applicant had entered Hong Kong illegally from Macau some years previously, and in the meantime had established a flourishing business. The authorities purported to expel him without an interview. The Privy Council held that, although the duty to act fairly might not generally extend to illegal immigrants, the Hong Kong authorities had by their assurances created a legitimate expectation of a hearing which should be enforced.

Instances of legitimate expectations derived from implied representations resting on the past conduct of the decision-maker include the *GCHQ* case[1] and *R. v Brent London Borough Council, ex p. McDonagh*.[2] In the latter, the applicant gypsies were held to have a legitimate expectation that the local authority would not evict them without first finding an alternative site on the basis of the authority's past practice of allowing the gypsies to remain on their land.

Akin to the implied representation cases are those where the **12–31** legitimate expectation is founded on the adoption of a policy by the decision-maker. This may be contained in primary legislation, as in *R. v Secretary of State for the Home Department, ex p. Ruddock*.[3] There, the relevant expectation was that the Home Secretary would adhere to the conditions of the Interception of Communications Act 1985 and guidelines setting out the manner in which the statutory discretion in relation to telephone tapping would be exercised. Alternatively, criteria contained in government circulars may generate a legitimate expectation that those criteria will be applied, as in *R. v Secretary of State for the Home Department, ex p. Khan*.[4] Relying on a circular issued by the Home

---

[97] *R. v Inland Revenue Commissioners, ex p. MFK Underwriting Agencies Ltd* [1990] 1 W.L.R. 1545 at 1570, *per* Bingham L.J. See to similar effect Lord Woolf C.J. in *R. v North and East Devon Health Authority, ex p. Coughlan* [2001] Q.B. 213 at 247. "What is required is a clear, unambiguous and unqualified representation that the authority concerned will act in a certain way and that the representation has been so understood." Thus, *e.g.* in *R. v S of S for the Home Dept, ex p. Sakala* [1994] Imm. A.R. 142, it was held that a ministerial statement in Parliament that the Secretary of State would "almost invariably" accept the recommendation of a special adjudicator did not give rise to a legitimate expectation that the adjudicator's recommendation would be followed.

[98] [1972] 2 Q.B. 299.

[99] [1983] 2 A.C. 629.

[1] *Council of Civil Service Unions v Minister for the Civil Service* [1985] A.C. 374.

[2] [1990] C.O.D. 3.

[3] [1987] 1 W.L.R. 1482.

[4] [1985] 1 All E.R. 40.

Office stating the criteria which the Home Secretary would apply in cases of international adoption, the applicant sought entry clearance for his nephew from Pakistan; on the basis of different criteria, clearance was refused. Parker L.J. held that the Home Secretary could not depart from his stated policy without "affording interested persons a hearing and only then if the overriding public interest demands it."

This reference to the public interest serves to emphasise that an individual's legitimate expectation may be outweighed by competing considerations. Again, the *GCHQ* case[5] provides an example: the unions had a legitimate expectation of consultation prior to changes being made in terms and conditions, but this was overridden by the public interest in national security, which the minister claimed was jeopardised by industrial action at GCHQ. In general terms, it is obviously important that, notwithstanding the creation of legitimate expectations, public bodies should be able to alter their policies and practices as the public interest requires. But the doctrine of legitimate expectations serves to remind government that, in so doing, it must, in fairness, treat individuals' legitimate expectations with the degree of respect that is compatible with the wider public interest.

12–32   A final issue in relation to legitimate expectations is whether they attract only procedural protection or whether the courts may go further and protect the substance of the expectation.[6] If the former, the courts can do no more than inquire whether the decision-maker has acted fairly towards the applicant, in view of his legitimate expectation, prior to making his decision; if the latter, the courts may test the substantive fairness to the applicant of the actual outcome.[7] In *R. v North and East Devon Health Authority,*

---

[5] *Council of Civil Service Unions v Minister for the Civil Service* [1985] A.C. 374.

[6] This is a distinction without a difference in some cases, such as *R. v S of S for the Home Dept, ex p. Ruddock* [1987] 1 W.L.R. 1482 and *Attorney-General of Hong Kong v Ng Yuen Shiu.* [1983] 2 A.C. 629, where the substance of the expectation is that a pre-ordained procedure would be followed and no more.

[7] Arguments for recognising the substantive dimension to legitimate expectations were rejected by Laws J. in *R. v S of S for Transport, ex p. Richmond upon Thames London BC* [1994] 1 All E.R. 577, but accepted by Sedley J. in *R. v Ministry of Agriculture, Fisheries and Food, ex p. Hamble (Offshore) Fisheries Ltd* [1995] 2 All E.R. 714. *Hamble Fisheries* was subsequently overruled by the Court of Appeal in *R. v S of S for the Home Dept, ex p. Hargreaves* [1997] 1 All E.R. 397, in which Pill L.J. held (at 416): "I cannot agree that the court can take and act upon an overall view of the fairness of the respondent's decision in substance. The court can quash the decision only if, in relation to the expectation and in all the circumstances, the decision to apply the new policy in the particular case was unreasonable in the *Wednesbury* sense. The claim to a broader power to judge the fairness of a decision in substance is in my view wrong in principle."

ex p. Coughlan,[8] the Court of Appeal confirmed that, in certain limited circumstances, a legitimate expectation of a substantive benefit could, as a matter of fairness, be enforced by the courts. There, the applicant had been grievously injured in a road traffic accident in 1971. In 1993, she was moved, together with other comparably disabled patients, to Mardon House, a purpose-built NHS facility. The patients were assured that Mardon House would be their home for life. In 1998, however, the health authority decided to close the facility. It was found that a clear promise had been made to the patients that Mardon House would be their permanent home; that a decision to break that promise, if unfair, would be equivalent to a breach of contract; that a public authority could reasonably resile from such a promise if the overriding public interest demanded it; but that the health authority here had failed to establish that there were such compelling circumstances justifying the closure. In his detailed analysis of the law on legitimate expectations, Lord Woolf noted that a given expectation might fall into any one of three categories:

"(a) The court may decide that the public authority is only required to bear in mind its previous policy or other representation, giving it the weight it thinks right, but no more, before deciding whether to change course. Here the court is confined to reviewing the decision on *Wednesbury* grounds. This has been held to be the effect of changes of policy involving the early release of prisoners. (b) On the other hand, the court may decide that the promise or practice induces a legitimate expectation of, for example, being consulted before a particular decision is taken. Here it is uncontentious that the court itself will require the opportunity for consultation to be given unless there is overriding reason to resile from it, in which case the court will itself judge the adequacy of the reason advanced for the change of policy, taking into account what fairness requires. (c) Where the court considers that a lawful promise or practice has induced a legitimate expectation of a benefit which is substantive, not simply procedural, authority now establishes that here too the court will in a proper case decide whether to frustrate the expectation is so unfair that to take a new and different course will amount to an abuse of power. Here, once the legitimacy of the expectation is established, the court will have the task of weighing the requirements of fairness against any overriding interest relied upon for the change of policy."

---

[8] [2001] Q.B. 213.

Lord Woolf then explained that the nature of the court's function varies according to the category into which the legitimate expectation contended for falls:

> "In the case of the first, the court is restricted to reviewing the decision on conventional grounds. The test will be rationality and whether the public body has given proper weight to the implications of not fulfilling the promise. In the case of the second category the court's task is the conventional one of determining whether the decision was procedurally fair. In the case of the third, the court has when necessary to determine whether there is a sufficient overriding interest to justify a departure from what has been previously promised."

Given the importance of what had been promised to the applicant, the fact that the promise was limited to a small class of persons and the fact that the consequences to the health authority of requiring it to honour its promise were "likely to be financial only", Lord Woolf placed the expectation here in the third category, noting that most cases of a legitimate expectation falling into the third category would tend to involve a promise or representation having the character of a contract, being made to only one person or a small number of people. The Court of Appeal was aware that it was taking a fairly bold step in so holding. Its authority for doing so was culled from the developing jurisprudence on unfairness as an abuse of power. Against this backdrop, the approach to legitimate expectations taken in cases such as *R. v Secretary of State for the Home Department, ex p. Hargreaves*[9] was inadequate in so far as it permitted review only on *Wednesbury* grounds in relation to a legitimate expectation of a substantive benefit. Most decisions survive *Wednesbury* scrutiny[10] and, once a rational decision relevantly directed to a proper purpose has been reached by lawful process, there is normally no further basis on which it may be impugned. Founding chiefly upon *Preston*[11] and *Unilever*,[12] Lord Woolf held that:

> "Unfairness in the purported exercise of a power can be such that it is an abuse or excess of the power . . . . Such an abuse

---

[9] [1997] 1 All E.R. 397

[10] As Lord Woolf put it: "[T]he health authority knew of the promise and its seriousness; it was aware of its new policies and the reasons for them; it knew that one had to yield, and it made a choice which, whatever else may be said of it, may not easily be challenged as irrational. . . . A decision to prioritise a policy change over legitimate expectations will almost always be rational from where the authority stands."

[11] *R. v Inland Revenue Commissioners, ex p. Preston* [1985] A.C. 835.

[12] *R. v Inland Revenue Commissioners, ex p. Unilever plc* [1996] S.T.C. 681.

of power may take the form of reneging without adequate justification, by an otherwise lawful decision, on a lawful promise or practice adopted towards a limited number of individuals. . . . Fairness in such a situation, if it is to mean anything, must include fairness of outcome. This is why the doctrine of legitimate expectation has emerged as a distinct application of the concept of abuse of power in relation to substantive as well as procedural benefits."

Duty to give reasons

Statutes often require that decisions made under them should be **12–33** supported by reasons. It is often said that, statute apart, there is no general common law duty to provide reasoned decisions. However, developments in this area have been such that the sum of the exceptions to the general principle probably outweighs the principle itself.

There are a number of rationales for requiring that reasons be provided. Reasons may be required where the effect of their absence is to frustrate a right of appeal or review.[13] In *Stefan v Health Committee of the General Medical Council*,[14] the Judicial Committee of the Privy Council considered the relevance of the existence of a right of appeal and/or the availability of judicial review to whether a duty to give reasons was to be implied into a statutory procedural code. Lord Clyde said:

"This factor [provision of a right of appeal] may operate in different directions. As Lord Donaldson of Lymington MR accepted in *R. v Civil Service Appeal Board, ex p. Cunningham*,[15] some judicial decisions, such as those of justices, do not call for reasons and that is because there is a right of appeal to the Crown Court which hears the matter *de novo* and also a right to have a case stated for the opinion of the High Court on a point of law. . . . In *Cunningham*, although there was no provision for appeal from the decision of the body in question it was susceptible to judicial review, and that appears to have been a factor pointing to the conclusion that reasons were required. In *R v Secretary of State for the Home Department, ex p. Doody*,[16] Lord Mustill regarded it as necessary for reasons to be disclosed where it was important for there to be an effective means of detecting the kind of error

[13] *Minister of National Revenue v Wright's Canadian Ropes Ltd* [1947] A.C. 109 (appeal); *R. v S of S for the Home Dept, ex p. Dannenberg* [1984] Q.B. 766 (review).
[14] [1999] 1 W.L.R. 1293.
[15] [1992] I.C.R. 817.
[16] [1994] 1 A.C. 531.

which would enable the court to intervene by way of judicial review. On the other hand the existence of a right of appeal has also been taken as a factor pointing towards a requirement for the giving of reasons. In *Norton Tool Co Ltd v Tewson*,[17] a requirement to give reasons was identified on the ground that otherwise the parties would in effect be deprived of their right of appeal on a question of law. So also in *Hadjianastassiou v Greece*,[18] it was observed that the grounds of a decision must be stated with sufficient clarity as that is one of the factors which makes it possible for an accused to exercise usefully the right of appeal open to him."

12–34 An alternative rationale rests on the decision of the House of Lords in *Padfield v Minister of Agriculture, Fisheries and Food*.[19] There it was held that, where all the facts and evidence before the court point in favour of a decision other than that which was actually taken, the court is entitled to infer, in the absence of reasons to the contrary, that the decision lacks a rational basis. But, as Lord Keith pointed out in *R. v Secretary of State for Trade and Industry, ex p. Lonrho plc*,[20] absence of reasons is not in itself a vitiating factor here: if at all, the decision will be quashed on the grounds of irrationality. As Latham J. put it in *R. v Secretary of State for Education, ex p. G*[21]:

"In a series of cases during the last year, it is apparent that, whilst there is a spectrum of factual situations ranging from those where no reasons are required at all on the one hand to those where the circumstances are such as to cry out for full and detailed reasons, the general approach has been to require there to be sufficient reasons to be given to determine whether or not the decision maker has asked the right question and approached it in a rational way."

In *R. v Civil Service Appeal Board, ex p. Cunningham*,[22] the applicant sought judicial review of the board's decision to award him by way of compensation for unfair dismissal a sum some two-thirds less than an industrial tribunal would have awarded. In quashing the decision, the Court of Appeal relied in part on the *Padfield* reasoning. But Lord Donaldson M.R. went further, stating that a "judicialised" tribunal is bound to provide outline reasons

---

[17] [1972] I.C.R. 505.
[18] (1992) 16 E.H.R.R. 219.
[19] [1968] A.C. 997.
[20] [1989] 1 W.L.R. 525.
[21] [1995] E.L.R. 58.
[22] [1992] I.C.R. 817.

for its decisions, sufficient to show to what it has directed its mind, and that failure to do so is a breach of natural justice.[23] Absence of reasons may conceal the basis of a decision and so frustrate the right of the person aggrieved by it to seek judicial review on some independent ground. However, as the House of Lords subsequently held in *R. v Secretary of State for the Home Department, ex p. Doody*,[24] the very importance of a decision to the individual affected by it may be such that, in fairness and without more, reasons should be provided for the decision. This serves not some instrumental end (although instrumental ends, such as ensuring that the decision-maker properly and conscientiously addresses his mind to the issues to be decided, are important) but the more abstract, non-instrumental goal of ensuring that administrators treat those subject to their decisions with the appropriate degree of respect. Thus the more important or fundamental the nature of the individual's right or interest in question, the more likely it is that the discipline of fairness will require reasons to be given.

It is not always appropriate, however, that the courts should impose this obligation on public authorities. In *R. v Higher Education Funding Council, ex p. Institute of Dental Surgery*,[25] the institute challenged the council's assessment of its research (upon which the level of government funding depended) because it was unsupported by reasons. Sedley J. held that the council was not required to recite the reasons for its decision as it depended on an unquantifiable exercise of "pure academic judgment". The courts are also conscious of the resource implications of duties to give reasons, and concede that the interests of the complainant must be balanced against administrative efficiency and convenience.[26] Thus

---

[23] In *Stefan v Health Committee of the General Medical Council* [1999] 1 W.L.R. 1293, Lord Clyde observed: "[The] distinction between administrative and judicial decisions as a factor in the susceptibility of a decision to review was destroyed by *Ridge v Baldwin* [1964] A.C. 40. Thus the fact that an administrative function is being performed does not exclude the possibility that reasons may require to be given for a decision (*R. v Higher Education Funding Council, ex p. Institute of Dental Surgery* [1994] 1 W.L.R. 242). But the carrying out of a judicial function remains, as was recognised by McCowan L.J. in *R. v Civil Service Appeal Board, ex p. Cunningham* [1992] ICR 817 and accepted by Hooper J. in *R. v Ministry of Defence, ex p. Murray* [1998] COD 134, a consideration in favour of a requirement to give reasons."

[24] [1994] 1 A.C. 531.

[25] [1994] 1 W.L.R. 242.

[26] A like balance is recognised in the jurisprudence of the ECHR. In *Helle v Finland* (1997) 26 E.H.R.R. 159, the ECHR held that "while Article 6(1) obliges the courts to give reasons for their judgments, it cannot be understood as requiring a detailed answer to every argument adduced by a litigant. The extent to which the duty to give reasons applies may vary according to the nature of the decision at issue. It is moreover necessary to take into account, *inter alia*, the diversity of the submissions that a litigant may bring before the courts and the

even where reasons are required, there may be an issue about the level of detail into which the decision-maker is obliged to go. The standard formulation, derived from *In re Poyser & Mills Arbitration*,[27] is that reasons must be "proper, adequate and intelligible." However, as was held in *R. v Immigration Appeal Tribunal, ex p. Patel*[28]:

> "[I]t is not only well established that the duty to give reasons requires reasons that are clear and adequate and deal with the substantial issues in the case, it is also well established that what are good reasons in any particular case depends on the circumstances of the case."

<h3 style="text-align:center">SUBSTANTIVE REVIEW</h3>

Wednesbury doctrine

12–35 Assume a decision is taken in the proper exercise of a public authority's powers, in accordance with a fair procedure and following consideration of all relevant factors. Still the individual affected by that decision insists that it is in some sense legally flawed. Until recently, the only possibility of redress would have rested on the *Wednesbury* test of unreasonableness (or irrationality, as Lord Diplock preferred to describe it in the *GCHQ* case[29]). According to Lord Greene M.R. in *Associated Provincial Picture Houses Ltd v Wednesbury Corporation*,[30] such a decision could only be impugned by the court if it was found to be "a decision no reasonable body could have come to"[31] or, as Lord Diplock put it, "so outrageous in its defiance of logic or of accepted moral standards that no sensible person who had applied his mind to the question to be decided could have arrived at it."[32] The reason why the threshold of unreasonableness necessary to attract judicial intervention was pitched at so high a level was explained by Lord Greene M.R. in the following terms:

---

differences existing in the Contracting States with regard to statutory provisions, customary rules, legal opinion and the presentation and drafting of judgments. That is why the question whether a court has failed to fulfil the obligation to state reasons, deriving from Article 6 of the Convention, can only be determined in the light of the circumstances of the case."

[27] [1964] 2 Q.B. 467.

[28] [1996] Imm. A.R. 161 at 169, *per* Carnwath J.

[29] *Council of Civil Service Unions v Minister for the Civil Service* [1985] A.C. 374.

[30] [1948] 2 K.B. 223.

[31] *ibid.*, at 231, *per* Lord Greene M.R.

[32] *Council of Civil Service Unions v Minister for the Civil Service* [1985] A.C. 374 at 410, *per* Lord Diplock.

"It is not what the court considers unreasonable. If it is what the court considers unreasonable, the court may very well have different views to that of a local authority on matters of high public policy of this kind. The effect of the legislation is not to set the court up as an arbiter of the correctness of one view over another. It is the local authority that are set in that position and, provided they act within the four corners of their jurisdiction, this court cannot interfere."[33]

Thus the *Wednesbury* principle expresses the courts' sensitivity to their constitutional position, in the context of review, in relation to Parliament and to the primary decision-maker entrusted by Parliament with discretionary powers. Certainly, the deference it denotes is appropriate to a matter such as a local authority's policy on the licensing of cinemas. But such pronounced deference is not appropriate across the board. In recent years, the courts have explicitly acknowledged this, freely insisting upon more compelling justification for decisions which affect fundamental rights.[34] But even prior to this, the courts would in certain cases apply a stricter standard of review than apparently countenanced by the *Wednesbury* test, either by finding the *Wednesbury* test to be established where in truth it was not,[35] or by simply reformulating the obligation of a decision-maker in terms of acting reasonably rather than refraining from acting in a manifestly unreasonable manner.[36]

Even on its own terms, *Wednesbury* unreasonableness can take a **12–36** variety of forms.[37] It may strike at decisions tainted by an element of fraud, dishonesty or bad faith.[38] It may also apply where a

---

[33] *Associated Provincial Picture Houses Ltd v Wednesbury Corp.* [1948] 1 K.B. 223 at 229, 230.

[34] See, in particular, *Bugdaycay v S of S for the Home Dept* [1987] A.C. 514; *R. v Ministry of Defence, ex p. Smith* [1996] Q.B. 517.

[35] See, *e.g. Hall & Co Ltd v Shoreham-by-Sea Urban DC* [1964] 1 W.L.R. 40; *R. v Hillingdon London BC, ex p. Royco Homes Ltd* [1974] Q.B. 720.

[36] See, *e.g. Roberts v Hopwood* [1925] A.C. 578 at 613, *per* Lord Wrenbury; *Tameside Metropolitan BC v S of S for Education* [1977] A.C. 1014 at 1064, *per* Lord Diplock; *R. v S of S for the Home Dept, ex p. Brind* [1991] 1 A.C. 696 at 749, *per* Lord Bridge; *R. v Chief Constable of Sussex, ex p. International Traders Ferry Ltd* [1999] 2 A.C. 418 at 452, *per* Lord Cooke (deploring the "admonitory circumlocutions" and "needless complexity" of the *Wednesbury* formula). On the basis of decisions such as these, there is much to be said for the view that the standard *Wednesbury* test tends only to be "paraded where the court has decided against intervening": see M. Fordham, *Judicial Review Handbook* (3rd ed., Hart Publishing, Oxford, 2001), para.57.1.

[37] Hence the argument that it is no more than a code for a number of substantive principles of review, which should in the interests of clarity be articulated explicitly: J. Jowell and A. Lester, "Beyond *Wednesbury*: Substantive principles of Administrative law" [1987] P.L. 368.

[38] See, *e.g. Roncarelli v Duplessis* (1959) 16 D.L.R. (2d) 689. The "boycott" cases

complaint is made, not that a public authority has failed to have regard to a relevant consideration, but that it has attributed excessive weight to one factor over others.[39] Decisions that are unduly oppressive or onerous in their effect on the citizen may also be struck down as unreasonable. Thus in *Mixnam's Properties Ltd v Chertsey Urban District Council*,[40] the House of Lords quashed conditions attached to caravan site licences as unreasonable, being "a gratuitous interference with the rights of the occupiers." The quasi-penalty cases of *Congreve v Home Office*[41] (where the Home Secretary revoked television licences which had been purchased just in advance of a substantial increase in their cost) and *Wheeler v Leicester City Council*[42] (where the council revoked the licence of a local rugby club to use council-owned recreation grounds because of the club's failure to stop four of its members from joining a tour to South Africa) are other illustrations of judicial intervention to control oppressiveness. Although the respondents had in both cases acted to achieve a legitimate aim, the manner of their actions was excessive and wrong in that it punished those who had done no wrong.[43] Arbitrariness, perversity or absurdity is liable to be condemned as unreasonable, not only where it is manifest but also where "there is an absence of logical connection between the evidence and the ostensible reasons for the decision, where the reasons display no adequate justification for the decision, or where there is an absence of evidence in support of the decision."[44]

Proportionality

12–37   Many of the decisions cited above could be taken as illustrating of a species of proportionality review (if not a very exacting one). In the *GCHQ* case,[45] Lord Diplock alluded to the possible future

---

may also fall into this category: see *R. v Ealing London BC, ex p. Times Newspapers Ltd* (1986) 85 L.G.R. 316 (where the council's ban on Murdoch newspapers, adopted to express councillors' disapproval of a "tyrannical employer", was quashed on *Wednesbury* grounds) and *R. v Derbyshire C, ex p. The Times Supplements Ltd* [1991] C.O.D. 129 (where a similar ban based on the publication by The Times of articles critical of councillors was struck down). In *R. v Lewisham London BC, ex p. Shell UK Ltd* [1988] 1 All E.R. 938, however, the council's boycott of Shell's products—motivated by a desire to pressurise the company to sever its links with South Africa—was held illegal but not unreasonable, although "very near the line."

[39] See, *e.g. R. v S of S for the Home Dept, ex p. Cox* [1992] C.O.D. 72; *R. v Office of Passenger Rail Franchising, ex p. Save our Railways, The Times*, Dec. 18, 1995 (CA).

[40] [1965] A.C. 735.

[41] [1976] 1 Q.B. 629.

[42] [1985] 1 A.C. 1054.

[43] See, also, *R. v Barnsley Metropolitan BC, ex p. Hook* [1976] 1 W.L.R. 1052.

[44] De Smith, Woolf and Jowell, *Principles of Judicial Review* (London, Sweet & Maxwell, 1999), para.12–018.

[45] *Council of Civil Service Unions v Minister for the Civil Service* [1991] 1 A.C. 696.

reception of a free-standing doctrine of proportionality, which not only had its academic advocates[46] but which also fell to be applied by the domestic courts when adjudicating on cases having a Community law dimension. In *R. v Secretary of State for the Home Department, ex p. Brind*,[47] the House of Lords declined to adopt a test of proportionality going beyond that of irrationality or unreasonableness as traditionally understood. But *Brind* did not, as is sometimes thought, rule out the reception of proportionality review altogether.[48] Indeed, it would have been passing strange had it done so, since the House of Lords had already accepted that "the court . . . must be entitled to subject an administrative decision to the most rigorous examination, to ensure that it is in no way flawed, *according to the gravity of the issue which the decision determines.*"[49] This doctrine of proto-proportionality was developed further by the Court of Appeal in *R. v Ministry of Defence, ex p. Smith*,[50] which accepted that "the more substantial the interference with human rights, the more the court will require by way of justification before it is satisfied that the decision is reasonable."[51] The point to notice is that, even in advance of the enactment of the Human Rights Act 1998, the courts had "in effect recognised proportionality" albeit "without so far daring to speak its name" in cases impinging on fundamental rights as enshrined in the Convention.[52] The converse of this higher-intensity review was adherence to the traditional *Wednesbury* standard in areas not touching upon fundamental rights, where the democratic imperative and/or considerations of relative expertise and institutional competence called for continued deference to the judgment of the primary decision-maker.[53]

---

[46] J. Jowell and A. Lester, "Proportionality: Neither Novel nor Dangerous" in *New Directions in Judicial Review* (Jowell and Oliver eds), p.51–73.

[47] [1991] 1 A.C. 696.

[48] Lord Ackner and Lord Lowry were concerned that to adopt such a test would "inevitably involve inquiry into and a decision upon the merits", but the view of the majority was that *R. v S of S for the Home Dept, ex p. Brind* [1991] 1 A.C. 696 simply was not an appropriate occasion for applying a stricter standard of scrutiny than *Wednesbury*.

[49] *Bugdaycay v S of S for the Home Dept* [1987] A.C. 514, at 531, *per* Lord Bridge (emphasis added).

[50] [1996] Q.B. 517.

[51] at 554, *per* Lord Bingham M.R. See also, *e.g. R. v Chief Constable of Sussex, ex p. International Traders Ferry Ltd* [1999] 2 A.C. 418 and, in Scotland, *Abdadou v S of S for the Home Dept*, 1998 S.C. 504.

[52] M. Hunt, *Using Human Rights Law in the English Courts* (Hart Publishing, Oxford, 1997), p.216.

[53] *R. v S of S for the Environment, ex p. Hammersmith and Fulham London BC* [1991] 1 A.C. 521; *East Kilbride DC v S of S for Scotland*, 1995 S.L.T. 1238. See in light of the HRA 1998 comparable deference to the choices of the legislature in matters of social and economic policy in *R. v S of S for the Environment, Transport and the Regions, ex p. Alconbury Developments Ltd* [2001] U.K.H.R.R. 728; *R. v Tower Hamlets London BC, ex p. Runa Begum (Begum)* [2003] 2 W.L.R. 388; *Wilson v First County Trust Ltd (No.2)* [2003] .

This is not to say that *Wednesbury* as adapted in *Bugdaycay Secretary of State for the Home Department*[54] and *Smith* is equivalent to fully-fledged proportionality review. When deciding on the lawfulness of a legislative restriction on constitutional rights, the court must ask "whether (i) the legislative objective is sufficiently important to justify limiting a fundamental right; (ii) the measures designed to meet the legislative objective are rationally connected to it; and (iii) the means used to impair the right or freedom are no more than is necessary to accomplish the objective."[55] As Lord Steyn observed in *R (Daly) v Secretary of State for the Home Department*,[56] this approach differs from the *Wednesbury* approach in at least three ways: first, it may require the reviewing court to assess the balance struck by the decision-maker, not merely whether it is within a range of rational or reasonable grounds; secondly, it may go further than *Wednesbury* in requiring attention to be directed to the relative weight accorded to specific rights and considerations; and thirdly, even the heightened scrutiny test developed in *Smith* may not be appropriate to the protection of human rights. Lord Steyn also recognised that in many cases, the two approaches would yield the same results. Outcomes can differ, as the *Smith* litigation itself shows.[57] But the distinction between proportionality and *Wednesbury* is one of degree rather than of kind.[58] "Simple" *Wednesbury*, "super" *Wednesbury* and proportionality mark rather points on a scale of substantive review than intrinsically different tests. What differs is the degree of latitude accorded to the primary decision-maker by each of the three tests. Which standard is appropriate will vary depending on the circumstances of the case at hand. But there is no warrant for supposing that the reception of proportionality will supplant *Wednesbury* review altogether. Although there is force in Lord Cooke's criticism of *Wednesbury* as an "unfortunately retrogressive decision . . . *in so far as it suggested* that there are degrees of unreasonableness and that only a very extreme degree can bring an administrative decision within the legitimate scope of judicial invalidation",[59]

---

[54] [1987] A.C. 514.

[55] *De Freitas v Permanent Secretary of the Ministry of Agriculture, Fisheries, Lands and Housing* [1999] A.C. 69 at 80, *per* Lord Clyde.

[56] [2001] 2 A.C. 532 at 546–548.

[57] The applicants in *R. v Ministry of Defence, ex p. Smith*, above, former members of the armed forces who had been discharged on the grounds of their sexual orientation, were unsuccessful in challenging the policy of the Ministry of Defence before the Court of Appeal, despite the court's recognition that the policy intruded upon their right to respect for their private lives; but succeeded before the ECHR: *Lustig-Prean v United Kingdom* (2000) 29 E.H.R.R. 548.

[58] M. Elliott, "The Human Rights Act 1998 and the Standard of Substantive Review" (2001) 60 C.L.J. 301 at 308.

[59] *R (Daly) v S of S for the Home Dept* [2001] 2 A.C. 532, para.32 (emphasis added to underscore the point that even if the *Wednesbury* test was couched in "one size fits all" language, it was never applied in such an unvarying way).

plainly full proportionality review is neither necessary nor appropriate in many cases. What recent developments have permitted is the explicit recognition of a more nuanced approach to substantive review, which requires thought to be given to the competing arguments for and against judicial intervention, than was countenanced by the traditional *Wednesbury* test (at least read literally).[60]

REMEDIES

In exercising its supervisory jurisdiction on an application for **12–38** judicial review, the court may grant or refuse the petition or any part of it, with or without conditions.[61] In particular, the court may:

"make such order in relation to the decision in question as it thinks fit, whether or not such order was sought in the petition, being an order that could be made if sought in any action or petition, including an order for reduction, declarator, suspension, interdict, implement, restitution, payment (whether of damages or otherwise) and any interim order."[62]

Generous as this is (and the remedies listed are not exhaustive), there are certain limitations on the court's remedial jurisdiction. The court cannot grant interdict against the Crown under rule 58.4(b), this being excluded by section 21 of the Crown Proceedings Act 1947.[63] In deciding whether to grant a particular remedy, the court should have regard to the wider interest in good

---

[60] Precisely the same variations in the intensity of substantive review are observable in other systems. The ECJ relaxes the rigour of its proportionality doctrine in certain contexts, such as market regulation: see G. de Burca, "The Proportionality Principle and its Application in EC Law" (1993) Y.E.L. 105; T. Tridimas, "Proportionality in European Community Law: Searching for the appropriate standard of scrutiny" in *The Principle of Proportionality in the Laws of Europe* (Ellis ed., Hart Publishing, Oxford, 1999). The US Supreme Court likewise applies a "strict scrutiny" test or a more relaxed "rational basis" test depending on the circumstances of the case; and in the ECHR too, the application of the proportionality doctrine differs in accordance with the nature of the Convention right founded on, on the one hand, and the nature of the countervailing public interests pleaded by the state by way of justification.

[61] Rules of the Court of Session, r.58.4(a).

[62] *ibid*. r.58.4(b).

[63] This exclusion is disapplied, however, where the Crown is said to infringe the applicant's rights under Community law: *Millar & Bryce Ltd v Keeper of the Registers of Scotland*, 1997 S.L.T. 1000. Whether the exclusion requires to be disapplied where a violation of the applicant's Convention rights is claimed is a question currently before the Court of Session: *Davidson v Scottish Ministers (No.2)*, 2003 S.C. 103.

administration,[64] and damages may be awarded only where their award would otherwise be competent.[65] There is no restriction in principle on the causes of action that may be pleaded against a public authority, although the prevailing approach of the courts is generally to limit the potential liability of such bodies.

As with any other employer, a public authority will be vicariously liable for actionable harm caused by the negligent acts of its employees.[66] But not all harm is necessarily actionable in negligence. It must be shown that the defender owed the pursuer a duty of care, and although this is easily established in cases involving the infliction of physical damage to the person or property, it is less easily established where, for example, the loss complained of is purely economic, or the complaint is that the defender omitted to take some action which would or might have prevented the loss caused to the pursuer. Moreover, however much loss it may cause, a public authority cannot be held liable in respect of a lawful, *intra vires* act or decision. It is thus a precondition of liability in negligence that what the authority did (or failed to do) was outwith the scope of its powers. The difficulty has been to reconcile public law criteria (when is an act or decision *ultra vires*?) with private law principles governing liability (when does an act or decision sound in damages?). The key device adopted to control the scope of the liability of public authorities in negligence has been the "policy/operational dichotomy", according to which policy matters, involving the exercise of discretion, can give rise to no duty of care unless the discretionary choice made was manifestly irrational, whereas operational matters may (or may not) give rise to a duty of care on ordinary principles.[67] This approach is not free of problems, but its essence was affirmed by the House of Lords in two strikingly restrictive decisions on the scope of public authorities' liability in negligence.[68] More recent decisions of the House of

---

[64] *King v East Ayrshire DC*, 1998 S.C. 182 at 196, *per* Lord Rodger. This raises a related question, namely whether the grant of remedies in the context of judicial review is purely discretionary. This is certainly true of English law, but the position in Scotland is more equivocal: see *Anderson v S of S for Work and Pensions*, 2002 S.L.T. 68.

[65] The reference to "payment (whether of damages or otherwise)" in r.58.4(b) appears to countenance the award of monetary redress even absent a cause of action, but if such power exists it appears only to have been exercised twice: *Kelly v Monklands DC*, 1986 S.L.T. 169 and *Mallon v Monklands DC*, 1986 S.L.T. 347.

[66] See *Lister v Hesley Hall Ltd* [2002] 1 A.C. 215.

[67] See *Dorset Yacht Co Ltd v Home Office* [1970] A.C. 1004 and *Anns v Merton London BC* [1978] A.C. 728. The policy/operational dichotomy survived the overruling of *Anns* by the House of Lords in *Murphy v Brentwood DC* [1991] 1 A.C. 398.

[68] *X v Bedfordshire C* [1995] 2 A.C. 633 and *Stovin v Wise (Norfolk CC: Third Party)* [1996] A.C. 923.

Lords indicate a relaxation in this approach,[69] a relaxation which owes much to the decision of the European Court of Human Rights in *Osman v United Kingdom*.[70] It should not however be thought that these recent developments signal a judicial willingness to countenance a general extension in the scope of public authorities' liability in negligence: the arguments from constitutional propriety and economy that have influenced the prevailing caution remain compelling.

Evidence of a like caution is observable in relation to the other, **12–39** typically "public", causes of action in delict, breach of statutory duty and misfeasance in public office. As to the first, whether a statutory duty gives rise, in the event of its breach, to a private law right of action in damages depends fundamentally on the intention of the legislature.[71] In keeping with this approach, the House of Lords in *X v Bedfordshire County Council*[72] and *Stovin v Wise*[73] indicated that, generally speaking, the conferment of discretion is incompatible with the existence of a cause of action, whether in breach of statutory duty or negligence. Again in *O'Rourke v Camden London Borough Council*,[74] the House of Lords held that a statutory duty consisting in the performance of a "public law function" (there, the provision of accommodation to the homeless) was enforceable, if at all, solely by way of judicial review. As for misfeasance in public office,[75] the conditions of liability here are

---

[69] See *Barrett v Enfield London BC* [1999] 3 W.L.R. 79 and *Phelps v Hillingdon London BC* [2000] 3 W.L.R. 776.

[70] (1999) 25 E.H.R.R. 245. There it was held that the Court of Appeal's striking out of applicants' claim against the Metropolitan Police (see *Osman v Ferguson* [1993] 4 All E.R. 344) amounted to a breach of their rights under ECHR, Art.6. It is a deeply flawed decision, as noted by Lord Browne-Wilkinson in *Barrett*, above; see also A. Bowen. "A Terrible Misunderstanding? *Osman v UK* and the Law of Negligence", 2001 S.L.T. (News) 59. The ECHR found no breach of Art.6 in *either TP and KM v UK*, App. No. 28945/95, *The Times*, May 31, 2001 or *Z v UK* (2002) 34 E.H.R.R. 3, but did find breaches of other Convention rights (respectively, the right to respect for private and family life and the right to freedom from inhuman and degrading treatment, together with, in both cases, a breach of the right to an effective remedy under ECHR, Art.13) in the striking out of the applicants' claims in negligence against public authorities. The applications in both cases were brought by the disappointed plaintiffs in two of the five joined appeals heard in *X v Bedfordshire C*, above.

[71] *R. v Deputy Governor of Parkhurst Prison, ex p. Hague* [1992] 1 A.C. 58. Thus, *e.g.* the fact that a statutory duty exists for the protection of a class of which the pursuer is a member may suggest that the statutory duty was intended to be actionable at the instance of such as the pursuer (see *Cutler v Wandsworth Stadium Ltd* [1949] A.C. 398); but, if the statute prescribes remedies for its breach, that is likely to preclude any finding of a right of action (see *Groves v Lord Wimborne* [1898] 2 Q.B. 402).

[72] [1995] 2 A.C. 633.

[73] [1996] A.C. 923.

[74] [1998] A.C. 188.

[75] A cause of action the existence of which in Scots law was only recognised in *Micosta SA v Shetland Islands Council*, 1986 S.L.T. 193.

more restrictive than in respect of negligence or breach of statutory duty.[76] The conduct complained of must be the conduct of a public officer and must have occurred in the course of the performance of a public function. It must then be shown that the conduct was specifically intended to cause injury to a person or persons ("targeted malice") or was performed by the official in the knowledge that he had no power to perform it and with reckless indifference to the consequences.[77]

---

[76] Although, if the constituent elements of liability are established, that liability is not affected by the nature of the damage complained of.

[77] *Three Rivers DC v Bank of England (No.3)* [2000] 2 W.L.R. 1220, HL. The elements of this cause of action are established in rather more cases than one might expect: apart from *Three Rivers* itself, see also, *e.g. Bourgoin SA v Ministry of Agriculture, Fisheries and Food* [1986] Q.B. 716; *Harmon CFEM Facades (UK) Ltd v Corporate Officer of the House of Commons* [2000] 72 Con. L.R. 29.

CHAPTER 13

OMBUDSMEN

The advances that have been made in the reach and intensity of the **13–01** principles of administrative law, both before and since the advent of the Human Rights Act, are rightly regarded as amongst the greatest achievements of the common law. Yet what is their real impact? Empirical studies have suggested that the practical influence of judicial review on actual decision making is limited, even in quasi-judicial contexts where one might expect its doctrines to have greater resonance, and that the contact between administrative law and the day-to-day business of administration remains sporadic and peripheral at best.[1] In any case, the concern of the aggrieved individual who applies for judicial review is less likely to be with the beauty of legal doctrine and rather more with whether or not he will win; and, if he wins, what this actually means. In particular, if he has suffered financial or other loss as a consequence of an unlawful decision, will he be restored to the position he would have been in but for that decision? As we saw in the previous chapter, the answer to that question is likely to be no, even still. An invalid decision may result in harm; but the same harm might flow from the same decision, lawfully retaken. In such circumstances, there is no actionable damage. Even if there is actionable damage, the available causes of action against public authorities—principally negligence, breach of statutory duty and misfeasance in public office—hold out little practical hope of success. In that respect, a successful application for judicial review may well feel, for the individual applicant, like a distinctly pyrrhic victory.

This state of affairs has been described as increasingly anomalous against the backdrop of developments in EU law and under the Human Rights Act, both of which have widened the potential liability of public authorities in damages; and, in particular, when contrasted with the developing practice of the Parliamentary Commissioner for Administration (PCA)—the Westminster

---

[1] See, *e.g.* S. Halliday, "The Influence of Judicial Review on Bureaucratic Decision Making" [2000] P.L. 110; G. Richardson and D. Machin, "Judicial Review and Tribunal Decision Making" [2000] P.L. 494; M. Sunkin and K. Pick, "The Changing Impact of Judicial Review: The independent review service of the social fund" [2001] P.L. 736.

Ombudsman.[2] Long regarded as something of a poor relation in our system of public law, lacking visibility, authority and coercive remedial power, the PCA has in more recent times emerged as a powerful and effective adjunct to mainstream administrative law. This chapter therefore examines the role and functions of the PCA, together with those of the Scottish Public Services Ombudsman, established by Act of the Scottish Parliament in 2002.

PARLIAMENTARY COMMISSIONER FOR ADMINISTRATION

13–02 The office of the PCA was established pursuant to the Parliamentary Commissioner Act 1967, and in the face of a good deal of parliamentary resistance.[3] His principal function is to investigate complaints by private persons that they have suffered injustice in consequence of maladministration[4] by government departments, agencies and non-departmental public bodies.[5] This general definition is then limited by reference to a list of matters excluded from the PCA's jurisdiction.[6] The Act also provides that the PCA may not normally investigate any action in respect of which the complainant has or had a right of recourse to a tribunal or a

---

[2] See M. Amos, "The PCA, Redress and Damages for Wrongful Administrative action" [2000] P.L. 21.

[3] The inspiration for the 1967 Act, in turn, was the 1961 report by JUSTICE, *The Citizen and the Administration: The redress of grievances* ("the Whyatt Report"), which identified the weaknesses of existing legal and political avenues of redress and advocated the establishment of an ombudsman as adopted in the Scandinavian countries.

[4] "Maladministration" is not defined in the 1967 Act. Reference is often made to the so-called "Crossman catalogue" of administrative sins, derived from the speech of the Leader of the House of Commons, Richard Crossman M.P., during the second reading debate on the Parliamentary Commissioner Bill: "bias, neglect, inattention, delay, incompetence, ineptitude, perversity and arbitrariness." Specific instances as found by the PCA include failure to adhere to departmental guidance, over-rigid adherence to departmental guidance, failure to honour assurances given to a citizen, failure to give correct advice, delay in dealing with an individual's case or claim, and "unwillingness to treat the complainant as a person with rights".

[5] 1967 Act, s.5. For the list of bodies subject to the PCA's jurisdiction, see Sch.2, as periodically updated by Order in Council under s.4. Note also that an important addition was made to the jurisdiction of the PCA in 1994, when he was given responsibility for complaints arising under the Code of Practice on Access to Government Information. When the Freedom of Information Act 2000 comes fully into force, this jurisdiction will cease, responsibility for enforcement of the duties contained in that Act falling on the Information Commissioner.

[6] s.5(3) and Sch.3. Thus the PCA may not investigate, *inter alia*, matters certified by the Secretary of State to affect relations between the UK government and other governments or international organisations; actions taken by or with the authority of the Secretary of State for investigating crime or protecting national security; and matters relating to contractual or other commercial transactions on behalf of central government.

remedy by way of proceedings in any court of law, unless it would be unreasonable to expect the person to have exercised that right.[7] Complaints must also be made within 12 months of the date on which the citizen first had notice of the matter complained of, subject to a discretion to accept a late complaint where there are special circumstances excusing the delay.[8]

One of the most frequently criticised aspects of the scheme contained in the 1967 Act is the absence of any right of direct access to the PCA. Complaints must be made in the first instance to an M.P. (not necessarily the complainant's own) and it is for the M.P. to decide whether or not to refer the complaint to the PCA.[9] It may no longer be the case that the M.P. filter actively obstructs access to the PCA, but that was certainly its effect even in the relatively recent past.[10] If, however, a complaint is referred, is found to be within the PCA's jurisdiction and if the PCA decides to undertake an investigation, it receives a treatment quite unlike that on offer through other, legal or political, channels of redress. An investigation is conducted in private, and the relevant department or body, together with any person named in the complaint, must be given an opportunity to comment on the allegations made. The PCA has wide powers of compelling the production of official documents and information, and the same powers as the Court of Session to compel a witness to give evidence.[11] Crown privilege, or public interest immunity, cannot be claimed in the context of an investigation by the PCA.[12] If the investigation is carried through to the point of completion (the PCA may discontinue an investigation if he manages to broker a settlement at some earlier stage), the PCA must send a report of his investigation to the referring M.P. and to the department concerned.[13] He must also report annually to Parliament, and may lay reports on selected cases at

---

[7] s.5(2).

[8] s.6(3).

[9] s.5(1). The presence of the "M.P. filter" served to assuage some of the more pronounced anxieties expressed by M.P.s during the passage of the Parliamentary Commissioner Bill, to the effect that the new office would usurp their traditional constitutional functions in relation to obtaining redress for their aggrieved constituents. Where a complaint is sent directly to the PCA and appears to be investigatable, the PCA may send it to the complainant's M.P. with a request that he formally refer it.

[10] See, *e.g.* L. Cohen, "The Parliamentary Commissioner and the MP Filter" [1972] P.L. 204; *Our Fettered Ombudsman* (JUSTICE, 1977); G. Drewry and C. Harlow, "A 'Cutting Edge'? The Parliamentary Commissioner and MPs" (1990) 53 M.L.R. 745.

[11] s.8. Contrast the position of select committees, which, at worst, may treat a refusal of a witness to attend and give evidence as a contempt of Parliament.

[12] s.8(3). Note however that privilege may be claimed for documents certified by the Cabinet Secretary, with the approval of the P.M., as relating to the proceedings of the Cabinet or Cabinet committees: s.8(4).

[13] s.10.

other times. The Select Committee on Public Administration is charged with considering the reports of the PCA, and is vocal in its support for his work.

The PCA has no coercive remedial power, and cannot change a departmental decision or require payment of compensation. He may, and does, recommend remedial action, and this may go beyond a recommendation for specific redress of the complainant's grievance, extending to improvements in systems and processes in order to minimise the risk of the same mistake recurring.[14] The pressure on the government to accede to the PCA's recommendations is considerable.[15] Where the PCA considers that an injustice has been caused through maladministration and has not been remedied, he may lay a special report before Parliament accordingly.[16]

13–03   Nowadays there is less concern about the PCA being underused than overburdened. Until recently, the holder of the office also held the offices of Health Service Commissioner for each of England, Scotland and Wales,[17] not to mention the transitional office of Scottish Parliamentary Commissioner for Administration.[18] Even as the PCA alone, his workload has increased considerably, from 801 complaints in 1990–91 to 2139 complaints in 2001–02.[19] But the utility of the present ombudsman system from the viewpoint of the citizen is questionable. Leaving aside the PCA in his various guises, there are also ombudsmen in local government, internal adjudicators established by public authorities on a voluntary basis to handle customer complaints, and a whole host of ombudsmen in the private sector. In this scenario, "it would take an exceptional citizen to know how and to whom he or she could refer complaints about officialdom."[20] The Select Committee on Public Administration first called for an overhaul of the existing structure of public sector ombudsmen in 1997,[21] and in 2000 the

---

[14] W. K. Reid, "What's the Good of Law in a Case o' the Kind?" [1993] P.L. 221.

[15] Thus even where the government is not prepared to accept the PCA's findings of maladministration, it may agree to pay *ex gratia* compensation. Such was the case in the Barlow Clowes débâcle, where a investment business, licensed and regulated by the Dept of Trade and Industry, collapsed causing financial loss to thousands of small investors: see HC 76 (1989–90) and HC 99 (1989–90).

[16] Section 10(3). The PCA has only laid special reports on two occasions: see HC 598 (1977–78) and HC 193 (1994–95).

[17] See the Health Service Commissioners Act 1993.

[18] Pursuant to the Scotland Act 1998 (Transitory and Transitional Provisions) (Complaints of Maladministration) Order 1999 (SI 1999/1351).

[19] HC 897 (2001–02). The Child Support Agency, the Immigration and Nationality Directorate and the Legal Services Commission between them accounted for 20% of the total number of complaints amungst them.

[20] A. W. Bradley and K. D. Ewing, *Constitutional and Administrative Law* (13th ed., Longmans, 2003), p.693.

[21] Third Report of the Select Committee on Public Administration, HC 398 (1997–98).

Cabinet Office published a review of that system as it operates in England.[22] The review, warmly endorsed by the Select Committee, recommended radical reform, including unification of the separate ombudsmen within a new, collegiate commission and the introduction of direct access across the board. But as the Select Committee noted (with some asperity) in its most recent treatment of the subject, the review has still to produce results.[23]

SCOTTISH PUBLIC SERVICES OMBUDSMAN

The story of ombudsman reform in Scotland is somewhat brighter. **13–04** Section 91(1) of the Scotland Act required the Scottish Parliament to make provision for the investigation of complaints in respect of any action taken by or on behalf of a member of the Scottish Executive or any other office holder in the Scottish Administration. In addition, section 91(3) gave the Parliament the power to provide for the investigation of complaints against other public authorities in Scotland, including the Parliamentary corporation, public authorities having mixed functions or no reserved functions, and cross-border public authorities so far as the complaint concerns their devolved functions in Scotland. The jurisdiction of the PCA was not thereby excluded: it extends still to Scotland so far as maladministration in reserved areas of government is concerned. Otherwise, however, it ceased with devolution (although, pending legislation by the Scottish Parliament, transitional provision was made conferring jurisdiction on a Scottish Parliamentary Commissioner for Administration).[24]

Following devolution, the Scottish Executive published two consultation documents[25] canvassing views on what sort of distinctively Scottish provision might be made for the resolution of complaints.[26] The result of this activity was the Scottish Public Services Ombudsman Act 2002. The new Scottish Ombudsman assumed the jurisdiction of the transitional Scottish Commissioner; she[27] also absorbed the responsibilities previously vested in the

---

[22] *Review of the Public Sector Ombudsmen in England* (Cabinet Office, Apr. 2000), and see M. Seneviratne, "Joining up the Ombudsmen" [2000] P.L. 582.
[23] Third Report of the Select Committee on Public Administration, *Ombudsman Issues*, HC 448 (2002–03).
[24] See n.18.
[25] *Modernising the Complaints System*, (Oct. 2000) and *A Modern Complaints System* (July 2001).
[26] Although the scope for innovation was restricted by the requirement in s.91 that in making any such provision, the Scottish Parliament should have regard (among other things) to the Parliamentary Commissioner Act 1967.
[27] The pronoun is deliberate: the first holder of the office of Scottish Public Services Ombudsman is Prof. Alice Brown.

Commissioner for Local Administration in Scotland, the Health Service Commissioner for Scotland, the Housing Association Ombudsman for Scotland, the External Adjudicators for Scottish Enterprise and Highlands and Islands Enterprise, and the Mental Welfare Commission.[28] The Ombudsman is appointed by the Queen on the nomination of the Scottish Parliament, and the Act makes provision for the appointment of up to three deputy ombudsmen (through whom, it is thought, the expertise developed by the specialist ombudsmen will be preserved).

Under section 2(1), the Ombudsman may investigate any matter, whenever arising, if the matter consists of action taken by or on behalf of a person "liable to investigation under this Act"; it is a matter which the Ombudsman is entitled to investigate; and a complaint in respect of it has been duly made to the Ombudsman. If the first two of these conditions are met, the person or body liable to be investigated may request the Ombudsman to investigate the matter.[29] Who, then, is liable to be investigated? The question is dealt with by section 3 and Schedule 2. Schedule 2 is divided into two parts. Part 1 contains a list of authorities which cannot be amended (other than by way of primary legislation); Part 2 contains a list of authorities which may be amended by Order in Council. In Part 1 we find, among others, the Scottish Parliamentary Corporate Body, members of the Scottish Executive and office holders in the Scottish Administration; health service bodies, including health boards and NHS trusts, family health service providers such as general practitioners, and even "independent providers" providing services under arrangements with the NHS; local authorities; police and fire boards; and registered social landlords. Part 2 presently contains a list of 77 Scottish public authorities and cross-border public authorities, together with reference to any local enterprise company and the holders of any offices established by or under any enactment.[30] New entries may be added to Part 2 but only in respect of Scottish public authorities with mixed functions or no reserved functions, publicly-owned companies or entities which are neither a Scottish public authority not a publicly-owned company but which appear to Her Majesty to exercise functions of a "public nature".[31]

---

[28] In the latter case, only the complaints-handling functions of the commission have been transferred to the Ombudsman.

[29] Scottish Public Services Ombudsman Act 2002, s.2(2).

[30] Only executive non-departmental public bodies are included in the list in Pt 2. The Scottish Ministers decided to exclude advisory non-departmental public bodies on the grounds that such bodies do not deal directly with the public, but exist to advise the Scottish Executive, which could, if necessary, be held to account by the Ombudsman for the quality of advice given.

[31] s.2(3), subject also to the restrictions in s.2(6) and to the requirement for consultation in s.2(5).

The definition of the Ombudsman's jurisdiction *ratione materiae* **13–05**
is complicated—unduly so, if the object of introducing a unified
system was to make it clearer and more user-friendly for complainants. Section 8 together with Schedule 4 *excludes* 15 categories of
subject-matter from the Ombudsman's jurisdiction altogether.[32]
Section 7 *restricts* the Ombudsman's jurisdiction in various respects,
inter alia by providing that she may not question the merits of
discretionary decisions taken without maladministration (except
where the decision was taken by a health care provider and
depended on the exercise of clinical judgment)[33]; investigate any
matter in respect of which the complainant has or had a right of
appeal to a Minister of the Crown, the Scottish Ministers or any
tribunal, or a remedy by way of legal proceedings[34]; or investigate
any action by a cross-border public authority which relates to
reserved matters.[35] What remains? Section 5 defines three different
categories of what may be investigated by the Ombudsman:
maladministration (action taken in the exercise of administrative
functions); "service failures"; and "any action". "Any action" may
be investigated where it is the action of a registered social landlord,
health service body, independent health care provider or family
health service provider (but, in the latter case, only in relation to
their provision of family health services). "Service failures" may be
investigated in relation to any entity within the Ombudsman's
jurisdiction except registered social landlords and family health
service providers. Maladministration may be investigated in relation to any listed authority.[36]

The Ombudsman may only proceed to investigate where she
receives a competent complaint from a member of the public,[37]

---

[32] Among them, action taken for the purposes of or in connection with the
investigation or prevention of crime or the protection of national security; the
commencement of civil or criminal proceedings; action taken in a judicial
capacity; action taken in matters relating to contractual or other commercial
transactions of a listed authority (other than a health care provider in certain
specified respects); and public service appointments and related issues).

[33] s.7(1), (2).

[34] s.7(8).

[35] s.7(5).

[36] The Explanatory Notes state (at para.20) that the differences enshrined in section
5 "reflect existing differences between the transitional Commissioner, the Health
Services Commissioners Act 1993 and the Local Government (Scotland) Act
1975 as respects the separate ombudsmen." So too they may. But it is difficult to
regard this as an especially forceful reason for retaining those differences given
the stated aims of the legislation, *viz.* the achievement of simplicity, effectiveness
and transparency.

[37] That is, any individual or body (corporate or unincorporated) other than the
Parliamentary corporation, a local authority or other authority constituted for
purposes of the public service or local government, nationalised industries or
undertakings; and any other body whose members are appointed by the Queen,
any Minister of the Crown, government department or member of the Scottish
Executive, or whose revenues consist wholly or mainly of moneys provided by the
UK Parliament or sums paid out of the Scottish consolidated fund: s.5(6).

provided that person claims to have sustained "injustice or hardship" in consequence of the maladministration or failure complained of.[38] This is in the nature of a "title and interest" test, designed to ensure that the Ombudsman does not receive (or may reject) abstract complaints of maladministration by persons, however well intentioned, who lack a direct personal interest in the matter. There is no MSP filter, although a complaint may be made on a person's behalf by any authorised person, including an MSP.[39] As with the PCA, complaints must be made within 12 months of the date on which the aggrieved person first had notice of the matter complained of, subject to a discretion to accept late complaints in special circumstances.[40]

The procedure for the conduct of investigations is modelled closely on that contained in the 1967 Act. Investigations must be conducted in private, and the authority (and any persons named in the complaint) must be given an opportunity to comment on the allegations made.[41] The Ombudsman has power under section 13 to compel the production of information or documents in connection with an investigation,[42] and has the same powers of the Court of Session to compel the attendance and examination of witnesses. No claim for Crown privilege or confidentiality may be made in respect of documents required for an investigation.[43] On concluding an investigation, the Ombudsman is required to report to the complainant, the authority and any person named in the complaint, and the Scottish Ministers,[44] and must lay a copy of the report before the Parliament. The report should not, unless the Ombudsman deems it necessary, identify any person other than the authority concerned.[45] Listed authorities are under a duty to make

---

[38] s.5(3). Where a listed authority requests the Ombudsman to undertake an investigation in terms of s.2(2), she may do so only if it has been publicly alleged that its actions have caused injustice or hardship and the authority concerned has taken all reasonable steps to deal with the matter to which the allegation relates: s.5(5).

[39] s.9(1), (2).

[40] s.10(1).

[41] s.12.

[42] Subject to s.13(7), which protects from disclosure documents or information "relating to proceedings of the Scottish Cabinet or any committees of the Scottish Cabinet." Here it would appear that the draftsman simply borrowed the wording contained in the 1967 Act, with the addition of the word "Scottish" where appropriate. The usual approach adopted in legislative drafting is to refer to the Scottish Ministers or a member of the Scottish Executive or a member of the Scottish Administration. At all events, while loose reference is sometimes made to the "Scottish Cabinet", there are no such things as "Scottish Cabinet committees".

[43] Obstruction of the Ombudsman in the performance of her duties may be certified to the Court of Session and punished as a contempt: s.14.

[44] s.15(1). Special provision is made where complaints are made on a person's behalf and in respect of complaints relating to a health care provider.

[45] s.15(3).

arrangement for the inspection and copying of reports, which arrangements must be adequately publicised. Like the PCA, however, the Ombudsman has no coercive remedial powers. She may recommend redress, and if she considers that the injustice or hardship identified in her reports has gone unremedied, she may lay a special report before the Parliament.[46] In any event, she is obliged to report annually to the Parliament on her activities.[47]

At this stage, it is difficult to predict with certainty what the **13–06** workload of the new Ombudsman will be. In his final report before demitting office, the transitional Ombudsman noted that in 2001–02 he received 67 new complaints (as against 60 in 2000–01),[48] but that in his capacity as Health Service Commissioner he received 225 complaints in the same period (as against 224 in the previous period).[49] As at Westminster, it seems a significant proportion of complaints are rejected as being outwith the Ombudsman's jurisdiction[50] (and this is perhaps less likely to improve than it should be, given the impenetrability of the definition of that jurisdiction in section 5 of the 2002 Act).

Value of ombudsmen

Perhaps the salient virtue of the public sector ombudsmen is that **13–07** they are not courts: "all the complainant has to do is complain; no expensive lawyers are necessary, no evidence has to be amassed and no case has to be proved."[51] Their investigative procedures are private and inquisitorial, enabling them to identify systemic flaws in administrative processes as well as the precise causes of individual injustice, and if they have no coercive remedial power, the political pressure exerted by findings of maladministration has tended to result in corrective action being taken and redress being conceded where it is found to be due.[52] There is a risk, however, that the

---

[46] s.16.
[47] s.17.
[48] The Scottish Legal Aid Board and the Scottish Executive's Rural Affairs Dept attracted the largest number of complaints in both periods.
[49] *Scottish PCA: Annual Report for 2001–2002*, S.P.P. 595 (2002).
[50] The 225 health-related complaints represent only 24% of the total number received, the remainder being rejected on jurisdictional grounds.
[51] C. Harlow and R. Rawlings, *Law and Administration* (2nd ed., Butterworth, London, 1997), p.400.
[52] Indeed, the PCA's Annual Report for 2001 (HC 598) stated that, despite large individual compensation payments sometimes being involved, there were no cases in which redress had been withheld contrary to the PCA's recommendations. The support lent to the PCA by the Select Committee on Public Administration may be helpful here, and the Scottish Parliament should perhaps give thought to setting up a committee with a comparable role in supporting the work of the Scottish Public Services Ombudsman.

ombudsmen could be victims of their own success. They are under no statutory duty to investigate every complaint made to them which falls within their jurisdiction, but it has been held that every statutory power contains within it an element of obligation, at least to the extent that proper consideration must be given to the exercise of the power.[53] That being so, questions may arise in the future about the basis on which the ombudsmen reject complaints they could competently have investigated. For it seems likely that resort to the ombudsmen will increase, yet they are resource-limited institutions with no power to charge for the investigative services they provide. If growing workloads force the ombudsmen to ration their investigations, disappointed complainants may want to know why their complaints have been rejected in favour of others, and may resort to legal action in order to extract an explanation.

On that score, it was held in *R v Parliamentary Commissioner for Administration, ex parte Dyer*[54] that the PCA was under no obligation to proceed with complaints which were trivial or inappropriate for investigation, and there may be hints here about the evolving nature of the ombudsmen's role. According to the PCA, his "touchstone remains that a person who has suffered an injustice due to maladministration should so far as possible be restored to the position he or she would have been in had the maladministration not occurred."[55] But many commentators have detected in the PCA's approach to his role less of a concern to uncover and investigate individual grievances than to provide an internal administrative audit (which is not to say that his inquiries are not extremely fruitful for a handful of lucky individuals).[56] As Harlow and Rawlings note, "where the PCA excels is in 'big inquiries'. Here his exhaustive investigatorial procedure, too costly, cumbersome and slow for trivial complaints, comes into its own." [57] On this view, forced by circumstances to be selective in their uptake of complaints, the ombudsmen will seek out those that give them the best opportunity to turn their admittedly intense searchlights on administrative shortcomings needing to be remedied. But there are risks in this strategy, as Harlow and Rawlings point out. Complainants are less willing to accept negative outcomes from the PCA, at least, which suggests that the courts will be invited to scrutinise the

---

[53] *Stovin v Wise (Norwich C (Third Party))* [1996] A.C. 923.

[54] *R. v Parliamentary Commissioner for Administration, ex p. Dyer* [1994] 1 W.L.R. 621.

[55] Annual Report of the Parliamentary Commissioner for Administration, HC 845, (1997–98), para.5.2.

[56] See, *e.g.* M. Seneviratne, *Ombudsmen in the Public Sector* (Open University Press, Buckingham, 1994), pp.52–58; Harlow and Rawlings, *Law and Administration, op.cit.*, pp.452–455.

[57] Harlow and Rawlings, *Law and Administration, op.cit.*

work of the ombudsmen—not only preliminary decisions as to whether to investigate a complaint, but also their procedures and substantive outcomes—with increasing frequency. The difficulty with this is that it introduces elements of adversarial civil procedure which are ill adapted to the essentially informal, inquisitorial approach of the ombudsmen.[58] It appears that, as the system of public sector ombudsmen has bedded down, its origins as an adjunct to political and parliamentary channels for the redress of grievances have been overshadowed; like the structure of administrative tribunals and inquiries before them,[59] it may be that they will increasingly be absorbed into the machinery of justice. Certainly, there is a tendency on the part of lawyers to regard the judicial process as the model against which all other (implicitly inferior) dispute resolution processes fall to be judged. We have noted elsewhere in this book manifestations of "juridification". In relation to the public sector ombudsmen, that tendency should be resisted, for it threatens what is distinctive and therefore valuable about the institution.

---

[58] The "creep" of judicial review has been most marked in relation to decisions of local government ombudsmen (see M. Jones, "The Local Ombudsmen and Judicial Review" [1988] P.L. 608) and private sector ombudsmen (see, *e.g. Seifert and Lynch v Pensions Ombudsman* [1997] 1 All E.R. 214). So far as the PCA is concerned, jurisdiction was established in *Dyer*, above, although the court there found in favour of the PCA; since then, decisions of the PCA have been overturned twice in *R. v Parliamentary Commissioner for Administration, ex p. Balchin* [1998] 1 P.L.R. 1 and *R. v Parliamentary Commissioner for Administration, ex p. Balchin (No.2)* [2000] R.V.R. 303, in the first case on grounds of investigative error of fact, in the second on grounds of defective reasoning.

[59] See in particular the Report of the Royal Commission on Administrative Tribunals and Inquiries (1957) ("the Franks Report").

INDEX